Rick Ste

GREAT

& IRELAND

2001

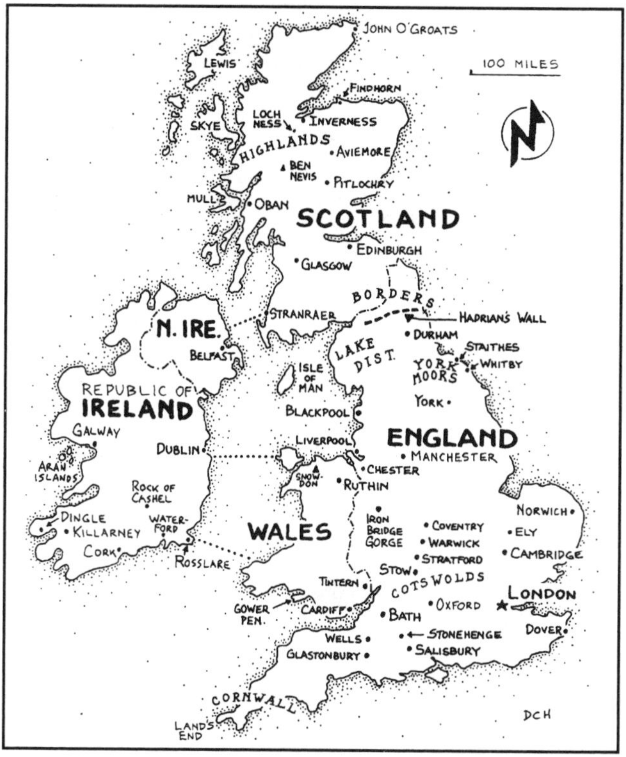

AVALON
TRAVEL
publishing

Other ATP travel guidebooks by Rick Steves
Rick Steves' Europe 101: History and Art for the Traveler (with Gene Openshaw)
Rick Steves' Mona Winks: Self-Guided Tours of Europe's Top Museums (with Gene Openshaw)
Rick Steves' Postcards from Europe
Rick Steves' Best of Europe
Rick Steves' Europe Through the Back Door
Rick Steves' France, Belgium & the Netherlands (with Steve Smith)
Rick Steves' Germany, Austria & Switzerland
Rick Steves' Italy
Rick Steves' Scandinavia
Rick Steves' Spain & Portugal
Rick Steves' London (with Gene Openshaw)
Rick Steves' Paris (with Steve Smith and Gene Openshaw)
Rick Steves' Rome (with Gene Openshaw)
Rick Steves' Phrase Books for: German, Italian, French, Spanish/Portuguese, and French/German/Italian

Thanks to my wife, Anne, for making "home" my favorite travel destination. Thanks also to Roy and Jodi Nicholls for their research help, to our readers for their input, and to local friends listed in this book who put the "Great" in Britain.

Avalon Travel Publishing, 5855 Beaudry Street, Emeryville, CA 94608

Printed in the United States of America
First printing December 2000

For the latest on Rick's lectures, guidebooks, tours, and public television series, contact Europe Through the Back Door, Box 2009, Edmonds, WA 98020, tel. 425/771-8303, fax 425/771-0833, www.ricksteves.com, or e-mail: rick@ricksteves.com.

ISSN 1090-6843
ISBN 1-56691-232-6

Europe Through the Back Door Editor Risa Laib
Avalon Travel Publishing Editor Kate Willis
Research Assistance Risa Laib, Brooke Burdick, Pat O'Connor, Robin Dority
Production & Typesetting Kathleen Sparkes, White Hart Design
Design Linda Braun
Cover Design Janine Lehmann
Maps David C. Hoerlein
Printer Publishers Press
Cover Photo Tower Bridge, London, England; Leo de Wys Inc./Steve Vidler

Distributed to the book trade by Publishers Group West, Berkeley, California

CONTENTS

The Best Destinations in Great Britain and Ireland

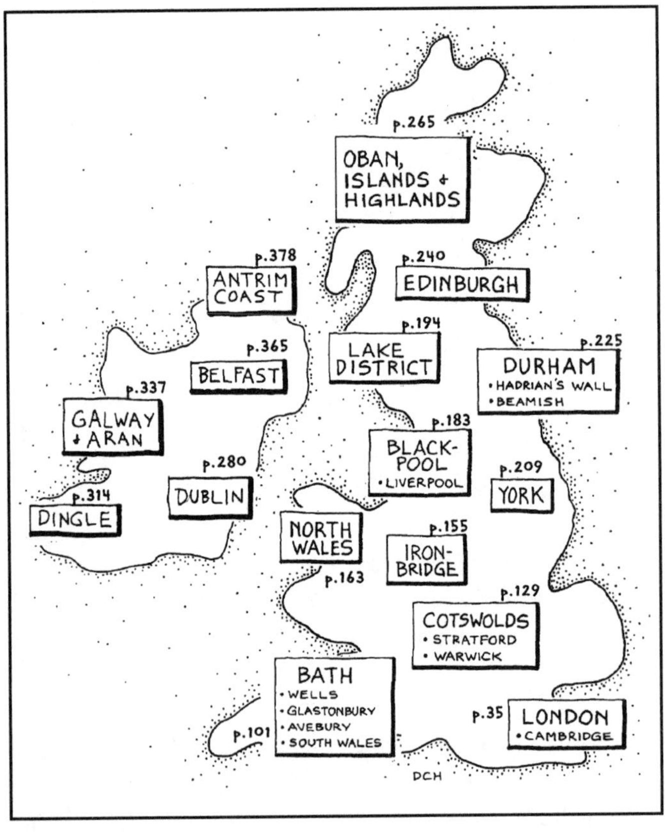

INTRODUCTION

This book breaks Britain and Ireland into their top big-city, small-town, and rural destinations. It gives you all the information and opinions necessary to wring the maximum value out of your limited time and money in each of these destinations. If you plan a month or less for Britain and Ireland and have a normal appetite for information, this lean and mean little book is all you need. If you're a travel info fiend, this book sorts through all the superlatives and provides a handy rack upon which to hang your supplemental information.

Experiencing British and Irish cultures, people, and natural wonders economically and hassle free has been my goal for more than 25 years of traveling, tour guiding, and travel writing. With this new edition I pass on to you the lessons I've learned, updated for your trip in 2001.

Rick Steves' Great Britain & Ireland is a personal tour guide in your pocket. The places I cover are balanced to include a comfortable mix of exciting big cities and great-to-be-alive-in small towns. While including the predictable biggies (such as Big Ben, Stratford, bagpipes, and the *Book of Kells*), the book also mixes in a healthy dose of Back Door intimacy (nearly edible Cotswold villages, Gaelic folk pubs, angelic boys' choirs, and windswept Roman lookouts). I've been selective. On a short trip, visiting both Oxford and Cambridge is redundant; I cover just the best (Cambridge). There are plenty of great countryside palaces; again, I recommend just the best (Blenheim).

The best is, of course, only my opinion. But after more than two busy decades of travel writing, lecturing, and tour guiding, I've developed a sixth sense for what tickles the traveler's fancy. The places featured in this book will knock your spots off.

This Information Is Accurate and Up-to-Date

Most publishers of guidebooks that cover a country from top to bottom can afford an update only every two or three years, and even then it's often by letter. Since this book is selective, covering only the top month of sightseeing, I'm able to update it each year. Even with an annual update, things change, but if you're traveling with the current edition of this book, I guarantee you're using the most up-to-date information available. This book will help you have an inexpensive, hassle-free trip.

Use this year's edition. I tell you, you're crazy to save a few bucks by traveling on old information. If you're packing an old book, you'll learn the seriousness of your mistake... once you start your trip. To rescue those of you who will inevitably travel with a two-year-old edition of this book (and realize your mistake too late), I've sent the latest edition to my lead B&Bs in each town for you to transcribe over breakfast. Your trip costs about $10 per waking hour. Your time is valuable. This guidebook saves lots of time.

Planning Your Trip

This book is organized by destinations, each one a mini-vacation on its own, filled with exciting sights and homey, affordable places to stay. In each chapter, you'll find the following:

Planning Your Time, a suggested schedule with thoughts on how to best use your limited time.

Orientation, including tourist information, city transportation, and an easy-to-read map designed to make the text clear and your entry smooth.

Sights, with ratings: ▲▲▲—Don't miss; ▲▲—Try hard to see; ▲—Worthwhile if you can make it; No rating—Worth knowing about.

Sleeping and **Eating,** with addresses and phone numbers of my favorite budget hotels and restaurants.

Transportation Connections to nearby destinations by train or bus and route tips for drivers.

The appendix is a traveler's tool kit, with information on history, architecture, TV, climate, telephoning, and a British-Yankee vocabulary list.

Browse through this book, choose your favorite destinations, and link them up. Then have a great trip! You'll travel like a temporary local, getting the absolute most out of every mile, minute, and dollar. You won't waste time on mediocre sights because, unlike others, this guidebook covers only the best. Since your major financial pitfall is lousy, expensive hotels, I've worked hard to assemble the best accommodation values for each stop. And as you travel the route I know and love, I'm happy you'll be meeting some of my favorite British and Irish people.

Trip Costs

Five components make up your trip costs: airfare, surface transportation, room and board, sightseeing/entertainment, and shopping/miscellany.

Airfare: Don't try to sort through the mess. Find a good travel agent. A round-trip U.S.A.-to-London flight costs $500 to $1,000, depending on where you fly from and when. Consider saving time and money in Europe by flying "open-jaw" (into one city and out of another; for instance, into London and out of Dublin).

Surface Transportation: For a three-week whirlwind trip of all my recommended British destinations, allow $450 per person for public transportation (train pass and key buses), or $500 per person (based on 2 people sharing) for a three-week car rental, gas, and insurance. About $150 more covers the ferry to Ireland and train and bus connections to its major sights. Car rental is cheapest if arranged from the United States. Train passes are normally available only outside of Europe. You may save money by simply buying tickets as you go (see "Transportation," below).

Room and Board: You can thrive in Britain and Ireland on $70 a day per person for room and board (allow $90 a day for London). A $70-a-day budget allows $10 for lunch, $15 for dinner, and $45 for lodging (based on two people splitting a $90 double room that includes breakfast). That's doable, particularly outside London. Students and tightwads can do it on $40 ($20 for a bed, $20 a day for meals and snacks). But budget sleeping and eating require the skills and information covered below (and in greater detail in my book *Rick Steves' Europe Through the Back Door*).

Sightseeing and Entertainment: In big cities, figure $5 to $10 per major sight (Imperial War Museum—$7.50; Edinburgh Castle—$9), $2 for minor ones (climbing church towers), $10 for guided walks, and $25 for bus tours and splurge experiences (Welsh and Scottish folk evenings). An overall average of $15 a day works for most. Don't skimp here. After all, this category directly powers most of the experiences all the other expenses are designed to make possible.

You will be tempted to buy the British Heritage Pass, which gets you into more than 500 British Heritage and National Trust properties (£32 for 7 days, £45 for 15 days, £60 for 30 days; sold at airport information desks and the Britain Visitors Centre on Regent Street in London). Of the 500 sights included (a list comes with the pass), here are the sights I describe and recommend for a three-week tour of Britain, along with their adult admission prices. A typical sightseer with three weeks will probably pay to see nearly all of these: Tower of London, £11 (London); Shakespeare's Birthplace and Anne Hathaway's Cottage, £9.50 (Stratford); Warwick Castle, £9.75 (near Stratford); Blenheim Palace, £9 (near the Cotswolds and Oxford); Roman and Medieval Baths, £6.90 (Bath); Stonehenge, £4 (near Bath); Caerphilly Castle, £2.50 and Tintern Abbey, £2.50 (South Wales); Caernarfon Castle, £4.20 (North Wales); Wordsworth's Dove Cottage, £4.80 (Lake District); Housesteads Roman Fort, £2.80 (Hadrian's Wall); Edinburgh Castle, £7.50, Georgian House, £5, Gladstone's Land, £3.50, and Holyrood Palace, £6 (Edinburgh); Culloden Battlefield, £3.50 (near Inverness); and Urquhart Castle, £3.80 (near Loch Ness). Your pass also saves you £1 on all Guide Friday bus tours (you'll probably take 4). This totals about £100; a pass takes the pain out of all these admissions with one big pill. People traveling by car—easily able to get to the more remote sights—are more likely to get their money's worth out of the pass.

Shopping and Miscellany: Figure $1 per postcard, tea, or ice cream cone and $2 per beer. Shopping can vary in cost from nearly nothing to a small fortune. Good budget travelers find that this category has little to do with assembling a trip full of lifelong and wonderful memories.

Exchange Rates

I list prices in pounds (£) throughout this book.

1 British pound (£1) = about $1.60
1 Irish pound (£1) = about $1.40

Britain: The British pound sterling (£), also called a "quid," is broken into 100 pence (p). Pence means "cents." You'll find coins ranging from 1p to £2 and bills from £5 to £50. To roughly convert pounds to dollars, add 50 percent to British prices: £6 is about $9 (actually $9.60), £3 is about $4.50, and 80p is about $1.20. Scotland and Northern Ireland issue their own currency in pounds, worth the same as an English pound. English, Scottish, and Northern Ireland's Ulster pounds are technically interchangeable in each region, although Scottish and Ulster pounds are "undesirable" in England. Banks in any of the three regions will convert your Scottish or Ulster pounds into English pounds at no charge. Don't worry about the coins, which are accepted throughout Britain.

Ireland: The Irish-English money relationship is like the Canadian-American one. The Irish call their pound a "punt." To roughly convert prices in punts into dollars, use the same formula as for Britain—add 50 percent to Irish prices: £6 is $9 (actually $8.40), £3 is about $4.50, and 80p is about $1.20. Use Irish, not English, money on the Emerald Isle. Ireland is a different country—treat it that way.

Euro: The euro, adopted as a currency by 11 countries in Europe, won't concern you until 2002, when it materializes into actual bills and coins. For a preview, Ireland will convert to euros while Britain refuses to shed its pounds.

Prices, Times, and Discounts

The prices in this book, as well as the hours and telephone numbers, are accurate as of late 2000. Britain and Ireland are always changing, and I know you'll understand that this guidebook, like any other, starts to yellow even before it's printed.

In Britain and Ireland you'll be using the 24-hour clock. After 12:00 noon, keep going—13:00, 14:00.... For anything over 12, subtract 12 and add p.m. (14:00 is 2 p.m.).

Peak season for most attractions is Easter through October (abbreviated in this book as Easter–Oct). Off-season, from November through Easter, expect shorter hours, more lunchtime breaks (especially at tourist information offices in smaller cities), and fewer activities. Some attractions are open only on weekends or are closed entirely in the winter. Confirm your sightseeing plans locally, especially when traveling between November and April.

While discounts (called "concessions" in Britain) are not listed in this book, nearly all British and Irish sights are discounted for seniors (loosely defined as anyone retired or willing to call themselves a "senior"), youths (ages 8–18), students, groups of 10 or more, and families.

When to Go

July and August are peak season—my favorite time—with very long days, the best weather, and the busiest schedule of tourist fun. Prices and crowds don't go up as dramatically in Britain as they do in much of Europe. Still, travel during "shoulder season" (May, early June, Sept, and early Oct) is easier and a bit less expensive. Shoulder-season travelers get minimal crowds, decent weather, the full range of sights and tourist fun spots, and the joy of being able to just grab a room almost whenever and wherever they like—often at a flexible price. Winter travelers find absolutely no crowds and soft room prices but shorter sightseeing hours. The weather can be cold and dreary, and nightfall draws the shades on sightseeing well before dinnertime. While England's rural charm falls with the leaves, city sightseeing is fine in the winter.

Plan for rain no matter when you go. Just keep going and take full advantage of "bright spells." In Ireland rainy weather is called "nice and soft." Conditions can change several times in a day, but rarely is the weather extreme. Daily averages throughout the year range between 42 and 70 degrees Fahrenheit. Temperatures below 32 or over 80 degrees are cause for headlines (see the climate chart in the appendix). July and August are not much better than shoulder months, though May and June can be lovely. While sunshine may be rare, summer days are very long. The summer sun is up from 6:30 until 22:30. It's not uncommon to have a gray day, eat dinner, and enjoy hours of sunshine afterward.

Sightseeing Priorities

Depending on the length of your trip, here are my recommended priorities:

Britain:

3 days:	London
5 days, add:	Bath, Cotswolds, Blenheim
7 days, add:	York
9 days, add:	Edinburgh
11 days, add:	Stratford, Warwick, Cambridge
14 days, add:	North Wales, Wells/Glastonbury/Avebury
17 days, add:	Lake District, Hadrian's Wall, Durham
21 days, add:	Ironbridge Gorge, Blackpool, Scottish Highlands
24 days, add:	South Wales

(The Whirlwind Tour map and three-week itinerary on the following pages include everything in the above 24 days. With 30 days you could slow down or add a five-day swing through Ireland.)

Best Three-Week Trip in Britain by Car

Day	Plan	Sleep in
1	Arrive in London, bus to Bath	Bath
2	Bath	Bath
3	Pick up car, Avebury, Wells, Glastonbury	Bath
4	South Wales, St. Fagans, Tintern	Chipping Camden
5	Explore the Cotswolds, Blenheim	Chipping Camden
6	Stratford, Warwick, Coventry	Ironbridge Gorge
7	Ironbridge Gorge, Ruthin banquet	Ruthin (if banquet) or Conwy
8	Highlights of North Wales	Ruthin or Conwy
9	Liverpool, Blackpool	Blackpool
10	Southern Lake District	Keswick area
11	Northern Lake District	Keswick area
12	Drive up west coast of Scotland	Oban
13	Highlands, Loch Ness, Scenic Highlands Drive	Edinburgh
14	More Highlands or Edinburgh	Edinburgh
15	Edinburgh	Edinburgh
16	Hadrian's Wall, Beamish, Durham evensong	Durham
17	York Moors, York, turn in car	York
18	York	York
19	Early train to London	London
20	London	London
21	London	London
22	Side trip to Cambridge or Greenwich, London	Whew!

While this three-week itinerary is designed to be done by car, it can be done by train and bus or, better yet, with a rail 'n' drive pass (best car days: Cotswolds, North Wales, Lake District, Scottish Highlands, Hadrian's Wall). For three weeks without a car, I'd probably cut back on the recommended sights with the most frustrating public transportation (South and North Wales, Ironbridge Gorge, the Highlands). Lacing together the cities by train is very slick. With more time, everything is workable without a car.

Whirlwind Three-Week Tour of Great Britain

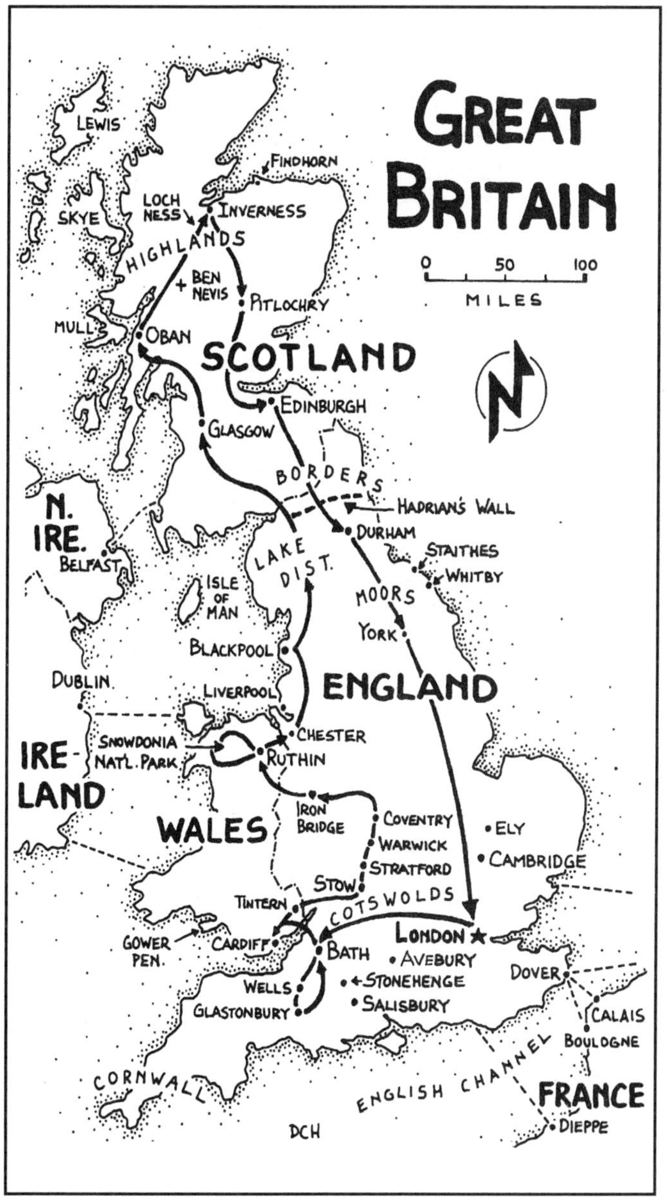

Ireland Itinerary

Ireland:

3 days:	Not worth the trouble
5 days:	Dublin, Dingle Peninsula
7 days, add:	Galway and a day in Belfast
9 days, add:	County Clare/Burren
11 days, add:	Northern Ireland's Antrim Coast
15 days, add:	Aran Islands, Wicklow area

Itinerary Tips

Most people fly into London and remain there for a few days. Instead, consider a gentler small-town start in Bath, and visit London at the end of your trip. You'll be more rested and ready to tackle Britain's greatest city. Heathrow Airport has direct connections to Bath and other cities.

To give yourself a little rootedness, minimize one-night stands. It's worth a long drive after dinner to be settled into a town for two nights. B&Bs are also more likely to give a good price to someone staying more than one night.

Many people save a couple of days and a lot of miles by going directly from the Lake District to Edinburgh and skipping the long joyride through Scotland. I consider a trip to Wales, rather than Scotland or Ireland, the best quick look at Celtic Britain.

Ireland, because of its nature and the expense and headaches involved in getting there, is not worth a very quick visit. It requires a minimum of five days. Don't overlook the handy ferry connections between Belfast and Scotland and between southeast Ireland and France. If you ask the Irish about ferries, they'll say, "I don't believe in them. But they're there."

Red Tape and Taxes

You need a passport, but no visa or shots, to travel in Britain and Ireland.

Sales Tax: Britain's and Ireland's sales tax—the "value added tax," or VAT (17.5 percent)—is built into the price of nearly everything you buy. Tourists can get this VAT refunded on souvenirs they take out of the country. But unless you buy something worth at least $100, your refund won't be worth the trouble. Before you make a substantial purchase of merchandise, ask the store clerk if you will be able to get a VAT refund. You'll likely get a "Tax-Free Shopping Cheque" which is redeemable for cash or credit-card credit at virtually any European airport before you fly home.

Banking

Throughout Britain and Ireland, cash machines are the way to go. Bring an ATM or debit card (with a 4-digit PIN) to withdraw funds from cash machines as you travel, and carry traveler's checks only as a backup.

Bring a credit card, handy for booking rooms and theater and transportation tickets over the phone—and necessary for renting a car. For cash advances you'll find that Barclays, National Westminster, and places displaying an Access or Eurocard sign accept MasterCard. Visa is accepted at Barclays and Midland banks. In general, Visa is far more widely accepted than American Express.

Traveler's checks work fine in Britain and Ireland, but banks commonly charge a commission fee of £2 to £4 or even more. While policies vary, some British banks favor various traveler's checks by waiving the commission: Barclays and Visa checks at Barclays banks, American Express checks at Lloyds banks, and Thomas Cook checks at Midland banks or Cook offices. American Express exchange offices don't charge a commission on their checks or any others. This can save you around 1.5 percent. But don't let this cloud your assessment of their exchange rates. Many people traveling exclusively in Great Britain buy traveler's checks in pounds sterling. Whether your checks are in pounds or dollars, save time and money by changing plenty of money at a time.

On my last trip I bought all my pounds in cash from a good

American foreign exchange service, stowed them safely in my money belt, and never needed a bank. Even in jolly olde England and friendly Ireland you should use a money belt (for our free newsletter/catalog, call 425/771-8303 or visit www.ricksteves.com). Thieves target tourists. A money belt provides peace of mind. You can carry lots of cash safely in a money belt—and, given the high bank fees, you should.

Bank holidays bring most businesses to a grinding halt on Christmas, December 26, New Year's Day, Good Friday, Easter Monday, the first and last Monday in May, and the last Monday in August.

Travel Smart

Upon arrival in a new town, lay the groundwork for a smooth departure. Reread this book as you travel and visit local tourist information offices. Buy a phone card and use it for reservations and confirmations. You speak the language—use it! Enjoy the friendliness of the local people. Ask questions. Most locals are eager to point you in their idea of the right direction. Bring along a pocket-size notebook to organize your thoughts. Those who expect to travel smart do. Plan ahead for banking, laundry, post office chores, and picnics. Mix intense and relaxed periods. Every trip (and every traveler) needs at least a few slack days. Pace yourself. Assume you will return.

As you read this book, make note of festivals, colorful market days, and days when sights are closed. Sundays have pros and cons, as they do for travelers in the United States (special events, limited hours, closed shops and banks, limited public transportation, no rush hours). Saturdays are virtually weekdays. Popular places are even more popular on weekends—especially sunny weekends, which are sufficient cause for an impromptu holiday in this soggy corner of Europe.

Consider making the travel arrangements and reservations listed below before your trip or within a few days of arrival.

Before You Go

- Reserve a room for your first night.
- If you'll be traveling in late June, July, or August and want to sleep in my lead listings, book your B&Bs (and the Ruthin Medieval Banquet) as soon as you're ready to commit to a date.
- Confirm car rental and pick-up plans with your rental agency (picking up a car on Saturday afternoon or Sunday may be difficult).
- If you'll be attending the Edinburgh Festival (Aug 12–Sept 1 in 2001), you can book tickets in advance (from mid-April on) by calling the festival office at 0131/473-2000 or ordering online (www.eif.co.uk). And while you're at it, book your Edinburgh room.
- If you want to attend the pageantry-filled Ceremony of the Keys

at the Tower of London, write for tickets (see details in the London chapter under "Sights—East London").

Within a Day or Two of Arrival

• If you'll be in London the last night of your trip, reserve a room and book tickets for a London play or concert. You can book a play from home (see details in the London chapter under "Entertainment and Theater in London"), but for simplicity, I book plays while in London.
• If the Royal Shakespeare Company will be performing at the Stratford Theater when you're in or near Stratford, consider booking a ticket (tel. 01789/295-623).

Tourist Information

Virtually every town in Britain has a helpful tourist information center (abbreviated "TI" in this book) eager to make your visit as smooth and enjoyable as possible. Take full advantage of this service. Arrive (or telephone) with a list of questions and a proposed sightseeing plan. Pick up maps, brochures, and walking-tour information. In London you can pick up everything you'll need for Britain in one stop at the Britain Visitors Centre.

The TIs in Ireland have lost their government funding and are now little more than sales outlets for the various hotels and gimmicky new attractions. They have little of value to give you except flyers printed by whoever wants your money. Avoid the room-finding service offered by TIs throughout Britain and Ireland (bloated prices, fees, no opinions, and they take a cut from your host).

Each country's national tourist office in the United States has a wealth of information. Before your trip request any information you may want (such as city maps and schedules of upcoming festivals).

British Tourist Authority (BTA): 551 Fifth Avenue, 7th floor, New York, NY 10176, tel. 800/462-2748, fax 212/986-1188, www.travelbritain.org. Meaty material, responsive to individual needs. Their free London and Britain maps are excellent (and the same maps are sold for £1.40 each at TIs in Britain).

Irish Tourist Board: 345 Park Avenue, 17th floor, New York, NY 10154, tel. 800/223-6470 or 212/418-0800, fax 212/371-9052, www.irelandvacations.com. For Ireland's Heritage sites (national monuments, parks, gardens, nature reserves), check www.heritageireland.ie.

Recommended Guidebooks

You may want some supplemental travel guidebooks, especially if you're traveling beyond my recommended destinations. I know it hurts to spend $25 or $35 on extra books and maps, but when you consider the money they'll save you and the improvements they'll make in your $3,000 vacation, not buying them would be penny-wise and pound-foolish.

While this book offers everything you'll need for the structure of your trip, each place you will visit has plenty of great little guidebooks to fill you in on local history. For cultural and sightseeing background in bigger chunks, Michelin and Cadogan guides to London, England, Britain, and Ireland are good. The best budget travel guides to Britain and Ireland are the Lonely Planet and Let's Go guidebooks. Lonely Planet's guidebook is more thorough and informative. Let's Go is youth oriented, with good coverage of nightlife, hosteling, and cheap transportation deals.

Rick Steves' Books and Videos

Rick Steves' Europe Through the Back Door 2001 gives you budget-travel skills, such as minimizing jet lag, packing light, planning your itinerary, traveling by car or train, finding beds without reservations, changing money, avoiding rip-offs, outsmarting thieves, hurdling the language barrier, staying healthy, taking great photographs, and much more. The book also includes chapters on 35 of my favorite "Back Doors," eight of which are in Great Britain and Ireland.

Rick Steves' Country Guides are a series of seven guidebooks—including this book—covering my favorite continent: Best of Europe; France/Belgium/Netherlands; Italy; Spain/Portugal; Scandinavia; and Germany/Austria/Switzerland. All are updated annually and come out in January.

My new **City Guides** cover London, Paris, and Rome. Updated annually (available in January), they offer in-depth coverage of the sights, hotels, restaurants, and nightlife in these grand cities, along with illustrated tours of their great museums.

Rick Steves' Europe 101: History and Art for the Traveler (co-written with Gene Openshaw, 2000) gives you the story of Europe's people, history, and art. Written for smart people who were sleeping in their history and art classes before they knew they were going to Europe, *101* helps Europe's sights come alive. However, this book focuses on the Continent, with just a chapter apiece for Britain and Ireland.

Rick Steves' Mona Winks (co-written with Gene Openshaw, 1998), provides fun, easy-to-follow, self-guided tours of Europe's top 20 museums. In London, *Mona* leads the way through the British Museum, British Library, National Gallery, Tate Britain, Westminster Abbey, and the historic Westminster neighborhood.

My PBS TV series, *Rick Steves' Europe*, airs in 2001 with 16 new shows; four are on Britain. Fifty-two episodes of my first series, *Travels in Europe with Rick Steves* (with 8 featuring Britain and Ireland) still air nationally on public television and the Travel Channel. These are also available in information-packed home videos, along with my two-hour slide-show lecture on Britain (for our free newsletter/catalog, call us at 425/771-8303 or visit www.ricksteves.com).

Rick Steves' Postcards from Europe (1999), my autobiographical book, packs more than 25 years of travel anecdotes and insights into the ultimate 3,000-mile European adventure. Through my guidebooks, I share my favorite European discoveries with you. *Postcards* introduces you to my favorite European friends.

All of my books are published by Avalon Travel Publishing (www.travelmatters.com).

Maps

The maps in this book, designed and drawn by Dave Hoerlein, are concise and simple. Dave, who is well traveled in Britain and Ireland, has designed the maps to help you locate recommended places and get to the tourist information office, where you'll find more in-depth, cheap (or free) maps of the city or region. For overall trip planning, consider my new Europe Planning Map, geared for the traveler, with sightseeing destinations featured prominently (tel. 425/771-8303, www.ricksteves.com).

Maps to buy in England: Train travelers can do fine with a simple rail map (such as the one that comes with your train pass) and city maps from TIs. (Get a free map of London and Britain from the BTA before you go; see "Tourist Information," above.) If you're driving, get a road atlas (1 inch equals 3 miles) covering all of Britain. Ordnance Survey, AA, and Bartholomew editions are available for about £7 in TIs, gas stations, and bookstores. Drivers, hikers, and bikers may want much more detailed maps for the Cotswolds, North Wales, and Lake District (easy to buy locally).

Tours of London, Britain, and Ireland

Travel agents can tell you about all the normal tours, but they won't tell you about ours. At Europe Through the Back Door (ETBD) we offer 20-day tours of Britain and 14-day tours of Ireland (departures April–Oct)—plus 7-day winter getaways to London—featuring the all-stars covered in this book (call us at 425/771-8303, www.ricksteves.com). And ETBD tour guides Roy and Jodi Nicholls lead a variety of their own tours in their spare time (call Roy and Jodi in England at 44/1749/812-873 or visit www.brittours.com).

Transportation in Britain and Ireland

By Car or Train?

Cars are best for three or more traveling together (especially families with small kids), those packing heavy, and those scouring the countryside. Trains and buses are best for solo travelers, blitz tourists, and city-to-city travelers.

Cost of Public Transportation

My free *Rick Steves' Guide to European Railpasses* has the latest on 2001 prices. To get the railpass guide, call us at 425/771-8303 or visit www.ricksteves.com/rail (you can order most passes online).

BRITRAIL CLASSIC PASS (2000)

	Adult first class	Adult standard	Senior (60+) first class	16-25 youth standard
8 consecutive days	$ 400	$ 265	$ 340	$ 215
15 consecutive days	600	400	510	280
22 consecutive days	760	505	645	355
1 month	900	600	765	420

"Standard" is the polite British term for "second" class. No senior discounts for standard class. For each adult pass you buy, one child (5-15) gets a free pass of the same type (ask for the "Family Pass"). Additional kids pay the normal half-adult rate. Kids under 5: free. These rules also apply to the Flexipasses listed below.

BRITRAIL FLEXIPASS (2000)

	Adult first class	Adult standard	Senior (60+) first class	16-25 youth standard
4 days in 2 months	$ 350	$ 235	$ 300	$ 185
8 days in 2 months	510	340	435	240
15 days in 2 months	770	515	655	360

BRITRAIL PASS 'N DRIVE (2000)

Any 3 rail days and 2 car days in 2 months.

	1st class	2nd class	extra car day
Mini car	$299	$219	$56
Compact car	319	235	75
Intermediate car	329	249	89

Prices are approximate per person for 2 traveling together. 3rd and 4th person sharing car pay $244 in 1st or $164 in 2nd class. Senior, child, and single adult rates also available. To order Britrail Pass 'N Drive, call your travel agent or Rail Europe at 800/438-7245.

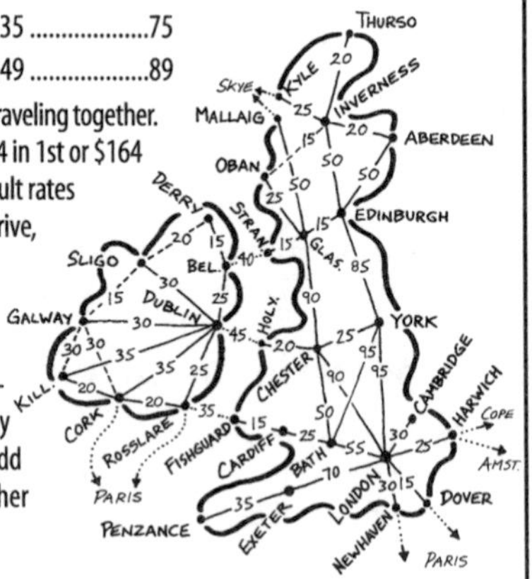

Britain & Ireland:

The map shows approximate point-to-point one-way 2nd-class fares in $US by rail (solid line) and bus (dashed line). Add up fares for your itinerary to see whether a railpass will save you money.

BritRail Routes

Britain has a great train-and-bus system, and travelers who don't want (or can't afford) to drive a rental car can enjoy an excellent tour using public transportation. Britain's 100-mph train system is one of Europe's best. Buses pick you up when the trains let you down.

In Britain, my choice is to connect big cities by train and to explore rural areas (the Cotswolds, North Wales, Lake District, and the Highlands) footloose and fancy-free by rental car. You might consider a BritRail Plus Car pass, which gives you various combinations of rail days and car days to use within a month's time. For a short swing through Ireland, it's easy to take trains and buses, buying tickets as you go.

Deals on Rails, Wheels, and Wings in Britain

Regular tickets on Britain's great train system (15,000 departures from 2,400 stations daily) are the most expensive per mile in all of Europe. Those who go round-trip (leaving after 9:30 in the morning), buy in advance, or ride the bus save big.

Buying Train Tickets in Advance: Either go direct to any station or call and book your ticket with a credit card. To book ahead, call 08457/484-950 (from the States call 011/44/8457-484-950) to find out the schedule and best fare for your journey; then you'll be referred to the appropriate number to call—depending on the particular rail company—to book your ticket (or book online; see below). Here are a few of the many deals. **Bargain Return** fares offer the greatest savings but must be booked at least seven days in advance and usually apply to journeys of about 250 miles (i.e., London–Edinburgh) or longer, but sometimes shorter journeys qualify—ask. Note that a Bargain Return is a round-trip ticket, but you can use it only one-way if you want. **Apex** fares, which must be booked at least seven days in advance, apply to journeys of about 100 miles (i.e., London–York) or longer. (You can book Apex and Bargain Return tickets as early as six to eight weeks before your journey; be warned that cheap fares go fast in summer, tickets have refund restrictions, and you'll need to pin down dates and times—for schedules, visit http://bahn.hafas.de/english.html or www.railtrack.co.uk). To save a few pounds, get a **Super Advance** ticket (for any journey on any day) by buying your ticket before 18:00 the day prior to your journey. To save a little less, purchase a **Super Saver** ticket the day you want to travel, leave after 9:30, and avoid traveling on Friday or summer Saturdays. There can be up to 30 different prices for the same journey. A clerk at any station (or the helpful folks at tel. 08457-484-950, 24 hours daily) can figure out the cheapest fare for your trip. Savings can be significant. For a London–Edinburgh round-trip (standard class), the regular fare is £77, Super Saver is £69, Super Advance is £63, Apex is £49, and Bargain Return is £36. For a York–London round-trip, the regular fare is

Sample Train Journey

Here is a typical example of a personalized train schedule printed out by Britain's train stations. At the Llandudno Junction station in North Wales, I told the clerk I wanted to leave after 16:30 for Moreton-in-Marsh, in the Cotswolds.

Stations	Arrive	Depart	Accom.
Llandudno Junction	——	16:41	Standard
Crewe	17:56	18:11	Standard
Smethwick	19:20	19:33	Standard
Worcester	20:20	20:58	1st/Std
Moreton-in-Marsh	21:37	——	

Even though the trip involved three transfers, this schedule allowed me to easily navigate the rails. It's helpful to ask at the info desk (or any conductor) for the final destination of your next train so you'll be able to quickly figure out the platform it's departing from (e.g., upon arrival at Worcester, look for "Oxford" on the station's overhead train schedule to determine where to catch your train to Moreton-in-Marsh; often the conductor on your previous train can even tell you the platform your next train will depart from, but it's wise to confirm). Note that on the smaller runs, only standard (second) class is available. If you're exploring Britain's backcountry with a Britrail pass, buy standard class—because that's how you'll travel.

£62, Super Saver is £53, Super Advance is £46, Apex is £36, and Bargain Return is £29.

You can book rail tickets online at www.thetrainline.com. Before ordering online, be sure you know what you want (it's tough to reach a person in case you want to change a ticket later). Note that you must pick up your ticket at the station; it's not mailed to you. Finally, Britrail passholders cannot use this site to make reservations.

Railpasses: Consider getting a railpass. The BritRail pass comes in "consecutive day" and "flexi" versions, with price breaks for youths, seniors, and second class ("standard" class, available to anyone). Standard class is a good choice since many of the smaller train lines don't even offer first-class cars. BritRail passes cover England, Scotland, and Wales. There are now Scotland passes, England/Ireland passes, southeast Britain passes, and BritRail Plus Car passes, which allow you to take a day of rail here and a day of Hertz car rental there. Any Brit pass or Eurailpass gives a discount on the Eurostar train that zips you to continental Europe under the English Channel. These passes are sold outside of Europe

Public Transportation in Ireland

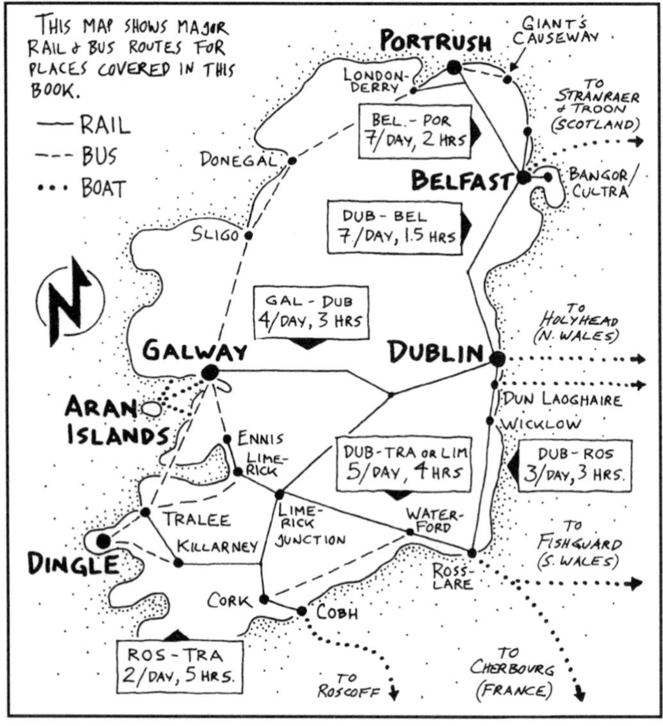

only. For specifics, contact your travel agent or Europe Through the Back Door (tel. 425/771-8303).

Senior, Youth, and Family Deals: To get a third off the price of most point-to-point rail tickets, seniors (aged 60 and over) can buy a Senior Railcard (www.senior-railcard.co.uk), and young people (aged 16–25, or full-time students 26 and over with a valid ISIC card) can buy a Young Persons Railcard. Each card costs £18. A Family Railcard (£20) allows adults to travel cheaper (about 20–33 percent) while their kids age 5 to 15 pay just £2 apiece for most trips. Any of these cards are valid for a year on virtually all trains except special runs like the Heathrow Express and Eurostar (fill out application at station, brochures on racks in info center, need to show passport). Youth also need to submit a passport-type photo for the Young Persons Card and have to pay a minimal fare for journeys starting before 10:00 on weekdays. Family cards are not valid on some busy commuter trains on weekday mornings during peak times.

Buses: Although buses are about 33 percent slower than trains, they're also a lot cheaper. Round-trip bus tickets usually cost less than two one-way fares (e.g., London–York one-way costs £17; round-trip costs £26). And buses go many places that trains don't. Budget travelers can save a wad with a bus pass. The National Express sells Tourist Trail bus passes (over the counter, tel. 08705-808-080, www.nationalexpress.co.uk); passes cost £49 (any 2 days out of 3 consecutive days), £85 (any 5 days within 10), £120 (any 7 days within 21), and £187 (any 14 days within 30). If you want to bus from your last destination to Heathrow, ask about the many National Express Flight Link buses. In Britain, bus stations are normally at or near train stations (in London, the bus station is a block southwest of Victoria Station). The British distinguish between "buses" (for local runs with lots of stops) and "coaches" (long-distance express runs).

A couple of companies offer **backpacker's bus circuits.** These hop-on hop-off bus circuits take mostly youth hostelers around the country super cheap and easy with the assumption that they'll be sleeping in the hostels along the way. For instance, **Stray Travel** network does a six-day-or-more "tour," making a 1,600-kilometer circle connecting London, Bath, Stratford, the lakes, Edinburgh, York, Cambridge, and London hostels (£129 for 6 days, 3 buses weekly, commentary from driver, also offers loop trips of Ireland—6 days by bus—and of Europe—20 days by train, tel. 020/7373-7737, www.straytravel.com). **Haggis Backpacker** offers a similar deal, with buses circling Scotland (£85, 1,000 km: Edinburgh, Oban, Glencoe, Fort William, Skye, Inverness, Edinburgh; buses run daily in summer, otherwise 4–6 buses weekly, ticket good for 3 months, tel. 0131/557-9393, www.radicaltravel.com).

Flights: If you've got more money than time, don't buy a ticket for a long train trip without considering a flight offered by one of the discount airlines. British Midland, which has been around the longest, offers reasonable flights such as Heathrow–Dublin (8/day, 75 min, about £128 one-way, as little as £99 round-trip with a stay over Sat) and Heathrow–Edinburgh (8/day, 75 min, as little as £70 round-trip with a stay over Sat). BM also offers decent fares to Paris (£139 one-way, £78 round-trip with a stay over Sat), Brussels (£85/£143), and Amsterdam (£91/£130). To get the lowest fares, book months in advance and go round-trip, leaving and returning on a weekday (Mon–Thu), and staying over a Saturday. For reservations and information, call 0870-607-0555. The U.S. office of British Midland sells Discover Europe air passes: flights out of London that are less than 500 miles—say, to Paris or Amsterdam—cost $109 plus tax; flights over 500 miles cost $159 plus tax (tel. 800/788-0555). For more information, visit www.britishmidland.com).

Other cut-rate airlines include Ryanair (Irish tel. 01/609-7800, British tel. 0870-333-1231, www.ryanair.com), Virgin Express (British tel. 020/7744-0004, www.virgin-express.com), and Easy Jet (British tel. 0870-600-0000, www.easyjet.com). Also consider www.cheapflights.co.uk. Returns can be cheaper than one-way—ask. To get the best prices, book far in advance, as soon as you have a date set. Each flight has an allotment of cheap seats; these sell fast, leaving the higher-priced seats for latecomers.

Transportation within Ireland

Ireland's train system matches its sparse population. Trains work like spokes, connecting Dublin with each corner of the country (Rosslare in the southeast, Cork in the south, Limerick and Tralee in the southeast, Galway in the west, and Belfast in the north). Between the bus and train systems you can get around the Emerald Isle quite handily. Departures are not as frequent as the European norm. The Bus Eireann Expressway Bus Timetable comes in handy (free, available at some bus stations, www.buseirann.ie). On many Irish buses, pop music or sports games are piped throughout the bus; have earplugs handy if you prefer silence.

Students can use their ISIC (student card) to get discounts on rail tickets (up to 50 percent), but only if they first purchase a "Travel Save" stamp (for about £15) at any major railway station in Ireland.

Ireland's various passes offer a better value than Britrail's pricey "Britrail plus Ireland" (e.g., any 5 days in 30—$396 second-class—2000 price includes round-trip ferry crossing between the countries). Irish passes can be purchased easily and cheapest in Ireland at major stations (Dublin info tel. 01/836-6111, London office on Bond Street at tel. 020/7493-3201).

Rail only: "Irish Explorer Rail Only" passes cover the Republic—any 5 days in 15 (£67). "Irish Rover Rail Only" passes cover all of Ireland—any 5 days in 15 (£83). Note that if you're traveling up or down Ireland's west coast, buses are best (or a combination of buses and trains); relying on "rail only" here is too time-consuming.

Bus only: "Irish Rambler Bus Only" passes cover the Republic—3 days in 8 (£30), 8 days in 15 (£70), and 15 days in 30 (£100). "Irish Rover Bus Only" passes cover all of Ireland—3 days in 8 (£40), 8 days in 15 (£90), and 15 days in 30 (£140).

Rail and bus: "Irish Explorer Rail/Bus" passes cover the Republic—8 days in 15 (£100). "Emerald Card Bus/Rail" passes cover all of Ireland—8 days in 15 (£115) and 15 days in 30 (£200).

Car Rental

Car rental for this tour is cheapest if arranged in advance through your hometown travel agent. The best rates are weekly with unlimited mileage or leasing (possible for rentals of over three weeks). You can pick up and drop off just about anywhere, anytime. For a trip covering both Britain and Ireland you're better off with two separate car rentals. If you pick up the car in a smaller city, such as Bath, you'll more likely survive your first day on the British roads. If you drop it off early or keep it longer, you'll be credited or charged at a fair, prorated price. Big companies have offices in most cities. (Ask to be picked up at your hotel.) Small local rental companies can be cheaper but aren't as flexible.

The Ford 1.3-liter Escort-category car costs about $50 per week more than the smallest cars but feels better on the motorways and safer on the small roads. Remember, minibuses are a great budget way to go for five to nine people.

For peace of mind, spring for the CDW insurance (Collision Damage Waiver, about $15 per day), which gives a zero (or low) deductible rather than the standard value-of-the-car "deductible." A few "gold" credit cards cover CDW insurance; quiz your credit-card company on the worst-case scenario.

Driving

Your U.S. license is all you need to drive in Britain and Ireland. Set your car up for a fun road trip. Establish a cardboard-box munchies pantry. Buy a rack of liter boxes of juice for the trunk. Buy some Windex and a roll of paper towels for cleaner sightseeing.

Britain: Driving in Britain is basically wonderful—once you remember to stay on the left and after you've mastered the "roundabouts." But be warned: Every year I get a few cards from traveling readers advising me that, for them, trying to drive Britain was a nerve-racking and regrettable mistake. If you want to get a little slack on the roads, drop by a gas station or auto shop and buy a green "L" (new driver with license) sign to put in your window (don't get the red "L" sign, which means you're a student driver without a license, prohibited from driving on motorways).

A British Automobile Association membership comes with most rentals. Understand its towing and emergency road service benefits. Gas (petrol) costs over $4 per gallon and is self-serve. Green pumps are unleaded. Seat belts are required by law. Speed limits are 30 mph in town, 70 mph on the motorways, and 50 or 60 mph elsewhere. The national sign for 60 mph is a white circle with a black slash. Note that road-surveillance cameras strictly enforce speed limits. Any driver (including foreigners renting cars) photographed speeding will get a nasty bill in the mail. (Cameras—you'll see the foreboding gray boxes—flash on your rear license plate in order not to invade the privacy of anyone sharing the front seat with someone who they shouldn't be with.) Avoid driving in big cities whenever possible. Most have modern ring roads to skirt the congestion. The shortest distance between

Standard European Road Signs

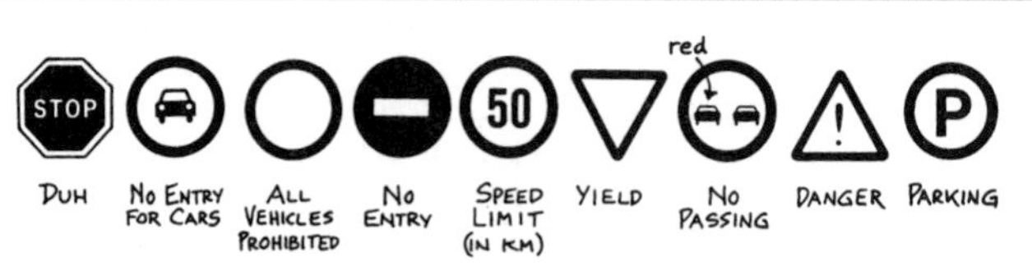

any two points is usually the motorway. Road signs can be confusing, too little, and too late. Study your map before taking off. Know the cities you'll be lacing together since road numbers are inconsistent. Miss a motorway exit and you can lose 30 minutes. A Britain road atlas (sold at gas stations and bookstores) is $10 well spent.

Parking is confusing. One yellow line marked on the pavement means no parking Monday through Saturday during work hours. Double yellow lines mean no parking at any time. Broken yellow lines mean short stops are OK, but you should always look for explicit signs or ask a passerby. White lines are good news.

Even in small towns, rather than fight it, I just pull into the most central and handy "pay and display" car park I can find. Rates are reasonable by U.S. standards. Locals love to share "pay and display" stickers. If you stand by the machine, invariably someone on their way out with time left on their sticker will give it to you. I keep a bag of 10p and 20p coins in the ashtray for parking meters.

Ireland: In Ireland you'll be dealing with the same left-hand drives and roundabouts. Traffic and parking are rarely a problem. Ireland's roads, while getting much better with the financial help of the European Union, are still among the worst in Europe. There simply aren't enough people to justify big, slick roads. Except for rush hour in the big cities, traffic is wonderfully sparse. But roads are so narrow that every passing car or truck comes with a slight adrenaline rush. Take things slowly. If you rush, you'll wear yourself out, hit a pothole, and blow a tire—or worse. In Ireland, a single yellow line means parking is regulated (look for a street sign explaining the hours or limits on that street). A double yellow line means parking is not permitted at any time. Some towns require a disk, which you can buy at the TI or newsstands. Parking lots are cheap and central. While theft is rare in Ireland, tourists' cars are likely targets. Don't tempt thieves needlessly.

Telephones, Mail, and E-mail

Use the telephone routinely. You can make long-distance calls directly, cheaply, and easily, and there's no language barrier. Call ahead to reserve or reconfirm rooms, check opening hours, confirm tour times, and reserve theater tickets.

To call long distance you'll need the correct area code. Britain and Ireland have about as many area codes as we do. For long distance you'll find area codes listed throughout this book, or you can get them from directory assistance (free and happy to help, dial 192 in Britain, 11811 in Ireland). Phone numbers and area codes rarely have a standard number of digits. For information on telephoning throughout Europe, see the appendix.

The British and Irish telephone systems are great. Easy-to-find public phone booths are either coin- or card-operated. Phones clearly list which coins they'll take (usually from 10p to £1), and a display shows how your money supply's doing. Only completely unused coins will be returned, so put in biggies with caution. (If money's left over, rather than hanging up, push the "make another call" button.) The more convenient phone-card booths are common only in cities. You can purchase phone cards for £3, £10, or £20 at newsstands, hotels, tourist offices, and post offices; insert the card into the phone and dial away. (Some "credit-card phones" have a slot that will take—but not accept—a British or Irish phone card.)

In Britain and Ireland, insertable phone cards are getting a lot of competition from the new, cheaper-per-minute PIN cards. These PIN cards, which have a scratch-off Personal Identification Number, allow you to call home at the rate of about five minutes per dollar. The main difference is that an insertable British (BT) or Irish phone card can only be used at a phone-card booth. PIN cards, which are not inserted into a phone, allow you to dial from virtually any phone, even from your hotel room. To use a PIN card, dial the toll-free access number listed on card; then, at the prompt, enter your Personal Identification Number (also listed on card), dial the number you want to call (for calls to the U.S., dial 00-1-area code-local number; for calls within Britain or Ireland, dial area code-local number; when using a PIN card, the area code must be dialed even if you're calling across the street). There are many different brands of PIN cards; simply ask for an "international calling card" (sold for £3, £5, £10, and £20 at most newsstands, exchange bureaus, and mini-marts). Because PIN cards occasionally malfunction, avoid the high denominations. To make numerous calls with a PIN card without having to redial the long access number each time, press the keys (see instructions on card) that allow you to launch directly into your next call. PIN cards work only within the country of purchase, with the exception of some of the Spirit brand cards, usable in both Britain and Ireland (confirm before purchase).

The only tricky British phones you'll use are the expensive Mickey Mouse coin-op ones in bars and B&Bs. Some require money before you dial, while others wait until after you've connected. Many have a button you must push before you begin talking. But all have clear instructions. Long distance in Britain and Ireland is most expensive from 8:00 to 13:00 and cheapest from 17:00 to 8:00. A short call is quite inexpensive; don't hesitate to call long distance. Remember that Northern Ireland is part of Britain and just a long-distance call away (simply dial the area code and local number).

Direct Dialing: When calling long distance within either Britain or Ireland, first dial the area code (which starts with zero), then the local number. When dialing internationally, dial the international access code of the country you're calling from (00 for Britain and Ireland, 011 for the U.S.), the country code of the country you're calling, the area code (without its initial zero if you're calling Britain or Ireland), and the local number. For example, London's area code is 020. To call one of my listed London B&Bs from New York, I dial 011 (U.S. international access code), 44 (Britain's country code), 20 (London's area code without its initial zero), then 7730-8191 (the B&B's number). To call it from Britain's old York, dial 020/7730-8191.

To call my office from Britain, I dial 00 (Britain's international access code), 1 (U.S. country code), 425 (Edmonds' area code), then 771-8303. For a listing of international access codes and country codes, see the Appendix.

USA Direct Services (with an AT&T, MCI, or Sprint calling card) are popular for calling the United States from any kind of phone. While these used to be a fine deal, direct-dial rates have since been cut in half, and now you can more cheaply call home using the new PIN cards, coins, or British or Irish phone cards. For a list of calling-card operators, see the appendix. It's a rip-off to use USA Direct for making calls between European countries—instead, call direct.

Mail: Get stamps at the neighborhood post office or at newsstands within fancy hotels (and, only in Britain, at some minimarts and card shops). To arrange for mail delivery, reserve a few hotels along your route in advance and give their addresses to friends or use American Express mail services (available to anyone who has at least one AmEx traveler's check). Allow 10 days for a letter to arrive. Phoning is so easy that I've dispensed with mail stops altogether.

E-mail: E-mail is getting more common among hoteliers. I've listed e-mail addresses where possible. Cybercafés, popular in the bigger cities, are now popping up in smaller towns.

Sleeping

In the interest of smart use of your time, I favor accommodations (and restaurants) handy to your sightseeing activities. Rather than list hotels scattered throughout a city, I choose two or three

Sleep Code

To give maximum information with a minimum of space, I use this code to describe accommodations listed in this book. *Prices in this book are listed per room, not per person.* Breakfast is included.

- **S** = Single room, or price for one person in a double.
- **D** = Double or twin room. (I specify double- and twin-bed rooms only if they are priced differently, or if a place has only one or the other. When reserving, you should specify.)
- **T** = Three-person room (often a double bed with a single).
- **Q** = Four-person room (adding an extra child's bed to a T is usually cheaper).
- **b** = Private bathroom with toilet and shower or tub.
- **t** = Private toilet only. (The shower is down the hall.)
- **s** = Private shower or tub only. (The toilet is down the hall.)
- **CC** = Accepts credit cards (**V** = Visa, **M** = MasterCard, **A** = American Express). If CC isn't mentioned, assume you'll need to pay cash.

No smoking—With this edition, about 80 percent of my recommended B&Bs are smoke free. While some places allow smoking in the sleeping rooms, breakfast rooms are nearly always smoke free.

Family deal—Indicates that parents with young children can easily get a room with an extra child's bed or a discount for larger rooms. Call to negotiate the price. Teenage kids are generally charged as adults. Little kids sleep almost free.

According to this code, a couple staying at a "Db-£55, CC:VM" hotel would pay a total of £55 (about $88) per night for a room with a private toilet and shower (or tub). The hotel accepts Visa, MasterCard, or cash.

favorite neighborhoods and recommend the best accommodations values in each, from $15 bunk beds to fancy-for-my-book $200 doubles. Outside of London you can expect to find good doubles for $60 to $100, including full-cooked breakfasts and tax.

I've described my recommended hotels and B&Bs with a standard code. Prices listed are for one-night stays in peak season, include a hearty breakfast (unless otherwise noted), and assume you're going direct and not through a TI. Prices can soften off-season, for stays of two nights or longer, or for payment in cash (rather than credit card). Particularly at nicer hotels in Britain and Ireland, ask about deals (usually offered for 2-night stays, sometimes midweek or weekends, often called Leisure Breaks in Britain); the room price doesn't drop dramatically, but the pricey breakfasts are usually included.

When establishing prices with a hotelier or B&B owner, confirm if the charge is per person or per room (if a price is too good to be true, it's probably per person). Because many places in Britain charge per person, small groups often pay the same for a single and a double as they would for a triple. Note: In this book, room prices are listed per room, not per person.

Most places have three floors of rooms, steep stairs, and no elevator. If you're concerned about stairs, call and ask about ground-floor rooms.

In Britain and Ireland, virtually all rooms have sinks. Rooms with a private bathroom (toilet plus shower and/or tub) are called "en suite"; rooms that lack private plumbing are "standard." As more rooms go en suite, the hallway bathroom is shared with fewer standard rooms. If money's tight, ask for standard rooms.

Both Britain and Ireland have rating systems for hotels and B&Bs. These diamonds, stars, and shamrocks are supposed to imply quality, but I find that they mean only that the place sporting symbols is paying dues to the tourist board. Rating systems often have little to do with value.

Bed-and-Breakfasts (B&Bs)

Compared to hotels, bed-and-breakfast places give you double the cultural intimacy for half the price. In 2001, you'll pay £20 to £35 ($32–56) per person for a B&B in Britain or Ireland. Prices include a big cooked breakfast. How much coziness, teddies, tea, and biscuits are tossed in varies tremendously.

If you have a reasonable but limited budget, skip hotels. Go the B&B way. If you can use a telephone and speak English, you'll enjoy homey, friendly, clean rooms at a great price by sticking to my listings. Always call first.

If you're traveling beyond my recommended destinations, you'll find B&Bs where you need them. Any town with tourists has a TI that books rooms or can give you a list and point you in the right direction. In the absence of a TI, ask people on the street for help.

"Twin" means two single beds, and "double" means one double bed. If you'll take either one, let them know or you might be needlessly turned away. "Standard" rooms come with just a sink (many better places have standard rooms that they don't even advertise). If you want a room that contains a private bathroom, specify "en suite"; B&B owners sometimes use the term "private bathroom" for a bathroom down the hall that only your room has the key for.

B&Bs range from large guest houses with 15 to 20 rooms to small homes renting out a spare bedroom. The philosophy of the management determines the character of a place more than its size and facilities offered. Avoid places run as a business by absentee owners. My top listings are run by couples who enjoy welcoming the world to their breakfast table.

The B&Bs I've recommended are nearly all stocking-feet comfortable and "homely," as they say in England. I look for a place that is friendly (i.e., enjoys Americans); located in a central, safe, quiet neighborhood; clean, with firm beds; a good value; not mentioned in other guidebooks (and therefore filled mostly by English or Irish travelers); and willing to hold a room until 16:00 or so without a deposit (though more and more places are requiring a deposit or credit-card number). In certain cases my recommendations don't meet all of these prerequisites. I'm more impressed by a handy location and a fun-loving philosophy than hair driers and shoe-shine machines.

A few tips: B&B proprietors are selective as to whom they invite in for the night. Risky-looking people (2 or more single men are often assumed to be troublemakers) find many places suddenly full. If you'll be staying for more than one night you are a "desirable." Sometimes staying several nights earns you a better price—ask about it. If you book through a TI, it takes a 10 percent commission. If you book direct, the B&B gets it all (and you'll have a better chance of getting a discount). I have negotiated special prices with this book (often for cash). You should find prices quoted here good through 2001 (except for major holidays and festivals). In popular weekend getaway spots you're unlikely to find a place to take you for Saturday night only. If my listings are full, ask for guidance. (Mentioning this book can help.) Owners usually work together and can call up an ally to land you a bed.

B&Bs are not hotels; if you want to ruin your relationship with your hostess, treat her like a hotel clerk. Americans often assume they'll get new towels each day. The British and Irish don't, and neither will you. Hang them up to dry and reuse. Electrical outlets sometimes come with switches on the outlet to turn the current on or off; if your electrical appliance isn't working, flip the switch. Some B&Bs stock rooms with a hot-water pot, cups, tea bags, and coffee packets (if you prefer decaf, buy a jar at a grocery, and dump into a baggie for easy packing). B&Bs have plenty of stairs. Expect good exercise and be happy you packed light.

In B&Bs, showers are like snowflakes; no two are alike. Sometimes you'll encounter "telephone" showers—a hand-held nozzle in a bathtub. Many B&Bs have been retrofitted with plumbing, and water is heated individually for each shower rather than by one central heating system. While the switch is generally left on, in some rooms you'll have a hot-water switch to consider. Any cord hanging from the ceiling is for lights (not emergencies). Once in the shower you'll find a multitude of overly clever mechanisms designed to somehow get the right amount and temperature of water. Good luck.

Cheap Modern Hotels

Hotel chains, offering predictably comfortable accommodations at reasonable prices, are popping up in the center of big cities in Britain and Ireland.

In Britain, the biggies are Travelodge (central reservations tel. 0870-905-6343, also has freeway locations for tired drivers, www.travelodge.co.uk), Travel Inn (reservations tel. 0870-242-8000, www.travelinn.co.uk), and Premier Lodge (their older ones are a little scruffy but OK, reservations tel. 0870-201-0203, www.premierlodge.com). In Ireland, it's Jurys Inn, which also has some hotels in Britain (reserve at Irish tel. 01/607-0000, call their hotels directly, or book online at www.jurys.com).

These superconvenient hotels offer simple, clean, and modern rooms for up to four people (2 adults/2 children) for £50 to £90, depending on the location. Most rooms have a double bed, single bed, five-foot trundle bed, private shower, WC, and TV. Hotels usually have an attached restaurant, good security, and a 24-hour staffed reception desk. Of course they are as cozy as a Motel 6, but they're great for families, and many travelers love them. You can book over the phone (or online) with a credit card, then pay when you check in. When you check out, just drop off the key, Lee.

Couples could also consider Holiday Inn Express, spreading throughout Britain. These are like a Holiday Inn Lite, with cheaper prices and no restaurant (Db-about £60–70, maximum 2 per room, reservations tel. 0800-897-121, make sure Express is part of name or you'll pay more for a regular Holiday Inn, www.holiday-inn.com).

Making Reservations

It's possible to travel at any time of year without reservations, but given the high stakes, erratic accommodations values, number of people traveling with this book, and the quality of the gems I've listed, I highly recommend calling ahead for rooms at least a few days in advance as you travel. When tourist crowds are down, you might make a habit of calling your hotel between 9:00 and 10:00 on the day you plan to arrive, when the hotel knows who'll be checking out and just which rooms will be available. I've taken great pains to list telephone numbers with long-distance instructions (see "Telephones, Mail, and E-mail" above; also see the appendix). Get a phone card and use it to confirm and reconfirm as you travel. A hotel receptionist will trust you and hold a room until 16:00 without a deposit, though some will ask for a credit-card number.

Honor your reservations or cancel by phone: Trusting travelers to show up is a huge, stressful issue and a financial risk for small B&B owners. I promised the owners of the places I list that you will be reliable when you make a telephone reservation; please don't let them (or me) down. If you'll be delayed or won't make it, simply call in. Americans are notorious for reserving B&Bs long in advance and never showing up (causing B&B owners to lose money—and respect for Americans). Being late is no problem if you are in telephone contact. Long distance is cheap and easy from public phone booths. While it's generally easy to find a room, a few national holidays jam things up (especially "bank holiday" Mondays) and merit reservations long in advance. Mark these dates in red on your travel calendar: Good Friday, Easter plus Easter Monday, the first and last Monday in May, the last Monday in August, Christmas, December 26, and New Year's Day. Monday bank holidays are preceded by busy weekends; book the entire weekend in advance.

If you know exactly which dates you need and really want a particular place, reserve a room before you leave home. To reserve from home, call, fax, e-mail, or write the hotel. To fax or e-mail, use the form in the Appendix (online at www.ricksteves.com/reservation). If you're writing, add the postal code and confirm the need and method for a deposit. A two-night stay in August would be "two nights, 16/8/01 to 18/8/01"—Europeans write the date day/month/year, and hotel jargon uses your day of departure. You'll often receive a letter back requesting one night's deposit. Your credit-card number and expiration date will usually be accepted as a deposit, though you may need to send a signed traveler's check or a bank draft in the local currency. If your credit card is the deposit, you can pay with your card or cash when you arrive; if you don't show up, you'll be billed for one night. Reconfirm your reservations a day in advance for safety (or you may be bumped—really). Also, don't just assume you can extend. Take the time to consider in advance how long you'll stay.

Hostels

Britain and Ireland have more than 400 hostels of all shapes and sizes. They can be historic castles or depressing huts, serene and comfy or overrun by noisy children. Unfortunately, many of the international youth hostels have become overpriced, and, in general, I no longer recommend them. The only time I do is if you're on a very tight budget, want to cook your own meals, or are traveling with a group that likes to sleep on bunk beds in big rooms. The informal private hostels are often more fun, easygoing, and cheaper. These alternatives to the International Youth Hostel Federation (IYHF) hostels are more common than ever. If you're traveling alone, hosteling is the best way to conquer hotel loneliness.

Hostels are also a tremendous source of local and budget travel information. If you hostel selectively, you'll enjoy historical and interesting buildings.

You'll pay an average of £10 for a bed, £1 for sheets, and £2 for breakfast. Anyone of any age can hostel in Britain and Ireland. While there are no membership concerns for private hostels, IYHF hostels require membership. Those without cards simply buy one-night guest memberships for £1.50. You can book online for many hostels (London: www.hostellondon.com, England and Wales: www.yha.org.uk, and Ireland: www.hostelireland.com).

Eating

I don't mind English food. But then, I liked dorm food. True, England isn't famous for its cuisine and probably never will be, but we tourists have to eat. If there's any good place to cut corners to stretch your budget in Britain and Ireland, it's in eating. Here are a few tips on budget eating.

In Britain and Ireland, the traditional "fry" is famous as a hearty way to start the day. Also known as a "heart attack on a plate," the breakfast is especially feasty if you've just come from the land of the skimpy continental breakfast across the Channel. Your standard fry gets off to a healthy start with juice and cereal or porridge. (Try Weetabix, a soggy English cousin of shredded wheat. Scotland serves great porridge.) Next, with tea or coffee, you get a heated plate with a fried egg, lean Canadian-style bacon, a bad sausage, a grilled tomato, and often a slice of delightfully greasy pan toast and sautéed mushrooms. Toast comes on a rack (to cool quickly and crisply) with butter and marmalade. Order kippers (herring filets smoked in an oak fire). This meal tides many travelers over until dinner. Order only what you'll eat. A B&B hostess, your temporary local mother, doesn't like to see food wasted. And there's nothing wrong with skipping the "fry"—few locals actually start their day with this heavy traditional breakfast.

These days, the best coffee is served in a *cafetiére* (also called a French press). When your coffee has steeped as long as you like, plunge down the filter and pour. To revitalize your brew, pump the plunger again.

Many B&Bs don't serve breakfast until 8:00. If you need an early start, ask politely if it's possible. While they may not make you a cooked breakfast, they can usually put out cereal, toast, juice, and coffee.

Picnicking saves time and money. Try boxes of orange juice (pure, by the liter), fresh bread (especially Irish soda bread), tasty English cheese, meat, a tube of Colman's English mustard, local eatin' apples, bananas, small tomatoes, a small tub of yogurt (they're drinkable), rice crackers, gorp or nuts, plain "Digestive Biscuits" (the chocolate-covered ones melt), and any local specialties.

At open-air markets and supermarkets you can get produce in small quantities (3 tomatoes and 2 bananas cost me 50p). Supermarkets often have good deli sections (even offering Indian dishes in Britain) and sometimes salad bars. Decent, packaged sandwiches (£2–3) are sold everywhere. I often munch a relaxed "meal on wheels" in a car, train, or bus to save 30 precious minutes for sightseeing.

Ireland's restaurants are plentiful, and compared to Britain, cheap. In both Britain and Ireland, look for "early bird specials" at the classier places, allowing you to eat well and affordably, but early (around 17:30–19:00, last order by 19:00). In Britain, where restaurants can be pricey, cheap alternatives abound: fish-and-chips joints, Chinese and Indian take-outs, cafeterias, pubs (see below), and your typical good old greasy-spoon cafés. At a sit-down place with table service (in either Britain or Ireland), tip around 10 percent—unless the service charge is already listed on the bill.

For fresh, fast, and cheap lunches in Britain, bakeries have meat pies (and microwaves), pastries, yogurt, and cartons of "semiskimmed" milk. Pasties (PASTE-eez) are "savory" (not sweet) meat pies that originated in the mining country. They had big crust handles so miners with filthy hands could eat them and toss the crust. For easy lunches in Ireland, try a small café, tea room, pub, or bakery.

In Britain, people of leisure punctuate their afternoon with a "cream tea" at a tea room. You'll get a pot of tea, two homemade scones, jam, and thick, creamy-as-honey clotted cream. For maximum pinkie-waving taste per calorie, slice your scone thin like a miniature loaf of bread. Tea rooms, which often serve appealing light meals, are usually open for lunch and close around 17:00, just before dinner.

Pub Grub and Beer

Pubs are a basic part of the British and Irish social scene, and whether you're a teetotaler or a beer guzzler they should be a part of your travel here. Pub is short for "public house." It's an extended living room where, if you don't mind the stickiness, you can feel the pulse of Britain and Ireland. Most traditional atmospheric pubs are in the countryside and smaller towns. Unfortunately, many city pubs have been afflicted with an excess of brass, ferns, and video games. In any case, smart travelers use the pubs to eat, drink, get out of the rain, watch the latest sporting event, and make new friends.

Pub grub gets better each year. It's Britain's and Ireland's best eating value. For £5 you'll get a basic budget hot lunch or dinner in friendly surroundings. The *Good Pub Guide*, published annually by the British Consumers Union, is excellent. Pubs attached to restaurants often have fresher food and a chef who knows how to cook.

I recommend certain pubs, but food can spoil, and your B&B

host is usually up-to-date on the best neighborhood pub grub. Ask for advice (but adjust for nepotism and cronyism, which run rampant). Locals will rarely recommend a rough pub that's a local hangout. If you want this experience (the food will be cheaper but not very good), ask for a "spit-and-sawdust" place. Big-city spit-and-sawdust places may not welcome tourists. Rural and village ones will. They are the most interesting.

Pubs generally serve assorted meat pies, such as steak and kidney pie or shepherd's pie, curried dishes, fish, quiche, vegetables, and (invariably) chips and peas. Better pubs let you substitute a "jacket potato" (baked potato) for your fries. Meals are usually served from 12:00 to 14:00 and 18:00 to 20:00, not throughout the day. Servings are hearty, service is quick, and you'll rarely spend more than £5 to £7 ($8–11). Your beer or cider adds another pound or two. Free tap water is always available. In Britain a "ploughman's lunch" is a modern "traditional English meal" that nearly every tourist tries... once. Pubs that advertise their food and are crowded with locals are less likely to be the kind that serve only lousy microwaved snacks.

In a pub you order your beer at the bar. Part of the experience is standing before a line of "hand pulls" and wondering which on-tap beer you want. The British and Irish take great pride in their beer. They think that drinking beer cold and carbonated, as Americans do, ruins the taste. At pubs, long hand pulls are used to pull the traditional rich-flavored "real ales" up from the cellar. These are the connoisseur's favorites: They're fermented naturally, vary from sweet to bitter, and often include a hoppy or nutty flavor. Notice the fun names. Experiment with the obscure local microbrews. Short "hand pulls" at the bar mean colder, fizzier, mass-produced, and less interesting keg beers. Mild beers are sweeter, with a creamy malt flavor. Stout is dark and more bitter, like Guinness. For a cold, refreshing, basic American-style beer, ask for a "lager." Try the draft cider (sweet or dry)... carefully. Proper English ladies like a half-beer and half-lemonade "shandy." Teetotalers can order a soft drink. Drinks are served by the pint or the half pint. (It's almost feminine for a man to order just a half; I order mine with quiche.) There's no table service in either British or Irish pubs. Order drinks and meals at the bar. Pay as you order and don't tip.

Pub hours vary. The strictly limited wartime hours (designed to keep the wartime working force sober and productive) finally ended a few years ago, and now pubs can serve beer from 11:00 to 23:00, and Sunday from noon to 22:30. Children are served food and soft drinks in pubs (sometimes in a courtyard or the restaurant section), and you must be 18 to order a beer. A cup of darts is free for the asking. People go to a "public house" to be social. They want to talk. Get vocal with a local. Pubs are the next best thing to relatives in every town.

Stranger in a Strange Land

We travel all the way to Europe to enjoy differences—to become temporary locals. You'll experience frustrations. There are certain truths that we find God-given and self-evident, such as cold beer, ice in drinks, bottomless cups of coffee, easy shower faucets, and driving on the right side of the road. One of the benefits of travel is the eye-opening realization that there are logical, civil, and even better alternatives. A willingness to go local ensures that you'll enjoy a full dose of hospitality.

Back Door Manners

While updating this book, I heard over and over again that my readers are considerate and fun to have as guests. Thank you for traveling as temporary locals who are sensitive to the culture. It's a joy to follow you in my travels.

Send Me a Postcard, Drop Me a Line

If you enjoy a successful trip with the help of this book and would like to share your discoveries, please fill out and send the survey at the end of this book to me at Europe Through the Back Door, Box 2009, Edmonds, WA 98020. I personally read and value all feedback. Thanks in advance—it helps a lot.

For our latest travel information, tap into www.ricksteves.com. To check on any updates for this book, visit www.ricksteves.com /update. My e-mail address is rick@ricksteves.com. Anyone can request a free issue of our newsletter.

Judging from the happy postcards I receive from travelers, it's safe to assume you're on your way to a great, affordable vacation—with the finesse of an independent, experienced traveler. Thanks, and happy travels!

BACK DOOR TRAVEL PHILOSOPHY

As Taught in *Rick Steves' Europe Through the Back Door*

Travel is intensified living—maximum thrills per minute and one of the last great sources of legal adventure. Travel is freedom. It's recess, and we need it.

Experiencing the real Europe requires catching it by surprise, going casual... "Through the Back Door."

Affording travel is a matter of priorities. (Make do with the old car.) You can travel—simply, safely, and comfortably—anywhere in Europe for $70 a day plus transportation costs. In many ways, spending more money only builds a thicker wall between you and what you came to see. Europe is a cultural carnival and, time after time, you'll find that its best acts are free and the best seats are the cheap ones.

A tight budget forces you to travel close to the ground, meeting and communicating with the people, not relying on service with a purchased smile. Never sacrifice sleep, nutrition, safety, or cleanliness in the name of budget. Simply enjoy the local-style alternatives to expensive hotels and restaurants.

Extroverts have more fun. If your trip is low on magic moments, kick yourself and make things happen. If you don't enjoy a place, maybe you don't know enough about it. Seek the truth. Recognize tourist traps. Give a culture the benefit of your open mind. See things as different but not better or worse. Any culture has much to share.

Of course, travel, like the world, is a series of hills and valleys. Be fanatically positive and militantly optimistic. If something's not to your liking, change your liking. Travel is addictive. It can make you a happier American as well as a citizen of the world. Our earth is home to 6 billion equally important people. It's humbling to travel and find that people don't envy Americans. They like us, but, with all due respect, they wouldn't trade passports.

Globetrotting destroys ethnocentricity. It helps you understand and appreciate different cultures. Travel changes people. It broadens perspectives and teaches new ways to measure quality of life. Many travelers toss aside their hometown blinders. Their prized souvenirs are the strands of different cultures they decide to knit into their own character. The world is a cultural yarn shop. And Back Door Travelers are weaving the ultimate tapestry. Come on, join in!

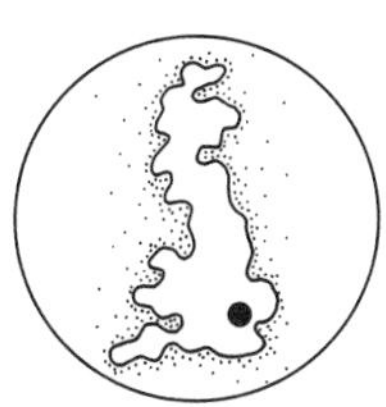

LONDON

London is more than 600 square miles of urban jungle. With 9 million struggling people—many of whom speak English—it's a world in itself and a barrage on all the senses. On my first visit I felt very, very small. London is much more than its museums and famous landmarks. It's a living, breathing, thriving organism.

London has changed dramatically in recent years, and many visitors are surprised to find how "un-English" it is. Whites are now a minority in major parts of the city that once symbolized white imperialism. Arabs have nearly bought out the area north of Hyde Park. Chinese take-outs outnumber fish-and-chips shops. Many hotels are run by people with foreign accents (who hire English chambermaids), while outlying suburbs are home to huge communities of Indians and Pakistanis. London is learning—sometimes fitfully—to live as a microcosm of its formerly vast empire. Many see the English Channel Tunnel as another foreign threat to the Britishness of Britain.

With just a few days here, you'll get no more than a quick splash in this teeming human tidal pool. But, with a quick orientation, you'll get a good taste of its top sights, history, and cultural entertainment, as well as its ever-changing human face.

Have fun in London. Blow through the city on the open deck of a double-decker orientation tour bus, and take a pinch-me-I'm-in-Britain walk through downtown. Ogle the crown jewels at the Tower of London, hear the chimes of Big Ben, and see the Houses of Parliament in action. Hobnob with the tombstones in Westminster Abbey, duck WWII bombs in Churchill's underground Cabinet War Rooms, and brave the earthshaking Imperial War Museum. Overfeed the pigeons at Trafalgar Square. Visit with Leonardo, Botticelli, and Rembrandt in the National Gallery.

The Party's Not Over

Last year, London was hell-bent on hosting the world's grandest millennium celebrations. The year 2000 brought London revamped museums, a huge Ferris wheel, and a giant dome at Greenwich.

After the stardust of the millennium settles, what's left?

Only Greenwich's Millennium Dome has been a disappointment. It needed to draw 35,000 people a day to recoup its huge costs. But its crowds kept away bigger crowds.

To celebrate the millennium, the British Museum opened its glass-domed Great Court, giving the museum a formal entry and offering visitors a classy place to hang out after the museum closes—to shop, dine, people watch, or attend a lecture. Marx (Karl not Groucho) enjoyed the museum's Round Reading Room, freshly restored and once again open to the public.

The striking Tate Modern, which opened in 2000, is as modern as its art. The new pedestrian Millennium Bridge links the old, sedate St. Paul's Cathedral with the new great Tate. Gracefully spanning the Thames, the Millennium Bridge connects old and new, religious and secular, the heart of London with the art of the world.

The London Eye Ferris Wheel, for the silly thrill of it, is a delightful way to see London from a 450-foot-high perch. The towering Wheel adds a carnival whirl to London's stodgy skyline.

London gambled big on the millennium, and you're the winner.

Whisper across the dome of St. Paul's Cathedral and rummage through our civilization's attic at the British Museum. Cruise down the Thames River. You'll enjoy some of Europe's best people watching at Covent Garden and snap to at Buckingham Palace's Changing of the Guard. Just sit in Victoria Station, at a major tube station, at Piccadilly Circus, or in Trafalgar Square, and observe. Spend one evening at a theater and the others catching your breath.

Planning Your Time

The sights of London alone could easily fill a trip to Britain. It's a great one-week getaway. On a three-week tour of Britain I'd give it three busy days. If you're flying in, consider starting your trip in Bath and make London your British finale. Especially if you hope to enjoy a play or concert, a night or two of jet lag is bad news.

Here's a suggested schedule:

Day 1: 9:00–Tower of London (Beefeater tour, crown jewels), 12:00–Munch a sandwich on the Thames while cruising from the Tower to Westminster Bridge, 13:00–Follow the self-guided Westminster Walk (see below) with a quick visit to the Cabinet War Rooms, 15:30–Trafalgar Square and National Gallery, 17:30–Visit the Britain Visitors Centre near Piccadilly, planning ahead for your trip, 18:30–Dinner in Soho. Take in a play or 19:30 concert at St. Martin-in-the-Fields.

Day 2: 8:30–If traveling around Britain, spend 30 minutes in a phone booth getting all essential elements of your trip nailed down. If you know where you'll be and when, call those B&Bs now. 9:00–Take the Round London bus tour (consider hopping off near the end for the 11:30 Changing of the Guard at Buckingham Palace), 12:30–Covent Gardens for lunch and people watching, 14:00–Tour the British Museum. Have a pub dinner before a play, concert, or evening walking tour.

Days 3 and 4: Choose among these remaining London highlights: Tour Westminster Abbey, British Library, Imperial War Museum, the two Tates (Tate Modern on the south bank for modern art, Tate Britain on the north bank for British art), St. Paul's Cathedral, Museum of London, or London Eye Ferris Wheel; cruise to Kew or Greenwich; do some serious shopping at one of London's elegant department stores or open-air markets; or consider another historic walking tour.

After considering nearly all of London's tourist sights, I have pruned them down to just the most important (or fun) for a first visit of up to seven days. You won't be able to see all of these, so don't try. You'll keep coming back to London. After 25 visits myself, I still enjoy a healthy list of excuses to return.

Orientation

(area code: 020)

To grasp London comfortably, see it as the old town without the modern, congested sprawl. Most of the visitor's London lies between the Tower of London and Hyde Park—about a three-mile walk. Mentally—maybe even physically—scissor down your map to include only the area between the Tower, King's Cross Station, Paddington Station, the Victoria and Albert Museum, and Victoria Station. With this focus and a good orientation, you'll find London manageable and even fun.

Tourist Information

The **Britain Visitors Centre** is the best information service in town (Mon-9:30–18:30, Tue–Fri 9:00–18:30, Sat–Sun 10:00–16:00, July–Sept until 17:00 on Sat, booking service, just off Piccadilly Circus at 1 Lower Regent Street, tel. 020/8846-9000, www.visitbritain.com). It's great for London information; buy your city map here (£1). If you're traveling beyond London, take advantage of its well-equipped London/England desk, Wales desk (tel. 020/7803-3838), Ireland desk (tel. 020/7493-3201), and Scotland desk. At the center's extensive bookshop, gather whatever guidebooks, hostel directories, maps, and information you'll need. If venturing beyond London, consider the *Michelin Green Guide* to London or Britain (£9.25), the Britain road atlas (£10), and Ordnance Survey maps for areas you'll be exploring by car. There's also a travel agency upstairs plus computers displaying only www.visitbritain.com (no Internet access).

Nearby you'll find the **Scottish Tourist Centre** (mid-June–mid-Sept Mon–Fri 9:00–18:00, Sat 10:00–17:00, otherwise Mon–Fri 9:30–17:30, Sat 12:00–16:00, Cockspur Street, tel. 020/7930-8661, www.holiday.scotland.net) and the slick **French National Tourist Office** (Mon–Sat 9:00–17:30, closed Sun, 178 Piccadilly Street, tel. 0891-244-123).

Unfortunately **London's Tourist Information Centres** (TIs) are now owned by the big hotels and are simply businesses selling advertising space to companies with fliers to distribute. They are reasonably helpful but biased; the London map they sell for £1.40 is littered with hotels. Avoid their 50p-per-minute telephone information service (instead try the **Britain Visitors Centre** at 020/8846-9000). Locations include Heathrow Airport's Terminal 3 (daily 6:00–23:00, most convenient and least crowded); Heathrow Airport's Terminal 1 and 2 tube station (daily 8:00–18:00); Victoria Station (daily 8:00–18:00, crowded and commercial); and Waterloo International Terminal Arrivals Hall (daily 8:30–22:30, serving trains from Paris; if you arrive by train when TI is mobbed, skip the TI, buy city map at a newsstand upstairs in station lobby, then return downstairs to catch tube to your hotel).

At any of the TIs, bring your itinerary and a checklist of questions. Pick up these publications: *London Planner* (a great free monthly that lists all the sights, events, and hours), walking-tour schedule fliers, a theater guide, and the Thames River Services brochure. Of all the TIs, only the Britain Visitors Centre on Regent Street sells a good city map (£1, free from British Tourist Authority in U.S.A.: tel. 800/462-2748, 551 Fifth Avenue, 7th floor, New York, NY 10176, www.travelbritain.org). Bensons Mapguide of London is the best map of London I've seen (£2, sold at newsstands).

TIs sell BT phone cards, long-distance bus tickets and passes, British Heritage Passes, and tickets to plays (steep booking fee). And they book rooms (avoid their £5 booking fee by calling hotels direct). Skip the pricey London Pass, which covers 50 mostly minor sights (1 day/£17.50).

TIs also sell "Fast Track" tickets to some of London's

attractions (at no extra cost), allowing you to skip the queue at the sights; these are worthwhile for places notorious for long ticket lines: Tower of London, London Eye Ferris Wheel, and Madame Tussaud's Wax Museum.

Helpful Hints

U.S. Embassy: 24 Grosvenor Square (for passport concerns, open Mon–Fri 8:30–11:30 plus Mon, Wed, Fri 14:00–16:00, tube: Bond Street, tel. 020/7499-9000).

Theft Alert: The Artful Dodger is alive and well in London. Be on guard, particularly on public transportation and in places crowded with tourists. Tourists, considered naive and rich, are targeted. Over 7,500 handbags are stolen annually at Covent Garden alone. Thieves paw you so you don't feel the pickpocketing.

Changing Money: ATMs are the way to go. For changing traveler's checks, standard transaction fees at banks are £2–4. American Express Offices offer a fair rate and change any brand of traveler's checks for no fee. Handy Amex offices are at Heathrow's Terminal 4 tube station (daily 7:00–19:00) and near Piccadilly (30 Haymarket, June–Sept Mon–Fri 8:30–20:00, Sat 9:00–18:30, Sun 10:00–17:00; Oct–May Mon–Sat 9:00–17:30, Sun 10:00–17:00; tel. 020/7484-9600). Avoid changing money at exchange bureaus. Their latest scam: they advertise very good rates with a same-as-the-banks fee of 2 percent. But the fine print explains that the fee of 2 percent is for buying pounds. The fee for *selling* pounds is 9.5 percent. Ouch!

What's Up: For the best listing of what's happening (plays, movies, restaurants, concerts, exhibitions, protests, walking tours, shopping, and children's activities) and a look at the trendy London scene, pick up a current copy of *Time Out* (£1.85, www.timeout.co.uk) or *What's On* at any newsstand. The TI's free monthly *London Planner* lists sights, plays, and events at least as well. For a chatty, *People* magazine–type Web site on London's entertainment, theater, restaurants, and news, go to www.thisislondon.com.

Free Sights: The British Museum, British Library, National Gallery, National Portrait Gallery, Tate Britain (British art), and Tate Modern (modern art) are always free—though special exhibitions cost extra. The following museums are free from 16:30 to closing (17:30 or 18:00), saving you £5 or so: The Imperial War Museum, Museum of London, Natural History Museum, and Victoria and Albert Museum. More museums will be free in the next few years.

Internet Access: The astonishing easyEverything offers up to 500 computers per store, 24 hours daily. Depending on demand, a mere £1 ticket buys anywhere from 40 minutes to six hours of computer time; the ticket is valid for four weeks and multiple visits at any of their five branches: Victoria Station (across from front of station, near taxis and buses), Trafalgar

Square, Tottenham Court Road, Oxford Street, and Kensington High Street.

Travel Bookstores: Stanfords Travel Bookstores is good and stocks current editions of my books at Covent Garden (12 Long Acre, tel. 020/7836-1321) and 156 Regent Street (tel. 020/7434-4744). Waterstones Bookstore, on the corner of Trafalgar Square, is also handy, with a fine travel selection next to the Coffee Republic café (WC upstairs, tel. 020/7839-4411).

Travel Agency: The student travel agency, USIT, across from Victoria Station, has great deals on flights for people of all ages (Mon–Fri 9:00–18:00, Sat–Sun 10:00–17:00, Internet access, Buckingham Palace Road, tel. 020/7823-5363, www.usitcampus.co.uk). Also, look in the Sunday *Times* travel section for great deals on flights.

Beatles: Fans of the still Fabulous Four can take one of the Beatles walks (5/weekly, offered by Original London Walks, under "Tours of London," below); visit the Beatles Shop (231 Baker Street, next to Sherlock Holmes Museum, tube: Baker Street); or go to Abbey Road and walk the famous crosswalk (at intersection with Carlton Hill, tube: St. John's Wood).

Arrival in London

By Train: London has eight train stations, all connected by the tube (subway), all with exchange offices and luggage storage. From any station, ride the tube or taxi to your hotel.

By Bus: The bus station is one block southwest of Victoria Station, which has a TI and tube entrance.

By Plane: For detailed information on getting from London's airports to downtown London, see "Transportation Connections" at the end of this chapter.

Getting around London

London's taxis, buses, and subway system make a private car unnecessary. To travel smart in a city this size, you must get comfortable with public transportation. For tube and bus information 24 hours a day, call 020/7222-1234 (www.londontransport.co.uk).

By Taxi: London is the best taxi town in Europe. Big, black, carefully regulated cabs are everywhere. I never met a crabby cabbie in London. They love to talk and know every nook and cranny in town. I ride in one a day just to get my London questions answered. Rides start at £1.50 and cost about £1.50 per tube stop. Connecting downtown sights is quick and easy and will cost you about £4 (e.g., St. Paul's to the Tower of London). For a short ride, three people in a cab travel at tube prices. Groups of four or five should taxi everywhere. If a cab's top light is on, just wave it down. (Drivers flash lights when they see you.) They have a tiny turning radius, so you can wave at cabs going both directions. If waving doesn't work, ask someone where you can find a taxi stand. Stick with metered cabs. While telephoning a cab gets one in minutes, it's generally not necessary and adds to the cost. London is such a great wave-'em-down taxi town that most cabs don't even have a radio phone.

By Bus: London's extensive bus system is easy to follow. Just pick up a free "Central London bus guide" map from a TI or tube station. Signs at stops list routes clearly. Conductors are terse but helpful. Ask to be reminded when it's your stop. Just hop on, tell the driver where you're going, pay what he says (usually £1) grab a ticket, take a seat, and relax. (The best views are upstairs.) If the driver is not taking money, hop in and grab a seat. The conductor will eventually sell you a ticket. If you have a Travel Card (see below), get in the habit of hopping buses for quick little straight shots, even just to get to a metro stop. During bump-and-grind rush hours (8:00–10:00 and 16:00–19:00), you'll go faster by tube.

By Tube: London's subway is one of this planet's great people movers and the fastest—and cheapest—long-distance transport in town (runs daily about 5:00–24:00). Any ride in the Central Zone (on or within the Circle Line, including virtually all my recommended sights and hotels) costs £1.50. You can avoid ticket window lines in tube stations by buying tickets from coin-op machines; practice on the punchboard to see how the system works (hit "adult single" and your destination). Again, nearly every ride will be £1.50. (These tickets are valid only on the day of purchase.) Beware: Overshooting your zone will get you a £10 fine.

Most city maps include a tube map with color-coded lines and names (free at any station window). Each line has a name (such as Circle, Northern, or Bakerloo) and two directions (indicated by end stop). In stations you'll have a choice of two platforms per line. Navigate by signs leading to the platforms (usually labeled north, south, east, or west) which clearly list the stops served by each line, or ask a local or an orange-vested staff person for help. All city maps have north on top. If you know which general direction you're heading, tube navigation suddenly becomes easier. Some tracks are shared by several lines, and electronic signboards announce which train is next and the minutes remaining until various arrivals. Each train has its final destination or line name above its windshield. Depending on the particular line, trains run roughly every 3 to 10 minutes. Bring something to do to make your wait productive. And always . . . mind the gap.

You can't leave the system without feeding your ticket to the turnstile. Save time by choosing the best street exit (look at the maps on the walls). "Subway" means pedestrian underpass in "English."

London Tube and Bus Passes: Consider using these passes, valid on both the tube and buses (all passes are available for more zones and are purchased as easily as a normal ticket at any station):

London

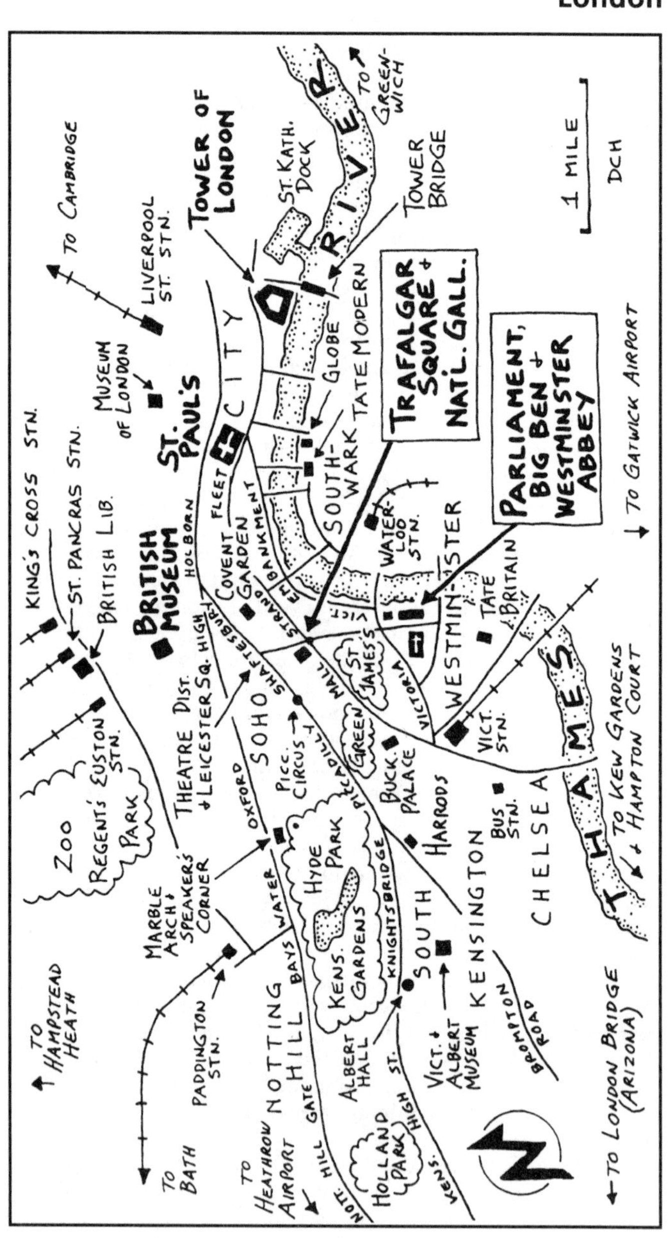
TO CAMBRIDGE
KING'S CROSS STN.
ST. PANCRAS STN.
BRITISH LIB.
EUSTON STN.
LIVERPOOL ST. STN.
MUSEUM OF LONDON
TOWER OF LONDON
ST. KATH. DOCK
TO GREENWICH
TOWER BRIDGE
RIVER
1 MILE
DCH
ZOO
REGENT'S PARK
BRITISH MUSEUM
HOLBORN
ST. PAUL'S
CITY
GLOBE
TATE MODERN
SOUTHWARK
FLEET
COVENT GARDEN
EMBANKMENT
STRAND
TRAFALGAR SQUARE + NATL. GALL.
PARLIAMENT, BIG BEN + WESTMINSTER ABBEY
TO GATWICK AIRPORT
WATERLOO STN.
WESTMINSTER
TATE BRITAIN
THEATRE DIST. + LEICESTER SQ.
HIGH
SHAFTESBURY
SOHO
OXFORD
PICC. CIRCUS
PICCADILLY
MALL
ST. JAMES'S
GREEN
VICT.
VICTORIA
VICT. STN.
BUCK. PALACE
HARRODS
BUS STN.
CHELSEA
THAMES
TO KEW GARDENS + HAMPTON COURT
MARBLE ARCH + SPEAKER'S CORNER
HYDE PARK
KENS. GARDENS
BAYS
WATER
KNIGHTSBRIDGE
SOUTH KENSINGTON
TO HAMPSTEAD HEATH
PADDINGTON STN.
NOTTING HILL
GATE
ALBERT HALL
VICT. + ALBERT MUSEUM
BROMPTON ROAD
TO LONDON BRIDGE (ARIZONA)
TO BATH
TO HEATHROW AIRPORT
HOLLAND PARK
NOTT. HILL
KENS. HIGH ST.
N

One Day passes: If you figure you'll take three rides in a day, a day pass is a good deal. The "One Day Travel Card," covering Zones 1 and 2, gives you unlimited travel for a day, starting after 9:30 and anytime on weekends, for £3.90. The all-zone version of this card costs £4.70 (and includes Heathrow airport). The "One Day LT Card," covering Zones 1 and 2 with no time restriction, costs £5. Families save with the one-day "Family Travel Card" (price varies depending on number in family).

Weekend pass: The "Weekend Travel Card," which covers Saturday, Sunday, and Zones 1 and 2 for £5.80, costs 25 percent less than two one-day cards.

Seven-day pass: The "7-Day Travel Card" costs £18, covers Zones 1 and 2, and requires a passport-type photo (cut one out of any snapshot and bring it from home).

Ten rides: If you want to travel a little each day or if you're part of a group, a £11 "carnet" is a great deal: you get 10 separate tickets for tube travel in Zone 1 (£1.10 per ride rather than £1.50). Wait for the machine to lay all 10 tickets.

Tours of London

▲▲▲Hop-on Hop-off Double-Decker Bus Tours—Two competitive companies ("Original" and "Big Bus") offer essentially the same tours, with buses that have live (English-only) guides as well as some marked buses with a tape-recorded, dial-a-language narration. This two-hour, once-over-lightly bus tour drives by all the most famous sights, providing a stressless way to get your bearings and at least see the biggies. You can sit back and enjoy the entire two-hour orientation tour (a good idea if you like the guide and the weather) or "hop on and hop off" at any of the nearly 30 stops and catch a later bus. Buses run about every 10 to 15 minutes in summer, every 20 minutes in winter. It's an inexpensive form of transport as well as an informative tour. Grab one of the maps from a TI and study it. Buses run daily except Christmas (from about 9:00 in summer—9:30 in winter—until early evening in summer, late afternoon in winter), stopping at Victoria Street (1 block north of Victoria Station), Marble Arch, Piccadilly Circus, Trafalgar Square, and so on. Each company offers a core two-hour overview tour and two other routes (buy ticket from driver, CC sometimes accepted at some major stops such as Victoria Station, ticket good for 24 hours, bring a sweater and extra film). Note: If you start at Victoria at 9:00, you can hop off near the end of the two-hour loop at the Buckingham Palace stop (Bressenden Place), a five-minute walk from the palace and the Changing of the Guard (at 11:30); ask your driver—who knows about current traffic diversions—if it makes more sense to walk to the palace from the Victoria Station stop. If it's important to you to get a close-up view of the Changing of the Guards or to take in the guards' inspection at 11:00 at

Wellington Barracks, save the bus tour for another day. Sunday morning, with light traffic and many museums closed, is a fine time for a tour.

Original London Sightseeing Bus Tour: Live guided buses have a Union Jack flag and a yellow triangle on the front of the bus. If the front has many flags or a green triangle, it's a tape-recorded multilingual tour—avoid it, unless you have kids who'd enjoy the more entertaining recorded kids' tour (£12.50, £2.50 off with this book—limit 2 discounts per book, they'll rip off the corner of this page, ticket good for 24 hours, tel. 020/8877-1722).

Big Bus Hop-on Hop-off London Tours: These are also good. For £15 you get the same basic tour plus coupons for three different one-hour London walks and the scenic and entertainingly guided Thames boat ride (normally £4.80) between Westminster Pier and the Tower of London. The pass and extras (which you could just barely do in a day) are valid for 24 hours. Buses with live guides are marked in front with a picture of a blue bus; buses with tape-recorded spiels display a picture of a yellow bus and headphones. While the price is steeper, Big Bus guides seem more dynamic than the Original guides, and the Big Bus system is probably better organized (office a block from Victoria Station at 48 Buckingham Palace Road, daily 8:30–17:30, CC accepted, or pay driver cash, tel. 020/7233-9533, www.bigbus.co.uk).

At Night: To do it at night, consider the London by Night Sightseeing Tour, which runs basically the same circuit as the other companies (£9, pay driver or buy tickets at Victoria Station TI, April–Oct, 2-hr tour with live guide, can hop on and off, leaves at 20:00, 21:00, and 22:00 from Victoria Station, Taxi Road, Stop E, at front of station, tel. 020/8646-1747).

▲▲Walking Tours—Many times a day top-notch local guides lead small groups through specific slices of London's past. Schedule fliers litter the desks of TIs, hotels, and pubs. *Time Out* lists many but not all scheduled walks. Simply show up at the announced location, pay £5, and enjoy two chatty hours of Dickens, the Plague, Shakespeare, Legal London, the Beatles, Jack the Ripper, or whatever is on the agenda. Original London Walks, the dominant company, lists their extensive daily schedule in a beefy, plain, black-and-white *Original London Walks* brochure; they also run Explorer day trips, a good option for those with limited time and transportation (different trip daily: Stonehenge/Salisbury, Oxford/Cotswolds, York, Bath, and so on; walks offered year-round—even Christmas, get schedule at hotel or TI, or call 020/7624-3978, private tours for £80, www.walks.com).

Here are a few private guides; for any of these, book well in advance: Robina Brown, who winters in Seattle (a bizarre concept), leads tours on foot or with small groups in her Toyota Previa. For car and guiding she charges £155 for three hours and about £275 to £360 per day trip per group (tel. & fax 020/7228-2238, e-mail: robina.brown@which.net). Brit Lonsdale, an energetic mother of twins, is another registered London guide (tel. 020/7386-9907, fax 020/7386-9807). Chris Salaman and his colleague, Rich Parks, both tailor specialty walks (Chris's favorite: industrial tours); their daylong private walks, including lunch, a tube travel card, and museum admissions, cost £120 for up to six people (Chris, tel. 020/8672-1270; Rich, tel. 020/8464-4369). For other guides call 020/7403-2962 (www.touristguides.org.uk); standard rates for registered guides: £83/4 hrs, £132/8 hrs.

▲▲Cruise the Thames—Boat tours with an entertaining commentary sail regularly from Westminster Pier (at the base of Westminster Bridge under Big Ben). You can cruise to the Tower of London (£4.80, only the one-way is included with Big Bus London tour, round-trip £6, 2/hrly, 10:20–21:00 April–Oct, until 15:45 Nov–March, 30 min, tel. 020/7930-9033), Greenwich (£6.30, round-trip £7.60, 2/hrly, 9:00–16:00, 50 min, tel. 020/7930-4097), and Kew Gardens (£7, round-trip £11, 5/day, 10:15–14:00, 90 min, 30 min narrated, some boats continue on to Hampton Court for extra £3, tel. 020/7930-2062). For pleasure and efficiency, consider combining a one-way cruise with a tube ride back.

Frog Tours—A bright yellow, amphibious vehicle takes you streetside past some famous sights (Big Ben, Buckingham Palace, Piccadilly Circus), then splashes into the Thames for a 30-minute cruise (£13, daily 10:00–18:00, live commentary, 80 min, departs from County Hall near London Eye Ferris Wheel, tube: Waterloo or Westminster, tel. 020/7928-3132, www.frogtours.com).

Sights—From Westminster Abbey to Trafalgar Square

▲▲Westminster Walk—Just about every visitor to London strolls the historic Whitehall boulevard from Big Ben to Trafalgar Square. Beneath London's modern traffic and big-city bustle lies 2,000 fascinating years of history. This three-quarter-mile, self-guided orientation walk (see map on next page) gives you a whirlwind tour and connects the sights listed in this section.

Start halfway across **Westminster Bridge** (#1 on map) for that "Wow, I'm really in London!" feeling. Get a close-up view of the **Houses of Parliament** and **Big Ben** (floodlit at night). Downstream (#2) you'll see the **London Eye Ferris Wheel**. Downstairs are boats to the Tower of London and Greenwich.

En route to Parliament Square, you'll pass a statue of Boadicea (#3), the Celtic queen defeated by Roman invaders in A.D. 60.

To thrill your loved ones (or bug the envious), call home from a pay phone near Big Ben at about three minutes before the hour. You'll find a phone on Great George Street, across from Parliament Square. As Big Ben chimes, stick the receiver outside

Westminster Walk

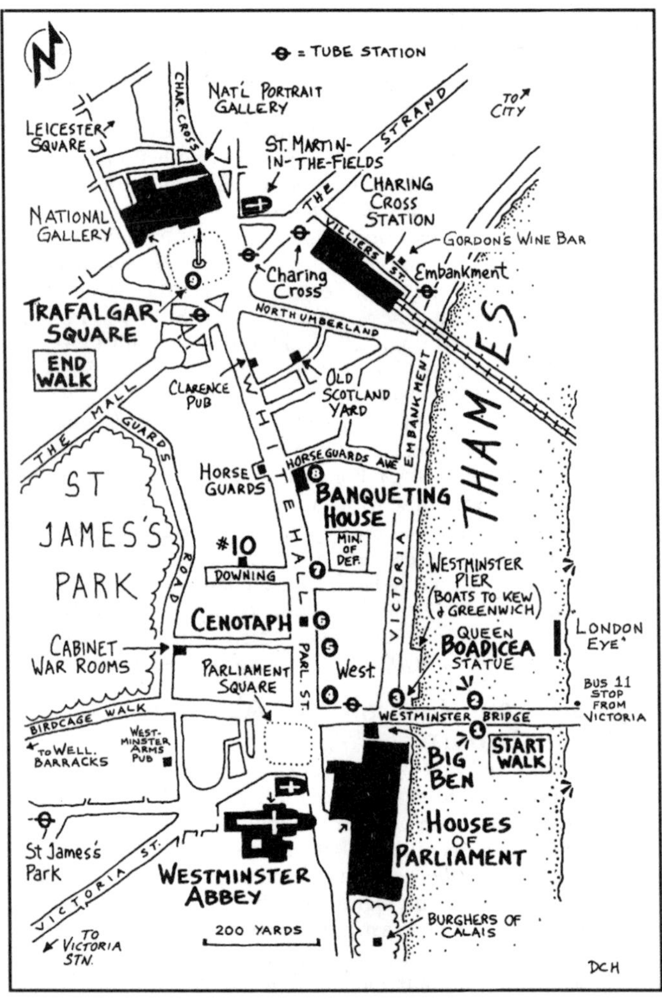

the booth and prove you're in London: Ding dong ding dong... dong ding ding dong.

Wave hello to Churchill in Parliament Square (#4). To his right is **Westminster Abbey** with its two stubby, elegant towers.

Walk north up Parliament Street (which turns into Whitehall) toward Trafalgar Square. You'll see the thought-provoking **Cenotaph** (#6) in the middle of the street, reminding passersby of Britain's many war dead. To visit the Cabinet War Rooms (see "Sights," below) take a left before the Cenotaph, on King Charles Street (#5).

Continuing on Whitehall, stop at the barricaded and guarded little **10 Downing Street** to see the British "White House" (#7), home of the prime minister. Break the bobby's boredom and ask him a question.

Nearing Trafalgar Square, look for the **Horse Guards** behind the gated fence (11:00 inspection Mon–Sat, 10:00 on Sun; dismounting ceremony daily at 16:00) and the 17th-century **Banqueting House** across the street (#8; see "Sights," below).

The column topped by Lord Nelson marks **Trafalgar Square** (#9). The stately domed building on the far side of the square is the **National Gallery** (free) which has a classy café (upstairs in the Sainsbury wing). To the right of the National Gallery is **St. Martin-in-the-Fields Church** and its Café in the Crypt.

To get to Piccadilly from Trafalgar Square, walk up Cockspur Street to Haymarket, then take a short left on Coventry Street to colorful **Piccadilly Circus.**

Near Piccadilly you'll find the **Britain Visitors Centre** and piles of theaters. **Leicester Square** (with its half-price ticket booth for plays) thrives just a few blocks away. Walk through seedy **Soho** (north of Shaftesbury Avenue) for its fun pubs (see "Eating," below, for "Food is Fun" Dinner Crawl). From Piccadilly or Oxford Circus, you can taxi, bus, or tube home.

▲▲▲Westminster Abbey—England's historic coronation church is a crowded collection of famous tombs. Like a stony refugee camp huddled outside St. Peter's gates, this is an English hall of fame. Consider a tour (audioguide-£2 or live-£3), an evensong service (weekdays except Wed at 17:00, Sat and Sun at 15:00), and the Sunday 17:45 organ recital (£5 for abbey entry, tours extra, Mon–Fri 9:15–16:45 plus Wed 18:00–19:45, Sat 9:00–14:45, technically no visitors on Sun, last admission 1 hr before closing, photography prohibited, lattés in cloister, tube: Westminster or St. James' Park, call for tour schedule, tel. 020/7222-7110). Since the church is often closed to the public for special services, it's wise to call first. Praying is free, thank God (in two chapels set aside for private prayer), but you must inform the marshal at the door of your intention.

▲▲Houses of Parliament (Palace of Westminster)—This neo-Gothic icon of London, the royal residence from 1042 to 1547, is now the meeting place of the legislative branch of government. While Parliament is too tempting to terrorists to be opened wide to tourists, you can view debates in either the bickering House of Commons or the genteel House of Lords if they're in session—indicated by a flag flying atop the Victoria Tower. It's not worth a long wait and the actual action is generally extremely dull, but it is a thrill to be inside and see the British government inaction

(House of Commons: Mon–Wed 14:30–22:30, Thu 11:30–19:30, Fri 9:30–15:00, generally less action and no lines after 18:00, use St. Stephen's entrance, tube: Westminster, tel. 020/7219-4272 for schedule, www.parliament.uk). The House of Lords has more pageantry, shorter lines, and less-interesting debates (Mon–Wed 14:30 until they finish, Thu from 15:00 on, sometimes Fri from 11:00 on, tel. 020/7219-3107 for schedule). If confronted with a too-long House of Commons line, see the House of Lords first. Once you've seen the Lords (hide your HOL flier), you can often slip directly to the Commons—joining the gang waiting in the lobby. If there's only one line outside, it's for the House of Commons. Go to the gate and tell the guard you want the Lords. You may pop right in.

After passing security, slip to the left and study the big dark **Westminster Hall,** which survived the 1834 fire. The hall is 11th century, and its famous self-supporting hammer-beam roof was added in 1397. The Houses of Parliament are located in what was once the Palace of Westminster, long the palace of England's medieval kings, until it was largely destroyed by fire in 1834. The palace was rebuilt in Victorian Gothic style (a move away from neoclassicism back to England's Christian and medieval heritage, true to the Romantic age). It was completed in 1860; only a few of its 1,000 rooms are open to the public.

The **Jewel Tower** is (along with Westminster Hall) about the only surviving part of the old Palace of Westminster. It contains a fine little exhibit on Parliament: first floor—history, second floor—Parliament today, with a 45-minute video and lonely picnic-friendly benches (£1.50, April–Sept daily 10:00–18:00, until 17:00 Oct, until 16:00 Nov–March, across street from St. Stephens Gate, tel. 020/7222-2219).

The clock tower (315 feet high) is named for its 13-ton bell, Ben. The light above the clock is lit when the House of Commons is sitting. For a hip HOP view, walk halfway over Westminster Bridge.

▲▲Cabinet War Rooms—This is a fascinating walk through the underground headquarters of the British government's fight against the Nazis in the darkest days of the Battle for Britain. The 21-room nerve center of the British war effort was used from 1939 to 1945. Churchill's room, the map room, and so on, are just as they were in 1945. For all the blood, sweat, toil, and tears details, pick up an audioguide at the entry and follow the included and excellent 30-minute tour; be patient—it's worth it (£5, April–Oct daily 9:30–18:00, Nov–March 10:00–17:15, last entry 45 min before closing, on King Charles Street 200 yards off Whitehall, follow the signs, tube: Westminster, tel. 020/7930-6961). For a nearby pub lunch, try theWestminster Arms (on Storey's Gate, a couple blocks south of War Rooms).

Horse Guards—The Horse Guards change daily at 11:00

(10:00 on Sun), and there's a colorful dismounting ceremony daily at 16:00. The rest of the day they just stand there—terrible for camcorders (on Whitehall, between Trafalgar Square and #10 Downing Street, tube: Westminster). While Buckingham Palace pageantry is canceled when it rains, the horse guards change regardless of the weather.

▲**Banqueting House**—England's first Renaissance building was designed by Inigo Jones around 1620. It's one of the few London landmarks spared by the 1666 fire and the only surviving part of the original Palace of Whitehall. Don't miss its Rubens ceiling, which, at Charles I's request, drove home the doctrine of the legitimacy of the divine right of kings. In 1649, divine right ignored, Charles I was beheaded on the balcony of this building by a Cromwellian parliament. Admission includes a restful 18-minute audiovisual history, which shows the place in banqueting action, a 30-minute tape-recorded tour that is interesting only to history buffs, and a look at a fancy banqueting hall (£3.80, Mon–Sat 10:00–17:00, last entry at 16:30, subject to closure for government functions, aristocratic WC, immediately across Whitehall from the Horse Guards, tube: Westminster, tel. 020/7930-4179). Just up the street is Trafalgar Square.

Sights—Trafalgar Square

▲▲**Trafalgar Square**—London's central square is a thrilling place to just hang out. Lord Nelson stands atop his 185-foot-tall fluted granite column, gazing out to Trafalgar, where he lost his life but defeated the French fleet. Part of this 1842 memorial is made from the melted-down cannons of his victims at Trafalgar. He's surrounded by giant lions, hordes of people, and even more pigeons. Buy a 25p cup of bird-pleasing seed. To make the birds explode into flight, you don't need to yell; simply toss a sweater into the air. (When bombed, resist the impulse to wipe immediately—it'll smear. Wait for it to dry and flake off gently.) This high-profile square is the climax of most marches and demonstrations (tube: Charing Cross).

▲▲▲**National Gallery**—Wonderfully renovated, displaying Britain's top collection of European paintings from 1250 to 1900 (works by Leonardo, Botticelli, Velázquez, Rembrandt, Turner, van Gogh, and the Impressionists), this is one of Europe's great galleries. While the collection is huge, following the 30-stop route suggested on the map on this page will give you my best quick tour. The audioguide tours are the best I've used in Europe (£4 donation requested). Don't miss the "Micro Gallery," a computer room even your dad could have fun in (closes 30 minutes earlier than museum); you can study any artist, style, or topic in the museum and even print out a tailor-made tour map (free, daily 10:00–18:00, Wed until 21:00, free one-hour overview tours daily

National Gallery Highlights

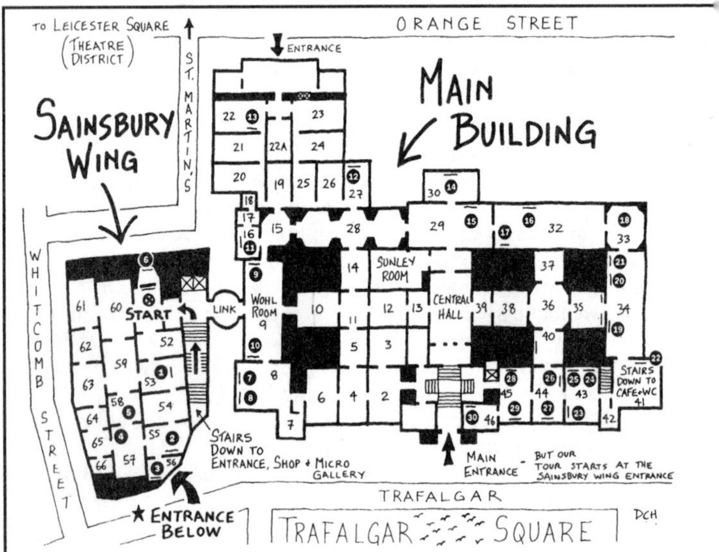

Medieval and Early Renaissance

1. Wilton Diptych
2. UCCELLO—Battle of San Romano
3. VAN EYCK—Arnolfini Marriage
4. CRIVELLI—Annunciation With St. Emidius
5. BOTTICELLI—Venus and Mars

at 11:30 and 14:30 plus Wed at 18:30, photography prohibited, on Trafalgar Square, tube: Charing Cross or Leicester Square, tel. 020/7747-2885).

▲National Portrait Gallery—Put off by halls of 19th-century characters who meant nothing to me, I used to call this "as interesting as someone else's yearbook." But a select walk through this five-centuries-long Who's Who of British history is quick and free and puts faces on the story of England. A bonus is the chance to admire some great art by painters such as Holbein, Van Dyck, Hogarth, Reynolds, and Gainsborough. The collection is well described, not huge, and in historical sequence, from the 16th century on the top floor to today's royal family on the bottom.

Some highlights: Henry VIII and wives; several fascinating portraits of the "Virgin Queen" Elizabeth I, Sir Francis Drake, and Sir Walter Raleigh; the only real-life portrait of Shakespeare; Oliver Cromwell and Charles I with his head on; self-portraits and

High Renaissance

6. LEONARDO DA VINCI—Virgin and Child (painting and cartoon)
7. MICHELANGELO—Entombment
8. RAPHAEL—Pope Julius II

Venetian Renaissance

9. TINTORETTO—Origin of the Milky Way
10. TITIAN—Bacchus and Ariadne

Northern Protestant Art

11. VERMEER—Young Woman Standing at a Virginal
12. REMBRANDT—Self Portrait
13. REMBRANDT—Belshazzar's Feast

Baroque and Rococo

14. RUBENS—The Judgment of Paris
15. VAN DYCK—Charles I on Horseback
16. VELÁZQUEZ—The Rokeby Venus
17. CARAVAGGIO—Supper at Emmaus
18. BOUCHER—Pan and Syrinx

British

19. CONSTABLE—The Hay Wain
20. TURNER—The Fighting Téméraire
21. TURNER—Rain, Steam, Speed

Impressionism and Beyond

22. DELAROCHE—The Execution of Lady Jane Grey
23. MONET—Gare St. Lazare
24. MANET—The Waitress (La Servante de Bocks)
25. DEGAS— Miss La La at the Cirque Fernando
26. RENOIR—The Umbrellas
27. SEURAT—Bathers at Asnieres
28. VAN GOGH—Sunflowers
29. CÉZANNE—Bathers
30. MONET—Water Lilies

other portraits by Gainsborough and Reynolds; the Romantics (Blake, Byron, Wordsworth, and company); Queen Victoria and her era; and the present royal family, including the late Princess Diana. For more information, follow the fine audioguide (£3 donation requested, tells more about history than art, hear actual interviews with 20th-century subjects) or get the 60p quick overview guidebooklet (free, Mon–Sat 10:00–18:00, Sun 12:00–18:00, entry 100 yards off Trafalgar Square, around the corner from the National Gallery, opposite Church of St. Martin-in-the-Fields, tel. 020/7306-0055).

▲**St. Martin-in-the-Fields**—This church, built in the 1720s, with a Gothic spire placed upon a Greek-type temple, is an oasis of peace on wild and noisy Trafalgar Square. St. Martin cared for the poor. "In the fields" was where the first church stood on this spot (in the 13th century), between Westminster and the City. Stepping inside, you still feel a compassion for the needs of the people in this community. The church is famous for its concerts. Consider a free lunchtime concert (Mon, Tue, and Fri at 13:05) or an evening concert (Thu, Fri, and Sat at 19:30, £6–16, CC:VM, box office tel. 020/7839-8362, church tel. 020/7930-0089). Downstairs you'll find a ticket office for concerts, a good shop, a brass-rubbing centre, and a fine budget support-the-church cafeteria (see "Eating," below).

More Top Squares: Piccadilly, Soho, and Covent Garden

▲▲Piccadilly Circus—London's touristy square got its name from the fancy ruffled shirts—picadils—made in the neighborhood long ago. Today the square is surrounded by fascinating streets and swimming with youth on the rampage. The Rock Circus offers a commercial but serious history of rock music with Madame Tussaud wax stars. While overpriced, it's an entertaining hour under radio earphones for rock 'n' roll romantics—many enter with a beer buzz and sing happily off-key under their headphones—nearly as entertaining as the exhibit itself (£8.25, daily 10:00–21:00, plenty of photo ops, tube: Piccadilly Circus, tel. 020/7734-8025). For overstimulation, drop by the extremely trashy Pepsi Trocadero Center's "theme park of the future" for its Segaworld virtual reality games, nine-screen cinema, and thundering IMAX theater (admission to Trocadero is free; individual attractions cost £2–8; find a discount ticket at brochure racks at TI or hotels before paying full price for IMAX; between Coventry and Shaftesbury, just off Piccadilly). Chinatown, to the east, has swollen since Hong Kong lost its independence. Nearby Shaftesbury Avenue and Leicester Square teem with fun seekers, theaters, Chinese restaurants, and street singers.

Soho—North of Piccadilly, seedy Soho is becoming trendy and is well worth a gawk. Soho is London's red-light district, where "friendly models" wait in tiny rooms up dreary stairways and scantily clad con artists sell strip shows. While venturing up a stairway to check out a model is interesting, anyone who goes into any one of the shows will be ripped off. Every time. Even a £3 show comes with a £100 cover or minimum (as it's printed on the drink menu) and a "security man." You may accidentally buy a £200 bottle of bubbly. And suddenly, the door has no handle. By the way, telephone sex is hard to avoid these days in London. Phone booths are littered with racy fliers of busty ladies "new in town." Some travelers gather six or eight phone booths' worth of fliers and take them home for kinky wallpaper.

▲▲Covent Garden—This boutique-ish shopping district is a people watcher's delight with cigarette eaters, Punch-and-Judy acts, food that's good for you (but not your wallet), trendy crafts, sweet whiffs of pot, two-tone hair (neither natural), and faces that

Central London

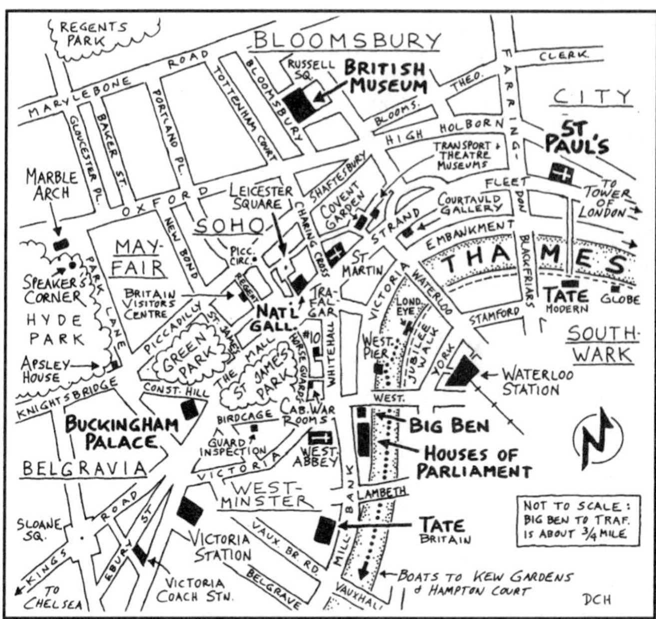

could set off a metal detector (tube: Covent Garden). For better Covent Garden lunch deals, walk a block or two away from the eye of this touristic hurricane (check out the places a block or two north of the tube station along Endell Street and Neal Street—try Food for Thought at #31), and for a "Food is Fun" dinner-crawl from Covent Garden to Soho, see "Eating," below.

Museums near Covent Garden

▲Courtauld Gallery—While far less impressive than the National Gallery, this generally overlooked yet wonderful collection of paintings is a joy. Part of the Courtauld Institute of Art, the thoughtful descriptions of each piece of art remind visitors that the gallery is still used for teaching. You'll see medieval European paintings, and works by Rubens, Impressionists (Manet, Monet, Degas, Seurat), and Post-Impressionists (Cezanne). An additional fee or combo ticket gets you into the Gilbert Collection, a glittering display of gold, silver, and tiny mosaics from the 15th to 19th centuries (£4 apiece, £7 combo includes Courtauld and Gilbert, both free Mon 10:00–14:00, Mon–Sat 10:00–18:00, Sun 12:00–18:00, located in Somerset House, near Waterloo Bridge, enter on Strand, tube: Temple or Covent Garden, tel. 020/7848-2526).

▲London Transport Museum—This wonderful museum is a delight for kids. Whether you're cursing or marveling at the buses and tube, the growth of Europe's biggest city has been made possible by its public transit system. Watch the growth of the tube, then sit in the simulator to "drive" a train (£5.50, Sat–Thu 10:00–18:00, Fri 11:00–18:00, 30 yards southeast of Covent Garden's marketplace, tel. 020/7836-8557).

Theatre Museum—This earnest museum, probably worthwhile only for theater buffs, traces the development of British theater from Shakespeare to today (£4.50, Tue–Sun 10:00–18:00, closed Mon, a block east of Covent Garden's marketplace down Russell Street, call about guided tours, makeup demos, and costume workshops, tel. 020/7943-4700).

Sights—North London

▲▲▲British Museum—This is the greatest chronicle of our civilization anywhere. Visiting this immense museum is like hiking through Encyclopedia Britannica National Park.

The museum has undergone a major transformation for the millennium and for its 250th birthday in 2003. With more than 6 million visitors a year, Britain's most popular museum was due for an upgrade.

Entering on Great Russell Street, you'll step into the **Great Court**, the new glass-domed hub of a two-acre cultural complex. This bustling people zone of shops, restaurants, and lecture halls stays open after the museum closes for the day. The Round Reading Room (Marx's hangout), located within the Great Court, has been restored and is once again public. The new Ethnographic Galleries contain collections on life in Africa, Asia, and the Americas.

After an overview ramble, cover just two or three sections of your choice more thoroughly. The Egyptian, Mesopotamian (Assyrian), and Greek (Parthenon) sections are highlights.

The huge winged lions (which guarded Assyrian palaces 800 years before Christ) guard the museum's three great ancient galleries. For a brief tour, connect these ancient dots:

Start with the **Egyptian.** Wander from the Rosetta Stone past the many statues. At the end of the hall, climb the stairs to mummy land.

Back at the winged lions, wander through the dark, violent, and mysterious **Assyrian** rooms. The Nimrud Gallery is lined with royal propaganda reliefs and wounded lions.

The most modern of the ancient art fills the **Greek** section. Find room 1 behind the winged lions and start your walk through Greek art history with the simple and primitive Cycladic fertility figures. Later, painted vases show a culture really into partying. The finale is the Elgin Marbles. The much-wrangled-over bits of the Athenian Parthenon (from 450 B.C.) are even more impressive than they look. To best appreciate these ancient carvings, take the free audioguide tour and read through the orientation material in the tiny area between rooms 7 and 8. (Free, £2 donation requested, Mon–Sat 10:00–17:00, Sun 12:00–18:00, least crowded weekday late afternoons, Great Russell Street, tube: Tottenham Court Road, tel. 020/7323-8000 or 020/7388-2227, www.thebritishmuseum.ac.uk.)

There are three types of **tours**: Highlights tours (£7, 4/day, 90 min), Focus tours (£5, 2/day, 60 min), and Eye Openers (free, nearly hrly, 50 min). For tour times, call ahead or check schedule and brochures at entry.

▲▲▲British Library—In the new and impressive British Library, wander through the manuscripts that have enlightened and brightened our lives for centuries. While the library contains 180 miles of bookshelves in London's deepest basement, one beautiful room filled with state-of-the-art glass display cases shows you the treasures: ancient maps, early Gospels on papyrus, illuminated manuscripts from the early Middle Ages, the Gutenberg Bible, the Magna Carta, pages from Leonardo's notebooks, and original writing by the titans of English literature, from Chaucer and Shakespeare to Dickens and Wordsworth. There's also a wall dedicated to music, with manuscripts from Beethoven to the Beatles. To virtually flip through the pages of a few precious books, drop by the "Turning the Pages" room (free, Mon–Fri 9:30–18:00, Tue 9:30–20:00, Sat 9:30–17:00, Sun 11:00–17:00; 60-minute tours for £4 usually offered Mon, Wed, and Fri–Sun at 15:00, also Tue 18:30, Sat 10:30, and Sun 11:30, call 020/7412-7332 to confirm schedule and reserve, great cafeteria/restaurant upstairs from café, tube: King's Cross, leaving station, turn right and walk a block to 96 Euston Road, library tel. 020/7412-7000, www.bl.uk).

▲Madame Tussaud's Waxworks—This is expensive but dang good. The original Madame Tussaud did wax casts of heads lopped off during the French Revolution (e.g., Marie Antoinette). She took her show on the road and ended up in London. And now it's much easier to be featured. The gallery is one big Who's Who photo op—a huge hit with the kind of travelers who skip the British Museum. Don't miss the "make a model" exhibit (showing Jerry Hall getting waxed) or the gallery of has-been heads that no longer merit a body (such as Sammy Davis Jr. and Nikita Khrushchev). After looking a hundred famous people in the glassy eyes and surviving a silly hall of horror, you'll board a Disney-type ride and cruise through a kid-pleasing "Spirit of London" time trip (£11.50, kids-£8, under age 5 free; combo ticket for Tussaud's and Planetarium-£14, kids-£9.50; Jan–Sept daily 9:00–17:30, Oct–Dec Mon–Fri 10:00–17:30, Sat–Sun 9:30–17:30, Marylebone Road, tube: Baker Street). Avoid a wait by either booking ahead to get a ticket with an entry time (tel. 0870/400 3000, online at www.madame-tussaud.com, or at TI) or arriving late in the day—90 minutes is plenty of time for the exhibit.

Sir John Soane's Museum—Architects and fans love this quirky place crammed with art and architectural bric-a-brac (free, Tue–Sat 10:00–17:00, also first Tue of month 18:00–21:00, closed Sun–Mon, 13 Lincoln's Inn Fields, 5 blocks east of British Museum, tube: Holborn, tel. 020/7405-2107).

Sights—Buckingham Palace

▲Buckingham Palace—This lavish home has been the royal residence since 1837. When the queen's at home, the royal standard flies; otherwise the Union Jack flaps in the wind (£10.50 for state apartments and throne room, open Aug and Sept only, daily 9:30–16:30, only 8,000 visitors a day—come early to get an appointed visit time or call 020/7321-2233 and reserve a ticket with CC, tube: Victoria).

▲▲Changing of the Guard at Buckingham Palace—The guards change with much fanfare at 11:30 daily May through August and generally every even-numbered day September through April (no band when wet; worth a 50p phone call any day to confirm that they'll change, tel. 0891-505-452). Join the mob at the back of the palace (the front faces a huge and extremely private park). You'll need to be early or tall to see much of the actual changing of the guard, but for the pageantry in the street you can pop by at 11:30. Stake out the high ground on the circular Victoria Monument for the best general views. The marching troops and bands are colorful and even stirring, but the actual changing of the guard is a non-event. It is interesting, however, to see nearly every tourist in London gathered in one place at the same time. Hop into a big black taxi and say, "Buck House, please." The show lasts about 30 minutes: three troops parade by, the guard changes with much shouting, the band plays a happy little concert, and then they march out. On a balmy day, it's a fun happening.

For all the color with none of the crowds, see the **Inspection of the Guard Ceremony** at 11:00 in front of the **Wellington Barracks**, 500 yards east of the palace on Birdcage Walk. Afterwards, stroll through nearby St. James' Park (tube: Victoria, St. James' Park, or Green Park).

Sights—West London

▲Hyde Park and Speakers' Corner—London's "Central Park"—originally Henry VIII's hunting ground—has more than 600 acres of lush greenery, a huge man-made lake, the royal Kensington Palace (not worth touring), and the ornate neo-Gothic Albert Memorial across from the Royal Albert Hall. Early afternoons on Sunday, Speakers' Corner offers soapbox oratory at its best (tube: Marble Arch). "The grass roots of democracy" is actually a holdover from when the gallows stood here and the criminal was allowed to say just about anything he wanted to before he swung. I dare you to raise your voice and gather a crowd—it's easy to do.

▲Apsley House (Wellington Museum)—Having beat Napoleon at Waterloo, the Duke of Wellington was the most famous man in Europe. He was given London's ultimate address, #1 London. His newly refurbished mansion offers one of London's best palace experiences. An 11-foot-tall marble statue (by Canova) of Napoleon clad only in a fig leaf greets you. Downstairs is a small gallery of Wellington memorabilia (including a 30-minute video and a pair of Wellington boots). The lavish upstairs shows off the duke's fine collection of paintings, including works by Velázquez and Steen (well described by included audioguide, £4.50, Tue–Sun 11:00–17:00, closed Mon, 20 yards from Hyde Park Corner tube station, tel. 020/7499-5676). Hyde Park's pleasant and picnic-wonderful rose garden is nearby.

▲▲Victoria and Albert Museum—The world's top collection of decorative arts is a gangly (150 rooms over 12 miles of corridors) but surprisingly interesting assortment of artistic stuff from the West as well as Asian and Islamic cultures. The V&A, which grew out of the Great Exhibition of 1851—that ultimate festival celebrating the Industrial Revolution and the greatness of Britain—was originally for manufactured art. But after much support from Queen Victoria and Prince Albert, it was renamed after the royal couple, and its present building was opened in 1909. The idealistic Victorian notion that anyone can be continually improved by education and example remains the driving force behind this museum.

While just wandering works well here, consider catching one of the regular 60-minute orientation tours, buying the fine £5 "Hundred Highlights" guidebook, or walking through these ground-floor highlights: Medieval Treasury (room 43, well-described treasury of Middle Age European art), the finest collection of Indian decorative art outside India (room 41), the Dress Gallery (room 40, 400 years of English fashion corseted into 40 display cases), the Raphael Gallery (room 48a, seven huge watercolor "cartoons" painted as designs for tapestries to hang in the Sistine Chapel, among the greatest art treasures in Britain and the best works of the High Renaissance), reliefs by the Renaissance sculptor Donatello (room 16), a close-up look at medieval stained glass (room 28, much more upstairs), the fascinating Cast Courts (rooms 46a and 46b, filled with plaster copies of the greatest art of our civilization—such as Trajan's Column and Michelangelo's *David*—made for the benefit of 19th-century art students who couldn't afford a railpass), and the hall of "great" fakes and forgeries (room 46). Upstairs you can walk through the British Galleries for centuries of aristocratic living rooms (£5, daily 10:00–18:00, free after 16:30, £3 admission on Wed 18:30–21:30, open Wed eve year-round except mid-Dec–mid-Jan; the museum café is in the delightfully ornate Gamble Room from

1868, just off room 14, tube: South Kensington, a long tunnel leads directly from the tube station to the museum, tel. 020/7938-8500).

▲**Natural History Museum**—Across the street from the Victoria and Albert Museum, this mammoth museum is housed in a giant and wonderful Victorian neo-Romanesque building. Built in the 1870s specifically to house the huge collection (50 million specimens), it presents itself in two halves: the Life Galleries (creepy-crawlies, human biology, the origin of the species, "our place in evolution," and awesome dinosaurs) and the Earth Galleries (meteors, volcanoes, earthquakes, and so on). Exhibits are wonderfully explained with lots of creative interactive displays (£7.50, children under 16 free, free to anyone after 16:30 on weekdays and after 17:00 on weekends—pop in if only for the wild collection of dinosaurs, Mon–Sat 10:00–17:50, Sun 11:00–17:50, a long tunnel leads directly from South Kensington tube station to museum, tel. 020/7938-9123, www.nhm.ac.uk).

Sights—East London: "The City"

▲▲**The City of London**—When Londoners say "The City," they mean the one-square-mile business, banking, and journalism center that 2,000 years ago was Roman Londinium. The outline of the Roman city walls can still be seen in the arc of roads from Blackfriars Bridge to Tower Bridge. Within the City are 24 churches designed by Christopher Wren, mostly just ornamentation around St. Paul's Cathedral. Today, while home to only 5,000 residents, the City thrives with over 500,000 office workers coming and going daily. It's a fascinating district to wander, but since almost nobody actually lives there, it's dull on Saturday and Sunday.

▲**Old Bailey**—To see the British legal system in action—lawyers in little blond wigs speaking legalese with a British accent—spend a few minutes in the visitors' gallery at "Old Bailey" (free, Mon–Fri 10:00–13:00, 14:00–14:30 most weeks, no kids under 14, no bags or cameras, purses OK, you can check your bag at the SPAR grocery across the street for £1, 2 blocks northwest of St. Paul's on Old Bailey Street, follow signs to public entrance, tube: St. Paul's, tel. 020/7248-3277).

▲▲▲**St. Paul's Cathedral**—Wren's most famous church is the great St. Paul's, its elaborate interior capped by a 365-foot dome. The crypt (included with admission) is a world of historic bones and memorials, including Admiral Nelson's tomb and interesting cathedral models. The great West Door is opened only for great occasions, such as the wedding of Prince Charles and the late Princess Diana in 1981. Stand at the back of the church and imagine how Diana felt before making the hike to the altar with the world watching. Sit under the second-largest dome in the world and eavesdrop on guided tours.

Since World War II, St. Paul's has been Britain's symbol of

East London: "The City"

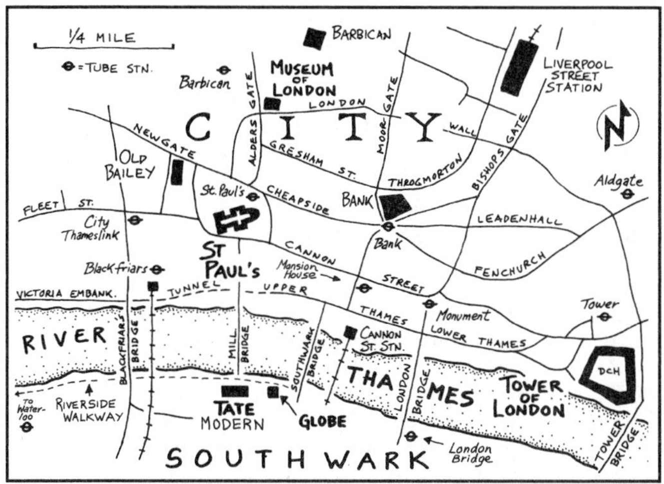

resistance. Despite 57 nights of bombing, the Nazis failed to destroy the cathedral, thanks to the St. Paul's volunteer fire watch who stayed on the dome. Climb the dome for a great city view and some fun in the whispering gallery—where the precisely designed barrel of the dome lets sweet nothings circle audibly around to the opposite side (£5 entry, Mon–Sat 8:30–16:30, last entry 16:00, closed Sun except for worship, allow an hour to climb up and down dome—closed Sun, no photography allowed within church, £2.50 for guided 90-minute "super tours" of cathedral and crypt offered at 11:00, 11:30, 13:30, and 14:00 or £3 for an audioguide tour anytime, Sun services at 8:00, 10:15, 11:30, and 15:15—evensong, good restaurant, and cheap and cheery café in the crypt, tube: St. Paul's, tel. 020/7236-8348).

The **evensong** services are free, though visitors are not allowed to linger afterward (Mon–Sat at 17:00, Sun at 15:15, 40 min).

▲Museum of London— London, a 2000-year-old city, is so littered with Roman ruins that when a London builder finds Roman antiquities he doesn't stop work. He simply documents the finds, moves the artifacts to a museum, and builds on. If you're asking, "Why did the Romans build their cities underground?," a trip to the creative and entertaining London Museum is a must. Stroll through London history from pre-Roman times through the Blitz up to today. This regular stop for the local schoolkids gives the best overview of London history in town (£5, free after 16:30, Mon–Sat 10:00–18:00, Sun 12:00–18:00, tube: Barbican or St. Paul's, tel. 020/7600-3699).

Geffrye Decorative Arts Museum—Walk through British front rooms from 1600 to 1990 (free, Tue–Sat 10:00–17:00, Sun 12:00–17:00, closed Mon, tube: Liverpool Street, then bus 149 or 242 north, tel. 020/7739-9893).

▲▲▲Tower of London—The Tower has served as a castle in wartime, a king's residence in peace, and, most notoriously, as the prison and execution site of rebels. This historic fortress is host to more than 3 million visitors a year. Enjoy the free, and riotously entertaining, 50-minute Beefeater tour (leaves regularly from inside the gate, last one is usually at 15:30 in summer, 14:30 off-season). The crown jewels, dating from the Restoration, are the best on earth—and come with hour-long lines for most of the day. To avoid the crowds, arrive at 9:00 and go straight for the jewels, doing the tour and tower later—or do the jewels after 16:30 (£11, one-day combo ticket with Hampton Court Palace-£18.50, March–Oct Mon–Sat 9:00–18:00, Sun 10:00–18:00, Nov–Feb Tue–Sat 9:00–17:00, Sun–Mon 10:00–17:00, last entry 1 hr before closing, the long but fast-moving ticket line is worst on Sun, no photography allowed of jewels or in chapels, tube: Tower Hill, tel. 020/7709-0765, recorded info: 020/7680-9004).

Ceremony of the Keys: Every night at 21:30, with pageantry-filled ceremony, the Tower of London is locked up (as it has been for the last 700 years). To attend this free 30-minute event, you need to request an invitation at least two to three months before your visit. Write to: Ceremony of the Keys, H.M. Tower of London, London EC3N 4AB. Include your name; the addresses, names, and ages of all people attending (up to 7 people, nontransferable, no kids under 8 allowed); requested date; alternative dates; and an international reply coupon (buy at U.S. post office).

Sights next to the Tower—The best remaining bit of London's **Roman Wall** is just north of the tower (at the Tower Hill tube station). Freshly painted and restored, **Tower Bridge**—the neo-Gothic maritime gateway to London—has an 1894 to 1994 history exhibit (£6.25, daily 10:00–18:30, last entry at 17:15, good view, poor value, tel. 020/7403-3761). The chic **St. Katherine Yacht Harbor**, just east of the Tower Bridge, has mod shops and the classic old Dickens Inn, fun for a drink or pub lunch. Across the bridge is the South Bank, with the upscale Butlers Wharf area, museums, and promenade.

Sights—South London, on the South Bank

The South Bank is a thriving arts and cultural center tied together by a riverside path. This trendy, pub-crawling walk—called the Jubilee Promenade—stretches from the Tower of London bridge past Westminster Bridge, where it offers grand views of the Houses of Parliament. (The promenade hugs the river except just east of London Bridge, where it cuts inland for a couple of blocks.)

The South Bank

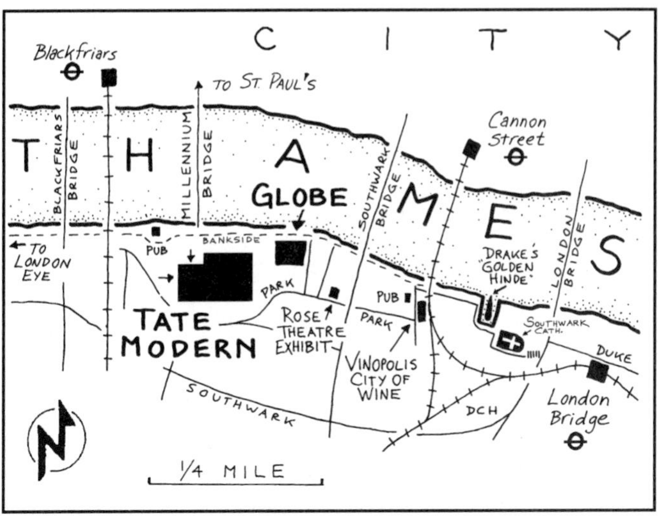

▲▲**Globe Theater**—The original Globe Theater has been rebuilt—half-timbered and thatched—exactly as it was in Shakespeare's time. Open as a museum and working theater, it hosts authentic old-time performances of Shakespeare's plays. The theater can be toured when there are no plays. The Globe's exhibition on Shakespeare is the world's largest, with interactive displays and film presentations, a sound lab, a script factory, and costumes (£7.50, mid-May–Sept daily 9:00–12:00, Oct–mid-May 10:00–17:00, includes guided 30-minute tour offered on the half hour, on the South Bank directly across the Thames over Southwark Bridge from St. Paul's, tube: Mansion House or London Bridge, tel. 020/7902-1500, www.shakespeares-globe.org, for details on seeing a play, see "Entertainment," below).

▲▲**Tate Modern**—Dedicated in spring of 2000, this striking new museum across the river from St. Paul's opened the new century with art from the old one (remember the 20th century?). Its powerhouse collection of Monet, Matisse, Dalí, Picasso, Warhol, and much more is displayed in a converted power house (museum free, fee for special exhibitions, daily 10:00–18:00, Fri–Sat until 22:00—a good time to visit, audioguide-£1, free guided tours, call for schedule, view café on top floor, walk the new Millennium Bridge from St. Paul's or tube: Southwark plus a 7-minute walk, tel. 020/7887-8008, www.tate.org.uk). From May through September, a river-bus service will connect Tate Modern with Tate Britain—ask for schedule at either Tate.

▲▲Millennium Bridge—This new pedestrian bridge links St. Paul's Cathedral and Tate Modern across the Thames. Its sleek minimalist design—370 meters long, 4 meters wide, stainless steel with teak planks—has clever aerodynamic handrails to deflect wind over the heads of pedestrians. This is London's only pedestrian bridge and its first new bridge in a century (free, always open).

▲▲▲London Eye Ferris Wheel—Towering above London opposite Big Ben, this is the world's highest observational wheel—and a chance to fly British Air without leaving London. Built like a giant bicycle wheel, it's a pan-European undertaking: British steel and Dutch engineering, with Czech, German, French, and Italian mechanical parts. It's also very "green," running extremely efficiently and virtually silently. Twenty-five people ride in each of its 32 air-conditioned capsules for the 30-minute rotation (each capsule has a bench, but most people stand).

The "flight" is as tame as an elevator ride, but fun for the grand views. From the top of this 450-foot-high wheel—the highest public viewpoint in the city, Big Ben looks small. You only go around once; save a shot on top for the glass capsule of people next to yours.

A big hit with Londoners and tourists alike, the ride gets booked up fast, especially on weekends. To save time and guarantee a spot, book a time slot a day ahead—at a London TI, in person at the office near the base of the wheel, at the Big Bus Information Centre (daily 8:30–17:30, 48 Buckingham Palace Road, a block from Victoria Station), or possibly through your hotel (ask). You can also book by phone, but allow at least five days before your ticket is available (pick up ticket at office at Wheel, 50p charge, automated booking tel. 0870-500-0600). Whether you book ahead or just stand in line, you'll be assigned—or you can request—a half-hour time slot (such as 9:00–9:30); you must arrive at the Wheel during this time (earlier is better) to ensure getting on. Advance booking, which costs nothing extra, allows you to skip the queue to buy tickets. No one escapes the second queue, the ticket-holders' line to get on the Wheel (line starts forming 10 minutes before your half-hour time slot begins; listen for announcement). The long line moves quickly; the many purple-shirted staff are there to help and herd you.

Freewheeling types who don't care for lines or prebooking will have the best luck spinning the Wheel at night; it's open until 22:00 in peak season (last boarding 21:30); if you're lucky, you can waltz right on (£8.50, April–mid-Sept 9:00–22:00, mid-Sept–March 10:00–18:00, at County Hall, WCs, coffee, shop that has binoculars for rent, on river Thames, with its own ferry dock, tube: Waterloo or Westminster, www.ba-londoneye.com). The Wheel is slated to be dismantled in 2005 and moved to a lower-profile location.

▲▲Imperial War Museum—This impressive museum covers the wars of this century, from heavy weaponry to love notes and Varga

Girls, from Monty's Africa campaign tank to Schwartzkopf's Desert Storm uniform. You can trace the development of the machine gun, watch footage of the first tank battles, hold your breath through the gruesome WWI trench experience, and buy WWII–era toys in the fun museum shop. Rather than glorify war, the museum does its best to shine a light on the powerful human side of one of mankind's most persistent traits (£5.50, free for kids under 16, daily 10:00–18:00, free for anyone after 16:30, 90 minutes is enough time for most visitors, tube: Lambeth North, tel. 020/7416-5000).

Bramah Tea and Coffee Museum—Aficionados of tea or coffee will find this small museum fascinating. It tells the story of each drink almost passionately. The owner, Mr. Bramah, comes from a big tea family and wants the world to know how the advent of commercial television, with breaks not long enough to brew a proper pot of tea, required a faster hot drink. In came the horrible English instant coffee. Tea countered with finely chopped leaves in tea bags, and it's gone downhill ever since. (£4, daily 10:00–18:00, in the Butlers Wharf complex just across the bridge from the Tower, behind the Design Museum, tel. 020/7378-0222). Its café, which serves more kinds of coffees and teas than cakes, is open to the public, not just museum goers (same hours as museum).

Sights—South London, on the North Bank

▲▲Tate Britain—One of Europe's great art houses, Tate Britain specializes in British painting: 16th century through the 20th, including Pre-Raphaelites. Commune with the mystical Blake and romantic Turner (free, daily 10:00–17:50, fine £3 audioguide, free tours: 11:30—Turner, 14:30 and 15:30—British Highlights, call to confirm schedule, no photography allowed, tube: Pimlico plus 7-minute walk, or arrive directly at museum by taking bus 88 from Oxford Circus or 77A from National Gallery, tel. 020/7887-8000, recorded info tel. 020/7887-8888, www.tate.org.uk).

Sights—Greater London

▲Kew Gardens—For a fine riverside park and a palatial greenhouse jungle to swing through, take the tube or the boat to every botanist's favorite escape, Kew Gardens. While to most visitors the Royal Botanic Gardens of Kew is simply a delightful opportunity to wander among 33,000 different types of plants, it's run by a hardworking organization committed to understanding and preserving the botanical diversity of our planet. The Kew tube station drops you in an herbal little business community a two-block walk from Victoria Gate (the main garden entry). Pick up a map brochure with a monthly listing of best blooms.

Garden lovers could spend days exploring Kew's 300 acres. For a quick visit, spend a fragrant hour wandering through three buildings: the Palm House—a humid Victorian world of iron,

Greater London

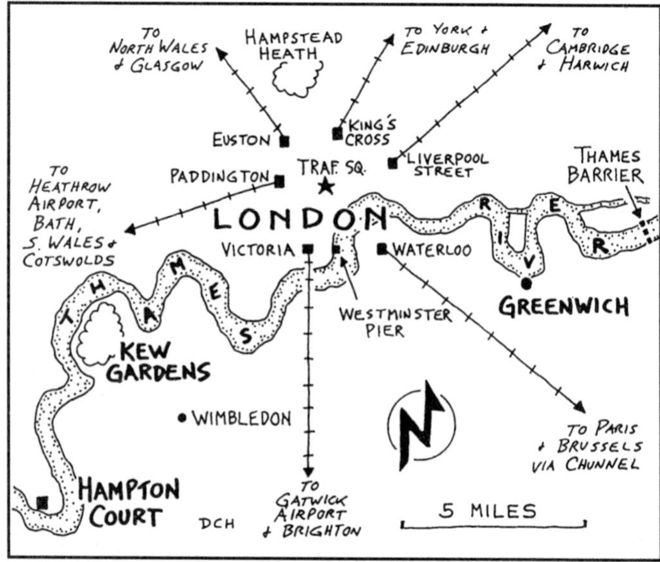

glass, and tropical plants—built in 1844; a Waterlily House—hottest in the gardens—that Monet would swim for; and the Princess of Wales Conservatory—a modern greenhouse with many different climate zones growing countless cacti, bug-munching carnivorous plants, and more (£5, Mon–Sat 9:30–18:00, Sun 9:30–19:30, until 16:30 or sunset off-season, galleries and conservatories close 45 minutes earlier, entry discounted to £3.50 at 45 minutes before closing, consider £2.50 narrated floral joyride on little train departing from Victoria Gate, tube: Kew Gardens, tel. 020/8332-5000). For a sun-dappled lunch, hike 10 minutes from the Palm House to the Orangery (£6 hot meals, daily 10:00–17:30). For tea, consider the Maids of Honor (280 Kew Road, near garden entrance, tel. 020/8940-2752).

▲**Hampton Court Palace**—Fifteen miles up the Thames from downtown (£15 taxi ride from Kew Gardens) is the 500-year-old palace of Henry VIII. Actually, it was the palace of his minister, Cardinal Wolsey. When Wolsey, a clever man, realized Henry VIII was experiencing a little palace envy, he gave it to his king. The Tudor palace was also home to Elizabeth I and Charles I. And parts were updated by Christopher Wren for William and Mary. The palace stands stately overlooking the Thames and includes some impressive Tudor rooms, including a Great Hall, with its magnificent hammer-beam ceiling. The industrial-strength Tudor kitchen was capable of keeping 600 schmoozing courtesans thoroughly—if not well—fed. The sculpted garden features a rare Tudor tennis court and a popular maze. The palace, fully restored since its 1986 fire, tries hard to please, but it doesn't quite sparkle. From the information center in the main courtyard, visitors book times for tours with tired costumed guides or grab audioguides for self-guided tours of various wings of the palace (all free). The Tudor Kitchens, Henry VIII's Apartments, and the King's Apartments are most interesting. The Georgian Rooms are pretty dull. The maze in the nearby garden is a curiosity some find fun (maze only-£2.50). The train (2/hrly, 30 min) from London's Waterloo station drops you just across the river from the palace (£10.50, one-day combo ticket with Tower of London-£18.50, Mon 10:00–18:00, Tue–Sun 9:30–18:00, Nov–March until 16:30, tel. 020/8781-9500).

RAF Museum—A hit with aviation enthusiasts, this huge aerodrome and airfield contain planes from World War I through the Battle of Britain up to the Gulf War. You can climb inside some of the planes, try your luck in a cockpit, and fly with the Red Arrows in a flight simulator (£7, daily 10:00–18:00, café, shop, car parking, Grahame Park Way, tube: Colindale—on the Northern Line, tel. 020/8205-2266, www.rafmuseum.org.uk).

Disappointments of London

The venerable BBC broadcasts from Broadcasting House. Of all its productions, its "BBC Experience" tour for visitors is among the worst. On the South Bank, the London Dungeon, a much-visited but amateurish attraction, is just a highly advertised, overpriced haunted house—certainly not worth the £10 admission, much less your valuable London time. It comes with long and rude lines. Wait for Halloween and see one in your hometown to support a better cause. The Design Museum (next to Bramah Tea and Coffee Museum) and "Winston Churchill's Britain at War Experience" (next to London Dungeon) waste your time. The Kensington Palace State Apartments are lifeless and not worth a visit.

Shopping in London

Harrods—Filled with wonderful displays, Harrods is London's most famous and touristy department store. Big yet classy, Harrods has everything from elephants to toothbrushes. The food halls are sights to savor, with cafeterias (Mon, Tue, and Sat 10:00–18:00, Wed–Fri 10:00–19:00, closed Sun, on Brompton Road, tube: Knightsbridge, tel. 020/7730-1234). Many readers report that Harrods is overpriced (its £1 toilets are the most expensive in Europe), snooty, and teeming with American and Japanese tourists. Still, it's the palace of department stores—an experience for even nonshoppers. The nearby Beauchamp Place is lined with classy and fascinating shops.

Harvey Nichols—The late Princess Diana's favorite, this is still the department store *du jour*. Its fifth floor is a food fest with a fancy restaurant and a Yo! Sushi bar. Consider a take-away tray of sushi to eat on a bench in the Hyde Park rose garden two blocks away (Mon–Tue and Sat 10:00–19:00, Wed–Fri 10:00–20:00, Sun 12:00–18:00, near Harrods, 109 Knightsbridge, tube: Knightsbridge).

Toys—The biggest toy store in Britain is **Hamley's** (Mon–Sat 10:00–20:00, Sun 12:00–18:00, 188 Regent Street, tube: Oxford Circus, tel. 020/7494-2000).

Street Markets—Antique buffs, people watchers, and folks who brake for garage sales love London's street markets. There's good early morning market activity somewhere any day of the week. The best are Portobello Road (Fri–Wed 9:00–18:00, Thu 9:00–13:00, go on Sat for antiques until 16:00—plus the regular junk, clothes, and produce; tube: Notting Hill Gate) and Camden Market (Sat–Sun 10:00–18:00, trendy arts and crafts, tube: Camden Town). The tourist office has a complete, up-to-date list. If you like to haggle, there are no holds barred in London's street markets. Warning: Markets attract two kinds of people—tourists and pickpockets.

Famous Auctions—London's famous auctioneers welcome the curious public for viewing and bidding. For schedules, call Sotheby's (Mon–Fri 9:00–16:30, 34 New Bond Street, tube: Oxford Circus or Bond Street, tel. 020/7293-5000, www.sothebys.com) or Christie's (Mon–Fri 9:00–17:00, 8 King Street, tube: Green Park, tel. 020/7839-9060, www.christies.com).

Entertainment and Theater in London

London bubbles with top-notch entertainment seven days a week. Everything's listed in the weekly entertainment magazines, available at newsstands. Choose from classical, jazz, rock, and far-out music, Gilbert and Sullivan, dance, comedy, Baha'i meetings, poetry readings, spectator sports, film, and theater.

London's theater rivals Broadway's in quality and beats it in price. Choose from the Royal Shakespeare Company, top musicals, comedy, thrillers, sex farces, and more. Performances are nightly except Sunday, usually with one matinee a week. Matinees (Wed, Thu, or Sat) are cheaper and rarely sold out. Tickets range from about £8 to £35.

Most theaters, marked on tourist maps, are in the Piccadilly-Trafalgar area. Box offices, hotels, and TIs have a handy "Theater Guide" brochure listing what's playing.

To book a seat, simply call the theater box office directly, ask about seats and dates available, and buy one with your credit card. You can call from the U.S.A. as easily as from England (photocopy your hometown library's London newspaper theater section or check out www.officiallondontheatre.co.uk). Pick up your ticket 15 minutes before the show.

Ticket agencies are scalpers with an address. Booking through an agency (at most TIs or scattered throughout London) is quick and easy, but prices are inflated by a standard 25 percent fee. If buying from an agency, look at the ticket carefully (your price should be no more than 30 percent over the printed face value; the 17 percent VAT tax is already included in the face value) and understand where you're sitting according to the floor plan (if your view is restricted it will state this on ticket). Agencies are worthwhile only if a show you've got to see is sold out at the box office. They scarf up hot tickets, planning to make a killing after the show is sold out. U.S. booking agencies get their tickets from another agency, adding even more to your expense by involving yet another middleman. Many tickets sold on the streets are forgeries. With cheap international phone calls and credit cards, there's no reason not to book direct.

Theater lingo: stalls (ground floor), dress circle (first balcony), upper circle (second balcony), balcony (sky-high third balcony).

Cheap theater tricks: Most theaters offer cheap returned tickets, standing room, matinee, and senior or student standby deals. These "concessions" are indicated with a *conc* or *s* in the listings. While theaters won't technically discount tickets, during slow times they'll offer to sell you a cheap seat and "upgrade" it to an expensive one for free—it doesn't hurt to ask. Picking up a late return can get you a great seat at a cheap-seat price. Standing room can be very cheap. If a show is "sold out," there's usually a way to get a seat. Call the theater box office and ask how. I buy the second-cheapest tickets directly from the theater box office.

The famous "half-price booth" in Leicester (pronounced "Lester") Square sells discounted tickets for good seats to shows on the push list the day of the show only (Mon–Sat 12:00–18:30). The real half-price booth is a free-standing kiosk at the edge of the garden actually in Leicester Square. Several dishonest outfits advertise "official half-price tickets" at agencies closer to the tube station. Avoid these.

Many theaters are so small that there's hardly a bad seat. After the lights go down, "scooting up" is less than a capital offense. Shakespeare did it.

Royal Shakespeare Company—If you'll ever enjoy Shakespeare, it'll be in Britain. The RSC performs at the Barbican Centre in London from December through May (box office open daily 9:00–20:00, call 020/7638-8891 to book with credit card, or for recorded information, call 020/7628-9760) and year-round at the Royal Shakespeare Theatre in Stratford (box office tel. 01789/ 295-623). To get a schedule, either request it by phone (tel. 020/7638-8891), write to the Royal Shakespeare Theatre

(Stratford-upon-Avon, CV37 6BB Warwickshire), or visit www.rsc.org.uk. Tickets for London performances range in price from £10 to £30. The best way to book is direct, by telephone and credit card. You can pick up your ticket at the door (Barbican Centre, Silk Street, tube: Barbican). Students, seniors, and those under 16 can get tickets for half price.

Shakespeare at the Globe Theater—To see Shakespeare in an exact replica of the theater for which he wrote his plays, attend a play at the Globe. This thatch-roofed, open-air round theater does the plays as Shakespeare intended (with no amplification). There are performances from mid-May through September (usually Tue–Sat 14:00 and 19:30, Sun at either 13:00 and 18:30 or at 16:00 only, and no plays on Mon). You'll pay £5 to stand and £10 to £26 to sit (usually on a backless bench; only a few rows and the pricier Gentlemen's Rooms have seats with backs). The £5 "yard" (or "groundling") tickets—while the only ones open to rain—are most fun. You're a crude peasant. You can walk around, munch a picnic dinner, lean your elbows on the stage, and even interact with the actors. I've never enjoyed Shakespeare as much as here, performed as it was meant to be in the "wooden O." The theater is on the South Bank directly across the Thames over Southwark Bridge from St. Paul's (tube: Mansion House, tel. 020/7902-1500, box office tel. 020/7401-9919). Plays are long. Many groundlings leave before the end. If you like, hang out an hour before the finish and beg or buy a ticket off someone leaving early (groundlings are allowed to come and go). The Globe is far from public transport, but the courtesy phone in the lobby gets a minicab in minutes. Confirm the cost, but they seem to be much cheaper than the official black cabs (£5–6 to Victoria Station).

Music—For easy, cheap, or free concerts in historic churches, check the TI's listings for lunch concerts (especially Wren's St. Bride's Church, tel. 020/7353-1301; St. James at Piccadilly; and St. Martin-in-the-Fields, Mon, Tue, and Fri at 13:05, church tel. 020/7930-0089). St. Martin-in-the-Fields also hosts fine evening concerts by candlelight (Thu, Fri, and Sat at 19:30, £6–16, CC:VM, box office tel. 020/7839-8362). For a fun classical event (mid-June–early Sept only), attend a "Prom Concert." This is an annual music festival with nightly concerts in the Royal Albert Hall at give-a-peasant-some-culture prices (£3 standing-room spots sold at the door; £5–65 seats, most £21.50, CC:VM, tube: South Kensington, tel. 020/7589-8212, www.royalalberthall.com).

Cruises—Of the Thames River evening cruises that offer four-course meals and dancing, London Showboat offers the best value (£45, 3.5 hrs, 4-course meal, April–Oct Wed–Sun departs 19:00 from Westminster Pier, tel. 020/7237-5134, www.citycruises.com). For more on cruising, get the Thames River Services brochure from a London TI.

London Day Trips

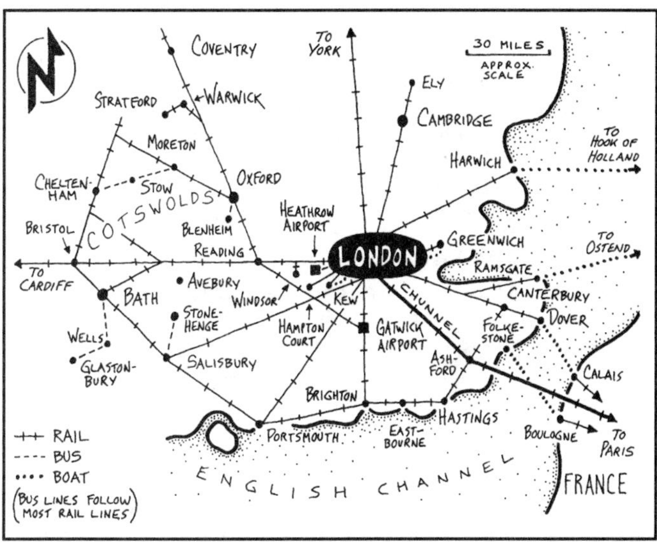

Day Trips from London

You could fill a book with the many easy and exciting day trips from London (Earl Steinbicker did: *Daytrips London: Fifty One-Day Adventures by Rail or Car, in and around London and Southern England*). Several tour companies take London-based travelers out and back every day. Original London Walks offers a variety of Explorer day trips using the train for about £10 plus transportation costs (see their walking-tour brochure, tel. 020/7624-3978, www.walks.com).

A big bus tour can be used by those without a car as a "free" way to get to Bath or Stow-on-the-Wold (saving you, for instance, the £31 London–Bath train ticket). Evan Evans' tours leave from the Victoria Coach Station daily every morning (with your bag stowed under the bus), include a day of sightseeing, and leave you in Bath before returning to London (£48 for fully guided version offered year-round; £33 for Low Cost version offered April–Oct—bus transportation only—there's a small chance this cheaper version won't be offered in 2001). You can book the tour at the Victoria Station TI, the Evan Evans' office (258 Vauxhall Bridge Road, near Victoria Station, tel. 020/7950-1777, www.evanevans.co.uk), or at Green Line Travel Office (4a Fountain Square, across from Victoria Coach Station, tel. 020/7950-1777)—please note that you have to specifically ask about the Low Cost version of the tour. Golden Tours also offers a similar, daily, fully guided tour of Stonehenge and Bath for similar prices (about £48, departs from Fountain Square, across from Victoria Coach Station, tel. 020/7233-6668, www.goldentours.co.uk).

The British rail system uses London as a hub and normally offers round-trip fares (after 9:30) that cost virtually the same as one-way fares. "Day return" tickets are best (and cheapest) for day trips. You can save a little money if you purchase Super Advance tickets before 18:00 on the day before your trip. But given the high cost of big-city living and the charm of small-town England, rather than side-tripping, I'd see London and get out.

Sleeping in London

(£1 = about $1.60, country code: 44, area code: 020)

Sleep Code: **S** = Single, **D** = Double/Twin, **T** = Triple, **Q** = Quad, **b** = bathroom, **t** = toilet only, **s** = shower only, **CC** = Credit Card (**V**isa, **M**asterCard, **A**mex). Unless otherwise noted, prices include a generous breakfast and all taxes.

London is expensive. For £50 ($80), you'll get a sleepable double with breakfast in a safe, cramped, and dreary place with minimal service. For £60 ($95) you'll get a basic, clean, reasonably cheery double in a usually cramped, cracked-plaster building or a soulless but comfortable room without breakfast in a huge Motel 6–type place. My London splurges, at £100 to £140 ($170–240), are spacious, thoughtfully appointed places you'd be happy to entertain or make love in. Hearty English or generous buffet breakfasts are included unless otherwise noted, and TVs are nearly standard in rooms.

Reserve your London room with a phone call or e-mail as soon as you can commit to a date. A few places will hold a room with no deposit if you promise to arrive by midday. Most take your credit-card number as security. Most have expensive cancellation policies. Some fancy £120 rooms rent for half price if you arrive late on a slow day and ask for a deal.

Sleeping in Victoria Station Neighborhood, Belgravia

The streets behind Victoria Station teem with budget B&Bs. It's a safe, surprisingly tidy, and decent area without a hint of the trashy touristy glitz of the streets in front of the station. Here in Belgravia, your neighbors include Andrew Lloyd Webber and Margaret Thatcher (her policeman stands outside 73 Chester Square). Decent eateries abound (see "Eating," below). The cheaper listings are dumpy. Don't expect £90 cheeriness in a £50 room. Off-season save money by arriving late without a reservation and checking around. Fierce competition softens prices, especially for multi-night stays. Particularly for Warwick Way hotels (and on hot summer nights), request a quiet back room. All are within a five-

London, Victoria Station Neighborhood

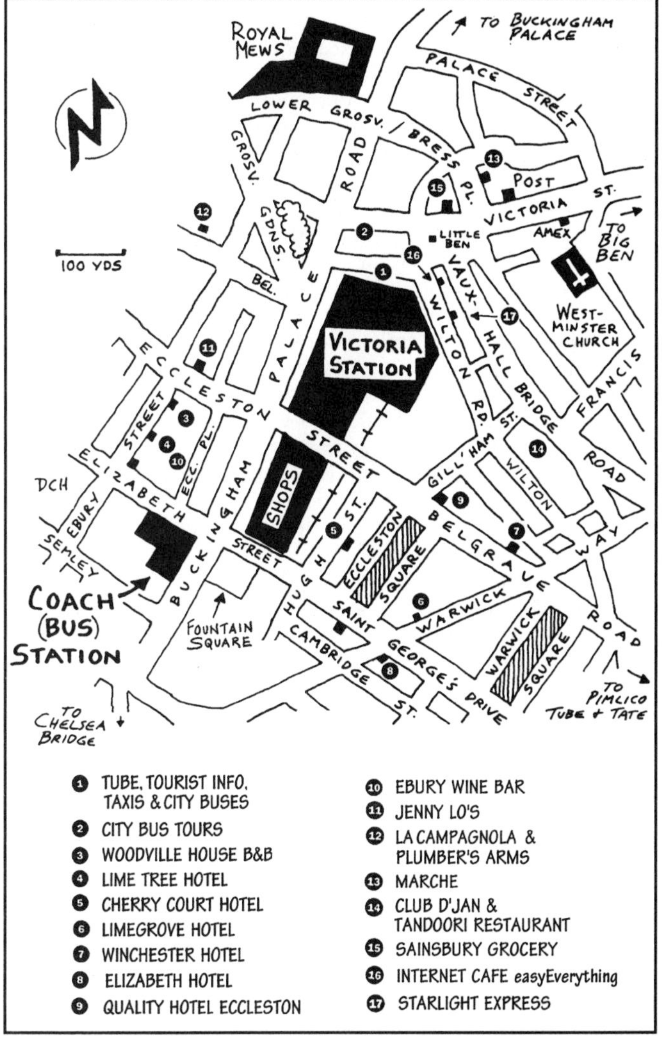

minute walk of the Victoria tube, bus, and train stations. There's an £8-per-day garage, a nearby launderette (daily 8:00–20:30, self-serve or full-serve, past Warwick Square at 3 Westmoreland Terrace, tel. 020/7821-8692), and an easygoing little dance club (Club D'Jan, £5 includes drink, Wed–Sat, 63 Wilton Road).

Winchester Hotel is family run and perhaps the best value, with 18 fine rooms, no claustrophobia, and a wise and caring management (Db-£80, Tb-£105, Qb-£125, no CC, no groups, no small children, 17 Belgrave Road, London SW1V 1RB, tel. 020/7828-2972, fax 020/7828-5191, run by Jimmy).

In **Woodville House,** the quarters are dollhouse tight, showers are down the hall, and several rooms are on the noisy street (doubles on quiet backside, twins and singles on street), but this well-run, well-worn place is a good value, with lots of travel tips and friendly chat—especially about the local rich and famous—from Rachel Joplin (S-£42, D-£62, bunky family deals-£80–110 for up to 5, CC:VM, 107 Ebury Street, SW1W 9QU, tel. 020/7730-1048, fax 020/7730-2574, www.woodvillehouse.co.uk, e-mail: woodville.house@cwcom.net).

Lime Tree Hotel, enthusiastically run by David and Marilyn Davies, comes with spacious and thoughtfully decorated rooms and a fun-loving breakfast room. While priced a bit steep, the place has character plus (Sb-£75, Db-£100–110, Tb-£140, family room-£145, David deals in slow times and is creative at helping travelers in a bind, CC:VM, 135 Ebury Street, SW1W 9RA, tel. 020/7730-8191, fax 020/7730-7865).

Elizabeth House feels institutional and a bit bland—as you might expect from a former YMCA—but the rooms are clean and bright, and the price is right (S-£30, D-£50, Db-£60, T-£75, Q-£85, CC:VM, 118 Warwick Way, SW1 4JB, tel. 020/7630-0741, fax 020/7630-0740, e-mail: elizabethhouse@compuserve.com).

Quality Hotel Eccleston is big, modern, well located, and a fine value for no-nonsense comfort (Db-£108, on slow days drop-ins can ask for "saver prices"—33 percent off on first night, breakfast extra, CC:VMA, nonsmoking floor, elevator, 82 Eccleston Square, SW1V 1PS, tel. 020/7834-8042, fax 020/7630-8942, e-mail: admin@gb614.u-net.com).

Astors Hotel has a helpful staff and 22 decent rooms, some with high ceilings (Db-£72, CC:VM, discount for payment in cash, 110 Ebury Street, SW1W 9QD, tel. 020/7730-3811, fax 020/7823-6728, www.astors.uk.com).

Georgian House Hotel has 50 pleasant rooms, with a cheaper annex that attracts backpackers (D-£40, Db-£66, annex Db-£55, CC:VM, small breakfast, Internet access, 35 St. George's Drive, SW1V 4DG, tel. 020/7834-1438, fax 020/7976-6085, www.georgianhousehotel.co.uk).

Enrico Hotel, with 26 simple rooms, is basic, older, clean, and affordable (S-£45, D-£55, Ds-£60, 77 Warwick Way, SW1V 1QP, tel. 020/7834-9583, fax 020/7233-9995, www.enricohotel.fsnet.co.uk).

These three places come with cramped rooms and claustrophobic halls. While they generate a lot of reader complaints, I list them because they offer cheap beds at youth hostel prices and are beautifully located a few minutes' walk from Victoria Station: **Cherry Court Hotel** is run by the friendly and industrious Patel family (S-£30, Sb-£42, Db-£48, T-£55, Tb-£70, price promised with this book, CC:VMA, using CC adds 5 percent extra, nonsmoking, Internet access, TV, phones, fruit basket breakfast in room, no twins—only double beds, 23 Hugh Street, SW1V 1QJ, tel. 020/7828-2840, fax 020/7828-0393, www.cherrycourthotel.co.uk). **Cedar Guest House,** run by a Polish organization to help Poles afford London, welcomes all (D-£40, Db-£50, T-£60, 30 Hugh Street, SW1V 1RP, tel. 020/7828-2625). **Limegrove Hotel,** run by harried Joyce, more musty and run-down, serves a humble breakfast in the room (S-£28, D-£38, Db-£50, T-£48, Tb-£60, cheaper off-season, lots of stairs, 101 Warwick Way, SW1V 1QL, tel. 020/7828-0458). Back rooms are quieter.

Big, Cheap, Modern Hotels

These places—popular with budget tour groups—are well run and offer elevators and all the modern comforts in a no-frills practical package. The doubles for £60 to £70 are a great value for London.

London County Hall Travel Inn, literally down the hall from a $400-a-night Marriott Hotel, fills one end of London's massive former City Hall. This place is wonderfully located, near the base of the London Eye Ferris Wheel, and across the Thames from Big Ben. Its 300 slick and no-frills rooms come with all the necessary comforts (Db-£70 for 2 adults and up to 2 kids under age 15, couples can request a bigger family room—same price, breakfast extra, book in advance, no-show rooms are released at 16:00, elevator, some smoke-free and easy-access rooms, CC:VMA, 500 yards from Westminster tube stop and Waterloo Station where the Chunnel train leaves for Paris, Belvedere Road, SE1 7PB, tel. 020/7902-1600, fax 020/7902-1619, www.travelinn.co.uk).

Other London Travel Inns charging about £60 per room include **London Euston** (141 Euston Road, NW1 2AU, tube: Euston), **Tower Bridge** (tube: London Bridge), and **London Putney Bridge** (farther out, tube: Putney Bridge). For any of these, contact tel. 0870-242-8000 (fax 0870-241-9000).

Hotel Ibis London Euston, which feels classier than a Travel Inn, is located on a quiet street a block behind Euston Station (Sb-£64, Db-£70, breakfast extra, CC:VMA, nonsmoking floor, 3 Cardington Street, NW1 2LW, tel. 020/7388-7777, fax 020/7388-0001, e-mail: h0921@accor-hotels.com).

Jurys Inn rents 200 mod, compact, and comfy rooms near King's Cross station (Db/Tb-£84, 2 adults and 2 kids—under age 12—can share one room, breakfast extra, CC:VMA, nonsmoking floors, 60 Pentonville Road, Islington, N1 9LA, tube: Angel, tel. 020/7282-5500, fax 020/7282-5511, www.jurys.com).

Premier Lodge opens in spring of 2001 near the Globe Theatre on the South Bank (55 rooms, Db for up to 2 adults and 2 kids-£64.50, Bankside, 34 Park Street, London SE1, tube: Canon, tel. 0870-201-0203, fax 0870-700-1457).

"South Kensington," She Said, Loosening His Cummerbund

To live on a quiet street so classy it doesn't allow hotel signs, surrounded by trendy shops and colorful restaurants, call "South Ken" your London home. Shoppers like being a short walk from Harrods and the designer shops of King's Road and Chelsea. When I splurge, I splurge here. Sumner Place is just off Old Brompton Road, 200 yards from the handy South Kensington tube station (on Circle Line, two stops from Victoria Station, direct Heathrow connection). There's a taxi rank in the meridian at the end of Harrington Road. The handy "Wash & Dry" Laundromat is on the corner of Queensberry Place and Harrington Road (daily 8:00–21:00, bring 20p and £1 coins).

Aster House Hotel—run by friendly and accommodating Simon and Leona Tan—has a sumptuous lobby, lounge, and breakfast room. Its newly renovated rooms are comfy and quiet, with TV, phone, air-conditioning, and fridge. Enjoy breakfast or just lounging in the whisper-elegant Orangery, a Victorian greenhouse (Sb-£65–85, Db-£125, deluxe four-poster Db-£145, CC:VM, entirely nonsmoking, 3 Sumner Place, SW7 3EE, tel. 020/7581-5888, fax 020/7584-4925, www.asterhouse.com).

Five Sumner Place Hotel was recently voted "the best small hotel in London." In this 150-year-old building, rooms are tastefully decorated and the breakfast room is a Victorian-style conservatory/greenhouse (13 rooms, Sb-£100, Db-£153, third bed-£22; CC:VMA, TV, phones, and fridge in rooms by request, nonsmoking rooms, elevator, 5 Sumner Place, South Kensington, SW7 3EE, tel. 020/7584–7586, fax 020/7823-9962, www.sumnerplace.com, e-mail: reservations@sumnerplace.com, run by Tom).

Sixteen Sumner Place—a lesser value for classier travelers—has over-the-top formality and class packed into its 37 unnumbered but pretentiously named rooms, plush lounges, and quiet garden (closed Jan–June for renovations, reopens in July, Db-£160 with showers, £185 with baths, CC:VMA, breakfast in your room, elevator, 16 Sumner Place, SW7 3EG, tel. 020/7589-5232, fax 020/7584-8615, U.S. tel. 800/592-5387, e-mail: reservations@numbersixteenhotel.co.uk).

Jurys Kensington Hotel is big and stately (Sb/Db/Tb-£100–170 depending upon "availability," ask for a deal, breakfast extra, CC:VMA, piano lounge, nonsmoking floor, elevator, Queen's Gate, South Kensington, SW7 5LR, tel. 020/7589-6300, fax 020/7581-1492).

South Kensington Neighborhood

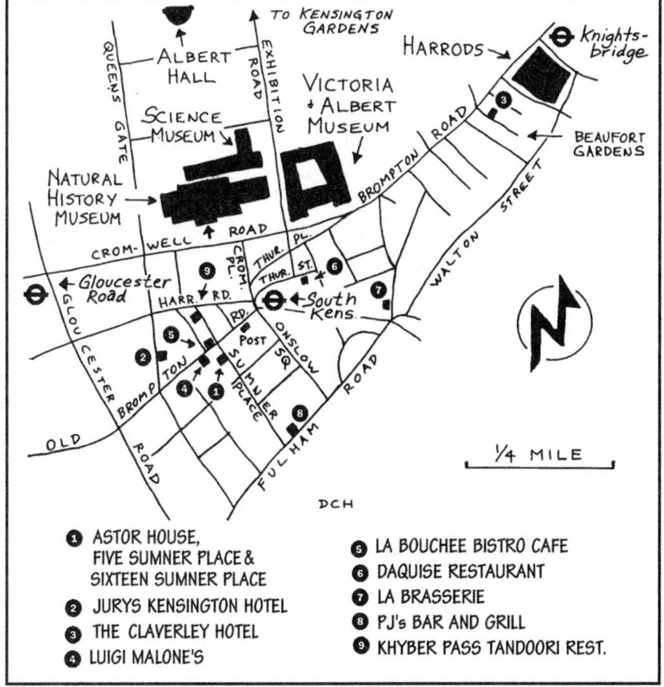

The Claverley, two blocks from Harrods, is on a quiet street similar to Sumner Place. The warmly furnished rooms come with all the comforts (S-£70, Sb-£85–115, Db-£130–155, sofa bed Tb-£160–215, flexible during slow times, CC:VMA, plush lounge, nonsmoking rooms, elevator, 13–14 Beaufort Gardens, SW3 1PS, tube: Knightsbridge, tel. 020/7589-8541, fax 020/7584-3410, U.S. tel. 800/747-0398, www.claverly.co.uk).

Sleeping in Notting Hill Gate Neighborhood

Residential Notting Hill Gate has quick bus and tube access to downtown, is on the A2 Airbus line from Heathrow, and, for London, is very "homely." It has a self-serve launderette, an artsy theater, a late-hours supermarket, and lots of fun budget eateries (see "Eating," below).

Westland Hotel is comfortable, convenient, and hotelesque, with a fine lounge and spacious 1970s-style rooms (Sb-£80, Db-£95, cavernous deluxe Db-£110, sprawling Tb-£120, gargantuan Qb-£135, 10 percent discount with this book through 2001 for

London, Notting Hill Gate Neighborhood

first stay only, CC:VMA, elevator, free garage—7 spaces, between Notting Hill Gate and Queensway tube stations, 154 Bayswater Road, W2 4HP, tel. 020/7229-9191, fax 020/7727-1054, www.westlandhotel.co.uk).

Vicarage Private Hotel, understandably popular, is family run and elegantly British in a quiet, classy neighborhood. It has 19 rooms furnished with taste and quality, a TV lounge, and facilities on each floor. Mandy, Richard, and Tere maintain a homey and caring atmosphere. Reserve long in advance. There's no better room for the price (S-£45, D-£74, Db-£98, T-£90, Q-£98, a 6-minute walk from the Notting Hill Gate and High Street Kensington tube stations, near Kensington Palace at 10 Vicarage Gate, Kensington, W8 4AG, tel. 020/7229-4030, fax 020/7792-5989, www.londonvicaragehotel.com).

Abbey House Hotel, next door, is similar, but—while also a fine value—it has no lounge and is less cozy (16 rooms, S-£45, D-£74, T-£90, Q-£100, Quint-£110, 11 Vicarage Gate, Kensington, W8 4AG, tel. 020/7727-2594, Rodrigo).

Norwegian YWCA (Norsk K.F.U.K.) is for women under 30 only (and men with Norwegian passports). Located on a quiet, stately street, it offers nonsmoking rooms, a study, TV room, piano lounge, and an open-face Norwegian ambience. They have mostly quads, so those willing to share with strangers are most likely to get a place (July–Aug: Ss-£27, bed in shared double-£25, shared triple-£21 apiece, shared quad-£18 apiece, with breakfast; Sept–June: same prices include dinner; CC:VMA, 52 Holland Park, W11 3RS, tel. & fax 020/7727-9897, www.kfuk.dial.pipex.com). With each visit I wonder which is easier to get—a sex change or a Norwegian passport?

Sleeping on Kensington Gardens

Several big old hotels line the quiet Victorian Kensington Gardens, a block off the bustling Queensway shopping street near the Bayswater tube station. Popular with young travelers from around the world, Queensway is a multicultural festival of commerce and lively eateries (such as Mr Wu's Chinese buffet, stuffing locals for £4.50, on Queensway, see "Eating," below). These hotels come with the least traffic noise of all my downtown recommendations. Brookford Wash & Dry is at Queensway and Bishop's Bridge Road (daily 7:00–19:30, service from 9:00–17:30, computerized pay point takes all coins).

Garden Court rents 34 large, comfortable rooms, offering one of London's best accommodations values. The breakfast room is sticky, and the public bathrooms are a bit unkempt, but it's friendly, with a great lounge and super prices (S-£34, Sb-£50, D-£54, Db-£82, T-£72, Tb-£90, Q-£80, Qb-£96, CC:VM, 30 Kensington Gardens Square, W2 4BG, tel. 020/7229-2553, fax 020/7727-2749, www.gardenhotel.co.uk, e-mail: gardencourthotel@londonw24bg.freeserve.co.uk).

Kensington Gardens Hotel laces 16 fine, fresh rooms together in a tall, skinny place with lots of stairs (S-£53, Sb-£58, Db-£79, 9 Kensington Gardens Square, W2 4BH, tel. 020/7221-7790, fax 020/7792-8612, www.kensingtongardenshotel.co.uk).

Vancouver Studios is a different concept, giving you a fully equipped kitchenette (utensils, stove, microwave, and fridge) rather than breakfast (Sb-£55–72, Db-£90–105, Tb-£123, Q-£160, CC:VMA, homey lounge and private garden, rooms with all the modern comforts, 30 Prince's Square, W2 4NJ, tel. 020/7243-1270, fax 020/7221-8678, www.vienna-group.co.uk, e-mail: hotels@vienna-group.co.uk).

Phoenix Hotel, a Best Western modernization of a 130-room hotel, offers American business-class comforts; spacious, plush public spaces; and big, fresh, modern-feeling rooms (Sb-£89, Db-£120, Tb-£145, CC:VMA, nonsmoking rooms, elevator, 1–8 Kensington Gardens Square, W2 4BH, tel. 020/7229-2494, fax 020/7727-1419, U.S. tel. 800/528-1234, www.phoenixhotel.co.uk).

London House Budget Hotel is a threadbare, nose-ringed slumbermill renting 220 beds in 76 stark but sleepable rooms (S-£40, twin-£54, dorm bed-£20, includes continental breakfast, CC:VMA, lots of school groups, 81 Kensington Gardens Square, W2 4DJ, tel. 020/7727-0696, fax 020/7243-8626).

Sleeping in Other Neighborhoods

Euston Station: The **Methodist International Centre** (new in 1998) is a youthful Christian residence, its lower floors filled with international students and its top floor open to travelers. Rooms are modern and simple yet comfortable, with fine bathrooms, phones, and desks. The atmosphere is friendly, safe, clean, and controlled, with a spacious lounge and game room (Sb-£38, Db-£58, Tb-£70, includes breakfast, three-course buffet dinner-£11, CC:VM, nonsmoking rooms, elevator, on a quiet street a block southwest of Euston Square, 81–103 Euston Street, not Euston Road, W1 2EZ, tube: Euston Station, tel. 020/7380-0001, fax 020/7387-5300, e-mail: sales@micentre.com).

Cottage Hotel is tucked away a block off the west exit of Euston Station. Established in 1950—a bit tired, cramped, and smoky—it feels like 1950. But it's cheap, quiet, and has a fine breakfast room (40 rooms, S-£35, Sb-£45, D-£45, Db-£55, T-£65, Tb-£75, Qb-£85, 67 Euston Street, tel. 020/7387-6785, fax 020/7383-0859).

Downtown near Baker Street: For a less hotelesque alternative in the center, consider renting one of 18 stark, hardwood, comfortable rooms in **22 York Street B&B** (Db-£94, Tb-£141, CC:VMA, strictly smoke free, inviting lounge, social breakfast, from Baker Street tube station walk 2 blocks down Baker Street and take a right, 22 York Street, tel. 020/7224-3990, fax 020/7224-1990, www.myrtle-cottage.co.uk/callis.htm, energetically run by Liz and Michael).

Near St. Paul's: The **City of London Youth Hostel** is clean, modern, friendly, and well run. You'll pay about £25 for a bed in three- to five-bed rooms, £26 in a single (hostel membership required, 200 beds, CC:VM, cheap meals, 36 Carter Lane, EC4V 5AD, tube: St. Paul's, tel. 020/7236-4965, fax 020/7236-7681).

South London: Caroline Cunningham's humble guest house is on a quiet street in a well-worn neighborhood south of Victoria Station near Clapham Common (3 rooms, S-£15, D-£30 with English breakfast, 98 Hambalt Road, Clapham Common, London SW4 9EJ, tel. 020/8673-1077). It's 15 minutes by tube to Clapham Common, then a bus ride or a 12-minute walk—exit left down Clapham

South Road, left on Elms, right on Abbeville Road, left on Hambalt. Rooms in Caroline's brother's house are a lesser value. A good, cheap Thai restaurant (the Pepper Tree) is near the tube station.

Near Gatwick Airport: The **Gatwick Travelodge** is a budget hotel two miles from the airport (Db-£50, free shuttle to/from south terminal, Church Road, Lowfield Heath, Crawley, tel. 0870-905-6343). These two B&Bs are both in the peaceful countryside and have tennis courts, small swimming pools, and a good pub within walking distance: **Barn Cottage,** a converted 17th-century barn, has two wood-beamed rooms, antique furniture, and a large garden that makes you forget Gatwick is 10 minutes away (S-£35, D-£50, can drive you to airport or train station for £5–6—a taxi costs £10—Leigh, Reigate, Surrey, RH2 8RF, tel. 01306/611-347, warmly run by Pat and Mike Comer). The idyllic **Crutchfield Farm B&B** offers three comfortable rooms, a great sitting room, and an elegant dining room in a 600-year-old renovated farmhouse surrounded by lots of greenery and a pond. Gillian Blok includes a ride to the airport and its train station, whether you're leaving Britain or day-tripping to London (Sb-£55, Db-£75, Tb-£85, Qb-£95, two miles from Gatwick Airport—£5 by taxi, 30 minutes by train from London, at Hookwood, Surrey, RH6 OHT, tel. 01293/863-110, fax 01293/863-233, e-mail: TonyBlok@compuserve.com).

Near Heathrow Airport: It's so easy to get to Heathrow from central London, I see no reason to sleep there. But for budget beds near the airport, consider the **Heathrow Ibis** (Db-£60, breakfast extra, CC:VMA, shuttle bus to terminals except to T-4, 112 Bath Road, tel. 020/8759-4888, fax 020/8564-7894, www.ibishotel.com). **Heathrow Airport Travelodge** is another option (300 rooms, Db-£70, free shuttle to/from all terminals, Bath Road, off A4, behind Le Meridien Excelsior Hotel, half mile from airport, tel. 0870-905-6343).

Eating in London

If you want to dine (as opposed to eat), check out the extensive listings in the weekly entertainment guides sold at London newsstands (or catch a train for Paris). The thought of a £30 meal in Britain generally ruins my appetite, so my London dining is limited mostly to easygoing, fun, but inexpensive alternatives. I've listed places by neighborhood—handy to your sightseeing or hotel.

Your £6 budget choices are pub grub, a café, fish and chips, pizza, ethnic, or picnic. Pub grub is the most atmospheric budget option. Many of London's 7,000 pubs serve fresh, tasty buffets under ancient timbers, with hearty lunches and dinners priced from £6 to £8. (While pubs are going strong, the new phenomenon is coffee shops: Starbucks and its competitors have sprouted up all over town providing cushy and social watering holes with comfy chairs, easy WCs, £1.50 lattes, and a nice break between sights.)

Ethnic restaurants from all over the world add spice to England's lackluster cuisine scene. Eating Indian or Chinese is "going local" in London. It's also going cheap (cheaper if you take out). Most large museums (and many churches) have inexpensive, cheery cafeterias. Sandwich shops are a hit with local workers eating on the run. Of course, picnicking is the fastest and cheapest way to go. Good grocery stores and sandwich shops, fine park benches, and polite pigeons abound in Britain's most expensive city.

Eating near Trafalgar Square

For a tasty meal on a monk's budget sitting on somebody's tomb in an ancient crypt, descend into the **St. Martin-in-the-Fields Café in the Crypt** (Mon–Sat 10:00–20:00, Sun 12:00–20:30, £5–7 cafeteria plates, cheaper sandwich bar, profits go to the church; underneath St. Martin-in-the-Fields on Trafalgar Square, tel. 020/7839-4342).

Chandos Bar's Opera Room floats amazingly apart from the tacky crush of tourism around Trafalgar Square. Look for the pub opposite the National Portrait Gallery (corner of William Street and St. Martin's Lane) and climb the stairs to the Opera Room. They serve £6 pub lunches and dinners (last orders at 19:00, 18:00 on weekends, tel. 020/7836-1401). This is a fine Tragalfar rendezvous point—smoky, but wonderfully local.

Gordon's Wine Bar is ripe with atmosphere. A simple steep staircase leads into a 14th-century cellar filled with candlelight, dusty old wine bottles, faded British memorabilia, and local nine-to-fivers (hot meals only for lunch, fine plate of cheeses or various cold cuts with salad buffet all day until 21:00—one plate of each feeds two for £7). While it's crowded, you can normally corral two chairs and grab the corner of a table (Mon–Sat 11:00–23:00, closed Sun, arrive before 18:00 to get a seat, 2 blocks from Trafalgar Square, bottom of Villiars Street at #47, near Embankment tube station, tel. 020/7930-1408).

Down Whitehall, a block south of Trafalgar Square, you'll find the touristy but atmospheric **Clarence Pub** (decent grub, lunch only) and cheaper cafeterias and pizza joints.

For a classy lunch in the National Gallery, eat at the moderately priced **Crizelli's Garden** (open daily, first floor of Sainsbury Wing).

Simpson's in the Strand serves a stuffy, aristocratic, old-time carvery dinner—where the chef slices your favorite red meat from a fancy trolley at your table—in their elegant smoky old dining room (£20, coat and tie required, Mon–Sat 12:15–14:30, 17:30–23:00, tel. 020/7836-9112).

Eating near Piccadilly

Hungry and broke in the theater district? Head for Panton Street (off Haymarket, 2 blocks southeast of Piccadilly Circus) for a line of decent eateries. **Stockpot** is a mushy-peas kind of place, famous and rightly popular for its edible, cheap meals (Mon–Sat 8:00–23:00, Sun 8:00–22:00, 38 Panton Street). The **West End Kitchen** (across the street at #5, same hours and menu) is a competitor that's just as good. The original **Stockpot,** a few blocks away, has better atmosphere (daily 12:00–23:00, a block north of Shaftesbury near Cambridge Circus at 18 Old Compton Street tel. 020/7287-1066).

The palatial **Criterion Brasserie** serves a special £15 two-course "Anglo-French" menu (or £18 for 3 courses) under gilded tiles and chandeliers in a dreamy Byzantine church setting from 1880. It's right on Piccadilly Circus but a world away from the punk junk. The house wine is great and so is the food (specials available Mon–Sat 12:00–14:30 and 17:30–18:30, pricier later, CC:VM, closed Sun, tel. 020/7930-0488).

Just off Leicester Square, **Luigi Malone's**, a chain restaurant, serves inexpensive salads and pasta (12 Irving Street, tel. 020/7925-0457).

Eating in the City, near St. Paul's

The **Counting House**, formerly an elegant old bank, offers great £7 lunches, nice homemade meat pies, fish, and fresh vegetables (gets really busy with the button-down 9–5 crowd after 12:15 Mon–Fri, 50 Cornhill, near Mansion House in the City, tel. 020/7283-7123).

The "Food Is Fun" Dinner Crawl: From Covent Garden to Soho

London has a trendy, generation X scene that most Beefeater seekers miss entirely. For a multicultural movable feast and a chance to sample some of London's most popular eateries, consider sampling these. Start around 18:00 to avoid lines, get in on early specials, and find waiters willing to let you split a meal. Prices, while reasonable by London standards, add up. Servings are large enough to share. All are open nightly.

Suggested nibbler's dinner crawl for two: Arrive before 18:00 at **Belgo** and split the early-bird dinner special: a kilo of mussels, fries, and dark Belgian beer; at **Yo! Sushi,** have beer or sake and a few dishes; slurp your last course at **Wagamama**; for dessert, people watch at Leicester Square, where the serf's always up.

Belgo Centraal is a space-station world overrun with Trappist monks serving hearty Belgian specialties. The classy restaurant section requires reservations, but just grabbing a bench in the boisterous beer hall is more fun. Belgians claim they eat as well as the French and as hearty as the Germans. Specialties include mussels, great fries, and a stunning array of dark, blond, and fruity Belgian beers. Belgo actually makes things Belgian trendy—a formidable feat (£14 meals; open daily until very late; Mon–Fri

From Covent Garden to Soho, "Food is Fun"

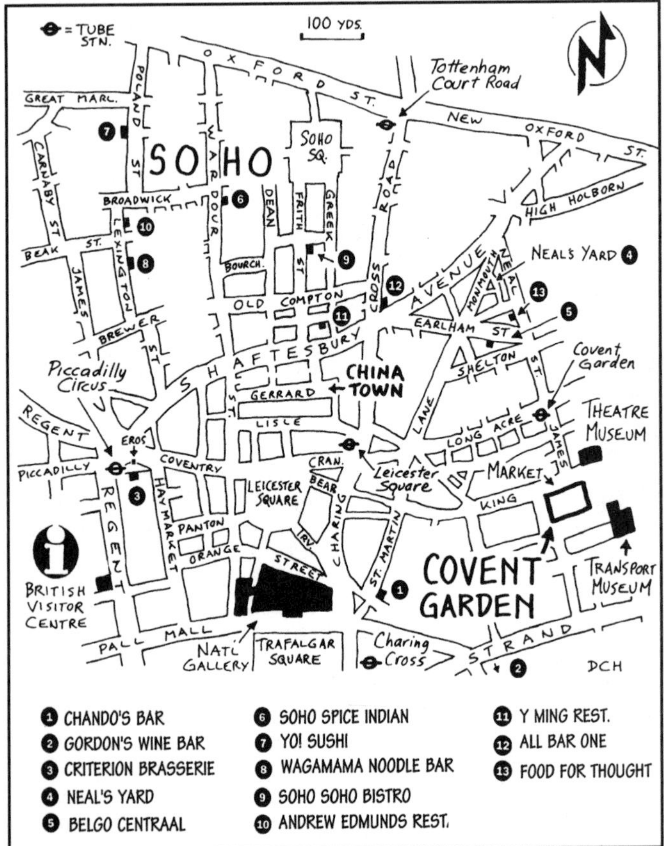

17:00–18:30 "beat the clock" meal specials cost only the time… £5 to £6.30, and you get mussels, fries, and beer; no meal splitting after 18:30; £5 lunch special daily, 12:00–17:00; one block north of Covent Garden tube station at intersection of Neal and Shelton Streets, 50 Earlham Street, tel. 020/7813-2233).

Soho Spice Indian is where modern Britain meets Indian tradition—fine Indian cuisine in a trendy jewel-tone ambience. The £15 "Tandoori selections" meal is the best "variety" dish and big enough for two (daily 11:30–24:00, nonsmoking section available Sun–Tue, CC:VM, 5 blocks due north of Piccadilly Circus at 124 Wardour Street, tel. 020/7434-0808).

Yo! Sushi is a futuristic Japanese food extravaganza

experience. With thumping rock music, Japanese cable TV, a 60-meter-long conveyor-belt sushi bar (the world's longest), automated sushi machines, and a robotic drink trolley, just sipping a sake on a bar stool here is a trip. For £1 you get unlimited tea (on request), water (from spigot at bar, with or without gas), or miso soup. Grab dishes as they rattle by (priced by color of dish; see their chart) and a drink off the trash-talking robot (daily 12:00–24:00, two blocks south of Oxford Street, where Lexington Street becomes Poland Street, 52 Poland Street, tel. 020/7287-0443). For more serious drinking on tatami mats, go downstairs into "Yo Below."

Wagamama Noodle Bar is a noisy, pan-Asian slurp-athon. As you enter, check out the kitchen and listen to the roar of the basement, where benches rock with happy eaters. Everything's organic—stand against the wall to feel the energy of all this "positive eating" (daily 12:00–23:00, crowded after 20:00, smoke free, 10A Lexington Street, tel. 020/7292-0990).

More possibilities: Soho Soho French Bistro-Rotisserie is a chance to go French in a Matisse-esque setting. The ground floor is a trendy wine bar and brasserie. Upstairs is an oasis of peace serving £16 three-course French "pretheater specials"—order from 17:30 to 19:00 (CC:VMA, near Cambridge Circus, 2 blocks east of Charing Cross Road at 11 Frith Street, tel. 020/7494-3491).

Near Covent Garden, the area around Neal's Yard is busy with fun cafés. One of the best is **Food for Thought** (serving until 20:15, Sun 12:00–16:15, good £5 vegetarian meals, non smoking, 2 blocks north of tube: Covent Garden, 31 Neal Street, tel. 020/7836-0239). Neal's Yard itself is a food circus of trendy, healthy eateries.

All Bar One, a modern English restaurant chain popular with the young black-clad crowd, offers good fast food in a rustic mod setting with plain wooden tables (£5 light meals, £8–10 meals). In Covent Garden, try the location at the intersection of Cross Road and Shaftesbury Avenue. Other locations include 19 Henrietta Street/Covent Garden, 84 Cambridge Circus, 36 Dean Street in Soho, 48 Leicester Square, 289 Regent Street, and 126 Notting Hill.

Y Ming Chinese Restaurant, across Shaftesbury Avenue from the ornate gates, clatter, and dim sum of Chinatown, has clean European decor, serious but helpful service, and authentic Northern Chinese cooking (good £10 meal deal offered 12:00–18:00, Mon–Sat 12:00–23:30, closed Sun, 35 Greek Street, tel. 020/7734-2721).

Andrew Edmunds Restaurant is a tiny candlelit place where you'll want to hide your camera and guidebook and act as local as possible. The modern-European cooking is worth the splurge (3 courses for £25, 12:30–15:00, 18:00–22:45, 46 Lexington Street in Soho, reservations are smart on weekends, tel. 020/7437-5708).

Eating near Recommended Victoria Station Accommodations

Here are places a couple of blocks southwest of Victoria Station where I've enjoyed eating (see map on page 71):

Jenny Lo's Tea House is a simple, for-the-joy-of-good-food kind of place serving up £5 Chinese-style meals to locals in the know (Mon–Sat 12:00–15:00, 18:00–22:00, 14 Eccleston Street, tel. 020/7259-0399).

For pub grub with good local atmosphere, consider the **Plumbers Arms** (filling £6 hot meals Mon–Fri, cheaper sandwiches anytime, indoor/outdoor seating, ask about the murdered nanny, 14 Lower Belgrave Street, tel. 020/7730-4067).

Next door, the small but classy **La Campagnola** is Belgravia's favorite budget Italian restaurant (£12–15, Mon–Sat 12:00–15:00, 18:00–23:30, closed Sun, 10 Lower Belgrave Street, tel. 020/7730-2057).

Across the street, the **Maestro Bar** is the closest thing to an English tapas bar I've seen, with salads, sandwiches, and 10 bar stools (very cheap, closed Sat).

The **Ebury Wine Bar** offers a French candlelit ambience and pricey but delicious meals (£15, daily 12:00–15:00, 18:00–22:30, CC:VM, 139 Ebury Street, at intersection with Elizabeth Street, near bus station, tel. 020/7730-5447). Several cheap places are around the corner on Elizabeth Street (#23 for take-out or eat-in fish and chips). **Goya**, a Spanish restaurant nearby, is popular for its fine tapas (Elizabeth Street).

The **Duke of Wellington** pub is good, if smoky, for dinner (£6 meals, Mon–Sat 12:00–15:00, 18:00–21:30, Sun 12:00–15:00, 63 Eaton Terrace, at intersection with Chester Row). **Peter's Restaurant** is the cabbie's hangout for cheap food, smoke, and chatter—men would feel more comfortable here than women (closed Sun, end of Ebury, at intersection with Pimlico).

The **Country Pub in London** lives up to its name and serves good £6 to £12 meals (12:00–15:00, 18:30–21:30, corner of Warwick and Cambridge Streets, tel. 020/7834-5281).

Jomuna Tandoori serves quality Indian cuisine (daily 12:00–15:00, 18:00–23:30, 74 Wilton Road, near Eccleston Hotel, tel. 020/7828-7509).

The **Marche** is an easy cafeteria a couple of blocks north of Victoria Station at Bressenden Place (Mon–Sat 7:30–23:00, Sun 11:00–21:00, CC:VM, tel. 020/7630-1733). If you miss America, there's a mall-type food circus at Victoria Place, upstairs in Victoria Station. **Cafe Rouge** is probably the best food there.

Groceries: The late-hours **Whistle Stop** at the station has decent sandwiches and a fine salad bar (daily, 24 hrs). A larger grocery, **Sainsbury Local**, is on Victoria Street in front of the station, just past the buses (daily 6:00–24:00).

Eating near Recommended Notting Hill Gate B&Bs and Bayswater Hotels

The exuberantly rustic and very English **Maggie Jones** serves my favorite £20 London dinner. You'll get solid English cuisine, with huge plates of crunchy vegetables, by candlelight (daily 18:30–23:00, CC:VMA, 6 Old Court Place, just east of Kensington Church Street, near High Street Kensington tube stop, reservations recommended, tel. 020/7937-6462). If you eat well once in London, eat here (and do it quick, before it burns down).

The **Churchill Arms** pub is a local hangout, with good beer and old English ambience in front and hearty £5 Thai plates in an enclosed patio in the back (you can bring the Thai food into the more atmospheric pub section, Mon–Sat 12:00–15:00, 18:00–21:30, closed Sun, 119 Kensington Church Street, tel. 020/7792-1246).

The friendly **Ladbroke Arms Pub** serves country-style meals that are one step above pub grub in quality and price (£10–12 meals, June–Sept daily 11:00–23:00, Oct–May daily 12:00–14:30, 19:00–22:00, great indoor/outdoor ambience, 54 Ladbroke Road, near Holland Park tube station, tel. 020/7727-6648).

For fish and chips, the almost-too-popular **Geale's** has long been considered one of London's best (£8, Mon–Sat 12:00–15:00, 18:00–23:00, Sun 18:00–23:00, 2 Farmer Street, just off Notting Hill Gate behind Gate Cinema, tel. 020/7727-7528). Get there early for a place to sit (they take no reservations) and the best selection of fish.

The **Modhubon** Indian restaurant is not too spicy, "vedy, vedy nice," and has cheap lunch specials (Sun–Fri 12:00–15:00, 18:00–24:00, Sat 12:00–24:00, 29 Pembridge Road, tel. 020/7727-3399). Next door is the cheap **Slowboat** Chinese take-out (daily 17:30–24:00, 19 Pembridge Road) and the tiny **Organic Restaurant** at #35, which busily keeps yuppie vegetarians as well as carnivores happy (£10, 100 percent organic, Mon–Fri 17:30–23:00, Sat–Sun 11:00–22:00, CC:VM, 35 Pembridge Road, tel. 020/7727-9620).

Cafe Diana is a healthy little sandwich shop decorated with photos of Princess Diana (daily 8:00–22:30, 5 Wellington Terrace, on Bayswater Road, opposite Kensington Palace Garden Gates, tel. 020/7792-9606).

Mr. Wu's Chinese Restaurant serves a 10-course buffet in a bright and cheery little place. Just grab a plate and help yourself (£4.50, daily 12:00–23:00, check quality of buffet—right inside entrance—before committing, pickings can get slim, across from Bayswater tube station, 54 Queensway, tel. 020/7243-1017). Queensway is lined with lively and inexpensive eateries.

Supermarket: Europa is a half-block from the Notting Hill Gate tube stop (Mon–Fri 8:00–23:00, Sun 12:00–18:00, 112 Notting Hill Gate, near intersection with Pembridge Road).

Eating near Recommended Accommodations in South Kensington

Popular eateries line Old Brompton Road and Thurloe Street (tube: South Kensington). See map on page 75.

Luigi Malone's is an Italian-food chain restaurant serving good £8 salads and pasta (73 Old Brompton Road, tel. 020/7584-4323). Its twin brother is just off Leicester Square at 12 Irving Street.

La Bouchee Bistro Café is a classy hole-in-the-wall touch of France serving early-bird, three-course, £11 meals before 19:30 and *plats du jour* for £8 all *jour* (daily 12:00–23:00, CC:VM, 56 Old Brompton Road, almost directly across street from Luigi Malone's, tel. 020/7589-1929).

Daquise, an authentic-feeling Polish place, is ideal if you're in the mood for kielbasa and kraut. It's fast, cheap, family run, and a part of the neighborhood (£8 meals, daily until 23:00, nonsmoking, 20 Thurloe Street, tel. 020/7589-6117).

La Brasserie fills a big, plain, tiled room with ceiling fans, a Parisian ambience, and good French-style food at reasonable prices (2-course £14 "regional menu," £12 bottle of house wine, CC:VMA, nightly until 24:00, 272 Brompton Road, tel. 020/7581-3089).

PJ's Bar and Grill is popular with the yuppie Chelsea crowd for a good reason. Traditional "New York Brasserie"–style yet trendy, it serves modern Mediterranean cuisine (£15 meals, nightly until 24:00, 52 Fulham Road, at intersection with Sydney Street, tel. 020/7581-0025).

For Indian food, the **Khyber Pass Tandoori Restaurant** is a nondescript but handy place serving good £12 dinners nightly (12:00–14:30, 18:00–23:30, CC:VM, 21 Bute Street, tel. 020/7589-7311).

Transportation Connections—London

Flying into London's Heathrow Airport

Heathrow Airport is the world's busiest. Think about it: 60 million passengers a year on 425,000 flights from 200 destinations riding 90 airlines... some kind of global maypole dance. While many complain about it, I like it. It's user-friendly. Read signs, ask questions. For Heathrow's airport, flight, and transfers information, call the switchboard at 0870-000-0123 (or 020/8759-4321). It has four terminals: T-1 (mostly domestic flights), T-2 (mostly European flights), T-3 (mostly flights from the U.S.), T-4 (British Air trans-Atlantic flights).

Each terminal has an airport information desk, car-rental agencies, exchange bureaus and ATMs, a pharmacy, a VAT refund desk (VAT info tel. 020/8910-3682; you must present the VAT claim form from the retailer here to get your 17.5 percent tax rebate on items purchased in Britain), and a £3.50/day baggage check desk (open 5:30–23:00). There's a post office in T-2 and T-4. Each terminal has cheap eateries (such as the cheery **Food Village** self-service cafeteria in T-3). The American Express desk, in the tube station at Terminal 4 (daily 7:00–19:00), has rates similar to the exchange bureaus upstairs, but they don't charge a commission (typically 1.5 percent) for cashing any type of traveler's check.

Heathrow's small TI gives you all the help that London's Victoria Station does, with none of the crowds (daily 8:30–18:00, a 5-minute walk from Terminal 3 in the tube station, follow signs to "underground"; bypass the queue for transit info to reach the window for London questions); if you're riding the Airbus into London, have your partner stay with the bags at the terminal. At the TI get a free simple map and brochures, and if you're taking the tube (subway) into London, buy a Travel Card day pass to cover the ride (see below).

Transportation to London from Heathrow Airport

By Tube (Subway): For £3.50, the tube takes you 14 miles to downtown London in 50 minutes (6/hrly, depending on your destination, may require one change). Even better, buy a £4.70 Travel Card that covers your trip into London and all your tube travel for the day (starting at 9:30). Buy it at the ticket window at the tube.

By Airport Bus: The Airbus, running between the airport and London's King's Cross station, serves the Notting Hill Gate and Bayswater neighborhoods—see recommended hotels, above (departs from each terminal, £7, 2/hrly 6:30–21:15, 60 min, buy ticket from driver, tel. 020/8571-2233). The tube works fine, but with baggage I prefer the Airbus—there are no connections underground and a lovely view from the top of the double-decker bus. Ask the driver to remind you when to get off. If you're going to the airport, exact pick-up times are clearly posted at each bus stop.

If you're staying in London's Victoria Station neighborhood, consider the National Express bus that runs between Heathrow's central bus station and Victoria Coach Station (£6, 2/hrly, 7:45–24:00 from Victoria, 5:40–21:45 from Heathrow, 40 min, tel. 08705-808-080).

By Taxi: Taxis from the airport cost about £35–50. Especially for four people traveling together this can be a deal. Hotels can often line up a cab back to the airport for £30. For the cheapest taxi to the airport don't order one from your hotel. Simply flag down a few and ask them for their best "off-meter" rate (I managed a ride for £25).

By Heathrow Express Train: This slick train service zips air travelers between Heathrow Airport and London's Paddington Station; at Paddington, you're in the thick of the tube system, with easy access to any of my recommended neighborhoods—Notting Hill Gate is just two stops away (£12 but ask about discount promos at Heathrow ticket desk, children under 16 ride free if you buy tickets before boarding, CC:VMA, covered by Britrail, 4/hrly, 5:10–23:30, 15 min to downtown from Terminals 1, 2, 3; 20 min from T-4; works as a free transfer between terminals, tel. 0845-600-1515, www.heathrowexpress.co.uk); a "Go Further" ticket for £13 includes one tube ride to get you to your hotel (valid only on same day and in Zone 1, saves 50p). For one person, combining the Heathrow Express with either a tube or taxi ride (between your hotel and Paddington) is as fast and half the cost of using solely a cab to (or from) the airport.

If you're flying out of Heathrow, check in at London's Paddington station. Take advantage of the calm, easy airline check-in at Paddington. If you're using any of the 26 represented airlines (including British Airways, British Midland, American, Lufthansa, SAS, Swiss Air, United Airlines, Air Canada, and Canadian Airlines), you can get a boarding pass and check your luggage (daily 5:00–21:00, last check-in 2 hrs before departure). You avoid the crowded chaos of check-in at Heathrow, and, even better, you'll have a little more time to sightsee instead of wasting three or four hours at the airport (on the morning of my departure, I checked my luggage at Paddington—6 hrs before my flight—then went on the London Eye Ferris Wheel, which I'd booked the day before). Catch your breath, then catch the Heathrow Express to arrive one hour before your plane leaves.

Buses from Heathrow to Destinations beyond London

The **National Express Central Bus Station** offers direct bus connections to **Cheltenham** (11/day, 2 hrs, £10.25), **Gatwick Airport** (2/hrly, 1 hr, £8), and **Bath** (11/day, at 8:40, 10:10, 11:40, 13:10, 14:40, 16:40, 18:10, 19:10, 20:10, 20:40, 21:40, 2.5 hrs, £11.25, direct, tel. 08705-808-080). Britrail passholders may prefer the 2.5-hour Heathrow–Bath bus/train connection via Reading (free with pass, otherwise £29.20, payable at desk in terminal, CC:VM); catch the twice-hourly RailAir Link shuttle bus to Reading (pron. RED-ing), then hop on the hourly express train to Bath. Most Heathrow buses depart from the common area serving terminals 1, 2, and 3, although some depart from T-4 (tel. 08705-747-777).

Flying into London's Gatwick Airport

More and more flights, especially charters, land at Gatwick Airport, halfway between London and the southern coast (airport tel. 01293/535-353). Trains—clearly the best way into London from here—shuttle conveniently between Gatwick and London's Victoria Station (£10.20, £19.50 round-trip, can purchase tickets on train at no extra charge, runs 24 hrs daily, 4/hrly during day, 1–2/hrly at night, 30 min, tel. 08705-301-530, www.gatwickexpress.co.uk).

London's Other Airports

If you're flying into or out of **Stansted** (airport tel. 01279/680-500), take the Airbus between the airport and downtown London's Victoria Coach Station (£8, 2/hrly, from 4:00–24:00, 1.75 hrs, picks up and stops throughout London, tel. 08705-747-777). For **Luton** (airport tel. 01582/405-100, www.london-luton.com), try Green Line's bus #757 to get to or from London's Victoria Station at Buckingham Palace Road—stop 6 (£7.50, 2/hrly, 1–1.25 hrs depending on time of day, from 4:30–24:00, tel. 0870-608-7261, www.greenline.co.uk).

Discounted Flights from London

With any of these discount airlines, the farther you book in advance (up to about 9–12 months or as few as 3 weeks), the cheaper the fares. Cheap seats sell out first, leaving more expensive seats for latecomers. British Midland has been around the longest, but Virgin Express and Ryanair generally offer cheaper flights.

British Midland, the local discount airline, is sometimes cheaper than the train. You can fly inexpensively to Edinburgh (as little as £70 round-trip if you stay over Sat); to Dublin, Ireland (as little as £99 round-trip over Sat); to Paris (as little as £78 round-trip over Sat); and more. For the latest, call British tel. 0870-607-0555 or U.S. tel. 800/788-0555 (www.britishmidland.com).

Virgin Express is a British-owned company with good rates (book by phone and pick up ticket at airport an hour before your flight, tel. 020/7744-0004, www.virgin-express.com). Virgin Express flies from London to Shannon, Ireland (£40 from Stansted) and to Brussels (£50 from Heathrow, £40 from Gatwick). From its hub in Brussels you can connect cheaply to Barcelona, Madrid, Nice, Berlin, Copenhagen, Rome, or Milan (e.g., London–Milan, £50).

Ryanair is a creative Irish airline that prides itself on offering the lowest fares. They fly from London (mostly Stansted airport) to Dublin, Glasgow, Frankfurt, Lyon, Stockholm, Oslo, Venice, Turin, and many others. Sample fares: London–Dublin—£40 round-trip, London–Frankfurt—£40 round-trip (Irish tel. 01/609-7800, British tel. 0870-333-1231, www.ryanair.com). If you're the spontaneous sort, this airline is probably the best choice to try first. Because they offer promotional deals any time of year, it's not as essential that you book long in advance to get the best deals.

Trains and Buses

London, Britain's major transportation hub, has a different train station for each region. Waterloo handles the Eurostar to Paris (tel. 800/EUROSTAR). King's Cross covers northeast England and Scotland (tel. 08457-225-225). Paddington covers west and southwest England (Bath) and South Wales (tel. 08457-000-125).

For the others, call 08457-484-950. Also see the BritRail map in the introduction.

National Express's excellent bus service is considerably cheaper than trains. (For a busy signal, call 08705-808-080, or visit www.nationalexpress.co.uk or the bus station a block southwest of Victoria Station.)

To Bath: Trains leave London's Paddington Station every hour (at a quarter after) for the 75-minute ride to Bath (costs roughly £31 if you leave after 9:30). As an alternative, consider taking a guided bus tour from London to Stonehenge and Bath and abandoning the tour in Bath. Evan Evans' tour comes fully guided, with admissions for £48, or ask about their Low Cost version, which runs from April through October only (and perhaps not at all in 2001) and provides just the bus transportation—with free time at Stonehenge and then in Bath—for £33 (can book at Victoria Station TI; at Evan Evans' office at 258 Vauxhall Bridge Road, near Victoria Station, tel. 020/7950-1777, www.evanevans.co.uk; or at Green Line Travel Office at 4a Fountain Square, across from Victoria Coach Station; tour departs from Victoria Coach Station). Golden Tours also runs a fully guided Stonehenge-Bath tour for a similar price (about £48, departs from Fountain Square, across from Victoria Coach Station, tel. 020/7233-6668, www.goldentours.co.uk).

To points north: Trains run hourly from London's King's Cross Station, stopping in York (2 hrs), Durham (3 hrs), and Edinburgh (5 hrs).

To Dublin, Ireland: The boat/rail journey takes 10–11 hours, all day or all night (7/day, £24–35, tel. 08705-143-219, www.eurolines.co.uk). Consider a cheap 70-minute Ryanair flight instead (see below).

Crossing the English Channel

By Eurostar Train: The fastest and most convenient way to get from Big Ben to the Eiffel Tower is by rail. In London, advertisements claim "more businessmen travel from London to Paris on the Eurostar than on all airlines combined." Eurostar is the speedy passenger train that zips you (and up to 800 others in 18 sleek cars) from downtown London to downtown Paris (12/day, 3 hrs) or Brussels (6/day, 3 hrs) faster and easier than flying. The train goes 80 mph in England and 190 mph on the Continent. (When the English segment gets up to speed the journey time will shrink to 2 hours.) The actual Tunnel crossing is a 20-minute black, silent, 100 mph nonevent. Your ears won't even pop. You can go direct to Disneyland Paris (1/day, more frequent with transfer at Lille) or change at Lille to catch a TGV to Paris' Charles de Gaulle airport.

Channel fares (essentially the same to Paris or Brussels) are reasonable but complicated. For the latest, call 800/EUROSTAR in the U.S. These are prices for 2000: The "Leisure Ticket" is cheap ($119 second class, $199 first class, 50 percent refundable up to 3 days before departure). "Full Fare" first class costs $239 and includes a meal (a dinner departure nets you more grub than breakfast); second class (or "standard") costs $159 (fully refundable even after departure date). Discounts for first- or second-class travel are available to railpass holders ($84 off "Full Fare"), youths under 26 ($80 off "Full Fare"), and children under 12 (about half the fare of your ticket).

Cheaper seats can sell out. Book from home if you're ready to commit to a date and time. Compare fares sold by U.S. rail agents (www.raileurope.com) and British agents (www.eurostar.co.uk). If you prefer the U.S. prices, book by calling 800/EUROSTAR, visit www.raileurope.com, or have your travel agent do it all for you (prices do not include FedEx ticket delivery). For the British fares, book by calling British tel. 08705-186-186 or 1233-61-75-75 or go online at www.eurostar.co.uk (inexpensive but nonrefundable round-trip ticket usually available with 7- or 14-day advance purchase, pick up ticket at station).

Buying your Eurostar ticket in London is easy. Here are some sample London–Paris standard—that's second-class—fares (London–Brussels fares are up to £20 less). Avoid the basic standard fare: one-way—£145, round-trip—£249. Those with a railpass pay £50 one-way, any day. Without a railpass, a same-day round-trip on a Saturday or Sunday costs £99. Those staying at least three nights pay £130 round-trip. Excursion fares (round-trip over a Sat) are cheaper: £100. "Saturday Night Away" tickets (round-trip, purchased a week in advance, and staying over a Sat) are the best deal: £90 standard, £160 first class. One-way tickets for departures after 14:00 Friday or anytime Saturday or Sunday cost £90. Youth tickets (for those under 26) are £80 to Paris, £65 to Brussels (round-trip any time and changeable). First-class and business-class fares are substantially higher. The only seven-day advance deal is the Saturday Night Away. Remember, round-trip tickets over a Saturday are much cheaper than the basic one-way fare... you know the trick.

In Europe, you can get your Eurostar ticket at any major train station (in any country) or at any travel agency that handles train tickets (expect a booking fee). In Britain, you can book and pay for tickets over the phone with a credit card by calling 08705-186-186; pick up your tickets at London's Waterloo station an hour before the Eurostar departure. Note: Britain's time zone is one hour earlier than the Continent's. Times listed on tickets are local times.

By Bus and Boat or Train and Boat: The old-fashioned way of crossing the Channel is competitive and cheaper than Eurostar; it's also twice as romantic, complicated, and time-consuming. You'll get better prices arranging your trip in London than you would in the U.S. Taking the bus is cheapest, and round-trips are a bargain. By bus to Paris, Brussels, or Amsterdam from Victoria Coach Station: £35 one-way, £51 round-trip; 8.5 hrs to Paris—6/day; 8.25 hrs to Brussels—5/day; 11.25 hrs to Amsterdam—6/day; day or overnight, on Eurolines (tel. 08705-143-219, www.eurolines.co.uk; for Hoverspeed ferry only, call 0870-240-8070, www.hoverspeed.co.uk). By train and ferry from London to Paris: £39 one-way, £49 round-trip with five-day return, £59 round-trip over more than five days (tel. 0870-600-0613).

By Plane: Typical fares are £110 regular, less for student standby. Call in London for the latest fares. Consider British Midland (see "Discounted Flights," above) for its cheap round-trip fares to Paris.

NEAR LONDON: GREENWICH AND CAMBRIDGE

GREENWICH

The palace at Greenwich was favored by the Tudor kings. Henry VIII was born here. Later kings commissioned Inigo Jones and Christopher Wren to beautify the town and palace. In spite of Greenwich's architectural and royal treats, this is England's maritime capital, and visitors go for things salty. Greenwich hosts historic ships, nautical shops, and—after a boost from last year's millennium hype—more tourists than ever.

See the two ships—*Cutty Sark* and *Gipsy Moth IV*—upon arrival. Then walk the shoreline promenade with a possible lunch or drink in the venerable Trafalgar Tavern before heading up to the National Maritime Museum and Old Royal Observatory.

The TI is a few paces from the *Cutty Sark* facing the riverside square (daily 10:00–17:00, may move in 2001 but will stay central, tel. 020/8858-6376). Most of Greenwich's sights are covered by combo tickets, a pricier one for nearly everything and sometimes a cheaper one for a couple of sights; each year the combination of sights is shuffled slightly and the prices go up. Greenwich throbs with day-trippers on weekends because of its arts-and-crafts and antique markets; to avoid crowds, visit on a weekday.

Sights—Greenwich

▲▲*Cutty Sark*—The Scottish-built *Cutty Sark* was the last of the great China tea clippers. Handsomely restored, she was the queen of the seas when first launched in 1869. With 32,000 square feet of sail, she could blow with the wind 300 miles in a day. Below deck you'll see the best collection of merchant-ship figureheads in Britain and exhibits giving a vivid peek into the lives of Victorian sailors back when Britain ruled the waves. Stand at the big wheel and look up at the still-rigged main mast towering 150 feet above. During summer afternoons costumed storytellers tell tales of the high seas (£3.50, £12 combo ticket covers most Greenwich sights,

Mon–Sat 10:00–17:00, Sun 12:00–17:00, tel. 020/8858-3445, www.cuttysark.org.uk).

▲*Gipsy Moth IV*—Tiny next to the *Cutty Sark*, the 53-foot *Gipsy Moth IV* is the boat Sir Francis Chichester used for the first solo circumnavigation of the world in 1966 and 1967. Upon Chichester's return, Queen Elizabeth II knighted him in Greenwich, using the same sword Elizabeth I had used to knight Francis Drake in 1582 (free, viewable anytime, but interior not open to public).

Stroll the Thames to Trafalgar Tavern—From the *Cutty Sark* and *Gipsy Moth*, pass the pier and wander east along the Thames on Five Foot Walk (the width of the path) for grand views in front of the Old Royal Naval College (listed below). Founded by William III as a naval hospital and designed by Wren, the college was split in two because Queen Mary didn't want the view from Queen's House blocked. The riverside view's good, too, with the twin-domed towers of the college (one giving the time, the other the direction of the wind) framing Queen's House and the Old Royal Observatory crowning the hill beyond.

Continuing downstream, just past the college, you'll see the Trafalgar Tavern. Dickens knew the pub well and even used it as the setting for the wedding breakfast in *Our Mutual Friend*. Built in 1837 in the Regency style to attract Londoners downriver, the tavern is still popular with Londoners for its fine lunches. And the upstairs Nelson Room is still used for weddings. Its formal moldings and elegant windows with balconies over the Thames are a step back in time (Mon–Sat 11:30–23:00, Sun 12:00–23:00, lunch 12:00–15:00, dinner 17:00–21:00, CC:VM, Park Row, tel. 020/8858-2437). From the pub, enjoy classic views of the Millennium Dome a mile downstream.

From the Trafalgar Tavern, you can walk the two long blocks up Park Row and turn right onto the park leading up to the Royal Observatory.

Old Royal Naval College—Now that the Royal Navy has moved out, the public is invited in to see the elaborate Painted Hall and Chapel, grandly designed by Wren and completed by other architects in the 1700s (£3, Mon–Sat 10:00–17:00, Sun 12:00–17:00, in the two college buildings farthest from river, choral service Sunday at 11:00 in chapel—all are welcome).

▲Queen's House—The building, the first Palladian-style villa in Britain, was designed in 1616 by Inigo Jones for James I's wife, Anne of Denmark. Exploring its Great Hall and Royal Apartments offers a sumptuous look at royal life in the 17th century—or lots of stairs if you're suffering from manor-house fatigue (£12 combo ticket covers most Greenwich sights, daily 10:00–17:00).

▲▲National Maritime Museum—Great for anyone interested in the sea, you'll see everything from Titanic tickets, to Captain Scott's reindeer hide sleeping bag from his 1910 Antarctic expedition, to the

Greenwich

uniform Admiral Nelson wore when he was killed at Trafalgar. The Nelson Gallery is the museum's highlight. While one-tenth of the floor space, it deserves at least half your time here. It offers an intimate look at his life, the Napoleonic threat, Nelson's rise to power, victory, and death at Trafalgar. Don't miss Turner's Battle of Trafalgar—his largest painting and only royal commission (£12 combo ticket covers most Greenwich town sights, daily 10:00–17:00, look for the events board at entrance: singing, treasure hunts, storytelling, particularly on weekends, tel. 020/8312-6565, www.nmm.ac.uk).

▲▲Old Royal Observatory—Whether you think the millennium started in 2000 or 2001, it happened/happens here first. The observatory is located on the prime meridian line—at longitude zero degrees—from where all time is measured. However, the observatory's early work had nothing to do with coordinating the world's clocks to GMT, Greenwich mean time. The observatory was founded in 1675 by Charles II to find a way to determine longitude at sea. Today the Greenwich time signal is linked with the BBC (which broadcasts the "pips" worldwide at the top of the hour). In the courtyard, set your wristwatch to the digital clock showing GMT to a 10th of a second and straddle the prime meridian (called the Times meridian at the observatory, in deference to the *London Times*, which paid for the courtyard sculpture and the inset meridian line that runs banner headlines of today's *Times*—I wish I were kidding). It's less commercial—and cheaper—to straddle the meridian marked on the path outside the museum's courtyard. Nearby (also outside the courtyard), see how your foot measures up to the foot where the public standards of length are cast in bronze. Look up to see the orange Time Ball, also visible from the Thames, which drops daily at 13:00. Inside, check out the historic astronomical instruments and camera obscura. Finally, enjoy the view: the symmetrical royal buildings; the Thames; the square-mile "City" of London, with its skyscrapers and the dome of St. Paul's; the Docklands, with its busy cranes; and the huge Millennium Dome—big news last year, old news this year (£12 combo ticket covers most Greenwich sights, daily 10:00–17:00). Planetarium shows twinkle on weekdays at 14:30, sometimes on weekends—ask (£2, buy tickets at the observatory, a 2-minute walk from the planetarium).

Greenwich Town—Save time to browse the town. Covered markets and outdoor stalls make weekends lively. The arts-and-crafts market is an entertaining mini–Covent Garden between College Approach and Nelson Road (Fri–Sun, best on Sun), and the antique market sells old ends and odds at high prices on Greenwich High Road near the post office. Wander beyond the touristy Church Street and Greenwich High Road to where flower stands spill into the side streets and antique shops sell brass nautical knickknacks. King William Walk, College Approach, Nelson Road, and Turnpin Lane are all worth a look.

Sights near Greenwich

Thames Barrier—East of Greenwich, the world's largest movable flood barrier welcomes visitors. You'll get a good video and exhibition on the river they claim is the cleanest urban waterway in the world, its floods, and how it was tamed (£3.40, Mon–Fri 10:00–17:00, Sat–Sun 10:30–17:30, tel. 020/8305-4188). To get to the Thames Barrier from London, catch a boat from Westminster Pier (70 min, first boat leaves about 10:15 in peak season, tel. 020/7930-3373) or take the train (a 20-minute ride from Charing

Cross station to Charlton, then a 15-minute walk). To reach the Barrier from Greenwich, take a 30-minute cruise (3/day, first boat leaves at 11:15 from Greenwich, tel. 020/8305-0300).

Transportation Connections—Greenwich

Getting to the town of Greenwich is a joy by boat or a snap by tube. From London, you have good choices: cruise down the Thames from central London's piers at Westminster, Charing Cross, or Tower of London; take the tube to Cutty Sark in Zone 2 (free with tube pass); or catch the train from Charing Cross station (2/hrly, £2.30).

CAMBRIDGE

Cambridge, 60 miles north of London, is world famous for its prestigious university. Wordsworth, Isaac Newton, Tennyson, Darwin, and Prince Charles are a few of its illustrious alumni. This historic town of 100,000 people is more pleasant than its rival, Oxford. Cambridge is the epitome of a university town, with busy bikers, stately residence halls, plenty of bookshops, and proud locals who can point out where electrons and DNA were discovered and where the first atom was split.

In medieval Europe, higher education was the domain of the Church and was limited to ecclesiastical schools. Scholars lived in "halls" on campus. This scholarly community of residential halls, chapels, and lecture halls connected by peaceful garden courtyards survives today in the colleges that make the universities at Cambridge and Oxford. By 1350 Cambridge had eight colleges (Oxford is roughly 100 years older), each with a monastic-type courtyard and lodgings. Today Cambridge has 31 colleges. While a student's life revolves around his or her independent college, the university organizes lectures, presents degrees, and promotes research.

The university dominates—and owns—most of Cambridge. The approximate term schedule is late January to late March (called Lent term), mid-April to mid-June (Easter term), and early October to early December (Michaelmas term). The colleges are closed to visitors during exams, from mid-April until late June, but King's College Chapel and the Trinity Library stay open, and the town is never sleepy.

Planning Your Time

Cambridge is worth most of a day but not an overnight. While Cambridge can be visited on your way from London to York, the cheap day-return train plan makes Cambridge easiest and economical as a side trip from London (from London's King's Cross Station, £14.60, 2/hrly, 1 hr, fast trains depart at :15 and :45 past each hour each way; the budget ticket requires a departure after 9:30 except on Sat and Sun). You can arrive in time for the 11:30 walking tour—an essential part of any visit—and spend the afternoon touring King's College and Fitzwilliam Museum (closed Mon) and simply enjoying the ambience of this stately old college town.

Orientation
(tel. code: 01223)

Cambridge is small but congested. There are two main streets separated from the river by the most interesting colleges. The town center, brimming with tearooms, has a TI and a colorful open-air market (daily 9:00–16:00 on Market Hill Square; on Sunday arts and crafts, otherwise clothes and produce). Also on the main square is a Marks & Spencer grocery (Mon–Sat 8:30–19:00, Sun 11:00–17:00). A J. Sainsbury supermarket, with longer hours and a better deli, is three blocks away on Sidney Street, just north of Green Street. A good picnic spot is Laundress Green, a grassy park on the river, at the end of Mill Lane near the Silver Street punts. Everything is within a pleasant walk.

Tourist Information: At the station, a Guide Friday TI dispenses free Guide Friday maps of Cambridge and sells more detailed ones. The official TI, well signed and just off Market Hill Square, is more harried than helpful (40p maps, Easter–Oct Mon–Fri 10:00–18:00, Sat 10:00–17:00, Sun 11:00–16:00; Nov–Easter Mon–Sat 10:00–17:00, Sun 11:00–16:00 except closed Sun in Jan; tel. 01223/322-640).

Arrival in Cambridge: To get to downtown Cambridge from the train station, take a 20-minute walk (the Guide Friday map is fine for this), a £4 taxi ride, or bus #5 (90p, every 10 min). Drivers can follow signs to any of the handy, central Short Stay Parking Lots.

Helpful Hints

The **Cambridge Shakespeare Festival** takes the stage for eight weeks in July and August with performances of the Bard's classics (tickets probably available at City Centre Box Office, Wheeler Street, tel. 01223/357-851 or check with TI). For Internet access, it's **Internet Exchange** (10p/minute, Mon–Sat 10:00–20:00, Sun 10:00–18:00, 2 St. Mary's Passage, tel. 01223/327-600, www.internet-exchange.co.uk). **Cambridge Cycles** rents bikes (by hour or day, 61 Newnham Road, 5-minute walk from TI, tel. 01223/506-035). Accommodations are frustrating in Cambridge, but if you need a place, consider Hamden Guest House (Db-£45, CC:VM, 89 High Street, 2.5 miles from center, catch #5 bus from train station, tel. 01223/413-263).

Tours of Cambridge

▲▲Walking Tour of the Colleges—A walking tour is the best way to understand Cambridge's mix of "town and gown." Walks give a good rundown on the historic and scenic highlights

Cambridge

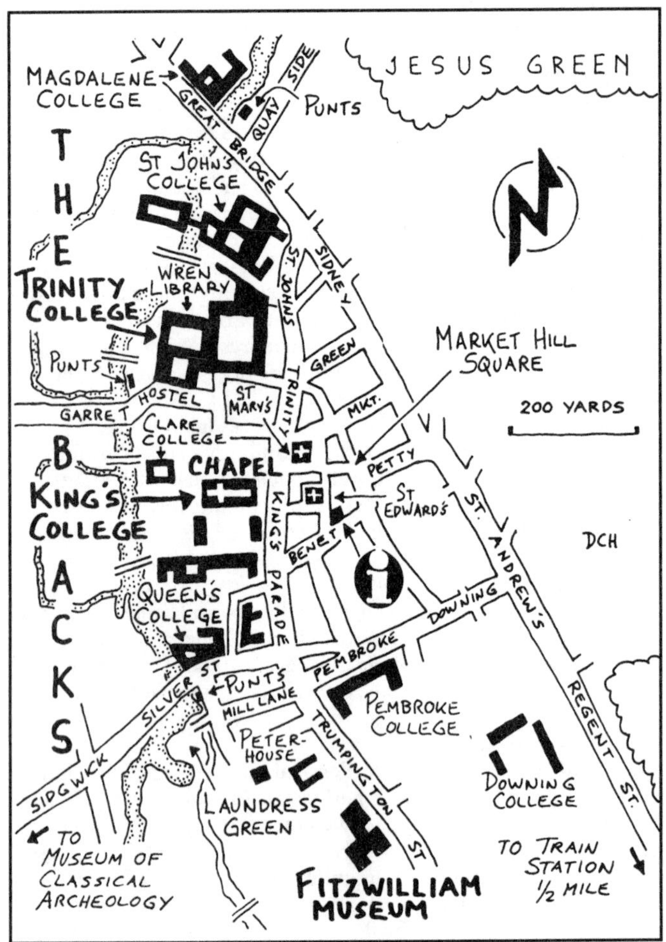

of the university as well as some fun local gossip. Walks are run by and leave from the tourist office. From mid-June through August, tours start at 10:30, 11:30, 13:30, and 14:30; September 10:30, 11:30, 13:30; the rest of the year often at 11:30 and always at 13:30. Tours cost £6.50 and include admission to King's College Chapel. Drop by the TI 60 minutes early to snare a spot (TI tel. 01223/322-640 or 01223/463-290). Particularly if you're coming from London, try calling at least to confirm that a tour is scheduled and not full. Private guides are also available.

Bus Tours—Guide Friday hop-on hop-off bus tours are informative and cover the outskirts (£8.50, departing every 15 minutes, can use CC if you buy tickets in train station office), but walking tours go where the buses can't—right into the center.

Sights—Cambridge

▲▲King's College Chapel—Built from 1446 to 1515 by Henrys VI through VIII, England's best example of Perpendicular Gothic is the single most impressive building in town. Stand inside, look up, and marvel, as Christopher Wren did, at what was the largest single span of vaulted roof anywhere—2,000 tons of incredible fan vaulting. Wander through the Old Testament via the 25 16th-century stained-glass windows (the most Renaissance stained glass anywhere in one spot; it was taken out for safety during World War II then painstakingly replaced). Walk to the altar and admire Rubens' masterful *Adoration of the Magi* (£3.50, erratic hours depending on school and events, but usually daily 9:30–15:30 in term, until 16:30 otherwise). During term you're welcome to enjoy an evensong service (Mon–Sat at 17:30, Sun at 15:30).

▲▲Trinity College—Half of Cambridge's 63 Nobel Prize winners came from this richest and biggest of the town's colleges, founded in 1546 by Henry VIII. Don't miss the Wren-designed library, with its wonderful carving and fascinating original manuscripts (£1.75, 10p leaflet, Mon–Fri 12:00–14:00, also Sat 10:30–12:30 during term). Just outside the library entrance, Sir Isaac Newton, who spent 30 years at Trinity, clapped his hands and timed the echo to measure the speed of sound as it raced down the side of the cloister and back. In the library's display cases (covered with brown cloth that you flip back), you'll see handwritten works by Newton, Milton, Byron, Tennyson, and Housman, alongside Milne's original *Winnie the Pooh* (the real Christopher Robin attended Trinity College).

▲▲Fitzwilliam Museum—Britain's best museum of antiquities and art outside of London is the Fitzwilliam. Enjoy its wonderful paintings (Old Masters and a fine English section featuring Gainsborough, Reynolds, Hogarth, and others, plus works by all the famous Impressionists), old manuscripts, and Greek, Egyptian, and Mesopotamian collections (free, £3 guided tour at 14:30 on Sun only, Tue–Sat 10:00–17:00, Sun 14:15–17:00, closed Mon, tel. 01223/332-900, www.fitzmuseum.cam.ac.uk).

Museum of Classical Archeology—While this museum contains no originals, it offers a unique chance to see accurate copies (19th-century casts of the originals) of virtually every famous ancient Greek and Roman statue. More than 450 statues are on display (free, Mon–Fri 10:00–17:00; sometimes also Sat 10:00–13:00 during term; Sidgwick Avenue, tel. 01223/335-153).

The museum is a five-minute walk west of Silver Street Bridge; after crossing the bridge, continue straight until you reach the sign "Sidgwick Site" (museum is on your right, its entrance away from street).

▲Punting on the Cam—For a little levity and probably more exercise than you really want, try hiring one of the traditional (and inexpensive) flat-bottom punts at the river and pole yourself up and down (around and around, more likely) the lazy Cam. Once you get the hang of it, it's a fine way to enjoy the scenic side of Cambridge. After 17:00 it's less crowded and less embarrassing. Three places, one at each bridge, rent punts (£25–50 deposit required, CC OK) and also offer chauffeured rides (minimum £30 for 40-minute ride). Trinity Punt, at Garrett Hostel Bridge near Trinity College, has the best prices (£8/hour rental, ask for short lesson, free). Scudamore's runs the other two locations: the central Silver Street (£10/hr rentals) and the less convenient Quayside at Great Bridge, at the north end of town (£8/hr, tel. 01223/359-750, www.scudamores.com). Depending on the weather, punting season runs daily Easter through October, with Silver Street open weekends year-round.

Transportation Connections—Cambridge

By train to: London's King's Cross or Liverpool Station (fast train departures at :15 and :45 past each hour, 45 min, one-way £15.60, cheap day-return for £14.60), **York** (hrly, 2.5 hrs, transfer in Petersborough), Birmingham (6/day, 3 hrs), **Liverpool** (5/day, 5 hrs), **Heathrow** (hrly buses, 3.5 hrs). Train info tel. 08457-484-950.

BATH

Any tour of Britain that skips Bath stinks. Two hundred years ago this city of 80,000 was the trendsetting Hollywood of Britain. If ever a city enjoyed looking in the mirror, Bath's the one. It has more "government-listed" or protected historic buildings per capita than any other town in England. The entire city, built of the creamy warm-tone limestone called "Bath stone," beams in its cover-girl complexion. An architectural chorus line, it's a triumph of the Georgian style. Proud locals remind visitors that the town is routinely banned from the "Britain in Bloom" contest to give other towns a chance to win. Bath's narcissism is justified. Even with its mobs of tourists, it's a joy to visit.

Long before the Romans arrived in the first century, Bath was known for its hot springs. What became the Roman spa town of Aquae Sulis has always been fueled by the healing allure of its 116-degree mineral hot springs. The town's importance carried through Saxon times, when it had a huge church on the site of the present-day Abbey and was considered the religious capital of Britain. Its influence peaked in 973, when England's first king, Edgar, was crowned in the Abbey. Bath prospered as a wool town.

Bath then declined until the mid-1600s, when it was just a huddle of huts around the Abbey and some hot springs, with 3,000 residents oblivious to the Roman ruins 18 feet below their dirt floors. Then, in 1687, Queen Mary, fighting infertility, bathed here. Within 10 months she gave birth to a son . . . and a new age of popularity for Bath.

The town boomed as a spa resort. Ninety percent of the buildings you'll see today are from the 18th century. Local architect John Wood was inspired by the Italian architect Palladio to build a "new Rome." The town bloomed in the neoclassical style, and streets were lined not with scrawny sidewalks but with wide "parades," upon which the women in their stylishly wide dresses could spread their fashionable tails.

Beau Nash (1673–1762) was Bath's "master of ceremonies." He organized both the daily regimen of the aristocratic visitors and the city, lighting and improving street security, banning swords, and opening the Pump Room. Under his fashionable baton, Bath became a city of balls, gaming, and concerts and the place to see and be seen in England. This most civilized place became even more so with the great neoclassical building spree that followed.

Planning Your Time

Bath needs two nights even on a quick trip. There's plenty to do, and it's a joy to do it. On a three-week British trip, spend three nights in Bath, with one day for the city and one for a side trip to Wells, Glastonbury, and Avebury. Bath could easily fill another day. Ideally, use Bath as your jet-lag recovery pillow and do London at the end of your trip.

Consider starting a three-week British vacation this way:

Day 1: Land at Heathrow. Catch the National Express bus to Bath (10/day, 2.5-hr trip). While you don't need or want a car in Bath, and most rental companies have an office there, those who pick up their cars at the airport can visit Stonehenge on their way to Bath on this day.

Day 2: 9:00–Tour the Roman Baths, 10:30-Catch the free city walking tour, 12:30–Picnic on the open deck of a Guide Friday bus tour, 14:30–Free time in the shopping center of old Bath, 16:00–Tour the Costume Museum.

Day 3: Pick up your rental car and tour Avebury, Glastonbury (Abbey and Tower), and Wells (17:15 evensong weekdays at the cathedral, 15:00 on Sun). Without a car, consider a one-day Avebury/Stonehenge/cute towns minibus tour from Bath ("Mad Max" tours are best; see "Near Bath," below).

Day 4: 9:00–Leave Bath for South Wales, 10:30–Tour Welsh Folk Museum, 15:00–Stop at Tintern Abbey, then drive to the Cotswolds, 18:00–Set up in your Cotswold home base.

Orientation (area code: 01225)

Bath's town square, three blocks in front of the bus and train station, is a bouquet of tourist landmarks, including the Abbey, Roman and medieval baths, and the royal Pump Room.

Tourist Information: The TI is in the Abbey churchyard (Mon–Sat 9:30–18:00, Sun 10:00–16:00; Oct–April Mon–Sat closes at 17:00, tel. 01225/477-101, www.visitbath.co.uk). Pick up the 50p Bath map/guide (called *Leisure Attractions in and around Bath*) and the free, info-packed *This Month in Bath*.

Browse through scads of fliers, books, and maps (including the Cotswolds). Skip their room-finding service (£3 fee for walk-ins, £5 for callers) and book direct. An American Express office is tucked into the TI (decent rates, no commission on any checks, open same hours as TI).

Arrival in Bath: The Bath train station is a pleasure (small-town charm, an international tickets desk, and a Guide Friday office masquerading as a TI). The bus station is immediately in front of the train station. To get to the TI, walk two blocks up Manvers Street from either station and turn left at the triangular "square," following the small TI arrow on signpost. My recommended B&Bs are all within a 10- or 15-minute walk or a £3.50 taxi ride from the station.

Driving within Bath is a nightmare of one-way streets. Nearly everyone gets lost. Ask for advice from your hotelier and minimize driving in town.

Helpful Hints

Festivals: The International Music Festival bursts into song from May 18 to June 3 in 2001(classical, folk, jazz, contemporary, tel. 01225/462-231) overlapped by the eclectic Fringe Festival from late May to mid-June (theatre, walks, talks, bus trips, tel. 01225/480-079, www.bathfringe.co.uk). The Mozart festival strikes a universal chord every November. Bath's box office sells tickets for most every event (2 Church Street, tel. 01225/463-362, www.bathfestivals.org.uk).

Internet Access: The best in town is Click Café, with two branches, one across from the railway station and the other on 19 Broad Street, near the YMCA (£2.50/30 min, daily 10:00–22:00, tel. 01225/337-711). Other places offering Internet access are the Itchy Feet Café & Travel Store (4 Bartlett Street, near Costume Museum) and the Bath Backpackers Hostel (13 Pierrepont Street; coming from train station, you pass hostel on your way to the TI).

Farmers' Market: First and third Saturday of the month at Green Park Station (9:00–15:00).

Car Rental: Avis (behind the station and over the river at Unit 4B Riverside Business Park, Lower Bristol Road, tel. 01225/446-680), Enterprise (Lower Bristol Road, tel. 01225/443-311), and Hertz (just outside the train station, tel. 01225/442-911) are all trying harder. Most offices are a 10-minute walk from most recommended accommodations. Consider hotel delivery (usually £5, free with Enterprise). Most offices close Saturday afternoon and all day Sunday, complicating weekend pickups. Ideally, pick up your car only on the way out and into the countryside. Take the train or bus from London to Bath and rent a car as you leave Bath rather than in London.

Tours of Bath

▲▲City Bus Tours—The Guide Friday green-and-cream open-top tour bus makes a 70-minute figure-eight circuit of Bath's main sights with an exhaustingly informative running commentary. For one £8.50 ticket (buy from driver), tourists can stop and go at will for a whole day. The buses cover the city center and the surrounding hills (17 signposted pick-up points, 3/hrly spring and fall—runs 9:30–17:00, 4/hrly in summer—9:30–18:00, hrly in winter—9:30–15:30, tel. 01225/464-446). This is great in sunny weather and a feast for photographers. You can munch a sandwich, work on a tan, and sightsee at the same time. Several competing hop-on hop-off tour bus companies offer basically the same tour, but in 45 minutes and without the swing through the countryside, for a couple pounds less. (Ask a local what he or she thinks about all of these city-tour buses.) Generally, the Guide Friday guides are better. Save your ticket to get a £1 discount on a Guide Friday tour in another town.

▲▲▲Walking Tours—These two-hour tours, offered free by trained local volunteers who want to share their love of Bath with its many visitors, are a chatty, historical, gossip-filled joy, essential for your understanding of this town's amazing Georgian social scene. How else will you learn that the old "chair ho" call for your sedan chair evolved into today's "cheerio" greeting? Tours leave from in front of the Pump Room (year-round daily at 10:30, plus May–Oct at 14:00 Mon–Fri, 14:30 Sun, and 19:00 on Tue, Fri, and Sat). For Ghost Walks and Bizarre Bath Comedy Walks, see "Nightlife," below. For a private walking tour from a local gentleman who's an excellent guide, contact Patrick Driscoll (£42/2 hrs, tel. 01225/462-010).

Sights—Bath

▲▲▲Roman and Medieval Baths—In ancient Roman times, high society enjoyed the mineral springs at Bath. From Londinium, Romans traveled so often to Aquae Sulis, as the city was called, to "take a bath" that finally it became known simply as Bath. Today a fine museum surrounds the ancient bath and is, with its well-documented displays, a one-way system leading you past Roman artifacts, mosaics, a temple pediment, and the actual mouth of the spring, piled high with Roman pennies. Enjoy some quality time looking into the eyes of Minerva, goddess of the hot springs. The included self-guided tour audio-wand makes the visit easy and plenty informative. For those with a big appetite for Roman history, in-depth 40-minute tours leave from the end of the museum at the edge of the actual bath (included, on the hour, a poolside clock is set for the next departure time). You can revisit the museum after the tour (£6.90, £8.90 combo ticket includes Costume Museum at a good savings, family combo-£23.50, combo

Bath

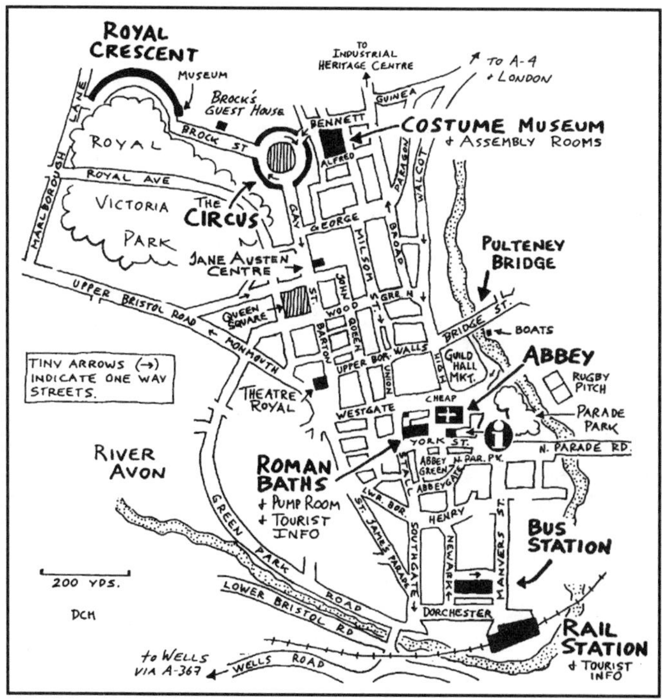

tickets good for 1 week; April–Sept daily 9:00–18:00, in Aug until 21:30, Oct–March until 17:00, tel. 01225/477-000). In 2002, when a new spa facility opens (near the museum), people will once again be able to bathe in the hot springs of Bath.

▲Pump Room—After a centuries-long cold spell, Bath was reheated when the previously barren Queen Mary bathed here and in due course bore a male heir to the throne (1687). Once Bath was back on the aristocratic map, high society soon turned the place into one big pleasure palace. The Pump Room, an elegant Georgian hall just above the Roman baths, offers the visitor's best chance to raise a pinky in this Chippendale elegance. Drop by to sip coffee or tea to the rhythm of a string trio or pianist (live music all year 10:00–12:00, summers until 17:00, tea/coffee and pastry available for £6 anytime except during lunch, a £9 traditional high tea served after 14:30). Above the newspaper table and sedan chairs a statue of Beau Nash himself sniffles down at you. Now's your chance to have a famous (but forgettable) "Bath bun" and split (and spit) a 50p drink of the awfully curative water.

Public WCs are in the entry hallway that connects the Pump Room with the Baths.

▲Abbey—Bath town wasn't much in the Middle Ages. But an important church has stood on this spot since Anglo-Saxon times. In 973, Edgar, the first king of England, was crowned here. Dominating the town center, the present church—the last great medieval church of England—is 500 years old and a fine example of Late Perpendicular Gothic, with breezy fan vaulting and enough stained glass to earn it the nickname "Lantern of the West" (worth the £2 donation, Mon–Sat 9:00–18:00, Sun 13:00–17:30, closes at 16:30 in winter, handy flier narrates a self-guided 18-stop tour). The schedule for concerts, services, and **evensong** (Sun at 15:15 year-round, plus most Sat in Aug at 17:00) is posted on the door. **Church bells** ring before services from 10:15 to 11:00 on Sunday; practice is usually on Monday evening (19:00–21:00; a glorious time to take an evening walk). Take a moment to really appreciate the Abbey's architecture from the Abbey Green square.

The Abbey's **Heritage Vaults**, a small but interesting exhibit, tells the story of Christianity in Bath since Roman times (£2, Mon–Sat 10:00–16:00, closed Sun, entrance just outside church, south side).

▲Pulteney Bridge and Cruises—Bath is inclined to compare its shop-lined Pulteney Bridge to Florence's Ponte Vecchio. That's pushing it. To best enjoy a sunny day, pay £1 to enter the Parade Gardens below the bridge (daily 10:00–19:00, until 20:00 June–Aug, free after 20:00, includes deck chairs, ask about the concerts held some Sun at 15:00 in summer).

Across the bridge at Pulteney Weir, tour boats run cruises from under the bridge (£4.50, up to 7/day if the weather's good, 50 minutes to Bathampton and back, WCs on board). Just take whatever boat is running. Avon Cruisers stop in Bathampton if you'd like to walk back; Pulteney Cruisers come with a sundeck ideal for picnics.

▲▲Royal Crescent and the Circus—If Bath is an architectural cancan, these are the kickers. These first elegant Georgian "condos" by John Wood (the Elder and the Younger) are well explained in the city walking tours. "Georgian" is British for "neoclassical," or dating from the 1770s. As you cruise the Crescent, pretend you're rich. Pretend you're poor. Notice the "ha ha fence," a drop in the front yard offering a barrier, invisible from the windows, to sheep and peasants. The round Circus is a colosseum turned inside out. Its Doric, Ionic, and Corinthian capital decorations pay homage to its Greco-Roman origin.

▲▲Georgian House at #1 Royal Crescent—This museum (on the corner of Brock Street and the Royal Crescent) offers your best look into a period house. It's worth the £4 admission to get behind one of those classy exteriors. The volunteers in each room are determined to fill you in on all the fascinating details of Georgian life . . . like how high-class women shaved their eyebrows and pasted on carefully trimmed strips of furry mouse skin in their place (Tue–Sun 10:30–17:00, closed Mon, closes at 16:00 in Nov, closed Dec–mid-Feb, "no stiletto heels, please," tel. 01225/428-126).

▲▲▲Costume Museum—One of Europe's great museums, displaying 400 years of fashion—one frilly decade at a time—is housed within Bath's Assembly Rooms. Follow the included, excellent audioguide tour (£4, an £8.90 combo ticket covers Roman Baths, family combo-£23.50, daily 10:00–17:00, tel. 01225/477-789). The Assembly Rooms, which you'll see en route to the museum, are big, elegant, empty rooms where card games, concerts, tea, and dances were held in the 18th century before the advent of fancy hotels with grand public spaces made them obsolete.

▲▲Museum of Bath at Work—This is the official title for Mr. Bowler's Business, a 1900s engineer's shop, brass foundry, and fizzy-drink factory with a Dickensian office. It's just a pile of meaningless old gadgets until a volunteer guide lovingly resurrects Mr. Bowler's creative genius. Fascinating hour-long tours go regularly; just join the one in session upon arrival. (£3.50, plus a few pence for a glass of genuine Victorian lemonade, April–Oct daily 10:00–17:00, weekends only in winter, 2 blocks up Russell Street from Assembly Rooms, call to be sure a volunteer is available to give a tour, café upstairs, tel. 01225/318-348.)

Jane Austen Centre—This new exhibition focuses on Jane Austen's five years in Bath (around 1800) and the influence Bath had on her writing. While the exhibit is thoughtfully done and is a hit with "Jane-ites," there is little of historic substance here. You'll walk through a Georgian townhouse which she didn't live in and see mostly enlarged reproductions of things associated with her writing. After a live intro explaining how this romantic but down-to-earth girl dealt with the silly, shallow, and arrogant aristocrat's world where "the doing of nothings all day prevents one from doing anything," you see a 13-minute video and wander through the rest of the exhibit (£4, Mon–Sat 10:00–17:30, Sunday 10:30–17:30, 40 Gay Street between Queen's Square and the Circus, tel. 01225/443-000, www.janeausten.co.uk).

The Building of Bath Museum—This offers a fascinating look behind the scenes at how the Georgian city was actually built. It's just one large room of exhibits, but those interested in construction find it worth the £4 (Tue–Sun 10:30–17:00, closed Mon, near the Circus on a street called "the Paragon," tel. 01225/333-895).

Microworld—This dark two-room museum glows with a couple dozen glass bubbles of light, containing the smallest sculptures you've ever seen—the creations of two artists. Ussa's work borders on hokey (flea riding a bicycle), but Wigan's work is remarkable. Wigan actually carves his minute work—out of a sugar grain, a match head, a bit of boxwood (look for the Statue of Liberty in the eye of a needle). As a dyslexic kid, labeled "nothing" by a racist teacher, he was determined to make something out of nothing (£3.50, daily 10:00–18:00, Kingsmead Square, near Theatre Royal, tel. 01225/333-003).

Royal Photographic Society—A hit with shutterbugs, this focuses on the earliest cameras, photos, and their development, (£4, daily 9:30–17:30, on Milsom Street, tel. 01225/462-841).

Views—For the best views of Bath, try Alexander Park (south of city, 10-minute walk from train station), Camden Crescent (10–15 minute walk north), or Becksford Tower (steep 20-minute walk north up Lansdown Road, www.bath-preservation-trust.org.uk).

▲American Museum—I know, you need this in Bath like you need a Big Mac. But this museum offers a fascinating look at colonial and early-American lifestyles. Each of 18 completely furnished rooms (from the 1600s to the 1800s) is hosted by an eager guide waiting to fill you in on the candles, maps, bedpans, and various religious sects that make domestic Yankee history surprisingly interesting. One room is a quilter's nirvana (£5.50, Tue–Sun 14:00–17:00, closed Mon and early Nov–late March, at Claverton Manor, tel. 01225/460-503). The museum is outside of town and a headache to reach if you don't have a car (15-minute walk from the nearest Guide Friday stop or a 10-minute walk from bus #18).

Activities in Bath

Walking, Biking, and Swimming—The Bath Skyline Walk is a six-mile wander around the hills surrounding Bath (70p leaflet at TI). For more options, get *Country Walks around Bath*, by Tim Mowls (£4.50 at TI).

Consider the idyllic walk up the canal path to Bathampton: from downtown, walk over Pulteney Bridge, through Sydney Gardens, turn left on canal, and in 30 minutes you'll hit Bathampton, with its much-loved Old George Pub. Sailors enjoy the river cruise up to Bathampton; hikers like walking back (see "Pulteney Bridge and Cruises," above). From Bathampton it's two hours along the canal to the fine old town of Bradford-on-Avon, from which you can train back to Bath. You can bike this route (rent bikes at Avon Valley Cyclery behind train station, £9/half day, £14/all day, tel. 01225/442-442). The scenic 12-mile path along the old Bath–Bristol train tracks is also popular.

The Bath Sports and Leisure Centre has a swimming pool and more (£2.50, daily 8:00–22:00, just across North Parade Bridge, call for free swim times, tel. 01225/462-563).

The Bath Boating Station, in an old Victorian boathouse, rents boats and punts (£4.50/first hr per person, then £1.50/hr,

April–Sept 10:00–18:00, tearoom, Forester Road, a mile northeast of center, tel. 01225/466-407).

Shopping—There's great browsing between the Abbey and the Assembly Rooms (Costume Museum). Shops close at 17:30, later on Thursday. Explore the antique center on Bartlett Street just below the Assembly Rooms. You'll find the most stalls open on Wednesday. Pick up the local paper (usually out on Friday) and shop with the dealers at estate sales and auctions listed in "What's On."

Nightlife in Bath

This Month in Bath (available at TI) lists events.

Plays—The Theatre Royal, newly restored and one of England's loveliest, offers a busy schedule of London West End–type plays, including many "pre-London" dress rehearsal runs (£11–25, cheaper matinees as low as £5, tel. 01225/448-844). Forty standby tickets per evening show go on sale starting at 12:00 on the day of the performance (either pay cash at box office or call and book with CC, 2 tickets maximum). Or you can buy a last-minute seat at a reduced price 30 minutes before "curtain up."

Evening Walks—For a walking comedy act "with absolutely no history or culture," follow J. J. or Noel Britten on their creative and entertaining **Bizarre Bath** walk. This 90-minute "tour," which plays off local passersby as well as tour members, is a kick (£4.50, 20:00 nightly April 9–Sept 30, heavy on magic, careful to insult all minorities and sensitivities, just racy enough but still good family fun; leave from Huntsman pub near the Abbey, confirm at TI or call 01225/335-124, www.bizarrebath.co.uk). **Ghost Walks** are another way to pass the after-dark hours (£4, 20:00, 2 hrs, unreliably Mon–Sat April–Oct; in winter Fridays only; leave from Garrick's Head pub near Theatre Royal, tel. 01225/463-618). Scholarly types can try the **free walking tours** offered several times a week (19:00 on Tue, Fri, and Sat, 2 hrs, May–Oct, leave from Pump Room, confirm at TI).

Sleeping in Bath

(£1 = about $1.60, country code: 44, area code: 01225)

Sleep Code: **S** = Single, **D** = Double/Twin, **T** = Triple, **Q** = Quad, **b** = bathroom, **t** = toilet only, **s** = shower only, **CC** = Credit Card (**V**isa, **M**asterCard, **A**mex).

Bath is a busy tourist town. To get a good B&B, make a telephone reservation in advance. Competition is stiff, and it's worth asking any of these places for a weekday, three-nights-in-a-row, or off-season deal. Friday and Saturday nights are tightest, especially if you're staying only one night, since B&Bs favor those staying longer. If staying only Saturday night, you're very bad news. At B&Bs (and cheaper hotels), expect lots of stairs and no lifts.

Laundrettes: The Spruce Goose Launderette is around the

corner from Brock's Guest House on the pedestrian lane called Margaret's Buildings (£4 self-serve, £7 full-service on same day if dropped off by 10:30, Sun–Fri 8:00–20:00, Sat 8:00–19:00, tel. 01225/483-309). The scruffier Monmouth Place Laundrette, closer to the Marlborough Lane listings, is on Upper Bristol Road (£4 self-serve, £6 full-service—drop off by noon for same-day return, daily 9:00–20:00, tel. 01225/429-378). East of Pulteney Bridge, the humble Lovely Wash is on Daniel Street (daily 9:00–21:00, self-serve only).

Sleeping in B&Bs near the Royal Crescent

From the train station, these listings are all a 10- to 15-minute uphill walk or an easy £3.50 taxi ride. Or take the Guide Friday bus tour from the station and get off at the stop nearest your B&B (for Brock's, Assembly Rooms; for Marlborough listings, Royal Avenue; for Armstrong's, Upper Bristol Road—confirm with driver), check in, then finish the tour later in the day. All of these B&Bs are nonsmoking.

Brock's Guest House will put bubbles in your Bath experience. Marion and Geoffrey Dodd have redone their Georgian townhouse (built by John Wood in 1765) in a way that would make the famous architect proud. It's located between the prestigious Royal Crescent and the elegant Circus (Db-£62–70, 1 deluxe Db-£72–75, Tb-£85–87, Qb-£99–105, reserve with a credit-card number far in advance, CC:VM, strictly nonsmoking, little library on top floor, 32 Brock Street, BA1 2LN, tel. 01225/338-374, fax 01225/334-245, www.brocksguesthouse.co.uk, e-mail: marion@brocks.force9.net). Marion can occasionally arrange a reasonable private car hire.

On Marlborough Lane: The **Woodville House** is run by Anne and Tom Toalster. This grandmotherly little house has three tidy, charming rooms, one shared shower/WC, an extra WC, and a TV lounge. Breakfast is served at a big, family-style table (D-£40, minimum 2 nights, strictly nonsmoking, below the Royal Crescent at 4 Marlborough Lane, BA1 2NQ, tel. & fax 01225/319-335, e-mail: toalster@compuserve.com).

Elgin Villa, also a fine value, has five comfy, well-maintained rooms (Ds-£45, Db-£50, discounts for 3-night stays, kids £15 extra, continental breakfast served in room, parking, nonsmoking, 6 Marlborough Lane, BA1 2NQ Bath, tel. & fax 01225/424-557, www.elginvilla.co.uk, Alwyn and Carol Landman).

Athelney Guest House, which also serves a continental breakfast in your room, has three spacious rooms with two shared bathrooms (D-£40–42, T-£60–63, nonsmoking, parking, 5 Marlborough Lane, BA1 2NQ, tel. & fax 01225/312-031, Sue and Colin Davies, e-mail: colin-davies@supanet.com).

Parkside Guest House is more upscale, renting four classy Edwardian rooms (Db-£65, nonsmoking, access to pleasant backyard, 11 Marlborough Lane, BA1 2NQ, tel. & fax 01225/429-444, e-mail: parkside@lynall.freeserve.co.uk, Erica and Inge Lynall).

Marlborough House is both Victorian and vegetarian, with seven comfortable rooms—well furnished with antiques—and optional £15 organic veggie dinners (Sb-£45–75, Db-£65–85 depending on season, CC:VM, varied breakfast menu, room service, nonsmoking,1 Marlborough Lane, BA1 2NQ, tel. 01225/318-175, fax 01225/466-127, www.s-h-systems.co.uk/hotels/marlbor1.html, Americans Laura and Charles).

Prior House B&B, with four well-kept rooms, is run by helpful Lynn and Keith Shearns (D-£40, Db-£45, CC:VM, nonsmoking, 3 Marlborough Lane, tel. 01225/313-587, fax 01225/443-543, e-mail: priorhouse@greatplaces.co.uk).

On Upper Bristol Road: The **Armstrong House B&B** is well run and closer to town on a busier road, with five pleasant rooms behind double-paned windows (Db-£55, continental breakfast in room, nonsmoking, 41 Crescent Gardens, Upper Bristol Road, BA1 2NB, tel. 01225/442-211, fax 01225/460-665, Tony Conradi).

Sleeping in B&Bs East of the River

These listings are about a 10-minute walk from the city center.

Near North Parade Road: The **Holly Villa Guest House,** with a cheery garden, six bright rooms, and a cozy TV lounge, is enthusiastically and thoughtfully run by Jill and Keith McGarrigle (Ds-£45, Db-£50, Tb-£70, strictly nonsmoking, easy parking, 8-minute walk from station and city center, 14 Pulteney Gardens, BA2 4HG, tel. 01225/310-331, fax 01225/339-334, e-mail: hollyvilla.bb@ukgateway.net). From the city center, walk over North Parade Bridge, take the first right, then the second left.

Near Pulteney Road: Muriel Guy's B&B is another good value, mixing Georgian elegance with homey warmth, artistic taste, and fine city views (5 rooms, 1 S with private bath upstairs-£25, Db-£50, nonsmoking, 10-minute walk from city center, go over bridge on North Parade Road, left on Pulteney Road, cross to church, Raby Place is first row of houses on hill, 14 Raby Place, BA2 4EH, tel. 01225/465-120, fax 01225/465-283).

The Ayrlington, next door to a lawn-bowling green, has attractive rooms that hint of a more genteel time. Though this well-maintained hotel fronts a busy street, it feels tranquil inside, with double-paned windows. Rooms in the back have pleasant views of sports greens and Bath beyond. For the best value, request a standard double with a view of Bath (standard Db-£80–95, superior Db-£90–110, deluxe Db with Jacuzzi-£99–125, prices decrease midweek and increase weekends, no Sat night only, CC:VMA, access to garden in back, easy parking, 10-minute walk from center, 24/25 Pulteney Road, BA2 4EZ, tel. 01225/425-495, fax 01225/469-029, www.ayrlington.com, Simon and Mee-Ling).

In Sydney Gardens: The **Sydney Gardens Hotel** is a classy Casablanca-type place with six tastefully decorated rooms, an elegant breakfast room, garden views, and an entrance to Sydney Gardens park (Db-£69/weekdays, £75/weekends, Tb-£95, CC:VM, 2 nights preferred, request garden view, located on busy road between park and canal, easy parking, 10-minute walk from center, Sydney Road, BA2 6NT, tel. 01225/464-818, fax 01225/484-347, Geraldine and Peter Beaven).

Sleeping East of Pulteney Bridge

These are just a few minutes' walk from the city center.

The **Kennard Hotel** is comfortable, with 14 charming Georgian rooms. Richard Ambler runs this place warmly, giving careful attention to guests (S-£48, Db-£88–98 depending upon size, CC:VMA, no kids under 12, nonsmoking, just over Pulteney Bridge, turn left at Henrietta, 11 Henrietta Street, BA2 6LL, tel. 01225/310-472, fax 01225/460-054, www.kennard.co.uk, e-mail: kennard@dircon.co.uk).

Laura Place Hotel is another elegant Georgian place (8 rooms, 2 on the ground floor, Db-£70–90 from small and high up to huge and palatial, 2-night minimum stay, must show this book to get 10 percent discount with cash, CC:VMA, family suite, nonsmoking, easy parking, 3 Laura Place, Great Pulteney Street, BA2 4BH, just over Pulteney Bridge, tel. 01225/463-815, fax 01225/310-222, Patricia Bull).

Villa Magdala, with 18 spacious rooms in a freestanding Victorian townhouse opposite a park, is centuries away from a Motel 6 (Db-£85–£105, depending on size, type of bed, and plumbing; nonsmoking, in quiet residential area, parking, Henrietta Road, Bath BA2 6LX, tel. 01225/466-329, fax 01225-483-207, www.villamagdala.co.uk).

Henrietta Hotel has simple, tidy, and decent rooms, giving you a budget hotel option in an elegant neighborhood (10 rooms, Db-£45–75, discounts for cash and 2-night stay Sun–Thu, CC:VM, 32 Henrietta Street, tel. 01225/447-779, fax 01225/444-150).

Sleeping in the City Center

Harington's of Bath Hotel, with 13 newly renovated rooms on a quiet street in the town center, is run by Susan and Desmond Pow (Db-£78–98, Tb-£110–120, prices decrease midweek and increase weekends, CC:VMA, nonsmoking, lots of stairs, attached restaurant/bar serves simple meals and pastries throughout day, extremely central at 10 Queen Street, BA1 1HE, tel. 01225/461-728, fax 01225/444-804, www.haringtonshotel.co.uk).

Parade Park Hotel, in a Georgian building, has a central

Hotels and Restaurants in Bath

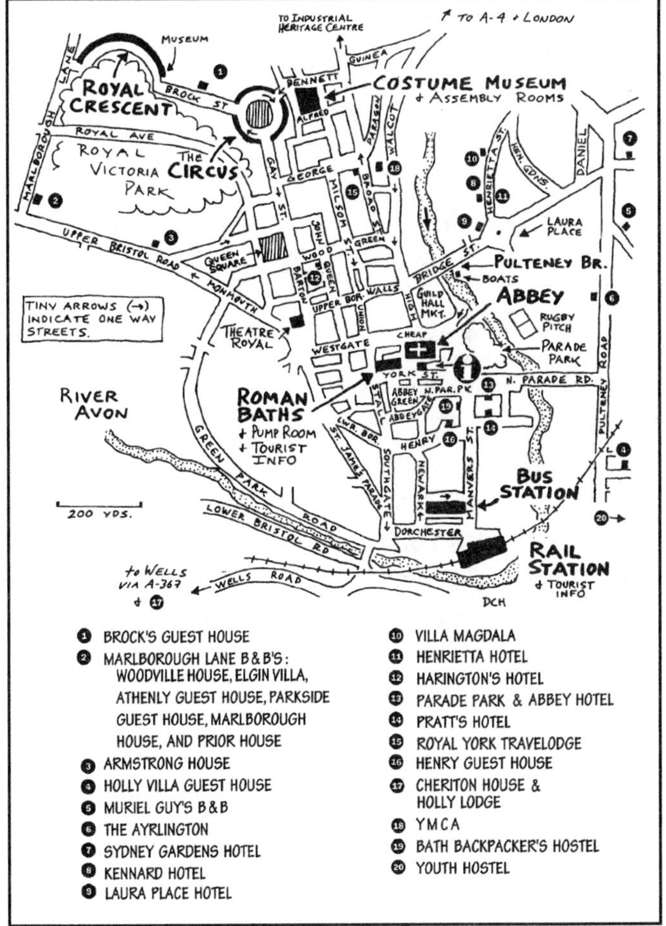

location, helpful owners, and comfortable rooms decorated in a modern style (35 rooms, Db-£60–65, 4-poster Db-£75, Tb-£80, Qb-£105, CC:VM, nonsmoking, beaucoup stairs, 10 North Parade, BA2 4AL, tel. 01225/463-384, fax 01225/442-322, www.paradepark.co.uk, Nita and David Derrick).

Pratt's Hotel is as proper and old English as you'll find in Bath. Its creaks and frays are aristocratic. Its public places make you want to sip a brandy, and its 46 rooms are bright, spacious, and come with all the comforts (Sb-£75, Db-£110, prices promised with this book in 2001, dogs £2.95 but children free, CC:VMA, attached restaurant/bar, elevator, 2 blocks immediately in front of the station on South Parade, BA2 4AB, tel. 01225/460-441, fax 01225/448-807, e-mail: admin@prattshotel.demon.co.uk).

The **Royal York Travelodge** offers American-style characterless, comfortable rooms, worrying B&Bs and hotels alike with its reasonable prices (Db-£69, 1 York Bldg, George Street, BA1 3EB, tel. 01225/448-999).

The Abbey Hotel, a Best Western hotel, has 60 good-quality rooms with a super location, and offers a rare elevator as well as some ground floor rooms (standard Db-£120, deluxe Db-£130, CC:VMA, attached restaurant, nonsmoking rooms available, North Parade, BA1 1LF, tel. 01225/461-603, fax 01225/447-758, e-mail: ahres@compasshotels.co.uk).

Henry Guest House is a plain, simple, old, vertical, eight-room, family-run place two blocks in front of the train station on a quiet side street. Nothing matches—not the curtains, wallpaper, carpeting, throw rugs, or bedspreads—but it is the cheapest hotel in the center (S-£22.50, D-£45, T-£67.50, TVs in rooms, lots of narrow stairs, 2 showers and WCs for all, 6 Henry Street, BA1 1JT, tel. 01225/424-052, e-mail: cox@thehenrybath.freeserve.co.uk).

Sleeping in B&Bs south of the Train Station

Up a hill an eight-minute walk south of the train station are a string of classy, upscale B&Bs with views of Bath. Here are two good ones (request a view room): **Cheriton House**, with nine well-furnished rooms (Db-£58–66, larger Db-£68–76, CC:VM, garden, 9 Upper Oldfield Park, BA2 3JX, tel. 01225/429-862, e-mail: cheriton @which.net, Mrs. Iris Wroe-Parker), and **Holly Lodge**, with six frilly, Victorian-style rooms and a view gazebo in the garden (Sb-£48–55, Db-£75–94, add £5 for 4-poster, CC:VM, no smoking, phones, tel. 01225/339-187, fax 01225/481-138, Mr. George Hall).

Sleeping in Dorms

The **YMCA,** wonderfully central on a leafy square down a tiny alley off Broad Street, has industrial-strength rooms and scuff-proof halls (S-£15, D-£28, T-£42, Q-£56, beds in big dorms-£11, cheaper for 2-night stays, includes continental breakfast, families offered a day nursery for kids under 5, cheap dinners, CC:VM, Broad Street Place, BA1 5LH, tel. 01225/460-471, fax 01225/462-065, e-mail: info@ymcabath.u-net.com).

Bath Backpackers Hostel bills itself as a totally fun-packed, mad place to stay. This Aussie-run dive/hostel rents bunk beds in 6- to 10-bed coed rooms (£12 per bed, 2 D-£30, no lockers, Internet access for nonguests as well, a couple of blocks toward the city center from the station, 13 Pierrepont Street, tel. 01225/446-787, fax 01225/446-305, e-mail: stayinbath@backpackers-uk.demon.co.uk).

The **Youth Hostel** is in a grand old building on Bathwick Hill outside of town (£11 per bed without breakfast in 2- to 12-bed rooms, bus #18 from station, tel. 01225/465-674).

Eating in Bath

While not a great pub grub town, Bath is bursting with quaint eateries. There's something for every appetite and budget—just stroll around the center of town. A picnic dinner of deli food or take-out fish 'n' chips in the Royal Crescent Park is ideal for aristocratic hobos.

Eating between the Abbey and the Station

Three fine and popular places share North Parade Passage, a block south of the Abbey: **Tilley's Bistro** serves healthy French, English, and vegetarian meals with ambience (£10 3-course lunches, £15–20 dinners, Mon–Sat 12:00–14:30, nightly 18:30–23:00, closed Sun lunch, CC:VM, nonsmoking, North Parade Passage, tel. 01225/484-200). **Sally Lunn's House** is a cutesy, quasi-historic place for expensive doily meals, tea, pink pillows, and lots of lace (£5–8, nightly, CC:VM, 4 North Parade Passage, tel. 01225 /461-634). It's fine for tea and buns, and customers get a free peek at the basement Kitchen Museum (otherwise 30p). Next door, **Demuth's Vegetarian Restaurant** serves good three-course £15 meals (daily 10:00–22:00, CC:VM, vegan options available, tel. 01225/446-059).

Crystal Palace Pub, with hearty meals under rustic timbers or in the sunny courtyard, is a handy standby (£6 meals, Mon–Fri 11:00–20:30, Sat 11:00–15:30, Sun 12:00–14:30; children welcome on patio, not indoors; 11 Abbey Green, tel. 01225/423-944).

Evans is considered the best fish 'n' chips joint in town, but it's mainly open only for lunch and is perpetually on the verge of being bought out (Mon–Fri 11:30–15:30, Sat 11:30–19:00, on Abbeygate, near Marks & Spencer). A good fallback is **Seafoods** (daily 12:00–23:00, 27 Kingsmeads Street, just off Kingsmead Square). For more cheap meals, try **Spike's Fish and Chips** (open very late) and the neighboring café just behind the bus station.

Eating between the Abbey and the Circus

George Street is lined with cheery eateries: Thai, Italian, wine bars, and so on. **Caffé Martini** is purely Italian with class (£10 entrees, £7 pizzas, daily 12:00–14:30, 18:00–22:00, CC:VM, 9 George Street, tel. 01225/460-818), while the **Mediterraneo,** also Italian, is homier (12 George Street, CC:VMA, tel. 01225/429-008).

Eastern Eye serves Indian food under the domes of a Georgian auction hall (£15 meals, £9 minimum, daily 12:00–14:30, 18:00–23:00, CC:VMA, 8a Quiet Street, tel. 01225/422-323).

Jamuna makes a mean curry (Mon–Sun 12:00–14:30, 18:00–24:00, Abbey views, 9–10 High Street, tel. 01225/464-631).

The **Old Green Tree Pub** on Green Street is a rare pub with good grub, locally brewed real ales, and a nonsmoking room (lunch only, served 12:00–14:30, no children, live jazz Sun–Mon 20:30 until closing, tel. 01225/448-259).

Browns, a popular, modern chain, offers affordable English food throughout the day (£6 lunch special, Mon-Sat 11:00–23:30, Sun 12:00–23:30, CC:VMA, half block east of Abbey, Orange Grove, tel. 01225/461-199).

The Moon and Sixpence, prized by locals, gives British cooking a needed international flair and flavor (£7 lunch, 3-course dinner menu for £18–22, daily 12:00–14:30, 17:30–22:30, CC:VM, indoor/outdoor seating, 6a Broad Street, tel. 01225/460-962).

All Bar One, offering inexpensive meals, is a trendy, modern-day pub popular with the younger crowd (12 High Street, tel. 01225/324-021).

Devon Savouries serves greasy, delicious take-out pasties, sausage rolls, and vegetable pies (Mon–Sat 9:00–17:30, hours vary on Sun; on Burton Street, the main walkway between New Bond Street and Upper Borough Walls).

Pasta Galore serves decent (sometimes so-so) Italian food and homemade pasta outside on a patio or inside—the ground floor beats the basement (daily 12:00–14:30, 18:00–22:30, CC:VM, 31 Barton Street, tel. 01225/463-861).

If you're missing California, try the popular **Firehouse Rotisserie** (daily 12:00–14:30, 18:00–23:00, reserve on weekends, John Street, tel. 01225/482-070).

Guildhall Market, across from Pulteney Bridge, is fun for browsing and picnic shopping, with an inexpensive Market Café if you'd like to sip tea surrounded by stacks of used books, bananas on the push list, and honest-to-goodness old-time locals (Mon–Sat 9:00–17:00, closed Sun, main entrance on High Street, a block north of Abbey).

The **Cornish Bakehouse**, near the Guildhall Market, has good take-away pasties (11a The Corridor, off High Street, tel. 01225/426-635).

Supermarkets: **Waitrose,** at the Podium shopping center, is great for groceries (Mon–Fri 8:30–20:00, Sat 8:30–19:00, Sun 11:00–17:00, salad bar, just west of Pulteney Bridge and across from post office on High Street). **Marks & Spencer,** near the train station, has a good grocery at the back of its department store (Mon–Sat 9:00–17:30, Sun 11:00–17:00, Stall Street).

Eating East of Pulteney Bridge

For a classy, intimate setting and "new English" cuisine worth the splurge, dine at **No. 5 Bistro** (main courses with vegetables

£12–15, Mon and Tue are "bring your own bottle of wine" nights—no corkage charge, Mon–Sat 18:30–22:00, closed Sun, just over Pulteney Bridge at 5 Argyle Street, smart to reserve, tel. 01225/444-499). **Rajpoot Tandoori,** next door to No. 5, serves good Indian food. **Cappeti's,** across the street from No. 5, is a pasta pleaser (Tue–Sat 12:00–14:00, 18:30–22:30, closed Mon, 12 Argyle Street, tel. 01225/442-299).

Eating near the Circus and Brock's Guest House

Circus Restaurant is intimate and a good value, with Mozartian ambience and candlelight prices: £17 for a three-course dinner special including great vegetables and a selection of fine desserts (daily 12:00–14:00, 18:30–22:00, CC:VM, 34 Brock Street, tel. 01225/318-918, Felix Rosenow).

Woods Restaurant serves modern English cuisine to well-dressed locals in a sprawling candlelit brasserie (lunches-£7, 3-course dinners-£13–25, daily 12:00–15:00, 18:00–22:30 except closed Sun eve, CC:VM, 9–13 Alfred Street, near Assembly Rooms, tel. 01225/314-812).

For real ale (but no food), try the **Star Pub** (top of Paragon Street).

Transportation Connections—Bath

To London's Paddington Station: By train (2/hrly, 75 min, £31 one-way after 9:30), or cheaper by National Express bus (nearly hrly, up to 3.25 hrs, £11.25 one-way, £19.50 round-trip but £23 on Fri, ask about £12 day returns). To get from London to Bath, consider an all-day Stonehenge-and-Bath organized bus tour from London. For about the same cost as the train ticket, you can see Stonehenge, tour Bath, and leave the tour before it returns to London (stow your bag underneath). Evan Evans offers daily Stonehenge/Bath day trips from London (£48 for fully guided version includes admissions, offered year-round; also has a £33 Low Cost version providing bus transportation only, offered April–Oct only, but may not run in 2001—ask, departs Victoria Coach Station, tel. 020/7950-1777, www.evanevans.co.uk). Golden Tours offers a similar fully guided tour at similar prices (about £48, departs from Fountain Square, across from Victoria Coach Station, tel. 020/7233-6668, www.goldentours.co.uk). Train info: tel. 08457-484-950.

To London's airports: By National Express bus to **Heathrow** Airport—and continuing on to London (10/day, leaving Bath at 5:00, 6:30, 7:30, 8:45, 10:00, 12:00, 13:30, 15:00, 16:30, and 18:30, 2.5 hrs, £11.50, tel. 08705-808-080), and to **Gatwick** (2/hrly, 4.5 hrs, £19.50, change at Heathrow). Trains are faster but more expensive (hrly, 2.5 hrs, £29.20, see "London Connections" section for details). Coming from Heathrow, you can take the Heathrow Express train from the airport to London's Paddington station, then catch the Exeter train to Bath (about £45 total).

To the Cotswolds: A handy Cotswold Link bus service runs twice daily in both directions between Bath and **Stratford,** stopping at 13 towns en route, including the Cotswold towns of **Chipping Campden, Stow-on-the-Wold,** and **Moreton-in-Marsh** (Bath–Stratford ticket costs £7.70 one-way; buy ticket on bus). You're allowed to break the journey within the same day and continue on the next bus; this allows you to easily day-trip from Bath to one Cotswold town or see one Cotswold town en route to another (e.g., see Stow, stay in Chipping Campden).

Other (lesser) Bath–Cotswolds options: By train to **Moreton-in-Marsh** (2.5 hrs, with either a transfer in Reading or transfers in Didcot Parkway and Oxford). By National Express bus to **Cheltenham** (1 direct bus a day, 1.75 hrs, more trips if you transfer), **Stratford** (1/day, 2.75 hrs, more with transfer), and **Oxford** (1/day, 2 hrs, more with transfer); bus info tel. 08705-808-080.

By train to: Oxford (hrly, 1 hr, change at Didcot Parkway), **Heathrow** (hrly, change at Reading to bus), **Gatwick** (hrly, 3 hrs), **Birmingham** (hrly, 2.5 hrs, transfer in Bristol), and **points north** (from Birmingham, a major transportation hub, trains depart for Blackpool, York, Durham, Scotland, and North Wales; use a train/bus combination to reach Ironbridge Gorge and the Lake District).

NEAR BATH: GLASTONBURY, WELLS, AVEBURY, STONEHENGE, AND SOUTH WALES

Oooo, mystery, history. Glastonbury is the ancient home of Avalon, King Arthur, and the Holy Grail. Nearby, medieval Wells gathers around its grand cathedral, where you can enjoy an evensong service. Then get neolithic at every Druid's favorite stone circles, Avebury and Stonehenge.

An hour east of Bath, at the Museum of Welsh Life, you'll find South Wales' story vividly told in a park full of restored houses. Relish the romantic ruins and poetic wax of Tintern Abbey, the lush Wye River Valley, and the quirky Forest of Dean.

Planning Your Time

Avebury, Glastonbury, and Wells make a wonderful day out from Bath. Splicing in Stonehenge is possible but stretching it. Everybody needs to see Stonehenge. But I'll tell you now, it looks just like it looks. You'll know what I mean when you pay to get in and rub up against the rope fence that keeps tourists at a distance. Avebury is the connoisseur's circle: more subtle and welcoming. Wells is simply a cute town, much smaller and more medieval than Bath, with a uniquely beautiful cathedral that's best experienced at the 17:15 evensong service. Glastonbury is normally done surgically,

Sights near Bath

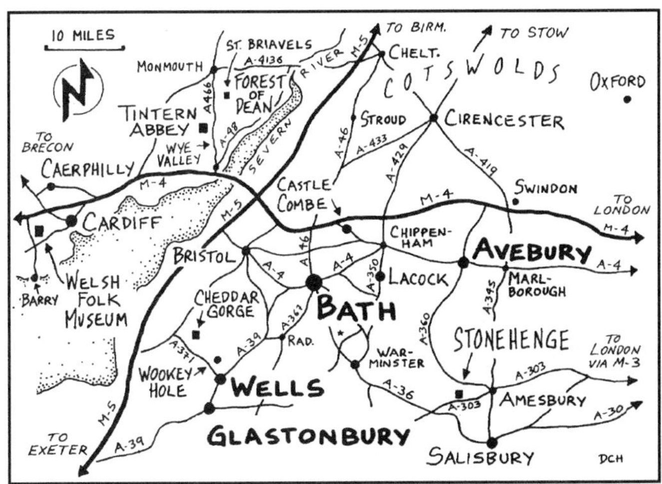

in two hours: See the abbey, climb the tower, ponder your hippie past (and where you are now), then scram.

Think of the South Wales sights as a different grouping. Ideally, they fill the day you leave Bath for the Cotswolds. Anyone interested in Welsh culture can spend four hours in the Museum of Welsh Life. Castle lovers and romantics will want to consider the Caerphilly Castle, Tintern Abbey, and Forest of Dean. See the beginning of this chapter for a day-by-day schedule.

Getting around near Bath

Wells and Glastonbury are easily accessible by bus from Bath; **Badgerline** offers several day tours from Bath as well as a "Day Rambler" ticket (£5.50, £11 per family, tel. 01225/464-446). You can get to South Wales by train via Bristol, connecting by bus from the Welsh train station to the various sights.

Avebury and Stonehenge are trickier. The most convenient and quickest way to see Avebury and Stonehenge if you don't have a car is to take an all-day bus tour. Of those tours leaving from Bath, "Mad Max" offers the cheapest and liveliest.

"Mad Max" minibus tours (£16, 6–14 people) are thoughtfully organized, informative, and inexpensive. They last from 8:45 to 16:40 and cover 110 miles with stops in Avebury, Stonehenge, and two cute villages—Lacock and Castle Combe. Castle Combe, the southernmost Cotswold village, is as cute as they come. The Mad Max bus picks up passengers at 8:45 at the statue on Cheap Street (behind Bath Abbey). To reserve a seat, call the Bath

YMCA (tel. 01225/325-900, please honor or cancel your seat reservation, e-mail: maddy@madmax.abel.co.uk).

If Mad Max is booked up, don't fret. Plenty of companies in Bath offer tours of varying lengths, prices, and destinations. Danwood Tours offers a daily daylong City Safari tour of the southern Cotswolds, Avebury, Stonehenge, Salisbury, and Longleat for £16.50 (departs outside Abbey Hotel at 10:00, book at Bath TI or call 07977-929-486 or 01373/461-135, private car hire also available). Another tour company is Andrews Country Tours (£15 for tour that includes Wells, Glastonbury, and more, 15-seat minivan, narrated trip, tel. 01761/416-362, Chris Andrews). The cost of admission to sites is usually not included with any tour.

Drivers can do a loop from Bath to Avebury (25 miles) to Glastonbury (56 miles) to Wells (6 miles) and back to Bath (20 miles). A loop from Bath to South Wales is 100 miles, mostly on the 80-mph motorway. Each of the Welsh sights is just off the motorway.

GLASTONBURY

Marked by its hill, or "tor," and located on England's most powerful line of prehistoric sights (called a "ley" line), the town of Glastonbury gurgles with history and mystery.

In A.D. 37, Joseph of Arimathea carried vessels containing the blood and sweat of Jesus to Glastonbury, and, with them, Christianity came to England. While this is "proven" by 4th-century writings and accepted by the Church, the Holy Grail legend that sprang from this in the Middle Ages isn't. Many think the Grail trail ends at the bottom of the Chalice Well (described below), a natural spring at the base of the Glastonbury Tor.

In the 12th century, England needed a morale-boosting folk hero for inspiration during a war with France. The 5th-century Celtic fort at Glastonbury was considered proof enough of the greatness of the fifth-century warlord Arthur. His supposed remains (along with those of Queen Guinevere) were dug up from the abbey floor, and Glastonbury became woven into the Arthurian legends. Reburied in the abbey choir, their grave site is a shrine today.

The Glastonbury Abbey was England's most powerful in the 10th century. By the year 1500, English monasteries owned one-sixth of all English land and had four times the income of the crown. Henry VIII dissolved the abbeys in 1536. He was particularly harsh on Glastonbury. He not only destroyed the abbey but also hung and quartered the abbot, sending the parts of his body on four different national tours . . . at the same time.

But Glastonbury rebounded. In an 18th-century tourism campaign, thousands signed affidavits stating that water from the Chalice Well healed them, and once again Glastonbury was on the tourist map. Today Glastonbury and its tor are a center for searchers, too creepy for the mainstream church but just right for those looking for a place to recharge their crystals.

Orientation
(area code: 01458)

The tourist information office (Sun–Thu 10:00–17:00, Fri–Sat 10:00–17:30, until 16:00 in winter, tel. 01458/832-954) is on High Street—as are many of the dreadlocked folks who walk it. The Lake Village Museum in the TI is nothing special (£2). Tuesday is market day—a combo crafts, flea, and produce gathering behind the TI (9:00–15:00).

Glastonbury, quickly becoming "the windy city," has no shortage of healthy eateries. The vegetarian **Rainbow's End** (next to TI, 17 High Street, tel. 01458/833-896) is one of several fine cafés for beans, salads, and New Age people watching. If you're looking for a midwife or a male-bonding tribal meeting, check their notice board. If this all causes you to wonder if you need spiritual guidance or just an odd rune read, wander through the **Glastonbury Experience,** a New Age mall at the bottom of High Street.

The **Tor Bus** shuttles visitors from the town center and abbey to the base of the tor, stopping at the Rural Life Museum and the Chalice Well (£1, 2/hrly, 9:30–17:00 throughout the summer). Their brochure outlines a good tor-to-town walk (a brisk, 10-minute walk).

Sights—Glastonbury

▲▲Glastonbury Abbey—The evocative ruins of the first Christian sanctuary in the British Isles stand mysteriously alive in a lush, 36-acre park. Start your visit in the museum, where a model shows the abbey in its pre–Henry VIII splendor, and exhibits tell the story of a place "grandly constructed to entice even the dullest minds to prayer." Today the abbey attracts people who find God within. Tie-dyed, starry-eyed pilgrims seem to float through the grounds naturally high. Others lie on the grave of King Arthur, whose burial site is marked off in the center of the abbey ruins. The only surviving building is the Abbot's conical kitchen, which often comes with a cheery singing monk demonstrating life in the abbey kitchen (£3, June–Aug daily 9:00–18:00, off-season 9:30 to dusk, tel. 01458/832-267).

Somerset Rural Life Museum—Exhibits include peat digging, cider making, and cheese making. The Abbey Farmhouse is now a collection of domestic and work mementos that illustrate the life of farmer John Hodges "from the cradle to the grave." The fine 14th-century barn, with its beautifully preserved wooden ceiling, is filled with Victorian farm tools (£2.50, Easter–Oct Tue–Fri

10:00–17:00, Sat–Sun 14:00–18:00, closed Mon and off-season, free car park, tel. 01458/831-197).

Chalice Well—The well is surrounded by a peaceful garden. According to tradition, Joseph of Arimathea brought the chalice of the Lord's Supper to Glastonbury in A.D. 37. Even if the chalice is not in the bottom of the well and the water is red from rust and not Jesus' blood, the tranquil setting is one where nature's harmony is a joy to ponder. Have a drink (£2, daily 10:00–18:00, in winter 13:00–16:00, tel. 01458/831-154, www.chalicewell.org.uk).

Glastonbury Tor—Seen by many as a Mother Goddess symbol, the tor, a natural plug of sandstone on clay, has an undeniable geological charisma. The tower is the remnant of a 14th-century church of St. Michael. A fine Somerset view rewards those who hike to its 520-foot summit.

Transportation Connections—Glastonbury

By bus to: Wells (2/hrly, 30 min, tel. 0117/955-3231) and **Bath** (hrly, 75 min). The nearest train station is in Bath.

WELLS

This wonderfully preserved little town has a cathedral, so it can be called a city. It's England's smallest cathedral city, with one of its most interesting cathedrals and more medieval buildings still doing what they were originally built to do than in any town you'll visit. Market day fills the town square on Wednesday and Saturday.

Tourist Information: The TI, on the main square, offers occasional £2 town walks in the summer at 14:30 (daily 9:30–17:30, in winter 10:00–16:00, tel. 01749/672-552, e-mail: wells.tic@ukonline.co.uk). Edie Westmoreland is a good local guide (tel. 01934/832-350).

Sights—Wells

▲▲Wells Cathedral—England's first completely Gothic cathedral (dating from about 1200) is the highlight of the city. The newly restored west front displays nearly 300 original 13th-century carvings (the *Last Judgment*, lots of kings, bottom row of niches empty—all too easily reached by Cromwell's men, who were hell-bent on destroying "graven images"). Stand back and imagine it as a grand Palm Sunday welcome with a cast of hundreds—all gaily painted back then, chorasters singing boldly from holes above the doors and trumpets tooting through the holes up by the 12 Apostles.

Inside you're immediately struck by the general lightness and the unique "scissors" or hourglass-shaped double arch (added in 1338 to transfer weight from the west, where the foundations were sinking under the tower's weight, to the east, where they were firm). You'll be warmly greeted, reminded how expensive it is to maintain the cathedral, and given a map of its highlights.

Don't miss the fine 14th-century stained glass (the "Golden Window" on the east wall). The medieval clock does a silly but much-loved joust on the quarter hour (north transept, its face dates from 1390). The embroidery work in the choir (the central zone where the daily services are sung) is worth a close look. Walk the well-worn steps up to the grand fan-vaulted chapter house—an intimate place for the theological equivalent of a huddle among church officials. The cathedral library (14:30–16:30 only, 50p), with a few old manuscripts, offers a peek into a real 15th-century library. The requested £4 donation for the cathedral is not intended to keep you out (daily 7:30–19:00 or dusk, 45-minute-long tours at 10:15, 11:15, 13:15, 14:15, and 15:15, £1 charge for photography, good shop and a handy restaurant, tel. 01749/674-483). See "Evensong," below.

Lined with perfectly pickled 14th-century houses, the oldest complete street in Europe is **Vicar's Close** (just a block north of the cathedral). It was built to house the vicar's choir, and it still houses church officials. The mediocre city museum is next door to the cathedral. For a fine cathedral-and-town view from your own leafy hilltop bench, hike 10 minutes up Tor Hill.

▲▲Cathedral Evensong Service—Weekdays at 17:15 and Sunday at 15:00, the cathedral choir takes full advantage of heavenly acoustics with a 45-minute entirely sung evensong service (boys' and men's voices, great pipe organ, you'll sit right in the old "quire." Note: generally not sung when school is out in July and August unless a visiting choir is performing, tel. 01749/674-483 to check). At 17:05 the verger ushers visitors to their seats. There's generally plenty of room. The last bus to Bath is at 17:43 (and you can't leave the service early), so on weekdays those without a car or a bed must take a tour; Danwood Tours offers a round-trip tour from Bath to Wells on weekdays expressly to allow tour members to attend the Wells evensong service (£7.50, leave Bath's Abbey Hotel at 16:30, return at 19:00, tel. 07977-929-486 or 01373/461-135).

Bishop's Palace—Next to the cathedral stands the moated Bishop's Palace. On the grounds (past the old-timers playing a proper game of croquet) is a fine garden with the idyllic springs that gave the city its name. The interior offers a look at elegant furniture and clothing (£3, Aug daily 10:30–18:00; April–Oct Tue–Fri 10:30–18:00, Sun 14:00–18:00, closed Mon; closed in winter, tel. 01749/678-691).

Cheddar Cheese—If you're in the mood for a picnic, drop by an aromatic cheese shop for a great selection of tasty Somerset cheeses. Real farmhouse cheddar puts "American" cheddar to Velveeta shame. The Laurelbank Dairy Company is a traditional cheese shop with all the local edibles (Mon–Sat 9:00–17:30, closed Sun, 14 Queen St., tel. 01749/679-803). Ask for a pound's worth of the most interesting mix. The Cheddar Gorge (and the Cheddar Gorge Cheese Company, which welcomes and educates guests) is six miles down the road.

Sleeping and Eating in Wells

(£1 = about $1.60, country code: 44, area code: 01749)

Wells is a pleasant overnight stop. The first two guest houses and the Fountain Inn are all within a block of each other behind (east of) the cathedral. Coming in on B3139 from Bath, they're just before the cathedral. The last B&B is idyllic and in the next village.

Furlong House B&B, a grand old house with a huge and peaceful garden, is more homey and laid-back (Db-£42, £46 on Friday and Saturday nights, nonsmoking, easy parking, a block from Fountain Inn, behind the gate at the end of Lorne Place, a tiny and quiet lane off St. Thomas Street just east of cathedral, Wells, BA5 2XF, tel. 01749/674-064, e-mail: howardwells @compuserve.com, by Lyn and John Howard).

Swan Hotel, an elegant old place facing the cathedral, is now run as a big, normal hotel by Best Western (Sb-£75, Db-£93, often cheaper if you just turn up, CC:VMA, Sadler Street, BA5 2RX, tel. 01749/678-877, fax 01749/677-647, e-mail: swan @heritagehotels.co.uk).

Manor Farm B&B in the village of Dulcote, a mile or so outside Wells, rents four fine rooms in a cozy 17th-century farmhouse (D-£40, Db-£46, huge ground floor easy-access Db suite-£55, nonsmoking, BA5 3PZ, tel. 01749/672-125, www.wells-accommodation.co.uk). The place comes complete with friendly farm animals and the good care and cooking of Rosalind Bufton (£6.50–8.50 lunches served 12:00–14:00). It's a peaceful 20-minute walk through wispy farmland to the Wells Cathedral.

Fountain Inn is great for pub grub (£6–10 meals nightly, creative vegetarian meals, real ales, and draft cider, CC:VMA, behind the cathedral on St. Thomas Street, tel. 01749/672-317). Their award-winning cheese plate lets you sample cheddar and its local cousins. For a good, traditional local dish, try their founders beef pie. In town, consider **Anton's Bistro** in the Crown Hotel. For a healthy lunch, consider the **Cathedral Cloister Restaurant** (in the cathedral) or the vegetarian **Good Earth** (Mon–Sat 9:30–17:30, closed Sun, Priory Road at bottom of Broad Street, tel. 01749/678-600).

Transportation Connections—Wells

By bus to: Bath (hrly, 75 min, Badgerline Buses, tel. 01749/673-084), **Glastonbury** (2/hrly, 30 min), **London** (£13, 2/hrly 7:00–19:00, 4 hrs, National Express, tel. 08705-808-080).

Sights—Near Wells

▲Wookey Hole—This lowbrow commercial venture, possibly worthwhile as family entertainment, is a real hodgepodge. It starts with a wookey-guided tour of some big but mediocre caves complete with history, geology lessons, and witch stories. Then you're free to wander through a traditional paper-making mill, with a demonstration, and into a 19th-century amusements room—a riot of color, funny mirrors, and old penny-arcade machines that visitors can actually play for as long as their pennies (on sale there) last. They even have old girlie shows. (£7.20 at the gate, £6.20 tickets available at the Wells TI, May–Sept daily 9:30–19:00, Oct–April daily 10:30–18:00, tickets sold until 2 hours before closing, 2 miles east of Wells, tel. 01749/672-243.)

Scrumpy Farms—Scrumpy is the wonderfully dangerous hard cider brewed in this part of England. You don't find it served in many pubs because of the unruly crowd it attracts. (The Beehive pub in Bath still serves its Scrumpy and seems to enjoy the consequences.) Scrumpy, 8 percent alcohol, will rot your socks. "Scrumpy Jack," carbonated mass-produced cider, is not real Scrumpy. The real stuff is "rough farmhouse cider." This is potent stuff. It's said some farmers throw a side of beef into the vat, and when fermentation is done only the teeth remain. TIs list local cider farms open to the public, such as Mr. Wilkins Land's End Cider Farm—a great "back door" travel experience (Mon–Sat 10:00–20:00, Sun 10:00–13:00, near Wells in Mudgeley a quarter mile off the B3151, 2 miles south of Wedmore—tough to find, get close and ask locals, tel. 01934/712-385). Glastonbury's Somerset Rural Life Museum has a cider exhibit. Apples are pressed from September through December. Hard cider, while not quite Scrumpy, is still West-country typical but more fashionable, decent, and accessible. You can have a pint drawn for you at nearly any pub.

AVEBURY

The stone circle at Avebury is bigger (16 times the size), less touristy, and, for many, more interesting than Stonehenge. You're free to wander among 100 stones, ditches, mounds, and curious patterns from the past, as well as the village of Avebury, which grew up in the middle of this fascinating, 1,400-foot-wide neolithic circle.

In the 14th century, in a kind of frenzy of religious paranoia, Avebury villagers buried many of these mysterious pagan stones. Their 18th-century descendants broke up the remaining stones and used them for building material. Today the buried stones have been resurrected, and concrete markers show where the broken-down stones once stood.

Take the mile walk around the circle. Visit the archaeology museum (£1.60, daily 10:00–18:00). Notice the pyramid-shaped Silbury Hill, a 130-foot-high, yet-to-be-explained mound of chalk just outside of Avebury. Nearly 5,000 years old, this mound is the largest man-made object in prehistoric Europe (with the surface area of London's Trafalgar Square and the height of the Nelson Memorial). It's a reminder that you've just scratched the surface of Britain's mysterious ancient and religious landscape.

The pleasant **Stones Café** serves nice and healthy vegetarian meals and unhealthy cream teas (daily in summer, weekends only in winter, check out their mouthwatering £18 cookbook, next to the National Trust store, tel. 01672/539-514). The **Red Lion Pub** has inexpensive pub grub, a creaky, well-worn, dart-throwing ambience, and a medieval well in its dining room (cooking daily, overpriced £60 rooms upstairs, CC:VM, tel. 01672/539-266).

Sleeping in Avebury makes lots of sense since the stones are lonely and wide open all night. **Mrs. Dixon's B&B,** directly across from Silbury Hill on the main road just beyond the tourist parking lot, rents three small but tidy rooms for a fine price (S-£30, D-£36, T-£50, 6 Beckhampton Road, Avebury, Wiltshire, SN8 1QT, tel. 01672/539-588).

For transportation connections, see "Getting around near Bath," above.

STONEHENGE

England's most famous stone circle, with parts older than the oldest pyramid, was built between 2800 and 1500 B.C. Many of these huge stones were rafted and then rolled on logs all the way from Wales to form a remarkably accurate celestial calendar. Even today, every summer solstice (around June 21) the sun sets in just the right slot, and Druids boogie. The monument is roped off, so even if you pay the £4.20 entry fee (which includes a worthwhile 1-hr audioguide, subject to availability), you're kept at a distance. Cheapskates see it free from the road (June–Aug daily 9:00–19:00, less off-season, tel. 01980/625-368, www.english-heritage.org.uk).

For transportation connections, see "Getting around near Bath," above.

SOUTH WALES

▲Cardiff—The Welsh capital (pop. 300,000) has a pleasant modern center across from its castle. A castle visit is interesting only if you catch one of the entertaining tours (every 30 minutes). The interior is a Victorian fantasy.

▲▲St. Fagans' Welsh Folk Museum—This best look at traditional Welsh folk life displays more than 30 carefully reconstructed old houses from all corners of this little country in a 100-acre park under a castle. Each is fully furnished and comes equipped with a local expert warming herself by a toasty fire and happy to tell you anything you want to know about life in this old cottage. Ask questions!

A highlight is the Rhyd-y-Car 1805 row house, which displays ironworker cottages as they might have looked in 1805, 1855, 1895, 1925, 1955, and 1985, offering a fascinating zip through Welsh domestic life. You'll see traditional crafts in action and a great gallery displaying crude washing machines, the earliest matches, elaborately carved "love spoons," an impressive costume exhibit, and even a case of memorabilia from the local man who pioneered cremation. While everything is well explained, the £2 museum guidebook is a good investment.

The museum has three sections: houses, museum, and castle/garden. If the sky's dry, see the scattering of houses first. Spend an hour in the large building's fascinating museum. The castle interior is royal enough and surrounded by a fine garden, but, if you're tired, it's not worth the hike. While the cafeteria near the entrance (Vale Restaurant) is handy, you'll eat light lunches better, cheaper, and with more atmosphere in the park at the Gwalia Tea Room. The Plymouth Arms pub just outside the museum serves the best food. (£5.50 admission, daily 10:00–18:00, until 17:00 off-season, tel. 01222/573-500.) City bus #56 runs hourly between Cardiff Castle and the Welsh Folk Museum (which is in the village of St. Fagans). Drivers leave the M4 at Junction 33 and follow the signs. Leaving the museum, jog left on the freeway, take the first exit, and circle back, following signs to the M4.

▲**Caerphilly Castle**—This impressive but gutted old castle is the second largest in Europe (after Windsor). With two concentric walls, it was considered to be a brilliant arrangement of defensive walls and moats (£2.50, daily June–Sept 9:30–18:00, May and Oct 9:30–17:00, Nov–April Mon–Sat 9:30–16:00, Sun 11:00–16:00, 9 miles north of Cardiff, 30 minutes by car from the Welsh Folk Museum, or take train from Cardiff to Caerphilly—3/hrly, 20 minutes—and walk 5 minutes, tel. 01222/883-143).

▲▲**Tintern Abbey**—Inspiring monks to prayer, Wordsworth to poetry, Turner to a famous painting, and rushed tourists to a thoughtful moment, this poem-worthy ruined-castle-of-an-abbey is worth a five-mile detour off the motorway. Founded in 1131 on a site chosen by Norman monks for its tranquility, it functioned as an austere Cistercian abbey until its dissolution in 1536 (£2.50, daily 9:30–18:00 in summer, 9:30–17:00 in spring and fall, Mon–Sat 9:30–16:00, Sun 11:00–16:00 in winter, tel. 01291/689-251, from Cardiff catch a bus or train to Chepstow—1.5 hrs, then bus from Chepstow to abbey—30 min). Visit late to miss crowds. The abbey's shop sells fine Celtic jewelry and other gifts. Take an easy 15-minute walk up to St. Mary's Church for a view of England just over the River Wye.

If seduced into spending the night, you'll find plenty of B&Bs near the abbey or in the charming castle-crowned town of Chepstow just down the road. The Tintern TI is helpful (April–Oct 10:30–17:30, closed Nov–March, tel. 01291/689-566).

▲**Wye River Valley and Forest of Dean**—This land is lush, mellow, and historic. Local tourist brochures explain the Forest of Dean's special dialect, its strange political autonomy, and its oaken ties to Trafalgar and Admiral Nelson.

For a medieval night, check into the **St. Briavels' Castle Youth Hostel** (£11 beds in 4- to 10-bed dorms, members only, tel. 01594/530-272). An 800-year-old Norman castle used by King John in 1215—the year he signed the Magna Carta, it's comfortable (as castles go), friendly, and in the center of the quiet village of St. Briavels just north of Tintern Abbey. For dinner, eat at the hostel or walk "just down the path and up the snyket" to the **Crown Pub** (decent food and local pub atmosphere).

Transportation Connections—Cardiff

By train to: Caerphilly (2/hrly, 20 min), **Bath** (hrly, 90 min, transfer in Bristol), **Birmingham** (8/day, 2 hrs), **London** (hrly, 2 hrs), **Chepstow** (hrly, 30 min, 6 miles to Tintern by bus). Train info: tel. 08457-484-950.

Route Tips for Drivers

Bath to South Wales: Leave Bath following signs for A4, then M4, then Stroud. It's 10 miles north (on A46 past a village called Pennsylvania) to the M4 superfreeway. Zip westward, crossing a huge suspension bridge into Wales (£4.20 toll westbound only). Stay on the M4 (not M48) past Cardiff, take exit 33, and follow the brown signs south to the Welsh Folk Museum. To get to Tintern Abbey, take the M4 to Exit 21 and get on M48. The abbey is six miles (up A466, signs to Chepstow then Tintern) off M48 at Exit 2, right where the northern bridge across the Severn hits Wales.

Cardiff to the Cotswolds via Forest of Dean: On the Welsh side of the big suspension bridge, take the Chepstow exit and follow signs up A466 to Tintern Abbey and the Wye River Valley. Carry on to Monmouth and, if you're running late, follow the A40 and the M50 to the Tewksebury exit, where small roads will take you into the Cotswolds.

THE COTSWOLDS

The Cotswold Hills, a 25-by-50-mile chunk of Gloucestershire, are dotted with villages and graced with England's greatest countryside palace, Blenheim.

As with many fairy-tale regions of Europe, the present-day beauty of the Cotswolds was the result of an economic disaster. Wool was a huge industry in medieval England, and Cotswold sheep grew the best wool. The region prospered. Wool money built fine towns and houses. Local "wool" churches are called "cathedrals" for their scale and wealth. Stained-glass slogans say things like "I thank my God and ever shall, it is the sheep hath paid for all."

With the rise of cotton and the Industrial Revolution, the woolen industry collapsed. Ba-a-a-ad news. The wealthy Cotswold towns fell into a depressed time warp, so poor that nobody even bothered to knock them down. Today visitors enjoy a harmonious blend of man and nature—the most pristine of English countrysides decorated with time-passed villages, rich wool churches, tell-me-a-story stone fences, kissing gates you wouldn't want to experience alone, and the gracefully dilapidated homes of an impoverished nobility. Appreciated by hordes of 21st-century romantics, the Cotswolds are enjoying new prosperity.

Planning Your Time

The Cotswolds are an absolute delight by car and, with the new Cotswold Link bus, enjoyable even without a car. On a three-week British trip, I'd spend two nights and a day in the Cotswolds (sleeping in Chipping Campden or Stow-in-the-Wold). The Cotswolds' charm has a softening effect on many tight itineraries. You could spend days of enjoyable walking from a home base here.

One-day driver's 100-mile Cotswold blitz (includes Blenheim; use a good map; reshuffle to fit your home base): 9:00–Browse through Chipping Campden; 10:00–Joyride through Snowshill, Stanway, Stanton, Guiting Power, the Slaughters, and Bourton; 13:00–Lunch and explore Stow-on-the-Wold; 15:00–Drive 30 miles to Blenheim Palace, take the hour-long tour (last tour departs at 16:45); 18:00–Drive home for a pub dinner in home village.

Orientation

The north Cotswolds are best. Two of the region's coziest towns, Chipping Campden and Stow-on-the-Wold, are eight and four miles, respectively, from workaday Moreton, the only Cotswold town with a train station. Any of these three towns, now connected by the useful Cotswold Link bus (running twice daily between Bath and Stratford), would make a fine home base for your exploration of the thatch-happiest of Cotswold villages and walks.

Cotswold Appreciation 101

Much history can be read into the names of the area. *Cotswold* could come from the Saxon phrase meaning "hills of sheeps' coats." Or it could mean shelter ("cot" like *cottage*) on the open upland ("wold").

In the Cotswolds, a town's main street (called High Street) needed to be wide to accommodate the sheep and cattle being marched to market (and today, to park tour buses). Some of the most picturesque cottages were once humble row houses of weavers' cottages, usually along a stream for their water wheels (Bibury, Castle Combe). The towns run on slow clocks and yellowed calendars. An entire village might not have a phone booth that accepts a telephone card.

Fields of yellow (rapeseed) and pale blue (linseed) separate pastures dotted with black and white sheep. In just about any B&B, when you open your window in the morning you'll hear sheep baa-ing. The decorative "toadstool" stones that litter front yards throughout the region are medieval staddle stones. Buildings were set upon these to keep the rodents out.

Cotswold walls and roofs are made of limestone. The limestone roof tiles hang by pegs. To make the weight more bearable, smaller, lighter tiles are higher up. An extremely strict building code keeps towns looking what many locals call "overly quaint."

The area is provincial and gossipy. People are ever so polite but commonly catch themselves saying, "It's all very... ummm... yyya." Rich people open their gardens to support their favorite charities, while—until recently—the less couth enjoyed "badger baiting" (a gambling cousin of cockfighting in which a badger, with his teeth and claws taken out, is mangled by right-wing dogs).

The Cotswolds

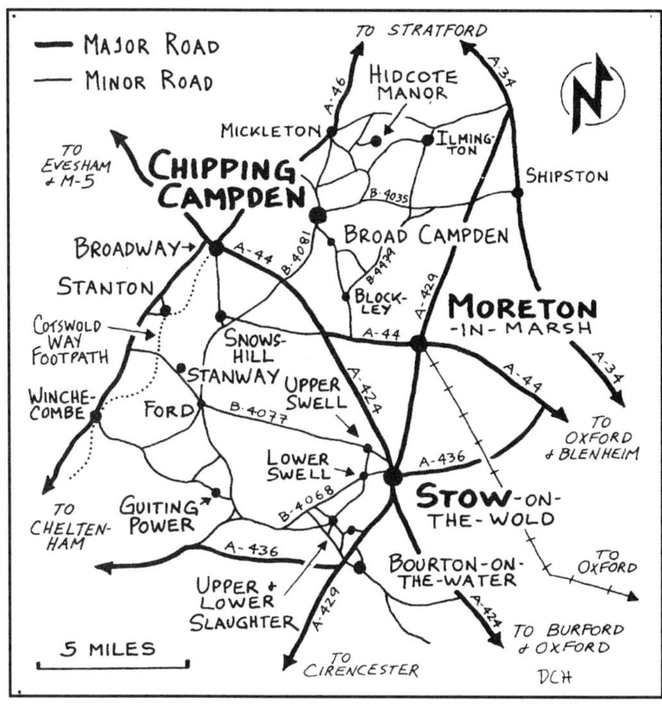

This is walking country. The English love their walks and vigorously defend their age-old right to free passage. Once a year the Rambling Society organizes a "Mass Trespass," when each of the country's 50,000 miles of public footpaths is walked. By assuring each path is used at least once a year, they stop landlords from putting up fences. Any paths found blocked are unceremoniously unblocked.

Questions to ask locals: Does badger-baiting survive? Do you approve of foxhunting with hounds? Who are the Morris men? What's a kissing gate?

Getting around the Cotswolds

By Bus: A handy Cotswold Link X55 bus service runs twice daily in both directions between Bath and Stratford, making up to 13 stops en route and hitting the highlights of the Cotswolds, including Chipping Campden, Stow-on-the-Wold, and Moreton-in-Marsh. You can use this service to day-trip from Bath to visit one Cotswold town, to travel through the Cotswolds (stopping where

Cotswold Link X55 Bus Schedule*

This schedule from 2000 is meant only to give you an idea of the route and approximate times. Get 2001 schedules locally.

From Bath to Stratford

Bath	9:30	15:30
Cirencester	10:44	16:44
Stow-on-the-Wold	11:35	17:35
Moreton-in-Marsh	11:48	17:48
Chipping Campden	12:12	18:12
Hidcote Manor	12:23	18:23
Stratford	12:44	18:44

From Stratford to Bath

Stratford	10:00	15:30
Hidcote Manor	10:23	15:53
Chipping Campden	10:34	16:04
Moreton-in-Marsh	10:58	16:28
Stow-on-the-Wold	11:11	16:41
Cirencester	12:02	17:32
Bath	13:16	18:46

you like for an overnight), or to day-trip from a Cotswold town to visit Stratford. A Bath–Stratford ticket costs £7.70 one-way (buy on bus; you can break journey within the same day; arrive early at bus stop and keep alert, stops are quick; buses are green and marked X55; Badgerline tel. 01225/464-446); the new Three-Day Rover Ticket, valid only on the Cotswold Link bus, isn't worth £15. Several other bus companies make different runs to different towns; ask for bus schedules at any local TI. Note that the Cotswold Link bus is virtually the only bus that runs on Sunday.

By Bike: In Moreton-in-Marsh, Country Lanes Cycle Centre rents 21-speed bikes for £15 a day and offers bike tours (Easter–Oct daily 9:30–17:30, includes helmets, at train station, free routes, £5 maps, reserve ahead, tel. 01608/650-065, www.countrylanes.co.uk). In Chipping Campden, try Cotswold Country Cycles (£10/day, daily 9:00–dusk, includes helmets, route maps, delivery for a fee, Longlands Farm Cottage, tel. 01386/438-706, cellular 0771-500-2972). Despite narrow roads and high hedgerows (blocking some views), it's still a pleasant ride, free from the constraints of bus schedules.

By Foot: Walking guidebooks abound, giving you a world of choices for each of my recommended stops (choose one with clear maps). Villages are generally no more than three miles apart, and most have pubs that would love to feed and water you. For a list of guided walks, ask at any TI for the free AONB (Area of Outstanding Natural Beauty) brochure. The walks are free, range from 2 to 12 miles, and often involve a stop at a pub or tearoom (April–Sept).

By Car: Robinson's car-rental company, near Moreton-in-Marsh, offers one-day rentals from £25 including everything but gas. Figure a delivery charge of £1/mile to just about anywhere in the Cotswolds (Mon–Fri 8:30–17:00, Sat 8:30–12:30, closed Sun, tel. 01608/661-681).

Car hiking is great. Distances are minuscule. In this chapter, I cover the postcard-perfect (but discovered) villages. With a car and the local Ordnance Survey map you can easily ramble about and find your own gems. The problem with having a car is that you are less likely to hike. Try to taxi or bus somewhere so you can hike back to your car and enjoy the scenery.

By Taxi: Two or three taxi trips can make more sense than renting a car. While taking a cab cross-country seems extravagant at £1.20 per mile, the distances are short (Stow–Moreton is 4 miles, Stow–Chipping Campden is 10), and one-way walks are lovely.

To scare up a taxi in Morton, call Four Shires (tel. 01608/650-463, cellular 077-4780-2555); in Stow, call Cotswold Country Cars (tel. 01451/832-226); in Chipping Campden, try Marnic Cars & Taxis (tel. 01386/840-014, cellular 046-845-4376).

By Tour: From Bath, take a Mad Max tour to Castle Combe, the charming southernmost Cotswold town (book by calling Bath YMCA at 01225/325-900). Another possibility from Bath: Cotswold Experience, which covers five Cotswold villages in a full-day trip (£19.50, April–Oct Tue, Thu, Sat, Sun, 10:00–18:00, 14-seat bus, 4-person minimum, book at Bath TI or call 01225/477-101 days or 01453/767-574 eves, www.cotswold-tours.co.uk).

From Stratford, catch the Guide Friday tour (£17, April–Oct daily 13:45–17:15, drive through 15 villages and stop briefly in Stanton, Chipping Campden, and Stow, depart from Civic Hall near Market Square, buy tickets at Guide Friday office in Civic Hall, tel. 01789/294-466).

Sights—North Cotswolds

▲▲Chipping Campden—Ten miles north of Stow-on-the-Wold and less touristy, Chipping Campden (pron. CAM-den) is a working market town, home of some incredibly beautiful thatched roofs and the richest Cotswold wool merchants. Both the great British historian Trevelyan and I call Chipping Campden's High Street the finest in England.

Walk the full length of High Street; its width is characteristic of market towns. Go around the block on both ends. On one end you'll find impressively thatched homes (out Sheep Street, past the public WC and ugly gas station, and right on Westington Street).

Walking north on High Street you'll pass the Market Hall (built in 1627), the wavy roof of the first great wool mansion (the house of William Grevel, from 1380, on left), a fine and free memorial garden (on right), and, finally, the town's famous 15th-century Perpendicular "wool" church, down Church Street.

Chipping Campden's TI, opposite the Ford dealer on High Street, may move in 2001 but will stay on High Street (daily 10:00–17:30, 10p town maps, tel. 01386/841-206). Stop by the Guild of Handicrafts Museum on Sheep Street for an endearing look at Cotswold crafts from the late 1800s (downstairs) to today (upstairs; watch silversmithing in action weekdays but not weekends; museum open Tue–Sun 11:00–17:00). For Internet access, try the library (High Street, near TI). For accommodations, see "Sleeping," below.

Stanton, Snowshill, and Guiting Power—Located between Chipping Campden and Stow, these are my nominations for the cutest Cotswold villages. Like marshmallows in hot chocolate, they nestle side by side, awaiting your arrival.

▲▲Stanway House—Stanway is notable for its manor house. Lord Neidpath, whose family tree charts relatives back to 1270, occasionally opens his melancholy home to visitors (£3, Aug–Sept Tue and Thu 14:00–17:00, tel. 01386/584-469). The 14th-century Tithe Barn predates the manor and was originally where monks—in the days before money—would accept one-tenth of whatever the peasants produced. Peek inside—this is a great hall for village hoedowns.

While the Tithe Barn is no longer used to greet motley peasants with their feudal "rents," the lord still collects rents from his vast landholdings. But the place feels musty and poor, even though the lord has recently remarried.

Ask the ticket taker (inside) to demonstrate the spinning rent-collection table. In the great hall marvel at the one-piece oak shuffleboard table and the 1780 Chippendale exercise chair (half an hour of bouncing on this was considered good for the liver).

The manor dogs have their own cutely painted "family tree," but Lord Neidpath admits that his current dog, CJ, is "all character and no breeding." The place has a story to tell. And so do the docents stationed in each room—modern-day peasants who, even without family trees, probably have relatives going back just as far in this village. Really. Talk to these people. Probe. Learn what you can about this side of England.

To get to Stanway, leave the B4077 at a statue of (Christian) George slaying the dragon (of pagan superstition); you'll round the corner and see the manor's fine 17th-century Jacobean gatehouse.

Stanway and Stanton are separated by a great oak forest and grazing land, with parallel waves echoing the furrows plowed by medieval farmers. Centuries ago, farmers were allotted long strips of land (called a "furlong"—an attempt to dole out good and bad land equitably). Over centuries of plowing these furrows were formed. Let someone else drive so you can sit on the roof under a canopy of oaks as you pass stone walls and sheep. The first building outside Stanway (on the left) is a thatched cricket pavilion overlooking the village cricket green. Dating only from 1930, it's raised up on rodent-resistant staddle stones, like in the Middle Ages. Stanton's just ahead.

▲▲Stanton—Pristine Cotswold charm cheers visitors down this village's main street. Stanton's Church of St. Michael betrays a pagan past. It's safe to assume any church dedicated to St. Michael (the archangel who fought the devil) sits upon a sacred pagan site. Stanton is actually at the intersection of two ley lines (lines of prehistoric sights). You'll see St. Michael's well-worn figure (with a sundial) above the door as you enter. Inside, above the capitals in the nave, find the pagan symbols for the sun and the moon. While the church probably dates back to the ninth century, today's building is mostly 15th century with 13th-century transepts. On the north transept, medieval frescoes weakly show through the 17th-century whitewash. (Once upon a time, medieval frescos were considered too "papist.") Imagine the church interior colorfully decorated throughout. There's original medieval glass behind the altar. The list of rectors (left side wall) goes back to 1269. Finger the grooves in the back pews, worn away by sheepdog leashes. A man's sheepdog accompanied him everywhere.

▲Snowshill Manor—Another nearly edible little bundle of cuteness, Snowshill (SNOWS-hill) has a photogenic triangular square with a fine pub at its base. The Snowshill Manor is a dark and mysterious old palace filled with the lifetime collection of Charles Paget Wade. It's one big, musty celebration of craftsmanship, from finely carved spinning wheels to frightening samurai armor to tiny elaborate figurines carved by prisoners from the bones of meat served at dinner. Taking seriously his family motto, "Let Nothing Perish," Wade dedicated his life and fortune to preserving things finely crafted. The house (whose management made me promise not to promote it as an eccentric collector's pile of curiosities) really shows off Mr. Wade's ability to recognize and acquire fine examples of craftsmanship. It's all very . . . ummm . . . yyya. The manor overlooks the town square, but, ridiculously—to stoke business for the overpriced manor shop 300 yards away—there's no direct access from the town square (£6, April–Oct Wed–Sun 12:00–17:00, closed Mon–Tue and Nov–March, car park and shop are a pleasant 500-yard walk from the house, tel. 01386/852-410, recorded info tel. 01684/855-376).

Broadway—This very crowded town is worth a drive-through but not a stop. There won't be a parking place anyway (a couple of miles west of Chipping Campden).

▲**Hidcote Manor**—If you like gardens, the grounds around this manor house are worth a look. Garden designers here pioneered the notion of creating a series of outdoor "rooms," each with a unique theme and separated by a yew-tree hedge. Follow your nose through a clever series of small gardens that lead delightfully from one to the next. Among the best in England, Hidcote gardens are at their fragrant peak in May, June, and July (£5.60, April–Oct 11:00–18:00, always closed Fri, also closed Tue except in June and July, last entrance 17:00, tearoom, 4 miles northeast of Chipping Campden, tel. 01386/438-333, www.ntrustsevern.org.uk).

Sights—Central Cotswolds

▲▲**Stow-on-the-Wold**—With a name that means "meeting place on the uplands," Stow-on-the-Wold is the highest point of the Cotswolds. Despite its crowds, it retains its charm. Most of the tourists are day-trippers, so even summer nights are peaceful. Stow has no real sights other than itself, some good pubs, antique stores, and cutesy shops draped seductively around a big town square. A visit to Stow is not complete until you've locked your partner in the stocks on the green.

At the helpful TI on the main square, get the handy little 25p walking-tour brochure called "Town Trail" and the free "Cotswold Events" guide (Mon–Sat 9:30–17:30, Sun 10:30–16:00; Nov–Easter Mon–Sat 9:30–16:30, closed Sun, tel. 01451/831-082). The TI also reserves tickets for events (Stratford plays) and rooms for a £2 fee (save money and book direct). For accommodations, see "Sleeping," below. You can generally find a parking spot on the main square (free for 2 hrs).

▲**Moreton-in-Marsh**—This work-a-day town is like Stow or Chipping Campden without the touristic sugar. Rather than gift and antique shops you'll find streets lined with real shops: iron-mongers selling cottage nameplates and carpet shops strewn with the remarkable patterns that decorate B&B floors. A traditional market with 260 stalls filling High Street gets the town shin-kicking each Tuesday as it has for the last 400 years (8:00–16:00). There is an economy outside of tourism in the Cotswolds, and you'll feel it here. Moreton has a tiny, sleepy train station two blocks from High Street (office open Mon–Sat 6:15–13:00), lots of bus connections, and a proficient TI (Mon–Fri 9:00–17:00, Thu 9:00–19:30, closed Sat–Sun, free "Town Trail" leaflet for self-guided walk, £1 luggage check, ticket booking, rail and bus schedules, and racks of flyers, tel. 01608/650-881). For accommodations, see "Sleeping," below. For Internet access, it's Compulight (Mon–Sat 9:00–13:00, 13:30–17:00 but closed Wed afternoon, High Street, nearly across from TI, tel. 01608/652-980). Public WCs are on Corders Lane, next to the Co-op on High Street (near bus stop).

For a pleasant walk from Moreton, hike 1.5 miles to the Arboretum and Cotswold Falconry Centre (£5.50 combo, otherwise £3.50 apiece, March–mid-Nov daily 10:00–17:00, tearoom; from Moreton, take Corders Lane off High Street to path).

Bourton-on-the-Water—I can't figure out if they call this "the Venice of the Cotswolds" because of its quaint canals or its miserable crowds. If you can avoid the midday and weekend crowds, it's worth a drive-through, a few cynical comments, and maybe a short stop. It's easiest to enjoy after dark. The Motor Museum shows off a lifetime's accumulation of vintage cars, old lacquered signs, a village life exhibit, threadbare toys, and prewar memorabilia (£2.25, daily 10:00–18:00, in the Old Mill facing the town center, tel. 01451/821-255). Bourton is four miles south of Stow and a mile from the Slaughters.

Upper and Lower Slaughter—Lower Slaughter is a classic village, with ducks, a working water mill, and usually an artist busy at her easel somewhere. Just behind the skippable Old Mill Museum, two kissing gates lead to the path that goes to nearby Upper Slaughter. In Upper Slaughter walk between the yew trees (sacred in pagan days) down a lane between the raised graveyard (a buildup of centuries of graves) to the peaceful church. In the back of the fine graveyard, a wistful woman looks over the tomb of an 18th-century rector (sculpted by his son). By the way, "Slaughter" has nothing to do with lamb chops. It comes from the sloe tree (the one used to make sloe gin). From June through August, Guide Friday buses do a handy 35-minute loop from Bourton to Upper and Lower Slaughter (£4, hrly in summer, handy for hikers who'd like to hop off here and on there, tel. 01789/269-890). These towns are an easy one-hour round-trip walk from Bourton. You could also walk from Bourton through the Slaughters to Stow. The small roads from Upper Slaughter to Ford and Kineton are some of England's most scenic.

Sights—South Cotswolds

▲Cirencester—Nearly 2,000 years ago, Cirencester (pron. SIGH-ren-ses-ter) was the ancient Roman city of Corinium. It's 20 miles from Stow down A429, which was called Foss Way in Roman times. In Cirencester, stop by the Corinium Museum to find out why they say, "If you scratch Gloucestershire, you'll find Rome" (£2.50, April–Oct Mon–Sat 10:00–17:00, Sun 14:00–17:00, Nov–March closed Mon, tel. 01285/655-611). Cirencester's church is the largest of the Cotswolds "wool" churches. The cutesy Brewery Art crafts center and workshops entertain visitors with traditional weaving and potting in action, an interesting gallery, and a good coffee shop. Monday and Friday are general market days, Tuesday is cattle market day, and Saturday is a craft market unless it's the fifth Saturday in a month. The TI is in the Cornhill Marketplace (Mon–Sat 9:30–17:00, tel. 01285/654-180).

Cotswold Heritage Center—Housed in an 18th-century prison, this simple museum features rural life, with re-creations of shops (blacksmith and wheelwright); loads of wagons; a Victorian laundry, dairy, and kitchen; and a prison cell (£2.50, April–Oct Mon–Sat 10:00–17:00, Sun 14:00–17:00, some demonstrations, tearoom, in town of Northleach, south of Stow, tel. 01451/860-715).

▲Bibury—Six miles northeast of Cirencester, this is an entertaining but money-grubbing and not-very-friendly village with a trout farm, a Cotswolds museum, a stream teeming with fat trout and proud ducks, a row of very old weavers' cottages, and a church surrounded by rosebushes, each tended by a volunteer of the parish. Don't miss the scenic Coln Valley drive from A429 to Bibury through the enigmatic villages of Coln St. Dennis, Coln Rogers, Coln Powell, and Winson.

▲▲▲Blenheim Palace—Too many palaces can send you into a furniture-wax coma. Visiting one is enough... as long as it's Blenheim. The Duke of Marlborough's home, the largest in England, is still lived in. And that's wonderfully obvious as you prowl through it. (Note: Americans who pronounce the place "blen-HEIM" are the butt of jokes. It's "BLEN-em.")

John Churchill, first duke of Marlborough, beat the French at the Battle of Blenheim in 1704. So the king built him this nice home, perhaps the finest Baroque building in England. Ten dukes of Marlborough later, it's as impressive as ever. The 2,000-acre yard, well designed by "Capability" Brown, is as impressive to some as the palace itself. The view just past the outer gate as you enter is a classic. (The current 11th Duke considers the 12th more of an error than an heir, and what to do about him is quite an issue.)

The well-organized palace tour begins with a fine Churchill exhibit centered around the bed in which Sir Winston was born in 1874 (prematurely... while his mother was at a Blenheim Palace party). Take your time in the Churchill exhibit. Then catch the guided tours (5/hrly, 1 hr, included with ticket, £9, family rates, CC:VM, mid-March–Oct 10:30–17:30, last tour at 16:45, gardens open year-round, recorded info tel. 01993/811-325, live tel. 01993/811-091).

For a more extensive visit, follow up the general tour with a 30-minute guided walk through the actual private apartments of the duke. Tours leave on the top and bottom of each hour (£4, 12:00–16:30, tickets are limited, buy from table in library—last room of main tour, enter in corner of courtyard to left of grand palace entry).

Kids enjoy the pleasure garden (a tiny train takes you from the palace parking lot to the garden, but, if you're driving, it's more efficient simply to drive there). A lush and humid greenhouse flutters with butterflies. A kid zone (£1) includes a few second-rate games and the "world's largest symbolic hedge maze."

The maze is worth a look if you haven't seen one and could use some exercise. It costs £1.50 to rent a rowboat for a half hour.

Churchill fans can visit his tomb, a short walk away, in the Bladon town churchyard. The train station nearest Blenheim Palace (Hanborough, 1.5 miles away) has no taxi or bus service. Your easiest train connection is to Oxford; then take a bus to Blenheim (from the Oxford train station it's a 5-minute walk to Gloucester Green bus station, then catch bus #20a, #20b, or #20c to the palace gate, 2/hrly, 30–40 min; Oxford TI: tel. 01865/726-871).

Blenheim Palace sits at the edge of the cute cobbled town of Woodstock. The grandmotherly Wishaw House B&B rents two big and comfortable rooms in a humble old house a five-minute walk from the palace (Db or D with private bath-£40, 2 Browns Lane, 0X20 1ST, tel. 01993/811-343, Pat Hillier).

Sleeping and Eating in the Cotswolds
(£1 = about $1.60, country code: 44)

Sleep Code: **S** = Single, **D** = Double/Twin, **T** = Triple, **Q** = Quad, **b** = bathroom, **t** = toilet only, **s** = shower only, **CC** = Credit Card (**V**isa, **M**asterCard, **A**mex).

Chipping Campden is the most quaint without being overrun. Stow is the most touristy but offers the widest range of accommodations. Workaday Moreton is the only one of the three with a train station.

Sleeping in Chipping Campden (area code: 01386)

Sandalwood House B&B is a big, comfy, modern home with a royal lounge and a sprawling back garden. Just a five-minute walk from the center of town, it's in a quiet, woodsy, pastoral setting. Its two cheery pastel rooms are bright and spacious (D-£49, private baths down the hall, cheaper for 3-night stays and families, no kids under 7, nonsmoking, GL55 6AU, go west on High Street; at church and Volunteer Inn turn right and right again; look for sign in hedge on left, head up long driveway, tel. & fax 01386/840-091, well run by Diana Bendall).

Kettle House B&B has four comfortable rooms (named by colors) above a furniture store in a 17th-century building. The sitting room and small deck have a lovely view. The hosts will pack picnic lunches for £6.50 and offer historical talks on the Cotswolds for £6 per person (D with private bath in hall-£55, Db-£60, CC:VMA, laundry-£10, nonsmoking, near old church, High Street, Leysbourne, GL55 6HN, tel. 01386/840-328, fax 01386/841-740, www.kettlehouse.co.uk, e-mail: info@kettlehouse.co.uk, run by gracious Charles and Susie Holdsworth Hunt). They also offer three en suite rooms above their Bantam Tea Rooms (opposite the Town Hall).

Dragon House B&B has two compact, tidy rooms—with medieval beams—right on the center of High Street, with parking

Chipping Campden

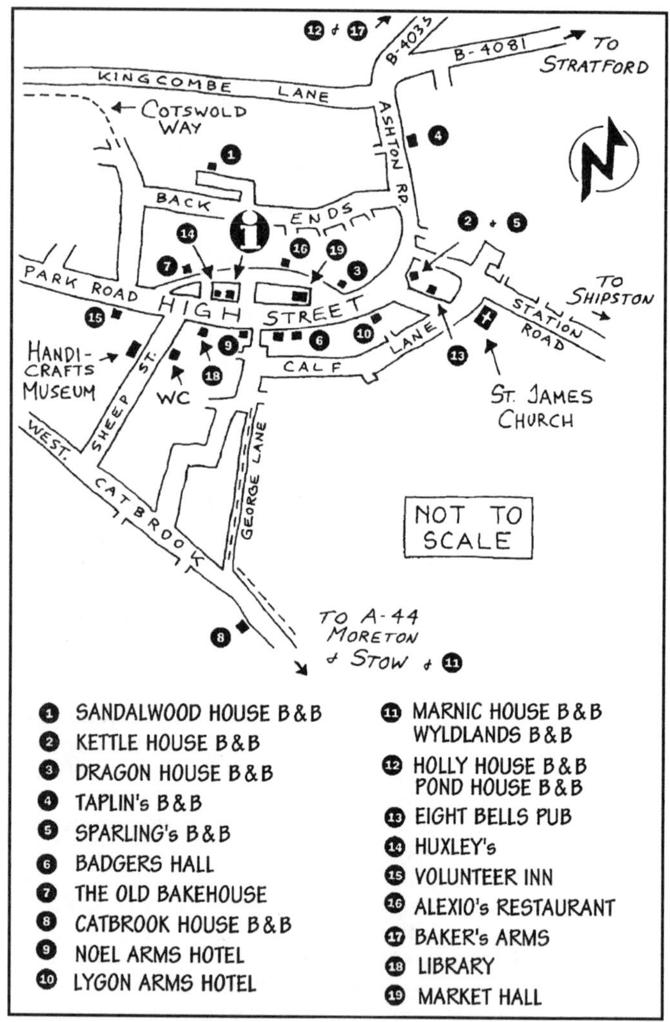

and a shady garden (Db-£48, near market hall, tel. & fax 01386/840-734, Valerie).

Taplins' B&B, a fine 100-year-old house a five-minute walk from the town center, rents a tastefully decorated double and twin, each with antique furniture and a fireplace (D-£44 with this book, nonsmoking, telephone shower, farm views, garden access, easy parking, 5 Aston Road, GL55 6HR, tel. 01386/840-927, e-mail: rachel.h@handbag.com, Rachel Hall).

Sparlings B&B, grandfather-clock tidy and run by the very proper Mr. Douglass, has two pleasant rooms in a smallish 17th-century townhouse with a conservatory (D-£50, Db-£53, nonsmoking, a bit musty, High Street, GL55 6HL, tel. 01386/840-505, fax 01386/841-676).

Badgers Hall Tea Room and B&B hides three cozy, wood-beamed rooms in its medieval attic (D with private bath in hall-£50, Db-£50, extra-large Db-£55, nonsmoking, personal check as deposit, center of High Street, tel. 01386/840-839, e-mail: badgershall@talk21.com, Karen Pinfold).

The Old Bakehouse rents five simple but pleasant rooms, most with beams, in a 600-year-old home (S-£30, Db or D with private bath down hall-£45, family deals, fun but dim attic room has beams running through it, small garden, parking, Lower High Street, GL55 6DZ, tel. 01386/840-979, www.sarah@vfit.co.uk, Sarah Drinkwater).

Catbrook House has several rooms about an eight-minute walk from the town center (2 D with private bath down hall-£41, Db-£49, nonsmoking, no kids under 9, Catbrook, GL55 6DE, tel. 01386/841-499, Anna and Mathias Klein).

Noel Arms Hotel is the characteristic old hotel on the main square, welcoming guests for 600 years. Its lobby is decorated with armor, guns, and heraldry; its medieval air is infused with complex, but not unpleasant, odors; and its 26 rooms are well furnished with antiques, including massive four-poster beds in smallish executive suites (Sb-£80, standard Db-£110, 4-poster Db-£120, executive 4-poster-£130, CC:VM, some ground-floor doubles, attached restaurant/bar, High Street, GL55 6AT, tel. 01386/840-317, fax 01386/841-136, www.cotswold-inns-hotels.co.uk).

Lygon Arms Hotel has dumpy public areas, but the rooms are decent and likely available when all else fails (D-£45, Db-£55, CC:VMA, High Street, tel. 01386/840-318).

Sleeping near Chipping Campden

A tiny village locally famous for its Baker's Arms pub, Broad Campden has two well-run B&Bs (just under a mile from Chipping Campden—addresses unnecessary, you'll see the signs, zip code: GL55 6UR). June Wadey's **Wyldlands** is a comfortable modern house with a breezy, relaxing mini-Hidcote of a garden (Db-£45, Db-£43 for 3 nights, nonsmoking, can loan maps, tel. 01386/840-478, fax 01386/849-031).

Holly House, in Ebrington—a mile from Chipping Campden—has three spacious rooms in a newish-style house (Sb-£25–40, Db-£40–42, laundry service-£5, parking, 6L55 6NL, tel. 01386/593-213, fax 01386/593-181, Mrs. Hutsby).

Pond House, in Bretforton—three miles from Chipping Campden—has four large rooms and a conservatory with countryside views (Db-£50–58, nonsmoking, WR11 5QA, near Evesham, tel. 01386/831-687, fax 01386/831-558).

Marnic House B&B is a 150-year-old stone cottage with three well-appointed rooms and a prize-winning garden, run by the entrepreneurial Janet Rawlings (Db-£44–46, keeps deposits if you cancel, non-smoking, tel. 01386/840-014, fax 01386/840-441, e-mail: marnic@zoom.co.uk).

Eating in Chipping Campden

Locals like **Eight Bells** (on Leysbourne), **Huxley's** (pricey, closed Mon, in town center on High Street), and Bantam Tea Rooms (opposite Town Hall). **Volunteer Inn** serves decent pub grub (grassy courtyard in back, Park Road). In the Cotswolds House Hotel, **Forbes Brasserie** (skip the formal restaurant) has good food, quick service, and vintage Cotswolds photos on its walls (12:00–20:00). **Lygon Pub** serves old English ...cuisine is not quite the right word. **Alexio's,** a fun Greek restaurant on High Street, breaks plates at closing every Saturday night (closed Sun to clean up, tel. 01386/840-826). The small **Your Store,** on High Street, is the town's main grocery (Mon–Sat 7:00–22:00, Sun 8:00–22:00).

In Broad Campden, a mile out of Chipping Campden, vegetarians and carnivores alike flock to the **Baker's Arms** for dinner (April–Oct daily 12:00–21:00, Nov–March daily 12:00–14:00, 18:00–21:00, can be smoky and crowded, slow service, indoor/outdoor seating, live folk music every third Tue, tel. 01386/840-515).

Sleeping in Stow-on-the-Wold (area code: 01451)

Hotels: The **Old Stocks Hotel,** facing the town square, is the best hotel value in town, even though the building itself is classier than its 18 big, simply furnished rooms. It's family run but professional as can be (Db-£75 promised through 2001 with this book, CC:VM, The Square, Stow-on-the-Wold, GL54 1AF, tel. 01451/830-666, fax 01451/870-014, Alan and Julie Rose).

Stow Lodge Hotel, on the town square in its own sprawling and peaceful garden, offers 21 large, thoughtfully appointed rooms and stately public spaces (Sb-£75–100, Db-£90–110, CC:VM, closed Jan, nonsmoking, The Square, GL54 1AB, tel. 01451/830-485, fax 01451/831-671, www.stowlodge.com, Hartley family).

Upscale B&Bs: **Crestow House** has four huge rooms in a grand manor house dating from the 16th to 19th centuries. Although on a busy street, the four-foot-thick manor walls keep it quiet inside. With a gracious spaciousness, antique furniture, a pool, and even exercise equipment, this place mixes charm and character with modern-day amenities (Db-£68–70, CC:VM, rooms in back have views, floral room in front has quirky bathtub

Stow-on-the-Wold

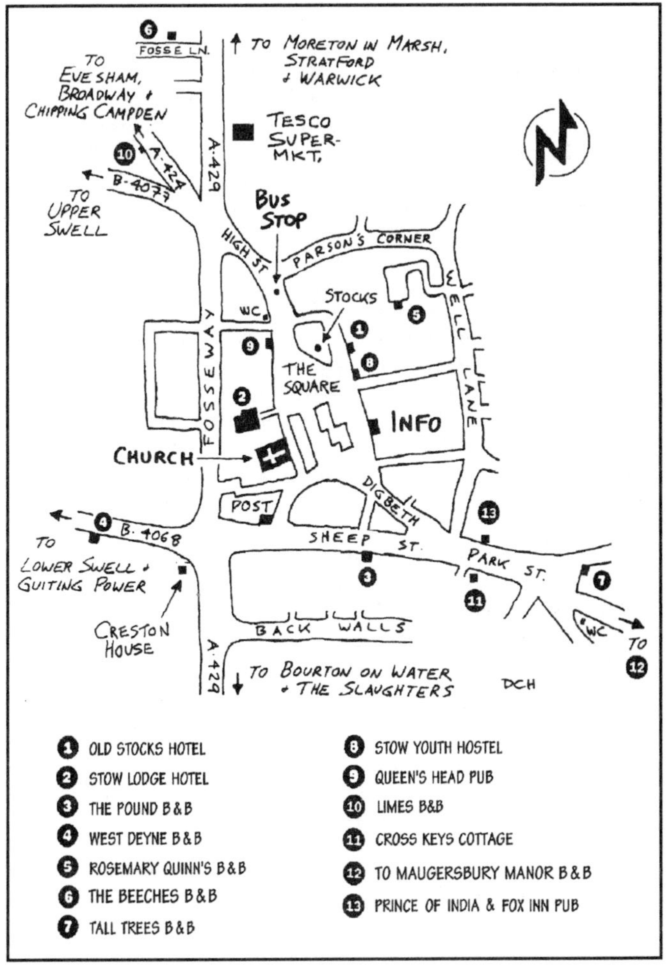

in painted closet, 2 blocks from square, intersection of A429 and B4068, GL54 1JX, tel. 01451/830-969, fax 01451/832-129, e-mail: fjsimon@compuserve.com, Jorge and Frank).

Cross Keys Cottage, offering three attractive, smallish rooms in a lovingly maintained 350-year-old beamed cottage, is a cover-girl B&B (D with private bath in hall-£45–48, Db-£52–55, Park Street, GL54 1AQ, tel. & fax 01451/831-128, e-mail: rogxmag@hotmail.com, Margaret and Roger Welton).

Number Nine has three large, well-furnished rooms in a 200-year-old home—with beamed ceilings, old wooden doors, and fresh flowers in every room (Db-£48–54, CC:VM, 9 Park Street, GL5 1AQ, tel. 01451/870-333, David and Connie).

Homey B&Bs: West Deyne B&B, with two cozy rooms, a peaceful garden, a fountain, and a small conservatory overlooking the countryside, has a comforting grandmotherly charm. This is a super place (D-£36, evening tea and biscuits, parking, Lower Swell Road, GL54 1LD, tel. 01451/831-011, run by thoughtful Joan Cave).

The Pound is the quaint, restored, 500-year-old, heavy-beamed home of Patricia Whitehead. She offers two bright, inviting twin-bedded rooms and a classic old fireplace lounge (D-£37, nonsmoking, downtown on Sheep Street, GL54 1AU, tel. & fax 01451/830-229, e-mail: brent.ford@zoom.co.uk).

Rosemary Quinn's B&B, on a peaceful cul-de-sac two blocks off the main square in a tidy modern building, rents two no-nonsense, comfy rooms (S-£18.50, D-£37, nonsmoking, 22 Glebe Close, GL54 1DJ, tel. 01451/830-042, ro@quinn39.freeserve.co.uk).

Tall Trees B&B, on the Oddington Road at the edge of Stow, rents six modern rooms in an old-style building overlooking a farm (Db-£50, family room, parking, tel. 01451/831-296, fax 01451/870-049, Jennifer).

The **Limes B&B,** in a Victorian home, has four pleasant rooms: three are spacious, the other has a high four-poster bed (D/Db-£42, family deals, pretty garden for guests to use, 2 blocks out of town on Evesham Road, tel. & fax 01451/830-034, friendly Helen and Graham).

The **Beeches,** with two comfortable rooms, is run by dear, older, congenial hosts who enjoy turning guests into friends (D-£36, nonsmoking, near town center on quiet street, Fosse Lane, GL54 1EH, tel. 01451/870-836, Ken and Marian Wilson). **Fifield Cottage,** also on Fosse Lane, rents three peaceful rooms (D with private bath in hall-£39, Db-£43, conservatory, garden, GL54 1EH, tel. 01451/831-056, Val and Tony Keyte).

In the hamlet of Maugersbury, an easy eight-minute walk from Stow, you'll find the peace Stow once had. The ivy-covered **Maugersbury Manor** rents two huge rooms, one with countryside views. The other is a sprawling ground-floor suite with a kitchen. Although it could use spiffing up, it's grand staying in a centuries-old manor house (Db-£40–45, March–Nov, nonsmoking, GL54 1HP, tel. 01451/830-581, Mrs. Martin). **Little Broom B&B,** a few doors down, has five tight rooms, a larger family room, and an open-air pool. Breakfast is served family-style at a round table. David and Brenda, who own 11 horses, have decorated their entire home with pictures of horses (S-£30, D-£50, Db-£55, family Db-£60, GL54 1HP, tel. 01451/830-510, e-mail: davidandbrenda@talk21.com). To get to either place, take the pedestrian footpath through the woods at the southeast edge of town or drive east on Park Street, taking the right fork to Maugersbury, then turning right on the road marked "No Through Road."

Hostel: The **Stow-on-the-Wold Youth Hostel,** on Stow's main square, has a friendly atmosphere, good hot meals, and a do-it-yourself members' kitchen (£11 dorm bed with sheets, nonmembers £2 extra, 50 beds in 9 rooms, some family rooms with private bathrooms, closed 10:00–17:00, laundry, no lockers, CC:VM, reserve long in advance, tel. 01451/830-497, fax 01451/870-102).

Sleeping near Stow-on-the-Wold

Holmleigh B&B, in a farmhouse in the nearby hamlet of Donnington, rents two rooms, the cheapest around (D-£25, tel. 01451/830-792, Mrs. Garbett).

Fairview Farmhouse B&B feels more like a countryside mansion than a farmhouse. It's regally situated a mile outside Stow, and its six rooms come with all the thoughtful touches (Db-£46, deluxe Db-£55, nonsmoking, just down Bledington Road, GL54 1JH, tel. & fax 01451/830-279, Susan and Andrew Davis).

Guiting Guest House, six miles west of Stow in the tiny village of Guiting Power, is my favorite sleepy-village alternative. Kindly Mrs. Yvonne Sylvester rents five modern, delightful doily rooms in her 400-year-old house. The owners make this place a winner (Sb-£32, Db-£56, CC:VM, Post Office Lane, Guiting Power, Cheltenham, GL54 5TZ, tel. 01451/850-470, fax 01451/850-034, www.information-britain.co.uk/bandbs/guiting/). If you're tired of pub grub, Yvonne serves a fine home-cooked dinner with the works for £18. Guiting Power is a great base for walking excursions.

Vine B&B, eight miles west of Stow in the postcard-pretty village of Stanton, is another idyllic hideaway. This classic Cotswolds home, run by Jill Gabb, is a block from the Stanton church. Jill's passion is horse riding. She rents horses by the hour (4 rooms, Ds/Db-£56, CC:VM, most rooms with 4-poster beds, WR12 7NE, tel. 01386/584-250, fax 01386/584-385, e-mail: luicarenza@msn.com).

Castlett Bank Cottage is a cottage suite with two themed bedrooms— medieval and Victorian (£27.50–30 per person, up to 4 people, Castlett Street, private entrance, garden, parking, tel. & fax 01451/850-300, www.accommodation-cotswolds.co.uk/castlett.html, Jan Wilderspin).

Eating in Stow-on-the-Wold

The formal but friendly bar in the **Stow Lodge** serves fine £7 lunches and £10 dinners (daily 12:00–14:00, 19:00–21:00, veggie options; they also have a pricier restaurant). Next door, the more pub-esque **Queen's Head** serves an inexpensive decent meal and the local Cotswold brew, Donnington Ale (Mon–Sat 11:00–14:30, 18:00–23:00). Consider **The Prince of India** for Indian food (nightly 18:00–23:30, CC:VM, Park Street) or the nearby **Fox Inn** for English food (daily 11:00–15:00, 17:30–21:30, courtyard, Digbeth Street, tel. 01451/831-609). Locals also like **The Unicorn** pub (daily 12:00–14:30, 19:00–21:30, Sheep Street). The prettiest restaurant in town is the **Grapevine,** which has a canopy of live grapevines above a modern, light, bright dining room (£10 lunch deals, pricier for dinner, daily 12:00–14:30, 19:00–21:15, Sheep Street, near park and Digbeth Street, tel. 01451/830-344).

Those with a car are likely to eat well at any of these pubs (all near Stow): **The Fox** in Oddington (2 miles from Stow, people love this place), **King's Head** in Bledington (pricier with more extensive menu than The Fox, closed Sun), **Plough Pub** in Ford, **Churchill Arms** at Paxford, and **The Plough** in Cold Aston (a 10-minute drive from Stow).

Sleeping in Moreton-in-Marsh (area code: 01608)

A handy laundrette is a block in front of the train station on New Road (Laundercentre, daily 7:30–20:00, £3.50 self-serve, or drop off Mon–Fri 9:00–12:30 for £1 extra and same-day service).

Treetops B&B is plush, with six spacious, attractive rooms, a sun lounge, and a three-quarter-acre backyard (large Db-£44, gigantic Db-£47, CC:VM, all rooms have sofas or easy chairs, ground-floor rooms have patios, easy parking, set far back from the busy road, London Road, GL56 0HE, tel. & fax 01608/651-036, e-mail: Treetops1@talk21.com, Liz and Brian Dean). It's a five-minute walk from town and an eight-minute walk from the railway station (exit station, keep left, go left over bridge over train tracks, look for sign, then long driveway).

Blue Cedar House has four comfortable rooms with an airy breakfast room full of plants. It's on a busy road but has double-paned windows and a pleasing setting, surrounded by a bright green half-acre garden (S-£21, D-£41, Db-£42, easy parking, 5-minute walk from center, Stow Road, GL56 0DW, tel. 01608/650-299, e-mail: gandsib@dialstart.net, Sandra and Graham Billinger).

The rest of the listings are within a few blocks of the station.

Townend Cottage and Coach House is a fun, 17th-century English-style hacienda. Two large rooms are in the main building, and two smaller rooms, including the upstairs treehouse, are across the courtyard (Sb-£32–35, D/Db-£40–45, nonsmoking, big garden, good breakfast, attached tearoom, near supermarket and park, end of High Street; 1 block from station; if arriving on foot from train station, exit station to right, take footpath by green iron fence to High Street; GL56 0AD, tel. 01608/650-846, new owners and probably new prices in 2001).

The Cottage dates back to 1620 and has low ceilings, a Cotswolds stone floor, inglenooky lounge, and lots of character (S-£22.50, D/Db-£45, no 1-nighters, nonsmoking, from station take Station Road to Oxford Street and turn right, GL56 0LA, tel. & fax 01608/651-740, e-mail: lcarter123@aol.com, Lorraine Carter).

Acacia B&B, with four small, clean, and cheery rooms on the third floor, is friendly and handy (S-£22, D-£36, Db-£40, less for 3-night stays and off-season, bunky family deals, nonsmoking, across from laundrette, when leaving station take right fork about a half block, New Road, GL56 0AS, tel. 01608/650-130, Dot and Mick Ellwood).

Moreton House Guest House offers 11 basic rooms above an Old World lounge on far end of High Street, away from the train station (Db-£50, CC:VM, High Street, GL56 0LQ, tel. 01608/650-747, fax 01608/652-747, new owners and prices likely for 2001).

Manor House Hotel is Moreton's most elegant hotel, dating from 1545 but sporting such modern amenities as an indoor pool, sauna, and Jacuzzi. Its 39 classy-for-the-Cotswolds rooms and garden invite relaxation (Sb-£85, Db-£100, 4-poster bed Db-£135, family suite-£145, CC:VMA, elevator, car park, log fire in winter, attached restaurant, on far end of High Street, away from train station, GL56 0LJ, tel. 01608/650-501, fax 01608/651-481).

Eating in Moreton-in-Marsh

A stroll up and down High Street lets you survey your small-town options. Consider the upscale but affordable **Marshmallow** (£8–11 entrees, 15 different teas, daily 10:00–17:00, Wed–Sun until 21:30, CC:VM, tel. 01608/651-536) or the **Black Bear Inn,** offering traditional English food (daily 12:00–14:00, 18:30–21:00, head to dining room on the left, not the smoky pub on the right, CC:VM, tel. 01608/652-992). The friendly **Hassan Balti,** with tasty Bangladeshi food, is a fine value for sit down or takeout (daily 12:00–14:00, 18:00–23:30, tel. 01608/650-798); **Mermaid Fish** is popular for its take-out fish; and the **Budgens** supermarket is indeed super (Mon–Sat 8:30–22:00, Sun 10:00–16:00, far end of High Street, near Townend Cottage). Across the busy street from the supermarket is pleasant Victoria Park with picnic tables. On Oxford Street, **Ice 'n' Slice** makes good sandwiches to go (Mon–Sat 9:00–16:00).

For a splurge, consider the **Marsh Goose** (closed Sun, High Street) or **Annie's** (closed Sun, Oxford Street).

Sleeping Elsewhere in the Cotswolds (for drivers only)

Didbrook Fields Farm, in Toddington near Broadway, offers four oak-beamed suites in a restored 19th-century barn surrounded by a 40-acre environmental farm complete with a wildflower meadow.

The kids' play area comes with little dogs, cats, and chickens. The indoor saltwater pool and sauna is rentable. Nearby is a steam railway, a pitch-and-putting green, and a riding stable with horses available (Db-£65–70, 7 miles southwest of Chipping Campden, Toddington, GL54 5PE, tel. & fax 01242/620-950, e-mail: TheKettle@aol.com, Frank and Jane Kennedy).

Transportation Connections—Cotswolds

Your best bus option, sans car, is the Cotswold Link bus, which runs daily, including Sunday, between Stratford and Bath, stopping at Moreton, Chipping Campden, and Stow (see "Getting around the Cotswolds," above). Only the Cotswold Link bus connects Bath by bus with the Cotswolds. The other bus companies connect the Cotswolds with Stratford and Cirencester. Here are some possibilities (available Mon–Sat, dead Sun—except for Cotswold Link bus):

Moreton by bus to: Chipping Campden and **Stratford** (6/day, same bus connects all 3 towns, Moreton–Chipping Campden 20 min, Moreton–Stratford 1.25 hrs, Stratford Blue bus company, tel. 01789/292-630), **Circencester** via **Stow** and **Burton** (13/day, Moreton–Cirencester 1 hr, Moreton–Stow 10 min, Stagecoach buses), **Cheltenham** (8/day, Moreton–Cheltenham 1 hr, with stops at a few untouristy towns, Pulham buses). Ask for specific schedules at a local TI; Moreton's TI has the most comprehensive.

Moreton by train to: London's Paddington Station (£21 one-way, £19 round-trip after 8:00, 10/day, 1.75 hrs; One-Day Travelcard for £22 includes round-trip and London tube travel), **Heathrow** (10/day, 2.5 hrs, train to Reading, then RailAir Link shuttle bus to airport), **Bath** (10/day, 2.5 hrs, transfers at Oxford and Didcot Parkway; Cotswold Link bus is easier), **Oxford** (10/day, 40 min), **Ironbridge Gorge** (3.5 hrs total, with train transfers at Worcester Forgate and Birmingham New Street, arrive Telford, catch bus or cab 7 miles to Ironbridge Gorge). Train info: tel. 08457-484-950.

Drivers' Tips: Distances are wonderfully short (but only if you invest in the Ordnance Survey map of the Cotswolds—sold locally at TIs and newsstands): Moreton to: Broadway (10 miles), Chipping Campden (8 miles), Stratford (17 miles), Warwick (23 miles), Stow (4 miles).

NEAR THE COTSWOLDS: STRATFORD, WARWICK, AND COVENTRY

Shakespeare's hometown, Stratford... to see or not to see? A walking tour with a play's the thing to bring the Bard to life in this touristy town. Explore Warwick, England's finest medieval castle, and stop by Coventry, a workaday town with a spirit that Nazi bombs couldn't destroy.

Cotswolds to North Wales

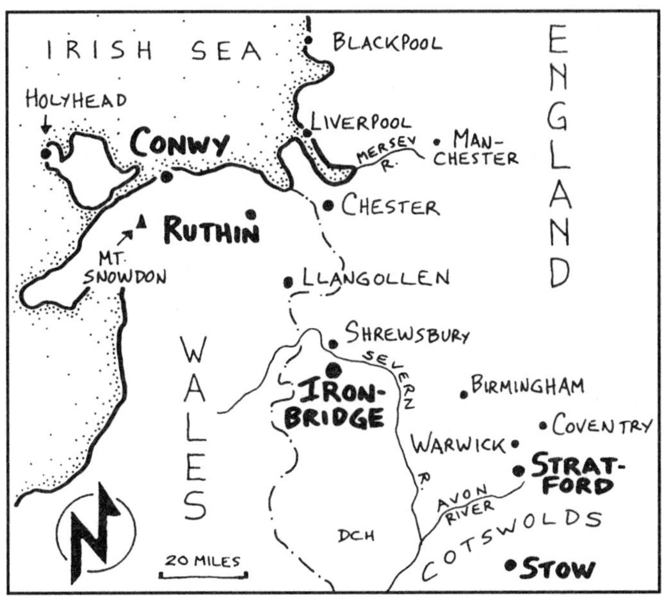

Planning Your Time

Stratford, Warwick, and Coventry are a made-to-order day for drivers connecting the Cotswolds with Ironbridge Gorge (IBG) or North Wales. While connections from the Cotswolds to IBG are tough, Stratford, Warwick, and Coventry are well served by public transportation.

Stratford is a classic tourist trap. But since you're passing through, it's worth a morning. (Don't spend the night.) Warwick is England's single most spectacular castle. It's very touristy but historic and fun for three hours. Lunch in Warwick town. Coventry, the least important stop on a quick trip, is most interesting as a chance to see a real, struggling, north-English industrial city (with some decent sightseeing).

The area is worth only a one-day drive-through. If you're speedy, hit all three sights. If you're more relaxed, do Stratford and Warwick and get to your Ironbridge Gorge B&B in time to enjoy the evening ambience of that more interesting stop.

STRATFORD-UPON-AVON

Stratford is the most overrated tourist magnet in England, but nobody back home would understand if you skipped Shakespeare's house. The old town is compact, with the TI and theater along the riverbank and Shakespeare's birthplace a few blocks off the river; you can walk easily to everything except Anne Hathaway's and Mary Arden's places. The river has an idyllic yet playful feel, with a park along the opposite bank, paddleboats, and an old, one-man, crank-powered ferry just beyond the theater.

Tourist Information: Pick up a free Attractions map at the TI (Mon–Sat 9:00–18:00, Sun 11:00–17:00, Nov–Mar 9:00–17:00 and closed Sun, has American Express office, tel. 01789/293-127).

Sights—Stratford-upon-Avon

▲Shakespeare's Birthplace—This half-timbered Elizabethan building—entirely rebuilt in the 1900s—is furnished as it was when young William was growing up and is filled with bits about his life and work. This is most worthwhile if you get the attendants in each room talking. Ask questions. The attached Shakespeare exhibition gives a fine historical background.

While William Shakespeare (1564–1616) was born in this house, he spent most of his career in London, where he taught his play-going public about human nature with plots that entertained the highest and the lowest minds at the same time. His tool was an unrivaled mastery of the English language. He retired—rich and famous—back in Stratford, spending his last five years at "New Place."

Little is known about Shakespeare the man. The scope of his brilliant work, his humble beginnings, and the fact that no original Shakespeare manuscripts survive raise a few scholarly eyebrows. But while some wonder who penned all these plays, most scholars accept his authorship (£5.50, Mon–Sat 9:00–17:00, Sun 9:30–17:00, last admission an hour before closing, mid-Oct–late March Mon–Sat 9:30–16:00, Sun 10:00–16:00, in the town center, tel. 01789/204-016, www.shakespeare.org.uk).

▲Four Other Shakespeare Properties—Shakespeare's hometown is blanketed with opportunities for "Bardolatry." There are four other "Shakespearian properties," all run by the Shakespeare Birthplace Trust, in and near Stratford. Each has a garden and helpful docents who love to tell a story. **Anne Hathaway's Cottage,** a mile out of town in Shottery, is a picturesque thatched 12-room farmhouse where the bard's wife grew up. It has little to do with Shakespeare but offers an intimate peek at lifestyles in Shakespeare's day. Guides in each room do their best to lecture to the stampeding hordes. **Mary Arden's House,** the girlhood home of William's mom, is in Wilmcote, about three miles from town. This 16th-century farmhouse sees far fewer tourists, so the guides in each room have a chance to do a little better guiding. A 19th-century farming exhibit and a falconry demonstration are on the grounds. **Hall's Croft,** the home of Shakespeare's daughter, who married a doctor, is in the town. This fine old Tudor house, the richest house of the group, is interesting only if you're into 16th-century medicine. **Nash's House,** where the Bard lived in retirement, is the least impressive of the properties. (Nash was the first husband of Shakespeare's granddaughter.) While Shakespeare's retirement home (New Place) is long gone, Nash's house has survived. It has the town's only general history exhibit—fascinating if you like chips of Roman pottery. Each property charges £3.50 to £5. Pilgrims save money buying combo tickets: £8.50 for three sights or £12 for all. (Anne Hathaway's Cottage has the same opening hours as Shakespeare's Birthplace; the other sights are open daily Mon–Sat 9:30–17:00, Sun 10:00–17:00; mid-Oct–mid-March Mon–Sat 10:00–16:00, Sun 10:30–16:00.) **Shakespeare's grave** is in the riverside Holy Trinity Church (a 10-minute walk past the theater).

Avon Riverfront—The River Avon is a playground with swans and canal boats. These canal boats, which saw their workhorse days during a short window of time between the start of the Industrial Revolution and the establishment of the railways, are now mostly pleasure boats. They are long and narrow, so two can pass in the narrow canals. There are 2,000 miles of canals here in the Midlands. These were built to connect centers of industry with seaports and provided vital transport during the early days of the Industrial Revolution.

▲▲Guide Friday Bus Tours—These open-top buses constantly make the rounds, allowing visitors to hop on and hop off at every sight in town. The full circuit takes about an hour and comes with a steady and informative live commentary (£9, buses leave from TI every 15 minutes 9:30–17:30, every half hour in winter, buy tickets on bus, tel. 01789/294-466).

Guide Friday offers longer tours of the Cotswolds (£18, 13:45–17:15, drive through 15 villages with brief stops in Stanton—15 min, Chipping Campden—20 min, and Stow—30 min, depart from Civic Hall near Market Square, buy tickets at Guide Friday office in Civic Hall, tel. 01789/294-466).

▲▲Royal Shakespeare Company—The RSC, undoubtedly the best Shakespeare company on earth, performs in Stratford year-round and in London in winter and spring (Dec–May). If you're a Shakespeare fan, see if the RSC schedule fits into your itinerary either here or in London. Tickets range from £5 to £50 (Mon–Sat at 19:30, Thu and Sat matinees at 13:30). You'll probably need to buy your tickets in advance, although 50 restricted-view and standing-room places are saved to be sold each morning (from 9:30, £5–15) and returned tickets can sometimes be picked up the evening of an otherwise-sold-out show (box office tel. 01789/295-623, Mon–Sat 9:00–20:00, closed Sun, www.rsc.org.uk). If you have a car, Stow and Chipping Campden are only 30 minutes from Stratford and an evening of classy entertainment.

Theater tours are given most days (£4, 13:30 and 17:30 if no matinee, sometimes 11:30 on matinee days, tours also given after performances, all tours must be booked in advance, Mon–Sat 9:30–17:30, Sun 11:30–16:00, tel. 01789/403-405). The theater sponsors Shakespeare's Life in Stratford walks (£6, Thu and Sat at 10:30 plus July–Sept Sun at 10:30, 2hrs).

Transportation Connections—Stratford-upon-Avon

To: London (4 trains/day, 2.5 hrs, direct from Paddington Station), **Chipping Campden** (6 buses/day, 60 min, on Stratford Blue bus, tel. 01789/292-630; plus 2 buses/day, 35 min, on Cotswold Link bus—continues to Moreton, Stow, and Bath), **Warwick** (hrly, 15 min, by bus or train), **Coventry** (hrly buses, 1 hr, tel. 01788/535-555). There is a Stratford–Warwick–Cambridge bus service (£12, 3/day, 2.5 hrs, tel. 01223/423-900). Train info: tel. 08457-484-950.

Driving is easy: Stow to Stratford (20 miles), Warwick (8 miles), Coventry (10 miles).

WARWICK AND COVENTRY

▲▲Warwick Castle—England's finest medieval castle is almost too groomed and organized, giving its hordes of visitors a decent value for the steep £9.75 entry fee. This cash-poor but enterprising lord hired the folks at Madame Tussaud's to wring maximum tourist dollars out of the castle. The latest marketing strategy is to build up the "kingmaker" reputation of the Earl of Warwick (WAR-ick).

With a lush, green, grassy moat and fairy-tale fornifications, Warwick will entertain you from dungeon to lookout. Standing inside the castle gate, you can see the mound where the original Norman castle of 1068 stood. Under this "motte," the wooden stockade, or "bailey," defined the courtyard as the castle walls do today. The castle is a 14th- and 15th-century fortified shell holding an 18th- and 19th-century royal residence surrounded by another dandy "Capability" Brown landscape job.

There's something for every taste—a fine and educational armory, a terrible torture chamber, a knight in shining armor on a horse that rotates with a merry band of musical jesters, a Madame Tussaud re-creation of a royal weekend party with an 1898 game of statue-maker, a grand garden, and a peacock-patrolled, picnic-perfect park. The Great Hall and Staterooms are the sumptuous highlights. The "King Maker" exhibit (It's 1471 and the town's folk are getting ready for battle...) is highly promoted but not quite as good as a Disney ride. Be warned: The tower is a one-way, no-return, 250-step climb offering a view not worth a heart attack. The £2 CD-ROM audio tour provides 60 easy-listening minutes of number-coded descriptions of the individual rooms (rent from kiosk on the lane after the turnstile). The £3.25 guidebook gives you nearly the same script in souvenir booklet form. Either is worthwhile if you want to understand the various rooms. If you tour without help, pick the brains of the earnest and talkative docents (£9.75, daily 10:00–18:00, Nov–March until 17:00, tel. 01926/406-600, 24-hour recorded message).

The Stables self-serve restaurant upstairs is much nicer than the cafeteria near the turnstiles. From the castle, a lane leads into the old town center, a block away, where you'll find the TI (daily 9:30–16:30, tel. 01926/492-212), doll museum, county museum, and several pubs serving fine lunches.

▲Coventry's Cathedral—The Germans bombed Coventry to smithereens in 1940. From that point on, the German phrase for "to really blast the heck out of a place" was "to coventrate" it. But Coventry rose from its ashes, and its message to our world is one of forgiveness and reconciliation. The symbol of Coventry is the bombed-out hulk of its old cathedral with the huge new one adjoining it. The inspirational complex welcomes visitors. Climb the tower (£1.50, 180 steps). If you're touring the church, first go downstairs to see the 18-minute audiovisual presentation, "Spirit of Coventry," on the cathedral's history (£1.25 for the movie, plus a requested £2 donation at the church door, Mon–Sat 10:00–16:00, closed Sun, tel. 02476/227-597).

Coventry's most famous hometown girl, Lady Godiva, rode bareback through the town in the 11th century to help lower taxes. You'll see her bronze statue a block from the cathedral (near Broadgate). Just beyond that is the Museum of British Road Transport—the first, fastest, and most famous cars and motorcycles came from this British "Detroit" (free, daily 10:00–17:00). Other sights include the Herbert Art Gallery and Museum, which cover the city's history (free, Mon–Sat 10:00–17:30, Sun 12:00–17:00), and St. Mary's Guildhall, with 14th-century tapestries, stained glass, and an ornate ceiling (free, Sun–Thu 10:00–16:00, closed if event scheduled and sometimes off-season).

Browse through Coventry, the closest thing to normal, workaday, urban England you'll see. Get a map at the TI (Mon–Fri 9:30–16:30, Sat–Sun 10:00–16:30, Bayley Lane, tel. 02476/832-303).

Route Tips for Drivers

Stratford to Ironbridge Gorge via Warwick and Coventry: Entering Stratford from the Cotswolds, you cross a bridge. Veer right (following "through traffic," "P," and "Wark" signs), go around the block, turning right and right and right over the speed humps, then enter the multistory garage (50p/hr, you'll find no place easier or cheaper). The TI and Guide Friday bus stop are a block away. Leaving the garage, circle to the right around the same block but stay on the "Wark" (Warwick, A439) road. Warwick is eight miles away. The castle is just south of town on the right. If the free castle lot is full, you'll be directed to a city lot. You might lurk across the street until someone leaves. After touring the castle, carry on through the center of Warwick, following signs to Coventry (still A439, then A46). If stopping in Coventry, follow signs painted on the road into the "city centre" and then to cathedral parking. Grab a place in the high-rise car park. Leaving Coventry, follow signs to Nuneaton and M6 North through lots of sprawl, and you're on your way. If skirting Coventry, M69 (Leicester) leads to M6. M6 threads through giant Birmingham. Try to avoid the 14:00-to-20:00 rush hour (see Ironbridge Gorge chapter for tips). From M6 (northwest), take M54 to the Telford/Ironbridge exit. Following the Ironbridge signs, you do-si-do through a long series of roundabouts until you're there.

IRONBRIDGE GORGE

The Industrial Revolution was born in the Severn River Valley. In its glory days, this valley (blessed with abundant deposits of iron ore and coal and a river for transport) gave the world its first iron wheels, steam-powered locomotive, and cast-iron bridge. The museums in Ironbridge Gorge (IBG) take you back into the days when Britain was racing into the modern age and pulling the rest of the West with her.

Planning Your Time

Without a car, IBG isn't worth the headache. Drivers can slip it in between the Cotswolds/Stratford/Warwick and North Wales. For a short, reasonable visit, arrive in the early evening to browse the town and spend the morning and early afternoon touring the sights before driving on to North Wales (10:00–Museum of the Gorge, 11:00–Blists Hill Victorian Town for lunch and sightseeing, 15:30–Drive to Wales).

Speed demons zip in for a midday tour of Blists Hill, look at the bridge, and speed out. With a month in Britain I'd spend two nights and a leisurely day: 9:30–Iron Bridge and the town, 10:30–Museum of the Gorge, 11:30–Coalbrookdale Museum of Iron, 14:30–Blists Hill, dinner at Coalbrookdale Inn.

Orientation (tel. code: 01952)

The town is just a few blocks gathered around the Iron Bridge, which spans the peaceful, tree-lined Severn River. While the smoke-belching bustle is long gone, knowing that this wooded, sleepy river valley was the Silicon Valley of the 19th century makes wandering its brick streets almost a pilgrimage. The actual museum sites are scattered over three miles. The modern cooling towers (for coal, not nuclear energy) that loom ominously over these red-brick remnants seem strangely appropriate.

Tourist Information: The TI is a block downhill from the Iron Bridge (Mon–Fri 9:00–17:00, Sat–Sun 10:00–17:00, room-finding service, tel. 01952/432-166). The TI has lots of booklets for sale; hikers like the home-grown *Walks in the Severn Gorge* (11 walks, £2.50) or the farther-ranging *Ten Walks That Changed the World* (£6).

Bike Rental: The nearest is Wenlock Bike Hire in Much Wenlock (£11/day, free delivery to IBG, helmets available, tours, 3 Sheinton Street, tel. 01952/727-089, Geoff and Mandy).

Sights—Ironbridge Gorge

▲▲Iron Bridge—This first iron bridge was built in 1779, while England was at war with her American colonies, to show off a wonderful new building material. Lacking experience with iron, the builders erred on the side of sturdiness and constructed it as if it was made out of wood. The valley's centerpiece is free, open all the time, and thought provoking. Walk across the bridge to the toll booth/gift shop/free museum. Read the fee schedule and notice the subtle slam against royalty (England was not immune to the revolutionary sentiment brewing in the colonies at this time). Pedestrians paid half a penny to cross (poor people crossed cheaper by coracle—a crude tublike wood-and-canvas shuttle ferry). Cross back to the town and walk downstream along the towpath; near the bridge, peek through the dirty cracked windows of a riverside shack to glimpse a couple of these coracles.

▲▲▲Ironbridge Gorge Industrial Revolution Museums—This group of widely scattered sites has varied admission charges (usually £2–4.50; Blists Hill is £7.50). The £10 Passport ticket (£30 for families) gets you into all the sights, which all have the same hours (April–Oct daily 10:00–17:00; from Nov–March, a few Coalbrookdale sights close, Blists Hill's hours are Sat–Wed 10:00–16:00, closed Thu–Fri, tel. 01952/433-522 or 01952/432-166, www.vtel.co.uk/igmt). Even though several of the sights may not be worth your time, seeing Blists Hill Victorian Town, the Museum of the Gorge, and the Coalbrookdale Museum of Iron costs £14.10 without the Passport ticket.

Museum of the Gorge: Orient yourself to the valley here in the Severn Warehouse (£2, daily 10:00–17:00, 500 yards upstream from the bridge, pay £1 to park). See the eight-minute introductory movie, check out the exhibit and the model of the gorge in its heyday, and buy a Blists Hill guidebook and Passport ticket. From the parking lot, a tiny tour boat sometimes does a 45-minute round-trip Severn River tour (£3.50, look for sign near WC, slow-moving taped commentary, peaceful photo opportunity for bridge and lazy fishermen along riverbanks, tel. 01952/418-

Ironbridge Gorge

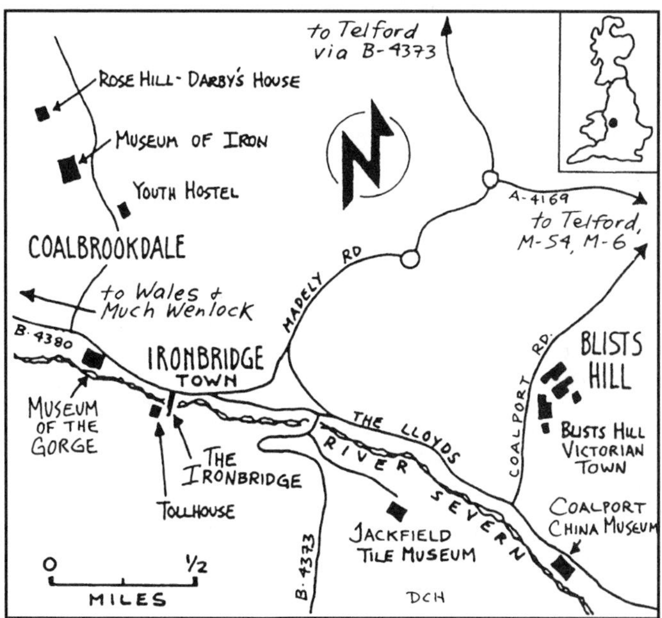

844). Farther upstream is the fine riverside Dale End Park, with picnic areas and a playground.

Blists Hill Victorian Town: Save most of your time and energy for this wonderful town. You'll wander through 50 acres of Victorian industry, factories, and a re-created community from the 1890s, complete with carriage rides, chemists, a candy shop, an ancient dentist's chair, candle makers, a working pub, a greengrocer's shop, a fascinating squatter's cottage, and a snorty, slippery pigsty. Don't miss the explanation of the winding machine at the Blists Hill Mine (first demonstration occurs 11:00–13:00, confirm time at entry). Walk along the canal to the "inclined plane." Grab lunch in the Victorian Pub or the cafeteria near the squatter's cottage and old-time children's rides. The board by the entry lists which exhibits are staffed and lively (with docents in Victorian dress). The £2 Blists Hill guidebook gives a good step-by-step rundown (£7.50, tel. 01952/583-003).

Coalbrookdale Museum of Iron: This does a fine job of explaining the original iron-smelting process (£4.60, opposite Darby's furnace—see below).

The Coalbrookdale neighborhood is the birthplace of the Industrial Revolution. Abraham Darby's blast furnace sits like a shrine inside a big glass pyramid (free), surrounded by the evocative Industrial Age ruins. This is where, in 1709, Darby first smelted iron using coke as fuel. If you're like me, "coke" is a drink, and "smelt" is the past tense of smell.... Nevertheless, this event kicked off the modern Industrial Age.

All the ingredients of the recipe for big industry were here in abundance—iron ore, top-grade coal, and water for power and shipping. Wander around Abraham Darby's furnace. Before this furnace was built, iron ore was laboriously melted by charcoal. With a huge waterwheel-powered billows, Darby burned top-grade coal super hot (burning off the impurities to make "coke"). Local iron ore was dumped into the furnace and melted. Impurities floated to the top, while the pure iron sank to the bottom of a clay tub in the bottom of the furnace. Twice a day the plugs were knocked off, allowing the "slag" to drain away on the top and the molten iron to drain out on the bottom. The low-grade slag was used locally on walls and paths. The high-grade iron trickled into molds formed in the sand below the furnace. It cooled into pig iron (named because the molds look like piglets suckling their mother). The pig iron "planks" were broken off by sledgehammers and shipped away. The Severn River became one of Europe's busiest, shipping pig iron to distant foundries, where it was remelted and made into cast iron (for projects such as the Iron Bridge), or to forges, where it was worked like toffee into wrought iron.

Rosehill House, just up the hill, is the 18th-century Darby mansion furnished as a Quaker ironmaster's home would have been in 1850 (daily 10:00–17:00). The adjacent Dale House from the 1780s is less interesting.

Coalport China Museum, Jackfield Tile Museum, and Broseley Pipeworks: Housed in their original factories, these showcase the region's porcelain, decorated tiles, and clay pipes. These industries were developed to pick up the slack when the iron industry shifted away from Severn Valley. Each museum features finely decorated pieces, and the china and tile museums offer low-energy workshops.

Skiing, Swimming, Fishing, and More—There's a small, brush-covered ski slope with two poma lifts at Telford Ski Centre in Madeley, which is two miles from Ironbridge Gorge; you'll see the signs for it as you drive into IBG (£8.60/hr including gear, less for kids, CC:VMA, Mon–Fri 10:00–22:00, Sat 10:00–18:00, Sun 10:00–20:00, tel. 01952/586-862). There's a public swimming pool next door. The Woodlands Farm, on Beech Road, runs a private fishing business where only barbless hooks are used and locals toss their catch back to hook again (kind of a fish hell). In IBG, a steam trains runs for fun most Sundays (get schedule at TI).

If you're looking for reasons to linger in IBG, these sights are all within a short drive: the medieval town of Shrewsbury, the abbey village of Much Wenlock, the scenic Long Mynd gorge at Church Stretton, the castle at Ludlow, and the steam railway at the river town of Bridgnorth. Shoppers like Chester (en route to North Wales).

Sleeping in Ironbridge Gorge

(£1 = about $1.60, country code: 44, area code: 01952)
Sleep Code: **S** = Single, **D** = Double/Twin, **T** = Triple, **Q** = Quad, **b** = bathroom, **t** = toilet only, **s** = shower only, **CC** = Credit Card (**V**isa, **M**asterCard, **A**mex).

Sleeping in Farmhouses

Hill View Farm is a peaceful, thrifty, brave, clean, and reverent B&B run by Rosemarie Hawkins while her husband John raises a "beef suckler herd." If you're looking for calm and country—Auntie Em–style—this is it, in a great rural setting overlooking the ruins of a 12th-century abbey (D-£36 for 1 night, less for longer stays, nonsmoking, Buildwas, Ironbridge, Shropshire, TF8 7BP, tel. 01952/432-228). It's just outside of Ironbridge on the Much Wenlock road (A4169); pass the huge power plants, take a left over the bridge, and go about a quarter mile (sign on right).

If you like the country and Hill View Farm is full, try **Grove Farm House B&B** (D-£38, Db-£42, less for 2 nights, nonsmoking, 3 miles from IBG on the road to Shrewsbury in Buildwas, tel. 01952/433-572, fax 01952/433-650, e-mail: clive@g-f-h.demon.co.uk, Pat and Clive Pygott).

Bridge House, two miles north of town, dates from 1620, with four warmly decorated rooms (S-from £40, Db-from £55, big garden, parking, on fairly busy road B4380, river views, near Buildwas Abbey, TF8 7BN, tel. 01952/432-105, fax 01952/432-105, e-mail: janethedges@talk21.com, Janet Hedges).

Sleeping in the Town Center

Library House is "better-homes-and-gardens" elegant. In the town center, a half block downhill from the bridge, it's classy, friendly, and a fine value. It's hard to stay just one night. Helpful Chris and George Maddocks run this smoke-free place, and their breakfast won a "healthy heartbeat" award. The complimentary drink upon arrival is a welcome touch (Sb-£45, Db-£55, Tb-£70, family room-£70, video library, free parking, 11 Severn Bank, Ironbridge Gorge, TF8 7AN, tel. 01952/432-299, fax 01952/433-967, www.libhouse.enta.net). George will pick you up from the Telford train station if you request it in advance.

Three places right in the town center overlook the bridge: **Eley's Bridge View B&B** rents five bright and comfy rooms (Db-£45 with this book through 2001, CC:VM, tel. 01952/432-541,

Jo or Rich). The **Post Office House B&B** is literally above the post office. The postmaster's wife, Janet Hunter, rents three spacious rooms (D-£38, Ds-£40, Db with tiny kitchenette-£44, 6 The Square, Ironbridge, Shropshire TF8 7AQ, tel. 01952/433-201, fax 01952/433-582, e-mail: hunter@pohouse-ironbridge.fsnet.co.uk). The **Tontine Hotel** is the town's big, musty, Industrial Age hotel (12 rooms, S-£22, D-£40, Db-£56, 10 percent discount promised with this book, CC:VMA, attached restaurant with set menu, tel. 01952/432-127, fax 01952/432-094). Check out the historic photos in the bar.

Malt House, near the Museum of the Gorge, rents out six new, sparsely furnished rooms (Sb-£49, Dd-£59, CC:VMA, a five-minute walk along the river from town, attached restaurant, parking, The Wharfage, TF8 7NH, tel. 01952/433-712, fax 01952/433-298, e-mail: malthse@globalnet.co.uk).

Hostels

Coalport Youth Hostel, plush for a hostel, fills an old factory at the China Museum in Coalport (most beds are in quads, but they have plenty of bunk-bed Ds for £20, including sheets). The **Ironbridge Gorge Youth Hostel,** built in 1859 as the grand Coalbrookdale Institute, is another fine hostel (a 20-minute walk from the Iron Bridge down A4169 toward Wellington, 4- to 6-bed rooms). Each hostel charges £10.15 per bed with sheets, serves meals, has a self-serve laundry, closes from 10:00 to 17:00, requires that you have a hostel membership (available for £11), and uses the same telephone number: tel. 01952/588-755.

Wilderhope Manor Youth Hostel, a beautifully remote and haunted 400-year-old manor house, is one of Europe's best hostels. On Saturdays, tourists actually pay to see what we hostelers sleep in for £9.80 (dinner served at 19:00, unreliable hours throughout year, phone first, tel. 01694/771-363). It's six miles from Much Wenlock down B4371 toward Church Stretton.

Eating in Ironbridge Gorge

The best values and most local crowds are found outside of the IBG town. For a local crowd, fine spit-and-sawdust ambience, excellent ales, and surprisingly good food, try the **Coalbrookdale Inn** (dinner 18:00–20:00 except Sun, folk music on third Sun every month, across the street from the Coalbrookdale Museum of Iron, a mile from IBG, tel. 01952/433-953, www.coalbrookdale-inn.com; run by Corrine and Mike, who are on the quest for the perfect pint). This former "best pub in Britain" (1995) has a tradition of offering free samples from a lineup of featured beers. Each is listed on a blackboard with its price and alcohol content. Ask a local to explain... or ask if he's ever tried a brew called the Prior's Piddle.

For a classier and more subdued atmosphere, eat well at the **Meadow Inn,** a local favorite with prizewinning pub grub (a pleasant 15-minute walk from the center, head upstream, at Dale End Park take the path along the river, the inn is just after the railway bridge, dinners nightly 18:00–21:45, CC:VMA, can get crowded, no reservations taken, tel. 01952/433-193).

For a break from pub grub, you have these options in the town center. **Oliver's** is a smoke-free vegetarian place with prices and meals that make you want to turn—or stay—vegetarian (£6.95 main course, using CC adds 4 percent, Tue–Sat 19:00–21:00, also Sat–Sun 12:00–14:00, High Street, reservations wise, tel. 01952/433-086). The **Ironbridge Brasserie & Wine Bar** is an inviting bistro with an imaginative menu and real ale (Tue–Sun 18:30–23:00, also Fri–Sun 12:00–15:00, closed Mon, plenty of indoor/outdoor seating, High Street, tel. 01952/432-716). **Da Vinci's** serves good, though pricey, Italian food (£12 main course, Tue–Sat 19:00–22:00, Sun 12:00–16:30, closed Mon, CC:VM, 26 High Street, tel. 01952/432-250). For Indian takeout, consider **Aftab** (nightly 17:30–24:00, 25 High Street, tel. 01952/432-055). The popular **Malt House,** located in an 18th-century beer house, offers an English menu with a European accent (£10 main course, daily 12:00–14:30, 18:30–21:30, CC:VMA, near Museum of the Gorge, five-minute walk from the center, also rents rooms—see above, tel. 01952/433-712).

For a pleasant evening, drive down Wenlock Edge on B4371. At the Wenlock Edge Inn, park and walk to the cliff for a marvelous view of Shropshire at sunset (made nearly famous by the poet A. E. Housman). Then drive farther to Much Wenlock and eat with a fun local crowd at the **George and Dragon Pub.**

Transportation Connections—Ironbridge Gorge

IBG is seven miles from Telford, which has the nearest train station. To get between IBG and Telford, take a bus (£1, hrly except Sun, 20 min) or taxi (£7.50). Although Telford's train and bus stations are an annoying 15-minute walk apart (or a £2 cab ride), the bus station is part of a large modern mall, an easy place to wait for a bus to IBG. Few buses run Sunday. For bus information, call Telford Travelink at 01952/200-005. If you need a taxi while in Ironbridge Gorge, call 01952/501-050.

Telford by train to: Birmingham (hrly, 45 min), **Conwy** in North Wales (4/day, 3 hrs, with transfer in Chester), **Blackpool** (hrly, 4.5 hrs, with several transfers), **Lake District** (allow up to 6.5 hrs total, with several transfers, at Penrith catch a bus to Keswick, hrly except Sun 3/day, 40 min), **Edinburgh** (8 hrs, with several transfers). Train info: tel. 08457-484-950.

By Car: Driving in from the Cotswolds and Stratford, take

M6 through Birmingham then M54 to the Telford/Ironbridge exit. Follow the brown Ironbridge signs through lots of roundabouts to Ironbridge Gorge. The traffic north through Birmingham is miserable from 14:00 to 20:00, especially on Fridays. From Warwick, consider the M40, M42, Kidderminster alternative, coming into IBG on the A442 via Bridgnorth to avoid the B'ham traffic. Driving from IBG to Ruthin in North Wales is an easy two hours. IBG to Conwy is 2.5 hours.

NORTH WALES

Wales' top historical, cultural, and natural wonders are found in the north. From towering Mount Snowdon to lush forests to desolate moor country, North Wales is a poem written in landscape. For sightseeing thrills and diversity, North Wales is Britain's most interesting slice of the Celtic crescent. But be careful not to be waylaid by the many gimmicky sights and bogus "best of" lists. The region's economy is poor, and they're wringing every possible pound out of the tourist trade. Sort carefully through your options.

Welsh

Language: The Welsh language, Cymru, has been a written language since about A.D. 600 and was spoken 300 years before French or German. It remains alive and well. Although English imperialism tried to kill it, today Welsh and those who speak it are protected by law. In Northwest Wales well over half the population is fluent in Welsh. It's either the first or the required second language in the public schools. Tourists hardly notice that the locals chatter away in Welsh and, as they turn to you, switch seamlessly to English. Listen in.

Welsh is a Celtic language (like Irish) and most closely related to the Breton language in western France. The common "ll" is pronounced as if you were ready to make an "l" sound and then blew it out. The language is phonetic but comes with a few tricks: the Welsh "dd" sounds like the English "th," f = v, ff = f, w = oo, and y = i. In a pub, impress your friends (or make some) by toasting the guy who just bought your drink. Say "Yeach-hid dah" ("Good health to you") and "Dee olch" ("Thank you") or "Dee olch un vowr" ("Thanks very much"). If the beer's bad, just make something up.

North Wales

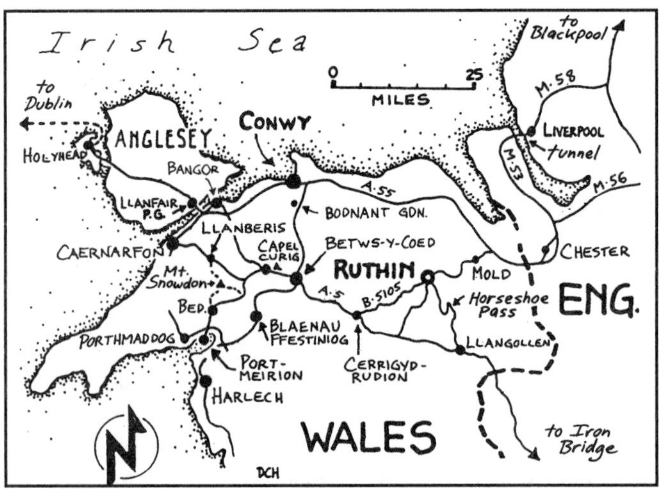

Choirs: Every town has a choir (men's or mixed) that practices weekly. Visitors are usually welcome to observe and very often follow the choir down to the pub afterward for a good, old-fashioned, beer-lubricated singsong. Choirs welcome visitors and practice weekly in the towns of Ruthin (mixed choir at the Tabernacle Church, Thu 19:30–21:30), Llangollen (men's choir Fri at 19:30 at the Hand Hotel, 21:00 pub singsong afterward, tel. 01978/860-303), Denbigh (men's choir Mon at 19:00 except in Aug), Llandudno (Sun 19:30–21:00, near Conwy), and Caernarfon (Tue 20:00–21:30 at the Conservative Club on High Street). Confirm choir schedules with your B&B hostess or a local TI.

Planning Your Time

Give North Wales two nights and a day (on a 3-week British trip), and it'll give you a medieval banquet, a mighty castle, a giant slate mine, and some of Britain's most beautiful scenery. Many visitors are charmed and find an extra day.

Drivers interested in the medieval banquet should set up in Ruthin and do this loop:

9:00–Drive over Llanberis mountain pass to Caernarfon (with possible short stops in Trefriw Mill, Betws-y-Coed, Pen-y-Gwryd Hotel, and Llanberis), 12:00–Caernarfon Castle. Catch noon tour and 13:00 movie in Eagle Tower. See Prince Charles (of Wales) exhibit. Climb to top for view. Walk through Caernarfon town, lunch, shop. 14:30–Drive the scenic road (A4085) to Blaenau Ffestiniog, 15:30–Tour Llechwedd Slate Mine, 17:30–Drive home to

Ruthin, 19:00–Arrive at home, 19:45–Medieval banquet at castle (if not last night).

With a car and no interest in the banquet, skip Ruthin and shorten your drive time by spending two nights in Conwy. Without a car, skip Ruthin. From Conwy you can tour Snowdonia and Caernarfon by bus and train.

With a second day, add the train up Snowdon (or take a hike) and visit Conwy. With more time and a desire to hike, consider using the mountain village of Beddgelert as a base.

Getting around North Wales

North Wales (except Ruthin) is well covered by a combination of buses and trains. A main train line zips along the north coast from Chester to Holyhead via Llandudno Junction, Conwy, and Bangor (hrly). From Llandudno Junction, the Conwy Valley line goes scenically south to Betws-y-Coed and Blaenau Ffestiniog (5/day, 1 hr). Without a car, you'll manage fine, using these two train lines; public buses (get the Gwynedd Public Transport Guide at any local TI); and Arriva buses, which circle Snowdonia National Park with the needs of hikers in mind (£5 Explorer day pass available, buy on bus, tel. 01492/592-968).

RUTHIN

Ruthin (rith-in) is a low-key, workaday market town whose charm is in its ordinary Welshness. The people are the sights. Admission is free if you start the conversation. The market square, castle, TI, bus station, and in-town accommodations are all within five blocks of each other. Ruthin is Welsh as can be, makes a handy base for drivers doing North Wales, and serves up a great medieval banquet. In the busy crafts center, you'll find the TI (June–Sept daily 10:00–17:30, Oct–May Mon–Sat 10:00–17:00, Sun 12:00–17:00, tel. 01824/703-992).

Sights—Ruthin

▲▲Ruthin Castle Welsh Medieval Banquet—English, Scottish, Irish, and Welsh medieval banquets are all variations on the same touristy theme. This one is fun, more culturally justifiable (if that's necessary), and less expensive than most. You'll be greeted with a chunk of bread dipped in salt, which the maiden explains will "guarantee your safety." Your medieval master of ceremonies then seats you, and the candlelit evening of food, drink, and music rolls gaily on. You'll enjoy harp music, angelic singing, and lots of entertainment, including insults slung at the Irish, Scots, English, and even us brash colonists. With fanfare (and historic explanation), wenches serve mead, spiced wine, and four hearty traditional courses. Drink from a pewter goblet, wear a bib, and eat with your fingers and a dagger. Food and mead are unlimited—just ask for

Ruthin

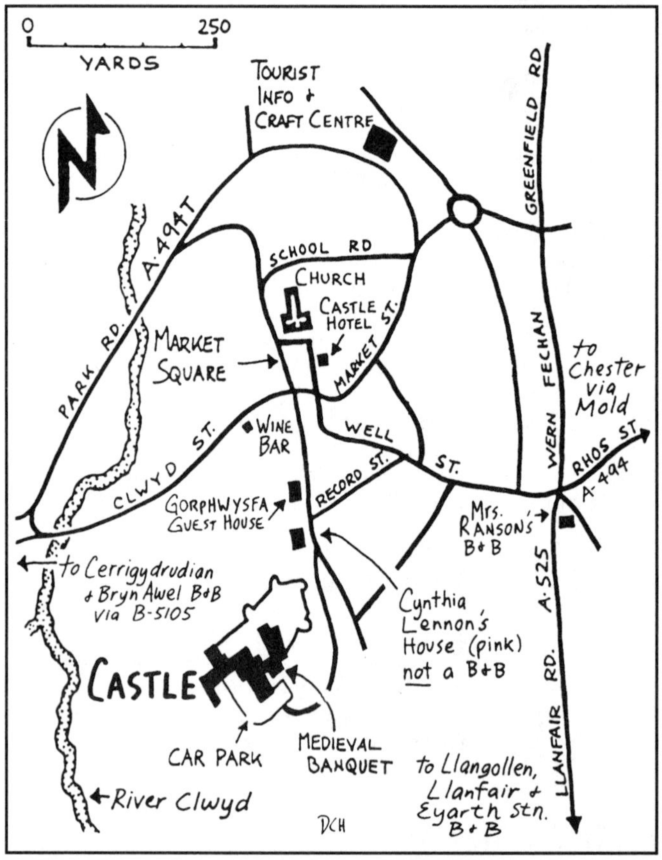

more (£28.95, CC:VMA, starts at 19:45, 2–5 nights weekly year-round, depending upon demand, vegetarian options, nonsmoking, easy doorstep parking, down Castle Street from the town square, call for reservations, tel. 01824/703-435 or, after hours, the hotel at 01824/702-664).

Walks—For a scenic and interesting one-hour walk, try the Offa's Dyke Path to Moel Famau (the "Jubilee Tower," a 200-year-old war memorial on a peak overlooking stark moorlands). The trail-head is a 10-minute drive from Ruthin.

▲▲Welsh Choir—The mixed choir performs at the Tabernacle Church on Thursday from 19:30 to 21:30 (except Aug, tel. 01824/703-757).

Sleeping in Ruthin

(£1 = about $1.60, country code: 44, area code: 01824)
Sleep Code: **S** = Single, **D** = Double/Twin, **T** = Triple, **Q** = Quad, **b** = bathroom, **t** = toilet only, **s** = shower only, **CC** = Credit Card (**V**isa, **M**asterCard, **A**mex).

Bryn Awel, a warm, traditional, charming farmhouse B&B with a paradise garden, is run by Beryl and John Jones in the hamlet of Bontuchel just outside of Ruthin (Db-£36–39, add £3 for 1-nighters, nonsmoking, LL15 2DE Bontuchel, tel. 01824/702-481, www.accomodata.co.uk/010797.htm). Beryl, a prizewinning quilter, is helpful with touring tips, nearby walks, restaurant recommendations, booking the medieval banquet, and key Welsh words. (From Ruthin, take Bala road, #494, then B5105 Cerrigydrudion road. Turn right after the church, at the Bontuchel/Cyffylliog sign. It's on the right, 1.8 fragrant miles down a narrow road. If you get to the Bridge Hotel, backtrack 200 yards.)

Gorphwysfa Guest House, in a cozy 16th-century Tudor home between the castle and the town square, serves a royal breakfast and has a library, a grand piano, and three huge, comfortable rooms (Db-£40, Ts-£54, Qs-£64, 8a Castle Street, LL15 1DP, tel. & fax 01824/707-529, Margaret O'Riain).

Margaret Ranson's B&B is friendly, comfortable, and moderately priced (3 rooms, Db-£38, strictly nonsmoking, Rhianfa, Ffordd Llanrhydd, Ruthin, Clwyd, LL15 1PP, a 10-minute walk from the castle; from Anchor Pub drive 100 yards toward the hospital; it's the first big red-brick house on right, Rhianfa sign on stone wall, tel. & fax 01824/702-971). Margaret's husband, John, a natural tour guide, will lend you an excellent North Wales road map. Or you can just play croquet in their sprawling backyard.

The Castle Hotel, not to be confused with the Ruthin Castle Hotel, is a worn, 24-room hotel on the town square (Db-£42 with this book through 2001, family suites, front rooms are larger and overlook the town square, some nonsmoking rooms, reasonable evening meals, CC:VM, St. Peter's Square, LL15 1AA, tel. 01824/702-479, fax 01824/703-488).

Moelfa B&B, on the busy Denbigh Road, is modern and nondescript but comfortable and friendly (D-£32 with this book, leave town on Denbigh Road, first B&B sign on left, tel. 01824/702-468, Meg Jones).

Ruthin Castle, the ultimate in creaky, faded, Old World elegance for North Wales, is actually not a castle but a hotel near castle ruins (Sb-from £79, Db-from £99, show this book for 10 percent off room rates or 10 percent off their two-nights-with-a-banquet-plus-restaurant-dinner deal, CC:VMA, tel. 01824/702-664, fax 01824/705-978, www.ruthincastle.co.uk). Enjoy lavish public places, armor, antlers, ghosts, and your private snooker table (giant billiards, £1/hr). Explore the fascinating grounds, complete with a drowning pool and 40 peacocks. You'll wake up to their cry thinking it's a loony-tune damsel in distress.

For cheap beds go to the **Llangollen Youth Hostel** (15 miles from Ruthin, see below).

Eating in Ruthin

Don't to rush home for dinner in Ruthin if you're not going to the medieval banquet. No one place is a clear winner, but you'll eat reasonably well at the **Anchor Pub,** the **Wynnstay Arms,** the **Middleton Arms Pub** on the main square, the classier **Manor House Hotel Restaurant** (pricey), or a mile out of town in Cyffylliog at the **Red Lion** pub. Or try a wine bar—**Da Vinci's** (The Mews, Well Street) or the bar above the Castle Hotel (£6 entrees). For fish and chips, locals paddle over to **Finns** on Clwyd Street (take-away only).

Transportation Connections—Ruthin

Ruthin to: Llangollen (15 miles, 4 buses/day but never on Sun, 60 min), **Betsw-y-Coed** (30 miles, allow 3–4 hrs, bus to Rhyl, train to Llandudno Junction, train to Betsw-y-Coed), **Conwy** (3 hrs by bus, with transfer at Llanrwst), **Chester** (6 buses/day, 30 min, or a £20 taxi).

LLANGOLLEN

Worth a stop if you have a car, Llangollen is famous for its musical **International Eisteddfod** (July 2–8 in 2001), a very popular and very crowded festival of folk songs and dance. Men's choir practice is held on Friday nights throughout the year (19:30 at the Hand Hotel, 21:00 pub singsong afterward, tel. 01978/860-303).

Walk or ride a horse-drawn boat down the old canal (£3.50, 45 min, 3-mile round-trip, March–Oct, tel. 01978/860-702) toward the lovely 13th-century **Cistercian Vale Crucis Abbey** near the even older cross called **Eliseg's Pillar.** TI: daily April–Oct 10:00–18:00, Nov–March 9:30–17:00, tel. 01978/860-828.

Llangollen has a handful of other amusements and attractions, including scenic steam train trips (daily Easter–Dec), the world's largest permanent exhibition of model railways, and the biggest "Doctor Who" exhibition anywhere.

Glasfryn B&B is good (D/Db-£35, Abbey Road, LL20 8SN, near bridge, tel. 01978/860-757, Eleanor Jones). **Gale's Hotel** is a decent value (Db-£58, £49 for 2 nights, good food, CC:VMA, Bridge Street 18, LL20 8PF, tel. 01978/860-089, fax 01978/861-313) and the **Llangollen Youth Hostel** is cheap (£11.80 per bed in 2- to 20-bed rooms, £2 less for members, tel. 01978/860-330).

Llangollen is a 30-minute drive from Ruthin or a bus ride (4/day, none on Sun, 60 min, year-round). Llangollen is connected by bus with train stations at Chirk (hrly), Ruabon (hrly), and Wrexham (2/hrly).

King Edward's Castles

In the 13th century the Welsh, under two great princes named Llywelyn, created a united and independent Wales. The English King Edward I fought hard to end this Welsh sovereignty. In 1282 Llywelyn was killed (and went to where everyone speaks Welsh). King Edward spent the next 20 years building or rebuilding 17 great castles to consolidate his English foothold in troublesome North Wales. The greatest of these (such as Conwy Castle) were masterpieces of medieval engineering, with round towers (tough to undermine by tunneling), a castle-within-a-castle defense (giving defenders a place to retreat and wreak havoc on the advancing enemy...or just wait for reinforcements), and sea access (safe to stock from England). These were English islands in the middle of angry Wales. Most were built with a fortified grid-plan town attached and were filled with English settlers. (With this blatant abuse of Wales, you have to wonder, where was Greenpeace 700 years ago?)

Castle lovers will want to tour each of Edward's five greatest castles. With a car and two days this makes one of Europe's best castle tours. I'd rate them in this order: **Caernarfon** is most entertaining and best presented (described below). **Conwy** is attached to the cutest medieval town and the best public transport (described below). **Harlech** is the most dramatic (£3, daily early April–late Oct 9:30–17:00 or 18:00, late Oct–early April Mon–Sat 9:30–16:00, Sun 11:00–16:00, tel. 01766/780-552; TI open Easter–Oct, tel. 01766/780-658). **Beaumaris,** surrounded by a swan-filled moat, was the last, largest, and most romantic (£2.20, same hours as Harlech, tel. 01248/810-361). **Criccieth** (KRICK-ith), built in 1230 by Llywelyn, is also dramatic and remote (£2.20, daily early April–late Sept 10:00–17:00 or 18:00, closed off-season, tel. 01766/522-227; TI open Easter–Oct, tel. 01766/523-633). For photos and more information on the castles, and Welsh historic monuments in general, check www.cadw.wales.gov.uk.

CONWY

This garrison town was built at the same time in the 1280s as the castle to give Edward I an English toehold in Wales (see above). What's left today are the best medieval walls in Britain surrounding a humble workaday town and crowned by the bleak and barren hulk of a castle awesome in its day. Conwy's charming High Street leads from Lancester Square (with the bus stop, unmanned train station, and a column honoring the town's founder, Welsh prince Llywelyn the Great) down to a fishy harbor that permitted Edward to safely restock his castle.

Tourist Information: The TI is supposed to move in 2001 from the castle entrance but will stay in the town center, likely near the harbor (April–Oct daily 9:30–18:00, Nov–March daily 9:30–16:00, tel. 01492/592-248). Ask about train or bus schedules for your departure (because Conwy doesn't have a staffed train or bus station—only a lonely train platform and bus stop). The TI sells books and maps on the area (such as *Footprints' Walks around Snowdonia*, £3.50, 16 walks with maps), books rooms for a £1 fee, and does theatre bookings. Don't confuse the TI with the tacky "Conwy Visitors Centre" near the station with its goofy little 80p video show.

Helpful Hints

Every Monday night, the gritty Malt Loaf pub hosts the Conwy Folk Music Club (across from the train station) from 20:30 on. Every Tuesday, a small market hums in the train station parking lot (year-round, but canceled if rainy). On weekends, when banks are closed, only cash machines are available for changing money.

Trains: Train schedules are posted outside the unstaffed station. Trains do drop off and pick up and stop in Conwy (if your train is listed with an "x," you'll need to flag down the train). The nearest "real" train station is in Llandudno Junction, a mile away.

Car Rental: The nearest car rental agencies are in the city of Llandudno, 1.5 miles away. Consider Aberconwy Car Hire (from £30/day, £3 fee to deliver car to your Conwy hotel or meet you at station, tel. 01492/874-669) or the pricier, "why try harder" Europcar (from £39/day, £10 delivery to hotel, tel. 01492/878-608).

Bike Rental: Conwy Outdoor rents bikes for £12/day, including helmets (daily 9:00–18:00, CC:VM, packed lunches available, 9 Castle Street, tel. 01492/593-390).

Sights—Conwy

▲Conwy Castle—Built dramatically on a rock overlooking the sea with eight linebacker towers, this castle has an interesting story to tell (£4, mid-May–Sept daily 9:30–18:00, Apr–mid-May and Oct daily 9:30–17:00, in winter Mon–Sat 10:00–16:00, Sun 11:00–16:00, tel. 01492/592-358). Guides wait inside to take you on a 60-minute, £1 tour. If the booth is empty, look for the group and join it. (These guides also do evening city tours; consider enthusiastic Neville Hortop, tel. 01492/878-209, who charges just £2 per person.)

City Wall—Much of the wall, with its 22 towers, is walkable and free, featuring castle and harbor views; start at Upper Gate (the highest point) or Berry Street (the lowest) or do the small section at the castle entrance.

Harbor—Since the highway was tunneled under the town, a

Conwy

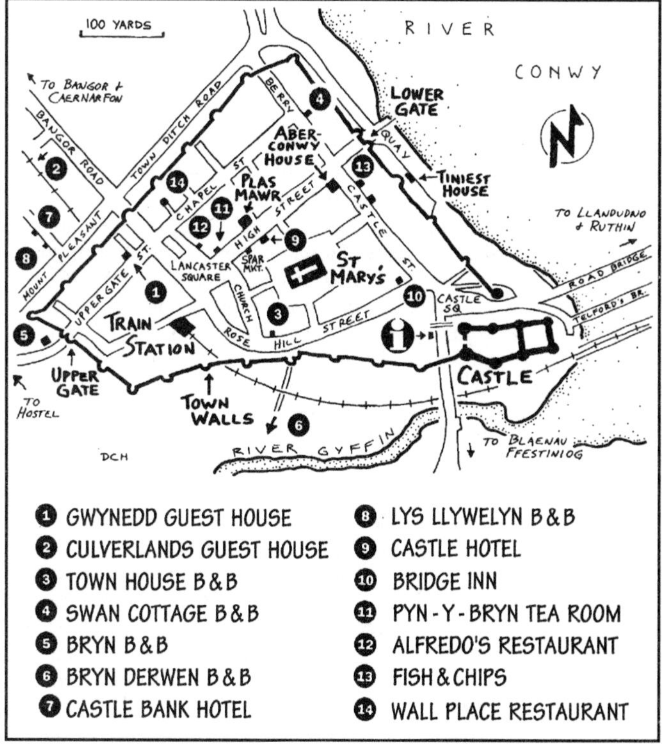

strolling ambience has returned to Conwy. Wander the harbor past Britain's smallest house (see below), the "Queen Victoria" tour boat (£3, 30-minute cruise, pay on boat), an aquarium, the town lifeboat house, and a fresh-fish trailer (Keith the Fish) selling 10p crab sticks. Beyond the castle, the mighty Telford suspension bridge is a 19th-century slice of English imperialism, built in 1826 to better connect (and control) the route to Ireland. The newly restored bridge is open to pedestrians only (£1).

Old Houses—On the harbor, the tiniest house in Britain is red, 72 inches wide, 122 inches high, and 50p to see. Two old houses on High Street may tempt you. Plas Mawr, billed as the oldest house in Wales, offers a frail look at domestic life in 16th-century Wales (£4, includes audio tour, Tue–Sun 9:30–17:00, closed Mon). The Aberconwy House—the oldest house in Conwy—at the bottom of the street, is even less exciting (£2, April–Oct daily 11:00–17:00).

St. Mary's Parish Church—Built in 1186, it's still the core of the town and worth a look for its fine interior and wispy graveyard. Originally a Cistercian church, it is actually older than the town.
Butterfly Jungle—Butterflies flutter in a steamy, lush greenhouse with tropical forest sounds. It's sweet, small, and too humid to linger long (£3.50, ticket valid all day—OK to return, 50p identification chart not necessary because charts posted inside, April–Sept daily 10:00–17:30, Oct 10:00–16:00, follow signs from harbor, pleasant 5-minute walk north, tel. 01492/593-149). If it's not busy, ask the owner why he started a butterfly house.
Pony Riding—Cowpokes mosey on down to Pinewood Riding Stables, a mile from Conwy (£11/60 min, longer and shorter rides possible, Sychnant Pass Road, past hostel, tel. 01492/592-256).
▲Bodnant Garden—This sumptuous 80-acre display of floral color is six miles south of Conwy. Set in the lush green of Snowdonia, this garden is one of Britain's best. It's famous for its magnolias, rhodies, camellias, and floral arch (£5, mid-March–Oct daily 10:00–17:00, café, best in spring, phone message tells what's blooming, tel. 01492/650-460).

Sleeping in Conwy

(£1 = about $1.60, country code: 44, area code: 01492)

Conwy has decent budget B&Bs, each located within a five-minute walk from the bus and train station. There's no launderette in town.

Gwynedd Guest House, spacious, thoughtfully decorated, and charmingly run by Margaret Young, is Conwy's best value in the city center (S-£18, D-£32, T/Q-£50, family deals, Internet access-£1/15 min, laundry-£5, parking, 2 blocks from bus stop and train station, 10 Upper Gate Street, LL32 8RF, tel. & fax 01492/596-537, cellular 0797-957-8389, e-mail: margaret.young1@virgin.net).

Culverlands Guest House has three slick, clean, woody rooms worth the five-minute walk from town (Db-£36, no kids, car park, big friendly dog, 7 Bryn Celyn, Cadnant Park, LL32 8PW, tel. 01492/596-744, Pauline and Peter Hobson). From Conwy's Lancaster Square, head west on Bangor Road, pass under city wall, turn left at Cadnant Park, cross bridge, then continue straight up Bryn Celyn cul-de-sac.

Bryn B&B offers five large, clutter-free rooms in a big 19th-century house with the city wall right in the backyard (Sb-£20–23, Db-£36–40, 1 ground-floor room, parking, use of backyard, travel recommendations, possible day tours, Sychnant Pass Road, LL32 8NS, immediately outside upper gate of wall, tel. 01492/592-449, www.bryn.org.uk, Janet Shaw).

Town House B&B rents six tidy, bright rooms—some with views—near the entrance of the castle (S-£16, D-£32, Db-£38, nonsmoking, parking, Rosehill Street 18, LL32 3LD, tel. 01492/596-454, cellular 0797-465-0609, Alan and Elaine Naughton).

Swan Cottage B&B is a homey place near the harborfront renting three comfortable rooms (D/Db-£32 with this book, both D rooms have harbor view, top floor best, 18 Berry Street, LL32 8DG, tel. 01492/596-840, Mr. and Mrs. Roberts).

Castle Bank Hotel has nine spacious rooms run by the gracious Karen Morton, who also serves optional dinners with the help of her kids, for £12.50 to £15 (Sb-£35, Db-£57, 10 percent discount with this book, CC:VM, nonsmoking, easy parking, Mount Pleasant, LL32 8NY, tel. 01492/593-888, fax 01492/596-466, e-mail: castlebank@bun.com).

Llys Llywelyn B&B, next door and faded in comparison, still has a stately feel, with nine rooms, a big lounge, and some castle views (Sb-£20, Db-£39, CC:VM, mention this book for a discount, nonsmoking rooms and veggie options available, can check e-mail, easy parking, will pick you up from station if you request it in advance, just outside the town wall at Mount Pleasant, LL32 8NY, tel. 01492/593-257, e-mail: llys-llewelyn@talk21.com, Alan Hughes).

The Bridge Inn rents six new, brightly decorated rooms above its pub. The floor just above the pub is noisy, particularly on weekend nights; the top floor is quieter (Sb-£35, Db-£60, cheaper off-season, CC:VM, some views, nonsmoking, separate entrance from pub, tel. 01492/573-482, www.bridge-conwy.co.uk).

Bryn Derwen, an eight-minute walk from town, is in a near-mansion atop a hill, set back from a busy road. Most of its six rooms are pink and frilly without being sugary (Db-£38, antlered breakfast room with medieval-type table; exit train station from its farthest and lowest corner, go through gate in city wall to busy road—Woodlands—and turn right, look for sign, then stiff 1-minute climb to hotel, Woodlands, LL32 8LT, tel. 01492/596-134). The **Glan Heulog Guest House,** next door in the other half of the mansion, isn't as nice for the same price (tel. 01492/593-845).

The big, old **Castle Hotel** in the town center rents 29 decent but pricey rooms (Sb-£60, Db-£80, cheaper for 2-night stays, Db-£50-76, CC:VMA, halls musty though rooms OK, nonsmoking rooms available, High Street, LL32 8DB, tel. 01492/592-324, fax 01492/583-351, e-mail: reply@marketsite.co.uk).

The **Conwy Hostel,** welcoming travelers of any age, has super views from all its rooms (including 12 bunk-bed doubles). Each room is equipped with either two or four bunk beds and a shower; WCs are down the hall. The airy dining hall and glorious rooftop deck make you feel you're in the majestic midst of Wales (Db-£30, bed in quad-£12, Internet access, laundry, lockers, dinners, elevator, parking, 10-minute uphill walk from upper gate of Conwy's wall, Larkhill, Sychnant Pass Road, book in advance for doubles, tel. 01492/593-571, fax 01492/593-580, e-mail: conwy@yha.org.uk).

Eating in Conwy

When hungry in Conwy, stroll down High Street comparing the cute teahouses and smoky pubs. At the top, on Lancaster Square, is **Alfredo's Restaurant,** a family-friendly place that serves good and reasonable Italian food (nightly 18:00–22:00, CC:VM, tel. 01492/592-381). At the bottom of High Street two fish-and-chips joints—**Galleon's** and **Fisherman's**—brag they're the best. Locals like **Anna's Tea Rooms,** located upstairs within the Conwy Outdoor shop (daily 10:00–17:00, CC:VM, near Fisherman's, 9 Castle Street, tel. 01492/580-908). The tiny **Wall Place** on Chapel Street has vegetarian cuisine and one chef; service is sloooow but everything is freshly made (June–Sept daily 12:00–15:00, 19:00–22:00, April–May open weekends and some weekdays, closed Oct–March, tel. 01492/596-326). **The Bridge** pub, at the intersection of Rosehill and Castle Streets, has good food (daily 12:00–14:30, until 19:30 Easter–Sept). The best cheap meal in town is either a picnic from the **Spar grocery** (daily 8:00–22:00, top of High Street) or fish and chips on the harborfront with the locals.

Transportation Connections—Conwy

Be proactive whether taking the bus or train; let the driver or conductor know you want to stop at Conwy. Consider getting train times and connections for your onward journey at a bigger station before you get to Conwy. For train information in Conwy, ask at the TI or call 08457-484-950. If you want to depart Conwy by train, flag down the train. For a quick pick of more frequent trains, catch a bus—or walk a mile—from Conwy to Llandudno Junction.

Conwy to: Llandudno Junction (2 buses/hrly, 5 min; 4 trains/day, 5 min), **Caernarfon** (hrly, 1 hr), **Trefriw–Betws-y-Coed–Penygwryd–Llanberis** (bus #19, hrly in summer).

Llandudno Junction by train to: Chester (2/hrly, 1 hr), **Birmingham** (2/hrly, 2.5 hrs), **London's Euston Station** (hrly, 3.5 hrs).

CAERNARFON

The small and lively little town of Caernarfon (kah-NAR-von) is famous for its striking castle—the place where the Prince of Wales is "invested." The old garrison town still marches out from the castle following the original medieval grid plan laid within its well-preserved ramparts.

But Caernarfon is mostly a 19th-century town. Then, the most important thing in town wasn't the castle but the area—now a parking lot—that sprawls below the castle. This was once a booming slate port shipping tidy bundles of slate from North Wales mining towns to roofs all over Europe.

The statue of local boy David Lloyd George looks over the

town square. A member of parliament from 1890 to 1945, he was the most important politician Wales ever sent to London and ultimately became Britain's prime minister. Boy George began his career as a noisy nonconformist liberal advocating Welsh rights. He ended up an eloquent spokesperson for the notion of Great Britain, convincing his slate-mining constituents that only as part of the Union would their slate industry boom.

A small but lively town, Caernarfon bustles with shops, cafés, and people. Market-day activities fill its main square on Saturdays year-round; a smaller, sleepy market yawns on Monday from late May to September. The charming grid-plan medieval town is worth a wander.

Tourist Information: The TI, across from the castle entrance, sells a wonderful town map/guide (50p), has train and bus schedules, sells hiking books, and books rooms here and elsewhere for a £1 fee (April–Oct daily 10:00–18:00, Nov–March daily 9:30–16:30 with a 13:00–13:30 lunch break, tel. 01286/672-232). Donna "Caernarfon is more than a castle" Goodman leads historic walks several times a week in July and August (£3, 1.5 hrs, call 01286/677-059 for her schedule).

Arrival in Caernarfon: If you arrive by bus, walk a few steps to Bridge Street, go left until you hit the main square and—bingo—there's the castle. The TI is opposite the entrance. Public WCs are off the main square, on the road down to the harbor parking lot. Drivers pay £2 to park.

Helpful Hints: Within a couple of blocks of the bus stop, you'll find an Internet café (Dimensiwm 4, Mon–Sat 10:00–18:00, closed Sun, Turf Square), the post office (main square), and Pete's Laundromat (£4 same-day full service, £3 self-serve, daily 9:00–17:30, Skinner Street).

The only car rental agency in town is Caernarfon Rent-a-Car (on the harbor, 2 Slate Quay, tel. 01286/676-171). Two shops rent bikes: Cycle Hire (£11/day, on the harbor, tel. 01286/676-804) and Beics Castell (£13/day, includes helmets, closed Thu and Sun, High Street, tel. 01286/677-400).

Ainsworth's, a fish-and-chips joint, is at 31 Bridge Street, and plenty of sandwich shops and tearooms line nearby High Street. The nearest supermarket is Kwik Save, with a larger Safeway a block beyond (a 5-minute walk from city center on Bangor Street).

Sights—Caernarfon

▲▲Caernarfon Castle—Edward I built this impressive castle 700 years ago to establish English rule over North Wales. Modeled after the striped and angular walls of ancient Constantinople, the castle—while impressive—was never finished and never really used. From the inner courtyard you can see the notched walls ready for more walls that were never built. Its fame is due to its physical grandeur and from its association with the Prince of Wales. The English king got the angry Welsh to agree that if he presented them with "a prince, born in Wales who spoke not a word of English," they would submit to the crown. In time, Edward had a son... born in Wales... who spoke not a word of English, Welsh, or any other language. In modern times, as another political maneuver, the Prince of Wales has been "invested" (given his title) here. This "tradition" actually dates only from the 20th century and only 2 of 21 Princes of Wales have taken part.

In spite of its disappointing history, it's a great castle to tour. An essential part of any visit is the guided tour (50-minute tours for £1.50 leave on the hour from the courtyard steps just beyond the ticket booth; if you're late, ask to join one in progress). In the huge Eagle Tower (on the seaward side) see the "Chieftains and Princes" history exhibit (ground floor), watch the 20-minute movie (a broad mix of Welsh legend and history, shown on the hour and half hour, upstairs, comfortable theater seats), and climb the tower for a great view. The tower at the opposite end of the castle has an exhibit about the investiture of Prince Charles in 1969 (£4.20, June–Sept daily 9:30–18:00, April–May and Oct daily 9:30–17:00, Nov–March Mon–Sat 9:30–16:00, Sun 11:00–16:00; CC:VM, can store luggage during visit, tel. 01286/677-617). Martin de Lewandowicz gives mind-bending tours of the castle (tel. 01286/674-369).

Distractions—A Welsh Highland **steam train** billows through the countryside to Waunfawr and back (£7.60, May–Sept daily, April and Oct weekends only, 4/day, 1.5 hrs, tel. 01766/512-340, www.restrail.co.uk). Narrated **harbor cruises** on the "Queen of the Sea" run daily in summer (June–Sept 11:00–18:00 or 19:00, depending on weather, tides, and demand, 40 min, castle views, tel. 01286/672-772). The **Segontium Roman Fort**, dating from A.D. 77, was manned for more than 300 years to keep the Welsh and the coast quiet. Little is left but foundations (small museum, 15-minute walk from town, tel. 01286/675-625). For **pony riding**, try Snowdonia Riding Stables (£12/1 hr, longer and shorter time available, 3 miles from Caernarfon, off the road to Beddgelert, bus #89 or #95 from Caernarfon, tel. 01286/650-342).

Men's Choir—If spending the night, consider dropping by the local men's choir practice (Tue 20:00–21:30, Conservative Club on High Street).

Sleeping in Caernarfon

(£1 = about $1.60, country code: 44, area code: 01286)

Isfryn B&B is just down the street from the castle and overlooks the water (6 rooms, S-£19, D-£37, Db-£42, family deals, 11 Church Street, LL5 51SW, tel. & fax 01286/675-628, Graham).

B&Bs cling to St. David's Road, past the roundabout and near the Safeway on the edge of town nearest Conwy. **Bryn Hyfryd** has five pleasant rooms and a light-wood design (Db-£34–40, St. David's Road, LL551EL, tel. 01286/673-840, cellular 0777-562-7299, Mrs. Royle). **Marianfa**, a few doors closer to town, charges the same but isn't quite as nice (tel. 01286/675-589, Mrs. Ashcroft). To reach St. David's Road from the bus stop, turn right on Bridge Street and follow it to the roundabout, then veer to the far right.

For a splurge, it's the **Celtic Royal Hotel**, with 110 comfortable rooms, a gym, pool, Jacuzzi, and sauna. Its grand, old-fashioned look comes with modern-day conveniences (Db-£70–90, deals for 2-night stays, CC:VM, nonsmoking rooms available, bar, restaurant; from bus stop, go right on Bridge Street, turns into Bangor Street, 5-minute walk; Bangor Street, LL55 1AY, tel. 01286/674-477, fax 01286/674-139, www.nwi.co.uk/celticroyal).

Totters Hostel is a creative little hostel well run by Bob and Henriette (30 beds in 5 dorm rooms, £10 per bed with sheets, includes continental breakfast; couples can have their own room when available; open all day, lockers, welcoming game room/lounge, use of kitchen, a block from the castle at 2 High Street, tel. 01286/672-963, www.applemaps.co.uk/totters).

Transportation Connections—Caernarfon

Caernarfon by bus to: Conwy (2/hrly, hrly on Sun, 1.25 hrs, buy ticket on bus), **Llanberis** (2/hrly, 30 min), **Beddgelert** (hrly, 30 min), **Blaenau-Ffestiniog** (hrly buses, 1.5 hrs), **Beddgelert–Penygwryd–Llanberis** (bus #95, every 2 hrs, 1.5 hrs, June–Sept only).

SNOWDONIA NATIONAL PARK

Snowdonia National Park is Britain's second-largest national park, with Mount Snowdon—the tallest mountain in England and Wales—as its centerpiece. Each year half a million people choose one of seven different paths to the top of 3,560-foot Snowdon (the small book *The Ascent of Snowdon*, by E. G. Bowland, describes the routes, £2, sold by local TIs). Hikes take from five to seven hours. If you're reasonably fit and the weather cooperates, it's an exciting day. Trail info abounds. As you explore the area, notice the slate roofs—they're the local specialty.

Sights—Snowdonia

Betws-y-Coed—The resort center of Snowdonia National Park, Betwys-y-Coed (BET-oos-uh-coyd) bursts with tour buses and souvenir shops. Its good national park, TI, and guided walks are the only reasons to stop here (April–Oct daily 10:00–18:00, Nov–March daily 9:30–13:00, 14:00–16:30, tel. 01690/710-426). Consider a long, guided walk (£3.50, April–Sept Thu–Sun, depart TI at 10:00, 6–8 mile hike, £5 ascent of Mt. Snowdon on Fri only, any public transport extra, booking in advance with TI is advisable but not necessary).

Snowdonia Area

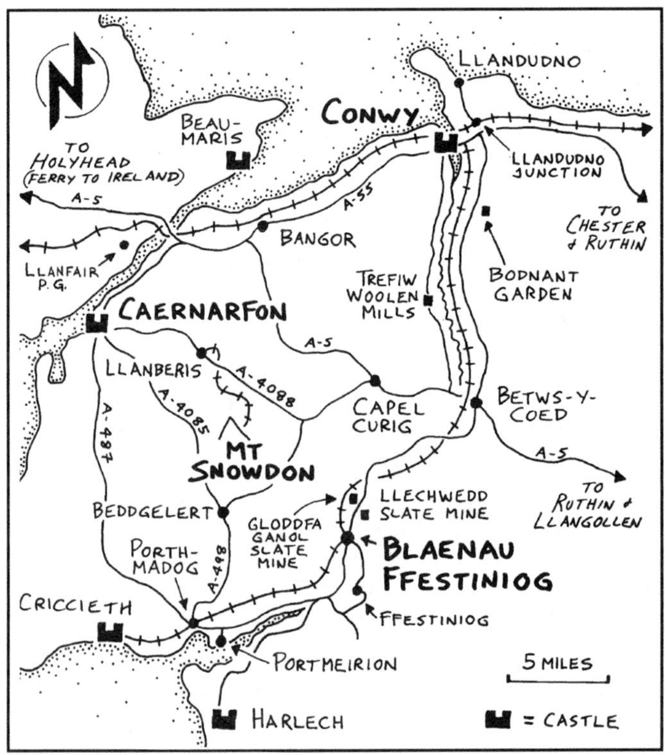

If you drive west out of town on A5, after two miles you'll see the car park for scenic Swallow Falls, a pleasant five-minute walk from the road. A half mile past the falls on the right you'll see "The Ugly House," built overnight to take advantage of a 15th-century law that let any quickie building avoid fees and taxes. Buses connect Conwy and Betws-y-Coed (#19, hrly June–Aug, 50 min). Trains run from the north coast through Betws-y-Coed to Blaenau (6/day).

Trefriw Woolen Mills—The mill in Trefriw (TREV-roo), five miles north of Betws-y-Coed, is free and surprisingly interesting if the machines are running (April–Oct Mon–Fri 10:00–13:00, 14:00–17:30, same hours off-season, but only weaving is demonstrated, tel. 01492/640-462). Follow the 11 stages of wool transformation: warping, weaving, carding, hanking, spanking, spinning, and so on. From June to September, the hand-spinning house (next to the WC) has a charming spinster and a petting cupboard filled with all the fibers that can be spun into cloth. Be sure to enjoy the fine woolen shop, the pleasant town (more so than Betws-y-Coed), and the coffee shop. The woolen mill at Penmachno (also near Betws-y-Coed) is smaller and less interesting.

Beddgelert—This is the quintessential Snowdon village, packing a scenic mountain punch without the tourist crowds (17 miles from Betws-y-Coed). Set on a river in the shadow of Snowdon and her sisters, with a fine variety of hikes from its doorstep and pretty good bus service, Beddgelert (BETH-geh-let) makes a good stop for those wanting to experience the peace of Snowdonia.

Locals can recommend walks. You can follow the lane along the river (3 miles round-trip), walk down the river and around the hill (3 hrs, 6 miles, 900-foot gain, via Cwm Bycham), hike along (or around) Llyn Gwynant Lake and four miles back to Beddgelert (ride the bus to the lake), or try the more dramatic higher ridge walks on Moel Hebog (Hawk Hill).

Sleeping in Bleddgelert: Plas Tan Y Graig Guest House, at the village bridge, is a good value (D-£35, Db-£45, CC:VM, family room, fine lounge, tea garden, LL55 4LT, tel. 01766/890-329, fax 01766/890-629, www.nwi.co.uk/plastanygraig/). Also just over the bridge, Brian Wheatley rents six rooms at **Plas-Gwyn,** a 19-century townhouse (Sb-£18, Db-£40, nonsmoking, tel. 01766/890-215, www.plas-gwyn.com). The **Royal Goat Hotel** offers well-worn, chandeliered, woody elegance in a grand hotel built for the rugged 19th-century aristocrat (Sb-£44, Db-£74, cheaper for 2-night stays, some nonsmoking rooms, CC:VMA, tel. 01766/890-224, fax 01766/890-422).

Mountaineers note that this area was used by Sir Edmund Hillary and his men as they practiced for the first ascent of Mount Everest. The **Pen-y-Gwryd Hotel Pub** (at the top of the pass north of Beddgelert) is strewn with fascinating Hillary and Everest memorabilia (D-£46, Db-£56, saggy beds, smoky, old-time-elegant public rooms, those in D rooms get to use museum-piece Victorian tubs, grand five-course dinners-£17, tel. 01286/870-211). With a crampon ambience, this is ideal for well-bred hikers.

Llanberis—A town of 2,000 people with as many tourists on a sunny day, Llanberis is a popular base for Snowdon activities. Along with the station for the Snowdon train, there is a good information center, a few touristy museums, pony trekking, and good bus connections (hrly buses to Beddgelert, 45 min).

Sleeping in Llanberis: Consider **Dolafon Hotel**, an 1860s Victorian building with seven traditionally furnished rooms (1 D with private bath down the hall-£40, Db-£48, large Db-£55, nonsmoking, garden, High Street, tel. & fax 01286/870-993, www.dolafon.co.uk).

▲▲Mount Snowdon and the Mountain Railway—The easiest and most popular ascent of Mount Snowdon is by the Snowdon

Mountain Railway, a rack-and-pinion railway from 1896 that climbs 3,500 feet over 4.5 miles from Llanberis to the summit (£16.50 round-trip, 2.5 hours, includes 30-minute stop at the summit, CC:VM, tel. 01286/870-223). Family discounts are offered all day except from mid-July through August, when discounts are given only for the early trains (up to and including 10:00 departure).

The first departure is usually at 9:00. While the schedule flexes with weather and demand, they try to run several trips a day mid-March through October (2/hrly in peak season). On sunny summer days, trains fill up (waits are longer in the afternoon; arrive by lunchtime and get a departure appointment time—usually a wait of an hour or two). Off-season trains often stop short of the summit (due to snow and high winds).

BLAENAU FFESTINIOG

This quintessential Welsh slate-mining town is notable for its slate-mine tour and its old steam train. The town—a dark, poor place—seems to struggle on, oblivious to the tourists who nip in and out. Take a walk. The shops are right out of the 1950s. Long rows of humble "two up and two down" houses (four rooms) feel pretty grim. There are some buses from the town to the slate mines; the road isn't pedestrian friendly. (TI, daily 10:00–13:00, 14:00–18:00, closed Oct–Easter, tel. 01766/830-360.)

Sights—Blaenau Ffestiniog

▲▲Llechwedd Slate-Mine Tour—Slate mining played a blockbuster role in Welsh heritage, and this mine on the northern edge of the bleak town of Blaenau Ffestiniog (BLIGH-nigh FES-tin-yog) does a fine job of explaining the mining culture of Victorian Wales. The Welsh mined and split most of the slate roofs of Europe. For every ton of usable slate found, 10 tons were mined. The exhibit has three parts: a tiny Victorian mining town (free and worthwhile) and two 30-minute tours. The "deep mine" tour features an audiovisual dramatization of social life, a serious descent, and a half mile of walking. The "tramway" tour is a level train ride with two stops, no walking, and a live guide; it focuses on working life and traditional mining techniques. Both are different and, considering the cheap combo-ticket, worthwhile. Don't miss the slate-splitting demonstration at the end of the tramway tour (£6.95 for 1 tour, £10.50 for both, March–Sept daily 10:00–18:00, Oct–Feb closes at 17:00, last tour starts 45 minutes before closing, tel. 01766/830-306). Dress warmly—I mean it. You'll freeze underground without a sweater.

▲Ffestiniog Railway—This 13-mile narrow-gauge train line was built in 1836 for small horse-drawn wagons to transport the slate from the Ffestiniog mines to the port of Porthmadog. In the 1860s horses gave way to steam trains. Today hikers and tourists enjoy these tiny titans (£13 round-trip, hrly, 2.5 hrs round-trip; diesel trains are £2 cheaper, first-class observation cars are £5 extra, tel. 01766/512-340). This is a novel steam train experience, but the full-size Llandudno–Blaenau Ffestiniog train is more scenic and works better for hikers.

Portmeirion—Ten miles southwest of Blaenau Ffestiniog, this "Italian Village" was the lifework of a rich local architect who began building it in 1925. Set idyllically on the coast just beyond the poverty of the slate-mine towns, flower-filled fantasy is extravagant. Surrounded by lush Welsh greenery and a windswept mudflat at low tide, the village is an artistic glob of palazzo arches, fountains, gardens, and promenades filled with cafés, tacky shops, a hotel, and local tourists who always wanted to go to Italy (or who are fans of the cultish British 1960s TV series *The Prisoner*). The architect explains his purpose in a videotaped slide presentation. Not worth the £5 (daily 9:30–17:30, 2 miles from Porthmadog, tel. 01766/770-228).

Transportation Connections—North Wales

Two major transfer points out of (or into) North Wales are Chester and Crewe.

Chester by train to: London (hrly, 3 hrs), **Liverpool** (2/hrly, 50 min), **Birmingham** (2/hrly, 2 hrs), points in **North Wales** (2/hrly).

Crewe by train to: London (2/hrly, 2 hrs), **Bristol**, near Bath (hrly, 2.5 hrs), **Cardiff** (hrly, 2.5 hrs), **Holyhead** (nearly hrly, 2.25 hrs), **Blackpool** (4/day, 2.5 hrs, more frequent with transfer in Preston), **Penrith**, near Lake District (hrly, 1.75 hrs), **Glasgow** (nearly hrly, 3.5 hrs).

Ferry Connections—North Wales and Ireland

Holyhead and Dun Laoghaire: Stena Line sails between Holyhead (North Wales) and Dun Laoghaire near Dublin (4/day, 2 hrs on *HSS Catamaran*, £36 one-way walk-on fare, reserve by phone—they book up long in advance on summer weekends, Dun Laoghaire tel. 01/204-7777, Holyhead tel. 01407/606-666, general reservations number for Stena Lines in Britain: 08705-707-070, can book online at www.stenaline.ie).

Holyhead and Dublin: Irish Ferries sail between Holyhead (North Wales) and Dublin (5/day—2 slow, 3 fast; slow boats-3.25 hrs, £20 one-way walk-on fare; fast boats-1.75 hrs, £25; car fares prohibitively expensive, Holyhead tel. 08705-329-129, Dublin tel. 01/661-0511, www.irishferries.ie).

Sleeping near Holyhead dock: The fine Monravon B&B has nine smoke-free rooms (Db-£35, CC:VM, family deals, 10-minute walk from dock, Porth-Y-Felin Road, LL65 1PL, tel. & fax 01407/762-944, e-mail: len@monravon.com).

Route Tips for Drivers

Ironbridge Gorge to Ruthin: Drive for an hour to Wales via A5 through Shrewsbury, crossing into Wales at the pretty castle town of Chirk. There, take A5 to Llangollen. Cross the bridge in Llangollen, turn left, and follow A542 and A525 past the romantic Valle Crucis abbey, over the scenic Horseshoe Pass, and into Ruthin. Driving to Conwy is faster via Wrexham and then the A55.

Ruthin to Caernarfon (56 miles) to Blaenau (34 miles) to Ruthin (35 miles): This route connects the top sights with the most scenic routes. From Ruthin take B5105 (steepest road off main square) and follow signs to Cerrigydrudion. Then follow A5 into Betws-y-Coed, with a possible quick detour to the Trefriw Woolen Mill (five miles north on B5106, well signposted). Climb west on A5 through Capel Curig, then take A4086 over the rugged Pass of Llanberis, under the summit of Mount Snowdon (to the south, behind those clouds), and on to Caernarfon. Park under the castle in the harborside car park (£2).

Leaving Caernarfon, take the lovely A4085 southeast through Beddgelert to Penrhyndeudraeth. (Make things even more beautiful by taking the little B4410 road from Garreg through Rhyd.) Then take A487 toward What Maentwrog and A496 to Blaenau Ffestiniog. Go through the dark, depressing mining town of Blaenau Ffestiniog on A470 into hills of slate and turn right into the Llechwedd Slate Mine.

After the mine, continue uphill on A470, snapping photos north through Dolwyddelan (passing a fine old Welsh castle ruin) and back to A5. For a high and desolate detour, return to Ruthin via the windy, curvy A543 road over the stark moors to the Sportsman's Arms Pub (the highest pub in Wales, good food), through Denbigh, and home.

BLACKPOOL

This is Britain's fun puddle. It's England's most-visited attraction, the private domain of its working class, a faded and sticky mix of Coney Island, Las Vegas, and Woolworth's. Juveniles of any age love it. My kids declared it better than Disneyland.

Blackpool grew up with the Industrial Revolution. In the mid-1800s entire mill towns would close down and take a two-week break in Blackpool. They came to drink in the fresh air—much needed after a hard year in the mills—and the seawater. (Back then they figured this was healthy.) Blackpool's heydays are past now, as more and more working people can afford the cheap charter flights to sunny Spain. Still, this is an accessible and affordable fun zone for the Anne and Andy Capps of northern England. People come year after year. They stay for a week, and they love it.

Most Americans don't even consider a stop in Blackpool. Many won't like it. It's an ears-pierced-while-you-wait, tipsy-toupee kind of place. Tacky, yes. Lowbrow, OK. But it's as English as can be, and that's what you're here for. An itinerary should feature as many facets of a culture as possible. Blackpool is as English as the queen—and considerably more fun.

Spend the day "muckin' about" the beach promenade of fortune-tellers, fish-and-chips joints, amusement piers, warped mirrors, and Englanders wearing hats with built-in ponytails. A million greedy doors try every trick to get you inside. Huge arcade halls advertise free toilets and broadcast bingo numbers into the streets; the wind machine under a wax Marilyn Monroe blows at a steady gale; and the smell of fries, tobacco, and sugar is everywhere. Milk comes in raspberry or banana in this land where people under incredibly bad wigs look normal. If you're bored in Blackpool, you're just too classy.

Planning Your Time

Ideally, get to Blackpool around lunchtime for a free afternoon and evening of making bubbles in this cultural mud puddle. For full effect, it's best to visit Blackpool during its peak season: June through early November. Blackpool's Illuminations (Aug 31–Nov 4 in 2001), when much of the waterfront is decorated with lights, draws crowds (particularly on weekends).

Blackpool is easy by car or train. Speed demons with a car can treat it as a midday break (it's just off the M6 on M55) and continue north. If you have kids, they'll want more time here (hey, it's cheaper than Disneyland). If you're into nightlife, this town delivers. If you're before or beyond kids and not into kitsch and greasy spoons, skip it. If the weather's great and you love nature, the lakes are just a few hours north. A visit to Blackpool does sharpen the wonders of Windermere.

Orientation
(area code: 01253)

Everything clusters along the six-mile beachfront promenade, a tacky, glittering strip mall of fun. The three amusement piers are the sedate North Pier (with theatre), the something-for-everyone Central Pier (rides plus theatre), and the rollicking South Pier (all rides; the theatre was replaced by a roller coaster). The piers were originally built for Victorian landlubbers who wanted to go to sea but were afraid of getting seasick. The Pleasure Beach rides are near the South Pier. Jutting up near the North Pier is Blackpool's stubby Eiffel-type tower. The most interesting shops, eateries, and theaters are inland from the North Pier. For a break from glitz, you can hike north along the waterfront path for, say, 20 miles or so.

Tourist Information: There are two TIs near the tower. The main one is on Clifton Street (April–early Nov Mon–Sat 9:00–17:00, Sun 10:00–16:00, early-Nov–March Mon–Sat 9:00–16:30 and closed Sun, tel. 01253/478-222, the same number gives recorded entertainment info after hours). The other TI is on the Promenade (June–early Nov). Get the city map (50p), pick up brochures on the amusement centers, and ask about special shows. The TIs do same-day room bookings for one-night stays for a £2 fee.

For a history fix, get the TI's *Heritage Trail* booklet, which takes you on an hour's walk through downtown Blackpool. Saying much about little, it's endearing (60p).

Arrival in Blackpool: The train station is just three blocks from the town center (no maps given but one is posted, no ATM in station but many in town). The motorway funnels you down Yeadon Way into a giant parking zone (formerly the central station).

Helpful Hints

Internet Access: Cafe Net has computers and munchies (£1.50/30 min, Mon–Sat 10:00–16:00, until 20:00 in summer, Deansgate 16, between TI and train station).

Post Office: The main P.O. is on Abingdon Street, a block inland from the TI (Mon–Sat 9:00–17:30).

Markets: At the work-a-day Abingdon Market, vendors sell fruit, bras, jewelry, eggs, and more (Mon–Sat 9:00–17:30, also Sun 10:00–16:00 during Illuminations, on Abingdon Street next to P.O). The Fleetwood Market, eight miles north, is huge, with two buildings full of produce, clothes, and crafts spilling out into the street (May–Oct: daily 9:00–17:00 except Wed and Sun; Nov–April: Tue, Fri, Sat only; catch trolley marked Fleetwood, 30 min, £1.60 one-way).

Car Rental: In case you decide to tour the Lake District by car, you'll find plenty of rental agencies in Blackpool, including Avis (292 Waterloo Road, tel. 01253/408-003), Budget (434 Waterloo Road, tel. 01253/691-632), and Hertz (181 Clifton Drive, tel. 01232/404-021).

Getting around Blackpool

Vintage trolley cars run 13 miles up and down the waterfront, connecting all the sights. This first electric tramway in Europe dates from 1885 (90p–£2, depending on length of trip, £4.50 for all-day pass, pay conductor, trolleys come every 5 minutes or so, Nov–May every 10–20 minutes, runs 6:00–24:00). Taxis are easy to snare in Blackpool.

Sights—Blackpool

▲Blackpool Tower—This mini–Eiffel Tower is a vertical fun center over 100 years old. You pay £10 to get in; after that, the fun is free. Work your way up from the bottom through layer after layer of noisy entertainment: circus (2–3 acts a day Sat–Thu, usually around 14:00 and 19:30, no circus on Fri, daredevil act instead), space world, dinosaur land, aquarium, and a wonderful old ballroom with barely live music and golden oldies dancing to golden oldies all day. Enjoy a break at the dance-floor-level pub or on a balcony perch. Kids love this place. With a little marijuana, adults would, too. Ride the elevator to the tip of the 500-foot-tall symbol of Blackpool for a smashing view, especially at sunset (Easter–May daily 10:00–18:00, June–early Nov daily 10:00–23:00, early Nov–Easter 10:00–18:00 weekends only, tower closed when windy, CC:VM, tel. 01253/622-242). If you want to leave the Tower and return, request a wristband.

▲Pleasure Beach—These 42 acres, littered with more than 145 rides (including "the best selection of white-knuckle rides in Europe"), ice-skating shows, cabarets, and amusements attract

Blackpool

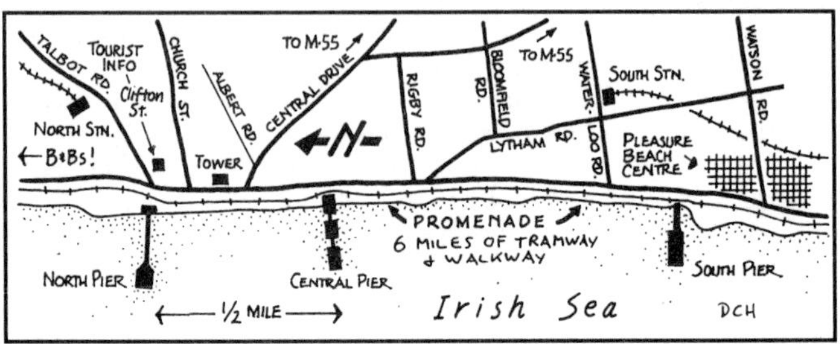

7 million people a year. The Pepsi Max Big One is "the world's fastest and highest" roller coaster (235 feet, 85 mph). Ice Blast rockets you straight up before letting you bungee down. Also memorable is the Passage de Terror and a frightening race called the Steeple Chase—imagine carousel horses stampeding down a roller-coaster track. The latest ride, Valhalla, zips you on a Viking boat in watery darkness past scary Nordic things like lutefisk. Admission is free. You can pay individually for rides (most are a couple of pounds each) or you can get ride tickets for about £22 for 12–16 rides (mid-April–early Nov daily, opens at 12:00 weekdays, 10:00 weekends, closes as early as 17:00 or as late as 24:00, depending on season, weather, and demand, tel. 01253/341-033 or 0870-444-5566). There are several other major amusement centers, including a popular water park called Sand Castle (across the street from Pleasure Beach, tel. 01253/343-602).

▲▲▲People Watching—Blackpool's top sight is its people. You'll see England here as nowhere else. Grab someone's hand and a big stick of "rock" (candy) and stroll. Grown men walk around with huge teddies looking for "bowlingo" places. Ponder the thought of actually retiring here and spending your last years, day after day, surrounded by Blackpool and wearing a hat with a built-in ponytail. Blackpool puts people in a talkative mood. Ask someone to explain the difference between tea and supper.

▲▲Variety Show—Blackpool always has a few razzle-dazzle music, dancing-girl, racy-humor, magic, and tumbling shows. Box offices around town can give you a rundown on what's available (tickets £7–15). I enjoy the old-time music-hall shows. They're corny—neither hip nor polished—but it's fascinating to be surrounded by hundreds of partying British seniors swooning and waving their hankies to the predictable beat. Busloads of happy widows come from all corners of North England to giggle at jokes I'd never tell my grandma. Your B&B has the latest.

For something more highbrow, try the Opera House for musicals (tel. 01253/292-029) and the Grand Theatre for drama and ballet (tel. 01253/290-190). Both are on Church Street, a couple of blocks behind the Tower.

▲▲**Funny Girls**—Blackpool's current hot bar is just a block from the North Pier. Every night from 20:30 to 23:30 Funny Girls puts on a "glam bam thank you ma'am" burlesque-in-drag show that delights footballers and grannies alike. Cover is only £3 (£4.50 on weekends). Get your drinks at the bar unless the transvestites are dancing on it. The show, while racy, is not raunchy. The music is very loud. The crowd is young, old, straight, gay, very down-to-earth, and fun loving. Go on a weeknight; Friday and Saturday are too jammed. You can pay £5 to £10 for VIP seats to avoid any weekend lines and look down on the show and crowded floor from a mezzanine level (to book, call 01253/624-901).

Blackpool's clubs and discos are cheap, with live bands and an interesting crowd (22:00–01:00). The pubs of Blackpool have a unique tradition of "and your own, luv." Say that here and your barmaid will add 20p to your bill and drop it into her tip jar. (Say it anywhere else and they won't know what you mean.)

▲**Illuminations**—Blackpool was the first town in England to "go electric" in 1879. Now, every fall (Aug 31–Nov 4 in 2001), Blackpool stretches its tourist season by illuminating its six miles of waterfront with countless lights, all blinking and twinkling. The American in me kept saying, "I've seen bigger, and I've seen better," but I filled his mouth with cotton candy and just had some simple fun like everyone else on my specially decorated tram. Look for the animated tableaux on North Shore.

Sleeping in Blackpool

(£1 = about $1.60, country code: 44, area code: 01253)

Sleep Code: **S** = Single, **D** = Double/Twin, **T** = Triple, **Q** = Quad, **b** = bathroom, **t** = toilet only, **s** = shower only, **CC** = Credit Card (**V**isa, **M**asterCard, **A**mex).

Blackpool's 140,000 people provide 120,000 beds in 3,500 mostly dumpy, cheap, nondescript hotels and B&Bs. Remember, the town's in the business of accommodating the people who can't afford to go to Spain. Most have the same design—minimal character, maximum number of springy beds—and charge £15 to £18 per person. Empty beds abound except September through November and summer weekends. It's only really tight on Illumination weekends. When a price range is given in these listings, the higher prices are charged during the Illuminations. Prices are soft off-season.

Laundry: There are a couple of laundrettes, neither central to my recommended accommodations (sorry): Albert Road Launderette (£4-you do it, £6-they do it, but they don't guarantee same-day service, Mon–Sat 9:00–18:00, Sat 9:00–16:00, Sun 10:00–14:00, downtown—7 blocks inland—at Albert Road and Regent Road, tel. 01253/293-305) and Central Laundry (£3-self-serve, £5–7 full-serve with same-day service, daily 8:30–16:00, 105 Central Drive, at intersection with Louise Street).

Sleeping North of the Tower

These listings are on the waterfront in the quiet area they call "the posh end," a mile or two north of the tower, with easy parking and easy access to the center by trolley. The last two listings (big hotels) are closer to the tower.

Robin Hood Hotel is a super place, cheery and family run, with a big, welcoming living room and 10 newly and tastefully refurbished rooms and the only sturdy beds I found (Sb-£21–26, Db-£36–42, less for two nights, family deals, CC:VM, entirely nonsmoking, trolley stop: St. Stevens Avenue and walk 1 block north; 1.5 miles north of tower across from a peaceful stretch of beach, 100 Queens Promenade, North Shore FY2 9NS, tel. 01253/351-599, Pam and Colin Webster).

Beechcliffe Private Hotel is clean, smoke free, and family run, with more charm than average (S-£15–17.50, D-£30–35, Dt-£33–38, Tt-£50–55, trolley stop: Uncle Tom's, walk a block away from the beach, can pick up from station if arranged in advance, 16 Shaftesbury Avenue, North Shore FY2 9QQ, tel. 01253/353-075, David and Brenda).

Prefect Hotel is all smiles and pink-flamingo pretty. Its 13 rooms are older but clean and spacious-for-Blackpool, with fun touches—ask to see the shoe collection. You can't miss the painted parking lot (Sb-£17–21, Db-£34–42, CC:VM, smoking allowed but not in breakfast room, request a view room, trolley to Bispham, 2 miles north of tower at 204 Queens Promenade, FY2 9JS, tel. 01253/352-699, www.chesbyte.co.uk/hotel, run with warmth by Bill and Pauline Acton).

At **Burlees Hotel,** look beyond the garishly carpeted hallway to find nine bright, comfy, sedately carpeted rooms (Db-£47–52, CC:VM, 2-night stays preferred in high season, deals for families and 2-night stays, most rooms nonsmoking, double-glazed windows, trolley stop: Uncle Tom's, from Queens Promenade walk 3 blocks inland, 40 Knowle Avenue, FY2 9TQ, tel. & fax 01253/354-535, www.btinternet.com/~burleeshotel, e-mail: burleeshotel@btinternet.com, Linda and Mike Lawrence).

The following hotels are within a 5- to 10-minute walk north of the tower. At either hotel, ask if they're offering any special deals.

The **Savoy Hotel,** in a stately Victorian building, has 131 rooms and more age-old elegance than the modern Hilton, below. Request a refurbished room, which costs the same as an unrefurbished room (Db-£80, £100 during Illumination weekends, includes breakfast, £20 extra for big-windowed sea view, CC:VM, non-smoking rooms, trolley stop: Gynn Square, Queens Promenade, tel. 01253/352-561, fax 01253/500-735).

I know, staying at the **Hilton** in Blackpool is like wearing a tux to eat a falafel. But if you need a splurge, this is a grand place with lots of views, a pool, sauna, kids' playground, and comfortable rooms (Db-£100, £150 during Illuminations, request sea view—no extra charge, includes breakfast, CC:VM, nonsmoking rooms, trolley stop: Stakis Hotel, North Promenade, FY1 2JQ, tel. 01253/623-434, fax 01253/627-864, www.hilton.com).

Sleeping near the Train Station

Valentine Private Hotel is a 15-room mix of renovated, attractive rooms (with bath added) and older, cheaper rooms with a bathroom down the hall. Smoking is allowed, but the breakfast room is smoke free (S-£12–14, D-£24–28, Db-£32–36, CC:VMA, family deals, plenty of showers, 3 blocks from station; with back to tracks, exit station far right, go up Springfield 3 blocks, turn right on Dickson: 35 Dickson Road, FY1 2AT, tel. 01253/622-775, Denise and Garry Hinchliffe).

Sleeping near the South Pier

Windsor Hotel, with 12 spiffy rooms, is one of the nicer B&Bs in Blackpool (Db-£36–40, 4-poster Db-£42–46, prices jump to £65 during Illumination weekends, CC:VM, one nonsmoking floor, tight bathrooms, trolley: South Pier, car park, 2 blocks inland, 53 Dean Street, FY4 1BP, tel. 01253/400-232, fax 01253/346-886, e-mail: hazel@windsorhotel.co.uk).

Eating in Blackpool

Your hotel may serve a cheap, early-evening meal. The following places are all between the tower and the North Pier: For mushy peas and good fish and chips, go to the "world famous" **Harry Ramsden's** near the tower (£4–8, daily 11:30–19:30, Fri–Sat until 21:00, 60 The Promenade, tel. 01253/294-386). **Robert's Oyster Bar** is a fixture that actually predates the resort—as do some of its employees (daily 9:30–22:00, at the corner of West Street and the Promenade, 1 block south of North Pier, tel. 01253/621-226). Around the corner from the Oyster Bar is the **Mitre Bar** on West Street—drop in to survey the great photos of old Blackpool (Mon–Sat 11:00–23:00, Sun 12:00–22:30). **The Scullery,** across the street from the bar, serves healthy, hearty food for great prices (open at owner's whim, 10 West Street). Food in the tower is terrible, but it's not much better elsewhere. Locals like **Kwizeen** (on King Street) and **September Brasserie** (on Queen Street).

Marks & Spencer has a big supermarket in its basement (Mon–Sat 9:00–17:30, Sun 10:30–16:30, near recommended eateries, on Coronation Street and Church Street). Picnic at the beach.

Transportation Connections—Blackpool

If you're heading to (or from) Blackpool by train, you'll usually need to transfer at **Preston** (3/hrly, 30 min). Train info: tel. 08457-484-950.

Preston to: Keswick, the Lake District (hrly trains, 30 min to Penrith, then catch a bus to Keswick, hrly except Sun 3/day, 40 min), **York** (hrly, 4.5 hrs), **Edinburgh** (8/day, 3 hrs).

Points south: To **Moreton-in-Marsh** in the Cotswolds (every 2 hrs, allow 5 hrs with 2 transfers), **Bath** (hrly, 4.5–5 hrs with 2 transfers), **Conwy** in North Wales (nearly hrly, allow 3 hrs with 2 transfers). Although you'll usually have transfers, you'll find fast and frequent trains. Some trains go direct from **Blackpool** to: **London** (1/day, 3.5-4 hrs), **Liverpool** (every 2 hrs, 1.5 hrs).

Drivers entering and leaving Blackpool: As you approach Blackpool, the motorway dumps you right onto Yeadon Way, which funnels you into a huge city parking lot. Day-trippers need to park here. The quickest way out of town is to drive the Promenade to the Central Pier and turn inland. Under the bridge take an immediate left (take the exit for M55). This gets you into the huge parking lot that leads directly to the motorway.

NEAR BLACKPOOL: LIVERPOOL

Liverpool, a gritty but surprisingly enjoyable city, is a fascinating stop for Beatles fans and those who would like to look urban England straight in its eyes.

Tourist Information: One of Liverpool's TIs is in the midst of most of the sights—on the huge, tidy Albert Dock (daily 10:00–17:30, tel. 0151/708-8854). Get a free, small map (also available at station for £1). In summer, guided tours leave daily from another TI, on Queen Square (£3, mid-June–Sept, call 0151/652-3692 for schedule, also offered Sun at 14:00 year-round, TI tel. 0151/928-0630).

Arrival in Liverpool: From the train station to the Dock, it's a 20-minute walk or short ride on a bus (#1), taxi (£3), or metro (get off at James Street). When returning to the center from the Dock, it's best to walk or take the bus (since the metro makes a long loop before returning to the station). Luggage storage at station: £2, daily 7:00–22:00.

Passes: A "NMGM Eight Pass," sold for £3 at participating museums, gets you into the Maritime and Liverpool Life Museum (along with a half dozen other Liverpool museums). The TI sells a different pass, called the Waterfront Pass, for £10, which covers a ferry cruise, Beatles' Story, Museum of Liverpool Life, and the Maritime Museum. The Waterfront Pass saves you about £3 if you're already planning to do the four covered sights.

Market: On Sunday, Heritage Market transforms Stanley Dock into a commotion of clothes, fruits, veggies, sweets, and furniture (9:30–16:00).

Planning Your Time

Here's an easy day plan: From the station, take the metro to Albert Dock. At the Dock, choose among museums, shops, cafés, and the Beatles' Story. Consider a 50-minute ferry cruise on the river (departs Mersey Ferry dock, a 5-minute walk from Albert Dock). Then walk back to the station, stopping at Mathew Street if you're a Beatle fan, and browsing the central pedestrian core (Church Street, Williamson Square, and more) on the way. You'll have seen the art and the heart of the city.

Sights—Liverpool

▲Albert Dock—Opened in 1852 by Prince Albert and enclosing seven acres of water, the dock is surrounded by five-story brick warehouses. In its day, Liverpool was England's greatest seaport. It prospered as one corner of the triangular commerce of the 18th-century slave trade. As England's economy boomed, so did the port of Liverpool. From 1830 to 1930, 9 million emigrants sailed from Liverpool to find their dreams in the New World. But the port was not deep enough for the big new ships; trade declined after 1890, and by 1972 it was closed entirely. Like Liverpool itself, the docks have enjoyed a renaissance, and today they are the featured attraction of the city. The city's main attractions are lined up here out of the rain and padded by lots of shopping mall–type distractions (daily 10:00–17:30, tel. 0151/708-8838). There's plenty of parking.

▲Merseyside Maritime Museum—This museum, which tells the story of this once-prosperous shipping center, gets an A for effort but feels designed for visiting school groups. The ships section is pretty dull, but the smuggling and customs, slavery, and emigration sections are interesting. The associated **Museum of Liverpool Life** offers a good look at the town's story (£3 "NMGM Eight Pass" covers both; daily 10:00–17:00).

Tate Gallery Liverpool—This prestigious gallery of modern art is next to the Maritime Museum. It won't entertain you as well as its London sister, but if you're into modern art, any Tate's great (free, Tue–Sun 10:00–18:00, closed Mon, tel. 0151/709-0507).

▲The Beatles Story—It's sad to think the Beatles are stuck in a museum (and Ringo's in reruns of *Shining Time Station*). While overpriced and not very creative, the story's a great one, and even an avid fan will pick up some new information (£7.50, CC:VM, daily 10:00–18:00, tel. 0151/709-1963). The shop is an impressive pile of Beatles buyables.

Tours: Die-hard Beatles fans may want to invest a couple of hours in one of several Beatles "Magical Mystery" bus tours (the lads' homes, Penny Lane, and so on, £9.50, 2 hrs). The TI has specifics on the big bus that goes daily. You may want a more fun and intimate three-hour minibus Beatles tour from Phil Hughes

(£11 per person, minimum £60 per group, includes 2-for-1 coupons to Beatles Story; if you take tour on Thu you'll meet John Lennon's Uncle Charlie; Phil also offers Liverpool and regional tours as far as North Wales; tel. & fax 0151/228-4565, cellular 07961-511-223).

Ferry Cruise—Mersey Ferries offer narrated cruises departing from Mersey Dock, an easy five-minute walk from Albert Dock. The cruise makes two brief stops on the other side of the river; you can hop off and catch the next boat back (£3.50, Mon–Fri 10:00–15:00, Sat–Sun 10:00–18:00, year-round, leaves at top of hour, café, WCs on board, tel. 0151/639-0609).

▲Mathew Street—Beatles fans will want to explore Mathew Street (a 15-minute walk into the center from Albert Dock), including the famous Cavern Club, the new Cavern Club nearby, a statue of the young John Lennon, and the Beatles Shop at #31.

Sleeping in Liverpool

(£1 = about $1.60, country code: 44, area code: 0151)

You can sleep on Albert Dock at the new **Holiday Inn Express,** which has 117 comfortable, American-style rooms, some with views and bits of the original brick warehouse arches and walls (Db-£59, includes breakfast, CC:VM, will order take-out for you, at Britannia Pavilion, next to Beatles' Story, Albert Dock, L3 4AD, best to book at least a week in advance, tel. 0151/709-1133, fax 0151/09-1144). Closer to the center of town is the older **Henry's Premier Lodge,** a budget hotel with 39 decent rooms that could use a little sprucing up (Db-£46, up to 2 adults and 2 kids OK, breakfast-£4–6, CC:VM, parallel to Mathew Street, 5 minutes' walk from station, 45 Victoria Street, L1 6JB, tel. 0870-700-1422, fax 0870-700-1423). Both hotels have plenty of nonsmoking rooms available. And both offer deals periodically—ask if there are any price breaks.

Transportation Connections—Liverpool

By train to: Blackpool (every 2 hrs, 1.5 hrs, more frequent with transfer at Preston), **York** (hrly, 2.5 hrs), **Edinburgh** (7/day, 4 hrs, can involve transfer), **London** (hrly, 2.5 hrs), **Crewe** (18/day, 45 min), **Chester** (2/hrly, 45 min). Train info: tel. 08457-484-950.

By ferry to Dublin, Ireland: Merchant Ferries sails most mornings (Tue–Sat) and every evening year-round (8 hrs, £25–35 one-way day crossing, £20–30 one-way overnight, cabins extra, can carry cars, British tel. 0870-600-4321, Dublin tel. 01/819-2999, www.merchant-ferries.com).

Route Tips for Drivers

Ruthin to Blackpool via Liverpool: From Ruthin, get to the M53, which tunnels under the Mersey River (£1). Once in

Liverpool, follow signs to City Center, Pier Head, and Albert Dock, where you'll find a huge car park next to all the sights. Leaving Liverpool, drive north along the waterfront, following signs to M58 (Preston), then M6, and finally M55 into Blackpool.

Ruthin to Blackpool (100 miles): From Ruthin, take A494 through the town of Mold and follow the blue signs to the motorway. M56 zips you to M6, where you'll turn north toward Preston and Lancaster. Don't miss your turnoff. A few minutes after Preston take the not-very-clearly signed next exit (#32, M55) into Blackpool and drive as close as you can to the stubby Eiffel-type tower in the town center. Downtown parking is terrible. If you're not spending the day, head for one of the huge £6/day garages. If you're spending the night, drive to the waterfront and head north. My top B&Bs are north on the promenade (easy parking).

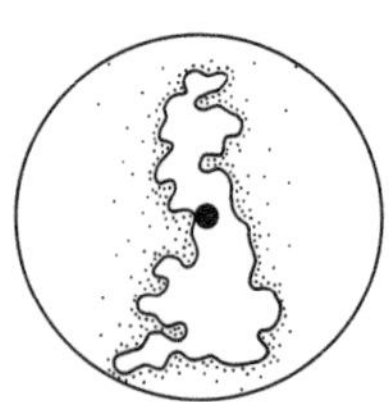

LAKE DISTRICT

In the pristine Lake District, Wordsworth's poems still shiver in trees and ripple on ponds. This is a land where nature rules and man keeps a wide-eyed but low profile. Relax, recharge, take a cruise or a hike, and maybe even write a poem. Renew your poetic license at Wordsworth's famous Dove Cottage.

The Lake District, about 30 miles long and 30 miles wide, is nature's lush, green playground. Explore it by foot, bike, bus, or car. While not impressive in sheer height (Scafell Pike, the tallest peak in England, is only 3,206 feet), there's a walking-stick charm about the way nature and the local culture mix. Walking along a windblown ridge or climbing over a rock fence to look into the eyes of a ragamuffin sheep, even tenderfeet get a chance to feel very outdoorsy.

You'll probably have rain mixed with brilliant bright spells. Drizzly days can be followed by delightful evenings. Pubs offer atmospheric shelter at every turn. As the locals are fond of saying, "There's no such thing as bad weather, only unsuitable clothing."

While the south lakes (Windermere, Bowness, Beatrix Potter's cottage) get the promotion and tour crowds and are closer to London, the north lakes (Ullswater, Derwentwater, Buttermere) are less touristy and at least as scenic.

The town of Keswick, the lake called Derwentwater, and the vast time-passed Newlands Valley will be our focus. The area works great by car or train/bus. And Wordsworth and Potter fans can easily side-trip south to see the authors' homes.

Planning Your Time

On a three-week trip in Britain, I'd spend two days and two nights in the area. The quickest way in is to leave the motorway or train line at Penrith.

Those without a car will use Keswick as a springboard. Cruise the lake and take one of the many hikes in the Cat Bells area. Nonhikers can take a minibus tour.

Here's the most exciting way for drivers to pack their day of arrival: Get an early start from Blackpool or North Wales, leave the motorway at Kendal by 10:30, drive along Windermere and through Ambleside, 11:30-Tour Dove Cottage, 12:30-Backtrack to Ambleside, where a small road leads up and over the dramatic Kirkstone Pass (far more scenic northbound than southbound, get out and bite the wind) and down to Glenridding on Ullswater. You could catch the 14:40 boat. Hike six miles (15:15–18:45) from Howtown back to Glenridding. Drive to your farmhouse B&B near Keswick, with a stop as the sun sets at Castlerigg Stone Circle.

On your second day, explore Buttermere Lake, drive over Honister Pass, explore Derwentwater, and do the Cat Bells High Ridge walk. Spend the evening at the same B&B.

If great scenery is commonplace in your life, the Lake District can be more soothing (and rainy) than exciting. If you're rushed, you could make this area a one-night stand—or even a quick drive-through.

Getting around the Lake District

Those based in Keswick without a car can manage fine. Be sure to pick up the excellent *Lakeland Explorer* magazine (free from TIs and hotels), which explains all the local bus and boat schedules and outlines some great walks for the first-time visitor.

By Foot: Piles of hiking information are available everywhere you turn. Consider buying a detailed map (such as Ordnance Survey). For easy hikes, the fliers at TIs and B&Bs detailing particular routes are helpful. The best ridge walk is immediately outside of town (see "Cat Bells High Ridge Hike," below). The Lake District's TIs advise hikers to check the weather before setting out (for an up-to-date weather report, ask at TI or call 017687/75757), wear suitable clothing, and bring a map.

By Boat: A circular boat service glides you easily around Derwentwater (for a sail/hike option, see "Derwentwater," below).

By Bus: Buses take you quickly and easily (if not always frequently) to all nearby points of interest. Pick up the free 30-page "Lakeland Explorer" bus brochure for schedules and suggested bus/hike outings.

By Bus Tour: Mountain Goat Tours runs an interesting variety of half-day (£14) and all-day (£25) minibus tours from Keswick (daily Easter–Oct). They are informative, off the beaten path, led by local guides, and great for people with bucks who'd like to see the area without hiking or messing with public transport (office at Keswick central car park, CC:VM, tel. 017687/73962, www.lakes-pages.co.uk).

Lake District

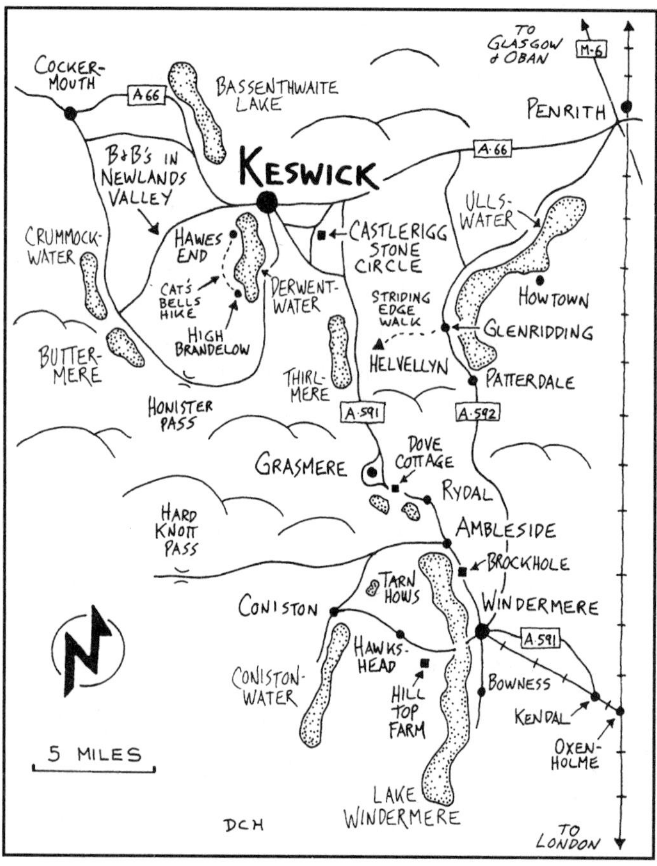

The National Trust offers more sedate, less expensive tours with an emphasis on conservation (£11/half day, £21/full day, book at TI or office at Keswick boat dock, CC:VM, tel. 017687/73780).

As a supercheap alternative to tours, take a round-trip on bus #77 from Keswick to Buttermere and back; it loops around Honister Pass (May–Oct, 2/day clockwise, 2/day "anticlockwise," 1.5 hrs).

By Bike: Several shops rent bikes in Keswick; the most central is Lake Pedlar (£13/day, daily 9:00–17:30, includes helmet, tandems available, CC:VMA, behind Bryson's Bakery on the main street, take alley to car park, tel. 017687/75752). The Keswick TI sells plasticized cycling maps and the leaflet "6 Cycle Routes from Keswick" (£1).

By Car: Nothing is very far from Keswick and Derwentwater. Get a good map, get off the big roads, and leave the car, at least occasionally, for some walking. In summer, the Keswick–Ambleside–Windermere–Bowness corridor (A591) suffers from congestion. If you want to rent a car in Keswick, Fiat is your only choice (from £32/day, Mon–Sat 8:30–17:30, closed Sun, Lake Road in town center, tel. 017687/72064).

KESWICK

As far as touristy Lake District centers go, Keswick (KEZZ-ick, pop. 5,000) is far more enjoyable than Windermere, Bowness, or Ambleside. An important mining center (slate, copper, lead) through the Middle Ages, Keswick became a resort in the 19th century. Its fine Victorian buildings recall those romantic days when city slickers first learned about "communing with nature." Today the compact town is lined with tearooms, pubs, gift shops, and hiking-gear shops. The lake is a pleasant five-minute walk from the town center.

Keswick is the ideal home base: plenty of good B&Bs (see "Sleeping," below), an easy bus connection to the nearest train station at Penrith, and a prime location near the best lake in the area, Derwentwater. In Keswick everything is within a five-minute walk of everything else: the market square, the TI, recommended B&Bs, a bike-rental shop, the municipal pitch-and-putt golf course, the bus stop, Mountain Goat minibus tour starting point, a lakeside boat dock, the post office (with Internet access), and a central car park. Saturday is market day, and the town square is packed and lively.

Keswick hosts an annual convention in July that books up a lot of rooms. Reserve well in advance if you plan to visit in July.

Tourist Information: The helpful TI is in Moot Hall right in the middle of the main square (daily 9:30–17:30, Nov–Easter 9:30–16:30, tel. 017687/72645). They sell great 50p–£1 brochures outlining nearby hikes (including a Keswick Town Trail for history buffs), help you figure out public transportation to out-lying sights, sell Lakeland Explorer bus passes (4-day £13.60 passes only, get £5.75 1-day passes on the bus), change money, book rooms, and sell discounted Derwentwater Launch tickets (£4; £5 at the lake).

Internet Access: Inside the P.O., just off the main square, is U-Compute (July–Sept Mon–Sat 8:30–20:00, Sun 10:30–16:30; Oct–Jun until 17:30 and closed Sun; head to computers at the back to the right, don't wait in P.O. queue).

Sights—Keswick

▲▲Daily Walks—Walks of varying levels of difficulty led by local guides depart from the Keswick TI daily at 10:15, regardless of the weather (£5, Easter–Oct, bring a lunch; sometimes taxi, bus, or boat fare required; return by 17:00, book through TI, tel. 017687/72645). For a list of free daily guided walks offered throughout the Lake District by "Voluntary Wardens," check the *Events 2001* booklet at any local TI. Many of the hikes start at Brockhole National Park Visitors Centre, which is an easy bus ride or a short drive from Keswick, but two hikes a week originate in Keswick (on Sun and Wed afternoons, July–Sept).

▲**Pencil Museum**—Graphite was first discovered centuries ago in Keswick. A hunk of the stuff proved great for marking sheep in the 15th century, and the rest is history (which you can learn all about here). While you can't tour the 150-year-old factory where the famous Derwent pencils are made, the charming museum on the edge of Keswick is a good way to pass a rainy hour (£2.50, daily 9:30–16:00, rentable headsets are not necessary, but the fine and free 20-minute film is; cheap brass rubbing in the shop, tel. 017687/73626).

▲**Plays**—Locals are proud of their new Theatre by the Lake, which offers events year-round and plays nearly nightly in summer. This is a fine opportunity to do something completely local (£9–16, tel. 017687/74411).

▲**Golf**—A lush nine-hole pitch 'n' putt golf course separates the town from the lake and offers a classy, cheap, and convenient chance to golf near the birthplace of the sport (daily 9:30–20:00, £3.50 for nine holes).

Swimming—The Leisure Center has a pool kids love, with a huge water slide (a short walk from the town center, tel. 017687/72760 for hours).

Sights—Derwentwater Area

▲▲**Derwentwater**—This is one of the region's most photographed and popular lakes. With four islands, good circular boat service, plenty of trails, and the pleasant town of Keswick at its north end, Derwentwater entertains.

The roadside views aren't much, so walk or cruise. You can walk around the lake (fine trail, but floods in heavy rains, 9 miles, 3 hours), cruise it (50 min), or do a hike/sail mix. I suggest a hike/sail trip around the lake. From mid-March to October, boats run from Keswick about every 30 minutes—alternating clockwise and "anticlockwise"—from 10:00 to 20:00 (during slow times until 15:30; in winter 3/day on weekends), making seven stops on each 50-minute round-trip. The best hour-long lakeside walk is the 1.5-mile path between the docks at High Brandlehow and Hawse End. You could continue on foot along the lake back into Keswick. Lodore is an easy stop for its Lodore Falls, a 10-minute walk from the dock (falls behind Lodore Hotel, which serves lunch). The boat trip costs £5 per circle (£4 if you book through the TI), with free stopovers, or 75p per segment. Stand on the pier or the boat

Keswick

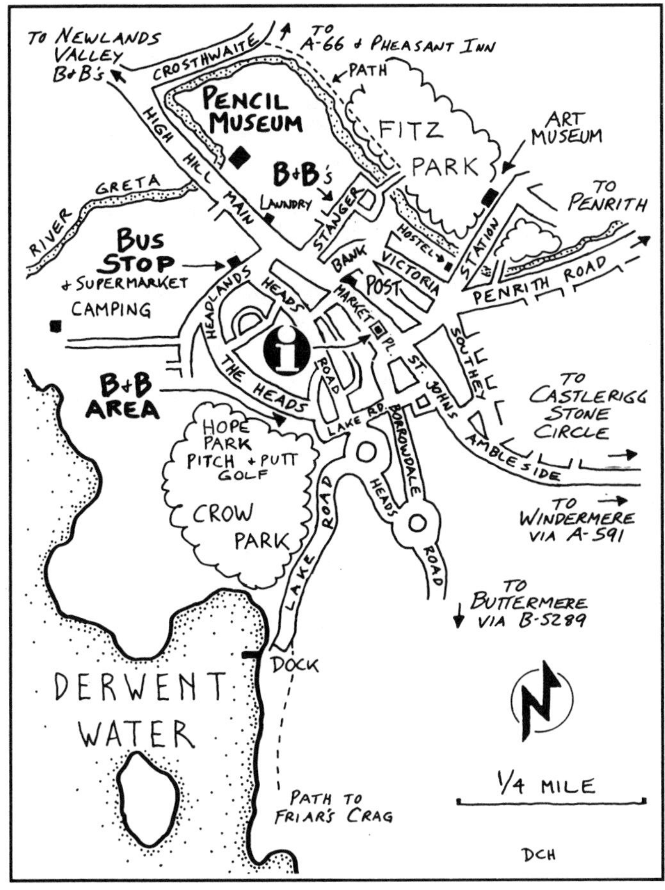

may not stop. The Keswick Launch also offers a 60-minute cruise every evening mid-June through September (£5.80) and rents rowboats (£3/hr, tel. 017687/72263).

▲▲Cat Bells High Ridge Hike—For a great (and fairly easy) "king of the mountain" feeling, sweeping views, and a close-up look at the weather blowing over the ridge, hike about two hours from Hawes End up along the ridge to Cat Bells (1,480 feet) and down to High Brandlehow. From there you can catch the boat or take the easy path along the shore of Derwentwater to your Hawes End starting point. This is probably the most dramatic family walk in the area. From Keswick, the lake, or your farmhouse B&B, you can see silhouetted stick figures hiking along this ridge. Drivers can park free at Hawes End (not particularly safe) or at the Littletown Farm on the Newlands Valley side of Cat Bells (£1). The Keswick TI sells a "Skiddaw & Cat Bells" brochure on the hike (50p).

Cat Bells is just the first of a series of peaks all connected by a fine ridge trail. Heartier hikers continue up to nine miles along this same ridge, enjoying valley and lake views as they arc around the Newlands Valley toward (and even down to) Buttermere. After High Spy you can descend an easy path into Newlands Valley. An ultimate day plan would be to bus to Buttermere, climb Robinson, and follow the ridge around to Cat Bells and back to Keswick.

▲▲Car Hiking from Keswick—Distances are short, roads are narrow and have turnouts, and views are rewarding. Ask your B&B host for advice. Particularly scenic drives include Latrigg (from a car park just north of Keswick walk a few minutes to the top of the hill for a commanding view of the town and lake). Two miles south of Keswick on the lakeside B5289 Borrowdale Valley Road, take the small road left (signposted Watendlath) for a half mile to a packhorse bridge (a quintessential Lake District scene) and, a half mile farther, to a car park and the "surprise view" of Derwentwater. Following the road to its end, you hit the idyllic farm hamlet of Watendlath, where you can ponder the tiny lake and lazy farm animals. (On summer Sundays, free shuttle buses—offered to minimize traffic congestion—run hourly between Keswick and Watendlath. Ride to the end and hike home.) Return down to B5289 and back to Keswick or farther south to scenic Borrowdale and over the dramatic pass to Buttermere.

▲▲Buttermere—This ideal little lake with a lovely, encircling four-mile stroll offers nonstop, no-sweat, Lake District beauty. If you're not a hiker but kind of wish you were, take this walk. If you're very short on time, at least stop here and get your shoes dirty. (Parking and pubs are in Buttermere village.) Buttermere is connected with Borrowdale and Derwentwater by a great road over the rugged Honister Pass, strewn with glacial debris and curious shaggy Swaledale sheep (looking more like goats with their curly horns). In the other direction you can explore the cruel Newlands Valley or carry on through gentler scenery along Crummock Water and through the forested Whinlatter Pass (fine Visitors Centre with a café the flying squirrels love) and back to Keswick. From May through October, bus #77 makes a round-trip loop between Keswick and Buttermere over Honister Pass (2/day in both directions, 1.5 hrs).

▲▲Castlerigg Stone Circle—These 38 stones, 90 feet across and 3,000 years old, are mysteriously laid out on a line between the two tallest peaks on the horizon. For maximum goose pimples (as they say here), show up at sunset (free, open all the time, 3 miles east of Keswick, follow brown signs, 3 minutes off A66, easy parking).

▲▲More Hikes—The area is riddled with wonderful hikes. B&Bs all have fine advice. From downtown Keswick you can walk the seven-mile Latrigg hike, which includes the Castlerigg Stone Circle (pick up 50p map/guide from TI). From the car park at Newlands Pass, at the top of Newlands Valley, an easy one-mile walk to Knottrigg probably offers more thrills per calorie burned than any walk in the region.

▲Lakeland Sheep & Wool Centre—If you're from farm country this is nothing special. But for a city slicker, the Sheep & Wool Centre offers an interesting and entertaining introduction to the region's most famous residents: its sheep. In the 50-minute show you'll meet 19 different breeds of sheep, watch one get sheared, and see sheepdogs do their impressive thing. Afterward you'll meet the stars of the show. It's a hands-on experience kids enjoy (£3, 4 shows daily: 10:30, 12:00, 14:00, and 15:30, only Wed–Sun in winter, unimpressive exhibition but good sheep-stuff shop, drive west from Keswick 15 minutes on A-66, at A-5086 roundabout you'll see the 300-seat auditorium on left).

Keswick Sheepdog Demonstration—Every Wednesday afternoon, five sheepdogs at various levels of training (some championship) round up sheep and ducks for this simple, down-home demonstration (£2, May–Sept 16:00–17:00, on Brundholme Road a mile northeast of Keswick off A66, tel. 017687/79603).

Sights—Windermere Area

▲Brockhole National Park Visitors Centre—Check the events board as you enter. The center offers a 15-minute introduction-to-the-lakes slide show (played upon request), an information desk, organized walks, exhibits, a bookshop, a good cafeteria, gardens, nature walks, and a large car park. It's in a stately old lakeside mansion between Ambleside and the town of Windermere on A591 (April–Oct daily 10:00–17:00, free entry but £3 to park, tel. 015394/46601). The bookshop has an excellent selection of maps and guidebooks. I enjoyed Hunter Davies' refreshingly opinionated (but now a bit dated) *Good Guide to the Lakes* (£6).

▲▲Dove Cottage—William Wordsworth, the poet whose appreciation of nature and back-to-basics lifestyle put this area on the map, spent his most productive years (1799–1808) in this well-preserved old cottage on the edge of Grasmere. Today it's the obligatory sight for any Lake District visit. Even if you're not a fan, Wordsworth's "plain living and high thinking," his appreciation of nature, his romanticism, and the ways his friends unleashed their creative talents are appealing. The 20-minute cottage tour (departures every few minutes) and adjoining museum are excellent. In dry weather the garden where the poet was much inspired is worth a wander. Even a speedy, jaded museum-goer will want at least an hour here (£5, includes voucher for 15 percent off Rydal

Mount, below, and Cockermouth, Wordsworth's birthplace, daily 9:30–17:30, tel. 015394/35544).

Rydal Mount—Wordsworth's final, higher-class home with a lovely garden and view lacks the charm of Dove Cottage. Just down the road from Dove Cottage, it's worthwhile only for Wordsworth fans (£3.75, includes voucher for 15 percent off Dove Cottage and Cockermouth, March–Oct daily 9:30–17:00; Nov–Feb Wed–Mon 10:00–16:00, closed Tue; tel. 015394/33002).

▲Beatrix Potter's Hill Top Farm and Other Sights—Many come to the lakes on a Beatrix Potter pilgrimage. Sensing that, entrepreneurial locals have dreamed up a number of BP sights. This can be confusing. Most important (and least advertised) is **Hill Top Farm,** the 17th-century cottage where Potter wrote many of her Peter Rabbit books (£4, April–Aug Sat–Wed 10:30–16:30, Sept–Oct Sat–Wed 11:00–16:00, closed Thu–Fri and Nov–March, next to Sawrey, 2 miles south of Hawkshead, tel. 015394/36269). Small, dark, and crowded, it gives a good look at her life and work.

The **Beatrix Potter Gallery** (in the neighboring, likeable town of Hawkshead) shows off BP's original drawings and watercolor illustrations used in her children's books and tells more about her life and work (£3, Sun–Thu 10:30–16:30, closed Fri–Sat and Nov–March, Main Street, tel. 015394/36355). The gimmicky **World of Beatrix Potter** tour—a hit with children—features a five-minute video trip into the world of Mrs. Tiggywinkle and company, a series of Lake District tableaus starring the same imaginary gang, and a 15-minute video biography of BP (not worth £3.50, daily 10:00–17:30, Sept–Easter 10:00–16:30, in Bowness near Windermere town, tel. 015394/88444).

Hard Knott Pass—Only 1,300 feet above sea level, this pass is a thriller, with a narrow, winding, steeply graded road. Just over the pass are the scant but evocative remains of the Hard Knott Roman fortress. There are great views but miserable rainstorms, and it can be very slow and frustrating when the one-lane road with turnouts is clogged by traffic (avoid in summer).

Sights—Ullswater Area

▲▲Ullswater Hike and Boat Ride—Long, narrow Ullswater offers eight miles of diverse and grand Lake District scenery. While you can drive it or cruise it, I'd ride the boat from the south tip halfway up and hike back. Boats leave Glenridding regularly—from four to nine a day, depending on the season (£3.40 one-way, £5.60 round-trip, daily 9:00–16:15, 35-minute ride to Howtown, cheap and safe parking lot, café, free timetable shows walking route, tel. 017684/82229 for schedule, arrive 20 minutes before departure in summer, www.ullswater-steamers.co.uk). Ride to the first stop, Howtown, halfway up the lake. Then spend four hours hiking and dawdling along the well-marked path by the lake south to Patterdale and then along the road back to Glenridding. This is a serious seven-mile walk with good views, varied terrain, and a few bridges and farms along the way. Wear good shoes and be prepared for rain. For a shorter hike from Howtown Pier, consider a three-mile loop around Hallin Fell.

Several steamer trips chug daily up and down Ullswater. A good rainy-day plan is to ride the covered boat up and down the lake (to the farthest point—Poorley Bridge, £6.60 round-trip, 2 hrs) or to Howtown and back (£5.60 round-trip, 1 hr). To reach Glenridding by bus from Keswick, allow two hours with a transfer at Penrith.

Helvellyn—Often considered the best high-mountain hike in the Lake District, this breathtaking, round-trip route from Glenridding includes the spectacular Striding Edge ridge walk. Be careful; do this six-hour hike only in good weather and get advice from the Glenridding TI (tel. 017684/82414). While there are shorter routes, the Glenridding ascent is best. The Keswick TI has a helpful "Helvellyn from Glenridding" leaflet on the hike (50p).

Sleeping in the Lake District
(£1 = about $1.60, country code: 44, area code: 017687)

Sleeping in Keswick

Sleep Code: **S** = Single, **D** = Double/Twin, **T** = Triple, **Q** = Quad, **b** = bathroom, **t** = toilet only, **s** = shower only, **CC** = Credit Card (**V**isa, **M**asterCard, **A**mex).

The Lake District abounds with attractive B&Bs, guest houses, and hostels. It needs them all when summer hordes threaten the serenity of this romantic mecca. Alert: Book well in advance if you plan to visit during Keswick's annual convention in July.

Outside of summer, if you have a car, you should have no trouble finding a room. But to get a particular place (especially on Sat), call ahead. Those using public transportation should stay in Keswick. With a car, drive into a remote farmhouse experience. Lakeland hostels are cheaper and filled with an interesting crowd. The Keswick TI can give you phone numbers of places with vacancies if you call or book you a room if you drop in.

In Keswick I've featured two streets, each within three blocks of the bus station and town square. "The Heads" is a classier street lined with proud Victorian houses, close to the lake and new theatre, overlooking a golf course. Stanger Street, a bit humbler but also quiet and handy, has smaller homes. All of my Keswick listings are strictly smoke free.

The launderette is around the corner from the bus station on Main Street (daily 7:30–19:30, £3 wash and dry, change machine and coin-op flake dispenser, £2 extra for full service by 10:00 or earlier; just leave clothes inside by rear door with a note and she'll do them for you).

Sleeping on The Heads

Berkeley Guest House, a big slate mansion enthusiastically run by Barbara Crompton, has a pleasant lounge, narrow hallways, and carefully appointed, comfortable rooms. The chirpy, skylight-bright £36 bathless double in the attic is a fine value if you don't mind the stairs (D-£34, Dt-£42, Db-£46, The Heads, Keswick, Cumbria, CA12 5ER, tel. 017687/74222, www.berkeley-keswick.homepage.com).

Parkfield is thoughtfully run and decorated by Fay and Bob Watson. This big Victorian house is bright and pastel, with a fine, restful view lounge (8 rooms, 1 on the ground floor, Db-£44–48 with this book through 2000, CC:VM, car park, strictly nonsmoking, vegetarian options, The Heads, CA12 5ES, tel. 017687/72328, www.kencomp.net/parkfield).

Howe Keld Lakeland Hotel offers more of a guest-house feel, with 15 attractive rooms, a wide variety of breakfast selections, £12.75 evening meals, and a bar (Sb-£30, budget Db-£45, Db-£52, clarify which kind of double you have, minimum 2 nights, prices with this book through 2001?, 2 ground-floor rooms, 5–7 The Heads, CA12 5ES, tel. & fax 017687/72417, www.howekeld.co.uk, David and Valerie Fisher plus their two adorable girls).

West View Guest House, next door to Parkfield, with seven tastefully furnished rooms, is pleasant and a decent value (Sb-£26, Db-£52, The Heads, CA12 5ES, tel. 017687/73638, run by friendly Carole and John Fullagar).

Sleeping on Stanger Street

Abacourt House is an old Victorian slate townhouse completely redone by Sheila and Bill Newman. Bill, who just finished climbing all the "Wainwright" peaks, is a wealth of Lake District sightseeing information and happy to point you in the most scenic direction. All five doubles have firm beds, TVs, and shiny, modern bathrooms (Db-£44, no children, 26 Stanger Street, Keswick, CA12 5JU, tel. 017687/72967, http://members.aol.com/abacourt).

Dunsford Guest House, a few doors down, has four cheery, inviting rooms run by an energetic couple who get their exercise fellrunning—running the mountain trails (Db-£39 with this book, veggie breakfast options, 16 Stanger Street, CA12 5JU, tel. 017687/75059, www.dunsford.net, run by Pat and photographer Peter Richards).

Fell House B&B, with six charming rooms, is run by Barbara Hossack, who serves tea and homemade cakes each evening and won a "healthy heartbeat" award in 1999 for her cooking (S-£18, D-£36, Db-£44, 28 Stanger Street, CA12 5JU, tel. & fax 017687/72669, e-mail: fellhouse@kencomp.net).

Badgers Wood B&B, at the top of the street, has six pastel, stocking-feet-comfortable rooms (S-£18, D-£36, Db-£42 with this book, 30 Stanger Street, CA12 5JU, tel. 017687/72621, www.badgers-wood.co.uk, Irene and David).

Ellergill Guest House has three pleasant rooms, one with a super view (Db-£39 with this book, 22 Stanger Street, CA12 5JU, tel. 017687/73347, www.ellergill.co.uk, Christine and Keith Taylor).

Two former hotels now operate as hostels with £10 dorm beds: **Keswick** (3- to 10-bed rooms, center of town just off Station Road, tel. 017687/72484) and **Derwentwater** (4- to 22-bedrooms, 2 miles south of Keswick, tel. 017687/77246).

Sleeping in Newlands Valley

With a car, I'd drive 10 minutes past Keswick down the majestic Newlands Valley. Hiking opportunities are wonderful. If the place had a lake it would be packed with tourists. But it doesn't—and it isn't. The valley is studded with 500-year-old farms that have been in the same family for centuries. Shearing day is reason to rush home from school. Sons get school out of the way ASAP and follow their dads. Neighbor girls marry sons and move in. Grandparents retire to the cottage next door. With the price of wool depressed, most of the wives supplement the family income by running B&Bs. The rooms are much plainer than in town. Traditionally, farmhouses lacked central heating, and, while they are now heated, you can still request a hot-water bottle to warm up your bed.

Newlands Valley is just over the Cat Bells ridge from Derwentwater between Keswick and Buttermere. Leave Keswick heading west on the Cockermouth Road (A66). For Birkrigg, Keskadale, Ellas Crag, and Uzzicar B&Bs, take the second Newlands Valley exit through Braithwaite and follow signs through Newlands Valley (drive toward Buttermere). You'll pass Uzzicar first, then Ellas Crag, then the curious purple house, then Birkrigg Farm B&B, and finally Keskadale Farm (about 4 miles before Buttermere). The road is one lane with passing turnouts. For the Low Skelgill Farm, take the first Newlands Valley exit, head through Portinscale on the Buttermere Road for three miles to Stair, then look for the sign.

Birkrigg Farm is the ideal farmhouse B&B. Mrs. Margaret Beaty offers visitors a comfy lounge, evening tea (good for socializing with her other guests), a classy breakfast, a territorial view, and perfect peace on this 220-acre working farm. Take your toast and last cup of tea out to the front yard bench (£17–18 per person in S, D, T, or Q, discounts for kids, 1 shower, 1 tub, and 3 WCs for 6 rooms, closed Dec–March, Newlands Pass Road, Keswick, Cumbria, CA12 5TS, tel. 017687/78278).

Keskadale Farm B&B is another great farmhouse experience, with valley views and ponderosa hospitality. This working farm has lots of curly horned sheep and three rooms to rent

(D/Db-£48–50, closed Dec–Feb, nonsmoking, 1 minute farther down Newlands Pass Road to Buttermere Road on a hairpin turn, Keskadale Farm, Newlands, Keswick CA12 5TS, tel. 017687/78544, fax 017687/78150, Margaret Harryman). One of the valley's oldest, it's made from 500-year-old ship beams.

Low Skelgill Farm, with three rooms sharing two bathrooms, is immediately under Cat Bells. This is ideal for hikers, since you can leave your car there for the Cat Bells ridge walk (S-£17, D-£34, less for 2 nights, take the Buttermere Road to Stair, then follow the "narrow-gated" road, look for Low Skelgill, not simply Skelgill, tel. 017687/78453, Ann Grave). She also runs a rustic "camping barn" with mattresses for £3.50 a night on weekdays (no bedding provided).

Ellas Crag B&B, in the same glorious setting, is a more comfortable stone house rather than a farm. This homey place, with a good mix of modern and traditional, is enthusiastically run by Tony, Jean, and Catherine Hartley, who cook up great gourmet-type breakfasts and £16.50 dinners with an emphasis on freshness (S-£22.50, Ds-£45; no twin beds, only doubles within house; separate Db chalet in garden has twin beds-£50; nonsmoking, veggie options, packed lunches, laundry possible, Stair, Newlands Valley, CA12 5TT, tel. 017687/78217, www.ellascragguesthouse.co.uk, e-mail: ellascrag@talk21.com).

Uzzicar rents two rooms in a 16-century farmhouse on a working sheep farm (Db-£36, families welcome, Newlands Valley, CA12 5TS, tel. 017687/78367).

Sleeping in Buttermere or Embleton

Buttermere: The **Bridge Hotel,** just beyond Newlands Valley at Buttermere, offers a classy, musty, Old World, countryside hotel experience (22 rooms, £60 per person with a 5-course dinner, cheaper for longer stays, £45 per person B&B only upon request, CC:VM, Buttermere, Cumbria, CA13 9UZ, tel. 017687/70252, fax 017687/70215). There are no shops within 10 miles—only peace and quiet a stone's throw from one of the region's most beautiful lakes. Buttermere also has a hostel (see below).

Embleton: Lambfoot House, run by Ruth and Howard Holden, has three cozy rooms named after sheep (Sb-£23, Db-£46, nonsmoking, near pub,10 miles from Keswick, in Embleton, CA13 9XL, tel. 017687/76424, fax 017687/76721, www.lambfoot.co.uk). From Keswick, take A66 (direction: Cockermouth), turn right at the second Embleton signpost and go 200 yards.

Lake District Hostels

The Lake District's inexpensive hostels (£11/bed), usually located in great old buildings, are handy sources of information and social fun. Local TIs have lists. The Lake District's free booking service

(Easter–Oct daily 9:00–18:00, tel. 015394/31117) will tell you which of the area's 30 hostels have available beds and can even book a place on your credit card (no more than 7 days in advance). Since most hostels don't answer their phones during the day and many are full, this is a helpful service. Hostelers need to be members or buy a £12 membership.

The **Buttermere King George VI Memorial Hostel,** a quarter-mile south of Buttermere village on Honister Pass Road, has good food, family rooms, and a royal setting (tel. 017687/70245). The well-run **Borrowdale Hostel** is secluded in Borrowdale Valley just south of Rosthwaite (drying rooms, tel. 017687/77257).

Eating in the Lake District

Eating in Keswick

The bus station faces a fine **supermarket** (Mon–Sat 9:00–19:00, Sun 10:00–16:00), which has a smoke-free **Coffee Shop Café** popular with locals. It features regional specialties and a menu that's healthy for your body and your pocketbook (Mon–Sat 9:30–17:00, until 18:00 July–Aug, Sun 10:00–16:00). **Maysons Whole Food Restaurant** is favored for its home cooking: curry, Cajun, vegetarian options, and not a chip in sight. It feels Californian (£6 meals, June–Oct daily 10:00–20:45, otherwise 10:30–16:30, family-friendly, on Lake Road, tel. 017687/74104). **Kitchins Cellar Bar** is the latest local favorite for its reasonable prices and good food, a cut above pub grub (daily 12:00–14:00, 18:00–21:00, same menu for restaurant or cellar bar, but "lite" meals available only in bar, CC:VM, 18 Lake Road, tel. 017687/72990). Another good bet is **The Four in Hand** (daily 12:00–14:30, 18:30–21:30, Lake Road, tel. 017687/72069).

Keswick Lodge Pub is popular for its fine pub meals and atmosphere (daily 12:00–21:00, just off main square on Main Street, tel. 017687/74584), the **Pheasant Inn** for its pub-simple country fare (Mon–Sat 12:00–14:00, 17:30–20:00, Sun 19:00–20:00, 10-min walk, at top of Stanger Street, angle right to cross river, turn left along riverside path to Crosthwaite Road, turn right). For fish and chips, Keswickians go to **The Old Keswickian** (daily 11:15–23:30, facing TI, take out or eat upstairs).

It's easy to find ready-made sandwiches for your hike: try the supermarket or **Bryson's Bakery** on the main square or get one freshly made at the **Coffee Lounge** (down a narrow alley to the right of Bryson's as you face it).

Eating in Newlands Valley

Since most farmhouses don't serve dinner to their guests, take the lovely 10-minute drive to Buttermere for your evening meal at the **Fish Hotel** pub (£5, nightly 18:00–21:00, family-friendly, limited menu, good fish, beaucoup chips, no vegetables) or the more expensive but much cozier and tastier **Bridge Hotel** pub (£6 or £7, nightly 18:00–21:30, more interesting menu, crunchy veggies). On the Keswick side of Newlands Valley, the **Farmer's Arms** pub in Portinscale also serves good pub grub. **Swinside Inn,** the only pub actually in Newlands Valley, is a little tatty but serves decent meals.

Transportation Connections—Lake District

Keswick by bus to: Buttermere (4/day via Whinlatter Forestry Centre and Crummock Water, 40 min), **Borrowdale** (8/day to the powerfully scenic valley south of Derwentwater, Grange, and Seatoller, 30 min), **Grasmere/Ambleside/Windermere** (hrly, 1 hr), **York** (1/day Mon–Sat in both directions, runs mid-April–early Sept only, nothing on Sun, Stagecoach X9 bus, leaves Keswick in morning, leaves York in afternoon, 4 hrs, also stops in Grasmere, Ambleside, and Windermere, tel. 01946/63222; this direct bus is far superior to taking the train with several transfers), **Penrith** (£3, hrly 7:00–21:50, only 3 on Sun, 40 min, Stagecoach X4 and X5 buses). Buses run from the Penrith train station to **Ullswater** and **Glenridding** (6/day, 1 hr, direction: Patterdale). Bus info: tel. 01946/63222.

Penrith by train to: Oban (hrly to Glasgow, 2 hrs; then to Oban, 3/day, 3 hrs), **Edinburgh** (8/day, 2 hrs), **Blackpool** (hrly, 2 hrs, transfer in Preston), **Liverpool** (hrly, 2.5 hrs), **Birmingham** (hrly, 3 hrs), **London's** Euston Station (hrly, 4.5 hrs). Train info: tel. 08457-484-950.

Route Tips for Drivers

North Wales or Blackpool to the Lake District: The direct, easy way to Keswick is to leave the M6 at Penrith and take the A66 highway 16 miles to Keswick. For the scenic sightseeing drive through the south lakes to Keswick, exit the super M6 on A590/A591 through the towns of Kendal and Windermere to reach Brockhole National Park Visitors Centre. From Brockhole, the A road to Keswick is fastest, but the high road—the tiny road over Kirkstone Pass to Glenridding and lovely Ullswater—is much more dramatic.

For the drive north to **Oban,** see the Highlands chapter.

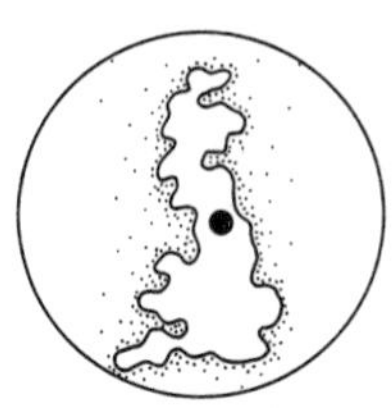

YORK

Historical York is loaded with world-class sights. Marvel at the York Minster, England's finest Gothic church. Ramble through the Shambles, York's wonderfully preserved medieval quarter. Enjoy a walking tour led by an old Yorker. Hop a train at Europe's greatest Railway Museum, travel to the 1800s in York Castle Museum, and head back a thousand years to Viking York at the Jorvik exhibit.

York has a rich history. In A.D. 71 it was Eboracum, a Roman provincial capital. Constantine was proclaimed emperor here in A.D. 306. In the 5th century, as Rome was toppling, a Roman emperor sent a letter telling England it was on its own, and York became Eoforwic, the capital of the Anglo-Saxon kingdom of Northumbria. A church was built here in 627, and the town was an early Christian center of learning. The Vikings later took the town, and from about 860 to 950 it was a Danish trading center called Jorvik. The invading and conquering Normans destroyed then rebuilt the city, giving it a castle and the walls you see today. Medieval York, with 9,000 inhabitants, grew rich on the wool trade and became England's second city. Henry VIII spared the city's fine Minster and used York as his Anglican church's northern capital. The Archbishop of York is second only to the Archbishop of Canterbury in the Anglican Church. In the Industrial Age, York was the railway hub of North England. When it was built, York's train station was the world's largest. Today, York's leading industry is tourism. Its leading drug? Starbucks and Costa are doing their best to turn high tea into high coffee.

Planning Your Time

York rivals Edinburgh as the best sightseeing city in Britain after London. On even a 10-day trip through Britain, it deserves two nights and a day. For the best 36 hours, follow this plan: Catch the 19:00 city walking tour on the evening of your arrival. The next morning be at Jorvik at 9:00 when it opens (to avoid the midday crowds—or prebook at least a day ahead; see Jorvik under "Sights," below). The nearby Castle Museum is worth the rest of the morning (10:00–noon, I could spend even more time here). Three options for your early afternoon: shoppers browse the Shambles, train buffs tour the National Railway Museum, and scholars do the Yorkshire Museum. Tour the Minster at 16:00 before catching the 17:00 evensong service. Finish your day with an early evening stroll along the wall and perhaps through the abbey gardens. This schedule assumes you're there in the summer (evening orientation walk) and that there's an evensong on. Confirm your plans with the TI.

Orientation (area code: 01904)

The sightseer's York is small. Virtually everything is within a few minutes' walk: the sights, train station, TI, and B&Bs. The longest walk a visitor might take (from a B&B across the old town to the Castle Museum) is 15 minutes.

Bootham Bar, a gate in the medieval town wall, is the hub of your York visit. At Bootham Bar (and on Exhibition Square facing it) you'll find the TI, the starting points for most walking tours and bus tours, handy access to the medieval town wall, Gillygate (pronounced "jilly-gate," lined with good eateries), and Bootham Street, which leads to the recommended B&Bs. (In York, a "bar" is a gate and a "gate" is a street. Go ahead, blame the Vikings.)

Tourist Information: The TI at Bootham Bar sells a 75p "York Map and Guide." Ask for the free monthly *What's On* guide and the monthly *Gig Guide* for live music (April–Oct Mon–Sat 9:00–18:00, Sun 9:00–16:00; July–Aug until 19:00; Nov–March Mon–Sat 9:00–17:30, Sun 10:00–16:00, tel. 01904/621-756, pay WCs next door). The TI books rooms for a £3 fee and sells theatre tickets and Guide Friday city bus tours (£8.50, CC:VM). The train station TI is smaller but provides all the same information and services (April–Sept Mon–Sat 9:00–20:00, Sun 9:30–17:00, shorter hours off-season).

Arrival in York: The station is a five-minute walk from town; turn left down Station Road and follow the crowd toward the Gothic towers of the Minster. After the bridge, a block before the Minster, signs to the TI send you left on St. Leonard's Place. Recommended B&Bs are a five-minute walk from there. (For a shortcut to B&B area from station, walk 1 block toward Minster, cut through parks to riverside, cross railway bridge/pedestrian walkway, cross parking lot for B&Bs on St. Mary's Street, or duck through pedestrian walkway under tracks to B&Bs on Sycamore and Queen Anne's Road.) With lots of luggage, consider a quick

York

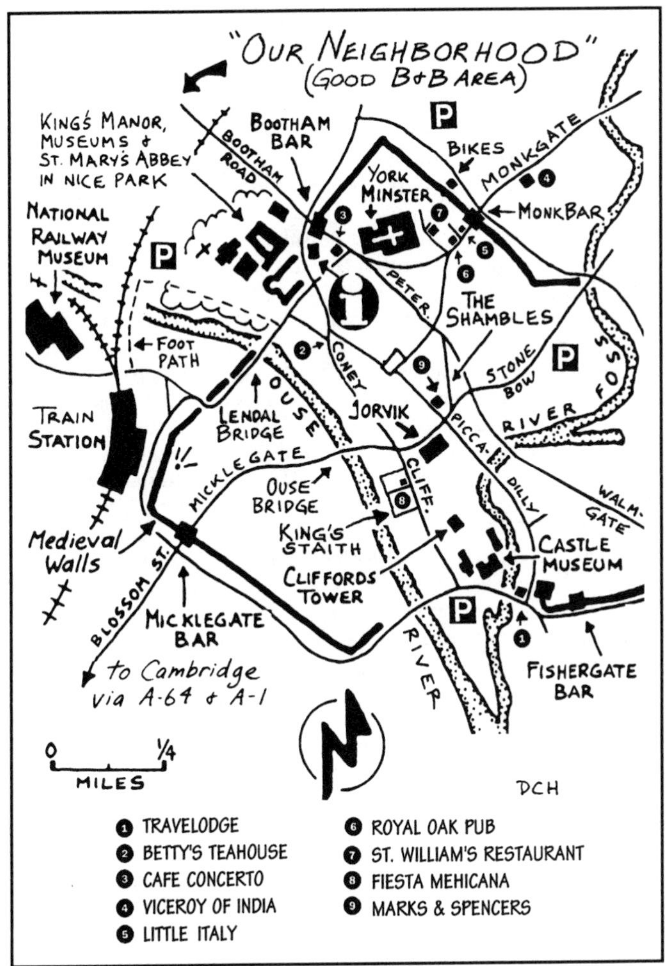

taxi ride (£3.50–4). Luggage storage at York's train station: £1.50 (Mon–Sat 8:30–20:30, Sun 9:00–20:30, platform 1).

Helpful Hints

Study Ahead: York has a great Web site: www.york.gov.uk.

Internet Access: Try Internet Exchange (Mon–Sat 8:00–20:00, Sun 10:00–18:00, 13 Stonegate), Gateway (Mon–Sat 10:00–20:00, Sun 12:00–16:00, 26 Swinegate), or comms.port

(Mon–Thu 8:00–18:00, Fri–Sat 8:00–20:00, Sun 10:00–17:00, on St. Helen's Square, above Costas coffee shop, near Betty's, Coney Street 2a, 1st floor, tel. 01904/658-270).

Festivals: The Viking Festival in late February (tentatively Feb 22–25 in 2001) is a lot of fun, with lur-blowing, warrior drills, and recreated battles. The Early Music Festival zings its strings in mid-July (July 6–15 in 2001). The York Festival of Food and Drink takes a 10-day bite out of the last half of September. Book a room well in advance during festival times and weekends any time of year.

Bike Rental: Trotters, just outside Monk Bar, has free cycle maps. The riverside path is fun (£8/day, helmets-£2, Mon–Sat 9:00–17:30, Sun 10:00–16:00, tel. 01904/622-868). Europcar at the train station also rents bikes (£7.50/day, platform 1).

Car Rental: If you're nearing the end of your trip, consider dropping your car upon arrival in York. The money saved by turning it in early nearly pays for the train ticket that whisks you effortlessly to Edinburgh or London. Avis (1 Layerthorpe, closed Sun, tel. 01904/610-460), Hertz (at train station, daily including Sun 9:00–13:00 April–Sept, tel. 01904/612-586), Kenning Car & Van Rental (Micklegate, closed Sun, tel. 01904/659-328), Budget (Leeman Road, next to National Railway Museum, daily including Sun 9:00–11:00, tel. 01904/644-919), and Europcar (train station, platform 1, also Sun 9:00–13:00, tel. 1904/656-161) all have offices in York. Beware, car rental agencies close Saturday afternoon and some close all day Sunday—when dropping off is OK but picking up is impossible.

Tours of York

▲▲▲Walking Tours—Charming local volunteer guides give energetic, entertaining, and free two-hour walks through York (daily 10:15 all year, plus 14:15 April–Oct, plus 19:00 June–Aug, from Exhibition Square across from TI). There are many other commercial York walking tours. YorkWalk Tours, for example, has reliable guides and many themes to choose from, such as Roman York, City Walls, or Snickleways—small alleys (£4.50, tel. 01904/622-303, TI has schedule). Most of the ghost tours, all offered after nightfall, are more fun than informative. Haunted Walk, though, relies on storytelling and history rather than masks and surprises (£3, April–Nov daily at 20:00, 90 min, just show up, depart from Exhibition Square, across street from TI, end in the Shambles, tel. 01904/621-003 or 01904/411-578).

▲Guide Friday Hop-on Hop-off Bus Tours—York's Guide Friday offers tour guides on speed who can talk enthusiastically to three sleeping tourists in a gale on a topless double-decker bus for an hour without stopping. Buses make the 60-minute circuit, covering secondary York sights that the city walking tours skip—

the workaday perimeter of town (£8.50, pay driver cash, can also buy from TI with CC, departures every 15 min from 9:15 until around 17:00, includes vouchers for discounts on York's sights, read brochure, tel. 01904/640-896). While you can hop on and off all day, the York route is of no value from a transportation-to-the-sights point of view. I'd catch it at the Bootham Bar TI and ride it for an orientation all the way around or get off at the Railway Museum, skipping the last five minutes. Guide Friday's competitors give you a little less for a little less.

Boat Cruise—The York Boat does a lazy 60-minute lap along the River Ouse (£4.50, daily Feb–Nov from 10:30 on, narrated cruise, leaves from Lendal Bridge and King's Staith landing), and also offers themed evening cruises: ghost, dinner, floodlit, and so on (boat rentals possible, tel. 01904/628-324, www.yorkboat.co.uk).

Sights—York Minster

▲▲▲Minster—The pride of York, this largest Gothic church north of the Alps (540 feet long, 200 feet tall) brilliantly shows that the High Middle Ages were far from dark. The word "minster" means a place from which people go out to minister or spread the word of God.

Your first impression might be the spaciousness and brightness of the nave (built 1280–1350). The nave—from the middle period of Gothic, called "Decorated Gothic"—is one of the widest Gothic naves in Europe. Notice the Great West Window (1338) above the entry. The heart in the tracery is called "the heart of Yorkshire."

Look down the nave. The mysterious gold-and-red dragon's head (in the middle of the nave, sticking out of the side) was probably used as a crane to lift a font cover.

The north and south transepts are the oldest part of today's church (1220–1270). The oldest complete window in the minster is the entire wall of glass in the north transcept (1260). Known as the Five Sister's Window, these 50-foot-high panels were made of modern-looking grisaille (gray-silver) glass.

The fanciful choir and the east end (high altar) is from the last stage of Gothic, Perpendicular (1360–1470). The Great East Window (1405), the largest medieval glass window in existence, shows the beginning and the end of the world, with scenes from Genesis and the book of Revelation. A chart (on the right, with a tiny, more helpful chart within) highlights the core Old Testament scenes in this hard-to-read masterpiece. Enjoy the art close up on the chart and then step back and find the real thing.

There are three more extra visits to consider. The **Chapter House,** an elaborately decorated 13th-century Gothic dome, features playful details carved in the stonework (pointed out in the flier that comes with the £1 admission, enter from north transept).

You can scale the 275-step **tower** for £3 and a great view (south transcept). The **Undercroft,** also in the south transcept, consists of the crypt, treasury, and foundations (£3). The crypt is an actual bit of the Romanesque church, featuring 12th-century Romanesque art, excavated in modern times. The foundations give you a chance to climb down—archaeologically and physically—through the centuries to see the roots of the much smaller, but still huge, Norman church (Romanesque, 1100) that stood on this spot and, below that, the Roman excavations. Constantine was proclaimed Roman emperor here in A.D. 306. Peek also at the modern concrete save-the-church foundations.

Hours and Tours: The cathedral opens daily at 7:00. The closing time flexes with the season (roughly 20:30 July–Aug, 19:30 May–June and Sept, 18:00 Oct–April, tel. 01904/624-426). The Chapter House, tower, and Undercroft have shorter hours, usually 9:30 to 18:00 (Oct–April 10:00–16:30). Activities are limited Sunday morning during services.

While a donation of £2.50 to visit the church is reasonably requested, by visiting all the small extra spots inside I give that (and more) in the form of those admissions. Just pay for and enjoy all the little extras. The recent £1 photography fee, which applies to everyone, may or may not last due to obvious problems of enforcement.

Follow the "Welcome to the York Minster" flyer and ask about a free guided tour at the reception desk at the entry (tours go frequently, even with just one or two people; you can join one in progress). The helpful blue-armbanded Minster guides are happy to answer your questions.

Evensong and Church Bells: To experience the cathedral in musical and spiritual action, attend an evensong (Tue–Sat 17:00, Sat–Sun 16:00); when the choir is off on school break (mid-July–Aug), visiting choirs usually fill in. If you're a fan of church bells, Sunday morning (around 10:00) and Tuesday evening practice (19:30–21:30) are heavenly.

Sights—York

▲City Walls—The historic walls of York provide a fine two-mile walk. Walk from Bootham Bar (gate) to Monk Bar for outstanding cathedral views. Open from dawn until dusk (barring attacks) and free.

▲The Shambles—This is the most colorful old York street in the half-timbered, traffic-free core of town. Ye olde downtown York, while very touristy, is a window-shopping, busker-filled, people-watcher's delight. Don't miss the more frumpy Newgate Market or the old-time candy store just opposite the bottom end of the Shambles. For a cheap lunch, consider the cute, tiny **St. Crux Parish Hall,** a medieval church now used by a medley of charities selling tea and simple snacks (Mon–Sat 10:00–16:00, at bottom end of the Shambles, at intersection with Pavement).

▲▲▲**York Castle Museum**—Truly one of Europe's top museums, this is a Victorian home show, the closest thing to a time-tunnel experience England has to offer. It includes the 19th-century Kirkgate, a fine collection of old shops well stocked exactly as they were 150 years ago, along with the new "From Cradle to Grave" exhibit, plus costumes, armor, and an eye-opening Anglo-Saxon helmet (from A.D. 750). The one-way plan allows you to see everything: a working water mill (April–Oct), prison cells, man traps, World War II fashions, and old toys (£5.25, daily 9:30–17:00, Nov–March daily 9:30–16:30, cafeteria midway through museum, shop, car park; the £2.50 guidebook, while not necessary, makes a nice souvenir; CC:VM, tel. 01904/653-611). Clifford's Tower (across from Castle Museum, not worth the £1.80, daily 10:00–18:00, until 16:00 Oct–March) is all that's left of York's castle (13th century, site of a 1190 massacre of local Jews—read about this at base of hill).

▲**Jorvik**—Sail the "Pirates of the Caribbean" north and back 800 years and you get Jorvik—more a ride than a museum. Innovative 10 years ago, the commercial success of Jorvik (yor-vik) inspired copycat ride/museums all over England. You'll ride a little Disney-type train car for 13 minutes through the recreated Viking street of Coppergate. It's the year 948, and you're in the village of Jorvik. Next your little train takes you through the actual excavation sight that inspired this. Finally you'll browse through a small gallery of Viking shoes, combs, locks, and other intimate glimpses of that red-headed culture (£6, daily 9:00–17:30, Nov–March closing varies from 15:30–16:30, last entry 30 minutes before closing, tel. 01904/643-211, www.jorvik-viking-centre.co.uk).

Midday lines can be an hour long, and even past the turnstile there's a 25-minute wait. Avoid the line by going very early or very late in the day or by prebooking (call 01904/543-403 at least a day ahead, Mon–Fri 9:00–17:00, office closed on weekends, CC:VM, you're given a time slot, add £1 per ticket for entry 10:00–16:00). Some love this "ride"; others call it a gimmicky rip-off. If you're looking for a serious museum, see the Viking exhibit at the Yorkshire Museum. It's better. If you're thinking Disneyland with a splash of history, Jorvik's great. I like Jorvik, but it's not worth a long line.

▲▲**National Railway Museum**—This thunderous museum shows 150 fascinating years of British railroad history. Fanning out from a grand roundhouse is an array of historic cars and engines, including Queen Victoria's lavish royal car and the very first "stagecoaches on rails." There's much more, including exhibits on dining cars, post cars, sleeping cars, train posters, and videos. This biggest and best railroad museum anywhere is interesting even to people who think "Pullman" is Japanese for "tug-o-war" (£6.50, kids under 17 free, CC:VM, daily 10:00–18:00, tel. 01904/621-261). Cute little "road trains" shuttle you between the Minster and the Railway Museum (£1.50, leaves Railway Museum every 30 minutes from 12:00–17:30 on the top and bottom of the hour, leaves Minster—from Duncombe Place—every 30 minutes at :15 and :45 after the hour).

▲**Yorkshire Museum**—Located in a lush and lazy park next to the stately ruins of St. Mary's Abbey, Yorkshire Museum is the city's forgotten serious "archaeology of York" museum. While the hordes line up at Jorvik, the best Viking artifacts are here—with no crowds and in a better historical context. You have to walk through this museum, but the stroll takes you through Roman, Saxon, Viking, Norman, and Gothic York. Its prize piece is the delicately etched 15th-century pendant called the Middleham Jewel. The video about the creation of the abbey is worth a look (£4, various exhibitions can increase price, daily 10:00–17:00, tel. 01904/629-745).

Theatre Royal—Fine plays, usually British comedies, entertain the locals (20:00 almost nightly, 19:30 Sept–May, tickets easy to get, £10–15, CC:VMA, closes for 6-week period starting in June, on St. Leonard's Place next to TI and a 5-minute walk from recommended B&Bs, recorded info tel. 01904/610-041, booking tel. 01904/623-568, www.theatre-royal-york.co.uk).

Honorable Mention

York has a number of other sights and activities (described in TI material) that, while interesting, pale in comparison to the biggies. **Fairfax House** is perfectly Georgian inside, with docents happy to talk with you (£4, Sat–Thu 11:00–17:00 except Sun 13:30–17:00, closed Fri except in Aug; guided tours offered at 11:00 and 14:00 on Friday during summer—confirm in advance at TI; a tour helps bring this well-furnished building to life; on Castlegate, near Jorvik, tel. 01904/655-543). The **Hall of the Merchant Adventurers** claims to be the finest medieval guildhall in Europe (from 1361). It's basically a vast half-timbered building with marvelous exposed beams and 15 minutes worth of interesting displays about life and commerce back in the days when York was England's second city (£2, daily 8:30–17:00, early Nov–mid-March until 15:30, below the Shambles off Piccadilly). The **Richard III "Museum"** is interesting only for Richard III enthusiasts (£1.50, daily 9:00–17:00, Nov–Feb until 16:00, Monk Bar). The **ARC, or Archaeological Resource Center,** is a big former church full of genuine archaeological artifacts that visitors—mostly school groups—can study as pretend archaeologists (£3.60, Mon–Fri 10:00–16:00, closed Sat–Sun, great for kids, welcomes adults, plenty of microscopes, hands-on fun, and helpful volunteers; just off Shambles on St. Saviourgate, tel. 01904/543-402). The **York Dungeon** is gimmicky but, if you insist on papier-mâché gore, is better than the London Dungeon (£6, daily 10:00–18:30, Oct–Mar until 17:30, 12 Clifford Street). The **antique shops** are a fun browse (41 Stonegate near the Minster, and 2 Lendal near Museum Garden). At the **bowling green** on Sycamore Place near the recommended B&Bs, visitors are welcome (tell them which B&B you're staying at) to buy a pint of beer and watch the action.

Sights—Near York

Eden Camp—Once an internment camp for German and Italian POWs during World War II, this is now a theme museum on Britain's war experience. Various barracks detail the rise of Hitler and the fury of the Blitz (with the sound of bombs, the acrid smell of burning, and quotes such as "Hitler will send no warning—so always carry your gas mask.") This award-winning museum energetically conveys the spirit of a country Hitler couldn't conquer (£3.50, daily 10:00–17:00, closed late-Dec–mid-Jan, mess-kitchen cafeteria, Malton, 18 miles northeast of York, tel. 01653/697-777, www.edencamp.co.uk). To get to the camp from York, catch the Coastliner bus at the York Railway Station (leaves from front of station, on station side of road). Buses are marked with the destination "Whitby" or "Pickering" and are numbered #840, #842, or #X40, depending on the time of day (Mon–Sat 11/day, 50 min, fewer on Sun, £4 round-trip).

Sleeping in York

(£1 = about $1.60, country code: 44, area code: 01904)

Sleep Code: **S** = Single, **D** = Double/Twin, **T** = Triple, **Q** = Quad, **b** = bathroom, **t** = toilet only, **s** = shower only, **CC** = Credit Card (**V**isa, **M**asterCard, **A**mex).

I've listed peak-season, book-direct prices. Don't use the TI. Outside of July and August some prices go soft. B&Bs will sometimes turn away one-night bookings, particularly for peak-season Saturdays. (York is worth two nights.)

Sleeping in B&Bs near Bootham

These recommendations are in the handiest B&B neighborhood, a quiet residential neighborhood just outside the old-town wall's Bootham gate, along the road called Bootham. All are within a five-minute walk of the Minster and TI and a 10-minute walk or taxi ride (£3.50–4) from the station. If driving, head for the cathedral and follow the medieval wall to the gate called Bootham Bar. Bootham "street" leads away from Bootham Bar.

These B&Bs are all small, nonsmoking, and family run and come with plenty of steep stairs but no traffic noise. For a good selection, call well in advance. B&Bs will generally hold a room

York, Our Neighborhood

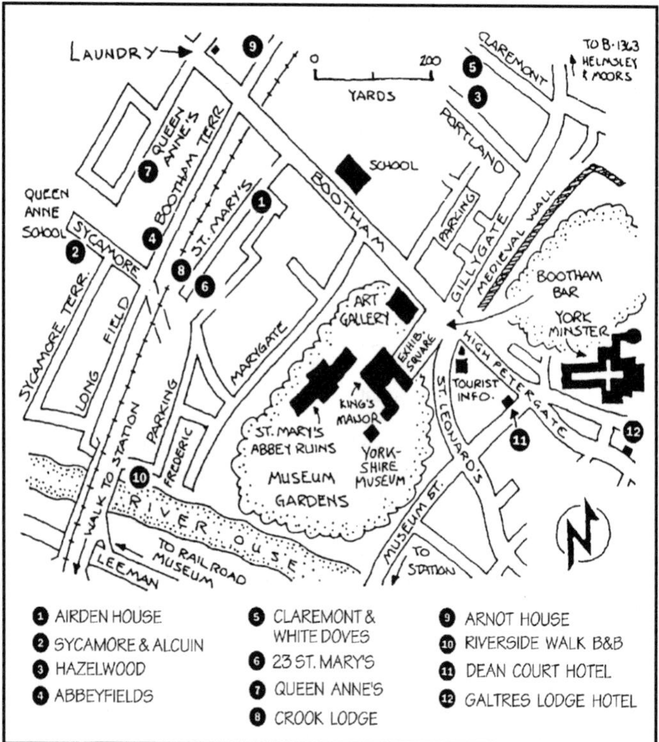

with a phone call and work hard to help their guests sightsee and eat smartly. Most have permits for street parking. And most don't take credit cards.

Laundry: Regency Dry Cleaning does small loads for £8 (drop off by 9:30 for same-day service, Mon–Fri 8:30–18:00, Sat 9:00–17:00, closed Sun, 75 Bootham, at intersection with Queen Anne's, tel. 01904/613-311). The cheaper Washeteria launderette is a 10 to 15 minute walk from the B&B neighborhood (£5 self-serve, £6 full-serve—drop off by 12:00 for same-day service, Mon–Fri 8:00–18:00, Sat 8:00–17:30, Sun 8:00–16:30, last wash 2 hrs before closing, 124 Haxby Road, at north end of Gillygate, continue on Clarence, then Haxby, tel. 01904/623-379).

Airden House, the most central of my Bootham-area listings, has eight spacious rooms, a grandfather clock–cozy TV lounge, and brightness and warmth throughout. Susan and Keith Burrows, a great source of local travel tips, keep their place simple, clean, comfortable, and friendly (D-£40–42, Db-£50–52, 1 St. Mary's, York Y030 7DD, tel. 01904/638-915). They also rent a fully equipped apartment and a house for weeklong stays starting Saturdays (Db-£210–250, Qb-£320–350, a 5-minute walk from the Minster).

The Sycamore, run by Margaret and David Tyce, is a fine value, with seven homey rooms strewn with silk flowers and personal touches. It's at the end of a dead end opposite a fun-to-watch bowling green (S-£20–24, D-£32–34, Db-£42–44, family deals, 19 Sycamore Place off Bootham Terrace, YO30 7DW, tel. & fax 01904/624-712, e-mail: thesycamore@talk21.com).

Abbeyfields Guest House has nine cozy, bright rooms and a quiet lounge. This doily-free place, which lacks the usual clutter, has been designed with care (S-£23, Sb-£33, Db-£52, 19 Boothham Terrace, YO30 7DH, tel. & fax 01904/636-471, www.abbeyfields.co.uk, Richard and Gwen Martin).

23 St. Mary's is extravagantly decorated. Mrs. Hudson has done everything supercorrectly and offers nine comfortable rooms, a classy lounge, and all the doily touches (Sb-£34–36, Db-£64–75 depending on season and size, 23 St. Mary's, YO30 7DD, tel. 01904/622-738, fax 01904/621-168).

Queen Anne's Guest House has seven pleasant, clean, and cheery rooms (May–Sept D-£34, Db-£36, Oct–April D-£30, Db-£32, prices good through 2001 with this book, CC:V, family deals, 24 Queen Anne's Road, Y030 7AA, tel. 01904/629-389, fax 01904/619-529, e-mail: info@queenannes.fsnet.co.uk, Phil and Debbie).

Crook Lodge B&B, with seven charming, tight rooms, is a bit more elegant than the rest (Db-£46–56, car park, quiet, 26 St. Mary's, Y030 7DD, tel. & fax 01904/655-614, Susan and John Arnott).

Alcuin Lodge is a good value, with seven flowery rooms and solid-wood furnishings (Db-£42–50, 1 small top-floor D-£35, no kids, CC:VM, 15 Sycamore Place, Y030 7DW, tel. 01904/632-222, fax 01904/626-630, e-mail: Alcuinlodg@aol.com, Susan Taylor).

Arnot House, run by a friendly daughter-and-mother team, is homey, cluttered, and lushly decorated with early 1900s memorabilia. The four well-furnished rooms have little libraries (Db-£52–56, CC:VM, minimum 2-night stay, nonsmoking, 17 Grosvenor Terrace, Y030 7AG, tel. & fax 01904/641-966, www.arnothouseyork.co.uk, Kim and Ann Robbins).

Riverside Walk B&B, on a pedestrian street along the river, has 14 small shipshape rooms, steep stairs, narrow hallways, and a breakfast room decorated in nautical green that feels like a fisherman's cottage. Request a river view or you'll overlook a car park (2 D-£45, Db-£52–57, nonsmoking, sun terrace on river, quiet, CC:VM for 3.5 percent extra, 8 Earlsborough Terrace, Y030 7BQ, tel. 01904/620-769, fax 01904/646-249, www.riversidewalkbb.demon.co.uk, Julie Mett).

York's Youth Hotel is well run, with lots of extras, like a kitchen, launderette, bar, and game room (S-£16, D-£30, £14 in 4- to 6-bed dorms, less for multinight stays, cheaper in larger dorms, same-sex or coed possible, continental breakfast-£2, CC:VM, 10-minute walk from station at 11 Bishophill Senior Road, YO1 1EF, tel. 01904/625-904, fax 01904/612-494, e-mail: info@yorkyouthhotel.demon.co.uk).

B&Bs nearer the Center

These are off Gillygate, a two minutes' walk to Bootham Bar.

Claremont Guest House is a friendly house offering two delightful rooms and many thoughtful touches, including £3 laundry service (D-£32–40, Db-£36–50, telephone shower, 18 Claremont Terrace off Gillygate, YO31 7EJ, tel. 01904/625-158, e-mail: claremont.york@dial.pipex.com, run by Gill—pronounced Jill—and Martyn Cornell).

White Doves is a cheery little Victorian place with a comfy lounge and three tastefully decorated rooms in soothing pastels (Db-£50–52, family deals, 20 Claremont Terrace off Gillygate, YO31 7EJ, tel. 01904/625-957, Pauline and David Pearce).

The Hazelwood, my most hotelesque listing in this neighborhood, is plush, though it lacks the friendly warmth of a B&B. This spacious house has 14 beautifully decorated rooms with modern furnishings (Db-£65–85 depending on room size, 2 ground-floor rooms, classy breakfast, CC:VM, quiet for being so central, laundry service-£5; a fridge, ice, and great travel library in the pleasant basement lounge; 24 Portland Street, Gillygate, YO31 7EH, tel. 01904/626-548, fax 01904/628-032, e-mail: hazwdyork@aol.com).

Sleeping in Hotels in the Center

Travelodge, newly opened, offers 90 identical, affordable rooms near the Castle Museum (Db-£60, CC:VM, attached restaurant, 1 Piccadilly, central reservations tel. 0870-905-6343).

Dean Court Hotel, facing the Minster, is a big, stately place marketed by Best Western that has classy lounges and 40 comfortable rooms (small Db-£105, standard Db-£130, superior Db-£145 includes fruit, spacious deluxe Db-£160, includes breakfast, CC:VMA, some nonsmoking rooms, tearoom, restaurant, elevator to most rooms, Duncombe Place, YO1 7EF, tel. 01904/625-082, fax 01904/620-305, www.deancourt-york.co.uk).

Galtres Lodge Hotel, a block from the Minster, offers comfy rooms above a restaurant in the old town center (S-£25, Sb-£35, Dt-£50, Db-£65, one refurbished Db-£75 and worth it, CC:VM, nonsmoking, 54 Low Petergate, Y01 7HZ, tel. 01904/622-478, fax 01904/627-804).

Eating in York

Traditional Tea

York is famous for its elegant teahouses. Drop into one around 16:00 for tea and cakes. Ladies love **Betty's Teahouse** (£5 cream tea, CC:VM, daily 9:00–21:00, piano music nightly 18:00–21:00, mostly nonsmoking, St. Helen's Square, fine people watching from a window seat on the main floor; downstairs near WC is a mirror signed by WWII bomber pilots). If there's a line for Betty's, it moves quickly. Or it's easy to come back at dinnertime, when the line disappears—because for the English, "tea time" is over, but tea time is any time at Betty's. If Betty's is just too crowded, many other tearooms can satisfy your king- or queen-for-a-day desires.

Eating near the Minster

Café Concerto, a French-style bistro, has a loyal following for good reason. Their food was the best I've had in York (daily 10:00–22:00, serves meals all day, CC:VM, Petergate 21, under Bootham Bar, smart to reserve at 01904/610-478).

The Viceroy of India—just outside Monk Bar and therefore outside the tourist zone—serves great Indian food at good prices to mostly locals; if you've yet to eat Indian on your trip, do it here (nightly 18:00–24:00, £8 plates, friendly staff, CC:VM, continue straight through Monk Bar to 26 Monkgate, notice the big old "Bile Beans keep you healthy, bright-eyed, and slim" sign on your left, tel. 01904/622-370). **Bengal Brasserie,** which serves Indian food, is also good (minimum charge-£8, Sun–Fri 12:00–14:30, 18:00–24:00, Sat 12:00–24:00, 21 Goodramgate, just inside Monk Bar, tel. 01904/640-066).

For Italian food, consider the popular **Little Italy** (£6–12, Tue–Sun 17:00–23:00, plus Sat 12:00–14:00, closed Mon, Goodramgate 12, just inside Monk Bar, tel. 01904/623-539).

There's a pub serving grub on every block. Eat where you see lots of food. The **Royal Oak** offers £5 pub grub throughout the day, a small nonsmoking room, and hand-pulled ale (daily 11:00–20:00, CC:VM, Goodramgate, a block from Monk Bar, a block east of the Minster, tel. 01904/653-856). The **Golden Slipper,** next door, is also good.

St. Williams Restaurant, just behind the great east window of the Minster in a wonderful half-timbered, 15th-century building, serves quick and tasty lunches and elegant candlelit dinners (daily 10:00–22:00, £10 early bird special 17:30–18:45, otherwise 2 courses-£13, 3 courses-£16, traditional and Mediterranean, CC:VM, College Street, tel. 01904/634-830).

For the closest you'll get to Mexico in Britain, try **Fiesta Mehicana** (nightly 18:00–22:00, take-out available and early bird discount for sit-down dinner before 19:00 except Sat, CC:VM, 14 Clifford Street, tel. 01904/610-243).

Eating near Bootham Bar and Your B&B

Walk along Gillygate and choose from an enjoyable array of eateries: For authentic Italian, consider **Mama Mia's** (£6–9, daily 11:30–14:00, 17:30–23:00, fun, leisurely Italian service, indoor/outdoor patio, CC:VM, 20 Gillygate, tel. 01904/622-020). **Gillygate Fisheries** is a wonderfully traditional little fish-and-chips joint where tattooed people eat in and housebound mothers take out (Mel serves £3–4 meals, "eat your mushy peas," Mon 17:00–23:30, Tue–Fri 11:30–13:30, 17:00–23:30, Sat 11:30–23:30, closed Sun, smoke-free seating, 59 Gillygate).

Pubs: The **Waggon and Horses** pub has local color and £5 meals (Mon–Sat 11:30–21:00, Sun 12:00–15:00, across from Fisheries joint, Gillygate 48, tel. 01904/654-103). The **Coach House** has consistently good quality (£8–11, CC:VM, nightly 18:30–21:30, 20 Marygate, tel. 01904/652-780). The **Grange Hotel's Brasserie** is easy, a couple of blocks from the B&Bs, and classier than a pub. Go downstairs—avoid the pricey ground-floor restaurant (£9 meals, Mon–Sat 12:00–14:00, 18:00–22:00, Sun 18:00–22:00, CC:VM, 1 Clifton, tel. 01904/644-744). The people who run your B&B know the latest on what's good.

Grocery stores: In the B&B neighborhood you'll find **Spar** (daily 9:00–21:00, on 61 Bootham, at intersection with Queen Anne's Road) and **Jacksons** (a little run-down but open late, daily 7:00–23:00, near Bootham Bar, on Bootham). In the old town is **Marks & Spencers** (Mon–Sat 9:30–18:00, Sun 11:00–17:00, on Parliament Street); go to the top floor for a striking view of the south wall of the Minster from the menswear department.

Most atmospheric picnic spot: In the Museum Gardens (near Bootham Bar), at the evocative 12th-century ruins of **St. Mary's Abbey**.

Transportation Connections—York

By train to: Durham (hrly, 60 min), **Edinburgh** (2/hrly, 2 hrs), **London** (2/hrly, 2 hrs), **Bath** (via Bristol, hrly, 5 hrs), **Cambridge** (nearly hrly, 2 hrs with a change in Petersborough), **Birmingham** (8/day, 3 hrs). Train info: tel. 08457/484-950.

By bus to: Keswick (1/day, 4 hrs, Stagecoach X9 bus runs mid-April–early Sept Mon–Sat, runs both directions, leaving York in afternoon, leaving Keswick in morning, also stops in Grasmere, Ambleside, and Windermere, tel. 01946/63222; off-season, when bus doesn't run, train is doable though tiring: allow 4 hrs, with transfers at Newcastle, Carlisle, and Penrith, then bus to Keswick).

The **York Bus Information Centre** is at 20 Hudson Street, near the train station (Mon–Fri 8:30–17:00, Sat 9:00–12:30, Sun

8:00–14:00, tel. 01904/551400, phone answered Mon–Sat 8:00–20:00, Sun 8:00–14:00).

Route Tips for Drivers

As you near York (and your B&B), you'll hit the A1237 ring road. Follow this to the A19/Thirsk roundabout (next to river on northeast side of town). From roundabout, follow signs for York City, traveling through Clifton into Bootham. All recommended B&Bs are four or five blocks before you hit the medieval city gate (see neighborhood map). If you're approaching York from the south, take M1 until it ends, then A64 for 10 miles until you reach York.

NEAR YORK: NORTH YORK MOORS

The North York Moors are a vacant lot compared with the Cumbrian Lake District. But that's unfair competition. In the lonesome North York Moors you can wander through the stark beauty of its time-passed villages, bored sheep, and powerful landscapes.

If you're driving, get a map. Without wheels, you have several choices: take a bus/steam train combination (below); choose one of several guided bus tours from York (focusing on Herriot or Brontë country, moors, Lake District, or Holy Island, different tour every day, offered by various companies for roughly £10 half day/£16 full day); or hire a private guide. John Smith, a licensed guide and driver, can take up to three people on one of his Yorkshire Tours—such as Herriot Country, a Castle Howard/steam train/Whitby combination, or a tour tailored to your interests (£15/hr, admissions extra, tel. 01904/636-653, cellular 0850-260-511).

Sights—North York Moors

▲**The Moors**—Car hike across the moors on any small road. You'll come upon tidy villages, old Roman roads, and maybe even a fox hunt. The Moors Visitors Centre provides the best orientation for exploring the moors. It's a grand old lodge offering exhibits, shows, nature walks, an information desk with plenty of books and maps, brass rubbing, a cheery cafeteria, and brochures on several good walks that start right there (free, April–Oct daily 10:00–17:00, Nov–Dec and March daily 11:00–16:00, Jan–Feb weekends only 11:00–16:00, a half mile from train station, tel. 01287/660-654, www.northyorkmoors-npa.gov.uk).

▲**North Yorkshire Moors Railway**—This 18-mile, one-hour steam-engine ride between Pickering and Grosmont (grow-mont) goes through some of the best parts of the moors almost hourly. Even with the windows small and dirty (wipe off the outside of yours before you roll) and the track mostly in a scenic gully, it's a good ride. You can stop along the way for a moors walk and catch the next train (£10 round-trip, May–Oct, first train departs Pickering about 9:20, last train departs Grosmount about 16:50, allow

3.5 hrs round-trip due to scheduling, CC:VM, tel. 01751/472-508, talking timetable 01751/473-535). It's not possible to leave luggage at any stop on the steam-train line—pack light if you decide to hike.

Pickering, with its rural-life museum, castle, and Monday market, is worth a stop. You could catch an early York–Pickering bus (hrly, 65 min, leaves from train station), see Pickering, and carry on to Grosmont, which is on a regular train line with good connections to Whitby and points north (or south).

▲Hutton-le-Hole—This postcard-pretty town is home of the fine Ryedale Folk Museum, which illustrates "farm life in the moors" through reconstructed and furnished 18th-century local buildings (£3.25, mid-March–Oct daily 10:00–17:30, tel. 01751/417-367).

Castle Howard—Especially popular since the filming of *Brideshead Revisited*, this fine, palatial 300-year-old home is about half as interesting as the Cotswolds' Blenheim Palace (£7.50, daily 11:00–17:00, closed early Nov–mid-March, 2 buses/day from York, 40 min, tel. 01653/648-333).

Rievaulx Abbey—Rievaulx (ree-voh) is a highlight of North York Moors and beautifully situated, but, if you've seen other fine old abbeys, this is a rerun (£3.40, April–Sept daily 10:00–18:00, July–Aug until 9:00, Oct until 17:00, Nov–March until 16:00, tel. 01439/798-228).

▲James Herriot Country—Herriot fans will be more interested in the Yorkshire Dales than the neighboring moors. Local booklets at the TI lay out the *All Creatures Great and Small* pilgrimage route for drivers, or you could consider a tour from York (see leaflets at TI).

Staithes/Whitby—See Durham and Northeast England chapter.

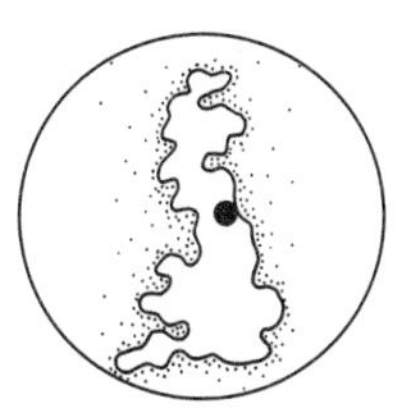

DURHAM AND NORTHEAST ENGLAND

Some of England's best history is harbored in the northeast. Hadrian's Wall reminds us that Britain was an important Roman colony 2,000 years ago. After a Roman ramble, you can make a pilgrimage to Holy Island, where Christianity gained its first toehold in Britain. At Durham, marvel at England's greatest Norman church and enjoy an evensong service. Travel back in time to spend a morning in the year 1913 at the Beamish Open-Air Folk Museum.

Planning Your Time

Of the sights described in this chapter, train travelers will find Durham the most convenient stop on a three-week British train trip. You can see Hadrian's Wall en route (doable with transfers, easiest late May–late Sept), a worthwhile visit for those inspired by Roman ruins. The Beamish Folk Museum is an easy day trip from Durham (hrly bus, 20 min).

By car you'll be driving right by Hadrian's Wall, Holy Island, Bamburgh, and the Beamish Folk Museum. Whitby and Staithes are seaside escapes worth a stop only for the seagulls and surf. Whitby is accessible by train, but Staithes makes sense only with a car.

By car, connect Edinburgh and York by this string of sights, spending a night near Hadrian's Wall and a night in Durham on a one-month trip, just a night in Durham on a three-week trip. For drivers (or train travelers) with 36 hours between Edinburgh and York, leave Edinburgh early, tour Hadrian's Wall and Housesteads Fort, take a walk and have lunch, and get to Durham in time to tour the cathedral and enjoy the evensong service (Tue–Sat 17:15, Sun 15:30). Sleep in Durham. Tour Beamish (15 minutes north of Durham by car or bus) or drive through the North York Moors the next day, arriving in York by late afternoon.

DURHAM

Without its cathedral it would hardly be noticed. But this magnificently situated cathedral is hard not to notice (even if you're zooming by on the train). Durham sits, seemingly happy to go nowhere, along its river and below its castle and famous cathedral. It has a workaday, medieval, cobbled atmosphere and a scraggly peasant's indoor market just off the main square (closed Sun). While Durham is the home of England's third-oldest university, the town feels working class, surrounded by newly closed coal mines and filled with tattooed and stapled people in search of job security. Yet Durham has a youthful vibrancy and a small-town warmth that shines especially on sunny days, when most everyone is licking an ice-cream cone or plans to.

Orientation (tel. code: 0191)

Tidy little Durham clusters everything safely under its castle within the tight, protective bend of its river. The longest walk you'd make would be a 15-minute walk from the train station to the cathedral.

Tourist Information: The TI, located on the town square, books rooms and local theater tickets, provides train times, and, from June through September, offers 90-minute city walks Wednesday and Saturday at 14:15 for £3 (June–Sept Mon–Sat 10:00–17:30, July–Aug also Sun 14:00–17:00; Oct–May Mon–Fri 10:00–17:00, Sat 10:00–13:00; public WC next door in indoor market, tel. 0191/384-3720). The brochure "Guided Walks in County Durham" lists themed walks led by local experts (£1, several times weekly, some hikes start in Durham).

Arrival in Durham: From the train station, follow the road downhill and take the second pedestrian turnoff (within sight of railway bridge), which leads almost immediately over a bridge above busy Alexander Crescent road; then take North Road into town or to the first couple of B&Bs (take Alexander Crescent to the other B&Bs). Day-trippers can store luggage at the station (£1.50, daily 7:00–20:00, ask at ticket window).

Helpful Hints

Internet Access: Reality-X is hard core, with 18 computers and no food (£5/hr, daily 10:00–22:00, at the west end of Framwelgate Bridge, might close in 2001, tel. 0191/384-5700); Saints Café has three computers as an afterthought (£2.50/30 min, daily 10:00–18:00, behind TI, from inside covered market go downstairs in the back, or reach from river, Market Vaults, tel. 0191/386-7700).

Car Rental: Embleton's of Durham is a few blocks off the city center (81 New Elvet, tel. 0191/384-777). The nearest brand names are in Newcastle (Avis: tel. 0191/232-5283, Budget: tel. 0191/261-8282, Hertz: tel. 0191/232-5313).

Durham

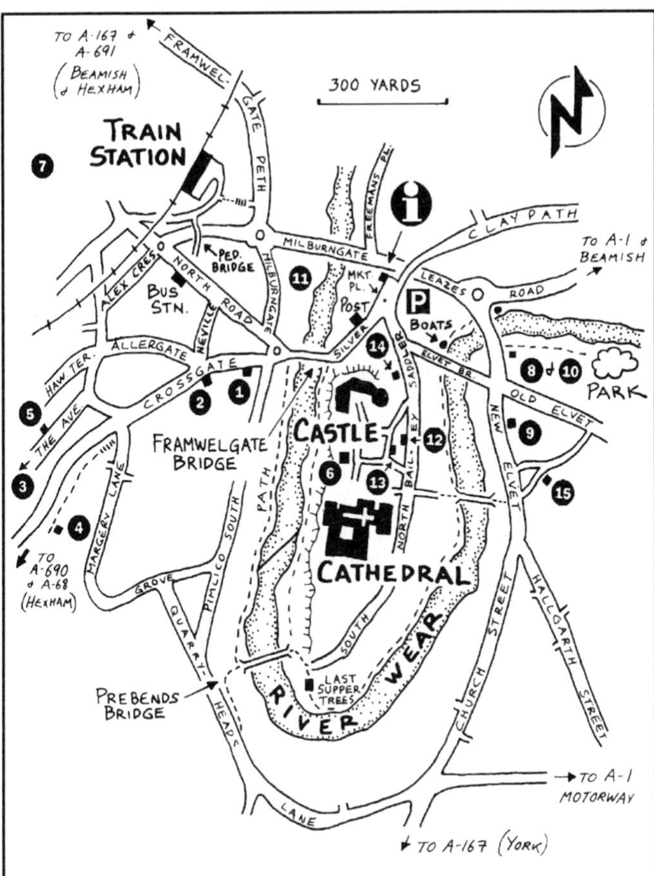

1. CASTLEVIEW GUEST HOUSE
2. GEORGIAN TOWN HOUSE
3. FARNLEY TOWER B&B
4. CASTLEDENE B&B
5. #12 B&B
6. DURHAM CASTLE HOUSING
7. BROMME FARM GUEST HOUSE
8. WATERSIDE HOTEL
9. SWALLOW THREE TUNS
10. SWALLOW ROYAL COUNTY
11. PIZZERIA VENEZIA & SAFEWAY
12. SHAHEEN'S RESTAURANT
13. THE ALMSHOUSES REST.
14. HOGSHEAD ALE HOUSE
15. COURT INN PUB

Sights—Durham

▲▲▲Cathedral—Built to house the much-venerated bones of St. Cuthbert from Lindisfarne, the cathedral is the best look at Norman architecture in England (free but £2.50 donation requested, daily 7:30–18:00, early Sept–Easter until 17:00, limited access Sun morning). For various fees, you can also climb the tower, ogle the treasury, and tour the Monk's Dormitory. I'd skip the A-V show on St. Cuthbert. Try to fit in some music (see "Evensong and Church Bells," below). No photos or videos are allowed. Tucked away in the cloisters you'll find a bookshop, cafeteria, and WC.

A Tour Plan: From the cathedral green, notice how this fortress of God stands boldly across from the Norman keep of Durham's fortress of man. (The castle, now part of the university, is not worth touring.)

As you stand at the cathedral door, notice the big, bronze, lion-faced knocker, a replica of the 12th-century original (in treasury), which was used by criminals seeking sanctuary (read the explanation).

Immediately inside you'll see the **information desk**. Church attendants happily answer questions. Ideally, follow a church tour (£3 donation, late May–early Sept Mon–Sat at 10:30 and 14:00, also at 11:30 in Aug; if one's in session you're welcome to join). The "A Walk Round Durham Cathedral" guide pamphlet is informative but dull (60p).

Notice the modern window with the novel depiction of the Last Supper (above and to the left of the entry door, given to the church by a local department store in 1984) and remember that the cathedral remains a living part of the community.

Near the entrance, the black marble strip on the floor was as close to the altar as women were allowed in the days when this was a Benedictine church (until 1540). Sit down (ignoring the black line) and let the fine proportions of England's best Norman (and arguably Europe's best Romanesque) nave stir you. Any frilly woodwork and stonework were added in later centuries.

The architecture of the **nave** is particularly harmonious because it was built in a mere 40 years (1093–1133). Few additions were made, and the bulk of what you see today is Norman (that's British for Romanesque). The round arches and zigzag carved decorations are textbook Norman. The church was also proto-Gothic, built by well-traveled French masons and architects who knew the latest innovations from Europe. Its stone and ribbed roof, Britain's first pointed arches, and first flying buttresses were revolutionary in this country. Notice the clean lines and simplicity. It's not as cluttered as other churches for several reasons. Out of respect for St. Cuthbert, for centuries no one else was buried here. During Reformation times, sumptuous Catholic decor was high risk. And subsequent fires and wars destroyed what Protestants didn't.

Durham Cathedral

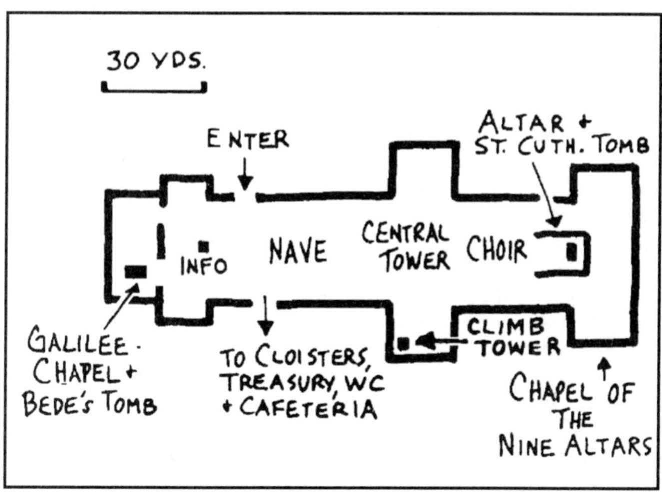

Enter the **Galilee Chapel** (late Norman, from 1175) in the back of the nave. Notice the paintings of St. Cuthbert and St. Oswald (seventh-century king of Northumbria) on the side walls of the side altar niche, rare examples of Romanesque or Norman paintings. Facing this altar, look above to your right to see more faint paintings on the upper walls above the columns. Near the center of the chapel, the upraised tomb topped with a black slab contains the remains of the Venerable Bede, an 8th-century Christian scholar who wrote the first history of England.

Back in the main church, stroll down the nave to the center, under the highest bell tower in Europe (218 feet). Gaze up. The ropes pull hammers that ring the bells. If you're stirred by the cheery ringing of **church bells,** tune into the cathedral on Sunday (9:30–10:00 and 14:30–15:00) or Thursday (19:30 practice) when the resounding notes pelt the entire town like rain.

Continuing east (all medieval churches faced east), you enter the **choir**. Monks worshiped many times a day, and the choir in the center of the church provided a cozier place to gather in this vast, dark, and cold building. This is the heart of the cathedral, where Mass has been said daily for 900 years. The fancy wooden chairs are from the 17th century. Behind the altar is the delicately carved stone Neville Screen (1380). Exit the choir from the far right side (south). Look for the millennium stained-glass window (to your right) commemorating the church's 1,000th anniversary in 1995. The colorful scenes depict England's history from coal miners to cows to computers.

Step down into the **apse,** the Gothic east end of the church. Go up a few stairs to the tomb of St. Cuthbert. An inspirational leader of the early Christian church in North England, St. Cuthbert lived in the Lindisfarne monastery on Holy Island (100 miles north of Durham). He died in 687. Eleven years later his body was exhumed and found to be miraculously preserved. This stoked the popularity of his shrine, and pilgrims came in growing numbers. When Vikings raided Lindisfarne in 875, the monks fled with his body (and the famous illuminated *Lindisfarne Gospels,* now in the British Library in London). After 120 years of roaming, in 995 they settled in Durham on an easy-to-defend hairpin bend in the Wear River. The cathedral was built over Cuthbert's tomb. His tomb is part of the larger 13th-century Gothic Chapel of the Nine Altars—taller, lighter, and relatively more extravagant than the Norman nave.

Consider the cathedral's other sights. The entry to the **tower** is in the south transept; the view from the tower will cost you 325 steps and £2 (Mon–Sat 10:00–16:00, Nov–March 10:00–15:00, closed Sun). The following sights are within the cloisters: The **treasury** (well worth £2), filled with medieval bits and holy pieces, fleshes out this otherwise stark building. The actual relics from St. Cuthbert's tomb are at the far end (Mon–Sat 10:00–16:30, Sun 14:00–16:00). The **Monks' Dormitory,** now a library with an original 14th-century timber roof filled with Anglo-Saxon stones, is worth 80p (Mon–Sat 10:00–15:30, Sun 12:30–15:00). The unexceptional A-V show in the unexceptional undercroft tells about St. Cuthbert (not worth 80p). The fine cafeteria (daily 10:00–16:30, lunch 12:00–14:30, nonsmoking), bookshop (in the old kitchen), and WCs are near the treasury.

Evensong: For a thousand years this cradle of English Christianity has been praising God. To really experience the cathedral, go for an evensong service. Arrive early and ask to be seated in the choir. It's a spiritual Oz, as 40 boys sing psalms—a red-and-white-robed pillow of praise, raised up by the powerful pipe organ. If you're lucky and the service went well, the organist runs a spiritual musical victory lap as the congregation breaks up (begins at 17:15 Tue–Sat, Sun at 15:30, 1 hr, normally not sung on Mon; when choir is off on school break during mid-July–August, visiting choirs often fill in; tel. 0191/386-2367).

Riverside Walk—For a 20-minute woodsy escape, walk Durham's riverside path from busy Framwelgate Bridge to sleepy Prebends Bridge. Just beyond the Prebends Bridge on the old-town side of the river, you'll find The Upper Room, a cluster of trees carved to show the Last Supper when seen from the tree-trunk throne provided. Where are the apostles? Count the tree trunks.

Boat Cruise and Rental—Captain Phil, known fondly in town as a "character," offers 60-minute narrated cruises of the river on the

"Prince Bishop" (£3.50, for schedule, call 0191/386-9525, check at TI, or go down to the dock at Brown's Boat House at Elvet Bridge, just east of old town). For his crocodile cruises for kids, he dresses up like a pirate and tows inflatable crocs.

You can also rent a rowboat at Brown's Boat House (£2.50/hr per person, £5 deposit, Easter–Sept daily 10:00–18:00, tel. 0191/386-3779).

Sleeping in Durham

(£1 = about $1.60, country code: 44, area code: 0191)

Sleep Code: **S** = Single, **D** = Double/Twin, **T** = Triple, **Q** = Quad, **b** = bathroom, **t** = toilet only, **s** = shower only, **CC** = Credit Card (**V**isa, **M**asterCard, **A**mex).

The B&Bs are a 5- or 10-minute walk from the station and the town center. Durham hosts a Rowing Regatta the second weekend in June; book ahead.

The only launderette in town is at Dunelm House, the Student Union building—a 10- to15-minute walk east of the B&B neighborhood (daily 8:00–21:00 during school term, otherwise 9:00–15:00, open to public, east end of Kingsgate Bridge, tel. 0191/374-3310).

Sleeping in B&Bs

Castleview Guest House, 400 yards off Framwelgate Bridge, is a good bet, with six airy, comfortable rooms (Sb-£40, Db-£55, nonsmoking, only garden has castle view, 4 Crossgate, DH1 4PS, tel. & fax 0191/386-8852, castle_view@hotmail.com, Mike and Anne Williams).

Georgian Town House, a few doors down, has a cheery bossa nova ambience with a breezy garden, plush sitting room, and bright rooms decorated with care and flair. The hearty breakfast is served in the conservatory (Db-£60 with this book, nonsmoking, tubs lack showers, some rooms with castle views, 10 Crossgate, DH1 4PS, tel. & fax 0191/386-8070, Jane Weil).

Farnley Tower, which bills itself as a "luxurious B&B," is indeed. Opened in mid-1999, it still feels like it just came out of the box. Its eleven doubles have all the comforts, and some have views. The hotel is on a quiet dead end at the top of a hill, a five-minute uphill walk (1 Sb-£40, Db-£60, superior Db-£70, CC:VM, nonsmoking, phones in rooms, pleasant bar, easy parking, 10-minute walk from station and city center, The Avenue, DH1 4DX, tel. 0191/375-0011, fax 0191/383-9694, e-mail: inquiries@farnleytowerhotel.fst.co.uk, John and Gail Khan).

Castledene B&B is tidy, simple, and friendly, with three twin-bedded rooms and double-glazed windows to keep the house quiet and warm (D-£40, top room has cathedral views; at inter section of Crossgate and Margery Lane, go up the stairs to the pedestrian-only walkway—running parallel to Crossgate Peth—to last house, 37 Nevilledale Terrace, DH1 4QG; drivers go south on Margery Lane a few yards past the intersection with Crossgate and turn right on Summerville, tel. & fax 0191/384-8386, Lorna and Brian Byrne, e-mail: lornabyrne@tinyworld.co.uk).

The low-key **Bed & Breakfast** has two simple rooms on a quiet dead-end street (small S-£20, D-£40, nonsmoking, no sign on door, close to train and bus station, 12 The Avenue, DH1 4ED, tel. 0191/384-1020, e-mail: jan.hanim@aol.com, run by kindly Jan Metcalfe).

Student Housing—Open to Anyone: Durham Castle, a student residence actually on the castle grounds facing the cathedral, rents 100 singles and 30 doubles (July–Sept only, £20.50 per person, £30.50 with private facilities, CC:VM, elegant breakfast hall; parking, with luck, on the cathedral green; University College, The Castle, Palace Green, DH1 3RW, can reserve long in advance, tel. 0191/374-3863, fax 0191/374-7470, Julie Marshall). Request a room in the classy old main building or you may get one of the few bomb shelter–style modern dorm rooms.

Away from the Center: Drivers could consider the **Bromme Farm Guest House,** which is good but two miles out of town (4 rooms, S-£20, D-£40, across from Love's Pub, Broom Park, DH7 7QX, tel. 0191/386-4755).

Hotels

These three hotels are Durham's most central, just a few blocks from the TI.

Waterside Private Hotel, perched on the river and hemmed in by the Royal County Hotel (below), offers 11 pleasant rooms, two on the ground floor and two with river views at no extra cost (Db-£75, CC:VM, publike restaurant, Elvet Waterside, DH1 3BW, tel. 0191/384-6660, fax 0191/384-6996).

Two big, pricey hotels, jointly owned, are virtually next door, near the river. Both offer "Breakaway" deals for two-night weekend stays: rooms are slightly discounted and dinner is thrown in. The cheaper **Swallow Three Tuns Hotel**, in a 19th-century building, has three stars and 50 comfortable rooms. Guests are welcome to use the Leisure Club at the sister hotel (Db-£120–145, includes breakfast, CC:VMA, New Elvet, DH1 3AQ, tel. 0191/386-4326, fax 0191/386-1406, www.swallowhotels.com). The **Swallow Royal County Hotel,** a four-star hotel, scatters its 151 posh rooms among several buildings sprawling along the river. The Leisure Club has a pool, sauna, Jacuzzi, and fitness equipment (Db-£150–175, includes breakfast, CC:VM, request larger standard double, 2 restaurants, bar, car park, Old Elvet, DH1 3JN, tel. 0191/386-6821, fax 0191/386-0704, www.swallowhotels.com). Personally, I'd rather pay less and stay at Farnley Tower (above).

Eating in Durham

Trust your host's advice, or stroll from Framwelgate Bridge through Market Place up Saddler and take what looks good. Consider **Pizzeria Venezia** for affordable Italian food (Mon–Sat 12:00–13:45, 18:00–21:45, early bird specials 18:00–19:00, west end of Framwelgate Bridge, tel. 0191/384-6777), **Bimbi's** for fish and chips (daily 11:00–22:30, on Market Place), **Shaheen's** for healthy Indian (nightly 18:00–23:30, CC:VM, up Saddler Street just past the turn-off to the cathedral, tel. 0191/386-0960), or **The Almshouses** on the cathedral green for tasty light meals (daily 9:00–20:00, Oct–Easter until 17:00, CC:VM, tel. 0191/386-1054). For healthy pub grub, consider **Hogshead Ale House** on Saddler Street in the old town (£-4–5, serving daily 12:00–19:00, wraps, salads, veggie menu, tel. 0191/386-9550). For more traditional pub grub, it's the **Court Inn** (daily 11:00–22:30, Court Lane, 5-minute walk east of old town, take Elvet or Kingsgate Bridge, tel. 0191/384-7350). Drivers looking for a nontouristy splurge can try **Bistro 21** (Mon–Sat 12:00–14:00, 18:00–22:00, closed Sun, CC:VM, Aykley Heads, 3 miles north of town, tel. 0191/384-4354).

Supermarkets: Of Durham's two supermarkets, **Safeway** has longer hours and is closer to the recommended B&Bs (Mon–Fri 8:30–20:00, Sat 8:00–18:00, in Millburngate Shopping Center, west end of Framwelgate Bridge). In the old town, try **Marks & Spencers,** just off the main square (Mon–Sat 9:00–17:30, on Silver Street, across from P.O., which has same hours). You can picnic on the benches and grass outside the cathedral entrance (but not on the Palace Green, unless the park police have gone home).

Transportation Connections—Durham

By train to: Edinburgh (nearly hrly, 2 hrs), **York** (1–3/hrly, 1 hr), **London** (hrly, 3 hrs), **Hadrian's Wall** (take train to Newcastle—1–4/hrly, 15 min; then a train/bus combination to Hadrian's Wall, see "Hadrian's Wall," below), **Bristol** (near Bath, 9/day, 5 hrs). Off-season, from September to May, only about half of the London–Edinburgh trains stop in little Durham; frequency drops to about six trains daily in winter (catch train to Newcastle for more options—1–4/hrly, 15 min). Train info: tel. 08457-484-950.

Parking in Durham: Parking in old Durham is nearly impossible. You're best off simply following the signs into the big public parking lots at the bottom end of town (£1.30/day in open lot, £10 in underground garage).

HADRIAN'S WALL

This is one of England's most thought-provoking sights. Around A.D. 130, during the reign of Emperor Hadrian, the Romans built this great stone wall. Its actual purpose is still debated. While Rome ruled Britain for 400 years, it never quite ruled its people.

The wall may have been used to define the northern edge of the empire, protect Roman Britain from invading Scottish tribes (or at least cut down on pesky border raids), monitor the movement of people, or simply give an otherwise bored army something to do. (Nothing's more dangerous than a bored army.) Stretching 74 miles coast to coast across the narrowest stretch of northern England, it was built and defended by nearly 20,000 troops. The wall was flanked by ditches, and a military road lies on the south side. At every mile of the wall a castle guards a gate, and two turrets stand between each castle. The mile castles are numbered. (Eighty of them cover the 74 miles because a Roman mile was slightly shorter than our mile.) Today, several chunks of the wall, ruined forts, and museums thrill history buffs. About a dozen Roman sites cling along the wall's route; the best are Housesteads Fort and Vindolanda. Housesteads shows you where the Romans lived; Vindolanda's museum shows you how they lived.

Sights—Hadrian's Wall

▲▲Housesteads Fort—With its tiny museum, powerful scenery, and the best-preserved segment of the wall, this is your best single stop. All Roman forts were the same rectangular shape and design, with the commander's headquarters, barracks, and latrines (lower end); this fort even has a hospital. The fort is built right up to the wall, which is on the far side (£2.80 for site and museum, June–Oct daily 10:00–18:00, Nov–May 10:00–17:00 or dusk, £1 car park, tel. 01434/344-363). At the car park are the WCs, snack bar, and a gift shop. You can leave your baggage at the gift shop, but confirm closing hours. From the car park, it's a half-mile, mostly uphill walk to the entrance of the miniscule museum and sprawling fort.

▲▲Hiking the Wall—From Housesteads, hike west along the wall speaking Latin. For a good, craggy, three-mile walk along the wall, hike between Housesteads and Steel Rigg. You'll pass a castle sitting in a nick in a crag (castle #39, called Castle Nick). There's a car park near Steel Rigg (take the little road up from Twice Brewed Pub).

▲Vindolanda—This larger Roman fort (which actually predates the wall by 40 years) and museum are just south of the wall. Although Housesteads has better ruins and the wall, Vinolanda has the better museum, revealing intimate details of Roman life. Eight forts were built on this spot. The Romans, by carefully sealing the foundations from each successive fort, left modern-day archaeologists seven yards of remarkably well-preserved artifacts to excavate: keys, coins, brooches, scales, pottery, glass, tools, leather shoes, bits of cloth, and even a wig. The earliest examples of Roman writing were recently discovered here. While the actual letters, written on thin wood, are in London's British Museum, see the interesting video here and read the translations—the first

Durham and Northeast England

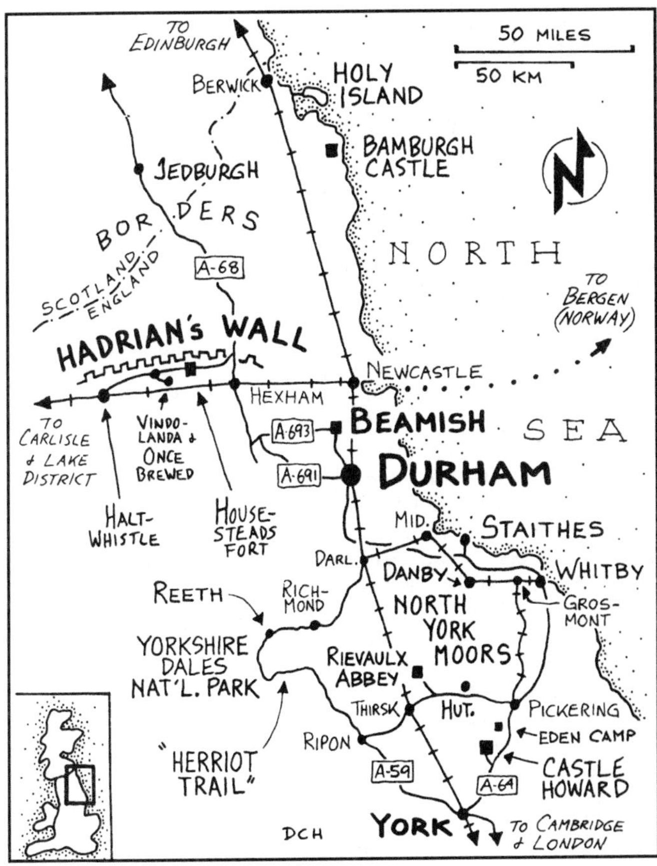

known example of a woman writing to a woman is an invitation to a birthday party. These varied letters, about parties held, money owed, and sympathy shared, brings Romans to life in a way that stones alone can't.

From the car park you'll walk through 600 yards of grassy parkland decorated by the foundation stones of the Roman fort and a full-size replica chunk of the wall. At the far side of the site is the museum, gift shop, and cafeteria (£3.80, £5.60 combo ticket includes Roman Army Museum, May–Aug daily 10:00–18:00, April/Sept closes at 17:30, March/Oct at 17:00, late-Feb/early-Nov at 16:00, closed late-Nov–early-Feb, can leave baggage at entrance, tel. 01434/344-277). The **Roman Army Museum,** a few miles farther west at Greenhead, is redundant if you've seen Vindolanda (£3, or buy combo ticket, above, same hours).

Walk the Wall—Mark your calendars. In 2003, it will be possible to walk along the wall's route on a new path stretching from coast to coast.

Sleeping and Eating near Hadrian's Wall

(£1 = about $1.60, country code: 44, area code: 01434)

Crindledykes Farm is a classy old farmhouse in an idyllic and peaceful setting a mile south of the wall (small D-£38, spacious twin room with view-£40, room for a child's bed, WC down the hall, nonsmoking, accessible by car only, signposted from the B6318 at Housesteads, Bardon Mill, Hexham, NE47 7AF, tel. 01434/344-316, Judy Davidson).

East Wharmley Farm rents two spacious rooms in a wonderfully rural setting; the farm's six miles from Housesteads on the A69, midway between Haydon Bridge and Hexham (D-£36, family deals, nonsmoking, Hexham, NE46 2PL, tel. & fax 01434/674-259, Dorothy and Harold Foster).

Crow's Nest B&B offers three rooms in a remodeled farmhouse a quarter mile from the wall (D-£36, on B6318 road 500 yards from the Once Brewed TI and hostel at East Twice Brewed, Bardon Mill, Hexham, tel. 01434/344-348, Jean Wanless).

The nearby **Mile Castle Pub** cooks up all sorts of exotic game and offers the best dinner around, according to hungry national park rangers. Two miles west of Housesteads, the **Twice Brewed Pub and Hotel** serves decent pub grub nightly to a local darts-and-pool crowd (S-£19, D-£37, Db-£45, dreary rooms, rarely full, tel. 01434/344-534). Next door to the Twice Brewed Pub is the comfortable **Once Brewed Youth Hostel** (£11 per bed with sheets, breakfast-£3.50, cheap lunches and dinners, 4–7 beds per room, Military Road, Bardon Mill, tel. 01434/344-360, fax 01434/344-045, e-mail: oncebrewed@yha.org.uk).

In Haltwhistle, consider the Old Schoolhouse B&B (3 Db-£40, Fairhill Road, also serves as writers' retreat, quiet, nonsmoking, 5-minute walk from Haltwhistle train station, tel. & fax 01434/322-595, cellular 077-1180-9180, www.oshouse.freeserve.co.uk).

Transportation Connections—Hadrian's Wall

By Car: Take B6318; it parallels the wall and passes several viewpoints, minor sights, and "severe dips." (If there's a certified nerd or bozo in the car, these road signs add a lot to a photo portrait.)

By Train and Bus: A train/bus combination (which operates with greatest frequency late May–late Sept) delivers you to the wall. From England's east coast, Newcastle is the gateway to the Newcastle–Carlisle train paralleling the wall (10/day, from Newcastle it's 30 min to Hexham, 20 more min to Haltwhistle). But the train only gets you near the wall. During peak season, take Hadrian's Wall bus #682 to get to the wall and all the Roman sights; get off the train at either Hexham or Haltwhistle to catch this bus (5 buses daily in each direction, late May–late Sept; Hexham–Housesteads 30 min, Housesteads–Vindolanda 10 min, Vindolanda–Haltwhistle 20 min). At Newcastle's train station, pick up a Hadrian's Wall bus schedule at the TI (Mon–Fri 9:30–17:30, until 20:00 June–Sept, Sat 9:30–17:00, Sun 10:00–16:00, can call for schedule, tel. 0191/261-0610) or call Haltwhistle's helpful TI for schedule information (Mon–Sat 10:00–13:00, 14:00–17:00, until 18:00 late-May–Sept, Sun 13:00–17:00; Nov–Easter Mon–Tue and Thu–Sat 10:00–12:30, 13:00–15:30, closed Wed and Sun, tel. 01434/322-002, www.hadrians-wall.org). If you start from Newcastle by at least 11:00 (earlier is better), you can fit in both Housesteads and Vindolanda.

To visit Housesteads off-season (late Sept–late May), first take a train to Haltwhistle. To continue to Housesteads, either catch the bus (bus #185, 2/day Mon–Sat, 20 min, call Haltwhistle's TI, above, for schedule) or take a taxi (taxi services: Sprouls 01434/321-064, Turnbulls 01434/320-105, £8 one-way; arrange for return pickup or have museum staff call a taxi).

Day-trippers can store luggage at Newcastle's train station (£2–3, daily 8:00–18:00, return by 18:00 or get it tomorrow). If you're staying on the wall, your B&B host can arrange a taxi.

By Tour: Consider Margaret Bond (based in Durham, tel. 0191/378-4700, www.escortedtoursuk.com).

Other Sights near Durham

▲▲Beamish Open-Air Museum—This huge museum, which recreates the year 1913 in northeast England, takes at least three hours to explore. A vintage tram shuttles visitors the four stations: Coal Mine Village, Home Farm, The Town, and an 1820s Manor House. This isn't wax. If you touch the exhibits, they may smack you. Attendants at each stop explain everything.

Start with the Coal Mine Village (company village around a coal mine), with a school, church, miners' homes, and a fascinating—if claustrophobic—20-minute tour into a real "drift" mine.

"The Town" (along with the mine tour) is the highlight. This bustling street features a 1913 candy shop, a dentist's office, a garage, a working pub (fun for a smoky beer), and a modern, smoke-free cafeteria. The old train station isn't much.

The Pockerley Manor, an 1820s manor house, is barely worth the climb, but the recreated first-ever passenger train from 1825—which takes modern-day visitors for a spin on 1825 tracks—draws railway buffs. The Home Farm is the least interesting section. (£10, daily 10:00–17:00; from Nov–March only "The Town" is open, 10:00–16:00, closed Mon and Fri; check events schedule as you enter, last tickets 2 hours before closing, tel. 01207/231-811.)

The museum is located between the villages of Stanley and Chester-le-Street. To get to Beamish from Durham, catch a #720 bus (marked "Stanley via Beamish," hrly, 20 min, stops 700 yards from museum) or drive north on the AI to the first exit (Chester-le-Street) and follow the signs.

▲**Whitby**—Whitby is a fun coastal resort town with a busy harbor and steep and salty old streets, a carousel of Coney Island–type amusements overseen by the stately ruins of its seventh-century abbey. Whitby has been an important port since the 12th century. The **Captain Cook Memorial Museum** offers an interesting look at the famous hometown sailor and his exotic voyages (£2.80, daily 9:45–17:00, closed Nov–March, in the old town just over the bridge). Two of Captain Cook's boats (*Resolution* and *Endeavour*) were built in the Whitby shipyards. The TI is on the harbor next to the train and bus stations (May–Sept daily 9:30–18:00, Oct–April daily 10:00–12:30, 13:00–16:30, tel. 01947/602-674).

Whitby has plenty of rooms. August is the only tight month. Most rooms at **Crescent House** come with sea views (Db-£44, family deals, nonsmoking, on the bluff just south of the harbor at 6 East Crescent, YO21 3HD, tel. & fax 01947/600-091, Janet and Mike Paget). **Dolphin Hotel,** in the old-town center at the bridge overlooking the harbor, is a pub with seven rooms upstairs (Db-£50, 3 blocks from train station, pub closes at 23:00, CC:VM, Bridge Street, Y022 4BG, tel. 01947/602-197). The **hostel** is next to the abbey above the town (bed-£10, 58 beds in 8 rooms, closed 10:00–17:00 for 1-nighters, tel. 01947/602-878).

Buses connect Whitby and York (4–6/day depending on season, 2 hrs, tel. 01653/692-556). Trains connect Durham with Middlesbrough (5/day, 50 min, more frequent with transfer in Darlington); the Middlesbrough–Whitby train (4/day, 90 min) stops at Grosmont (where you can catch the Moors steam train—see "North York Moors," previous chapter) and Danby (a half mile from the Moors info center).

▲**Staithes**—Staithes is a short drive north of Whitby and worthwhile by car (hrly Whitby–Staithes buses; 30 min). A poor and not particularly pretty village where the boy who became Capt. James Cook got his first taste of the sea, Staithes is a salty tumble of cottages bunny-hopping down a ravine into a tiny harbor. Ten years ago the town supported 20 fishing boats—today, only three. But fishermen (who pronounce their town "steerths") still outnumber tourists in undiscovered Staithes. There's nothing to do but drop by the lifeboat house (a big deal in England; page through the history book, read the not-quite-stirring accounts of the boats being called to duty; drop a coin in the box), stroll the beach, and relax to the tune of seagulls singing its praise.

I sleep in Staithes. The town is struggling. Tourists just aren't coming. It's changed little since Captain Cook's days. There are no fancy rooms. Each of these three- or four-bedroom places is cramped, with old carpets, bad wallpaper, lumpy beds, and tangled floor plans that make you feel like a stowaway. The first is on the harborfront (worth it for the view but not the rooms). **Harborside Guest House** provides basic beds, three sea-view rooms, breakfast in a café, and the sound of waves to lull you to sleep (D-£42, Seaton Garth, tel. 01947/841-296). Also consider the **Endeavour Restaurant B&B** (D/Db-£55, serves great food—see below, 1 High Street, tel. 01947/840-825, Lisa Chapman) and **Salmon Cottage** (a £40 twin and a family room, High Street, tel. 01947/841-193, Isabel Elliott). Staithes' zip code is TS13 5BH.

The oddly classy-for-this-town **Endeavour Restaurant** offers excellent £20 dinners (seafood, vegetarian, reservations at 01947/840-825). The **Cod and Lobster** pub serves dinner and overlooks the harbor, with outdoor benches and a cozy living room warmed by a coal fire. **Royal George** on High Street has bar food (dinners daily 19:00–21:00, throw darts while you wait).

▲Holy Island and Bamburgh—This "Holy Island" was Christianity's toehold on England 1,200 years ago. It was the home of St. Cuthbert. We know it today for the *Lindisfarne Gospels*, decorated by monks in the seventh century with some of the finest art from Europe's "Dark Ages" (now in the British Museum). It's a pleasant visit, a quiet town with an evocative priory and striking castle (not worth touring), reached by a two-mile causeway that's cut off daily by high tides. Tidal charts are posted, warning you when this holy place becomes Holy Island and you become stranded (for TI and tide information, call Berwick TI at 01289/330-733, Mon–Sat 10:00–17:00, Sun 11:00–16:00, Oct–April Mon–Sat until 16:00, closed Sun). For a peaceful overnight, a few good B&Bs cluster in the town center (Britannia Guest House, D-£36, Db-£40, tel. 01289/389-218, Mrs. Patterson).

A few miles farther south of Holy Island is the grand **Bamburgh Castle,** overlooking Britain's loveliest beach. Its interior is worth touring (£4, daily 11:00–17:00, closed Nov–March, tel. 01668/214-515). This area is only worthwhile for those with a car.

EDINBURGH

Edinburgh, the colorful city of Robert Louis Stevenson, Sir Walter Scott, and Robert Burns, is Scotland's showpiece and one of Europe's most entertaining cities. Historical, monumental, fun, and well organized, it's a tourist's delight.

Promenade down the Royal Mile through the Old Town. Historic buildings pack the Royal Mile between the castle (on the top) and Holyrood Palace (on the bottom). Medieval skyscrapers stand shoulder to shoulder, hiding peaceful courtyards connected to High Street by narrow lanes or even tunnels. This colorful jumble—in its day the most crowded city in the world—is the tourist's Edinburgh.

Edinburgh (ED'n-burah) was once two towns divided by a lake. To alleviate crowding, the lake was drained, and a magnificent Georgian city, today's New Town, was laid out to the north. Georgian Edinburgh, like the city of Bath, shines with broad boulevards, straight streets, square squares, circular circuses, and elegant mansions decked out in colonnades, pediments, and sphinxes in the proud, neoclassical style of 200 years ago.

While the Georgian city celebrated the union of Scotland and England (with streets and squares named after English kings and emblems), "devolution" is the latest craze. In a 1998 election the Scots voted for more autonomy and to bring their parliament home. Though Edinburgh has been the historic capital of Scotland for centuries, parliament has not met in Scotland since 1707. In 2000—while London still calls the strategic shots—Edinburgh resumed its position as home to the Scottish Parliament. And a strikingly modern new parliament building, opening in 2003, will be one more jewel in Edinburgh's crown.

Planning Your Time

While the major sights can be seen in a day, on a three-week tour of Britain I'd give Edinburgh two days and three nights.

Day 1: Tour the castle. Then consider catching one of the city bus tours (from castle parking lot) for a 60-minute loop, returning to the castle. Explore the Royal Mile, going downhill—lunching, museum-going, shopping, taking a walking tour (leaves at 14:00 from Mercat Cross). If you tour Holyrood Palace, do it near the end of the day and the bottom of the Mile. Evening–Scottish show, folk music at pub, literary pub crawl, or haunted walk.

Day 2: Tour the National Gallery and stroll the adjacent Princes Street Gardens. After lunch, choose among browsing the New Town/Georgian House, touring the Museum of Scotland (tours at 14:15), visiting the ship *Britannia* (booking advisable), or hiking up King Arthur's Seat. Evening–Show, pubs, walks, whatever you didn't do last night.

Orientation (area code: 0131)

The center of Edinburgh holds the Princes Street Gardens park and Waverley Bridge, where you'll find the TI, Waverley Shopping and Eating Center, train station, bus info office (starting point for most city bus tours), National Gallery, and a covered dance-and-music pavilion. Weather blows in and out—bring your sweater.

Tourist Information: The crowded TI is as central as can be atop the Waverley Market on Princes Street (May–June & Sept: Mon–Sat 9:00–19:00, Sun 10:00–19:00; July–Aug: daily until 20:00; Nov–March: daily until 17:00, ATM outside entrance, tel. 0131/473-3800). Buy a map (£1) and ask for the free monthly entertainment *Gig Guide* if you're interested in late-night music. For a longer visit, consider the *Essential Guide to Edinburgh* (£1), which lists additional sights and services. Book your room direct without the TI's help (and £3 charge). Browse the racks (tucked away in hallway at back of TI) for brochures on the various Scottish folk shows, walking tours, and regional bus tours. Connect@edinburgh, a small Internet café, is beyond the brochure racks (see "Hints," below). The best monthly entertainment listing, *The List*, is sold for £1.95 at newsstands.

Haggis Backpackers Ltd has budget travel information (Mon–Sat 8:00–18:00, Sun 14:00–18:00, 60 High Street, at Blackfriars Street, tel. 0131/557-9393).

Arrival in Edinburgh: Arriving by train at Waverley Station puts you in the city center and below the TI (go up the many stairs until you surface at street level, TI to your left) and the city bus to my recommended B&Bs (see "Sleeping," below, for directions to B&B neighborhood by bus). Both Scottish Citylink and National Express buses use the bus station two blocks north of the train station on St. Andrew Square in the New Town.

Edinburgh

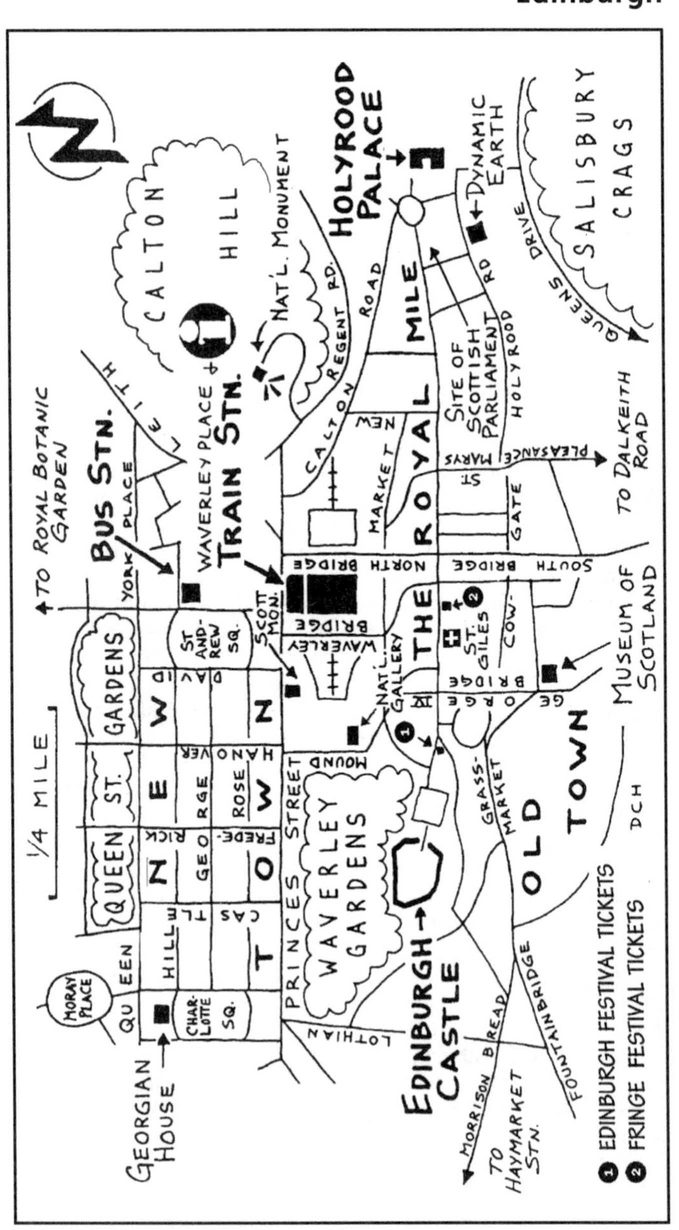
1/4 MILE
TO ROYAL BOTANIC GARDEN
BUS STN.
WAVERLEY PLACE
TRAIN STN.
CALTON HILL
NAT'L. MONUMENT
HOLYROOD PALACE
DYNAMIC EARTH
SALISBURY CRAGS
QUEENS DRIVE
REGENT RD.
CALTON ROAD
ROYAL MILE
THE ROYAL MILE
SITE OF SCOTTISH PARLIAMENT
HOLYROOD RD
PLEASANCE
ST. MARYS
TO DALKEITH ROAD
GATE
NEW
MARKET
NORTH BRIDGE
SOUTH BRIDGE
MUSEUM OF SCOTLAND
ST. GILES
COW-
BRIDGE
GEORGE
YORK PLACE
LEITH
ST. ANDREW SQ.
SCOTT MON.
WAVERLEY BRIDGE
NAT'L. GALLERY
QUEEN ST. GARDENS
NEW TOWN
DAVID
HANOVER
FREDERICK
GEORGE
ROSE
CASTLE
HILL
QUEEN
PRINCES STREET
MOUND
WAVERLEY GARDENS
EDINBURGH CASTLE
GRASSMARKET
OLD TOWN
MORAY PLACE
GEORGIAN HOUSE
CHARLOTTE SQ.
LOTHIAN
MORRISON
BREAD
FOUNTAINBRIDGE
TO HAYMARKET STN.
DCH
1 EDINBURGH FESTIVAL TICKETS
2 FRINGE FESTIVAL TICKETS

Edinburgh's slingshot-of-an-airport is 10 miles northwest of the center and well connected by shuttle buses with Waverley Bridge (LRT "Airline" bus #100, £3.30 or £4.20 with all-day "Airsaver" city bus pass, 4/hrly, 30 min, roughly 6:00_22:00). Flight info: tel. 0131/333-1000, British Midland tel. 0870-607-0555, British Air tel. 0345-222-111). Taxi to airport: £15.

Helpful Hints

Sunday Activities: Many sights close on Sunday, but there's still a lot to do: Royal Mile walking tour, Edinburgh Castle, St. Giles Cathedral, Holyrood Palace, Royal Botanic Gardens, Arthur's Seat hike, and city bus tour. An open-air market including antiques is held every Sunday from 10:00 to 16:00 at New Street Car Park near Waverley Center. The Georgian House and National Gallery open Sunday afternoon.

Internet Access: It's a cinch to get plugged in. Try connect @edinburgh at the TI (£1/20 min, Mon–Sat 9:00–18:00, Sun 10:00–18:00, as you enter TI head back to the left down a corridor, tel. 0131/473-3600); International Telecom Centre on the Royal Mile (£1/15 min, daily 8:00–23:00, also has cheap phones with rare sit-down booths, 52 High Street, half block east of Tron Kirk and South Bridge); or Café Cyberia in the New Town (£1.50/30 min, daily 10:00–22:00, 88 Hanover Street, near recommended restaurants, a few blocks northeast of TI).

Car Rental: Avis is at 100 Dairy Road in Haymarket suburb (tel. 0131/337-6363).

Getting around Edinburgh

Nearly all Edinburgh sights are within walking distance. City buses are handy and inexpensive (average fare-80p, LRT office, Old Town end of Waverley Bridge, tel. 0131/555-6363). Tell the driver where you're going, have change handy (most buses require exact change; you lose any excess), take your ticket as you board, push the stop button as you near your stop (so your stop isn't skipped), and exit from the middle door. Two companies handle the city routes: Lothian (or LRT) does most of it and First does the rest (e.g., route #C3 and #86). Day passes sold by each company are valid only on their buses (£2.20, or £1.50 after 9:30 weekdays and all day weekends, buy from driver). Buses run from about 6:00 to 23:00. Taxis are reasonable (easy to flag down, average ride between downtown and B&B district-£5).

Bus Tours of Edinburgh

▲Hop-on Hop-off City Bus Tours—Three companies offer 60-minute bus tours that circle the town center stopping at the biggies—Waverley Bridge, the castle, Royal Mile, Georgian New Town, and Princes Street—with pickups about every 10 to 15 minutes and an informative narration. You can hop on and off with one ticket all day, not 24 hours. Hop on at any stop or go to Waverley Bridge to comparison shop.

Guide Friday has a live guide (£8.50; can use CC if you buy ticket at TI, at office at 133 Canongate—near bottom of Royal Mile, or possibly at Waverley Bridge, tel. 0131/556-2244). LRT's "Edinburgh Classic Tour," which runs a little more frequently, uses headphones with a recorded narration (£7.50, usually includes price break on trip to Britannia, tel. 0131/555-6363). Mac Tours' "Edinburgh by Vintage Bus" has a live guide, fewer buses, and a shorter route (£7.50, 3/hrly, 50 min, ticket bought after 17:00 also valid the next day).

On sunny days they go topless (the buses) but can suffer from traffic noise and congestion. Buses run year-round. First and last buses leave Waverley Bridge around 9:00 through 19:00 mid-June through early September (off-season, last buses leave at 17:15).

Sights—Edinburgh

▲▲▲Edinburgh Castle—The fortified birthplace of the city 1,300 years ago, this imposing symbol of Edinburgh sits proudly on a rock high above the city. While the castle has been both a fort and a royal residence since the 11th century, most of the buildings today are from its more recent use as a military garrison (£7.50, CC:VM, daily 9:30–18:00, Oct–March until 17:00, cafeteria, tel. 0131/225-9846; consider avoiding the long uphill walk from the nearest city bus stop by taking a cab to the castle gate).

Entry Gate: Start with the wonderfully droll 30-minute guided introduction tour (free with admission, departs every 15 minutes from entry, see clock for the next departure; few tours run off-season). The CD-ROM audio guide is excellent, with four hours of quick digital dial descriptions (free with admission, pick up at entry gate before meeting the live guide). The clean WC at the entry annually wins "British Loo of the Year" awards (see plaques near men's room), but they use a one-way mirror showing the sink area in the women's room (women: pop your head into office near men's room to complain or make sure mirror is curtained).

In the castle there are four essential stops: Crown Jewels, Great Hall, National War Memorial, and St. Margaret's Chapel with city view. The newly refurbished National War Museum of Scotland is also worth considering. All are at the highest and most secure point—on or near the castle square, where your guided tour ends.

The **Royal Palace** (facing castle square under the flag pole) has two unimpressive rooms (through door reading 1566). Remember, Scottish royalty only lived here when safety or protocol required. They preferred the **Holyrood Palace** at the bottom of the Royal Mile. The line of tourists leads from the square directly to the jewels. Skip this line and enter the building around to the left where you'll get to the jewels via a wonderful *Honors of Scotland* exhibition about the crown jewels.

Scotland's **Crown Jewels** are older than England's. While Cromwell destroyed England's, the Scots hid theirs successfully. Longtime symbols of Scottish nationalism, they were made in Edinburgh—of Scottish gold, diamonds, and gems—in 1540 for a 1543 coronation. They were last used to crown Charles II in 1651. Apparently there was some anxiety about the Act of Union, which dissolved Scotland's parliament into England's to create the United Kingdom in 1707—the Scots locked up and hid their jewels. In 1818 Walter Scott and a royal commission rediscovered the jewels intact.

The **Stone of Scone** sits plain and strong next to the jewels. This big gray chunk of rock is the coronation stone of Scotland's ancient kings (ninth century). Swiped by the English, it sat under the coronation chair at Westminster Abbey from 1296 until 1996. With major fanfare, Scotland's treasured Stone of Scone returned to Edinburgh on November 15, 1996. Talk to the guard for more details.

Enter the **Mary Queen of Scots room**, where in 1666 the queen gave birth to James VI of Scotland, who later became King James I of England. The **Presence Chamber** leads into **Laich Hall** (Lower Hall), the dining room of the royal family.

The **Great Hall** was the castle's ceremonial meeting place in the 16th and 17th centuries. In modern times it was a barracks and a hospital. While most of what you see is Victorian, two medieval elements survive: the fine hammer-beam roof and the iron-barred peephole (above fireplace on right). This allowed the king to spy on his partying subjects.

The imposing **Scottish National War Memorial** commemorates the 148,000 Scottish soldiers lost in World War I, the 57,000 lost in World War II, and the 750 lost in British battles since. Each bay is dedicated to a particular Scottish regiment. The main shrine, featuring a green Italian-marble memorial containing the original WWI rolls of honor, actually sits upon an exposed chunk of the castle rock. Above you, the archangel Michael is busy slaying the dragon. The bronze frieze accurately shows the attire of various wings of Scotland's military. The stained glass starts with Cain and Abel on the left and finishes with a celebration of peace on the right.

St. Margaret's Chapel, the oldest building in Edinburgh, is dedicated to Queen Margaret, who died here in 1093 and was sainted in 1250. Built in 1130 in the Romanesque style of the Norman invaders, it is wonderfully simple, with classic Norman zigzags decorating the round arch that separates the tiny nave from the sacristy. Used as a powder magazine for 400 years, very little survives. You'll see an 11th-century Gospel book of St. Margaret's and small windows featuring St. Margaret, St. Columba (who brought Christianity to Scotland via Iona), and William Wallace (the brave defender of Scotland). The place is popular for weddings and, since it seats only 20, particularly popular with brides' fathers.

Belly up to the bannister (across the terrace outside the chapel) to enjoy the great view. Below you are the guns—which fire the one o'clock salute—and a sweet little line of doggie tombstones, the **soldier's pet cemetery**. Beyond stretches the **Georgian New Town** (read the informative plaque).

The **National War Museum of Scotland**, reopened after renovation, thoughtfully covers the last 400 years of Scottish military history. Instead of the usual musty, dusty displays of endless armor, this museum has an interesting mix of short films, uniforms, weapons, medals, mementos, and eloquent excerpts from soldiers' letters.

The castle has more to offer (for instance, below, in the vaults, you can see Mons Meg—a huge 15th-century siege cannon that fired 500-pound stones nearly 2 miles), but you've seen the essentials.

When leaving the castle, turn around and look back at the gate. There stand King Robert the Bruce (on the left, 1274–1329) and Sir William Wallace (Braveheart—on the right, 1270–1305). Wallace (newly famous, thanks to Mel Gibson) fought long and hard against English domination before being executed in London—his body cut to pieces and paraded through the far corners of jolly olde England. Bruce beat the English at Bannockburn in 1314. Bruce and Wallace still defend the spirit of Scotland.

Sights—Along the Royal Mile

These are listed in walking order, from top to bottom. (Bus #35 runs along the Mile, handy for going up after you've hit bottom.)

▲▲▲Royal Mile—This is one of Europe's most interesting historic walks. Start at the top and amble down to the palace. The Royal Mile, which consists of a series of four different streets—Castlehill, Lawnmarket, High Street, and Canongate—is actually 100 yards longer than a mile. And every inch is packed with shops, cafés, and lanes leading to tiny squares. By poking down the many side alleys, you'll find a few rough edges of a town well on its way to becoming a touristic mall. See it now. In a few years tourists will be slaloming through the postcard racks on bagpipe skateboards.

Royal Mile Terminology: A "close" is a tiny alley between two buildings (originally with a door that closed it at night). A close usually leads to a "court" or courtyard. A "land" is a tenement block of apartments. A "pend" is an arched gateway. A "wynd" is a narrow winding lane. And "gate" is from an old Scandinavian word for street.

Royal Mile Walking Tours: Mercat Tours offers two-hour guided walks of the Mile—more entertaining than historic (£6, April–Sept daily at 11:00 and 14:00, Oct–March daily 11:15 only,

Royal Mile

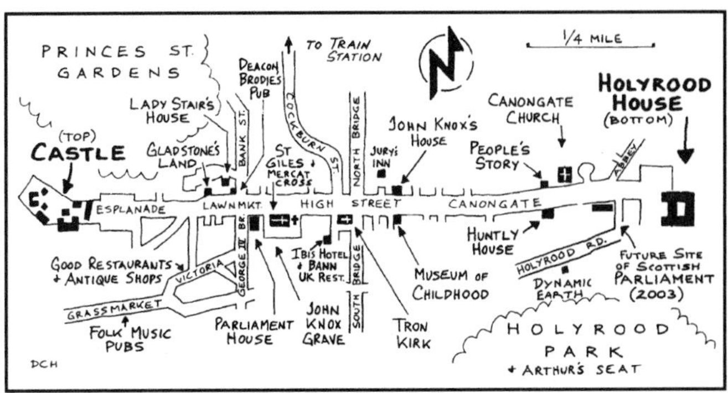

from Mercat Cross on the Royal Mile, tel. 0131/557-6464). The guides, who enjoy making a short story long, ignore the big sights, taking you behind the scenes with piles of barely historic gossip, bully-pulpit Scottish pride, and fun but forgettable trivia. They also offer a variety of other tours. In August only, the Voluntary Guides Association leads free tours of Edinburgh; call for schedule (tel. 0131/664-7180).

Castle Esplanade—At the top of the Royal Mile, the big parking lot leading up to the castle was once a military parade ground. It's often cluttered with bleachers under construction for the military tattoo—a spectacular massing of the bands that fills the square nightly for most of August (see "Edinburgh Festival," below). At the bottom, on the left, the tiny witch's fountain memorializes 300 women who were accused of witchcraft and burned here. Scotland burned more witches per capita than any other country—17,000 between 1479 and 1722. But in a humanitarian gesture, rather than burning them alive as was the custom in the rest of Europe, Scottish "witches" were strangled to death before they were burned. The plaque shows two witches: one good and one bad. (For 90 minutes of this kind of Royal Mile trivia, take the guided tour described above.)

Scotch Whiskey Heritage Centre—This touristy ambush is designed only to distill £5.50 out of your pocket. You get a free sample, video history, short talk, and a little whiskey-keg train-car ride before finding yourself in the shop 45 minutes later. If you say you're in a hurry, you'll likely be offered the unadvertised quickie—a sample and a whiskey-keg ride for £3.60. People do seem to enjoy it, but that might have something to do with the sample (tel. 0131/220-0441). The Camera Obscura, across the street, is just as rewarding.

▲▲Gladstone's Land—Take a good look at this typical

16th- to 17th-century merchant's house, complete with a lived-in furnished interior and guides in each room who love to talk (£3.50, Mon–Sat 10:00–17:00, Sun 14:00–17:00, last entry at 16:30). For a good Royal Mile photo, lean out the upper-floor window (or simply climb the curved stairway outside the museum to the left of the entrance).

▲**Writers' Museum at Lady Stair's House**—This interesting house, built in 1622, is filled with manuscripts and knickknacks of Scotland's three greatest literary figures: Robert Burns, Sir Walter Scott, and Robert Louis Stevenson. It's worth a few minutes for anyone and is fascinating for fans (free, Mon–Sat 10:00–17:00, closed Sun). Wander around the courtyard here. Edinburgh was a wonder in the 17th and 18th centuries. Tourists came here to see its skyscrapers, which towered 10 stories and higher. No city in Europe was so densely populated as "Auld Reekie."

Deacon Brodie's Tavern—This is a decent place for a light meal (see "Eating," below). Read the story of its notorious namesake on the wall facing Bank Street.

Visitors Centre of the Scottish Parliament—This new center, at the southwest corner of High Street and George IV Bridge, proudly introduces the new Scottish Parliament, with exhibits explaining how it works and models showing the building where it will work (currently an expensive hole in the ground near Holyrood Palace). At the Visitors Centre, you can sign up (free) to witness the new Parliament debating and creating Scottish history in their temporary quarters, a few steps off the Royal Mile, tucked away in Mylnes Court, across from The Hub (debates Wed 14:30–17:30, Thu 9:30–12:30, 14:30–17:30, day bags allowed after scanning, tel. 0131/348-5411).

▲**St. Giles Cathedral**—Wander through Scotland's most important church. Stepping inside, find John Knox's statue. Look into his eyes from 10 inches away. Knox, the great reformer and founder of austere Scottish Presbyterianism, first preached here in 1559. His insistence that every person should be able to read the word of God gave Scotland an educational system 300 years ahead of the rest of Europe. For this reason it was Scottish minds that led the way in math, science, medicine, engineering, and so on. Voltaire called Scotland "the intellectual capital of Europe."

The neo-Gothic **Chapel of the Knights of the Thistle** (from 1911, in far right corner), with its intricate wood carving, was built in two years entirely with Scottish material and labor. Find the angel tooting the bagpipes (from inside chapel, look above the door to the right). The Scottish crown steeple from 1495 is a proud part of Edinburgh's skyline (April–Sept daily 9:00–19:00, Oct–March until 17:00; ask about concerts—some are free, usually Thu at 13:00; fine café downstairs; see "Eating," below).

Scottish Words

aye	yes	**inch, innis**	island
ben	mountain	**inver**	river, mouth
bonnie	beautiful	**kyle**	strait
carn	heap of stones	**loch**	lake
creag	rock, cliff	**neeps**	turnips
tattie	potato		
haggis	rich assortment of oats and sheep organs stuffed into a chunk of sheep intestine, liberally seasoned, boiled, and eaten mostly by tourists. Usually served with "neeps and tatties." Tastier than it sounds.		

John Knox is buried out back—austerely, under the parking lot, at spot 44. The statue among the cars shows King Charles II riding to a toga party back in 1685.

Parliament House—Stop in to see the grand hall with its fine 1639 hammer-beam ceiling and stained glass. This hall housed the Scottish Parliament until the Act of Union in 1707 (explained in history exhibition adjacent) and now holds the law courts. Today it's busy with wigged and robed lawyers hard at work in the old library (peek through the door) or pacing the hall deep in discussion. Greater eminence . . . longer wig. The friendly doorman is helpful (free, public welcome Mon–Fri 9:00–16:30, best action midmornings Tue–Fri, open-to-the-public trials 10:00–16:00—doorman has day's docket, entry behind St. Giles Cathedral near parking spot 21).

Mercat Cross—This chunky pedestal, on the downhill side of St. Giles, holds a slender column topped with a white unicorn. Royal proclamations were read from here in the 14th century. Today it's the meeting point of various walking tours. Pop into the police information center, a few doors downhill, for a little local law-and-order history (free, daily 10:00–22:00).

▲Tron Kirk—This fine old building (staffed by volunteers and open at irregular times) houses a free, interesting Old Town history display and sometimes a TI.

▲Museum of Childhood—This five-story playground of historical toys and games—called the noisiest museum in the world because of its delighted tiny visitors—is rich in nostalgia and history (free, Mon–Sat 10:00–16:30, closed Sun). Just downhill is a fragrant fudge shop offering free samples.

▲John Knox House—Fascinating for Reformation buffs, this fine 16th-century house offers a well-explained look at the life of the great reformer (£2, Mon–Sat 10:00–16:30, closed Sun, 43 High

Street). While Knox never actually lived here, it was called "his house" to save it from the wrecking ball in 1850.

▲**People's Story**—This interesting exhibition traces the lot of the working class through the 18th, 19th, and 20th centuries (free, Mon–Sat 10:00–17:00, closed Sun). Curiously, while this museum is dedicated to the proletariat, immediately around the back is the tomb of Adam Smith—the author of *Wealth of Nations* and the father of modern capitalism (1723–1790).

▲**Huntly House**—Another old house full of old stuff, Huntly is worth a look for its early Edinburgh history and handy ground-floor WC. Don't miss the original copy of the National Covenant (written in 1638 on an animal skin) or the sketches of pre-Georgian Edinburgh with its lake still wet (free, Mon–Sat 10:00–17:00, closed Sun). Just a toot farther downhill is Bagpipes Galore.

White Horse Close—Step into this 17th-century courtyard (bottom of Canongate, on the left, a block before Holyrood Palace). It was from here that the Edinburgh stagecoach left for London. Eight days later, the horse-drawn carriage pulled into its destination: Scotland Yard.

▲**Holyrood Palace**—The palace marks the end of the Royal Mile. The queen spends a week in Scotland each summer, during which this is her official residence and office. The abbey—part of a 12th-century Augustinian monastery—stood here first. It was named for a piece of the cross brought here as a relic by queen-then-saint Margaret. Scotland's royalty preferred living here to the blustery castle on the rock, and, gradually, the palace grew. The building is rich in history and decor. But without information or a guided tour ("there's none of either," snickered the guy who sells the boring £3.70 museum guidebooks), you're just another peasant in the dark. Docents in each room are happy to give you the answer if you know the question. After wandering through the elegantly furnished rooms and a few dark older rooms filled with glass cases of historic bits and Scottish pieces that must be fascinating, you're free to wander through the ruined abbey and the queen's gardens (£6, CC:VM, daily 9:30–18:00, Nov–April until 16:30—guided tour mandatory off-season, last admission 45 minutes before closing; closed last 2 weeks in May, 10 days in early July, when the queen's home, and whenever a prince drops in; tel. 0131/556-7371).

The building lot near the palace entrance is the site of the new Scottish Parliament, slated for completion in 2003. As a conversation starter, ask a local what he/she thinks about the building's architect, expense, design, and so on.

More Bonnie Wee Sights

▲**Georgian New Town**—Cross Waverley Bridge and walk through Georgian Edinburgh. The grand George Street, connecting St. Andrew and Charlotte Squares, was the centerpiece of the elegantly planned New Town. The entire city plan—laid out in the late 18th century when George was king—celebrates the notion of the United Kingdom. Look at the map. You'll see George Street, Queen Street, and Hanover (the royal family surname) Street. Even Thistle and Rose Streets are emblems of the two happily paired nations. Rose Street, mostly pedestrian-only, is fun to wander. Where it hits St. Andrew's Square, Rose Street is flanked by the venerable Jenners department store and a Sainsbury supermarket. Sprinkled with popular restaurants and bars, the stately New Town is turning trendy.

▲▲Georgian House—This refurbished Georgian house, set on Edinburgh's finest Georgian square, is a trip back to 1796. A volunteer guide in each room is trained in the force-feeding of stories and trivia. Start your visit with two interesting videos (architecture/Georgian lifestyles) totaling 30 minutes (£5, Mon–Sat 10:00–17:00, Sun 14:00–17:00, new touch screens provide extra info, 7 Charlotte Square, tel. 0131/225-2160).

Princes Street Gardens—This grassy park, a former lake bed, separates Edinburgh's New and Old Towns and offers a wonderful escape from the city. There are plenty of free concerts and country dances in the summer and the oldest floral clock in the world. Join the local office workers for a picnic lunch break.

▲National Gallery—This elegant neoclassical building has a small but impressive collection of European masterpieces, from Raphael to van Gogh, and offers the best look you'll get at Scottish paintings (free, Mon–Sat 10:00–17:00, Sun 12:00–17:00, tel. 0131/624-6200).

▲Walter Scott Monument—Built in 1840, this elaborate, neo-Gothic monument honors the great author, one of Edinburgh's many illustrious sons. The 200-foot monument shelters a marble statue of Scott, surrounded by busts of 16 great Scottish poets and 64 characters from his books. Climb 287 steps for a fine view of the city (£2.50, Mon–Sat 9:00–18:00, Nov–Feb until 16:00, closed Sun).

Museum of Scotland—Learn the story of Scotland, from 2,400 million years ago through today. Take advantage of their free 60-minute tours, usually offered daily at 14:15 (orientation) and 15:15 (on a theme), plus Tuesday at 18:00 (orientation). Or take the included audioguide tour (£3, free Tue 16:30–20:00; Mon–Sat 10:00–17:00, Tue until 20:00, Sun 12:00–17:00, Chambers Street, off George IV bridge, 2 long blocks south of Royal Mile, tel. 0131/247-4422, www.nms.ac.uk). Admission includes entry to the Royal Museum, next door.

Dynamic Earth—Best for younger kids, this is a little tame for Americans raised on a steady diet of computers and science museums. The museum's grand goal is to showcase the power of the planet. Standing in a time tunnel, you watch time rewind from Churchill to dinosaurs to that first big poof. After several short films on stars, tectonic plates (interesting), and ice caps, you're freed to wander past salty pools, a recreated rain forest, and various TV screens, ending your visit with a 12-minute continuous film shown on the domed ceiling of a room with few seats (£7, family deals, April–Oct daily 10:00–18:00, Nov–March Wed–Sun 10:00–17:00, last ticket sold 1.25 hrs before closing, on Holyrood Road, near palace and park, tel. 0131/550-7800).

Royal Botanic Garden—Britain's second-oldest botanical garden, established in 1670 for medicinal herbs, is now one of Europe's best (free, Feb/Oct 9:30–17:00, March/Sept 9:30–18:00, April–Aug 9:30–19:00, Nov–Jan 9:30–16:00, 90-minute "rain forest to desert" tours daily at 11:00 and 14:00 for £2 April–Sept, 1 mile north of center at Inverleith Row, tel. 0131/552-7171).

Sights—Near Edinburgh

Britannia—This elegant vessel, which has carted around Britain's royal family for over 40 years and 900 voyages, is moored at Edinburgh's Port of Leith and open to the public. After watching a video about the ship, wander through the museum. Then, armed with the included audioguide, take the stairs or elevator up to the ship (BYO crown). Enjoy views of the Firth of Forth from the deck. Tour the bridge, dining room, and living quarters, following in the historic footsteps of such notables as Churchill, Gandhi, and Reagan. Book in advance—or risk a wait on site—by calling 0131/555-5566 (CC:VM); weekends are busiest (£8, April–Oct daily 9:30–18:00, in Aug Fri–Sun until 21:00, Nov–March 10:30–17:00, last ticket sold 1.5 hrs before closing; to get to ship from Edinburgh, catch city bus X50 bus at Waverley Bridge—£3 round-trip—or take the Guide Friday bus—£3.50 round-trip; cheap café on site, www.royalyachtbritannia.co.uk).

Edinburgh Crystal—Blowing, molding, cutting, polishing, and engraving, the Edinburgh Crystal Company glassworks tour smashes anything you'll see in Venice (£3, 35-minute tours offered year-round Mon–Fri 9:15–15:30, April–Sept weekends 11:00–14:30, kids under 8 not admitted). There is a shop full of "bargain" second-quality pieces, a video show, and a cafeteria. A free minibus shuttle service from Waverley Bridge departs at the top of the hour (April–Sept Mon–Fri 10:00–15:00, Sat–Sun 11:00–14:00), or you can drive 10 miles south of town on A701 to Penicuik. You can schedule a more expensive supertour where you actually blow and cut glass (tel. 01968/675-128).

Activities in Edinburgh

▲▲Arthur's Seat Hike—A 45-minute hike up the 822-foot volcanic mountain (surrounded by a fine park overlooking Edinburgh), starting from the Holyrood Palace, gives you a rewarding view. You can drive up most of the way from behind (follow the one-way street from the palace, park by the little lake) or run up like they did in *Chariots of Fire*. From the parking lot (immediately south of Holyrood Palace), you'll see two trails going up. For an easier grade, take the wide path to the left and skip the steeper path that begins with steps and skirts the base of the cliffs. You can also hike up to the Seat from the Dalkeith B&B neighborhood. Take the road (Holyrood Park Road) that borders the Commonwealth pool, turn right (on Queen's Drive), and continue to a small car park. From here, it's a 20-minute hike.

Brush Skiing—If you'd rather be skiing, the Midlothian Ski Centre in Hillend has a hill on the edge of town with a chairlift, two slopes plus jump slope, and rentable skis, boots, and poles (£6.50/first hr, then £2.60/hr, includes gear, Mon–Sat 9:30–21:00, Sun 9:30–19:00, closed last 2 weeks of June, probably closed if it snows, LRT bus #4 from Princes Street—garden side, tel. 0131/445-4433).

▲Royal Commonwealth Games Swimming Pool—The biggest pool I've ever seen is open to the public, with a well-equipped fitness center (£5.10, includes swim), sauna (£6.50 extra), and a cafeteria overlooking the pool (£2.70 for pool admission only, Mon–Fri 6:00–21:00, Sat–Sun 10:00–16:00, closed 9:00–10:00 every Wed, no towels or suit rentals, tel. 0131/667-7211).

More Hikes—You can hike along the river (called Water of Leith) through Edinburgh. Locals favor the stretch between Roseburn and Dean Village, but the 1.5-mile walk from Dean Village to the Royal Botanic Garden is also good. This and other hikes are described in the TI's "Walks in and around Edinburgh" (ask for the free one-page flyer, not their £2 guide to walks).

Shopping—The best shopping is along Princes Street (look for elegant old Jenners department store), Victoria Street (antiques galore), and the Royal Mile (touristy but competitively priced, shops usually open 9:00–17:30, later on Thu, some closed Sun).

Bus Tours to Countryside—Many companies offer day trips to regional sights (such as Loch Ness). Comparison-shop at the brochure rack at the TI.

Edinburgh Festival

One of Europe's great cultural events, Edinburgh's annual festival turns the city into a carnival of culture. There are enough music, dance, art, drama, and multicultural events to make even the most jaded traveler drool with excitement. Every day is jammed with formal and spontaneous fun. A number of festivals—official, fringe, book, film, and jazz and blues—rage simultaneously for about three weeks each August, with the Military Tattoo starting a week earlier (the best overall Web site is www.edinburghfestivals.co.uk). Many city sights run on extended hours, and those that normally close on Sunday (Writers' Museum, Huntly House, People's Story, and

Museum of Childhood) open in the afternoon. It's a glorious time to be in Edinburgh.

The official festival (August 12–September 1 in 2001) is the original, more formal and likely to get booked up first. Major events sell out well in advance. The ticket office is at The Hub, a churchlike building (with café, ATM, and WC), located near the top of the Royal Mile as you approach the castle (tickets-£4–55, CC:VMA, booking from mid-April on, office open Mon–Sat 9:30–17:30, in Aug until 20:00 plus Sun 10:00–17:00, tel. 0131/473-2000, fax 0131/473-2003, can book online, www.eif.co.uk).

The less-formal **Fringe Festival** features "on the edge" comedy and theater (CC:VM, Aug 5–27 in 2001, ticket/info office just below St. Giles Cathedral on the Royal Mile, 180 High Street, tel. 0131/226-5257, bookings tel. 0131/226-5138, can book online from mid-June on, www.edfringe.com). Tickets are usually available at the door, but popular shows can sell out.

Other festivals in August: jazz and blues (tel. 0131/467-5200, info@assemblydirect.ednet.co.uk), film (tel. 0131/229-2550, e-mail: info@edfilmfest.org.uk), and book (tel. 0131/228-5444, e-mail: admin@edbookfest.co.uk).

The **Military Tattoo** is a massing of the bands, drums, and bagpipes with groups from all over what was the British Empire. Displaying military finesse with a stirring lone-piper finale, this grand spectacle fills the castle esplanade nightly except Sunday, normally from a week before the festival starts until a week before it finishes: August 3 to 25 in 2001 (£10–27, CC:VMA, booking starts in Jan, Fri–Sat shows sell out first, office open Mon–Fri 10:00–16:30, 33 Market Street, behind—and south of—Waverley train station, tel. 0131/225-1188, www.edintattoo.co.uk). If nothing else, it is a really big show.

If you do manage to hit Edinburgh during the festival, book a room far in advance and extend your stay by a day or two. While Fringe tickets and most Tattoo tickets are available the day of the show, you may want to book a couple of official events in advance. Do it directly by telephone, leaving your credit-card number. Pick up your ticket at the office the day of the show. Several publications—including the festival's official schedule, the *Edinburgh Festivals Guide Daily*, *The List*, the *Fringe Program*, and the *Daily Diary*—list and evaluate festival events.

Nightlife in Edinburgh

▲▲Evening Walking Tours—These walks, more than a pile of ghost stories, are an entertaining and cheap night out (offered nightly, usually 19:00 and 21:00, easy socializing for solo travelers). The theatrical and creatively staged **Witchery Tours,** the most established of the ghost tours, offer two different walks: "Ghosts and Gore" and "Murder and Mystery" (£7, 90 min, leave from the Royal

Mile, reservations required, book your spot by calling 0131/225-6745). The fascinating-for-those-who-care **Literary Pub Tour** leaves from the Beehive Pub on Grassmarket, lasts two hours, and includes two actors and four pub stops (£7, April–May and Oct at 19:30 from Thu–Sun; July–Aug daily at 14:00,18:00, and 20:30; Nov–March Fri only at 19:30; tel. 0131/226-6665).

▲Scottish Folk Evenings—These £35 to £40 dinner shows, generally for tour groups, are held in huge halls of expensive hotels. (Prices are bloated to include 20 percent commissions.) Your "traditional" meal is followed by a full slate of swirling kilts, blaring bagpipes, and Scottish folk dancing with an "old-time music hall"–type emcee. You can often see the show without dinner for about half price. The TI has fliers on all the latest venues. **Carlton Highland Hotel** offers its Scottish folk evening with or without dinner, nearly nightly—ask when the next show is scheduled (£19.50 for show at 20:45–22:30, £39.50 includes dinner at 19:30, CC:VM, at High Street and North Bridge, tel. 0131/556-7277).

▲▲Folk Music in Pubs—Edinburgh is a good place for folk music. There's always a pub or two with a folk evening on. The monthly *Gig Guide* (free at TI and various pubs, www.gigguide.co.uk) lists most of the live music action. **Whistle Binkies** offers nightly ad-lib traditional music, which can start as early as 19:30 or as late as 22:30 and goes until the wee hours (just off the Royal Mile on South Bridge, another entrance on Niddry Street, tel. 0131/557-5114).

Grassmarket Street (below the castle) is sloppy with live music—mostly folk. This noisy nightlife center is fun to just wander through late at night. **Finnigan's Wake** has live music—often Irish folk songs—nightly (starts at 22:00, a block off Grassmarket at 9 Victoria Street, tel. 0131/226-3816). The **Fiddlers Arms, Biddy Mulligan,** and **White Hart Inn,** among others, all feature live folk music. By the noise and crowds you'll know where to go and where not to. Have a beer and follow your ear.

Theater—Even outside of festival time, Edinburgh is a fine place for lively and affordable theater. Pick up *The List* for a complete rundown of what's on.

Sleeping in Edinburgh

(£1 = about $1.60, country code: 44, area code: 0131)

Sleep Code: **S** = Single, **D** = Double/Twin, **T** = Triple, **Q** = Quad, **b** = bathroom, **t** = toilet only, **s** = shower only, **CC** = Credit Card (**V**isa, **M**asterCard, **A**mex).

Book ahead! The annual festival fills Edinburgh each August—when prices for accommodations are at their peak. Conventions, school holidays, and weekends can make finding a room tough at almost any time of year. Call in advance or pay 30 percent extra for a relative dump. For the best prices, book directly rather than through the TI, which charges a £3 booking fee. "Standard" rooms, with toilets and showers a tissue-toss away, save you £10 a night.

Room prices in this section are usually listed as a range, from low season (winter) to high season (July–Sept), though prices can go even higher during the August festival. Prices get soft off-season, for longer visits, and sometimes for midweek stays outside of summer.

Sleeping off Dalkeith Road

These recommendations are south of town near the Royal Commonwealth Pool, just off Dalkeith Road. This comfortably safe neighborhood is a 20-minute walk or 10-minute bus ride from the Royal Mile. All listings are nonsmoking, on quiet streets, a two-minute walk from a bus stop, and well served by city buses. B&Bs are unlikely to accept bookings for one-night stays in August.

Near the B&Bs you'll find plenty of eateries (see "Eating," below), easy free parking, and the handy Capital Laundrette (Mon–Sat 8:30–17:00, £4 for self-serve, £5.50 if they do it, drop off by 11:00 for same-day service, June–Sept they'll deliver your clean clothes to your B&B for free, 208 Dalkeith Road, tel. 0131/667-0825).

To reach the hotel neighborhood from the train station, TI, or Scott Monument, cross Princes Street and wait at the bus stop under the small C&A sign on the department store (80p, buses #C3, #14, #21, #33, #82, or #86; tell driver your destination is "Dalkeith Road," red bus: exact change or pay more; green bus: makes change; ride 10 minutes to first stop 100 yards after the pool, push the button, exit middle door). These buses also stop at the corner of North Bridge and High Street on the Royal Mile. Buses generally run from about 6:00 to 23:00, except on Sunday morning—buses don't start running from Dalkeith Road into town until 9:00. Taxi fare between the station or Royal Mile and the B&Bs is about £5.

Plusher B&Bs off Dalkeith Road

Turret Guest House is teddy-on-the-beddy cozy, with a great bay-windowed family room and a vast breakfast menu that includes haggis and vegetarian options (7 rooms, S-£20–23, S-£23–28, D-£46–56, Db-£44–58, £2-per-person discount with this book and cash, 8 Kilmaurs Terrace, EH16 5DR, tel. 0131/667-6704, www.turret.clara.net, Mrs. Jackie Cameron).

Amaragua Guest House, next door to Turret, is an inviting Victorian home away from home, decorated with a Malaysian twist—art and some furniture accumulated when the English owners lived in Kuala Lumpur (7 rooms, S-£18–25, Db-£36–55, £2-per-person discount with this book, 10 Kilmaurs Terrace, EH16 5DR, tel. & fax 0131/667-6775, cell 0789-987-8722, e-mail: amaragua @cableinet.co.uk, run by gracious Helen and Dave Butterworth).

Edinburgh, Our Neighborhood

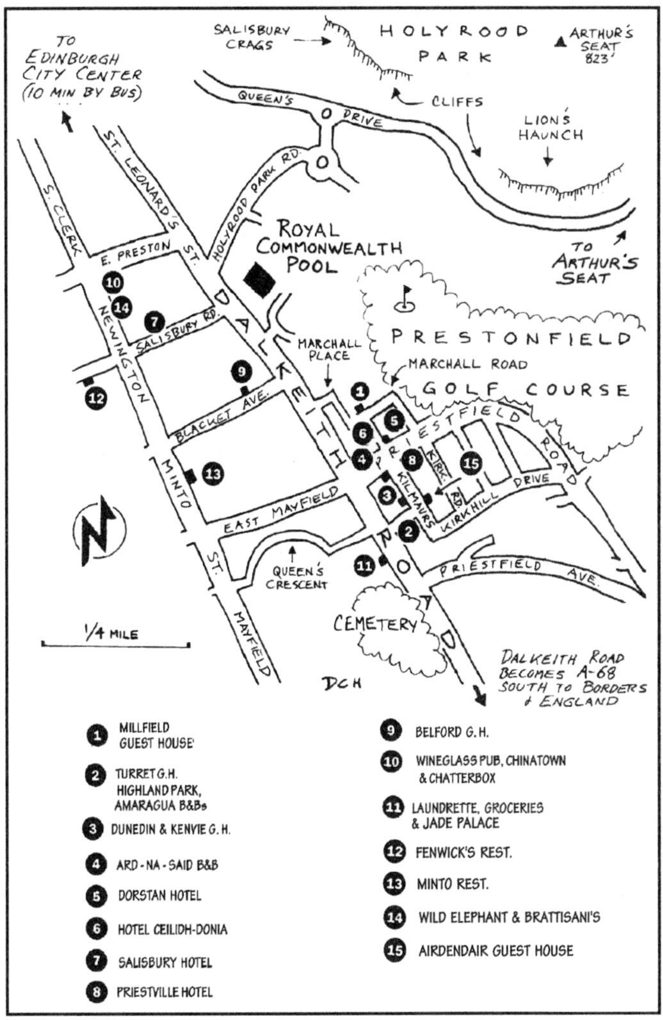

Dunedin Guest House (pron. dun-EE-din) is bright, plush, Scottish, and a good value (7 rooms, 1 S-£20–30, Db-£40–70, family rooms and deals, strong showers, good lighting, TVs with satellite channels, no 1-nights stays in Aug, 8 Priestfield Road, EH16 5HH, tel. 0131/668-1949, fax 0131/668-3636, e-mail: dunedin-guesthouse@edinburgh-EH16.freeserve.co.uk, Marcella Bowen).

Dorstan Private Hotel is personable but professional and hotelesque, with all the comforts. Several of its 14 thoughtfully decorated rooms are on the ground floor (2 Ds-£60, Db-£66, family rooms, no clothes washing except for "smalls," CC:VMA, 7 Priestfield Road, EH16 5HJ, tel. 0131/667-6721, fax 0131/668-4644, e-mail: reservations@dorstan-hotel.demon.co.uk, Mairae Campbell).

Hotel Ceilidh-Donia (pron. caledonia) has 13 rooms: half are state-of-the-art new and comfortable, and the other half—slated for renovation—are decent. Owners Max and Annette Preston offer dinner (£6–7), run a bar, and have a high-tech security system (2 D-£40–50, standard Db-£43–55, deluxe Db-£55–70, CC:VM, Internet access, nonsmoking except in part of bar, minibus tours possible, 14 Marchhall Crescent, EH16 5HL, tel. 0131/667-2743, fax 0131/668-2181, www.hotelceilidh-donia.freeserve.co.uk).

Ard-Na-Said B&B is an elegant 1875 Victorian house with a comfy lounge and classy rooms (reconfirm your reservation, 1 S-£22–28, Db-£44–60, family deals, 5 Priestfield Road, EH16 5HH, tel. 0131/667-8754, fax 0131/271-0960, www.ardnasaid.freeserve.co.uk, enthusiastically run by Jim and Olive Lyons).

Simpler B&Bs off Dalkeith Road

Millfield Guest House, run graciously by Liz and Ed Broomfield, is thoughtfully furnished with antique class, a rare sit-and-chat ambience, and a comfy TV lounge. Since the showers are down the hall, you'll get spacious rooms and great prices (S-£21–23, D-£38–40, T-£48–52, CC:VM, CC reservation allows for late arrival, 12 Marchhall Road, EH16 5HR, tel. & fax 0131/667-4428). Decipher the breakfast prayer by Robert Burns. Then try the "Taste of Scotland" breakfast option. See how many stone (14 pounds) you weigh in the elegant throne room. This place is worth calling well in advance.

Kenvie Guest House, well and warmly run by Dorothy Vidler, comes with six pleasant rooms and lots of personal touches (1 small twin-£40, D-£42, Db-£50, family deals, 3 percent more with CC, 16 Kilmaurs Road, EH16 5DA, tel. 0131/668-1964, fax 0131/668-1926, www.kenvie.co.uk, e-mail: dorothy@kenvie.co.uk).

Airdenair Guest House, offering views and homemade scones, has five attractive rooms with a lofty above-it-all feeling (Sb-£25–35, Db-£40–50, CC:VM, 29 Kilmaurs Road, EH16 5DB, tel. 0131/668-2336, http://airdenair.edinburghnet.co.uk/, Jill McLennan).

Highland Park House, bright and friendly, has homey rooms with double-glazed windows to shut out noise and keep in warmth (S-£20–25, D-£40–44, Db-£44–52 with this book, family deals, 16 Kilmaurs Terrace, EH16 5DR, tel. & fax 0131/667-9204, e-mail: highlandparkhouse@hotmail.com, Margaret and Brian Love).

Colquhoun Guest House, in an elegant building, has seven fine rooms, several on the ground floor (S-£22–25, D-£40, Db-£50, across street from Millfield House, 5 Marchhall Road, EH16 5HR, tel. 0131-667-8481, cell 0411-561066, run by amazing Grace McAinsh).

Priestville B&B, a spacious place, has six cozy rooms, each with a VCR and access to a video library (D-£40–50, Db-£45–60, CC:VM with 3 percent charge, family deals, Internet access, small fridge per floor, 10 Priestfield Road, EH16 5HJ, tel. & fax 0131/667-2435, e-mail: priestville@hotmail.com, Angela and Alan Aberdein).

Belford House is a tidy, homey place offering seven good rooms and a warm welcome (D-£40–44, Db-£50–54, family deals, CC:VM, 13 Blacket Avenue, tel. 0131/667-2422, fax 0131/667-7508, Isa and Tom Borthwick).

The Salisbury, more like a hotel than its neighbors, fills a classy old Georgian building with 12 rooms, a large lounge, tired carpeting, and even a dumbwaiter in the breakfast room (D-£44–56, Db-£50–62, 5 percent off with cash and this book, CC:VM, 45 Salisbury Road, EH16 5AA, tel. & fax 0131/667-1264, http://members.edinburgh.org/salisbury/, Brenda Wright).

Big, Modern Hotels

Four of these listings are cheap as hotels go, and offer more comfort than character; book in advance. One's a splurge. In each case, I'd skip the pricey breakfast and eat out.

Sleeping cheap near the Royal Mile: Travelodge, the cheapest hotel in the center, has 193 no-nonsense, central rooms all decorated in dark blue decor (Db-£50–70, breakfast-£8, CC:VMA, most rooms nonsmoking, 33 St. Mary's Street, a block off the Royal Mile, tel. 0870-905-6343, www.travelodge.co.uk).

Ibis Hotel, mid–Royal Mile behind Tron Church, is perfectly located and has 98 soulless but clean and comfy rooms and American charm (Sb-£54–70, Db-£62–70, continental breakfast-£4.50, CC:VMA, nonsmoking rooms available, elevator, 6 Hunter Square, EH1 1QW, tel. 0131/240-7000, fax 0131/240-7007, e-mail: H2039@accor-hotels.com).

Jurys Inn is another cookie-cutter place, with 186 dependably comfortable rooms. Prices fluctuate wildly, dropping in winter and soaring in August (Db-£39–82, CC:VM, breakfast-£7.50, nonsmoking rooms available, some views, pub/restaurant, on quiet street just off Royal Mile, 43 Jeffrey Street, EH1 1DG, tel. 0131/200-3300, fax 0131/200-0400, www.jurys.com).

Splurge near the Royal Mile: MacDonald, my only fancy listing, offers its best value outside of August. With its classy marble-and-wood decor, fitness center, and pool, it's hard to leave. On a gray winter day in Edinburgh, this could be worth it. Prices vary wildly (standard Db: £75 in winter, £90–110 May–July, up to £200 in Aug, breakfast-£11, CC:VM, near bottom of Mile, across from Dynamic Earth, Holyrood Road, EH8 6AE, tel. 0131/550-4500, fax 0131/528-8191, www.macdonaldhotels.co.uk). If you call, mention you're on holiday—not business—and ask if there's a Leisure Break (prices usually don't drop, but breakfast is thrown in).

Away from the center: Travel Inn, the biggest hotel in Edinburgh, has even less character but a great price and a mediocre location about a mile west of the Mile. Each of its 280 rooms is modern and comfortable, with a sofa that folds out for two kids if necessary (Db-£50 for 2 adults and up to 2 kids under 15, breakfast is extra, CC:VMA, elevators, nonsmoking rooms, weekends booked long in advance, near Haymarket station west of the castle at 1 Mor-rison Link, EH3 8DN, tel. 0131/228-9819, fax 0131/228-9836, www.travelinn.co.uk).

Hostels

Although Edinburgh's hostels are open to all and well run, providing Internet access, laundry facilities, and £12 bunk beds (about a £9–12 savings over B&Bs), they are scruffy and don't include breakfast.

Castle Rock Hostel is hip and easygoing, offering cheap beds, plenty of friends, and a great central location just below the castle and above the pubs with all the folk music (15 Johnston Terrace, tel. 0131/225-9666). Their sister hostels are nearly across the street from each other: **High Street Hostel** (laundry-£2.50, kitchen, 8 Blackfriars Street, just off High Street/Royal Mile, tel. 0131/557-3984) and **Royal Mile Backpackers** (105 High Street, tel. 0131/557-6120).

For more regulations and less color, try the IYH hostels: **Bruntsfield Hostel** (near golf course, 6–12 beds per room, 7 Bruntsfield Crescent, buses #11, #15, and #16 from Princes Street, tel. 0131/447-2994) and **Edinburgh Hostel** (4–10 beds per room, 18 Eglinton Crescent, 5-minute walk from Haymarket station, tel. 0131/337-1120).

Eating in Edinburgh

Eating along the Royal Mile

Historic pubs and doily cafés with reasonable, unremarkable meals abound. Here are some handy, affordable places for a good bite to eat (listed in downhill order). **Deacon Brodie's Pub** serves soup, sandwiches, and snacks on the ground floor and good £7 meals upstairs in the restaurant. As in all Edinburgh pubs, kids are allowed only in the restaurant section (daily 12:00–22:00, CC:VM, tel. 0131/225-6531). Or munch prayerfully in the **Lower Aisle** restaurant under St. Giles Cathedral (Mon–Fri 8:30–16:30; July–Sept also Sun 11:00–14:00). The **Filling Station** makes good burgers (daily

12:00–22:30, 235 High Street, near North Bridge, tel. 0131/226-2488). **Bann UK,** an upscale vegetarian café, serves carnivore-pleasing cuisine that goes way beyond tofu and granola (daily 11:00–23:00, CC:VM, just off South Bridge behind the Tron Church at 5 Hunter Square, tel. 0131/226-1112). **Food Plantation** has good, inexpensive, fresh sandwiches to eat in or take out (Mon–Fri 8:30–15:30, 274 Canongate). **Brambles Tea Room** serves light lunches and Starbucks coffee (Mon–Sat 10:30–16:45, Sun 11:00–16:45, next to Huntly House at 158 Canongate). **Clarinda's Tea Room,** near the bottom of the Royal Mile, is a charming and tasty place for a break after touring the Mile or palace (daily 9:30–16:45).

For a break from the touristic grind, consider the **Elephant House,** where locals browse newspapers, listen to classic rock, and sip coffee or munch a light meal (Mon–Fri 8:00–23:00, Sat–Sun 9:00–23:00, 3 blocks south of Royal Mile at 21 George IV Bridge, tel. 0131/220-5355).

Grassmarket Street, below the castle, is lined with sloppy eateries and noisy pubs. This is the place for live folk music. If you want dinner to melt into your beer, eat here.

Eating in the New Town

Waverley Center Food Court, below the TI and above the station, is a food circus of sticky fast-food joints littered with paper plates and shoppers (Mon–Sat 8:30–18:00, Thu until 19:00, Sun 11:00–17:00). If you'd prefer pubs, browse Rose Street.

The **Undercroft,** in the basement of St. Andrew's church, is the cheapest place in town for lunch (£1 sandwich or soup and roll, Mon–Fri 12:00–14:00, on George Street, just off St. Andrew's Square).

For a generation, New Town vegetarians have munched hearty cuisine and salads at **Henderson's Salad Table and Wine Bar** (£5–6, CC:VM, Mon–Sat 8:00–22:45, closed Sun, nonsmoking section, strictly vegetarian, pleasant live music nightly, between Queen and George Streets at 94 Hanover Street, tel. 0131/225-2131).

Local office workers pile into the friendly and family-run **La Lanterna** for good Italian food (Mon–Sat 12:00–14:00, 17:15–22:00, closed Sun, CC:VMA, 83 Hanover Street, 2 blocks off Princes Street, dinner reservations wise, tel. 0131/226-3090).

Browns, a chain restaurant that's like an upscale Denny's, offers predictably good food throughout the day (£8–11, daily 12:00–22:30, family scene at dinner, nonsmoking section, CC:VMA, at west end of George Street, near Georgian House, intersection with Charlotte Street, 131 George Street, tel. 0131/225-4442).

All Bar One, the hip, mod chain of light-wood pubs offering pasta and quesadillas, bumps and grinds on the corner of George and Hanover Streets (£4 meals, Mon–Sat 12:00–24:00, Sun 12:30–23:00, order at bar, 29 George Street).

Edinburgh's New Town

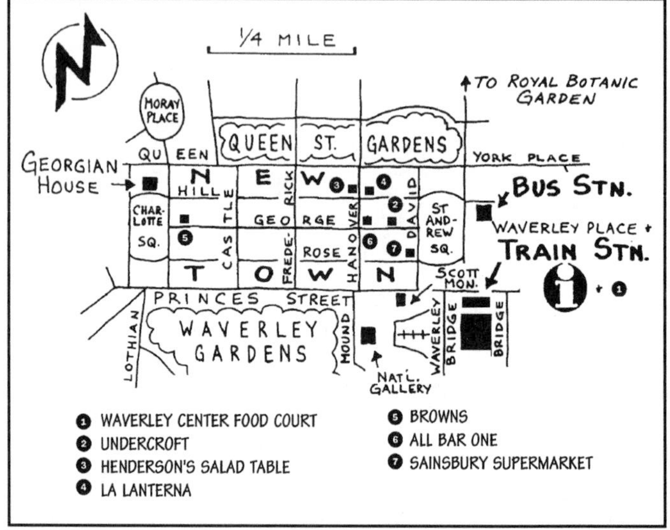

Supermarket: The glorious **Sainsbury** supermarket, with a tasty assortment of take-away food and specialty coffee, is just one block from the Walter Scott Monument and the lovely picnic-perfect Princes Street Gardens (Mon–Sat 7:00–21:00, Sun 10:00–19:00, CC:VM, on corner of Rose Street, on St. Andrew's Square). Across the street is Jenners, the classy department store.

Eating in Dalkeith Road Area, near Your B&B

All of these places except Howie's are within a five-minute walk of the recommended B&Bs. The following eateries are on or near the intersection of Newington and East Preston Streets. For a fun local atmosphere, the smoky **Wine Glass Pub** serves filling meals (£4, daily 12:00–14:30, 17:00–20:00 but no dinner on Fri, closes 19:30 on Sat). **Chinatown,** next to the Wine Glass, is a delightful—though not cheap—Chinese restaurant (£7–10, Tue–Fri 12:00–14:00, 17:30–23:00, Sat–Sun 17:30–23:00, closed Mon, CC:VM, reservations smart on weekend nights, tel. 0131/662-0555). The **Wild Elephant,** a few doors down on the same block, serves decent Thai food (£4–6, Tue–Sun 16:30–22:30, closed Mon, CC:VM, also does take-away, 21 Newington Road, tel. 0131/662-8822). **Chatterbox,** on the other side of the Wine Glass Pub, is fine for a light meal with tea (£4 meals, Mon–Fri 8:30–18:00, Sat 9:00–18:00, Sun 11:00–18:00). **Brattisanis** is your basic fish-and-chips joint serving lousy milk-shakes and great haggis (daily 11:30–24:00, 87 Newington Road).

Two affordable splurges feature Scottish cooking with a French flair, are open daily, and charge about £5 to £7 for lunch and £17 for a three-course dinner. **Fenwicks** is cozy and reliable, with tasty food (daily 12:00–14:00, dinner 18:00–late, all day Sunday, CC:VM, 15 Salisbury Place, tel. 0131/667-4265). **Howies,** with a more adventurous menu, is a bit pricier and a longer walk, about 10 minutes north of the B&B neighborhood; you could get off the bus at the Clerk Street stop on the way home (Tue–Sun 12:00–14:00, daily 18:00–22:00, can bring own wine for £2 corkage fee, 75 St. Leonard's Street, tel. 0131/668-2917).

Hotel Ceilidh-Donia, one of the recommended hotels, serves dinner (£6–7, Mon–Fri eves plus Sun lunch 12:00–14:30), runs a bar with a nonsmoking section, and is open to the public (CC:VM, Internet access, 14 Marchhall Crescent, tel. 0131/667-2743).

On Dalkeith Road, the huge Commonwealth Pool's noisy **cafeteria** is for hungry swimmers and budget travelers alike (pass the entry without paying, Mon–Fri 10:00–20:00, Sat–Sun 10:00–17:00).

Jade Palace, several blocks south of the pool, has tasty Chinese food—takeout only (Wed–Mon 16:30–23:00, closed Tue, 212 Dalkeith Road, tel. 0131/667-9030).

Minto Hotel's bar/restaurant serves a filling high tea—hot meaty dinner with tea and scones—for £7 to £10 (Mon–Sat 17:00–21:15, Sun 16:00–21:15, CC:VM, on Minto Street just north of intersection with Mayfield Terrace, tel. 0131/668-1234).

Supermarket: The nearest supermarket, **Tesco,** is located between the Royal Mile and B&B neighborhood (Mon–Sat 8:00–21:00, Sun 9:00–19:00, on Nicolson, just south of intersection with W. Richmond Street, 5 long blocks south of the Royal Mile).

Transportation Connections—Edinburgh

By train to: Inverness (7/day, 4 hrs), **Oban** (3/day, change in Glasgow, 4.5 hrs), **York** (hrly, 2.5 hrs), **London** (hrly, 5 hrs), **Durham** (hrly, 2 hrs, less frequent in winter), **Newcastle** (hrly, 1.5 hrs), **Lake District** (south past Carlisle to Penrith, catch bus to Keswick; hrly except Sun 3/day, 40 min), **Birmingham** (6/day, 4.5 hrs), **Crewe** (6/day, 3.5 hrs), **Bristol**, near Bath (hrly, 6–7 hrs). Train info: tel. 08457-484-950.

By bus to: Oban (1/day, 4 hrs), **Fort William** (1/day, 4 hrs), **Inverness** (hrly, 4 hrs), **Blackpool** (1/day, 5 hrs), **York** (1/day, 5 hrs). For bus info, call Scottish Citylink (tel. 08705-505-050, www.citylink.co.uk) or National Express (tel. 08705-808-080).

Route Tips for Drivers

Arriving in Edinburgh from the north: Rather than drive through downtown Edinburgh to the recommended B&Bs, circle the city on the A720 City Bypass road. Approaching Edinburgh on the M-9, take the M-8 (direction: Glasgow) and quickly get onto the A720 City Bypass (direction: Edinburgh South). After four miles you'll hit a roundabout. Ignore signs directing you into Edinburgh North and stay on A720 for 10 more miles to the next roundabout, named Sheriffhall. Exit the roundabout on the first left (A7 Edinburgh). From here it's four miles to the B&B neighborhood (see "Arriving from the south," below, and B&B neighborhood map).

Arriving from the south: Coming into town on A68 from the south, take the "A7 Edinburgh" exit off the roundabout. A7 becomes Dalkeith Road. If you see the huge swimming pool, you've gone a couple of blocks too far (avoid this by referring to B&B neighborhood map above).

Leaving Edinburgh, heading south: Edinburgh to Hadrian's Wall is 100 miles; to Durham it's another 50 miles. From Edinburgh, Dalkeith Road leads south and eventually becomes A68 (handy Cameron Toll supermarket with cheap gas is on the left as you leave Dalkeith Town, 10 minutes south of Edinburgh; gas and parking behind store). A68 takes you to Hadrian's Wall in two hours. You'll pass Jedburgh and its abbey after one hour. (For one last shot of shop-Scotland, there's a coach tour's delight just before Jedburgh, with kilt makers, woolens, and a sheepskin shop.) Across from Jedburgh's lovely abbey is a free parking lot, a good visitors centre, and public toilets (20p to pee). The England/Scotland border is a fun, quick stop (great view, ice cream, and tea caravan). Before Hexham, roller-coaster two miles down A6079 to B6318, following the Roman wall westward. (See "Hadrian's Wall" in the Durham chapter for more driving instructions.)

OBAN, ISLANDS, AND HIGHLANDS

Filled with more natural and historical mystique than people, the Highlands are where Scottish dreams are set. Legends of Bonnie Prince Charlie swirl around crumbling castles as pipers and kilts swirl around tourists. The harbor of Oban is a fruit crate of Scottish traditions, and the wind-bitten Hebrides are just an island hop, skip, and jump away.

The Highlands are cut in two by the impressive Caledonian Canal, with Oban at one end and Inverness at the other. The major sights cluster along the scenic 120-mile stretch between these two towns. Oban is a fine home base for western Scotland, and Inverness makes a good overnight stop on your way through eastern Scotland.

Planning Your Time

While Ireland has more charm and Wales has better sights, this area provides your best look at rural Scottish culture. There are a lot of miles, but they're scenic, the roads are good, and the traffic's light. In two days you can get a feel for the area with the car hike described below. To do the islands, you'll need more time. Iona is worthwhile but adds a day to your trip. Generally, the region is hungry for the tourist dollar, and everything overtly Scottish is designed to woo the tourist. You'll need more than this quick visit to get away from that.

The charm of the Highlands deserves more time and a trip farther north (ideally to the Isle of Skye). But with a car and two days to connect the Lake District and Edinburgh, this blitz tour is more interesting than two more days in England.

Day 1: 9:00–Leave Lake District (see Castlerigg Stone Circle if you haven't yet), 12:00–Rest stop on Loch Lomond, then joyride

on, 13:00–Lunch in Inveraray, 16:00–Arrive in Oban, tour whiskey distillery, and drop by the TI, 20:30–Have dinner with music at McTavish's Kitchen or dinner with class at The Studio.
Day 2: 9:00–Leave Oban, 10:00–Visit Glencoe museum and the valley's Visitors Centre, 12:00–Drive to Fort William and follow Caledonian Canal to Inverness, stopping at Fort Augustus for a wander around the locks and at Loch Ness to take care of any monster business, 16:00–Visit the evocative Culloden Battlefield near Inverness, 17:00–Drive south, 20:00–Set up in Edinburgh.

With more time, spend a second night in Oban and tour Iona, get to know Arthur Smith at Glencoe, or sleep in Inverness or Pitlochry, both fun and entertaining towns.

OBAN

Oban, called the "gateway to the isles," is a busy little ferry-and-train terminal with no important "sights" but a charming shiver-and-bustle vitality that gives you a feel for small-town Scotland. Wind, boats, gulls, layers of islands, and the promise of a wide-open Atlantic beyond give it a rugged and salty charm.

Orientation (area code: 01631)

Oban's business action, just a couple of streets deep, stretches along the harbor and its promenade. Everything's close together, and the town seems eager to please its many visitors. There's live, touristy music nightly in several bars and restaurants; woolen and tweed are perpetually on sale (shops open until 20:00 and on Sunday); and posters announce a variety of day tours to Scotland's wild and rabbit-strewn western islands.

Tourist Information: The TI has brochures on everything from saunas to launderettes to horseback riding to rainy-day activities as well as a fine bookshop (Mon–Sat 9:00–21:00, Sun 9:00–19:00, less Sept–June, on Argyll Square, just off the harbor a block from the train station, tel. 01631/563-122). Wander through their exhibit on the area and pick up a few phones to hear old-timers talk about their life on the west edge of Scotland. Check the TI's "What's On" board for the latest on Oban's small-town evening scene (free live entertainment nightly at the Great Western Hotel, with a Scottish Night every Wednesday, tug-of-war on the pier, American line dancing, and so on, tel. 01631/563-101).

Helpful Hints

Oban Cycles rents bikes across from the Tesco supermarket on Lochside Road (£6/half day, £12/day, Mon–Sat 9:00–17:30, closed Sun, tel. 01631/566-996). There's a laundrette downtown on Stevenson Street (Mon--Sat 9:00–17:00, closed Sun, self-serve or £5 for full-serve, tel. 01631/566-866). Café na Lusan on Craigard Road provides Internet access (£3.50/hr, tel. 01631-567-268).

Oban

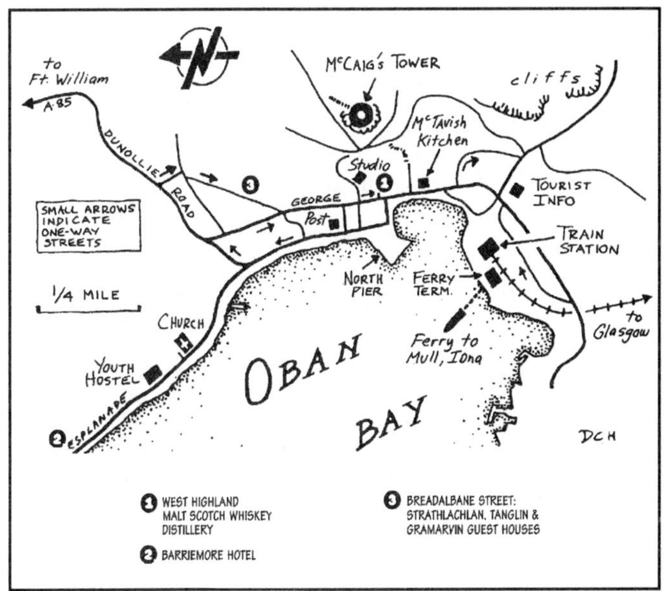

The Oban Lawn Bowling Club has welcomed visitors since 1869. This elegant green is the scene of a wonderfully British spectacle of old men tiptoeing wishfully after their balls. It's fun to watch, and—if there's no match and the weather's dry—for £2 each you can rent shoes and balls and actually play (2 blocks above the recommended B&Bs on Dalriach Road, tel. 01631/570-808).

Sights—Oban

▲West Highland Malt Scotch Whiskey Distillery Tours—The 200-year-old Oban Whiskey Distillery produces over 14,000 liters a week. They offer serious and fragrant 40-minute, £3 tours explaining the process from start to finish, with a free, smooth sample and a discount coupon for the shop. The exhibition preceding the tour gives a quick, whiskey-centric history of Scotland. This is the handiest whiskey tour you'll see, just a block off the harbor and better than anything in Edinburgh (Mon–Fri, in season Sat 9:30–17:00, last tour at 16:00, July–Sept last tour 19:30, to avoid a wait, call to reserve a place, tel. 01631/572-004).

McCaig's Tower—The unfinished "colosseum" on the hill overlooking the town was an "employ-the-workers-and-build-me-a-fine-memorial" project undertaken by an early Oban tycoon in 1900. While the structure itself is nothing to see close-up, a

10-minute hike through a Victorian residential neighborhood gets you to a peaceful garden and a mediocre view.

Sights—Near Oban

▲▲Day Trip to the Islands of Iona and Mull—See below.

Kerrera—This stark but very green island, nearly opposite Oban, offers a quick, easy opportunity to get that romantic island experience (ferry-£2.50 round-trip, 50p for bikes, sails upon request, at Gallanach's dock 2 miles south of Oban, tel. 01631/563-665).

Isle of Seil—Enjoy a drive, a walk, some solitude, and the sea. Drive 15 miles south of Oban on A816 to B844 to the Isle of Seil, connected to the mainland by a bridge. Just over the bridge on the Isle of Seil is a pub called Tigh-an-Truish ("House of Trousers"). After a 1745 English law forbade the wearing of kilts on the mainland, Highlanders used this pub to change from kilts to trousers before crossing the bridge. The pub serves great meals to those in kilts or pants (daily 12:00–14:15, 18:00–20:30, darts anytime, good seafood dish, crispy vegetables, tel. 01852/300-242). Five miles across the island, on a tiny second island, is Easdale, a historic, touristy, windy, little slate-mining town facing the open Atlantic (shuttle ferry goes the 300 yards; slate-town museum, incredibly tacky egomaniac's "Highland Arts" shop).

Sleeping in Oban

(£1 = about $1.60, country code: 44, area code: 01631)

Sleep Code: **S** = Single, **D** = Double/Twin, **T** = Triple, **Q** = Quad, **b** = bathroom, **t** = toilet only, **s** = shower only, **CC** = Credit Card (**V**isa, **M**asterCard, **A**mEx).

The first five places are well located on a quiet street two blocks off the harbor, three blocks from the center, and a 10-minute walk from the train station. By car, as you enter town, turn left after King's Knoll Hotel and take first right onto Breadalbane. Each has parking from an alley behind the buildings.

Strathlachlan Guest House is a winner. Mrs. Rena Anderson's place is stocking-feet cozy, crackerjack friendly, and chocolate-box tidy. Each of its four rooms has a private bathroom next door, and they share a rest-awhile TV lounge (S-£15, D-£30, family deals, entirely smoke free, 2 Breadalbane Street, Oban, Argyll, tel. 01631/563-861).

Tanglin B&B, next door, is another fine value. Liz and Jim Montgomery offer a bright, nonsmoking, and homey place with an easygoing atmosphere (S-£15, D-£29, Db-£36, off-season rates and family deals, 3 Strathaven Terrace, Breadalbane Street, tel. 01631/563-247, e-mail: jimtanglin@aol.com).

Gramarvin Guest House is also comfy, friendly, quiet, and a great value (small D-£25, D-£30, Db-£37, nonsmoking, Breadalbane Street, tel. 01631/564-622, Mrs. Hill).

Sand Villa Guest House rents five cheery rooms (D-£26–30, Db-£35, Tb-£45, Breadalbane Street, tel. 01631/562-803, Joyce).

Raniven Guest House is also good but a lesser value (Db-£35–40, Strathlachlan Terrace, tel. 01631/562-713, Jessie Turnbull).

Glenburnie Hotel is a stately Victorian home on Oban's waterfront (Sb-£26–35, Db-£52–60, good breakfast, nonsmoking, closed mid-Nov–mid-March, The Esplanade, PA34 5AQ, tel. & fax 01631/562-089, e-mail: graeme.strachan@btinternet.com, Graeme and Allyson).

Barriemore Hotel is the last place (and best value) on Oban's grand waterfront esplanade. It has a plush, dark, woody, equestrian feel and 13 spacious and comfortable nonsmoking rooms furnished like living rooms (Db-£44–56, grand views, CC:VM, The Esplanade, PA34 5AQ, tel. & fax 01631/566-356, e-mail: barriemore.hotel@dnet.co.uk, Evelyn and Jim McLean).

Sleeping in Hotels

I found only tired and smoky hotels in Oban. Most have unrealistically high "rack rates" with cheaper drop-in prices most of the year. The weary old **Caledonian Hotel** dominates the center of town (Db-£84 with specials as low as £61, tel. 01631/563-133). The **Balmoral Hotel** is smaller but also very central, with street noise (Db-£50–66, CC:VMA, 4 Craigard Road, tel. 01631/562-731, fax 01631/566-810, e-mail: balmoral@oban.org.uk). **Rowan Tree Hotel** is a group-friendly place with 24 basic rooms and a central but quiet locale (Sb-£38–50, Db-£62–70, group prices, CC:VMA, easy parking, George Street, tel. 01631/562-954, fax 01631/565-071).

Sleeping in Hostels and Dorms

Oban offers plenty of £10 dorm beds. Your choice: orderly, fun, or spacey. The orderly **IYHF hostel,** on the waterfront esplanade, is in a grand building with smashing views of the harbor and islands (4- to 12-bed rooms, great facilities and public rooms, tel. 01631/562-025). **Oban Backpackers** is central, laid-back, and fun, with 6 to 12 bunks per room and a wonderful sprawling public living room (Internet access, 5-minute walk from the station on Breadalbane Street, tel. 01631/562-107). **Jeremy Inglis'** spacey B&B, a block from the TI and train station, is least expensive and feels more like a commune than a youth hostel (21 Airds Crescent, tel. 01631/565-065).

Eating in Oban

Oban has plenty of fun options. Downtown is full of cheap eateries and pubs serving decent grub: consider the harborfront **Oban Inn** (the oldest building in town) or **Coasters.**

To mix a sappy folk show inexpensively with dinner, gum haggis at **McTavish's Kitchen.** This huge eating hall is an Oban institution featuring live but tired folk music and dancing. Like anything so clichédly Scottish, this is your basic tourist trap filled with English vacationers. The food is inexpensive and edible (£6 basic plate; £7 for haggis, neeps, and tatties; £13 for a super Scottish multicourse menu). The piping, dancing, and singing happen nightly May through September (20:30–22:30, mostly a fiddle and 2 accordions, with precious little dancing and bagpiping, the last hour is most interesting, tel. 01631/563-064). The show costs £4.50 without a meal, £1.50 with dinner, or free with dinner with a coupon from your B&B. No reservations required. Nonsmokers get the best harbor views. Smokers sit closest to the stage.

Everyone's favorite "nice dinner out" is at **The Studio,** a small, candlelit restaurant featuring serious, first-class Scottish cooking (£12 for a full Scottish meal, nightly 17:00–22:00, meals £1 off until 18:30, always make a reservation, tel. 01631/562-030). It has great trout, salmon, and a prawn-and-clam chowder that hits the spot on a stormy day.

For a genteel dining experience—pricey but worthwhile for a waterfront splurge—eat at the **Manor House Hotel** (£25 set meal, nouveau cuisine, a short drive or taxi ride south of town on the waterfront, Gallanach Road, tel. 01631/562-087).

For creative continental and vegetarian cuisine, consider the **Boxtree Restaurant** (£10 meals, nightly until 22:00, 108 George Street, tel. 01631/563-542). You'll eat good but pricey seafood at **The Waterfront Restaurant** (#1 The Pier, tel. 01631/563-110).

For a seafood appetizer drop by the **Local Shellfish** shack at the ferry dock (often free salmon samples, inexpensive coffee, meal-sized salmon sandwiches, open until the 18:00 boat unloads from Mull—a pleasant way to cap off your day trip to the islands).

Transportation Connections—Oban

The nearest transportation hub is Glasgow (see below).

Oban to: Inverness (6 buses/day, 4 hrs), **Glasgow** (3 trains/day, 3 hrs). Ferries fan out from Oban to the **southern Hebrides** (see "The Islands," below). Train info: tel. 08457-484-950. Bus info: tel. 01631/562-856. Caledonian MacBrayne Ferry info: tel. 01631/566-688.

Transportation Connections—Glasgow

Glasgow, one of the region's major transportation hubs, has a bus station and two train stations, a five minutes' walk apart. Train info: tel. 08457-484-950.

Glasgow's Central Station by train to: Penrith (9/day, 2 hrs; from Penrith, frequent buses except Sun to Keswick, Lake District), **Stranraer**/ferry to Belfast (6/day, 3 hrs), **Troon**/ferry to Belfast (2/hrly, 40 min), **Preston** (hrly, 3 hrs, easy 30-minute connection to Blackpool), **York** (8/day, 3.5 hrs), **London** (8/day, 6 hrs).

Glasgow's Queen Street Station by train to: Oban (3/day, 3 hrs), **Inverness** (2/day, 3.25 hrs, more frequent with change in Perth), **Edinburgh** (4/hrly, 1 hr).

Glasgow by bus to: Oban (3/day, 3 hrs), **Inverness** (hrly, 4.5 hrs), **Edinburgh** (3/hrly, 1.25 hrs; from Buchanan Bus Station on Killermont Street, 2 blocks from Queen Street Station, bus info: tel. 0141/332-7133).

THE ISLANDS OF IONA AND MULL

▲▲Day Trip to the Islands of Iona and Mull—For the best one-day look at the dramatic and historic Hebrides island scenery around Oban, take the Iona/Mull tour from Oban (£19, daily 10:00–17:40—but always confirm schedule). Bowman & MacDougall is the dominant and most established outfit. They offer a 10 percent discount on tours for anyone with this book (buy your ticket at the "Iona & Mull Tours" office, 3 Stafford Street facing the harbor next to the Oban Inn, tel. 01631/563-221).

Each morning travelers gather on the Oban pier and pile onto the huge Oban–Mull ferry (40 min). On board, if it's a clear day, ask a local to point out Ben Nevis, the tallest mountain in Great Britain. The ferry has a fine cafeteria and a bookshop (though guidebooks are cheaper in Oban). Five minutes before landing on Mull, you'll see the striking Duart castle on the left.

Upon arrival in Mull, you'll find your tour company's bus for the entertaining and informative 35-mile bus ride across the Isle of Mull (75 min, single-lane road). All drivers spend the entire ride chattering away about life on Mull. They are hardworking local boys who know how to spin a yarn, making historical trivia fascinating—or at least fun.

The Isle of Mull, the third-largest in Scotland, has 300 scenic miles of coastline and castles and a 3,169-foot-high mountain. Called Ben More ("big hill" in Gaelic), it was once much bigger. The last active volcano in northern Europe, it was 10,000 feet tall—the entire island of Mull—before it blew. Calmer now, Mull has a notably laid-back population. My bus driver reported there are no deaths from stress and only a few from boredom.

On the far side of Mull the caravan of tour buses unloads at a tiny ferry town. The ferry takes about 200 walk-ons. (Confirm clearly with bus driver when to catch the boat off Iona for your return. Hustle quickly off the bus and to the dock to avoid the 30-minute delay if you don't make the first trip over.) After the 10-minute ride, you wash ashore on sleepy Iona.

Tiny Iona, just three miles by 1.5 miles, with a population of about a hundred, is famous as the birthplace of Christianity in Scotland. You'll have about two hours here on your own before you retrace your steps, docking back in Oban by about 17:40. While the day is spectacular when it's sunny, it's worthwhile in any weather.

Iona's history: St. Columba, an Irish scholar, soldier, priest, and founder of monasteries, got into a small war over the possession of an illegally copied psalm book. Victorious but sickened by the bloodshed, Columba left Ireland, vowing never to return. According to legend, the first bit of land out of sight of his homeland was Iona. He stopped here in 563 and established the abbey.

Columba's monastic community flourished, and Iona became the center of Celtic Christianity. Iona missionaries spread the gospel through Scotland and North England, while scholarly monks established Iona as a center of art and learning. The *Book of Kells*—perhaps the finest piece of art from "Dark Age" Europe—was probably made on Iona in the eighth century. The island was so important that it was the legendary burial place for ancient Scottish and even Scandinavian kings (including Shakespeare's Macbeth).

Slowly the importance of Iona ebbed. Vikings massacred 68 monks in 806. Fearing more raids, the monks evacuated most of Iona's treasures (including the *Book of Kells*, which is now in Dublin) to Ireland. Much later, with the Reformation, the abbey was abandoned, and most of its finely carved crosses were destroyed. In the 17th century locals used the abbey only as a handy quarry for other building projects.

Iona's population peaked at about 500 in the 1830s. In the 1840s a potato famine hit. In the 1850s a third of the islanders emigrated to Canada or Australia. By 1900 the population was down to 210, and today it's only around 100.

But in our generation a new religious community has given the abbey new life. The Iona community is an ecumenical gathering of men and women seeking new ways of living the Gospel in today's world, with a focus on worship, peace and justice issues, and reconciliation (£2.50 entry, tel. 01681/700-512).

A pristine light and a thoughtful peace pervade the stark, car-free island and its tiny community. While the present abbey, nunnery, and graveyard go back to the 13th century, much of what you'll see was rebuilt in the 19th century. But with buoyant clouds bouncing playfully off of distant bluffs, sparkling white sand crescents, and lone tourists camped thoughtfully atop huge rocks just looking out to sea, it's a place perfect for meditation. Climb a peak—nothing's higher than 300 feet above the sea.

The village, Baile Mor, has a shop, tiny eateries, enough beds, and a meager heritage center. The Finlay Ross Shop rents bikes (near ferry dock, £4.50/half day, £8/day).

Sleeping in Iona: Enjoy the serenity of Iona by spending the night. When the day-trippers leave, you'll find that special peace. **Argyll Hotel,** built in 1867, sits proud and classy overlooking the waterfront, with basic rooms above a fine grassy yard and public spaces (15 rooms, Db-£60–116, dinner deals, CC:VM, tel. 01681/700-334, fax 01681/700-510, www.argyllhoteliona.co.uk). **Finlay**

B&B rents 11 no-charm rooms in front of the ferry dock (D-£42, Db-£46, reception at Finlay Ross Shop, tel. 01681/700-357, fax 01681/700-562).

Other Island Tours—The Oban tour companies offer an array of tours. You can spend an entire day on Mull. Those more interested in nature than church history will enjoy trips to the wildly scenic Isle of Staffa with Fingal's Cave. Trips to Treshnish Island brim with puffins, seals, and other sea critters.

THE HIGHLANDS: OBAN TO INVERNESS

Discover Glencoe's dark secrets in the Weeping Glen, where Britain's highest peak, Ben Nevis, keeps its head in the clouds. Explore the locks and lochs of the Caledonian Canal while the Loch Ness monster plays hide-and-seek. Hear the music of the Highlands in Inverness and the echo of muskets in Culloden, where the English put down Bonnie Prince Charlie and conquered the clans of the Highlands.

Getting around the Highlands

The trains are scenic, but if schedules frustrate, take the bus. Six buses a day connect the towns from Oban to Inverness (4 hrs). Ask at the station to see how schedules work for sight hopping. One great option is to ride with the mail carrier on the post bus. While locals do this to get somewhere, tourists do it to chat with the mail carrier—great gossip on the entire neighborhood! This costs only a few pounds and works well in remote spots like Glencoe.

GLENCOE

This valley is the essence of the wild, powerful, and stark beauty of the Highlands (and, I think, excuses the hurried tourist from needing to go north of Inverness). Along with its scenery, Glencoe offers a good dose of bloody clan history.

Glencoe town is just a line of houses. One is a tiny thatched building jammed with local history. The huggable Glencoe and North Lorn Folk Museum, purely a homegrown effort, is filled with humble exhibits gleaned from the town's old closets and attics (which come to life when explained by a local). When one house was being rethatched, its owner found a cache of old rifles hidden there from the British Redcoats after the disastrous battle of Culloden (£2, Mon–Sat 10:00–17:30, closed Sun).

A couple of miles into the dramatic valley you'll find the Visitors Centre. While little more than a café, WC, and bookshop, it does show a 14-minute video about the 1692 massacre when the Redcoats killed the sleeping MacDonalds and the valley got its nickname, "The Weeping Glen" (50p, April–Sept daily 9:30–17:00, closed Oct–March, just east of town on A82, tel. 01855/811-307). The nearest TI is in Ballachulish (tel. 01855/811-296).

Oban, Islands, and Highlands

Walks: For a steep one-mile hike, climb the Devil's Staircase (trail leaves from A82, 8 miles east of Glencoe). For a three-hour hike, ask at the Visitors Centre about the Lost Valley of the MacDonalds (trail leaves from A82, 3 miles east of Glencoe). For an easy walk from Glencoe, head to the mansion on the hill (over the bridge, turn left, fine loch views). Above Glencoe is a mansion built by a local big shot for his love—a Canadian Indian. She was homesick, so he actually replicated a Canadian garden/forest. It didn't work, and they eventually returned to British Columbia.

Glencoe's Burial Island and Island of Discussion: In the loch just outside Glencoe notice the burial island—where the souls of those who "take the low road" are piped home. (Ask a local about "You take the high road, and I'll take the low road.") The next island was the Island of Discussion—where those with disputes were put until they came to an agreement.

Sleeping in Glencoe

(£1 = about $1.60, country code: 44, area code: 01855)

Many find Glencoe more interesting than Oban for an overnight stop. In Glencoe village, Arthur Smith runs the **Cala Sona B&B,**

aptly named "haven of happiness" in Gaelic. He entertains his guests with a peat fire, ghost stories, and tales of the Glencoe massacre (S-£15, D-£30, on the main street, tel. 01855/811-314, e-mail: calasona@talk21.com). If Arthur's place is full, try the **Mack-Leven House B&B** (D-£30, Db-£32 with this book, family deals, smoke-free rooms, homey lounge, conservatory, Lorn Drive, Glencoe, tel. 01855/811-215, Mackintosh family) or **Tulachgorm B&B** (D-£30, flexible on price when slow, nonsmoking, just before Cala Sona B&B, tel. 01855/811-391, Ann Blake).

While nearby hotels and pubs serve food, **Mrs. Matheson's Tea Room Restaurant** (right in the village) is your best bet for good home-cooked meals (£8 meals, daily 11:00–21:00, tel. 01855/811-590). For evening fun, chat with your B&B host, take a walk, or drop by the "Wee Ceilidh" for music and dancing at the **Glencoe Hotel** (Mon and Fri at 20:00).

More Sights—Scottish Highlands

Ben Nevis—From Fort William, take a peek at Britain's highest peak, Ben Nevis (over 4,400 feet). Thousands walk to its summit each year. On a clear day you can admire it from a distance. Scotland's only mountain cable cars can take you to a not-very-lofty 2,150-foot perch for a closer look (£6.50, daily 10:00–17:00, later in summer, 15-minute ride, signposted on A82, tel. 01397/705-825).

▲Caledonian Canal—Three lochs and a series of canals cut Scotland in two. Oich, Lochy, and Ness were connected in the early 1800s by the great British engineer Thomas Telford. Traveling between Fort William and Inverness (60 miles), you'll follow Telford's work—20 miles of canals and locks between 40 miles of lakes, raising ships from sea level to 51 feet (Ness), to 93 feet (Lochy), and to 106 feet (Oich).

While "Neptune's Staircase," a series of locks near Fort William, is cleverly named, the best lock stop is Fort Augustus, where the canal hits Loch Ness. In Fort Augustus, the Caledonian Canal Heritage Centre, three locks above the main road, gives a good rundown on Telford's work (free). Stroll to the top of the locks past several shops and eateries for a fine view.

Loch Ness—I'll admit it. I had my zoom lens out and my eyes on the water. The local tourist industry thrives on the legend of the Loch Ness Monster. It's a thrilling thought, and there have been several seemingly reliable "sightings" (monks, policemen, and sonar images). The loch, 24 miles long, less than a mile wide, and the third deepest in Europe, is deepest near the Urquhart Castle. Most monster sightings are in this area.

The Nessie commercialization is so tacky that there are two "official" Loch Ness Exhibition Centres within 100 yards of each other. Each has a tour-bus parking lot and more square footage devoted to their kitschy shop than to the exhibit. The exhibits, while fascinating, are overpriced. The exhibition in the big stone mansion (closest to Inverness) is the better one, with a 40-minute series of video bits on the geological and historical environment that bred the monster story and the various searches (£5.95, daily 9:00–20:00, tel. 01456/450-573). The other (closest to Oban), is a high school–quality photo report followed by the 30-minute *We Believe in the Loch Ness Monster* movie, featuring credible-sounding locals explaining what they saw and a review of modern Nessie searches (£3.50, daily 9:00–19:30, until 21:00 in summer, tel. 01456/450-342).

The nearby Urquhart Castle ruins are gloriously situated with a view of virtually the entire lake (£3.80, daily 9:30–18:30, July–Aug until 20:30, tel. 01456/450-551). It's an empty shell of a castle with crowds and parking problems.

▲Culloden Battlefield—Scottish troops under Bonnie Prince Charlie were defeated here by the English in 1746. This last land battle fought on British soil spelled the end of Jacobite resistance and the fall of the clans. Wandering the battlefield, you feel that something terrible occurred here. Locals still bring flowers and speak of "46" as if it just happened.

The excellent Visitors Centre shows a stirring 16-minute audiovisual (3/hrly). Wander through a furnished old cottage and the battlegrounds (£3.50, April–Oct daily 9:00–18:00, otherwise daily 10:00–16:00, closed Jan, good tearoom, tel. 01463/790-607).

INVERNESS

The only sizable town in the north of Scotland, with 42,000 people, Inverness is pleasantly located on a river at the base of a castle (not worth a look) and has a free little museum (worth a look, cheap café). Check out the bustling pedestrian downtown and central TI (Mon–Sat 9:00–17:30, Sun 10:00–16:00, Castle Wynd, tel. 01463/234-353).

Balnain House Highland Music traces local music from heroic warrior songs to Gaelic rock. The bagpiper in residence will let you tootle a bagpipe (£2.50 to scan 6 hours of music, daily 10:00–17:00, July–Aug until 20:00; in summer live bagpiping at 17:30 and live music most weekday eves until 22:00; Balnain House, tel. 01463/715-757, www.balnain.com).

For day trips, consider taking a Guide Friday bus to the Culloden battlefield or any of the daily tours to Loch Ness for a monster hunt.

The Scottish Showtime evening is a fun-loving, hardworking, Lawrence Welk–ish show giving you all the clichés in a clap-along two-hour package. I prefer it to the big hotel spectacles in Edinburgh (usually June–Sept Mon–Fri at 20:30, no meals, £12 but £2 off with this book, Spectrum Centre, Margaret Street, tel. 0800-015-8001).

Sleeping and Eating in Inverness

(£1 = about $1.60, country code: 44, area code: 01463)

These rooms are all a short walk from the train station and town center (just up the steps from the pedestrian High Street).

Craigside Lodge B&B is a winner. Its six spacious, cheery rooms share a stay-awhile lounge with a great city view (Db-£40–42, CC:VM, just above Castle Street at 4 Gordon Terrace, IV2 3HD, tel. 01463/231-576, fax 01463/713-409, Wilf and Janette Skinner).

Ardconnel House, with six rooms, is tasteful, bright, spacious, and classy (Sb-£23–26, D-£40–44, Db-£44–50, CC:VM, family deals, nonsmoking, TVs in rooms, 21 Ardconnel Street, IV2 3EU, tel. & fax 01463/240-455, www.scotland-info.co.uk/ardconnel, Isabel and Richard Cowe).

Kinloch Lodge B&B is a minimal place renting four small but cheery double rooms (no twins, S-£20, D-£40, Db-£44, 13 Ardconnel Street, tel. 01463/716-005, Mrs. MacDonald).

Melness Guest House has fine rooms and a cozy lounge but is a bit overpriced (D-£42, Db-£52, less off-season, completely smoke free, at 8 Old Edinburgh Road, tel. 01463/220-963, www.melnessie.co.uk).

For £11 beds in six-bed rooms downtown and a 10-minute walk from the train station, consider the friendly and laid-back **Inverness Student Hotel** (8 Culduthel Road, tel. 01463/236-556).

Rajah Indian Restaurant provides a tasty break from pub grub (£6–10 meals, nightly until 23:00, just off Church Street at 2 Post Office Avenue, tel. 01463/237-190). Near the recommended B&B, **Redcliff Hotel** lounge is popular for its pub-style dinners. Several inviting eateries—including **Number 27**—line Castle Street.

Transportation Connections—Inverness

Trains link Inverness, **Pitlochry** (9/day, 1.5 hrs) and **Edinburgh** (9/day, 3.5 hrs, tel. 01463/238-924 or tel. 08457-484-950), and buses run between Inverness and **Oban** (6/day, 4 hrs, tel. 01463/233-371). Scottish Rail does a great 20:30–7:30 sleeper service to **London** (£95 for a private compartment with breakfast, www.scotrail.co.uk). Consider dropping your car in Inverness and riding to London by train.

PITLOCHRY

This likable tourist town, famous for its whiskey, makes an enjoyable overnight stop. Its cute **Edradour Scotch Distillery**—the smallest in Scotland—offers a free one-hour guided tour, a 10-minute audio-visual show, and, of course, a tasting (3/hrly, Mon–Sat 9:30–16:45 plus March–Oct Sun 12:00–16:45, a lovely 40-minute walk through the forest from downtown, tel. 01796/472-095). The big **Blair Athol Distillery** gives £3 hour-long tours with a sample at the end

(2/hrly, Mon–Sat 9:30–16:00, Sun 12:00–16:00, last tour starts at 16:00, half mile from town, tel. 01796/472-234). Pitlochry also has plenty of forest walks and a salmon ladder (free viewing area—best in May, 3-minute walk from town). From May through October, the town theater offers a different play every night (£16). For a unique look at jewelry made of pressed heather stems, tour **Heather-gems** (behind the TI). The TI is helpful (May–Sept daily 9:00–20:00, less off-season, Atholl Road, tel. 01796/472-215).

Sleeping in Pitlochry

(£1 = about $1.60, country code: 44, area code: 01796)

Try **Craigroyston House,** a big Victorian country house with eight smoke-free, Laura Ashley–style rooms run by charming Gretta Maxwell (Db-£40–52, flexing with demand, next to church and TI at 2 Lower Oakfield, PH16 5HQ, tel. & fax 01796/472-053, http://web.ukonline.co.uk/craigroyston, e-mail: craigroyston@ukonline.co.uk). She can find you another B&B if her place is full. For a simpler, more rural option, drive two miles south of town on the old A9 to **Donavourd Farmhouse B&B** (D-£34–44, dinner, near distillery, tel. 01796/472-254, Mrs. Shepley). Pitlochry's fine **hostel** is on Knockard Road (£11.25 bunks, above the main street, tel. 01796/472-308).

Route Tips for Drivers

Lake District to Oban (220 miles): From Keswick, take A66 for 18 miles to M6 and speed nonstop north (via Penrith and Carlisle), crossing Hadrian's Wall into Scotland. The road becomes the M74 south of Glasgow. To slip quickly through Glasgow, leave M74 at Junction 4 onto M73, following signs to M8/Glasgow. Leave M73 at Junction 2, exiting onto M8. Stay on M8 west through Glasgow, exit on Junction 30, cross Erskine Bridge (60p), and turn left on A82, following signs to Crianlarich and Loch Lomond. (For a scenic drive through Glasgow, take exit 17 off M8 and stay on A82 toward Dumbarton.) You'll soon be driving along scenic Loch Lomond. The first picnic turnout has the best lake views, benches, a park, and a playground. Halfway up the loch, at Tarbet, take the "tourist route" left onto A83, drive along Loch Long toward Inveraray via Rest-and-Be-Thankful Pass. (This colorful name comes from the 1880s, when second- and third-class coach passengers got out and pushed the coach and first-class passengers up the hill.) Stop in Inveraray, a lovely castle town on Loch Fyne. Park near the pier. (TI open July–Aug 9:00–18:00, Sept–June Mon–Sat 9:00–16:00, Sun 11:00–16:00, tel. 01499/302-063.) The town jail, now a museum, is a "19th-century living prison" (£4.75, daily 9:30–18:00, tel. 01499/302-381). Leaving Inveraray, drive through a gate (at the Woolen Mill) to A819, through Glen Aray, and along Loch Awe. A85 takes you into Oban.

Oban to Glencoe (45 miles) to Loch Ness (75 miles) to Inverness (20 miles) to Edinburgh (150 miles): Barring traffic, you'll make great time on good, mostly two-lane roads. Be careful, but if you're timid about passing, diesel fumes and large trucks might be your memory of this drive. From Oban, follow the coastal A828 toward Fort William. After about 20 miles you'll see the photogenic Castle Staulker marooned on a lonely island. At Loch Leven and Ballachulish Village, leave A828, taking A82 into Glencoe. Drive through the village up the valley (Glencoe) for 10 minutes for a grand view and a chance to hear a bagpiper in the wind—Highland buskers. If you play the recorder (and no other tourists are there), ask to finger a tune while the piper does the hard work.

At the top of the valley you hit the vast Rannoch Moor—500 square and desolate miles with barely enough decent land to graze a sheep. Then make a U-turn and return through Glencoe. Continue north on A82, over the bridge, past Fort William toward Loch Ness. Follow the Caledonian Canal on A82 for 60 miles, stop at Loch Ness, and then continuing on A82 to Inverness.

Leaving Inverness, follow signs to A9 (south toward Perth). Just as you leave Inverness, detour four miles east off A9 on B9006 to the Culloden Battlefield Visitors Centre. Back on A9 it's a wonderfully speedy, scenic highway (A9, M90, A90) all the way to Edinburgh (Inverness–Edinburgh, minimum 3 hrs).

For a scenic shortcut, head north only as far as Glencoe and then cut to Edinburgh via Rannoch Moor and Tyndrum. For directions to B&Bs, see "Edinburgh" chapter.

DUBLIN

With reminders of its stirring history and rich culture on every corner, Ireland's capital and largest city is a sightseer's delight. Dublin's fair city will have you humming "Alive, alive-O."

Founded as a Viking trading settlement in the ninth century, Dublin grew to be a center of wealth and commerce second only to London in the British Empire. Dublin, the seat of English rule in Ireland for 700 years, was the heart of a "civilized" Anglo-Irish area (eastern Ireland) known as "the Pale." Anything "beyond the Pale" was considered uncultured and almost barbaric... purely Irish.

The Golden Age of English Dublin was the 18th century. Britain was on a roll, and Dublin was Britain's second city. Largely rebuilt during this Georgian era, Dublin—even with its "tale of two cities" miserable underbelly—became an elegant and cultured capital.

Then nationalism and human rights got in the way. The ideas of the French Revolution inspired Irish intellectuals to buck British rule, and after the revolt of 1798, life in Dublin was never quite the same. But the 18th century left a lasting imprint on the city. Georgian (that's British for neoclassical) squares and boulevards gave the city a grandness. The National Museum, National Gallery, and many government buildings are in the Georgian section of town. Few buildings (notably Christchurch Cathedral and St. Patrick's Cathedral) predate this Georgian period.

In the 19th century, with the closing of the Irish Parliament, the famine, and the beginnings of the struggle for independence, Dublin was treated—and felt—more like a colony than a partner. The tension culminated in the Rising of 1916, independence, and the tragic civil war. With many of Dublin's grand streets left in ruins, the city emerged as the capital of the only former colony in Europe.

While bullet-pocked buildings and dramatic statues keep memories of Ireland's recent struggle for independence alive, it's boom time now, and the city is looking to a bright future. Locals are enjoying the "Celtic Tiger" economy—the best in Europe—while visitors enjoy a big-town cultural scene wrapped in a small-town smile.

Planning Your Time

On a two-week trip through Ireland, Dublin deserves three nights and two days. Consider this sightseeing plan:

Day 1: 10:00–Trinity College walk, 11:00–*Book of Kells* and Old Library, 12:00–Browse Grafton Street, lunch there or picnic on St. Stephen's Green, 13:30–National Museum, 15:00–Historical town walk, 17:00–Return to hotel, rest, dinner—eat well for less during "early-bird specials," 19:30–Evening walk (musical or literary), 22:00–Irish music in Temple Bar area.

Day 2: 10:00–Kilmainham Jail, 12:00–Guinness Brewery tour, 13:30–Lunch (with a faint buzz), 15:00–Tour Dublin Castle, Evening–Catch a play or concert.

Dublin

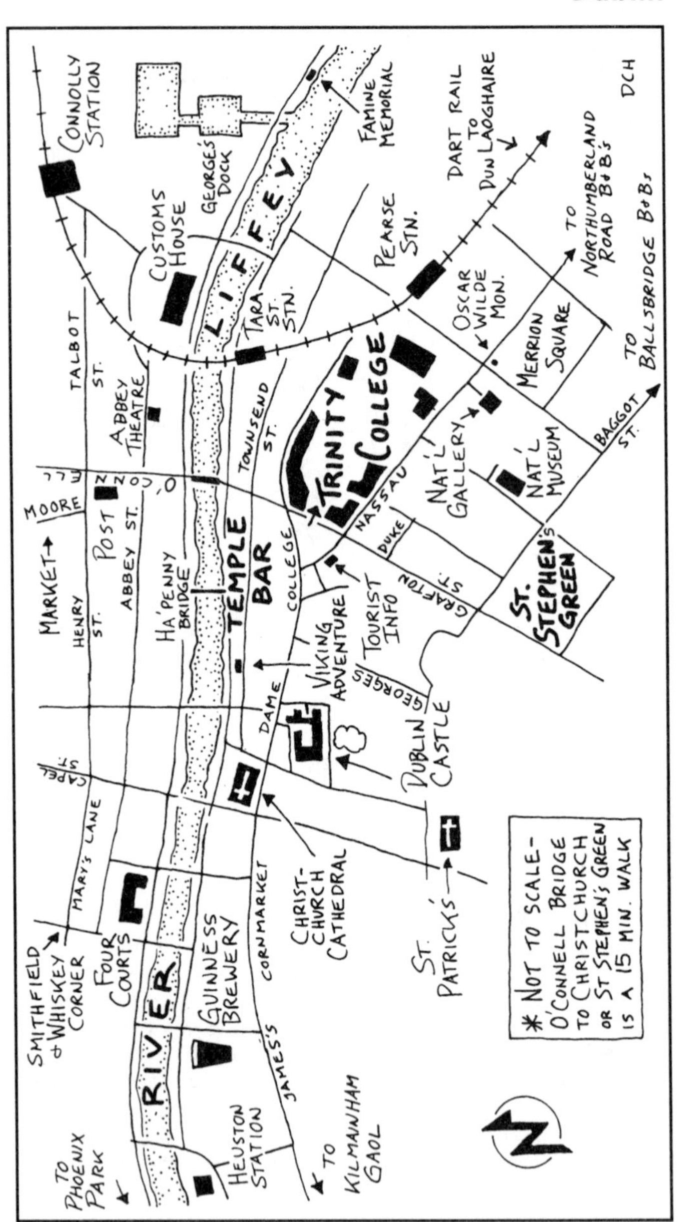
CONNOLLY STATION
CUSTOMS HOUSE
GEORGE'S DOCK
RIVER LIFFEY
FAMINE MEMORIAL
DART RAIL TO DUN LAOGHAIRE
PEARSE STN.
TARA ST. STN.
TO NORTHUMBERLAND ROAD B&Bs
TO BALLSBRIDGE B&Bs
DCH
OSCAR WILDE MON.
MERRION SQUARE
TALBOT ST.
ABBEY THEATRE
TOWNSEND ST.
TRINITY COLLEGE
BAGGOT ST.
NAT'L GALLERY
NAT'L MUSEUM
NASSAU
MOORE
POST O
ABBEY ST.
MARKET
HENRY ST.
HA'PENNY BRIDGE
TEMPLE BAR
COLLEGE
DUKE
GRAFTON ST.
ST. STEPHEN'S GREEN
TOURIST INFO
VIKING ADVENTURE
GEORGES
DAME
DUBLIN CASTLE
CAPEL ST.
MARY'S LANE
SMITHFIELD & WHISKEY CORNER
FOUR COURTS
GUINNESS BREWERY
CORNMARKET
CHRIST-CHURCH CATHEDRAL
ST. PATRICK'S
JAMES'S
TO KILMAINHAM GAOL
HEUSTON STATION
TO PHOENIX PARK
* NOT TO SCALE - O'CONNELL BRIDGE TO CHRISTCHURCH OR ST STEPHEN'S GREEN IS A 15 MIN. WALK

Orientation (area code: 01)

Greater Dublin sprawls with over a million people—nearly a third of the country's population. But the center of touristic interest is a tight triangle between O'Connell Bridge, St. Stephen's Green, and Christchurch Cathedral. Within this triangle you'll find Trinity College (*Book of Kells*), Grafton Street (top pedestrian shopping zone), Temple Bar (trendy nightlife center), Dublin Castle, and the hub of most city tours and buses.

The River Liffey cuts the town in two. Focus on the southern half (where nearly all your sightseeing will take place). Dublin's main drag, O'Connell Street (near Abbey Theater and the outdoor produce market) runs north of the river to the central O'Connell Bridge then continues as the main city axis—mostly as Grafton Street—to St. Stephen's Green. The only major sights outside your easy-to-walk triangle are the Kilmainham Jail and the Guinness Brewery (both west of the center).

Tourist Information

The main TI fills an old church on Suffolk Street (a block off Grafton Street, Mon–Sat 9:30–17:30, Sun 9:30–14:30, closed off-season Sun, Internet access, WC upstairs off café, tel. 01/605-7700; if calling from Britain dial simply 020/7493-3201; www.visitdublin.com). Packed with tourists, promotional brochures, an American Express office, car rental agency, bus info desk, café, and traditional knickknacks, it's helpful if you don't mind a long wait. Less crowded TIs are the low-key branch on Baggot Street (at bridge in unmarked glass building with tiny sign—Bord Failte—on door, Mon–Fri 9:30–17:00, tel. 01/602-4000) and a perky office at the airport (daily 8:00–22:00). The TI can give you a free newspaper (*The Guide to Dublin*) with a lousy map, a list of events, lots of advertisements, and the same fliers that fill racks all over town. The Dublin Map for 50p is decent, but the pricier maps are more detailed (sold at main TI or most newsstands). The handy *Dublin's Top Visitor Attractions* booklet has a small map and the latest on all of the town's sights—many more than I list here (£2.50, sold at TI bookshop without any wait). For a schedule of happenings in town, check the minimal calendar of events inside the free *The Guide to Dublin* newspaper (from TI), or, better, buy the excellent *In Dublin* at any newsstand (fortnightly, £2).

Arrival in Dublin

By Train: Trains arrive at Heuston Station (serving the west and southwest) on the west end of town. Dublin's second train station, Connolly Station (serving the north, northwest, and Rosslare), is closer to the center—a 10-minute walk from O'Connell Bridge. Each station has a luggage-check facility and cash machines. Bus #90 runs along the river, connecting both train stations, the bus station, and the city center (65p flat fee, 6/hrly).

By Bus: Bus Eireann, Ireland's national bus company, uses the Busaras Central Bus Station next to Connolly Station (10-minute walk or short ride on bus #90 to the city center).

By Ferry: Irish Ferries dock at the mouth of the River Liffey (near the town center), while the Stena Line docks at Dun Laoghaire (easy DART train connections into Dublin, at least 3/hrly, 15 min).

By Plane: The airport has ATMs, change bureaus, car rental agencies, baggage check, a café, and a supermarket at the car park. Taxis from the airport into Dublin cost about £13, to Dun Laoghaire about £30.

Airport Buses: Consider buying a bus pass that covers the Airlink bus into town (see "Getting Around Dublin," below), but read this first. To get to the recommended accommodations in the **city center**, take Airlink bus #748 (not #747); ask the driver which stop is closest to your hotel (£3.50, £2 with Aer Lingus boarding pass, pay driver, 4/hrly, 30 min, connects airport with Heuston train station and Central Bus Station near Connolly train station). For the **St. Stephen's Green** neighborhood, the Aircoach is a better bet (£4, 4/hrly, runs 5:30–22:30; pay driver and confirm best stop for your hotel; for some it's a short walk). If you're staying in **Dun Laoghaire**, take Airlink bus #746 direct to Dun Laoghaire.

City Bus: To get to Dublin cheaply, take the city bus from the airport; buses marked #41A, #41B, and #41C go to Marlborough Street, a five-minute walk from O'Connell Bridge (£1.15, exact change required, 3/hrly, 40 min).

Helpful Hints

U.S. Consulate: 42 Elgin Road, Ballsbridge (Mon–Fri 8:30–12:00 for passport concerns, tel. 01/668-7122).

Internet Access: Try Planet Cybercafé (£5/hr, daily 10:00–22:00, off Dame Street below the castle at 23 South Great George's Street, tel. 01/679-0583), Central Cybercafe (6 Grafton Street, tel. 01/677-8298), Cyberia (Temple Lane, tel. 01/679-7607), or the main TI off Grafton.

Laundry: Capricorn Laundrette, a block southwest of Jury's Christchurch on Patrick Street, is full-service only. Allow four hours and about £6 (Mon–Fri 7:30–20:00, Sat 9:00–18:00, Sun 10:00–16:00, tel. 01/473-1779). The All-American Laundrette offers self-service and full-service (Mon–Sat 8:30–19:00, Sun 10:00–18:00, 40 South George's Street, tel. 01/677-2779).

Festivals: St. Patrick's Day is a five-day extravaganza in Dublin (www.stpatricksday.ie). June 16 is Bloomsday, dedicated to James Joyce, featuring the Messenger Bike Rally. On rugby weekends (about 4 a year), hotels are the winners. Book ahead during festival times and for any weekend.

Getting around Dublin

You'll do most of Dublin on foot. Big green buses are cheap and cover the city thoroughly. Most lines start at the four quays nearest O'Connell Bridge. If you're away from the center, nearly any bus takes you back downtown. Tell the driver where you're going, and he'll ask for 65p, 85p, or £1.05, depending on the number of stops. Exact change is required (you'll lose any excess). If you're heading to the bus or train stations from the city center, catch bus #90 on the south side of river to get to Heuston, on the north side of the river to reach Connolly and the bus station.

Passes: The bus office at 59 Upper O'Connell Street has free "route network" maps and sells city bus passes: 3-day Rambler-£6 (covers Airlink airport bus but not DART trains) or 4-day adult Explorer pass-£10 (includes DART but not Airlink; passes are also sold at desks in airport and main TI, bus info tel. 01/873-4222).

DART: These speedy trains connect Dublin with Dun Laoghaire (ferry terminal and recommended B&Bs, at least 3/hrly, 15 min, £1.15).

Taxi: Taxis are honest, plentiful, friendly, and good sources of information (under £4 for most downtown rides, £20 per hour for a guided joyride available from most any cab).

Tours of Dublin

While the physical treasures of Dublin are mediocre by European standards, the city has a fine story to tell and people with a natural knack for telling it. It's a good town for walking tours—and the competition is fierce. Pamphlets touting creative walks are posted all over town. There are medieval walks, literary walks, Georgian Dublin walks, and more. The evening walks are great ways to meet other travelers.

▲▲Historical Walking Tour—This is your best introductory walk. A group of hardworking history graduates—many of whom claim to have done more than just kiss the Blarney Stone—fill Dublin's basic historic strip (Trinity College, Old Parliament House, Dublin Castle, and Christchurch Cathedral) with the story of their city, from its Viking origin to the present. As you listen to your guide's story, you stand in front of buildings that aren't much to see but are lots to talk about. Guides speak at length about the roots of Ireland's struggle with Britain (£6, 2 hrs, depart from front gate of Trinity College, May–Sept daily 11:00 and 15:00 plus Sun–Mon, Wed, and Fri–Sat at 12:00; Oct–April only Fri, Sat, and Sun at 12:00; specialty and private walks also available, tel. 01/878-0227, www.historicalinsights.ie).

▲Jameson Literary Pub Crawl—Two actors take 30 or so tourists on a walk, stopping at four pubs. Half the time is spent enjoying their entertaining banter, which introduces the novice to the high craic (conversation) of Joyce, O'Casey, and Yeats. The

2.25-hour tour is punctuated with 20-minute pub breaks (free time). While the beer lubricates the social fun, it dilutes the content of the evening. From April through October, meet any night at 19:30 (plus Sun at noon) in the Duke Pub off Grafton on Duke Street (£6.50, Nov–March only Thu–Sun, tel. 01/670-5602, www.dublinpubcrawl.com).

▲▲Traditional Irish-Music Pub Crawl—This is like the Literary Pub Crawl but features music. You meet upstairs at 19:30 at Gogarty's Pub (in the Temple Bar area at the corner of Fleet and Anglesea) and spend 40 minutes in the upstairs rooms of four pubs listening to two musicians talk about, play, and sing traditional Irish music. While having only two musicians makes the music a bit thin (Irish music aficionados will tell you you're better off just finding a good session), the evening—while touristy—is not gimmicky. The musicians demonstrate four instruments and really enjoy introducing rookies to their art (£6, boss Vinnie offers a £1 discount with this book, beer extra, nightly from May 4–Oct 27 in 2001; Nov and Feb–April on Fri–Sat only, allow 2.5 hours, expect up to 50 tourists, tel. 01/478-0193).

▲Bus Tours—Several companies offer the basic center-of-Dublin orientation (3 hrs, £10, departing 10:15 and 14:15, from 59 Upper O'Connell Street, tel. 01/873-4222).

Three companies offer hop-on hop-off bus tours of Dublin, doing virtually identical 90-minute circuits, allowing you to hop on and hop off at your choice of about 12 stops (mostly topless—with running commentaries; they go to Guinness Brewery but not to Kilmainham Jail).

For maximum hopping, go with either **Guide Friday** (£8.50, black-and-gold buses, tel. 01/676-5377) or **The Old Dublin Tour** (£8.50, maroon-and-cream buses, tel. 01/458-0054) because the same ticket works on either company's buses (minimizing your wait at stops). **Dublin City Tour** uses green-and-cream buses, charges less (£7), and does less (75 min, lops off Phoenix Park, tickets not valid on other companys' buses, tel. 01/873-4222).

Buy your ticket on board or in advance at the TI (each company's map, free with ticket, details various discounts you'll get on Dublin's sights). Your ticket's valid the entire day. Buses, which leave every 15 minutes from about 9:30 to 17:30 April through October (Nov–March 2/hrly 9:30–15:30) are especially enjoyable for photographers on sunny days.

▲Viking Splash Tours—If you'd like to ride in a WWII amphibious vehicle—driven by a Viking-costumed guide who is as liable to spout history as he is to growl—this is for you. The tour starts with a group roar from the Viking within us all. At first the guide talks as if he were a Viking ("When we came here in 841 . . . "), but quickly the patriot emerges as he tags Irish history to the sights you pass. Near the end of the 1.25-hour tour (punctuated by occasional group roars at passersby), you don a life jacket for a slow spin up and down a boring canal. Kids who expect a Viking splash may feel they've been trapped in a classroom, but historians will enjoy the talk more than the gimmick (£9, mid-March–Oct Tue–Sun 10:00–17:00, maybe later in summer, closed Mon, 2/hrly, depart from Bull Alley, beside St. Patrick's Cathedral, on gray days boat is covered but still breezy—dress warmly, tel. 01/296-6047, www.vikingsplashtours.com).

Dublin Bike Tours—A three-hour guided tour of Dublin's quieter streets costs £12 (includes bikes, April–Oct at 9:45 and 13:45, meet at front gate of Christchurch Cathedral, book ahead at TI; call 01/679-0899 or cellular 087-284-0799, or drop by office behind Kinlay House, 2–12 Lord Edward Street).

Sights—Dublin's Trinity College

▲Trinity College—Started in 1592 by Queen Elizabeth I to establish a Protestant way of thinking about God, Trinity has long been Ireland's most prestigious college. Originally the student body was limited to rich, Protestant males. Women were admitted in 1903, and Catholics, while allowed entrance by the school much earlier, were given formal permission to study at Trinity in the 1970s. Today half of Trinity's 12,500 students are women, and 70 percent are culturally Catholic (although only about 20 percent of Irish youth are churchgoing).

▲Trinity College Tour—Inside the gate of Trinity, students organize and lead 30-minute tours of their campus. You'll get a rundown on the mostly Georgian architecture; a peek at student life, both in the early days and today; and enjoy a chance to hang out with a witty Irish college kid as he talks about his school (late May–Sept daily 10:00–15:30; Oct–late May usually weekends only, weather permitting; look for small blue kiosk inside gate, the £5.50 tour fee includes the £4.50 fee to see the *Book of Kells*, where the tour leaves you).

▲▲▲*Book of Kells* in the Trinity Old Library—The only Trinity campus interior welcoming tourists—just follow the signs—is the Old Library with its precious *Book of Kells*. The first-class *Turning Darkness into Light* exhibit puts the 680-page illuminated manuscript in its historical and cultural context and prepares you for the original book and other precious manuscripts in the treasury. The exhibit is a one-way affair leading to the actual treasury, which shows only four books under glass in one display case (which everyone crowds around). Take your time in the exhibit.

Written on vellum (baby calfskin) in the eighth or early ninth century—probably by Irish monks in Iona, Scotland—this enthusiastically decorated copy of the four Gospels was taken to the Irish monastery at Kells in 806 after a series of Viking raids. Arguably the finest piece of art from what is generally called the Dark Ages,

Dublin Center

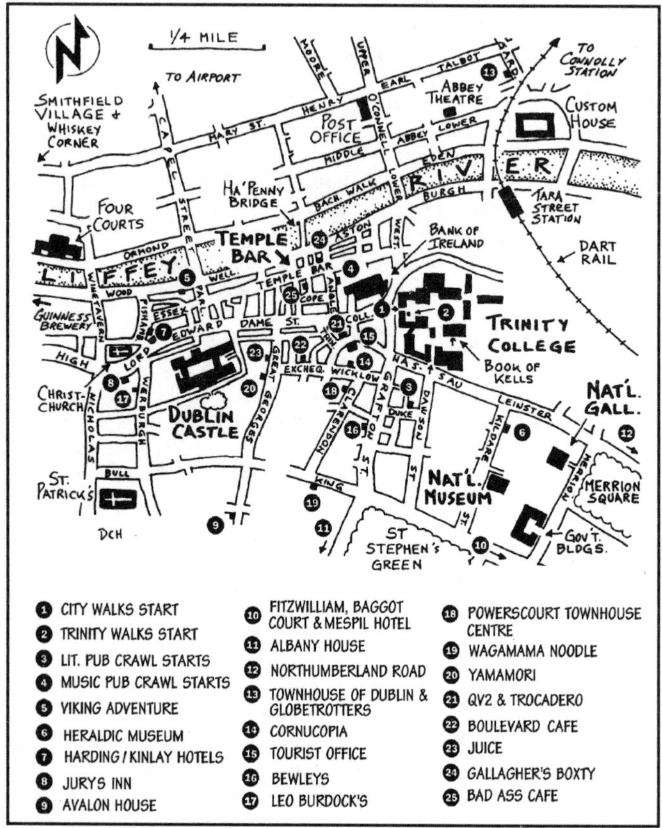

the *Book of Kells* shows that monastic life in this far fringe of Europe was far from dark. It has been bound into four separate volumes. At any given time, two of the gospels are on display. You'll see four richly decorated 1,200-year-old pages—two text and two decorated cover pages. The library treasury also displays the *Book of Armagh* (A.D. 807) and the *Book of Durrow* (A.D. 680), neither of which can be checked out.

Next, a stairway leads to the 65-yard-long main chamber of the Old Library (from 1732), stacked to its towering ceiling with 200,000 of the library's oldest books. Here you'll find one of a dozen surviving original copies of the 1916 Proclamation of the Irish Republic. Patrick Pearse read these words outside the

General Post Office on April 24 to start the Easter Rising that led to Irish Independence. Read the entire thing... imagining it was yours. Notice the inclusive opening phrase. (The seven signatories were each executed.) Another national icon is nearby—the oldest surviving Irish harp. From the 15th century, it's the one featured on Irish coins. Crowds thin out near the end of the day (£4.50, at Trinity College Library, Mon–Sat 9:30–17:00 year-round, Sun 9:30–16:30, Oct–May Sun 12:00–16:30, tel. 01/608-2308).

▲▲The Dublin Experience—This 40-minute video giving a historic introduction to Dublin is one more tourist movie with the sound turned up. It's good—offering a fine sweeping introduction to the story of Ireland—but pricey and riding on the coattails of the *Book of Kells* (£3, or discounted with a combo Kells/video ticket, daily June–Sept 10:00–17:00 on the hour, in modern arts building next to Trinity Old Library).

Sights—Dublin, South of the River Liffey

▲▲Dublin Castle—Built on the spot of the first Viking fortress, this castle was the seat of British rule in Ireland for 700 years (until 1922). Located where the Poddle and Liffey Rivers came together making a black pool ("dubh linn" in Irish), Dublin Castle was the official residence of the viceroy, who implemented the will of the British royalty. Today it's used for fancy state and charity functions. The 45-minute tours offer a room-by-room walk through the lavish state apartments of this most English of Irish palaces (£3, about 4 tours/hrly, Mon–Fri 10:00–17:00, Sat–Sun 14:00–17:00, 50p leaflet, tel. 01/677-7129). The tour finishes with a look at the foundations of the Norman tower and the best remaining chunk of the 13th-century town wall.

▲Dublin's Viking Adventure—This really is an adventure. You start in a box of seats that transforms into a Viking ship. Your chieftain—who hasn't washed since Norway—joins you, and suddenly you're in a storm, waves splash, smoke rolls, and you land in a kind of Viking summer camp, where you spend 30 minutes being shuttled from one friendly original Dubliner to the next (a trader, a sassy maiden, a monk building a church, and so on). After a guide takes you through a reconstructed excavation sight, you'll see a replica of a Viking ship and watch a film on shipbuilding, then tour a small museum. It feels hokey, but the cast is certainly hardworking, and you leave feeling as though you'd visited if not a Viking town, at least the set for a B-grade Viking movie. It's on Essex Street a block off the riverside Essex Quay in Temple Bar—where the Vikings established their first Dublin settlement in 841 (£4.95, Tue–Sat 10:00–16:30, last tour at 16:30, allow an hour total, closed Sun–Mon, tel. 01/679-6040).

Dublinia—This tries valiantly but fails to be a "bridge to Dublin's medieval past." The amateurish look at the medieval town starts with a goofy 12-minute audioguide tour through dim rooms of tableaus, followed by several rooms of medieval exhibits, a scale model of old Dublin (with a good, recorded explanation), and an interesting room devoted to medieval fairs. Then, after piles of stairs, you get a tower-top skyline view of Dublin's churches and breweries. Historians will find this museum worthwhile, others a waste of time (£4, £5 includes Christchurch Cathedral—saving you £1—daily 10:00–17:00, Oct–March 11:00–16:00, brass rubbing, coffee shop, tel. 01/679-4611).

Christchurch Cathedral—The oldest building in Dublin, the cathedral stands where the Vikings once did. The first church here was built of wood in 1038 by King Sitric. The present structure dates from a mix of periods: Norman and Gothic but mostly Victorian neo-Gothic (1870s restoration work). The unusually large crypt contains stocks, statues, and even a mummified cat and mouse (£2 admission to church, free brochure with self-guided tour, daily 10:00–17:00). Because of its British past, neither of Dublin's top two churches is Catholic. Christchurch Cathedral and the nearby St. Patrick's Cathedral are both from the Church of Ireland. In Catholic Ireland they feel hollow and are more famous than visit-worthy.

Evensong: At Christchurch, a 45-minute evensong service is sung at 18:00 on Wednesday and Thursday and 17:00 on Saturday. The 13th century St. Patrick's Cathedral, which had Jonathan Swift (author of *Gulliver's Travels*) as its dean in the 18th century, also offers evensong (Sun 15:15, Mon–Fri 17:30 but not on Wed in July–Aug).

▲▲▲National Museum—Showing off the treasures of Ireland from the Stone Age to modern times, this museum is wonderfully digestible under one dome. Ireland's Bronze Age gold fills the center. The prehistoric Ireland exhibit rings the gold, and in a corner you'll find the treasury with the most famous pieces (brooches, chalices, and other examples of Celtic metalwork) and an 18-minute video giving an overview of Irish art through the 13th century. The collection's superstar: the gold, enamel, and amber eighth-century Tara Brooch. Jumping way ahead, a special corridor features "The Road to Independence," with guns, letters, and death masks recalling the fitful birth of the "Terrible Beauty" (1900–1921, with a focus on the Easter Rising of 1916). The best Viking artifacts in town are upstairs (museum is free, Tue–Sat 10:00–17:00, Sun 14:00–17:00, closed Mon, between Trinity College and St. Stephen's Green on Kildare Street, tel. 01/677-7444). Greatest-hits tours are given several times a day (£1, 40 min, call in morning for schedule).

Heraldic Museum and Genealogical Office—This small gallery, near the National Museum, displays family coats of arms. It's popular for its resource center among those tracing their Irish roots. For a worthwhile visit, come with some family details (free, behind Trinity College at 2 Kildare Street, Mon–Fri 11:00–17:00, Sat 10:00–12:00, tel. 01/603-0311, www.heanet.ie/natlib/herald).

National Gallery—Along with a hall featuring the work of top Irish painters, this has Ireland's best collection of paintings by the European masters. It's impressive—unless you've been to London or Paris (free, Mon–Sat 10:00–17:30, Thu until 20:30, Sun 14:00–17:00, guided tours on Sat and Sun at 15:00, plus Sun at 14:15 and 16:00, Merrion Square West, tel. 01/661-5133, www.nationalgallery.ie).

▲▲Grafton Street—Once filled with noisy traffic, today Grafton Street is Dublin's liveliest pedestrian shopping mall. A five-minute people- and busker-filled stroll takes you from Trinity College up to St. Stephen's Green (and makes you wonder why American merchants are so terrified of a car-free street). Walking by a buxom statue of "sweet" Molly Malone (known by locals as "the tart with the cart"), you'll soon pass two venerable department stores: the Irish Brown Thomas and the English Marks & Spencer. An alley leads to the Powerscourt Townhouse Shopping Centre, tastefully filling a converted Georgian mansion. The huge, glass-covered St. Stephen's Green Shopping Centre and the peaceful and green green itself mark the top of Grafton Street.

▲St. Stephen's Green—This city park, originally a medieval commons, was enclosed in 1664 and gradually surrounded with fine Georgian buildings. Today it provides 22 acres of grassy refuge for Dubliners. On a sunny afternoon, it's a wonderful world apart from the big city.

Number Twenty-Nine—Tour the carefully restored house at Number 29 Lower Fitzwilliam Street for a walk through a Dublin home in 1790 (£2.50, Tue–Sat 10:00–17:00, Sun 14:00–17:00, closed Mon and last half of Dec, includes introductory video and eager-to-teach guides scattered throughout, tearoom, tel. 01/702-6165). Nearby Merrion Square is decorated with fine doors—a Dublin trademark—and elegant Georgian knobs and knockers.

▲Temple Bar—This was a Georgian center of craftsmen and merchants. When it grew poor in the 19th century, lower rents attracted students and artists, giving the neighborhood a bohemian flair. With recent government tax incentives and lots of development money, the Temple Bar district has become a thriving cultural (and beer-drinking) hot spot. Today, this much-promoted center of trendy shops, cafés, theaters, galleries, pubs with live music, and restaurants feels like the heart of Dublin. Dublin's "Left Bank" (actually on the right bank) fills the cobbled streets between Dame Street and the river. The central **Meeting House Square** (just off Essex Street) hosts free street theater, a lively organic produce market (Sat 9:30–15:00), and a book market (Sat 11:00–18:00). The square is surrounded by interesting cultural centers. For a listing of events and galleries, visit the **Temple Bar Information Centre** (Eustace Street, tel. 01/671-5717, www.temple-bar.ie). Rather than follow particular pub or restaurant recommendations (mine are below under "Eating"), venture down a few side lanes off the main drag to see what looks good. The pedestrian-only **Ha' Penny Bridge,** named for the half-pence toll people used to pay to cross it, leads over the Liffey to Temple Bar. ("Bar" means a walkway along the river.)

Sights—Dublin, North of the River Liffey

▲▲O'Connell Bridge—The bridge crosses the River Liffey, which has historically divided the town into the wealthy and cultivated south side and the poorer, cruder north side. While there's plenty of culture on the north, even today "the north" is considered rougher and less safe.

From the bridge look upriver (west). The high point, near Christchurch (marked by the eyesore of the city planning commission building), is where the Vikings established Dublin in the ninth century. Across the river (north), the green dome marks the Four Courts, today's Supreme Court building—tragically bombed and burned in 1922 during the civil war that followed Irish independence. Between you and the dome is the elegant iron Ha' Penny Bridge, leading into the Temple Bar district. Looking downstream you'll see the tall ugly union headquarters—for now the tallest building in the Republic—and lots of cranes. Booming Dublin is developing downstream. The Irish (forever clever tax fiddlers) have subsidized and revitalized this formerly dreary quarter with great success. A short walk downstream along the north bank leads to a powerful series of modern statues memorializing the great famine of 1845.

▲O'Connell Street—Dublin's grandest street leads from O'Connell Bridge through the heart of north Dublin. Since the 1740s it's been a 45-yard-wide promenade. Ever since the first O'Connell Bridge connected it to the Trinity side of town in 1794, it's been Dublin's main drag. The street, while lined with fast-food and souvenir shops, echoes with history. Much of the fighting during the 1916 Easter Rising and the civil war a few years later took place here. The imposing **General Post Office** is where Patrick Pearse read the Proclamation of Irish Independence. The GPO building itself—a kind of Irish Alamo—was the rebel headquarters and scene of a five-day bloody siege during the Rising. While there's little to see, its facade remains pockmarked with bullet holes (open for business and sightseers Mon–Sat 8:00–20:00, Sun 10:00–18:00). Up the street from the GPO on the median strip is a statue of Anna Livia, the mythological being who represents the spirit of the city. Dubliners have dubbed her "the floozie in the Jacuzzi."

Statues lining O'Connell Street celebrate great figures in

Ireland's fight for independence. Daniel O'Connell (1775–1847), known as "the Liberator," founded the Irish Labor Party and was a strong voice for Irish Catholic rights in the British parliament. James Larkin founded the Irish Workers' Union. One monument that didn't wave an Irish flag—a tall column crowned by a statue of the British hero of Trafalgar, Admiral Nelson—was blown up in 1966 as locals celebrated the 50th anniversary of the Rising.

More Sights North of the River—Make a point to get away from tourists' Dublin by strolling the smaller streets. Just a block west of O'Connell Street, the **Moore Street Market** is a colorful commotion of produce and hawkers (Mon–Sat). For workaday Dublin, the long pedestrian mall of Mary Street, Henry Street, and Talbot Street is a people-watchers' delight.

The prestigious **Abbey Theatre,** now a modern, ugly building, is still the much-loved home of the Irish National Theater (a block off the river on Abbey Street). **St. Mary's Pro-Cathedral** is the leading Catholic church in town but curiously is not a cathedral since Christchurch was made one in the 12th century (the Vatican has chosen to ignore the fact that it hasn't been Catholic for centuries). The **Georgian Parnell Square** has a Garden of Remembrance honoring the victims of the 1916 Rising.

The **Dublin Writers' Museum** fills a splendidly restored Georgian mansion. No country so small produced such a wealth of literature. As interesting to those interested in Irish literature as it is boring to those who aren't, this museum features the lives and works of Dublin's great writers (£3.10, includes slow-moving audioguide, Mon–Sat 10:00–17:00, Sun 11:00–17:00, June–Aug Mon–Fri until 18:00, 18 Parnell Square North, tel. 01/872-2077). With hometown wits such as Swift, Yeats, Joyce, and Shaw, literary fans will have a checklist of residences and memorials to see.

Sights—Dublin's Smithfield Village

Until recently a run-down industrial area, huge investments promise to make Smithfield Village the next Temple Bar. It's worth a look for "Cobblestores" (a redeveloped Duck Lane lined with fancy crafts and gift shops), the Ceol music museum, Old Jameson whiskey tour, and a chimney observatory with great Dublin views. The sights are clustered close together, two blocks north of the river behind the Four Courts—the Supreme Court building (www.smithfieldvillage.com).

▲▲Ceol Interactive Irish Music Encounter—Ceol (pron. kee-ol) means "music" in Gaelic. Throughout Ireland, musicians—lost in the traditional beat—are closing their eyes to commune with their heritage. A visit here before heading into the countryside will make your small-town pub-going more fun. Anyone interested in "trad" music will enjoy a stop at this clever introduction to Irish music. In this place filled with headphones, touch–computer screens, and music-filled TV screens, you'll go as deep as you like into the history, instruments, and regional differences of Irish music. The finale: a great 18-minute scenic and musical video tour of Ireland (£5, combo ticket with distillery available, Mon–Sat 9:30–18:00, Sun 11:00–19:00, Smithfield Village, tel. 01/817-3820, www.ceol.ie).

The Old Jameson Distillery—Whiskey fans enjoy visiting the old distillery. You get a 10-minute video, 20-minute tour, and a free shot in the pub. Unfortunately, the "distillery" feels fake and put together for tourism. The Old Bushmills tour in Northern Ireland, in a working factory, is a better experience. If you do take this tour, volunteer energetically when offered the chance to take the whiskey taste test at the end (£4, combo ticket with Ceol museum available, daily 10:00–18:00, last tour at 17:00, Sow Street, tel. 01/807-2355).

The Chimney—Built in 1895 for the distillery, the chimney is now an observatory with a restaurant. Ride the elevator 175 feet up for an unrivaled Dublin panorama (£5, daily 10:00–18:00, tel. 01/817-3820).

Sights—Outer Dublin

The Jail and the Guinness Brewery are the main sights outside of the old center. Combine these in one visit.

▲▲▲Kilmainham Gaol (Jail)—Opened in 1796 as the Dublin County Jail and a debtors' prison and considered a model in its day, it was used frequently as a political prison by the British. Many of those who fought for Irish independence were held or executed here, including leaders of the rebellions of 1798, 1803, 1848, 1867, and 1916. National heroes Robert Emmett and Charles Stewart Parnell each did time here. The last prisoner to be held here was Eamon de Valera (later president of Ireland). He was released on July 16, 1924, the day Kilmainham was finally shut down. The buildings, virtually in ruins, were restored in the 1960s. Today it's a shrine to the Nathan Hales of Ireland.

Start your visit with a guided tour (60 min, including 25 min in the prison chapel for a rebellion-packed video). It's touching to tour the cells and places of execution while hearing tales of terrible colonialism and heroic patriotism—alongside Irish schoolkids who know these names well. Then browse through the excellent exhibit on Victorian prison life and Ireland's fight for independence. Don't miss the dimly lit hall off the second floor displaying the stirring l ast letters patriots sent to loved ones hours before facing the firing squad (£3.50, daily 9:30–16:45, 2 tours/hrly, last admission 1 hr before closing; Oct–March Sun–Fri 9:30–16:45, closed Sat; £5 taxi, bus #51b, #78a, or #79 from Aston Quay, tel. 01/453-5984).

▲Guinness Brewery—A visit to the Guinness Hop Store is, for many, a pilgrimage. The home of Ireland's national beer welcomes

Charles Stewart Parnell (1846–1891)

Parnell, who led the Irish movement for home rule, did time in Kilmainham Jail. A Cambridge-educated Protestant and member of Parliament, he had a vision of a modern and free Irish Republic filled mostly with Catholics but not set up as a religious state. Momentum seemed to be on his side. With the British Prime Minister of the time, Gladstone, in favor of a similar form of home rule, it looked like all Ireland was ripe for independence. Then a sex scandal broke around Parnell and his mistress. The press, egged on by the powerful Catholic bishops (who didn't want a free but secular Irish state), battered and battered away at the scandal until finally Parnell was driven from office. Sadly, after that, Ireland became mired in the troubles of the 20th century: an awkward independence (1921) featuring a divided island, a bloody civil war, and sectarian violence ever since. It's said Parnell died of a broken heart. Before he did, perhaps the greatest Irish statesman requested to be buried outside of Ireland.

visitors (for £5) with a museum, video, and drink. Arthur Guinness began brewing the famous stout here in 1759. By 1868 it was the biggest brewery in the world. Today the sprawling brewery fills several city blocks. Around the world Guinness brews more than 10 million glasses a day. You can learn as much or as little about the brewing process as you like. Highlights are the cooperage (with old film clips showing the master wood-keg makers plying their now-extinct trade) and a display of the brewery's clever ads. The video is a well-done ad for the brew that makes you feel almost patriotic as you run down to the sample bar to turn in your coupons for a pint of the real thing (£5, April–Sept Mon–Sat 9:30–17:00, Sun 10:30–16:30, Oct–March Mon–Fri 9:30–16:30, Sun 12:00–16:00, enter on Crane Street off Thomas Street, bus #78A from Aston Quay near O'Connell Bridge, or bus #123 from Dame Street and O'Connell Street, tel. 01/408-4800). Hop-on hop-off bus tours stop here. (Why is there no museum of Irish alcoholism, which is a serious but rarely discussed problem in this land where the social world seems to float in a sea of beer?)

▲**Gaelic Athletic Association Museum**—The GAA was founded in 1884 as an expression of an Irish cultural awakening. While created to foster the development of Gaelic sports—specifically Irish football and hurling (and ban English sports such as cricket and rugby)—it played an important part in the fight for independence. This new museum, at the newly expanded 97,000-seat Croke Park Stadium, offers a high-tech, interactive introduction to Ireland's favorite games. Relive the greatest moments in hurling and Irish football history. Then get involved. Pick up a stick and try hurling, kick a football, and test your speed and balance. A 15-minute film clarifies the connection between sports and Irish politics (£3, May–Sept daily 9:30–17:00; Oct–April Tue–Sat 10:00–17:00, Sun 12:00–17:00, closed Mon; game Sundays open 12:00–17:00 to new-stand ticket holders only; under the new stand at Croke Park, from O'Connell Street catch bus 3, 11, 11a, 16, 16a, or 23; tel. 01/855-8176).

Hurling or Irish Football at Croke Park—Actually seeing a match here, surrounded by incredibly spirited Irish fans, is a fun experience. Hurling is like airborne hockey with no injury timeouts, and Irish football is a rugged form of soccer (matches most Sunday afternoons outside of winter, tickets—£10–20—are available at the stadium except during championships).

Greyhound Racing—For an interesting lowbrow look at local life, consider going to the dog races and doing a little gambling (£5, races generally Mon, Wed, Thu, and Sat at 20:00, Shelbourne Park, tel. 01/668-3502).

Day Trips from Dublin—See "Near Dublin," at the end of the chapter, for information on Newgrange, the Wicklow Mountains, and more.

Shopping

Shops are open roughly Monday to Saturday from 9:00 to 18:00, until 20:00 on Thursday, with shorter hours on Sunday (if open at all). The best shopping area is Grafton, with its neighboring streets and arcades (such as the fun Great George's Arcade between Great George's and Drury Streets), and nearby shopping centers (Powerscourt and St. Stephen's Green). For antiques, try Francis Street. For a street market, consider Mother Redcaps (all day Fri, Sat, Sun, bric-a-brac, antiques, crafts, Back Lane, Christchurch). For produce, noise, and color, visit Moore Street (Mon–Sat, near General Post Office). For raw fish, get a whiff of Michan Street (Tue–Sat 7:00–15:00, behind Four Courts building). At Temple Bar's Meeting House Square on Saturday, it's food in the morning (from 9:00) and books in the afternoon (until 18:00). Temple Bar is worth a browse any day for its art, jewelry, new-age paraphernalia, books, music, and gift shops.

Entertainment and Theater in Dublin

Ireland produced some of the finest writers in both English and Gaelic, and Dublin houses some of Europe's finest theaters. While Handel's *Messiah* was first performed in Dublin (1742), these days Dublin is famous for its rock bands (U2, Thin Lizzie, and Sinead O'Connor all got started here).

You have much from which to choose. **Abbey Theatre** is

Ireland's national theater, founded by W. B. Yeats in 1904 to preserve Irish culture during British rule (Lower Street, tel. 01/878-7222). **Gate Theatre** does foreign plays as well as Irish classics (Cavendish Row, tel. 01/874-4045). **Point Theatre,** once a railway terminus, is now the country's top live music venue (North Wall quay, tel. 01/836-3633). At the **National Concert Hall,** the National Symphony Orchestra performs most Friday evenings (Earlsfort Terrace, off St. Stephen's Green, tel. 01/475-1666, www.nch.ie). Street theater takes the stage in Temple Bar on summer evenings. Folk music rings in the pubs, and street entertainers are everywhere. For the latest on live theater, music, cultural happenings, restaurant reviews, pubs, and current museum hours, pick up a copy of the twice-monthly *In Dublin* (£2, any newsstand).

Irish Music in nearby Dun Laoghaire

For an evening of pure Irish music, song, and dance, check out the **Comhaltas Ceoltoiri Eireann,** an association working to preserve this traditional slice of Irish culture. It got started when Elvis and company threatened to steal the musical heart of the new generation. Judging by the pop status of traditional Irish music these days, Comhaltas accomplished its mission. Their "Fonntrai" evening is a costumed stage show mixing traditional music, song, and dance (£6, mid-June–Aug Mon–Thu at 21:00, followed by informal music session at 22:30). Fridays all year long they have a ceilidh (kay-lee) where everyone dances (£5, 21:30–00:30). Saturday nights feature an informal session by the fireside. Performances are held in the Cuturlann na Eireann, near the Seapoint DART stop or a 20-minute walk from Dun Laoghaire, at 32 Belgrave Square, Monkstown (tel. 01/280-0295). Their bar is free and often filled with music.

Sleeping in Dublin

(£1 = about $1.40, country code: 353, area code: 01)

Sleep Code: **S** = Single, **D** = Double/Twin, **T** = Triple, **Q** = Quad, **b** = bathroom, **t** = toilet only, **s** = shower only, **CC** = Credit Card (**V**isa, **M**asterCard, **A**mex). Breakfast is included unless otherwise noted.

Dublin is popular and rooms can be tight. Book ahead for weekends anytime of year, particularly in summer. On rugby weekends (Feb 16–17 and March 23–24 in 2001, plus several others not yet scheduled), many hotels increase their prices by £20 or more.

Big and practical places (both cheap and moderate) are most central at Christchurch on the edge of Temple Bar. For classy, older Dublin accommodations you'll pay more and stay a bit farther out (east of St. Stephen's Green). For a small-town escape with the best budget values, side-trip by the convenient DART train (at least 3/hrly, 15 min) from nearby Dun Laoghaire (see below).

Sleeping in the Center

Sleeping at Christchurch: These places face Christchurch Cathedral, a great locale a five-minute walk from the best evening scene at Temple Bar and 10 minutes from the sightseeing center (Trinity College and Grafton Street). Full Irish breakfasts, which cost £6 at the hotels, are nearly half the price at the many small cafés. You could try the recommended eateries in the center (such as Bewley's) for breakfast, but, if you prefer to stay close to home, consider Applewood (1b Werburgh Street, next to Burdoch's Fish & Chips) or Tasty Bites or Munchies (both on Dame Street, across from Kinlay House).

Harding Hotel is a hardwood, 21st-century, Viking-style place with 53 quiet, hotelesque rooms. The rooms are simpler than Jurys' (below), but it's more intimate, without the tour-group mob scenes (Sb-£45, Db/Tb-£69, full breakfast-£6, CC:VM, Internet access-£5/hr, talking elevator for blind guests, Copper Alley across the street from Christchurch, tel. 01/679-6500, fax 01/679-6504, www.iol.ie/usitaccm/, e-mail: hotel.harding@usitworld.com).

Jurys Christchurch Inn (like its sisters across town, in Galway, and in Belfast) is central and offers business-class comfort in all of its identical rooms. This no-nonsense, modern, American-style hotel chain has a winning keep-it-simple-and-affordable formula. If old is getting old (and you don't mind big bus-tour groups), you won't find a better value in town. All 182 rooms cost the same: £69 for one, two, or three adults or two adults and two kids (breakfast-£6). Each room has a modern bathroom, direct-dial telephone, and TV. Two floors are strictly non-smoking. Request a room far from the noisy elevator (book 5–6 months in advance for weekends, CC:VMA, Christchurch Place, Dublin 8, tel. 01/454-0000, fax 01/454-0012, U.S. tel. 800/843-3311, www.jurys.com, e-mail: info@jurys.com). Another Jurys is near the Connelly train station (see below).

Kinlay House, across the square from Jurys Christchurch Inn, is its backpackers' equivalent—definitely the place to go for cheap beds in a central location and an all-ages-welcome atmosphere. This huge, red-brick, 19th-century Victorian building has 149 metal, prison-style beds in spartan, smoke-free rooms: singles, doubles, four- to six-bed coed dorms (good for families), and a few giant dorms. It fills up most days. Call well in advance, especially for singles, doubles, and summer weekends (S-£25, D-£39, Db-£43, dorm beds-£11–17.50, cheaper off-season, includes continental breakfast, kitchen for guests to use, laundrette-£5, Internet access-£5/hr, left luggage, travel desk, TV lounge, small lockers, and lots of stairs, Christchurch, 2–12 Lord Edward Street, Dublin 2, tel. 01/679-6644, fax 01/679-7437, e-mail: kinlay.dublin@usitworld.com).

Sleeping near Grafton Street: Avalon House is 280 beds of backpacker heaven. Well located, cheap, safe, and institutional, it's much like Kinlay House (above). Book well in advance (S-£20, Sb-£25, D-£36, Db-£40, dorm beds-£9.50–15, includes continental breakfast, CC:VMA, elevator, Ireland bus tickets, Internet access, laundrette across street, a few minutes off Grafton Street at 55 Aungier Street, tel. 01/475-0001, fax 01/475-0303, can book online at www.avalon-house.ie).

Sleeping in Temple Bar: This is a noisy but central neighborhood. **Bewley's Principal Hotel** has 70 simple but comfy rooms with double-glazed windows and two nonsmoking floors. For its size, it has an intimate feel, with character (Sb-£86, Db-£108, full breakfast-£6.50—eat in Bewley's cafe downstairs or get voucher for their café on Grafton where breakfast is served all day, CC:VMA, ask about deals for 2-night stays with breakfast, 19–20 Fleet Street, tel. 01/670-8122, fax 01/670-8103, www.bewleysprincipalhotel.com). Adams Trinity, another three-star, isn't as nice (Db–£120, £99 for 2-night stay, 28 Dame Street, tel. 01/670-7100).

Sleeping near St. Stephen's Green

Four small luxurious guest houses are near St. Stephen's Green. All include a fine cooked breakfast, are run with class, and offer the best value for Georgian elegance with modern comforts near the center. The first two are on fashionable Baggot Street, a five minutes' walk east of St. Stephen's Green.

The Fitzwilliam rents 13 delightful rooms (Sb-£50, Db-£84, CC:VMA, 10 percent discount with cash, children under 16 sleep free, 41 Upper Fitzwilliam Street, Dublin 2, tel. 01/662-5155, fax 01/676-7488). **Baggot Court Accommodations** rents 11 similarly elegant rooms a block farther away (prices vary with size of room and season, Sb-£55–65, Db-£80–100, two Db with kitchenette-£100–120, Tb-£120–150, CC:VMA, nonsmoking, free car park, 92 Lower Baggot St, Dublin 2, tel. 01/661-2819, fax 01/661-0253, e-mail: baggot@indigo.ie).

The next two are just off St. Stephen's Green. **Harcourt Inn** has a classy lobby and 15 comfortable, well-appointed rooms with cheery bedspreads (Sb-£55–65, Db-£80–100, Tb-£120–150, CC:VMA, 27 Harcourt Street, tel. 01/478-3927, fax 01/478-2550, e-mail: harcourt@indigo.ie, run by owners of Baggot Court, above).

Albany House's 33 rooms come with Georgian elegance, modern comfort, and street noise. Request the huge "superior" rooms, which are the same price (Sb-£70, Db-£110, £80 in slow times, includes breakfast, CC:VMA, back rooms are quieter, smoke free, just 1 block south of St. Stephen's Green at 84 Harcourt Street, Dublin 2, tel. 01/475-1092, fax 01/475-1093, e-mail: albany@indigo.ie).

Sleeping Away from the Center, East of St. Stephen's Green

Mespil Hotel is a huge, modern, business-class hotel renting 260 identical three-star rooms (each with a double and single bed, phone, TV, voicemail, and modem hookup) at a good price with all the comforts. Some of the rooms overlook a canal greenbelt (Sb, Db, or Tb-£85, continental breakfast-£6, Irish breakfast-£9, CC:VMA, elevator, 1 nonsmoking floor, apartments for weeklong stays, 10-minute walk southeast of St. Stephen's Green or bus #10, Mespil Road, Dublin 4, tel. 01/667-1222, fax 01/667-1244, www.leehotels.ie, e-mail: mespil@leehotels.ie).

The next two listings are on Northumberland Road, southeast of the city center. Trinity College is a 15-minute walk away, or catch bus #5, #6, #7, #8, or #45 (to O'Connell Street) which lumber down Northumberland Road to downtown Dublin every 10 minutes.

Northumberland Lodge has eight elegant rooms in a quiet mansion (Sb-£45–55, Db-£70–90, highest on weekends and in summer, CC:VM, 68 Northumberland Road, Ballsbridge, Dublin 4, tel. 01/660-5270, fax 01/668-8679). **Glenveagh Town House** has 13 classy rooms with character—Victorian upstairs, modern downstairs (Sb-£50–55, Db-£75–80, less in slow times, includes breakfast, CC:VM, car park, 31 Northumberland Road, tel. 01/668-4612, fax 01/668-4559, e-mail: glenveagh@eircom.net).

Sleeping near Connolly Train Station

Jurys Custom House Inn, on Custom House Quay, offers the same value as the Jurys at Christchurch. Bigger (with 234 rooms) and not quite as well located (in a boring neighborhood, a 10-minute riverside hike from O'Connell Bridge), this Jurys is more likely to have rooms available (Db-£69, tel. 01/607-5000, fax 01/829-0400, U.S. tel. 800/843-3311, e-mail: info@jurys.com).

The following two places—one nice, one cheap—are adjacent, run by the same owners, have (minimal) Internet access, include a full breakfast (in the same breakfast room), offer discounts for three-night stays, and are located in a handy but grotty area midway between the train station and O'Connell Bridge. A good pub with live music in this neighborhood is the Celtic Pub (82 Talbot Road, off Lower Gardiner Street, near Abbey Theatre, tel. 01/878-8655).

The **Townhouse of Dublin** is a smartly run hotel with 80 smallish but comfortable rooms filling the richly decorated, carpeted, and furnished home of a 19th-century playwright (Sb-£38–47, D-£50–60, Db-£60–80, T-£65–70, depending on season and day of week, weekends are most expensive, CC:VMA, attractive mezzanine overlooks breakfast room, nonsmoking floor,

47 Lower Gardiner Street, Dublin 1, tel. 01/878-8808, fax 01/878-8787, e-mail: grotter@indigo.ie).

Globetrotters is a fine slumber mill with 94 beds in 6- to 12-bed coed dorms (£12–15 per bed, all with private bathrooms and lockers; same phone, fax, and e-mail as Townhouse).

Sleeping and Eating in nearby Dun Laoghaire (tel. code: 01, mail: County Dublin)

Dun Laoghaire (pron: dun leary) is seven miles south of Dublin. This beach resort, with the ferry terminal for Wales and easy connections to downtown Dublin by DART commuter train, is a great small-town base for the big city (from Dublin, catch a DART train marked "Bray" and get off at Sandy Cove or Dun Laoghaire, depending on the B&B you choose; from Dun Laoghaire, catch a train marked "Howth" to go to Dublin—get off at the central Tara Street station).

Dun Laoghaire harbor was strategic enough to merit a line of Martello Towers (built to defend against an expected Napoleonic invasion). By the mid-19th century, the huge breakwaters—reaching like two muscular arms into the Irish Sea—were completed, protecting a huge harbor. Ships sailed regularly to Wales (60 miles away), and the first train line in Ireland connected the terminal with Dublin. While still a busy transportation hub, today the nearly mile-long breakwaters are also popular with strollers, bikers, birders, and fishermen. Hike out to the lighthouse at the end of the more interesting East Pier.

While buses go into Dublin, the DART is much faster (6/hrly in peak times, at least 3/hrly otherwise, 15 min, runs Mon–Sat about 6:30–23:15, Sun from 9:00, £1.15 one-way, £2.20 round-trip, Eurail valid but uses day of flexipass; for a longer stay consider the £10 4-day Explorer ticket covering DART and Dublin buses). The **Dun Laoghaire TI** is in the ferry terminal (Mon–Sat 10:00–18:00 year-round, closed Sun). The Society of the Preservation of Irish Folk Music has a lively branch in Dun Laoghaire (see above). Taxi fare from Dun Laoghaire to central Dublin is about £10, to the airport about £30. With easy free parking and DART access into Dublin, this area is ideal for those with cars. A washerette is in the Sandycove "Village" (self- and full-serve, 2 Glasthule).

The first five listings are within several blocks of the Sandycove DART station and a seven-minute walk to the Dun Laoghaire DART station/ferry landing. The rest are closer to the Dun Laoghaire DART station. Except for the Mrs. Kane's B&B and Rathoe B&B, most are a bit tattered around the edges.

Mrs. Kane's Seaview B&B is a modern house with three big, cheery rooms and a welcoming guests' lounge. While a few blocks farther out than the others, it's worth the walk for its great,

Dun Laoghaire

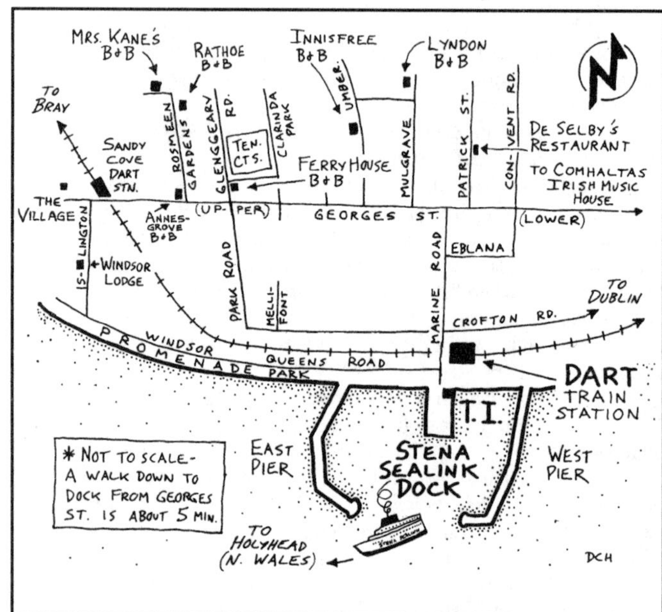

bright, and friendly feeling (Db-£46, strictly smoke free, just above Rosmeen Gardens at 2 Granite Hall, tel. & fax 01/280-9105, e-mail: seaviewbedandbreakfast@hotmail.com).

Windsor Lodge rents four fresh and cheery rooms on a quiet street a block off the harbor and a block from the DART station (Db-£44–50, family deals, CC:VM, nonsmoking, 3 Islington Avenue, Sandycove, Dun Laoghaire, tel. & fax 01/284-6952, e-mail: winlodge@eircom.net, Mary O'Farrell).

Rathoe B&B is lovingly run by Mrs. Valerie Fitzgibbon, who makes the fresh bread she serves at breakfast and refuses to mar her impeccable rooms by adding private bathrooms (S-£25–30, D-£40, conservatory, 12 Rosmeen Gardens, tel. 01/280-8070).

Annesgrove has four tidy rooms decorated in beige and brown (D-£44, Db-£50, includes breakfast, parking, close to park and beach, 28 Rosmeen Gardens, tel. 01/280-9801).

Ferry House B&B, a once-upon-a-time-stately old place near a quiet square with a tennis court, rents nine rooms. Pauline, Eamond, and family give the place a homey feel (Db-£46 with this book, CC:VM, house is kept warm, 15 Clarinda Park North, tel. 01/280-8301, fax 01/284-6530).

The following are closer to the Dun Laoghaire Dart station.

Lynden B&B, with a classy 150-year-old interior hiding behind a somber front, rents four big rooms. The owners Stephen and Maria Gavin get rave reviews from readers (one S-£17, D-£34, Db-£40, past Mulgrave Street to 2 Mulgrave Terrace, tel. 01/280-6404). Next door, the similar **Belmont B&B** rents three decent rooms (D-£34, Db-£39, tel. 01/280-1422, e-mail: cdifelice@esatclear.ie).

Innisfree B&B has a fine lounge and six big, bright, and comfy rooms (D-£33, Db-£37, CC:VM, from George Street follow the mysterious "Yellow Fever Vaccination Centre" sign up the plain but quiet Northumberland Avenue to #31, tel. 01/280-5598, fax 01/280-3093, e-mail: djsmith@club1.ie, Brendan and Mary Smith). **Mrs. Howard's B&B,** on the same street, rents several big rooms that look like they came out of grandma's house (S-£21, D-£35, TV lounge, 36 Northumberland Avenue, tel. 01/280-3262).

Eating in Dun Laoghaire: Local diners enjoy the local "Gourmet Mile"—several fine little restaurants within a few minutes' walk of these B&Bs.

Down the street from the Sandycove DART station is Glasthule (called simply "The Village" locally). **Bistro Vino** is the rage lately, with cozy candlelit Mediterranean ambiance and great food (£8–14 meals, seafood, pasta, arrive early or have a reservation, nightly early-bird special 17:00–19:00, tel. 01/280-6097). Across the street and a half block away, the big red-and-yellow **Eagle House** pub serves hearty inexpensive pub grub in a smoky atmosphere. The nearby **Daniel's Restaurant and Wine Bar** is also good (£15 meals, closed Mon, 34 Glasthule Road, tel. 01/284-1027).

The **Brasserie Na Mara** serves good contemporary Irish cuisine in a fancy, former train station setting (located in Dun Laoghaire DART station, tel. 01/280-6767). A good bet for families is the kid-friendly **De Selby's Restaurant**, serving traditional Irish food, stew, and seafood (£10 meals, nightly 17:00–22:00, Sun from 12:00, a block off George's Street at 17 Patrick Street, tel. 01/284-1761). **George's Street,** Dun Laoghaire's main drag and three blocks inland, has plenty of eateries and pubs, many with live music.

Eating in Dublin

As Dublin does its boom-time jig, fine and creative eateries are popping up all over town. While you can get decent pub grub for £6 on just about any corner, consider holding off on pub grub for the more spit-and-potatoes countryside. And there's no pressing reason to eat Irish in cosmopolitan Dublin. Dublin's good restaurants are packed from 20:00 on, especially on weekends. Eating early (18:00–19:00) saves time and usually money (as many better places offer an early-bird special).

Eating Quick and Easy around Grafton Street

Cornucopia is a small, earth-momma, vegetarian, self-serve place a block off Grafton. It's friendly, smoke free, and youthful, with great breakfasts, hearty £5 lunches, and £7 dinner specials (Mon–Fri 9:00–20:00, Thu until 21:00, Sat 9:00–18:00, closed Sun, 19 Wicklow Street, tel. 01/677-7583).

Graham O'Sullivan Restaurant and Coffee Shop is a cheap and cheery cafeteria serving soup, sandwiches, and a salad bar in unpretentious ambience (Mon–Fri 8:00–18:30, Sat 9:00–17:00, closed Sun, 12 Duke Street). Two pubs on the same street—**The Duke** and **Davy Burns**—serve pub lunches. The **Cathach Rare Books** shop (10 Duke Street) displays a rare first edition of *Ulysses* among other treasures in its window.

Bewleys Restaurant is an old-time local favorite serving traditional Irish and contemporary food in a big, fresh, and bright space decorated by local art students. Light meals start at £3.50, full meals from £6.50. Choose from three settings, all open daily: the classy ground floor (self-service 7:30–19:00, table service 19:00–23:00), atrium (simple cafeteria upstairs, 7:30–19:00), and mezzanine (table service only, 10:00–19:00, CC:VMA, 78 Grafton Street, tel. 01/635-5470). Bewley's also has branches in Temple Bar (on Fleet Street and Westmoreland, just south of O'Connell bridge) and on Mary's Street (shopping street north of River Liffey).

Blazing Salads, a crowd-pleasing vegetarian place, is just off Grafton Street, upstairs in the trendy Powerscourt Townhouse Centre (£5 meals, Mon–Sat 9:00–17:00, closed Sun, tel. 01/671-9669). Its new take-out deli is a block away (same hours, 42 Drury Street, tel. 01/671-9552).

Wagamama Noodle Bar, like its popular sisters in London, is a pan-Asian slurp-athon with great, healthy, £5 noodle and rice dishes served by walkie-talkie-toting waiters on long communal tables (daily 12:00–23:00, nonsmoking, CC:VMA, South King Street, underneath St. Stephen's Green Shopping Centre, tel. 01/478-2152).

Yamamori is a plain, bright, and mod Japanese place serving seas of sushi and noodles (£5 lunch deal served daily 12:30–17:30, £6–10 dinner 17:30–23:00, CC:VM, 71 South Great Georges Street, tel. 01/475-5001).

Marks & Spencer department store (on Grafton Street) has a fancy grocery store in the basement with fine take-away sandwiches and salads (Mon–Fri 9:00–19:00, Thu until 21:00, Sat 9:00–18:00, Sun 12:00–18:00). Locals prefer **Dunne's** department store for its lower prices (same hours, grocery in basement, in St. Stephen's Green Shopping Centre).

Eating Fast and Cheap near Christchurch

Many of Dublin's **late-night grocery stores** (along Dame Street at top of Temple Bar near Christchurch hotels and elsewhere) sell fine cheap salads, microwaved meat pies, and made-to-order sandwiches. A £3 picnic dinner back at the hotel might be a good option after a busy day of sightseeing.

Leo Burdocks Fish & Chips is popular with locals (takeout only, Mon–Sat 12:00–24:00, Sun 16:00–24:00, 2 Werburgh Street, off Christchurch square).

Dining at Classy Restaurants and Cafés

These three restaurants are located within a block of each other, just south of Temple Bar and Dame Street, near the main TI.

QV2 Restaurant serves "international with an Irish twist"—great cooking at reasonable prices with an elegant yet comfy atmosphere (£25 meals, Mon–Sat 12:00–15:00, 18:00–24:00, closed Sun, nonsmoking section, CC:VMA, 14 St. Andrew Street, tel. 01/677-3363, run by John Count McCormack). They offer a quick £7.95 lunch special and an 18:00–19:30 early-bird special for £16.

Trocadero, across the street, serves beefy European cuisine to locals interested in a slow romantic meal. The dressy red-velvet interior is draped with photos of local actors. Come early or make a reservation (£20 meals, Mon–Sat 18:00–24:00, closed Sun, nonsmoking section, CC:VMA, 3 St. Andrew Street, tel. 01/677-5545). The three-course early-bird special at £12.50 is a fine value (18:00–19:15, leave by 20:30).

Boulevard Cafe is a mod, local, and likeably trendy place serving Mediterranean cuisine heavy on the Italian. They serve salads, pasta, and sandwiches for around £5, three-course business lunch specials for £8 (Mon–Sat 12:00–15:00), and dinner plates for £7 to £10 (nightly 18:00–24:00, CC:VMA, 27 Exchequer Street, tel. 01/679-2131).

Eating at Temple Bar

Gallagher's Boxty House is touristy and traditional, with good, basic value in a fun old Dublin ambience (£8 meals, stews, corned beef, and boxties—the traditional Irish potato pancake filled and rolled with various meats, veggies, and sauces; daily 12:00–23:30, nonsmoking section, CC:VMA, 20 Temple Bar, tel. 01/677-2762). Gallagher's, which is extremely popular, takes same-day reservations only. To reserve for dinner, stop by between 12:00 and 15:00.

Bad Ass Café is a grunge diner serving cowboy/Mex/veggie/pizzas to old and new hippies. No need to dress up (£5 lunch and £11 dinner deals, kids' specials, daily 11:30–24:00, CC:VMA, Crown Alley, just off Meeting House Square, tel. 01/671-2596).

Luigi Malone's, popular in London, has settled in Dublin with its winning menu of pizza, ribs, pasta, sandwiches, and fajitas (£6–13, corner of Cecila and Fownes streets).

The Shack is a bit pricey but has a reputation for quality, serving traditional Irish, chicken, seafood, and steak dishes

(£10–15 entrees, CC:VMA, No. 3 Cork Hill, Dame Street, tel. 01/670-9785).

The Brazen Head, famous as Dublin's oldest pub, is a hit for dinner early and live music late. A sprawling complex of smoky atmospheric rooms with a courtyard made to order for balmy evenings, it overlooks the River Liffey (on Bridge Street, a 10-minute walk upstream from Temple Bar, tel. 01/677-9549).

Transportation Connections—Dublin

By bus to: Belfast (7/day, 3 hrs), **Ennis** (7/day, 4.5 hrs), **Galway** (10/day, 3.5 hrs, some depart from Dublin airport), **Limerick** (10/day, 3 hrs), **Tralee** (5/day, 6 hrs), **Dingle** (4/day, 8 hrs, £17, transfer at Tralee). Bus info: tel. 01/836-6111.

By train from Heuston Station to: Tralee (6/day, 4 hrs, talking timetable tel. 805-4266), **Ennis** (2/day, 4 hrs), **Galway** (5/day, 3 hrs, talking timetable tel. 01/805-4222).

By train from Connolly Station to: Rosslare (3/day, 3 hrs), **Portrush** (6/day, 5 hrs, £22.50 one-way, £31 round-trip, transfer in Belfast or Portadown), **Belfast** (8/day, 2 hrs, talking timetable tel. 01/855-4277). The **Dublin–Belfast train** connects the two Irish capitals in two hours at 90 mph on one continuous welded rail (£19 one-way, £29 round-trip; round-trip the same day only £19 except Fri and Sun; from the border to Belfast one-way £10, £13 round-trip). Train info: tel. 01/836-6222.

The **Dublin Airport** is well connected to the city center, seven miles away (airport info: tel. 01/814-1111; also see "Arrival in Dublin," above). Ryanair is an Irish cut-rate airline with cheap fares to London (£40 round-trip) and other European destinations (Irish tel. 01/609-7800, www.ryanair.com). British Air offers pricier flights to London's Gatwick Airport (5/day, from £109 round-trip, Irish tel. 01/814-5201 or toll-free tel. 1-800-626-747 in Ireland, U.S. tel. 800/247-9297, www.britishairways.com), as do Aer Lingus (Irish tel. 01/886-8888, www.aerlingus.ie) and British Midland (Irish tel. 01/283-8833, U.S. tel. 800/788-0555, www.britishmidland.co.uk).

Transportation Connections—Ireland and Britain

Dublin and London: The journey by boat plus train or bus takes 10 to 11 hours, all day or all night (bus: 4/day, £24–35, British tel. 08705-143-219, www.eurolines.co.uk; train: 4/day, £40–75, Dublin train info: tel. 01/836-6222). If going directly to London, flying is your best bet.

Dublin and Holyhead: Irish Ferries sails between Dublin and Holyhead in North Wales (dock a mile from O'Connell Bridge, 5/day—2 slow, 3 fast; slow boats-3.25 hrs, £20 one-way walk-on fare; fast boats-1.75 hrs, £25; Dublin tel. 01/661-0511, Holyhead tel. 08705-329-129, www.irishferries.ie).

Dublin and Liverpool: Merchant Ferries sails most mornings (Tue–Sat) and every evening year-round (8 hrs, £25–35 one way by day, £20–30 one-way overnight, cabins extra, car transport possible, Dublin tel. 01/819-2999, British tel. 0870-800-4321, www.merchant-ferries.com).

Dun Laoghaire and Holyhead: Stena Line sails between Dun Laoghaire (near Dublin) and Holyhead in North Wales (4/day, 2 hrs on HSS *Catamaran*, £36 one-way walk-on fare, reserve by phone—they book up long in advance on summer weekends, Dun Laoghaire tel. 01/204-7777, recorded info tel. 01/204-7799, can book online at www.stenaline.ie).

Ferry Connections—Ireland and France

Irish Ferries connect Ireland (Rosslare) with France (Cherbourg and Roscoff) every other day (less Jan–Mar). While Cherbourg has the quickest connection to Paris, your overall time between Ireland and Paris is about the same (18 hrs) regardless of which port is used on the day you sail. One-way fares vary from £40 to £80. Eurailers go half price. In both directions departures are generally between 16:00 and 18:00 and arrive late the next morning. While passengers can nearly always get on, reservations are wise in summer and easy by phone. If you anticipate a crowded departure you can reserve a seat for £6. Doubles (or singles) start at £34. The easiest way to get a bed (except during summer) is from the information desk upon boarding. The cafeteria serves bad food at reasonable prices. Upon arrival in France, buses and taxis connect you to your Paris-bound train (Irish Ferries: Dublin tel. 01/313-131 or 01/661-0511, recorded info tel. 01/661-0715, Paris tel. 01 44 94 20 40, www.irishferries.com, e-mail: info@irishferries.com, European Ferry Guide: www.youra.com/ferry/intlferries.html).

NEAR DUBLIN: NEWGRANGE, WICKLOW MOUNTAINS, KILKENNY, AND CASHEL

Newgrange, an hour's drive north of Dublin, is one of the world's most important, and one of Ireland's most talked-about, new tourist attractions.

The Wicklow Mountains, while only 10 miles south of Dublin, feel remote—remote enough to have provided a handy refuge for opponents to English rule. Rebels who took part in the 1798 Irish uprising hid out here for years. When the frustrated British built a military road in 1800 to help flush out the rebels, the area became more accessible. Now known as the R115, this same road takes you through the Wicklow area to Glendalough at its south end. While the darling of the Dublin day-trip tour organizers, the valley itself doesn't live up to its hype. But two blockbuster sights make a visit worth considering.

Dublin Area

If you're driving west to the west coast (Dingle), the best two stops to break the long journey are Kilkenny, often called Ireland's finest medieval town, and the Rock of Cashel, a thought-provoking early Christian site crowning the Tipperary Plain.

NEWGRANGE

The famous archaeological site commonly referred to as Newgrange (one of the tombs) is more properly known as Bru na Boinne—"dwelling place of the Boyne." The well-organized site is centered around a state-of-the-art museum. Visitors are given appointments for shuttle buses that ferry small groups five minutes away to one of two 5,000-year-old passage tombs, where a guide gives them a 30-minute tour. Newgrange is more famous and allows you inside. Knowth was opened more recently and is more extensive, but you can't go inside the tomb. Each is different enough, but for many, seeing one site is adequate.

Newgrange is one single mound, the most restored of the Bru na Boinne sites. Dating from 3200 B.C., it's 500 years older than the pyramids of Giza. While we know nothing of these people, this most certainly was a sacred spot dealing with some kind of sun god ritual. During your tour you'll squeeze down a narrow passageway to a cross-shaped central chamber under a 20-foot-high igloo-type stone dome. Bones and ashes were placed here under 200,000 tons of stone and dirt to wait for a special moment. As the sun rose on the shortest day of the year (winter solstice, December 21), a ray of sunlight would creep slowly down the 60-foot-long passageway. For 17 minutes it would light the center of the sacred chamber. Perhaps this was the moment when the souls of the dead would be transported to the afterlife via that mysterious ray of life-giving and life-taking light.

Knowth is a necropolis of several grassy mounds around one 85-yard-wide grand tomb. The big mound, covering 1.5 acres, has two passages (neither open to public). They are aligned so that on the spring and fall equinox, rays from the rising and setting sun shine down the passageways to the center chamber. The Knowth site thrived from 3000 to 2000 B.C., was the domain of fairies and myths for the next 2,000 years, and became an Iron Age fortress in the early centuries after Christ. Around 1000 it was an all-Ireland political center, and later a Norman fortress was built atop the mound. You'll see plenty of mysteriously carved stones, new-feeling grassy mounds, and a huge crane as the excavations continue.

Allow an hour for the excellent museum and an hour for each of the tombs you visit (Visitors Centre's museum is included in following prices: Newgrange-£4, Knowth-£3, both tombs-£7, May–Sept 9:00–18:30 or 19:00, hours a little shorter off-season, Newgrange is open year-round, Knowth only May–Oct, tel. 041/24488). The last shuttle bus leaves 1.75 hours before closing. Visits are limited, and on busy summer days those arriving in the afternoon may not get a spot (no reservations possible). In peak season, try to arrive by 9:30 for no wait. Generally, upon arrival you'll get a bus departure time for one or both of the passage tomb sites. Spend your wait in the museum, watching the video, and munching lunch in the cheery cafeteria. Don't try to drive to the actual passage tombs. From Dublin drive north on N1 to Drogheda, where signs direct you to the Bru na Boinne Visitors Centre.

WICKLOW MOUNTAINS

By car or tour, it's easy. If you lack wheels, take a tour. It's not worth the trouble on public transport.

By Car: It's a joy. Consider a scenic detour through the Wicklow area as you drive between Dublin and the west coast. Speed demons take the freeway south to Enniskerry, your gateway to the Wicklow Mountains. Signs direct you to the gardens and on to Glendalough. From Glendalough you can leave the valley (and pick up the highway to the west) over the famous but dull mountain pass called the Wicklow Gap.

By Tour: Wild Wicklow Tours covers the region with an entertaining guide packing every minute with information and fun craic. With a gang of 26 packed into tight but comfortable mountain-gripping buses, the guide kicks into gear from the first pickup in Dublin. Tours cover Dublin's embassy row, Dun Laoghaire, the Bay of Dublin with the mansions of Ireland's rich and famous, the windy Military Road over scenic Sally Gap, and the Glendalough monasteries (£22, year-round, 9:10 pickup at Dublin TI, 10:00 pickup at Dun Laoghaire TI, stop for lunch at a pub—not included, home by 17:30, Dun Laoghaire-ites can use the bus to get into Dublin for the evening, tel. 01/280-1899, www.wildcoachtours.com).

Several other tour companies run day trips through the Wicklow Mountains from Dublin (Dublin Bus is cheapest). Mary Gibbon's Tours visit both the monastery and the gardens in a five-hour trip (£17, be careful—they spend an hour picking up tourists at Dublin hotels before leaving, tel. 01/460-4464, e-mail: marygibbonstours@tinet.ie).

Sights—Wicklow Mountains

▲▲Gardens of Powerscourt—While the mansion's interior—restored after a 1974 fire—isn't much, its meticulously kept aristocratic gardens are Ireland's best. Commissioned in the 1730s by Richard Wingfield, first viscount of Powerscourt, the gardens are called "the grand finale of Europe's formal gardening tradition... probably the last garden of its size and quality ever to be created." I'll buy that.

Upon entry you'll get a flyer laying out 40-minute and 60-minute walks. The "hour walk" takes 30 minutes at a slow amble. With the impressive summit of the Great Sugar Loaf Mountain as a backdrop and a fine Japanese garden, Italian garden, and a goofy pet cemetery along the way, this garden provides the scenic greenery I hoped to find in the rest of the Wicklow area. The lush movie *Barry Lyndon* was filmed in this well-watered aristocratic fantasy.

Powerscourt Gardens, a mile above the village of Enniskerry, cover several thousand acres within the 16,000-acre estate. The dreamy driveway alone is a mile long (£2.50 Nov–Feb, £4 March–Oct, daily 9:30–17:30, great cafeteria, tel. 01/204-6000). Skip the associated waterfall (£2, 3 miles away).

▲▲Military Road over Sally Gap—This is only for those with a car. From Powerscourt Gardens and Enniskerry, go to Glencree, where you ride the tiny military road over Sally Gap and through the best scenery of the Wicklow Mountains. Look for the German military cemetery—built for U-boat sailors who washed ashore in World War II. Near Sally Gap notice the peat bogs and the freshly cut peat bricks drying in the wind. Many locals are nostalgic for the "good old days," when homes were peat-fire heated. At the Sally Gap junction, turn left, where a road winds through the vast Guinness estate. Look down on the glacial lake "Lough Tay" and the Guinness mansion (famous for jet-set parties). Nicknamed the Guinness Lake, the water looks like Ireland's favorite dark brown stout, and the sand of the beach actually looks like the head of a Guinness beer. From here the road winds scenically down into the village of Roundwood and on to Glendalough.

▲▲Glendalough—The steep wooded slopes of Glendalough (glen-da-lock, which means "valley of the two lakes"), at the south end of Wicklow's military road, hides Ireland's most impressive monastic settlement. Founded by St. Kevin in the 6th century, the monastery flourished (despite repeated Viking raids) throughout the "Age of Saints and Scholars" until the English destroyed it in 1398. While it was finally abandoned during the Dissolution of the Monasteries in 1539, pilgrims kept coming, especially on St. Kevin's Day, June 3. (This might have something to do with the fact that a pope said seven visits to Glendalough had the same indulgence value as one visit to Rome.) While much restoration was done in the 1870s, most of the buildings date from the 8th through the 12th centuries.

The valley sights are split between the two lakes. The lower lake has the Visitors Centre and the best buildings. The upper lake, with scant ruins, feels like a state park with a grassy lakeside picnic area, school groups, and fine walks.

General Glendalough plan: Park free at the Visitors Centre. For a complete visit, begin with the video and history exhibit in the center (£2, daily 9:00–18:30 in summer, closes earlier off-season, tel. 0404/45325), wander the ruins (free) around the Round Tower, walk the traffic-free Green Road one mile to the upper lake, and then walk back to your car. (You can drive to the upper lake—parking £1.50.) If you're rushed, skip the upper lake. Summer tour-bus crowds are terrible all day on weekends and from 11:00 to 14:00 on weekdays.

Glendalough Visitors Centre: Start your visit here. The 20-minute video provides a good thumbnail background on the monastic society in medieval Ireland. While the video is more general than specific to Glendalough, the adjacent museum room features this particular monastic settlement. The model in the center of the room recreates the fortified village in the year 1050 (although there were no black-and-white Frisian cows in Ireland back then—they would have been red cows). A browse here shows the contribution these monks made to intellectual life in Dark Age Europe (such as Irish minuscule, a more compact alphabet developed in the 7th century, and illuminated manuscripts, like the *Book of Kells* from the 9th century). From the center, a short and scenic walk along the Green Road takes you to the Round Tower.

The Monastic Village: Easily the best ruins of Glendalough gather around its famous 110-foot-tall Round Tower. Towers like this (60–110 feet tall, standard features in such settlements) functioned as beacons for pilgrims, bell towers, storage lofts, and places of final refuge during Viking raids. They had a high door with a pull-up ladder. Several ruined churches (8th–12th centuries) and a sea of grave markers complete this evocative scene. Markers give short descriptions of the ruined buildings.

In an Ireland without cities, these monastic communities were mainstays of civilization. They were remote outposts where ascetics (with a taste for scenic settings) gathered to commune with God. In the 12th century, with the arrival of grander monastic orders such as the Franciscans and the Dominicans and with the growth of cities, these monastic communities were eclipsed. Today Ireland is dotted with the reminders of this age—illuminated manuscripts, simple churches, carved crosses, and about 100 round towers.

Upper Lake: The Green Road continues one mile farther up the valley to the upper lake (where the marriage scene from *Braveheart* was filmed). The oldest ruins—scant and hard to find—lie near this lake. If you want a scenic Wicklow walk, start here.

KILKENNY

Famous as "Ireland's loveliest inland city," Kilkenny is a good overnight for drivers wanting to break the journey from Dublin to Dingle (necessary if you want to spend more time in the Wicklow area and at the Rock of Cashel). A night in Kilkenny comes with plenty of traditional folk music in the pubs (hike over the river and up John Street). While a small town today (under 20,000), Kilkenny has a big history. Way back, it was an important center—occasionally even capital of Ireland in the Middle Ages.

Kilkenny gives you a feel for salt-of-the-earth Ireland. A workaday town, its castle and cathedral stand like historic bookends between a higgledy-piggledy High Street of colorful shops and medieval facades.

Kilkenny Castle, dominating the town, is a stony reminder of how the Anglo-Norman Butler family dominated the town for 500 years (£3.50, daily 10:00–19:00 in summer, closes earlier off season, tel. 056/21450). A local crafts center weaves and warbles across the street from the castle.

The early English Gothic St. Canice's Cathedral (13th century) is rich with stained glass, medieval carvings, and floors paved in history (daily 10:00–18:00. tel. 056/64971). The 100-foot-tall round tower, built as part of a long-gone pre-Norman church here, recalls the need for a watchtower and refuge. The fun ladder-climb to the top for £1 affords a grand view of the countryside (Easter–Sept Mon–Sat 9:00–13:00, 14:00–18:00, Sun 14:00–18:00; Oct–Easter Mon–Sat 10:00–13:00, 14:00–16:00, Sun 14:00–16:00).

The train/bus station is four blocks from John's Bridge, which marks the center of town. The TI, a block off the bridge, offers hour-long guided town walks (£3, 6/day, first one at 9:15, tel. 056/51500, private guide, Pat Tynan, at tel. & fax 056/65929, cellular 087/265-1745).

Sleeping in Kilkenny: Kilkenny Tourist Hostel, filling a fine Georgian townhouse in the town center, offers a friendly family room, a well-equipped members' kitchen, a wealth of local information, and cheap beds (£9 dorm beds, D-£24, Q-£42, 2 blocks from cathedral at 35 Parliament Street, tel. 056/63541, fax 056/23397, e-mail: kilkennyhostel@tinet.ie).

The **Club House Hotel** is perfectly central. Originally a gentleman's sporting club, it comes with old-time Georgian elegance; a palatial, well-antlered breakfast room; and 35 large, comfy bedrooms (Sb-£38, Db-£75, CC:VMA, Patrick Street, tel. 056/21994, fax 056/71920, e-mail: clubhse@iol.ie).

Berkeley House, across the street from Club House Hotel, is smaller, less expensive, and comfortable (10 rooms, Db-£65, CC:VM, 5 Lower Patrick Street, tel. 056/64848, fax 056/64829).

Rock of Cashel

Rising high above the fertile plain of Tipperary, the Rock of Cashel is one of Ireland's most historic and evocative sites. Seat of the ancient kings of Munster (about 400–1100), this is the site where St. Patrick baptised King Aengus in about A.D. 450. In about 1100 Cashel became Church-run—an ecclesiastical center of the region. On this 200-foot-high outcrop of limestone you'll find a round tower, an early Christian cross, a delightful Romanesque chapel, and a ruined Gothic cathedral, all surrounded by my favorite Celtic cross graveyard. Begin your visit with the 15-minute video (shown every half hour) and the tiny museum (£3.50, mid-June–mid-Sept daily 9:00–19:30, closes earlier off-season, site tel. 062/61437).

Picture the Rock with just its 12th-century round tower (nearly 100 feet tall) and the small Romanesque chapel. Cormac's Chapel was built in about 1130 by the king and bishop of Cashel, Cormac MacCarthy. Study its misty old carvings.

Outside the chapel, notice the replica of St. Patrick's high cross (the 12th-century original is in the museum where you entered). Wander through the ruined 13th-century Gothic cathedral. Then tiptoe through the tombstones. Look out over the Plain of Tipperary. Called the Golden Veil, its rich soil makes it Ireland's most prosperous farm land. A path leads to the ruined 13th-century Cistercian Hore Abbey in the fields below (free, always open and peaceful).

The huggable town of Cashel at the base of the Rock affords a good break on the long drive from Dublin to Dingle (great cafés, plenty of B&Bs, and 2 fine hostels, TI tel. 062/62511).

DINGLE PENINSULA

Dingle Peninsula, the westernmost tip of Ireland, offers just the right mix of far-and-away beauty, ancient archaeological wonders, and desolate walks or bike rides all within convenient reach of its main town. Dingle Town is just big enough to have all the necessary tourist services and a steady nocturnal beat of Irish folk music.

While the big tour buses clog the neighboring Ring of Kerry before heading east to slobber all over the Blarney Stone, Dingle—while crowded in the summer—still feels like the fish and the farm really matter. Forty fishing boats sail from Dingle, and a faint whiff of peat fills its nighttime streets.

For 20 years my Irish dreams have been set here on this sparse but lush peninsula where locals are fond of saying "The next parish is Boston." There's a closeness to the land on Dingle. When I asked a local if he was born here, he thought for a second and said, "No, it was about six miles down the road." When I told him where I was from, a faraway smile filled his eyes, he looked out to sea and sighed, "Ah, the shores of Americay."

Dingle feels so traditionally Irish because it's a Gaeltacht, a region where the government subsidizes the survival of the Irish language and culture. While English is always there, the signs, menus, and songs come in Gaelic. Children carry hurling sticks o class, and even the local preschool brags "ALL Gaelic."

Of the peninsula's 10,000 residents, 1,300 live in Dingle Town. Its few streets, lined with ramshackle but gaily painted shops and pubs, run up from a rain-stung harbor always busy with fishing boats and yachts. Traditionally, the buildings were drab gray or whitewashed. Thirty years ago Ireland's "tidy town" competition started everyone painting their buildings in playful pastels.

It's a peaceful town. The court house (1832) is open one hour a month. The judge does his best to wrap up business within a half hour. During the day you'll see teenagers—already working on ruddy beer-glow cheeks—roll kegs up the streets and into the pubs in preparation for another night of music and *craic* (fun conversation).

Dingle History

The wet sod of Dingle is soaked with medieval history. In the darkest depths of the Dark Ages, peace-loving, bookwormish monks fled the chaos of the Continent and its barbarian raids. They sailed to the drizzly fringe of the known world—places like Dingle. These monks kept literacy alive in Europe. Charlemagne, who ruled much of Europe in the year 800, imported Irish monks to be his scribes.

It was from this peninsula that the semi-mythical explorer monk, St. Brandon, is said to have set sail in the 6th century in search of a legendary western paradise. Some think he beat Columbus to North America by nearly a thousand years.

Dingle (An Daingean in Gaelic) was a busy seaport in the late Middle Ages. Along with Tralee, it was the only walled town in Kerry—castles stood at the low and high ends of Main Street, protecting the Normans from the angry and dispossessed Irish outside. Dingle was a gateway to northern Spain—a three-day sail due south. Many 14th- and 15th-century pilgrimages left from Dingle for Santiago di Compostela.

In Dingle's medieval heydays, locals traded cowhides for wine. When Dingle's position as a trading center ended, the town faded in importance. In the 19th century it was a linen-weaving center. Until 1970 fishing dominated. The only visitors were scholars and students of old Irish ways. In 1970 the movie *Ryan's Daughter* introduced the world to Dingle. The trickle of Dingle fans has grown to a flood as word of its musical, historical, gastronomical, and scenic charms—not to mention its friendly dolphin—has spread.

Planning Your Time

For the shortest visit, give Dingle two nights and a day. It takes six to eight hours to get there from Dublin, Galway, or the boat dock in Rosslare. I like two nights because you feel more like a local on your second evening in the pubs. You'll need the better part of a day to explore the 30-mile loop around the peninsula by bike, car, or tour bus (see "Circular Tour," below). To do any serious walking or relaxing you'll need two or three days. It's not uncommon to find Americans slowing way, way down in Dingle.

Orientation (area code: 066)

Dingle—extremely comfortable on foot—hangs on a medieval grid of streets between the harborfront (where the Tralee bus stops)

Southwest Ireland

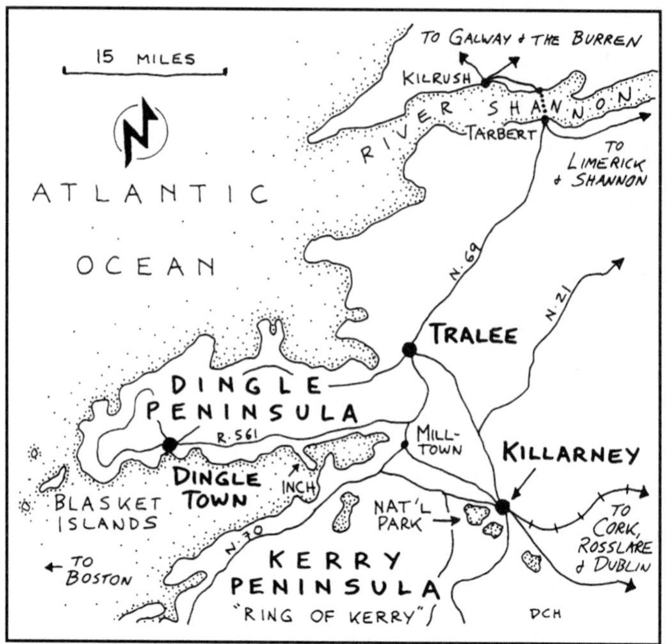

and Main Street (3 blocks inland). Nothing in town is more than a five-minute walk away. Street numbers are used only when more than one place is run by a family of the same name. Most locals know most locals, and people on the street are fine sources of information. Remember, locals love their soda bread, and tourism provides the butter. You'll find a warm and sincere welcome.

Tourist Information: The Bord Failte (TI) is on Strand Street by the water (June–Sept Mon–Sat 9:00–19:00 all day, Sun 10:00–18:00 with lunch break at 13:00; March–May and Oct–Nov Mon–Sat 9:15–17:30 with lunch break, closed Sun, closed Dec–Feb; tel. 066/915-1188). Ask about town walks in summer. The TI, which still seems new at its job, doesn't give out free maps or even post Tralee bus schedules (though you can buy a £1.50 map and borrow the TI's timetable). For more creative help, drop by the Mountain Man shop (on Strand Street, see below).

Helpful Hints

Before You Go: The local Web site (www.dingle-peninsula.ie) lists festivals and events. Look up old issues of *National Geographic* (April '76, Sept '94, and for the Aran Islands, April '81).

Crowds: Crowds trample Dingle's charm for the first three weeks in August. The absolute craziest are the Dingle Races (second weekend in Aug), Dingle Regatta (third weekend in Aug), and the Blessing of the Boats (end of Aug, beginning of Sept). July is also packed. Dingle's metabolism (prices, schedules, activities) rises and falls with the tourist crowds—October through April is sleepy.

Banking: Two banks in town, both uphill from the TI on Main Street, offer the same rates (Mon 10:00–17:00, Tue–Fri 10:00–16:00). Both have cash machines. The TI happily changes cash and traveler's checks at mediocre rates. Expect to use cash (rather than credit cards) to pay for most peninsula activities.

Supermarket: The Super Valu supermarket/department store, at the base of town, has everything and is ideal for assembling a peninsula picnic (Mon–Sat 8:00–21:00, Sun 8:00–19:00, until 22:00 in summer). Smaller groceries are scattered throughout the town, such as Centra on Main Street (Mon–Sat 8:00–21:00, Sun 8:00–18:00).

Launderette: Full-service only—drop off a load and pick it up dry and folded three hours later (tiny-£4.50, regular load-£6, Mon–Sat 9:00–17:30; Oct–April only Mon, Wed, Fri 9:00–17:00, on Green Street down alley opposite church, tel. 066/915-1837).

Post Office: It's on Main Street near Brenners Hotel (Mon–Fri 9:00–17:30, Sat 9:00–13:00).

Internet Access: Dingleweb is on Main Street (£5/hour, £1.50 per quarter hour, cheaper before noon, Mon–Sat 10:00–18:00, until 21:00 June–Aug, closed Sun, tel. 066/915-2478, e-mail: cafe@dingleweb.com).

Bike Rental: Bike rental shops abound. Consider Paddy's Bike Hire (£6/day, £8 for better bikes, £7–9/24 hrs, daily 9:00–19:00, includes helmets, on Dykegate next to Grapevine Hostel, tel. 066/915-2311), Foxy John's (Main Street), Mountain Man, or the Ballintaggert Hostel. If you're biking the peninsula, get a bike with skinny street tires, not slow and fat mountain-bike tires. Plan on leaving a credit card, driver's license, or passport as security.

Dingle Activities: The Mountain Man, a hiking shop run by a local guide, Mike Shea, is a clearinghouse for information, local tours, and excursions (May–Aug daily 9:00–21:00, Sept–April 9:00–18:00, just off harbor at Strand Street, tel. & fax 066/915-2400, fax 066/915-2396, e-mail: irasc@eircom.net). Stop by for bike rentals and ideas on biking, hiking, horse riding, climbing, peninsula tours (which they offer), and trips to the Blaskets. They are the Dingle Town contact for the Dunquin–Blasket Islands boats and shuttle bus rides to the harbor (see "Blasket Islands," below).

Travel Agency: Maurice O'Connor at Galvin's Travel Agency can book train, long-distance bus, plane tickets, and boat rides to France (Mon–Fri 9:30–18:00, Sat 9:30–17:00, John Street, tel. 066/915-1409).

Dingle Town

Sights—Dingle Town

▲**Oceanworld**—The only place charging admission in Dingle is worth considering. This aquarium offers a little peninsula history, 300 different species of local fish in thoughtfully described tanks, and the easiest way to see Fungi the dolphin . . . on video. Walk through the tunnel while fish swim overhead. The only creatures not local—other than you—are the sharks. The aquarium's mission is to teach and you're welcome to ask questions. The petting pool is fun. Splashing attracts the rays—they're unplugged (£5, families-£12, July–Aug daily 10:00–20:30, until 17:30 Sept–June, cafeteria, just past the harbor on the west edge of town, tel. 066/915-2111).

▲Fungi—In 1983 a dolphin moved into Dingle Harbor and became a local celebrity. Fungi (pronounced foon-gee, with hard "g") is now the darling of the town's tourist trade and one reason you'll find so many tour buses parked along the harbor. With a close look at Fungi as bait, tour boats are thriving. The hardy little boats motor 4 to 30 passengers out to the mouth of the harbor, where they troll around looking for Fungi. You're virtually assured of seeing the dolphin, but you don't pay unless you do (£6, kids-£3, 1-hr trips depart 10:00–19:00 depending upon demand, book behind TI at Dolphin Trips office, tel. 066/915-2626). To actually swim with Fungi, rent wetsuits and catch the early morning trip from 8:00 to 10:00 (£24 includes wetsuits—unless you've brought your own).

Eco-Cruises—Dingle Marine Eco Tours offers two-hour, guided, scenic boat tours of the peninsula, sailing either east toward Minard Castle or west toward the Blaskets, depending on the wind (£10, less for kids, daily April–Oct in afternoon if at least 10 people sign up and the weather is decent, book in office behind TI, cellular 086-285-8802, Elaine Garvey). In contrast to Eco Tours, Sea Thrill's 40-minute speedboat tours of the bay are bad news; please shun them.

▲Short Harbor Walk from Dingle—For an easy stroll along the harbor out of town (and a chance to see Fungi, 90-minute round-trip), head east from the roundabout past the Esso station. Just after Bambury's B&B, take a right following signs to Skelligs Hotel. At the beach, climb the steps over the wall and follow the seashore path to the mouth of Dingle harbor (marked by a tower—some 19th-century fat cat's folly). Ten minutes beyond that is a lighthouse. This is Fungi's neighborhood. If you see tourist boats out, you're likely to see him. The trail continues to a dramatic cliff.

The Harbor: The harbor was built on land reclaimed (with imported Dutch expertise) in 1992. The string of old stone shops facing the harbor was the loading station for the narrow-gauge railway that hauled the fish from Dingle to Tralee (1891–1953). The Esk Tower on the distant hill is a marker built in 1847 during the famine as a make-work project. In pre-radar days, it helped ships locate Dingle's hidden harbor. The fancy mansion across the harbor is Lord Ventry's 17th-century manor house.

Sailing—The Dingle Marina Center offers diving, sailing, and traditional currach rowing. One-man sailboats can be lent—subject to availability—to those wanting to blow around the bay with a day membership in the Sailing Club (£15, July–Aug, tel. 066/915-1984). Currachs—stacked behind the building—

are Ireland's traditional lightweight fishing boats, easy to haul and easy to make—cover a wooden frame with canvas and paint with tar. The currachs, owned by the Dingle Rowing Club, go out many summer evenings.

Dingle Pitch & Putt—For 18 scenic holes and a driving range, hike 10 minutes past Oceanworld (£3 with gear, driving range £3 for 100 balls, daily 10:00–20:00, over bridge take first left and follow signs, Milltown, tel. 066/915-1819).

Nightlife in Dingle Town

▲▲▲Folk Music in Dingle Pubs—Even if you're not into pubs, take a nap and then give these a whirl. Dingle is renowned among traditional musicians as a place to get work ("£30 a day, tax free, plus drink"). The town has 50 pubs. There's music every night and rarely a cover charge. The scene is a decent mix of locals, Americans, and Germans. Music normally starts around 21:30, and the last call for drinks is "half eleven" (23:30), sometimes later on weekends. For a seat near the music, arrive early. If the place is chockablock, power in and find breathing room in the back. By midnight the door is usually closed and the chairs are stacked. For more information, see "Irish Traditional Music," in the Appendix.)

While two pubs, the Small Bridge Bar (An Droighead Beag) and O'Flahertys are the most famous for their good beer and folk music, make a point to wander the town and follow your ear. Smaller pubs may feel a bit foreboding to a tourist, but people—locals as well as travelers—are out for the craic. Irish culture is so accessible in the pubs—highly interactive museums waiting to be explored. Have a glass in an empty no-name pub and chat up the publican. Pubs are smoky and hot (leave your coat home). The more offbeat pubs are more likely to erupt into leprechaun karaoke.

Pub crawl: The best pub crawl is along Strand Street to O'Flaherty's. Murphy's is liveliest, offering rock as well as ballads and traditional music. O'Flaherty's, with a high ceiling and less smoke, dripping in old-time photos and town memorabilia, is touristy but lots of fun, with nightly music in the summer.

Then head up Green Street. Dick Mack, across from the church, is nicknamed "the last pew." This is a tiny leather shop by day, expanding into a pub at night, with several rooms, a fine snug (private booth, originally designed to allow women to drink discreetly), reliably good beer, and a smoky and strangely fascinating ambience. Notice the Hollywood-type stars on the sidewalk recalling famous visitors. Established in 1899, the original Dick Mack's grandson now runs the place. A painting in the window shows Dick Mack II with the local gang.

Wander Main Street from top to bottom. MacCarthy's Pub, a smoke-stained relic at the top, is less touristy and has some fine traditional music sessions (plus occasional plays on its small stage, tel. 066/915-1205). The Small Bridge Bar at the bottom—with live music nightly—is popular for good reason (cover charge of £5 only if well-known musicians play). Finally, head up Spa Road a few doors to An Conair—a.k.a. John Benny's, a clean, modern pub attracting a more alternative Celtic folk talent (often less crowded but with good music, tel. 066/915-2011). Further up Spa Road, the big hotel has late-night dancing (see below).

For a touristy but less smoky alternative to a pub crawl, consider the Dingle Bay Caberet, an evening of music, song, dancing, and storytelling (£5, June–Aug Mon only, 20:00–23:00, might not run in 2001—ask at TI, CC:VM, at Skellig's Hotel, near Bambury's Guesthouse, tel. 066/915-1144).

Music info: The music office (Oifig an Cheoil) has the latest on musical happenings (Mon–Fri 10:00–14:00, on Dykegate next to Grapevine Hostel, tel. 066/915-2772, e-mail: oac@eircom.net).

Off-season: From October through May, the bands play on, though at fewer pubs: Small Bridge (live music nightly), An Conair (Mon, Wed, Thu), McCarthy's (Fri, Sat), and Murphy's (Sat).

Music shops: Danlann Gallery sells musical instruments and woodcrafts (Mon–Sat 10:00–18:00, until 22:00 in summer, Sun 11:00–18:00, CC:VM, owner makes violins, Dykegate Street). Siopa an Phiobaire, exclusively a music shop, sells traditional wind instruments, drums, and CDs (Mon–Sat 9:30–18:00, closed Sun, CC:VMA, Craft Centre, on edge of town a few minutes' walk past Oceanworld, tel. 066/915-1778). Dingle Bodhrans sells homemade traditional goatskin drums and gives lessons (Mon–Sat 10:30–18:00, Green Street, enter red iron gate of small alley opposite church, cellular 087-245-7689).

Dancing—Some pubs host "Set Dancing," with live music (An Conair Bar on Mon at 21:30, Small Bridge Bar on Thu). Hillgrove Hotel, up Spa Road a few hundred yards, is a modern hotel with traditional dances every Thursday at 23:00 and pop dancing other nights in summer. Locals say the Hillgrove "is a good time if you're pissed."

Theater—Dingle's great little theater is The Phoenix on Dykegate. Its film club (50 or 60 locals) meets here Tuesdays year-round at 20:30 for coffee and cookies, followed by a film at 21:00 (£4 for film, anyone is welcome). The leader runs it almost like a religion, with a homily on the film before he rolls it.

Sleeping in Dingle Town

(£1 = about $1.40, country code: 353, area code: 066, mail: Dingle, County Kerry)

Sleep Code: **S** = Single, **D** = Double/Twin, **T** = Triple, **Q** = Quad, **b** = bathroom, **t** = toilet only, **s** = shower only, **CC** = Credit Card (**V**isa, **M**asterCard, **A**mex). Prices vary with the season, with winter cheap and August tops.

Good B&Bs

Sraid Eoin B&B, on the quiet end of town, has four spacious and modern pastel rooms and giant bathrooms and is warmly run by Kathleen and Maurice O'Connor (Db-£36–42, family deals, 10 percent discount with this book and cash, CC:VM, smoke free, John Street, tel. 066/915-1409, fax 066/915-2156). Maurice runs Galvin's Travel Agency on the ground floor (same phone number).

Kellihers Ballyegan House is a big, plain building with six fresh, comfortable rooms on the edge of town and great harbor views. It's run by friendly Hannah and James Kelliher, who provide strictly smoke-free rooms (Db-£36–42, Tb-£60, family deals, 10 percent off with this book Dec–April, no CC, parking, TVs in rooms, Upper John Street, tel. 066/915-1702).

O'Neill's B&B is a homey, friendly place with six decent rooms (Db-£38–40, family deals, strictly nonsmoking, parking, John Street, tel. 066/915-1639, Mary O'Neill).

Corner House B&B is my longtime Dingle home. It's a simple, traditional place with five rooms run with a twinkle and a grandmotherly smile by Kathleen Farrell (S-£20, D-£36, T-£51, plenty of plumbing, but it's down the hall, no CC, reserve with a phone call and reconfirm a day or two ahead or risk losing your bed, central as can be on Dykegate Street, tel. 066/915-1516).

The two following B&Bs, which take up a quiet corner in the town center, are run by the same Collins—Coileain in Gaelic—family that does archeological tours of the peninsula (below). Both offer pleasant rooms (O Coileain's are a bit bigger), bike rental (£6), identical prices (Db-£40), and a homey friendliness: **O Coileain B&B** (tel. & fax 066/915-1937, e-mail: arch@iol.ie) and **Kirrary B&B** (tel. & fax066/915-1606, e-mail: collinskirrary@eircom.net). Nearby, **Connor's B&B,** with 15 basic rooms, is a lesser value (Db-£40–50, CC:VMA, quiet and central on Dykegate Street, tel. 066/915-1598, fax 066/915-2376, Mrs. Connor).

Ard Na Greine House B&B is a charming, windblown, modern house on the edge of town. Mrs. Mary Houlihan rents four well-equipped, comfortable rooms (with fridges) to nonsmokers only (Sb-£25–30, Db-£38–44, Tb-£51–57, CC:VM, car park, on the edge of town an 8-minute walk up Spa Road, 3 doors beyond Hillgrove Hotel, tel. 066/915-1113, fax 066/915-1898).

Ocean View B&B rents three tidy rooms (2 with views) in a little waterfront row house overlooking the bay (S-£16, D-£28, CC:VMA, welcome treat on arrival, 5-minute walk from the center, 100 yards past Oceanworld at 133 The Wood, tel. 066/915-1659, e-mail: thewood@gofree.indigo.ie, Mrs. Brosnan).

Finer B&Bs and Guest Houses

Greenmount House sits among palm trees at the top of town, in the countryside, with a commanding view of the bay and mountains, a five-minute hike up from the town center. John and Mary Curran run one of Ireland's best B&Bs, with five superb rooms (Db-£45–55) and seven sprawling suites (Db-£60–80) in a modern building with lavish public areas and breakfast in a solarium (CC:VM, no singles during high season or children under 8, most rooms at ground level, car park, top of John Street, reserve in advance, tel. 066/915-1414, fax 066/915-1974, e-mail: mary@greenmounthouse.com).

Captain's House B&B is a shipshape place fit for an admiral in the town center, with eight classy rooms and a stay-awhile garden (Sb-£35, Db-£60, great suite-£90, super breakfast in conservatory, CC:VMA, the Mall, tel. 066/915-1531, fax 066/915-1079, e-mail: captigh@eircom.net, Jim and Mary Milhench).

Alpine Guest House looks like a monopoly hotel, but that means comfortable and efficient. Its 13 spacious, bright, and fresh rooms come with wonderful sheep and harbor views, a cozy lounge, great breakfast, and friendly owners (Db-£40–56, Tb-£60–80, prices vary with room size and season, 10 percent discount with this book, CC:VM, car park, Mail Road, tel. 066/915-1250, fax 066/915-1966, www.alpineguesthouse.com, e-mail: alpinedingle@eircom.net). Driving into town from Tralee, you'll see this a block uphill from the Dingle roundabout and Esso station.

Bambury's Guesthouse, another big, modern place with views of sheep and the harbor, rents 12 big, airy, comfy rooms with a family-friendly feeling (Db-£40–60, depending on size and season, family deals, CC:VM, on your left coming in from Tralee on Mail Road 2 blocks before Esso station, tel. 066/915-1244, fax 066/915-1786, e-mail: bamburysguesthouse@eircom.net).

The next two places, virtually next door, are located on the water just west of town at the end of Dingle Bay—a five-minute walk past Oceanworld on The Wood. Both are great.

Coastline Guesthouse has seven bright, spacious rooms, all with at least a partial view of the water. Recently built, welcoming and elegant, this is a winner (Sb-£40, Db-£40–60, Tb-£78, deals for 3-night stays, CC:VM, nonsmoking, car park, The Wood, tel. 066/915-2494, fax 066/915-2493, www.coastlineguesthouse.com, e-mail: coastlinedingle@eircom.net, Vivienne O'Shea).

Heatons Guesthouse is big and peaceful. Their 12 classy rooms—most with views—are thoughtfully appointed with all the comforts (Db-£50–75, CC:VM, creative breakfasts, car park, tel. 066/915-2288, fax 066/915-2324, e-mail: heatons@iol.ie, Cameron and Nuala Heaton).

Barr Na Sraide Inn, central and hotelesque, has 22 comfortable rooms (Db-£40–70, CC:VM, self-service laundry, bar, car park,

Upper Main Street, past McCarthy's pub, tel. 066/915-1331, fax 066/915-1446).

Benners Hotel was the only place in town a hundred years ago. It stands bewildered by the modern world on Main Street, with abundant public spaces and sprawling hallways leading to 52 slightly musty, decent, overpriced rooms (Db-£130 July–Aug, £100 May–June, £70–90 Sept–May, kids under 7-£15 extra, CC:VMA, tel. 066/915-1638, fax 066/915-1412, e-mail: benners@eircom.net).

Hostels in Dingle Town

Ballintaggart Hostel, a backpacker's complex, is housed in a stylish old manor house used by Protestants during the famine as a soup kitchen (for those hungry enough to renounce their Catholicism). It comes complete with laundry service (£4), café, classy study, family room with a fireplace, and a resident ghost (148 beds, £8 in 10-bed dorms, £10 in Qbs, Db-£30, no breakfast but there's a kitchen, a mile east of town on Tralee Road, tel. 066/915-1454, fax 066/915-2207, e-mail: info@dingleaccommodation.com). Their shuttle bus meets each arriving intercity bus and does a nightly pub run—into town at 21:30, back at 23:30.

Grapevine Hostel is a clean and friendly establishment with a cozy fireplace lounge and a fine members' kitchen. Each four- to eight-bed dorm has its own bathroom. Dorms are coed, but there's usually a girls' room established (32 beds, £8–9.50 each, laundry-£4, open all day, Dykegate Lane, tel. 066/915-1434, e-mail: grapevine@dingleweb.com, run by Siobhan).

Eating in Dingle Town

For a rustic little village, Dingle is swimming in good food. Budget tips: The **supermarket** stays open late nightly, fancy restaurants serve early-bird specials from 18:00–19:00, many "cheap and cheery" places close at 18:00, and pubs do amazing £5 dinners all over town. Most pubs stop serving food around 21:00 (to make room for maximum beer).

Adam's Bar and Restaurant is a tight, smoky place popular with locals for traditional food at great prices. Try their corned beef and cabbage (£5 meals, last meal at 20:30 in summer, 17:30 off-season, closed Sun, Upper Main Street).

Maire De Barra's pub serves perhaps the best £5 dinners in town—traditional and seafood (daily 12:30–21:30, music after 21:30, the Pier). **Paudie Brosnan's** pub, a few doors down, is also good.

An Cafe Litearta, a popular and friendly eatery hiding behind an inviting bookstore, has tasty snacks and sandwiches (daily 10:00–17:30, Dykegate Street).

Vittle's Restaurant offers good food and prices with an early-bird special (18:00–19:00, 3-course meal-£13) and vegetarian selections (£13–16 entrees, Tue–Sun 18:00–20:00, closed Mon, CC:VMA, near the roundabout at Holyground, tel. 066/915-2502).

The **Global Village Restaurant** is where Martin Bealin serves his favorite dishes, gleaned from travels around the world. It's a smoky and eclectic healthy meat-eaters place popular with locals for its interesting cuisine (£5 lunches, £10 dinners, daily 9:30–21:30, the Thai curry is great, CC:VMA, top of Main Street, tel. 066/915-2325).

The Mystic Celt is new, run by husband-and-wife chefs with a passion for preserving ancient Irish recipes. Portions are huge, excellent, and lovingly prepared (£5 lunches, £10–15 dinners, daily 18:00–21:30, closed Wed off-season and Nov–Feb, veggie options, dietary restrictions taken into account, CC:VM, Main Street, tel. 066/915-2117, Paul and Sylvia Smith).

El Toro offers a candlelit splash of the Mediterranean, with good seafood, salads, and pizzas (£7–15 meals, daily 18:00–22:00, Oct–April closed Tue–Wed, Green Street, tel. 066/915-1820).

Dingle's long-established top-notch restaurants are neighbors on John Street: **Doyle's Seafood Bar** (more famous, tel. 066/915-1174) and the **Half Door** (heartier portions, tel. 066/915-1600). Both take credit cards, have the same hours (Mon–Sat 18:00–22:00, closed Sun), offer an early-bird special (18:00–19:00, 3-course meal-£20), and take reservations (wise).

Transportation Connections—Dingle Town

The nearest train station is in Tralee.

By bus from Dingle to: Galway (4/day, 6.5 hrs), **Dublin** (3/day, 8 hrs), **Rosslare** (2/day, 9 hrs), **Tralee** (4/day, 75 min, £6), fewer departures on Sundays. Most bus trips out of Dingle require at least one or two (easy) transfers. Dingle has no bus station and only one stop, on the waterfront by Super Valu supermarket (bus info tel. 01/830-2222 or Tralee station at 066/712-3566). See "Tralee Transportation Connections," below, for more information.

Drivers choose two roads into town, the easy southern route or the much more dramatic and treacherous Conor Pass (see "Tralee Transportation Connections," below). It's 30 miles from Tralee either way.

Dingle Peninsula: Circular Tour by Bike or Car

A ▲▲▲ sight, the Dingle Peninsula loop trip is about 30 miles long (7 hrs by bike, 3 hrs by car, including stops; do only in clockwise direction). While you can take a guided tour of the peninsula (below), it's not necessary with the route described in this section. A fancy map is also unnecessary with my instructions. I've keyed in mileage to help locate points of interest. If you're driving, as you leave Dingle, reset your odometer at Oceanworld. Even if

Dingle Peninsula Tour

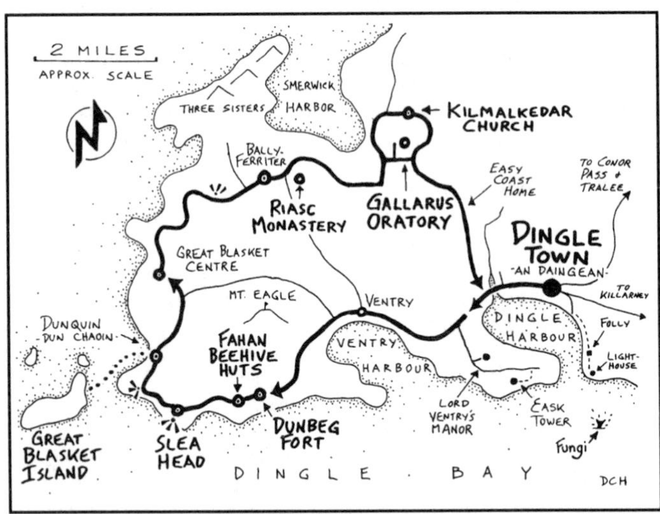

you get off track or are biking, derive distances between points from these numbers. To get the most out of your circle, read through this entire section before departing. Then go step by step (staying on R559 and following "The Slea Head Drive" signs). Note: Roads are very congested in August.

The Dingle Peninsula is 10 miles wide and runs 40 miles from Tralee to Slea Head. The top of its mountainous spine is Mount Brandon—at 3,130 feet, the second-tallest mountain in Ireland. While only tiny villages lie west of Dingle Town, the peninsula is home to 500,000 sheep.

Leave Dingle Town west along the waterfront (0.0 miles at Oceanworld). There's an eight-foot tide here. The seaweed was used to nourish reclaimed land. Across the water, the fancy Milltown House B&B (with flags) was Robert Mitchum's home for a year during the filming of *Ryan's Daughter*. Look back out the harbor to see the narrow mouth of this blind harbor. (That's where Fungi frolics.) Dingle Bay is so hidden, ships needed the tower (1847) on the hill to find its mouth.

0.4 miles: Turn left over the bridge. The building on the right was a corn-grinding mill in the 18th century.

0.8 miles: The Milestone B&B is named for the pillar stone (Gallaun in Gaelic) in its front yard. This may have been a prehistoric grave marker or a boundary marker between two tribes. The stone goes down as far as it sticks up. The peninsula, literally an open-air museum, is dotted with more than 2,000 monuments dating from the Bronze Age through early Christian times. Another pillar stone stands in the field across the street in the direction of the yellow manor house of Lord Ventry.

Lord Ventry, whose family came to Dingle as post–Cromwell War landlords in 1666, built this mansion about 1750. Today it houses an all-Gaelic boarding school for 140 high school–age girls.

As you drive along the Ventry estate and beyond, you'll pass palms, magnolias, fuschias, and exotic flora introduced to Dingle by Ventry. Because of the mild climate (cradled by the gulf stream), fuschias—imported from Chile and spreading like weeds—line the roads all over the peninsula and fill the countryside with red from June to September. The mild climate—it never snows—is fine for subtropical plants.

3 miles: Stay off the "soft margin" as you enjoy views of Ventry Bay and its four-mile-long beach (to your right as you face the water). Mount Eagle (1,660 feet), rising across the bay, marks the end of Ireland. In the village of Ventry, Gaelic is the first language.

4.7 miles: The rushes on either side of the road are the kind used to make the local thatched roofs. Thatching, which nearly died out because of the fire danger, is more popular now that a ntiflame treatments are available. Magpies fly.

5.3 miles: The Irish football star Paidi O Se (Paddy O'Shea) is a household name in Ireland. He now trains the Kerry team and runs the pub on the left.

5.6 miles: The blue house hiding in the trees 100 yards off the road on the left (view through the white gate) was kept cozy by Tom Cruise and Nicole Kidman during the filming of *Far and Away*.

6.6 miles: "Taisteaal go Mall" means "go slowly"; there's a peach-colored schoolhouse on the right. On the left is the small Celtic and Prehistoric Museum, a strange private collection of dinosaur eggs, Celtic and Viking tools, coins, weapons, and an odd mechanical sheep (overpriced at £3, Tue–Sun 9:00–18:00, closed Mon).

6.9 miles: The circular mound on the right is a late–Stone Age ring fort. In 500 B.C. it was a petty Celtic chieftain's headquarters, a stone-and-earth stockade filled with little stone houses. These survived untouched through the centuries because of superstitious beliefs that they were "fairy forts." While this is unexcavated, recent digging has shown that people have lived on this peninsula since 4000 B.C.

7.3 miles: Look ahead up Mount Eagle at the patchwork fields created by the stone fences.

7.7 miles: Dunbeg Fort, a series of defensive ramparts and ditches around a central clochan, while ready to fall into the sea, is open to tourists. Though there are no carvings to be seen, the small (beg) fort (dun) is dramatic (£1, daily 9:30–20:00, descriptive handout). Forts like this are the most important relics left from Ireland's Iron Age (500 B.C. to A.D. 500). Since erosion will someday take this fort, it has been excavated. Alongside the road, the new stone-roofed house was built to blend in with the landscape and the region's ancient rock slab architecture.

8.2 miles: A group of beehive huts, or clochans, is a short walk uphill. These mysterious stone igloos, which cluster together within a circular wall (£1, daily 9:30–19:00, WC), are a better sight than the similar group of beehive huts a mile down the road. Look over the water to the distant islands. The one jutting up like France's Mont St. Michel is Skellig Rock, which contains the rocky remains of an eighth-century monastic settlement. Next to it is a smaller island, Little Skellig, a breeding ground for gannets, birds with huge six-foot wingspans.

Farther on, you'll ford a stream. There has never been a bridge here; the road was designed as a ford.

9.2 miles: Pull off to the left at this second group of beehive huts. Look downhill at the scant remains of the scant home that was burned as the movie equivalent of Lord Ventry tried to evict the tenants in *Far and Away*. Even without Hollywood, this is a bleak and godforsaken land. Look above at the patches of land slowly reclaimed by the inhabitants of this westernmost piece of Europe. Rocks were cleared and piled into fences. Sand and seaweed were laid on the clay, and in time it was good for grass. The created land was generally not tillable. Much has fallen out of use now. Look behind at the Ring of Kerry in the distance and ahead at the Blasket Islands.

9.9 miles: At Slea Head, marked by a crucifix, a pullout, and great views of the Blasket Islands (described below), you turn the corner on this tour.

10.4 miles: Pull into the little parking lot (signed "Dunchaoin) to view the Blaskets and Dunmore Head (the westernmost point in Europe) and to review the roadside map (which traces your route) posted in the parking lot. The scattered village of Dunquin has many ruined rock homes—abandoned during the famine. They were built with small windows to minimize taxation. Some are fixed up, as this is a popular place these days for summer homes. You can see more good examples of land reclamation, patch by patch, climbing up the hillside. Mount Eagle was the first bit of land Charles Lindberg saw after crossing the Atlantic on his way to Paris. Villagers here were as excited as he was. Ahead, down a road on the left, a plaque celebrates the 30th anniversary of the filming of *Ryan's Daughter*.

11.9 miles: The Blasket Islanders had no church or cemetery on the island. This was their cemetery. The famous Blasket storyteller Peig Sayers (1873–1958) is buried in the center. Just past a washed-out bit of road, drive down the little lane that leads left

(100 yards) to a marker remembering the 1588 shipwreck of the *Santa Maria de la Rosa* of the Spanish Armada. Below that is the often-tempestuous Dunquin Harbor, from which the Blasket ferry departs. Island farmers—who on a calm day could row across in 20 minutes—would dock here and hike 12 miles into Dingle to sell their produce.

12 miles: Back on the main road, follow signs to the Great Blasket Centre.

13.1 miles: In the little town of Dunquin, fans of the Cranberries rock group pause and look inland, uphill to the brown house with the circular window, the home of the lead singer.

13.5 miles: Leave the Slea Head Road left for the Great Blasket Centre (described below).

13.7 miles: Back at the turnoff, head left (sign to Louis Mulcahy Pottery).

14.5 miles: Passing land that was never reclaimed, think of the work it took to pick out the stones, pile them into fences, and bring up sand and seaweed to nourish the clay and make soil for growing potatoes. Look over the water to the island aptly named the "Sleeping Giant"—hand resting happily on his beer belly.

15.1 miles: The view is spectacular, especially when the waves are "racing in like white horses." Ahead, on the right, study the top fields, untouched since the planting of 1845, when the potatoes didn't grow, but rotted in the ground. The vertical ridges of the potato beds can still be seen—a reminder of the famine. Before the famine, 60,000 people lived on this peninsula. Today it's home to only 10,000.

18.3 miles: Ballyferriter (Baile an Fheirtearaigh), established by a Norman family in the 12th century, is the largest town on this side of Dingle. The pubs serve grub, and the old schoolhouse is a museum (£1.50, Easter–Sept daily 10:00–16:30, closed off-season). The early Christian cross next to the schoolhouse looks real. Tap it…it's fiberglass—a prop from *Ryan's Daughter*.

19.1 miles: At the T junction, signs direct you to Dingle (An Daingean, 11 km) either way. Go left, via Gallarus. Take a right over the bridge, still following signs to Gallarus.

19.5 miles: Just beyond the bridge and a few yards before the sign to Mainistir Riaise (Reask Monastic enclosure), detour right up the lane. After 0.2 miles (the unsigned turnout on your right), you find the scant remains of the walled Riasc Monastery (dating from the 6th to 12th centuries). The inner wall divided the community into work and religious sections. The layer of black felt marks where the original rocks stop and the excavators' reconstruction begins. The pillar stone is Celtic (from 1000 B.C.). When the Christians arrived in the fifth century, they didn't throw out the Celtic society. Instead, they carved a Maltese-type cross over the Celtic scrollwork. The square building was an oratory (church—

you'll see an intact oratory at the next stop). The round buildings would have been stone igloo-type dwellings. The monasteries had cottage industries. Just outside the wall (opposite the oratory), find a stone hole with a passage facing the southwest wind. This was a kiln. Locals would bring their grain to be dried and ground, and the monks would keep a "tithe." With the arrival of the Normans in the 12th century, these small religious communities were replaced by relatively big-time state and church governments.

20 miles: Back on the main road, continue to the right.

21.1 miles: At the big hotel (Smerwick Harbor), turn left following the sign to Gallarus Oratory.

21.8 miles: At the big building (with camping sign), go right up a short one-lane road marked with a sign for the Oratory. Park. A small tourist center—with a shop, WC, and video theater—charges £1.50; you get a 17-minute video overview of Dingle Peninsula's historic sights.

The Gallarus Oratory, built about 1,300 years ago, is one of Ireland's best-preserved early-Christian churches. Shaped like an upturned boat, its finely fitted dry-stone walls are still waterproof. Notice the holes for some covering at the door and the fine alternating stonework on the corners. Pulling out of the parking lot, you could continue left up the rugged one-lane road and crest the hill to return to Dingle, but it's safer and more interesting to take a slightly longer route (and wider road) that adds a couple more sights.

Leaving the parking lot, turn right, then go straight through the T junction (following sign to An Mhuirioch).

22.9 miles: Turn right at the fork and immediately take a right at the next fork. Soon you'll soon pass a ninth-century church built next to the road; it's now a residence.

24.2 miles: The ruined Kilmalkedar church was the Norman center of worship for this end of the peninsula when England replaced the old monastic settlements in an attempt to centralize their rule.

24.3 miles: Overlooking the water, you'll pass another " fairy fort" (Ciher Dorgan) dating back to 1000 B.C. (free).

25.5 miles: At the crest of the hill, enjoy a three-mile coast back into Dingle Town (in the direction of the Eask Tower).

28.3 miles: At the T junction, turn left. Then take right at the roundabout.

29 miles: You're back into Dingle Town. Well done.

Dingle Peninsula Tours

▲▲Sciuird Archaeology Tours—These tours are offered by a father-son team with Dingle history—and a knack for sharing it—in its blood. Tim Collins (a retired Dingle policeman) and his son Michael give serious 2.5-hour minibus tours (£10, departing at 10:30 and 14:00, depending upon demand). Drop by the Kirrary

B&B (Dykegate and Grey's Lane) or call 066/915-1937 or 066/915-1606 to put your name on the list. Call early. Tours fill quickly in summer. Off-season (Oct–April) you may have to call back to see if the necessary four people signed up to make a bus go. While skipping the folk legends and the famous sights (such as Slea Head), your guide will drive down tiny farm roads (the Gaelic word for road means "cow path"), over hedges, and up ridges to hidden Celtic forts, mysterious stone tombs, and forgotten castles with sweeping seaside views. The running commentary gives an intimate peek into the history of Dingle. Sit as close to the driver as possible to get all the information. They do two completely different tours: west (Gallarus Oratory) and east (Minard Castle and a wedge tomb). I enjoyed both. Dress for the weather. In a literal gale with horizontal winds, Tim kept saying, "You'll survive it."

Moran's Tour does two different guided minibus trips of the peninsula with a more contemporary slant—on local life, fishing, sea life, etc. (£8 to Slea's Head, £7 to Conor Pass, 3 hrs, normally May–Sept at 10:00 and 14:00 from Dingle TI; Moran's is at Esso station at roundabout, tel. 066/915-1155 or 087/275-3333). There are always enough seats. But if no one shows up, consider a private Moran taxi trip around the peninsula (3 people, £25, cabby narrates ride). The **Mountain Man** also offers three-hour minibus tours of the peninsula (£8, 3 tours daily June–Aug, tel. 066/915-2400).

Blasket Islands

This rugged group of six islands off the tip of Dingle Peninsula seems particularly close to the soul of Ireland. The population of Great Blasket Island, home to as many as 160 people, dwindled until the government moved the last handful of residents to the mainland in 1953. Life here was hard. Each family had a cow, a few sheep, and a plot of potatoes. They cut their peat from the high ridge and harvested fish from the sea. There was no priest, pub, or doctor. These people formed the most traditional Irish community of the 20th century—the symbol of antique Gaelic culture.

Their special closeness to their island—combined with their knack for vivid storytelling—is inspirational. From this primitive but proud fishing/farming community came three writers of international repute whose Gaelic work—basically tales of life on Great Blasket—is translated into many languages. You'll find *Peig* (by Peig Sayers), *Twenty Years a-Growing* (Maurice O'Sullivan), and *The Islander* (Thomas O'Crohan) in shops everywhere.

In the summer there may be a café, shop, and hostel on the island, but it's little more than a ghost town overrun with rabbits on a peaceful, grassy, three-mile-long poem. The Blasket ferry runs hourly, and in summer every half hour, depending on weather and demand (£12, May–Sept, sometimes into Oct). In 2001 there should be two buses a day from Dingle Town to

Dunquin—both leave in the morning, and pick up in the late afternoon—coordinated with the ferry schedule (£3 each way by bus; one bus offered by Mountain Man, tel. 066/915-2400; the other by Moran, tel. 066/915-1155, who can add more as needed; Dunquin ferry tel. 066/915-6422). Dunquin has a fine hostel (tel. 066/915-6121).

▲▲**Great Blasket Centre**—This state-of-the-art Blasket and Gaelic heritage center gives visitors the best look possible at the language, literature, and way of life of the Blasket Islanders. See the fine 20-minute video (shows on the half hour), hear the sounds, read the poems, browse through old photos, and then gaze out the big windows at those rugged islands and imagine. Even if you never got past limericks, the poetry of these people—so pure and close to each other and nature—will have you dipping your pen into the cry of the birds (£2.50, Easter–Oct daily 10:00–18:00, until 19:00 July–Aug, cafeteria, on the mainland facing the islands, well signposted, tel. 066/915-6444). Visit this center before visiting the islands.

▲▲**Blasket Islands Adventure Cruise**—Three-hour cruises take visitors among the islands and provide a wild Atlantic dose of bird, fish, and natural scenery (£20, May–Sept 2/day: late morning and afternoon, weather permitting; bring barf bag, pack for rain and cold, coffee and snacks included, booking required, departs from Dunquin Pier, reach harbor from Dingle via shuttle bus—£6 round-trip—with Moran or Mountain Man, tel. 066/915-6533 or 066/915-6422, cellular 087-228-0460, www.blaskettours.com).

Sights—East of Dingle Town

▲**Minard Castle**—Three miles southwest of Annascaul (off Lispole Road) is Minard Castle, the largest fortress on the peninsula. Built by the Norman Knights of Kerry in 1551, it was destroyed by Cromwell in about 1650.

Wander around the castle. With its corners undermined by Cromwellian explosives, it looks ready to split. Look up the garbage/toilet chute. As you enter the ruins, find the faint scallop in the doorway—the symbol of St. James. The castle had a connection to Santiago de Compostela in Spain. Medieval pilgrims would leave from here on a seafaring pilgrimage to northern Spain. Inside, after admiring the wall flowers, recreate the floor plan: ground floor for animals and storage; main floor with fireplace; thin living-quarters floor; and, on top, the defensive level.

The setting is dramatic, with the Ring of Kerry across the way and Storm Beach below. Storm Beach is notable for its sandstone boulders that fell from the nearby cliffs. Grinding against each other because of the wave and tidal action, the boulders eroded into cigar-shaped rocks.

Next to the fortress, look for the "fairy fort," a Stone-Age fort from about 500 B.C.

▲Puicin Wedge Tomb—While pretty obscure, this is worth the trouble for its evocative setting. Above the hamlet of Lispole in Doonties, park your car and hike 10 minutes up a ridge. At the summit is a pile of rocks made into a little room with one of the finest views on the peninsula. Beyond the Ring of Kerry you may just make out the jagged Skellig Rock, noted for its eighth-century monastery.

Inch Strand—This four-mile sandy beach, shaped like a half moon, was made famous by *Ryan's Daughter*.

TRALEE

While Killarney is the tour-bus capital of county Kerry, Tralee is its true leading city. Except for the tourist complex around the TI and during a few festivals, Tralee feels like a bustling Irish town. A little outdoor market combusts on The Square (Thu–Sat).

Tralee's famous Rose of Tralee International Festival (Aug. 18–22 in 2001), while a celebration of arts and music, climaxes with the election of the "Rose of Tralee"—the most beautiful woman at the festival. While the rose garden in the Castle Gardens surrounding the TI is in bloom from summer through October, Tralee's finest roses are going about their lives in the busy streets of this workaday town.

Orientation (area code: 066)

For the tourist, the heart of Tralee is Ashe Memorial Hall, housing the TI and Kerry the Kingdom, located near the rose garden and surrounded by the city park. Beyond the park is the Aqua Dome and steam railway that, if you were here 50 years ago, would chug-chug you to Dingle. Today it goes only to the touristy windmill.

Tourist Information: The TI is in Ashe Memorial Hall (July–Aug daily 9:00–19:00, otherwise 9:00–17:00, tel. 066/721-288).

Arrival in Tralee: From the train and bus station (located in the same building, with bike rental available), the Ashe Memorial Hall is a 10-minute walk through the center of town. From the station head down Edward Street, then turn right on Castle Street and left on Denny. It's at the end of Denny. Drivers should knock around the town center until they find a sign to the TI. Parking on the street requires a disk (50p per hour, sold at TI and newsstands—have them date it for you—or from machines on the street).

Sights—Tralee

▲▲Kerry the Kingdom—This is the place to learn about life in Kerry. The museum has three parts: Kerry slide show, museum, and medieval town train ride. Get in the mood by relaxing for 15 minutes through the Enya-style, continuous slide show of Kerry's spectacular scenery, then wander through 7,000 years of Kerry history in the museum (well described, no need for £1 rentable headphones). The Irish say that when a particularly stupid guy moved from Cork to Kerry, he raised the I.Q. in both counties—but this is pretty well done. The museum starts with good background on the archaeological sights of Dingle and goes right up to a video showing highlights of the Kerry football team (a fun look at Irish football). The attempted finale is a 12-minute, four-person train ride down Tralee's Main Street in 1450 (£5.50, daily 10:00–18:00, until 19:00 in Aug, closed Jan–Feb, 50p disk at TI for one-hour parking, tel. 066/712-7777). Before leaving, garden enthusiasts will want to ramble through the rose garden in the adjacent park.

Blennerville Windmill—On the edge of Tralee, just off the Dingle road, spins a restored mill originally built in 1800. Its eight-minute video tells of the famine (£3, April–Oct daily 10:00–18:00, closed Nov–March, tel. 066/712-1064). A restored narrow-gauge steam railway runs hourly from Tralee's Ballyard Station to the windmill (£2.75 round-trip, tel. 066/712-1064). In the 19th century, Blennerville was a major port for America-bound emigrants.

Blennerville's *Jeanie Johnston* Shipyard—At this shipyard, a life-size replica was recently built of the *Jeanie Johnston*, the tall ship that made 16 successful voyages ferrying Irish refuges to North America (1847–1858) during and after the famine. Last year the ship set sail for America, where it's docking at many ports before returning to Tralee in 2002. Until it returns, you'll see only an exhibition and video about the making of the ship, a progress report on its American jaunt, and woodworking demonstrations (£3, daily 9:00–18:00, tel. 066/712-9999).

Siamsa Tire Theatre—The National Folk Theater of Ireland, Siamsa Tire (pron: shee-em-sah tee-rah), stages two-hour dance and theater performances based on Gaelic folk traditions. The songs are in Irish, but there's no dialogue (£11, 20:30 performance, virtually every evening mid-May–Oct, next to Kingdom of Kerry building in park, tel. 066/712-3055, e-mail: siamsatire@eircom.net).

Swimming—The Aqua Dome is a modern-yet-fortified swim center—the largest indoor waterworld in Ireland—at the Dingle end of town, near the Ashe Memorial Hall. Families enjoy the huge slide, wave pool, and other wet amusements (£6, £4 for kids, locker-50p, June–Aug daily 10:00–22:00, less off-season, tel. 066/712-8899 or 24-hr tel. 066/712-9150).

Music and Other Distractions—Tralee has a fine pub scene, with several pubs within a few blocks of each other (on Castle Street and Rock Street) offering live traditional music most evenings. There's greyhound racing (10 30-second races every 15 minutes, 20:00–22:15, Tue and Fri year-round plus Sat in summer, 10-min walk from station or town center, tel. 066/718-0008). It costs £4 plus what you lose gambling (kids free). At just about any time of day you can drop into a betting office to see the local gambling scene.

Sleeping and Eating in Tralee

(£1 = about $1.40, country code: 353, area code: 066, mail: Tralee, County Kerry)

The first two places—a pleasant B&B and a fancy guest house—are located a 10-minute walk from the station up Oakpark Road (which turns into Oakpark Drive). A cab runs £4.

O'Shea's B&B, a simple, tidy, modern house, rents four comfy rooms (Sb-£25, Db-£36–44, Tb-£45, leaving the station, walk up Oakpark Road to #2 Oakpark Drive, tel. 066/718-0123, fax 066/718-0188, Mairead O'Shea).

Meadowlands is a classy 27-room guest house that's fortunately too small for tour groups. If you want to splurge in Tralee, do it here (Db-£90–120, suites-£130–150, CC:VM, Oakpark Drive, nearly across street from O'Shea's B&B—above, tel. 066/718-0444, fax 066/718-0964, e-mail: medlands@iol.ie).

Cheap accommodations abound in Tralee, such as these two good, central hostels with some £25 doubles and lots of £10 dorm beds: The **Courthouse Lodge,** just opened last year, is on 5 Church Street (CC:VM, 5-minute walk from station toward town center, take Ashe Street, tel. & fax 066/712-7199). **Finnegan's Hostel,** in a stately Georgian house from 1826, is a block in front of TI at 17 Denny Street (rustic cellar restaurant serving fine meals, CC:VM, tel. 066/712-7610).

A mile out of town—in different directions—you'll find the homey **Lisnagree Hostel** (£10 beds in shared quads, D-£22, Db-£24, a mile east of center just off N21, follow Boherboy to Ballinorig Road, tel. 066/712-7133) and the **Collis-Sandes House**, a run-down, neo-Gothic mansion in a peaceful forest with 100 cheap beds (£7 beds in 4- to 8-bed rooms, D-£24, Db-from £30, includes sheets, breakfast-£1, CC:VMA, a mile north of station and town center; from the station head up Oakpark Drive, after about 8 blocks you'll see sign on left, tel. & fax 066/712-8658, e-mail: colsands@indigo.ie; they have a free shuttle service from station—ring upon arrival—and a Tralee pub run on summer evenings).

Eating: The Cookery is good (£5 lunches Tue–Sat 12:30–14:30, £10–15 dinners Tue–Sun from 18:00, CC:VM, 16 Abbey Street, a block off The Square, tel. 066/712-8833), but it's a lot cheaper to shop for a picnic at **Tesco,** the big grocery off The Square (Mon–Sat 8:30–20:00, Sun 10:00–18:00).

Transportation Connections—Tralee

Day-trippers, beware: The station has lockers, but not enough.

By train to: Dublin (4/day, 3/day on Sun, 4 hrs), **Rosslare** (1/day, 5 hrs). Train info: tel. 066/712-3522.

By bus to: Dingle (7/day, less off-season and on Sun, 75 min, £6 one-way, £9 round-trip), **Galway** (6/day, 4 hrs), **Limerick** (5/day, 2 hrs), **Doolin/Cliffs of Moher** (1–2/day, 4 hrs), **Ennis** (5/day, 3 hrs), **Rosslare** (2–3/day, 7 hrs, £17), **Shannon** (5/day, 2.5 hrs). Tralee's bus station is at the train station. Bus info: tel. 066/712-3566.

Car Rental: Duggan's Garage Practical Car Hire rents Fiat Puntos (£38/24 hours, £75/48 hours, includes everything but gas, CC:VM, 2 blocks from train station on Ashe Street, tel. 066/712-1124, fax 066/712-7527).

Kerry Airport, a 45-minute drive from Dingle Town, offers direct flights to **Dublin** and **London** (daily, £86; airport tel. 066/976-4644 or 066/976-4350, Ryanair tel. 01/609-7878).

Shannon Airport, the major airport in western Ireland, has direct flights to **Dublin** (2–3/day, 30 min) and **London** (6/day, 1 hr), plus easy bus connections to **Limerick** (nearly hrly, 1 hr, continue to Tralee—2 hrs, and Dingle—1.25 hrs more), **Ennis** (nearly hrly, 1 hr) and **Galway** (every 2 hrs, 2 hrs). Aer Lingus, Ryanair, and Virgin Express fly out of Shannon. Airport info: tel. 061/471-444. Shannon Airport TI: tel. 061/471-664 (daily 6:30–17:30, June–Sept until 19:00).

Route Tips for Drivers

From Tralee to Dingle: Drivers choose between the narrow, but very exciting, Conor Pass road or the faster, easier, but still narrow N86 through Lougher and Anascaul. On a clear day Conor Pass comes with incredible views over Tralee Bay and Brandon Bay, the Blasket Islands, and the open Atlantic. Pull over at the summit viewpoint to look down on Dingle Town and the harbor. While in Kerry listen to Radio Kerry FM 97. To practice your Gaelic, tune into FM 94.4.

Between Tralee and Galway/Burren/Doolin: The Killimer–Tarbert ferry connection allows those heading northbound for the Cliffs of Moher (or southbound for Dingle) to avoid the 80-mile detour around the Shannon River. If you're going to Galway, the Limerick route is faster, but the ferry route is more scenic (hrly trips, 20 min, £9/carload, leaves on the half hour going north and top of the hour going south, until 21:00 April–Sept, until 19:00 Oct–March, no need to reserve, tel. 065/905-3124).

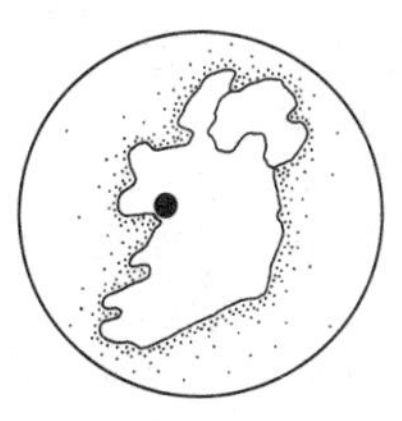

GALWAY, ARAN ISLANDS, AND COUNTY CLARE

GALWAY

Galway feels like a boomtown—rare in western Ireland. With 60,000 people, it's the area's main city—a lively university town and the county's industrial and administrative center. Amid the traditional regions of Connemara, James Joyce country, and the Aran Islands, it's also a Gaelic cultural center.

Galway offers tourists plenty of traditional music, easy bus connections to Dublin (hrly, 3.5 hrs, £7–9), and a convenient jumping-off point for a visit to the Aran Islands.

While Galway has a long and interesting history, its British overlords (who ruled here until 1922) had little use for anything important to the Irish heritage. Consequently, precious little from old Galway survives. What does survive has the interesting disadvantage of being built in the local limestone, which, even if medieval, looks like modern stone construction. A spirit of preservation came with the city's quincentennial celebration in 1984.

What Galway lacks in sights it makes up for in ambience. Spend an afternoon just wandering its medieval streets, with their delightful mix of colorful facades, labyrinthine pubs, weather-resistant buskers, and steamy eateries.

Blustery Galway heats up after dark, with fine theaters and a pub scene Dubliners travel for. Visitors mix with old-timers and students as the traditional music goes round and round.

If you hear a strange language on the streets and wonder where those people are from... it's Irish, and so are they.

Galway History

The medieval fishing village of Galway went big time when the Normans captured the territory from the O'Flaherty family in 1234.

Galway, Aran Islands, and County Clare

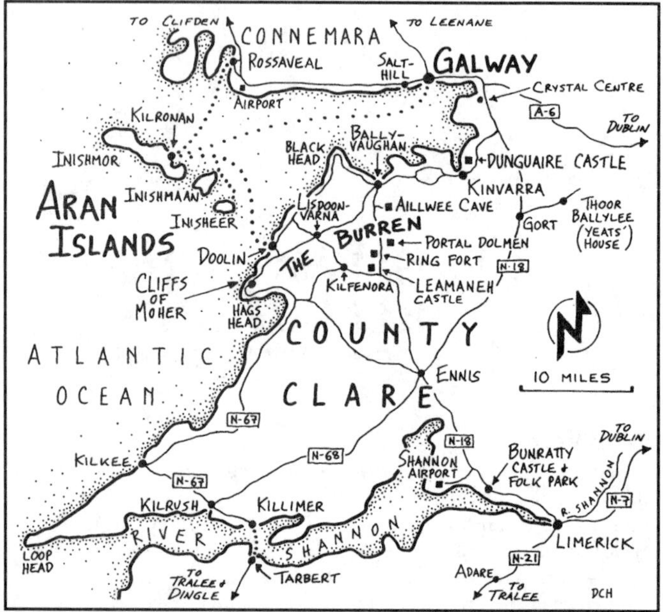

Making the town a base, they invited in their Anglo friends, built a wall (1270), and kicked out the Irish. Galway's Celtic name (Gaillimh) comes from an old Irish word, *gall*, which means "foreigner." Except for a small section in the Eyre Square Shopping Center and a chunk at the Spanish Arch, that Norman wall is gone.

In the 14th century, 14 merchant families, or "tribes," controlled Galway's commercial traffic, including the lucrative wine trade with Spain and France. These English families constantly clashed with the local Irish. While the wall was built to "keep out the O's and the Macs," it didn't always work. A favorite prayer at the time was "From the fury of the O'Flaherty's good Lord deliver us."

Galway's support of the English king helped it prosper. But with the rise of Oliver Cromwell, Galway paid a price. After sieges in 1651 by Cromwell and in 1691 by the Protestant King William, Galway declined. It wasn't until the last half of the 20th century that it regained some of its importance and wealth.

Galway Legends

Because of the dearth of physical old stuff, the town milks its legends. Here are a few you'll encounter repeatedly:

In the 15th century, the mayor, one of the Lynch tribe, condemned his son to death for the murder of a Spaniard. When no one in town could be found to hang the popular boy, the dad—who loved justice more than his son—did it himself.

Columbus is said to have stopped in Galway in 1477. He may have been inspired by tales of the voyage of St. Brandon, the Irish monk who is thought by some (mostly Irish) to have beaten Columbus to the New World by nearly a thousand years.

On the main drag you'll find a pub called the King's Head. It was originally given to the man who chopped the head off of King Charles I in 1649. For his safety he settled in Galway, about as far from London as an Englishman could go back then.

Every sight in town finds a way to tell you the story about the Claddagh ring—so I won't.

Planning Your Time

Galway's sights are little more than pins on which to hang the old town. The joy of Galway is its street scene. You could see its "sights" in three hours, but without an evening in town, you missed the best. Many spend three nights here and two days: one for the town and another for a side trip to Connemara, the Burren, or the Aran Islands. Tour companies make day trips to all three regions cheap and easy.

Orientation (area code: 091)

The center of Galway is Eyre Square. Within two blocks of the square you'll find the TI, Aran boat offices, a bike rental shop, a tour pick-up point, the best cheap beds, and the train station. The train and bus station butt up against the Great Southern Hotel, a huge gray railroad hotel that overlooks and dominates Eyre Square. The lively old town lies between Eyre Square and the river. From Eyre Square, Williamsgate Street leads right through the old town (changing names several times) to Wolfe Tone Bridge. Nearly everything you'll see and do is within a few minutes' walk of this spine.

Tourist Information: The TI, located a block from the bus/train station in the ground floor of the Forster Court Hotel, has a bookshop and many booking services (Mon–Sat 9:00–17:45, Sun 9:00–12:45, July–Aug daily 9:00–20:00, tel. 091/563-081, www.irelandwest.travel.ie). Pick up the TI's *Galway Magazine* (£1.50, persistent readers will find several maps and walking tours amid the ads).

Arrival in Galway: Trains and most buses share the same station, virtually on Eyre Square (which has the nearest ATMs). To get to the TI, turn right on Forster Street as you exit the bus/train station. Some buses from Dublin and Dublin's airport arrive at Forster Street Bus Park, next to the TI.

Helpful Hints

Crowd Control: Expect huge crowds—and higher prices—during the Galway Arts Festival (last half of July), Galway Oyster Festival (4 days near end of Sept), and Galway Races (a week in late July/early Aug, 3 days in mid-Sept, and 3 days in late Oct).

Bike Rental: Celtic Rent-a-Bike has good bikes and long hours—from sunrise to sunset (£10/day, if no one's there, buzz Celtic Tourist Hostel next door, on Queen Street, a block past Kinlay House, 2 blocks off Eyre Square, tel. 091/566-606).

Laundry: Prospect Hill Launderette (Mon–Fri 8:30–18:00, Sat 8:30–17:00, closed Sun, £5 self-serve, £8 drop-off, 44 Prospect Hill, 100 yards from town square, tel. 091/568-343).

Markets: A fun market clusters around St. Nicholas' Church all day on Saturday (best from 9:00–12:00). An antique market clinks and clanks at the base of the medieval wall in the Eyre Square Shopping Centre (daily, best Thu–Sat).

Internet Access: Try Internet Arcade in FunWorld at the top of Eyre Square (£4/hr, Mon–Sat 10:00–23:00, Sun 11:00–23:00, tel. 091/561-415).

Tours of Galway

▲Walking Tour—Kay Davis enjoys taking small groups on grandmotherly two-hour walks through old Galway. Starting at the TI, she covers Eyre Square, the cathedral, and the old town, and then finishes up at the Spanish Arch (£3.50 tickets at TI, June–Sept Mon–Fri at 11:30, Kay also does private walks, tel. 091/792-431).

▲Hop-on Hop-off City Bus Tours—Several companies run guided, 60-minute, hop-on hop-off double-decker buses from Eyre Square, making nine stops—including the cathedral, Salthill, and the Spanish Arch—allowing you to get off to explore and hop back on later (£5, daily 10:30–16:30, longer hours in summer, 2–3/hrly, buses usually depart from top of Eyre Square—near Hooker's Monument, sometimes elsewhere on square, different companies honor other company's tickets).

Sights—Medieval Galway's "Latin Quarter"

From the top of Eyre Square, **Williamsgate Street** (named for the old main gate of the Norman town wall that once stood here) is the spine of medieval Galway, leading downhill straight to the Corrib River. While the road changes names several times (William, Shop, High, and Quay Streets), it leads generally downhill and straight past these sights:

Lynch's Castle (now a bank), Galway's best surviving 16th-century fortified townhouse, was the home of the Lynch family—the most powerful of the town's 14 tribes. More than 60 Lynch mayors ruled Galway in the 16th and 17th centuries.

Galway

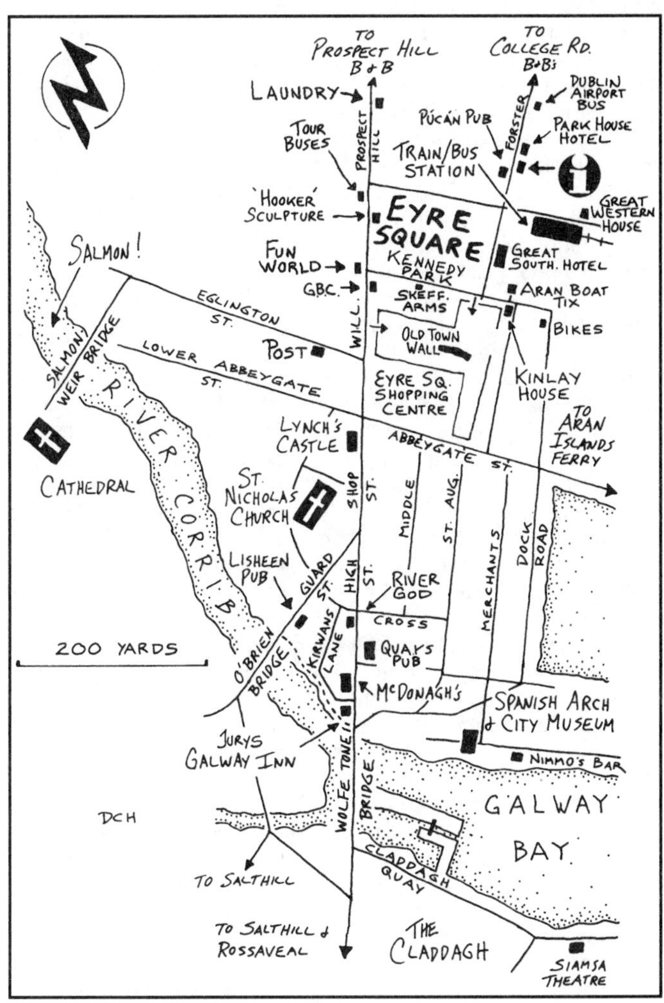

St. Nicholas' Church (half a block off the main street on the right) is the finest surviving medieval building in town (1320) and is dedicated to St. Nicholas of Myra, the patron saint of sailors. Columbus is said to have worshiped here in 1477 while undoubtedly contemplating a scary voyage. Its interior is littered with obscure town history (£1.50 donation for admission). On Saturday a wonderful market surrounds the church.

The Quay Pub, once owned by "Humanity Dick," an 18th-century member of Parliament who was the original animal-rights activist, is worth a peek inside for its lively interior. The lane just before it leads to the 100-seat Druid Theatre. Drop by to see if anything's playing tonight (£10 tickets for top-notch contemporary Irish theater, CC:VM).

The **Spanish Arch** and **City Museum,** overlooking the Corrib River, make up the best surviving chunk of the old city wall. The Spanish Arch (1584), the place where Spanish ships would unload their cargo, is a reminder of the trading importance Galway once enjoyed. The tiny museum is humble—but if it's fragments of old Galway you're looking for, this is where they're kept (£1, April–Oct daily 10:00–13:00, 14:00–17:00, closed off-season, tel. 091/567-641).

At the **Corrib River** you'll find a riverside park perfect for a picnic (or get take-out from the town's best chippie, McDonagh's, across the street). Over the river (southeast of the bridge) is the modern housing project that, in the 1930s, replaced the original Claddagh. The Claddagh was a picturesque Gaelic-speaking fishing village with a strong tradition of independence—and open sewers. This gaggle of thatched cottages actually functioned as an independent community with its own "king" until early in the 1900s. Nothing survives today except for the tradition of the popular Claddagh ring—two hands holding a heart—which comes with a fascinating story.

Notice the monument (just before the bridge), given to Galway by the people of Genoa, celebrating Columbus' visit here in 1477. (That acknowledgment, from a town known in Italy for its stinginess, helps to substantiate the murky visit.) From the bridge look up the river. The green copper dome marks the new city cathedral. Down the river is a tiny harbor with a few of Galway's famous square-rigged "hooker" fishing ships tied up and on display. Beyond that a huge park of reclaimed land is popular with the local kids for Irish football and hurling. From there the promenade leads to the resort town of Salthill.

Sights—Galway

▲Eyre Square—In the Middle Ages this was a green just outside the town wall. The square is named for the mayor who, in 1710, gave the land to the city. While still called Eyre Square, it now contains John F. Kennedy Park—established in memory of the Irish-descended president's visit in 1963, a few months before he was assassinated. (While Kennedy is celebrated as the first Irish Catholic president, there have been a dozen Irish presidents of Protestant Ulster stock.) On a sunny day Eyre Square is a popular grassy hangout. Walk to the rust-colored Quincentennial Fountain (built in 1984 to celebrate the 500th anniversary of the incorporation of the city). The sails represent Galway's "hooker" fishing ships and the trading vessels that made Galway a trading center so long ago. The Browne Doorway, from a 1627 fortified townhouse, is a reminder of the 14 family "tribes" that once ruled the town. Each had a town castle—much like the towers that characterize the towns of Tuscany with their feuding noble families. So little survives of medieval Galway that the town makes a huge deal of any surviving window or crest. The cannons are from the Crimean War (1854). The statue is of Patrick O'Connor, Galway's favorite Gaelic poet, who'd sit on a limestone wall, as sculpted, recording the local life.

The Eyre Square Shopping Centre (arcaded entry from the square) leads to a surviving piece of the old town wall that includes two reconstructed towers (and an antique market). Today it's a busy, modern shopping mall.

▲▲Cathedral—Opened by American Cardinal Cushing in 1965, this is one of the last great stone churches built in Europe. The interior is a treat: mahogany pews set on green Connemara marble floors under a Canadian cedar ceiling. The acoustically correct cedar accompanies the church's fine pipe organ. Two thousand worshipers sit in the round facing the central altar. A Dublin woman carved 14 larger-than-life stations of the cross. The carving above the chapel (left of entry) is from the old St. Nicholas church. Explore the modern stained glass. Find the Irish holy family—with Mary knitting and Jesus offering Joseph a cup of tea. The window depicting the Last Supper is particularly creative—find the 12 apostles. Church bulletins at the doorway tell of upcoming masses and concerts (located across Salmon Weir Bridge on outskirts of town, tel. 091/563-577).

Salmon Weir Bridge—This bridge was the local bridge of sighs. It led from the courthouse (opposite the church) to the prison (torn down to build the church—unlikely in the U.S.). Today the bridge provides a fun view of the fishing action. Salmon run up this river most of the summer (look for them). Fishermen, who wear waders and carry walking sticks to withstand the strong current, book long in advance to get half-day appointments for a casting spot.

Canals multiplied in this city (sometimes called the Venice of Ireland) to power more water mills.

Sights—Outer Galway

▲Galway Irish Crystal Heritage Center—This is a grand-sounding name in a grand new building for a sight made to order for big bus groups. Still, this cheap and handy (for drivers) tour is the place to see the making of Irish crystal. Tours go every half hour. After a guided tour through the museum and a quick look at craftsmen cutting crystal (Mon–Fri only), you sit for 10 minutes while a video subliminally sells you crystal while wowing you with Galway sights. The museum, more interesting than Galway's City Museum, gives you a good rundown on the Claddagh Village and a chance to see a large "hooker" named *Fiona* (£2, July–Aug Mon–Fri 9:00–19:00, Sat–Sun 10:00–18:00, Sept–June Mon–Sat 9:00–17:30, Sun 10:00–17:30, good cafeteria, 5 minutes out of Galway on Dublin road N6, or take Merlin Park bus—every 20 minutes—from Eyre Square, tel. 091/757-311).

▲**Salthill**—This small resort packs pubs, discos, a splashy water park, amusement centers, and a fairground up against a fine mile-long beach promenade. At the new Atlantaquaria aquarium, which features solely Irish water life, kids can help feed the fish at 15:00 (£5, daily 10:00–17:00, touch tanks, Toft Park, tel. 091/585-100). For sunny time on the beach, a relaxing sunset stroll, late-night traditional music, or later-night disco action, Salthill hops. To get to Salthill, catch bus #1 from Eyre Square in front of the IAB bank next to the Great Southern Hotel (80p, runs 7:00–23:00).

Dog Racing—Join the locals and cheer on the greyhounds on Tuesday and Friday evenings from 20:15 to 22:00 (£3, barking distance from my recommended B&Bs, a 10-minute walk from Eyre Square, tel. 091/562-273).

Tours to the Burren and Connemara—Two companies (Lally and O'Neachtain) do all-day, £13 tours of nearby regions. Tours of Connemara (northwest of Galway) include the Quiet Man Cottage, Kylemore Abbey, Clifden, and the Famine Village. Tours to the Burren do a loop south of Galway, covering Kinvarra, Aillwee Cave, Poulnabrone Dolmen, and Cliffs of Moher (tours go most days about 10:00–17:00, depart near TI, Lally tel. 091/562-905, O'Neachtain tel. 091/553-188). Drivers take cash only; to pay with a credit card, book at the TI.

Nightlife in Galway

Folk Theatre—Galway's folk theatre, **Siamsa,** features Irish music, folk drama, singing, and dancing—including the step-dancing popularized by Riverdance (late-June–Aug Mon–Fri at 20:45, Claddagh Hall, Nimmos Pier, tel. 091/755-479).

▲**Traditional Irish Music in Pubs**—Galway (like Dingle and Doolin) is a mecca for good Irish music (nightly 21:30–23:30). Unlike Dingle and Doolin, this is a university town (enrollment: 12,000), and many pubs are often overrun with noisy students. Still, the chances of landing a seat close to a churning band surrounded by new Irish friends are good any evening of the year. Touristy and student pubs are found and filled along the main drag down from Eyre Square to the Spanish Arch and across Wolfe Tone Bridge along William Street West and Dominick Street. Across the bridge start at **Monroe's** with its vast and music-filled interior (live music nightly, set dancing on Tue,

Dominick Street, tel. 091/583-397). Several other pubs feature almost-nightly traditional music within earshot.

Pubs along the main drag known for Irish music include **Taaffe's** (nightly music, plus Thu, Fri, and Sat at 17:00, Shop Street, across from St. Nicholas Church, tel. 091/564-066) and **The Quays** (traditional music at 21:30 on Mon, Tue, and Thu; at 17:00 Fri–Sun, young scene, Quay Street, tel. 091/568-347).

For a place with an older crowd, I like **The Lisheen**—with live traditional music nightly at 21:30 plus a 13:00 session on Sunday. Enjoy the large painting of the firelit "crossroads dance," an event that still takes place (good food, 5 Bridge Street, tel. 091/563-804). **Pucan Pub,** a smoky cauldron of music and beer drinking with an older crowd—including lots of tourists—is also worth a look (music nightly—sometimes traditional, just off Eyre Square on Forster Street, tel. 091/561-528).

Sleeping in Galway

(£1 = about $1.40, country code: 44, area code: 091)
Sleep Code: **S** = Single, **D** = Double/Twin, **T** = Triple, **Q** = Quad, **b** = bathroom, **t** = toilet only, **s** = shower only, **CC** = Credit Card (**V**isa, **M**asterCard, **A**mEx).

There are three price tiers for most beds in Galway: high season (Easter–October), off-season, and charge-what-you-like festival times (e.g., race weekends and the last three weeks in July). 've listed high-season rates. B&Bs simply play the market. If you're on a tight budget, call a few and see what the prices do. All B&Bs include a full fried breakfast.

Sleeping in Hotels

For a fancy hotel, Park House Hotel offers the best value; for a budget hotel, it's Jurys.

Park House Hotel, a plush, business-class hotel, is ideally located a block from the train station and Eyre Square. Its 57 spacious rooms come with all the comforts you'd expect (Db-£100 is the "corporate rate" you should get most of the year, ask if there's a discount, Sun night is slow and rooms can rent for Db-£85, includes breakfast, CC:VMA, good restaurant, elevator, free garage, helpful staff, Forster Street, tel. 091/564-924, fax 091/569-219, e-mail: parkhouse@eircom.net).

Jurys Galway Inn offers 128 American-style rooms in a modern hotel centrally located where the old town hits the river. Big bright rooms have two double beds and huge modern bathrooms (£61–91 per room, depending on season, whether filled by a single, a couple, 3 adults, or a family of 4, breakfast-£-6.50, elevator, lots of tour groups, parking-£5.50, CC:VMA, nonsmoking floor, Quay Street, tel. 091/566-444, fax 091/568-415, U.S. tel. 800/843-3311, www.jurys.com, e-mail: info@jurys.com).

The Skeffington Arms Hotel, which feels more Irish (and a bit smokier) than the Park House or Jurys, escapes most of the tour-group scene because it has only 24 rooms. Centrally located on Eyre Square, it's furnished in a dark wood Victorian style (Db-£80–90, CC:VMA, pub downstairs, Eyre Square, tel. 091/563-173, fax 091/561-679, e-mail: info@skeffington.ie).

Great Southern Hotel, filled with palatial Old World elegance and 116 rooms, marks the end of the Dublin–Galway train line and the beginning of Galway. Since 1845, it's been Galway's landmark hotel (Db-£165–190, some discounts during slow times, breakfast extra, CC:VMA, sauna, indoor rooftop pool, stuffy staff, at the head of Eyre Square, tel. 091/564-041, fax 091/566-704, e-mail: res@galway.gsh.ie).

Sleeping in B&Bs on College Road

Drivers, following city center signs into Galway, drive right by a string of B&Bs just after the greyhound racing stadium. These are a five-minute walk from Eyre Square (from the station, walk up Forster Street, which turns into College Road). The first two B&Bs listed are the best values. The last one is cheapest and is equally central, but it's in a different area.

College Crest Guest House is a proud establishment with 10 big, fresh rooms and a cushy lounge (Sb-£30, Db-£40–60, Tb-£70, CC:VM, nonsmoking, closest to town at 5 College Road, tel. & fax 091/564-744). Marion Fitzgerald enjoys her work and runs this place with flair, offering the best value on the street.

Petra House, a peaceful-feeling brick building, rents six great rooms, including a family room. The owners, Joan and Frank Maher, keep everything lovingly maintained (Sb-£37.50, Db-£55, CC:VMA, elegant sitting room, second door from stadium on right at 29 College Road, tel. & fax 091/566-580, e-mail: petrahouse@eircom.net).

Ardawn House is yet another classy B&B, with nine comfortable rooms (Db-£60–70, CC:VMA, College Road, next to Petra House, tel. 091/568-833, fax 091/563-454, e-mail: ardawn@iol.ie).

Balcony House B&B rents nine pleasant rooms (Db-£50–60, family deals in quads, 27 College Road, tel. & fax 091/563-438, Michael and Teresa Coyne).

Copper Beech House B&B rents seven rooms a bit cheaper than its neighbors but with no lounge, tight quarters, and an absentee owner (Db-£36–50, CC:VM, 26 College Road, tel. 091/569-544, e-mail: oceanbb@iol.ie).

Aaron House B&B rents 14 decent rooms (Sb-£20–25, Db-£45–50, CC:VM, 25 College Road, tel. & fax 091/563-315, e-mail: aaron@indigo.ie).

Lynfield House B&B rents five plain, practical rooms

(Db-£45–50, CC:VM, 9 College Road, tel. 091/567-845, e-mail: lynfield@eircom.net).

Prospect Hill Road (leaving Eyre Square from Richardson's Bar on Prospect Hill Road) is lined with small row houses, many of which do B&B. **Mrs. Bridie Flanagan's B&B** is a humble, friendly old home with a welcoming living room and four rooms—two big and two cramped (tiny D-£35, fine Db-£40, T-£45, 85 Prospect Hill, tel. 091/561-515).

Sleeping out of Town in Salthill

Carraig Beag B&B, the classiest, friendliest, and most peaceful of all, is a big brick home on a residential street a block off the beach just beyond the resort town of Salthill. Catherine Lydon, with the help of her husband Paddy, rents six big, bright, fresh, and comfy rooms with a welcoming living room and a social breakfast table (Sb-£30–38, Db-£40–50, family room-£50–65; 8-minute drive from Galway, follow the beach past Salthill, take second right after golf course on Knocknacarra Road, and go 2 blocks to 1 Burren View Heights; tel. 091/521-696). The #2 bus (80p, 3/hrly) goes from Eyre Square (picks up in front of Skeffington pub) to the Knocknacarra stop at the B&B's doorstep. Catherine can arrange for tour pickups at her place.

Sleeping in Hostels

Easygoing people of any age feel comfortable in either of these hostels, centrally located near the train station. If you want a double, book well in advance (several months in advance for weekends).

Great Western House is central, plain, cheap, and big, with 50 doubles and lots of dorm beds (270 beds, Db-£30, Qb-£12.50 per bed, dorm bed-£10, includes continental breakfast, CC:VM, lockers free with deposit, elevator, kitchen, almost entirely nonsmoking except in TV lounge, Frenchville Lane, across from train station, tel. 091/561-150, e-mail: shaungwh@iol.ie).

Kinlay House is a no-nonsense place just 100 yards from the train station, with 180 beds (1–8 beds per room) in bare, clean, and simple rooms, including 15 doubles. The lounge/reception area is enveloped in a haze of smoke, but the rooms are smoke free (Sb-£20, Db-£30, dorm bed-£10, CC:VM, includes continental breakfast, elevator, self-service kitchen, Internet access, launderette, luggage storage, on Merchants Road, just off Eyre Square, tel. 091/565-244, fax 091/565-245, e-mail: kingal@usit.ie).

Eating in Galway

Being a tourist and college town, the city is filled with colorful, inexpensive eateries. People everywhere seem to be enjoying their food. Each of these places is at the bottom of the old town within a block or two of Jurys Inn.

River God is a bistro/restaurant passionately run by Patric Juillet, who cooks fine "world French" cuisine. He slices, dices, and prices as if his bottom line is filling people with very good food (£5 lunch deals, £12 3-course dinners, Mon–Sat 12:00–22:00, closed Sun, CC:VM, reservations recommended; if you come early, nip into the great corner pub downstairs to enjoy an ancient snug and a fresh beer until your table's ready, you can bring your beer to dinner, 2 Quay Street, tel. 091/565-811).

Kirwan's Lane Creative Cuisine, considered Galway's best restaurant, is a dressy place where reservations are required (£15 lunches, £25 dinners, Mon–Sat 12:00–14:30 and dinner from 18:00, Kirwan's Lane a block from Jurys, tel. 091/568-266).

Busker Brownes has three eateries in a smoky, sprawling, pubby place popular for its good cheap food. Enter on Cross Street for the restaurant (and walk to the back for better seating) or enter on Kirwan's Lane for the ground-floor pub; upstairs from the pub is the third and smokiest section (£6 meals, daily 11:00–20:30, "Sunday morning jazz session" at 13:00, Cross Street and Kirwan's Lane, tel. 091/563-377).

The Lisheen, mentioned above as offering traditional music nightly, has good pub grub. Consider staying for the music—starts at 21:30 (5 Bridge Street, tel. 091/563-804).

McDonagh's Fish and Chips is a favorite chippie. They have a fast, cheap section and a classier restaurant. If you're determined to try Galway oysters, remember that they're in season September through April only. Other times you'll eat Pacific oysters—which doesn't make much sense to me (£4 cheap lunch, £10–15 in restaurant, Mon–Sat 12:00–23:00, Sun 17:00–23:00, nonsmoking section, 22 Quay Street, tel. 091/565-001).

The **Galway Bakery Company (GBC)** is a popular and basic place for a quick Irish meal (£3–6 meals in the ground-floor cafeteria, more pricey restaurant upstairs, Mon–Sat 8:00–21:00, Sun 9:00–21:00, CC:VMA, 9 Williamsgate Street, near Eyre Square, tel. 091/563-087).

Supermarkets: A Super Valu is in Eyre Square Shopping Centre (Mon–Sat 9:00–18:30, Thu–Fri until 21:00, closed Sun) and Dunne's is just moments away, accessed through the Eyre Square Shopping Centre or around the corner at tiny Castle Street, off the pedestrian street, Williamsgate (Mon–Sat 9:00–18:30, Thu until 21:00, Sun 12:00–18:00, supermarket in basement). Lots of smaller grocery shops are scattered throughout town.

Medieval Banquet: If you have a car, consider a **Dunguaire Medieval Castle Banquet** in Kinvarra, a 30-minute drive south of Galway (for more information, see "Kinvarra," near end of chapter). The 17:30 banquet can be done very efficiently as you're driving into or out of Galway (B&Bs are accustomed to late arrivals if you call).

Transportation Connections—Galway

By train to: Dublin (4/day, 3 hrs). For **Belfast, Limerick, Tralee,** and **Rosslare,** you'll change in or near Dublin. Train info: tel. 091/564-222.

By bus to: Ennis (5/day, 1.25 hr), **Doolin/Cliffs** (2–3/day, 1.5 hrs), **Rosslare** (2/day, 6.5 hrs), **Belfast** (5/day, 6.5 hrs, £18.50), **Dublin** (13/day, 3.5 hrs, £7 before 10:30, otherwise £9). Bus info: tel. 091/562-000. Nestor Travel and Citylink, among other companies, run cheap and fast bus services from Galway (Forster Street Bus Park) to Dublin (Tara Street Dart Station at George's Quay) and the Dublin airport (7/day, £7 and 3 hrs for Dublin, £10 and 3.5 hrs for airport, Nestor tel. 091/797-144, Citylink tel. 091/564-163).

ARAN ISLANDS

The Arans—an extension of the Burren—are made up of three limestone islands: Inishmor, Inishmaan, and Inisheer. The largest, Inishmor (eight miles by two miles), is by far the most populated, interesting, and visited. The landscape of all three islands is harsh—windswept, rocky fields divided by stone walls and steep, rugged cliffs. During the winter severe gales sweep the islands; because of this, most of the settlements on Inishmor are found on its more peaceful eastern side.

There's a stark beauty about these islands and the simple lives its inhabitants eke out of six inches of topsoil and a mean sea. Precious little of the land is productive; in the past its people made a precarious living from fishing and farming. The layers of limestone rock meant that there was little natural soil. Farming soil has been built up by the islanders—the result of centuries of layering seaweed and sand together. The fields are small, divided by several thousand miles of dry-stone wall. Most of these are built in the Aran "gap" style, where angled upright stones are filled with smaller stones. This allows a farmer who wants to move stock to dismantle and rebuild the walls easily. Nowadays tourism boosts the local economy.

The islands are a Gaeltacht area. While the islanders speak Irish among themselves, they happily speak English for their visitors. Many of them have direct or personal connections with America and will ask you if you know their cousin Paddy in Boston.

Today the 800 people of Inishmor (literally, "the big island") greet as many as 2,000 visitors a day. The vast majority of these are day-trippers. They'll hop on a minibus at the dock for a 2.5-hour tour to the Dun Aengus fort, then spend an hour or two browsing through the few shops or sitting at a picnic table outside a pub with their Guinnesses.

The other islands, Inishmaan and Inisheer, are smaller, much less populated, and less touristed. While extremely quiet, they have B&Bs, daily flights, and ferry service. For most, the big island is quiet enough.

Kilronan, on Inishmor

By far the Aran Islands' largest town, Kilronan is still just a village. Groups of backpackers wash ashore with the landing of each ferry. Minibuses, bike shops, and a few men in pony carts sop up the tourists. There are 9 or 10 shops and about as many pubs, restaurants, and B&Bs. Most of Kilronan huddles around the pier. A few blocks inland you'll find the Heritage Center, the best folk-music pubs, post office, and bank (open only on Wed, plus Thu June–Aug). The huge SPAR supermarket, two blocks inland from the harbor, seems too big for the tiny community. Several huts near the pier rent bikes (£5/day). Bring cash: Some B&Bs and other businesses don't accept credit cards. There are no ATMs on the island, and the bank is rarely open.

Tourist Information: The TI is helpful, but don't rely on them for accommodations. The only people who work with them are out of town and desperate (daily 10:00–17:00, until 19:00 June–Aug, faces the harbor, public WCs next door, tel. 099/61263).

Getting around Inishmor

Just about anything rolling functions as a taxi. A trip from Kilronan to Dun Aengus costs £2–3 in a shared minibus. Flag them down and don't hesitate to bargain. Pony carts cost about £20 for two people (£30 for 4) for a trip to the west end of the island. Biking is great though hilly (30 minutes to Dun Aengus). Bikers take the high road over and the low road back—fewer hills, scenic shoreline, and, at low tide, 50 seals sunbathing.

Sights—Inishmor

▲Aran's Heritage Center—This little museum, while nothing impressive, offers a worthwhile introduction to the island that covers the island's geology, its archeological wonders, and the traditional lifestyle (£2.50, or £4 combo ticket with movie, daily 10:00–17:00, until 19:00 June–Aug, tel. 099/61355).

Man of Aran: The 1934 movie *Man of Aran*, giving a good look at traditional island life with an all-local cast, is shown at the Heritage Center (£2.50, 1 hr, 6 shows/day in summer). The movie features currachs (canoelike boats) in a storm, fishing for sharks with hand-held harpoons, how the fields were made from bare rock, and life in the early 1900s when you couldn't rent bikes.

▲Island Minibus Tours—There couldn't be more than 100 vehicles on the island, and the majority of them seem to be minibuses. A line of buses, awaiting the arrival of each ferry, offer 2.5-hour, £5 island tours. Talk with several to find a driver who likes to talk. I learned that 800 islanders live in 14 villages, with three elementary

Inishmor Island

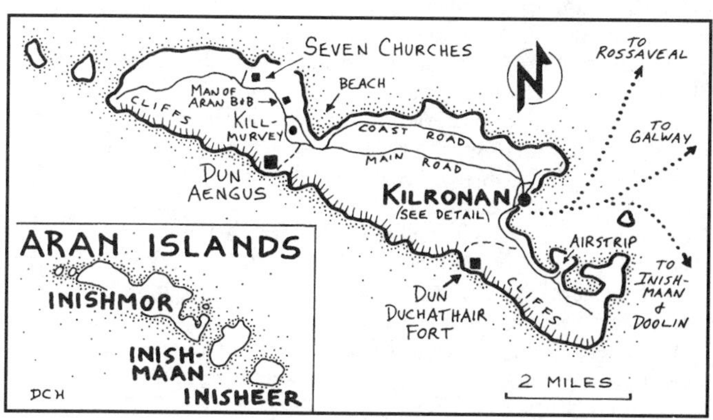

schools and three churches. Most own a small detached field where they keep a couple of cows (sheep are too much trouble). When pressured for more information, my guide explained that there are 400 different flowers and 19 different types of bees on the island. The tour, a convenient time-saver, zips you to the end of the island for a quick stroll in the desolate fields, gives you 10 minutes to wander through the historic but visually unimpressive "seven churches," and then drops you for 90 minutes at Dun Aengus (20 min to hike up, 30 min at the fort, 20 min back, 20 min in café or shops at drop-off point) before running you back to Kilronan. Ask your driver to take you back along the smaller coastal road (scenic beaches and sunbathing seals at low tide).

▲▲▲Dun Aengus—This is the island's blockbuster sight. The stone fortress hangs spectacularly and precariously on the edge of a cliff 300 feet above the Atlantic. The crashing waves seem to say, "You've come to the end of the world." Little is known about this 2,000-year-old Celtic fort. Its concentric walls are 13 feet thick and 10 feet high. As an added defense, the fort is ringed with a commotion of spiky stones sticking up like lances called a *chevaux-de-frise* (literally, "Frisian horses," named for the Frisian soldiers who used pikes like these to stop a charging cavalry). Slowly, as the cliff erodes, hunks of the fort fall into the sea. Dun Aengus (Dun Aonghasa in Gaelic) doesn't get crowded until after 11:00. I enjoyed a half hour completely alone at 10:00 in the tourist season. Be there early or late if you can (£1, daily April–Sept 10:00–18:00, Oct–March 10:00–16:00, guides at fort June–Aug answer questions and sometimes give free tours, 5.5 miles from Kilronan, tel. 099/61008). A small museum displays findings from recent digs and tells the story of the fort. Advice from rangers: Wear walking shoes and watch your kids closely; there's no fence.

Seven Churches (Na Seacht Teampaill)—Close to the western tip of the island, this gathering of ruined chapels, monastic houses, and fragments of a high cross dates from the 8th to 11th centuries. The island is dotted with early Christian reminders that, in the fifth century, Christianity was brought to the islands by St. Enda, who established a monastery on the island. Many great monks studied under Enda. Among these "Irish apostles," who started Ireland's "Age of Saints and Scholars" (A.D. 500–900), was Columba, the founder of the monastery of Iona in Scotland.

Kilmurvey—The island's second village sits below Dun Aengus. With a gaggle of homes, a laid-back hostel (listed below), a B&B, a great sheltered beach, and a pub, this is the place for solitude (except for the folk music in the pub).

Pub Music—Several pubs in Kilronan offer live music nearly nightly in summer. Off-season you're likely to find music on Wednesday, Friday, and Saturday evenings. Joe Watty's Pub, just past the post office, has reliably good Irish folk music. Tigh Fitz, on the airport road, has folk music and dancing on Friday, Saturday, and Sunday.

Other pubs offer Irish tunes but with musical detours beyond the tin whistle. The town hall (Halla Ronain) becomes a dance hall on most Saturday and Sunday nights, when from midnight to 02:00 locals have a *ceilidh* (kay-lee), the Irish equivalent of a hoedown.

Sleeping in Kilronan, Inishmor

(£1 = about $1.40, country code: 353, area code: 099, mail: Kilronan, Aran Islands)

Remember, this is a poor island. Most rooms are plain with sparse plumbing. Few places take credit cards.

The Pier House stands solidly a hundred yards beyond the pier offering 13 decent rooms, a cozy sitting room with a fireplace, a dramatic setting, and sea views from most of its rooms (Db-£50, CC:VM, tel. 099/61417, fax 099/61122).

Clai Ban, about the only really cheery place in town, is worth the 10-minute walk from the pier (D-£32, Db-£36, walk past the bank out of town and down a lane on the left, tel. 099/61111, fax 099/61423, Marion Hernon).

St. Brendan's B&B, hiding a cozy living room behind ivy-covered walls and a wind-blown garden, rents eight rooms (D-£30, Db-£34, about £2 less per person off-season, save £2 if you take a continental breakfast, tel. 099/61149).

Bayview House, the biggest place in town overlooking the harbor, rents eight simple, pleasant rooms in need of fresh paint (D-£38, Db-£42 in July–Aug, less otherwise, CC:VM, café, most rooms have views, a minute uphill from TI, tel. 099/61260, www.inismor.com).

Kilronan

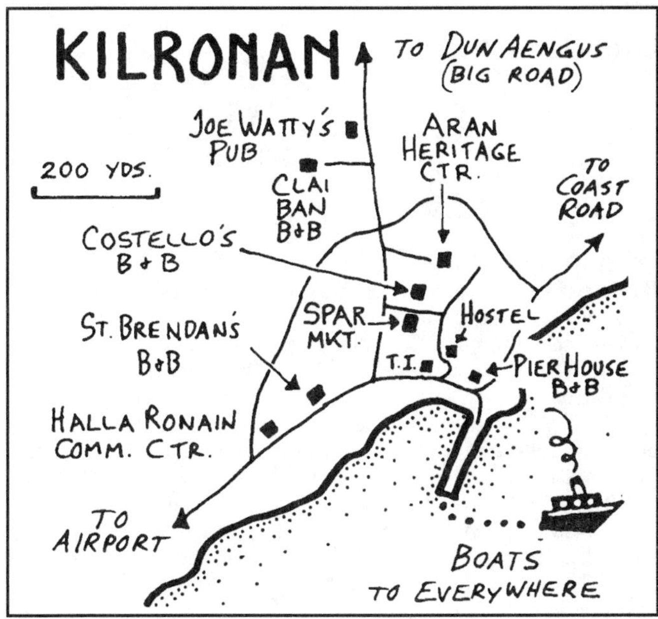

Costello's B&B has four plain rooms in a plain home in a fine garden setting (D-£30, Db-£36, with your back to Spar's entrance, take little alley at 1:00—ahead slightly to right—to last house, tel. 099/61241, Sally Costello).

Kilronan Hostel, overlooking the harbor above TI and the Joe Mac Pub, is cheap but noisy (£9 beds, 4- to 6-bed rooms, includes breakfast, self-service kitchen, laundry service, tel. 099/61255).

Dun Aengus Hostel is for those who really want to get away from things. It's located near Dun Aengus in Kilmurvey (5 miles from Kilronan) and is surrounded by birds, stone walls, and vast views. It's also near a pub (with good music), a restaurant, and a fine beach (£10 per bed in 2- and 8-bed rooms, communal kitchen, small shop, sometimes a free pickup upon arrival if you call, tel. 099/61318).

While Kilronan is getting pretty touristy, you can get out in to the Aran countryside and find true peace. The **Man of Aran B&B** is as classy as a thatched cottage can be. Rooms are quiet and rustic and have fireplaces. The restaurant uses all organic, homegrown vegetables and herbs (£17 meals), and the setting is pristine (this is where the movie was filmed, D-£40, Db-£50,

CC:VM, reserve well in advance, 100 yards past Dun Aengus turnoff, 4 miles out of Kilronan, tel. & fax 099/61301).

Eating in Kilronan

Kilronan's cafés dish up soup, soda bread, sandwiches, and tea. **Joe Watty's Bar** does hot pub lunches. **Sein Ceibh** is popular for its take-away fish and chips. **Aran Fisherman** does a good dinner (daily 10:00–16:00 for lunch, 16:00–22:00 for dinner, CC:VM, tel. 099/61363). The SPAR **supermarket** has all the groceries you'll need (Mon–Sat 9:00–20:00, Sun 10:00–17:00).

Transportation Connections—Aran Islands

By ferry from Rossaveal: Island Ferries sails to Inishmor from Rossaveal, a port 20 miles west of Galway (3/day April–Oct, 2/day Nov–March, 40-minute crossing, but if you're coming from Galway, allow 2 hours one-way including 45-minute bus ride, £15 round-trip boat crossing plus £4 round-trip for Galway–Rossaveal shuttle bus, CC:VM). Shuttle buses depart from Galway 75 minutes before the boat sails and return to Galway immediately after each boat arrives. Schedule for April–Oct: from Rossaveal at 10:30, 13:30, and 18:30; from Inishmor at 9:00, 12:00, and 17:00 (plus 19:30 in summer, WCs on board). Island Ferries has two offices, one at the Galway TI and the other in a little alley across from Kinlay House on Merchant Street (tel. 091/568-903). Boats go in anything less than a gale (only a couple departures a year are canceled). Don't worry about seat availability; buses and boats are added as needed. For drivers, there's a £2 car park at the dock.

By ferry from Doolin: This ferry is handy if you're in Doolin, but it's notorious for being canceled because of wind or tides (for specifics, see "Doolin," below).

By plane: Aer Arann, a friendly and flexible little airline, flies four planes a day and stops at all three islands (£35 round-trip, groups of 4 or more: £29 each, CC:VM, 10-minute flight); these flights get booked up—reserve a day or two in advance with a credit card. Their nine-seat planes take off from the Connemara Regional Airport, 20 miles west of Galway (not the Galway airport). A minibus shuttle—£5 round-trip—runs from Galway an hour before each flight. The Kilronan airport is small (baggage is transported from the plane to the "gate" in a shopping cart). A minibus shuttle to and from Kilronan costs £2 round-trip (2 miles from the airport). For reservations and late seat availability, tel. 091/593-034, fax 091/593-238. Ask for a 10 percent discount—they have lots of coupons out.

COUNTY CLARE AND THE BURREN

Those connecting Dingle in the south with Galway, the urban center of the west, can entertain themselves along the way by skipping through the fascinating landscape and tidy villages of County Clare. Ennis, the major city of the county, with a medieval history and a market bustle, is a workaday Irish town ideal for anyone tired of the tourist crowds. The Cliffs of Moher, a series of dramatic cliffs overlooking the Atlantic, offer tenderfeet a thrilling hike. The Burren is a unique, windblown, limestone wasteland that hides an abundance of flora, fauna, caves, and history. For your evening entertainment you can join a tour bus in a castle for a medieval banquet at Kinvarra or join traditional Irish music enthusiasts from around Europe at tin-whistling Doolin.

Planning Your Time

By train and bus, your gateway to this region is Ennis on the south and Galway from the north. By car the region can be an enjoyable daylong drive-through or a destination in itself. None of the sights has to take much time. But do get out and hike a bit.

If driving between Dingle/Tralee in the south and Galway/Aran Islands in the north, here's a day I'd prefer to the fast road via Limerick: north from Tralee to catch the Tarbert–Killimer car ferry (avoiding the 80-mile drive around the Shannon estuary, see "Route Tips" at the end of Dingle chapter), then drive the scenic coastal route to the Cliffs of Moher for an hour break. The scenic drive through the Burren, with a couple of stops and a tour of the caves, takes about two hours. There's a 17:30 medieval banquet at the Dunguaire Castle near Kinvarra (just 30 minutes south of Galway).

Skip the Bunratty Castle and Folk Museum. I'd leave this most commercial and least lively of all European open-air folk museums to the jet-laggy big bus American tour groups (located just a potty stop from the Shannon Airport past Limerick on the road to Ennis).

Cliffs of Moher

A visit to the Cliffs of Moher, worth ▲▲▲, is one of Ireland's great natural thrills. For five miles the dramatic cliffs soar as high as 700 feet above the Atlantic. Drivers park at the Visitors Centre (£1.50; TI office—daily at least 9:30–17:30, until 20:30 July–Aug; shop, cafeteria; 3 public buses stop here daily in summer; tel. 065/708-1171). From the center, walk 200 yards past harpists and accordion players along a low wall of the local Liscannor slate (notice the squiggles made by worms, eels, and snails a few years ago when the slate was still mud on the sea floor) to the cliff edge. O'Brien's Tower (1853) marks the highest point (£1).

For the best thrill, read the warning, consider the risk, then step over the slate barrier and down onto the stone platform. Here there are no crowds. If you're a risk-taking fool, gingerly belly out to peek over the ledge. You'll find yourself in a dramatic world

The Burren

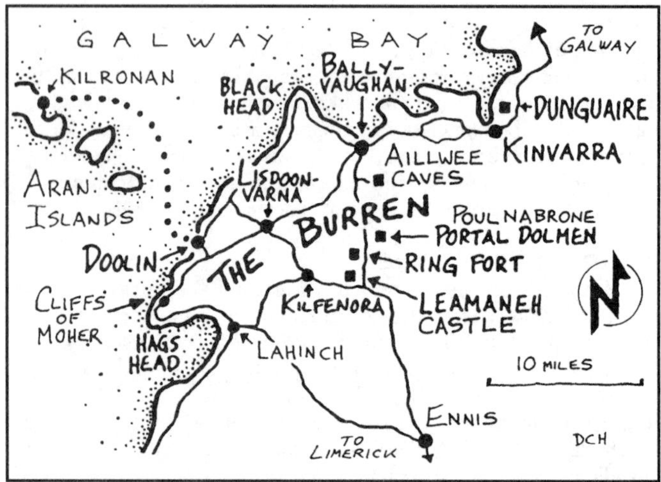

where the only sounds are the waves, the wind, the gulls, and your stomach signaling frantically for help. There's a particularly peaceful corner of the platform over on the far right. On the far left, watch the birds play in the updrafts. In the distance, on windy days, the Aran Islands can be seen wearing their white necklace.

Doolin

This town is a strange phenomenon. Tourists go directly from Paris or Munich to Doolin. It's on the touristic map for its three pubs that feature Irish folk music nightly. A few years ago, this was a mecca. Irish musicians came together here to jam before a few lucky aficionados. But now the crowds and the foreigners are overwhelming the musicians, and the quality of music is not as reliable. Still, Irish as well as European music lovers crowd the pubs, and the bodhran beat goes on. The Michael Russell Heritage Center, which just opened last year, may eventually become a museum of traditional music. As for now, some dances (ceilidh) are held here. Ask at a pub if anything's scheduled.

Doolin has plenty of accommodations, several good restaurants, and a Greek island-without-the-sun ambience. Each pub serves decent dinners before the music starts. The "town" is just a few homes and shops strung out along a valley road from the tiny harbor. Nearest the harbor, the Lower Village (Fisherstreet) has **O'Connor's Pub** (tel. 065/707-4168) and is the closest thing to a commercial center. A mile farther up the road, the Upper Village (Roadford) straddles a bridge with the other two destination pubs,

McGann's (tel. 065/707-4133) and **McDermott's** (tel. 065/707-4328). Music starts around 21:30 and finishes around midnight. On my last trip I hit Doolin on a mediocre music night. The craic is fine regardless.

From Doolin you can hike or bike (rentals in town) up the Burren Way for three miles to the Cliffs of Moher. (Get advice locally on the trail condition and safety.)

Ferries: The boats from Doolin to the Aran Islands can be handy but are often canceled. Even a balmy day can be too windy (or the tide can be too low) to allow for a sailing from Doolin's crude little port. If you are traveling by car and have time limits, don't risk sailing from Doolin. Without a car you can travel on from the Aran Islands by the bigger boats, so Doolin might work for you (£20 return, l/day, 60 min, leaving at 10:00 or 11:00, depending on season, returning at 16:00, CC:VM, tel. 065/707-4455 to see what's sailing).

Sleeping in Doolin (area code: 065): Harbour View B&B is a fine modern house a mile from the Doolin fiddles overlooking the valley. Mrs. Cullinan keeps the guests' living room stocked with touring books and games (4 rooms, Sb-£25.50, Db-£38, Tb-£51, larger family room deals, classy breakfast, CC:VM, on the main road halfway between Lisdoonvarna and the Cliffs of Moher next to the Statoil gas station, tel. 065/707-4154, fax 065/707-4935, e-mail: kathlen@eircom.net). **Doolin Hostel,** right in Doolin's Lower Village, caters creatively to all the needs of backpackers there for the music (dorm bed-£8, Db-£21, Qb-£36, bed in Qb-£9, Lower Village, tel. 065/707-4006, fax 065/707-4421, www.kingsway.ie/doolinhostel, e-mail: doolinhostel@eircom.net).

Lisdoonvarna

This town of 1,000 was known for centuries for its spa and its matchmakers. Today, except for a couple of September weeks during its Matchmaking Festival, it's pretty sleepy. (The bank is open one day a week.) Still, it's more of a town than Doolin and, apart from festival time, less touristy. Lisdoonvarna has reliably good traditional music in its pubs. I'd stay here rather than in Doolin and commute.

Sleeping in Lisdoonvarna (area code: 065): Each of these three places is on the main "Galway" road near the center square and church. **Marchmont B&B** rents two large twin/family rooms and two small doubles in a fine old house (Db-£36–38, just past post office, tel. 065/707-4050, Eileen Barrett). **Banner County Lodge** (S-£15, D/Db-£32, tel. 065/707-4340) and **St. Genevieve's B&B** (D-£26–30, Db-£30–34, T-£36, CC:VM, open May–Sept only, tel. 065/707-4074) are closer to the square but bigger, scruffier, and less personal.

The Burren

Literally, the "rocky place," the Burren is just that. The 50-square-mile limestone plateau, a ▲▲ sight, is so barren a disappointed Cromwell surveyor described it as "a savage land, yielding neither water enough to drown a man, nor a tree to hang him, nor soil enough to bury him." But he wasn't much of a botanist, because the Burren is a unique ecosystem, with flora that has changed little since the last Ice Age 10,000 years ago. It's also rich in prehistoric and early Christian sights. The first human inhabitants of the Burren came about 6,000 years ago. Today this "Limestone Land" is littered with more than 2,000 historic sites, including about 500 Iron Age stone forts.

Botany of the Burren in Brief: The Burren is a story of water, rock, geological force, and time. It supports the greatest diversity of plants in Ireland. Like nowhere else, Mediterranean and Arctic wildflowers bloom side by side in the Burren. It's an orgy of cross-pollination that attracts more insects than Doolin does music lovers—even beetles help out. Limestone, created from layers of sea mud, is the basis of the Burren. (This same basic slab resurfaces 10 miles or so out to sea to form the Aran Islands.) The earth's crust heaved it up. The glaciers swept it bare—dropping boulders as they receded. Rain slowly drilled potholes into the surface. Rainwater cut through weak parts in the limestone, leaving crevices on the surface and Europe's most extensive system of caves below. These puddles grew algae, which dried into a powder. That, combined with bug parts and rabbit turds (Irish hares abound in the Burren), creates a very special soil. Plants and flowers fill the cracks in the limestone. Grasses and shrubs don't do well here, and wild goats eat down any trees that try to grow, giving tender little flowers a chance to enjoy the sun. Different flowers appear in different months, sharing space rather than competing. The flowers are best in June and July.

Sightseeing the Burren: The drive from Kilfenora to Ballyvaughan offers the best quick swing through the historic Burren.

Kilfenora (5 miles southeast of Lisdoonvarna) is a good starting point. Its humble but hardworking community-run Burren Centre gives a quick tour of its one-room museum followed by an intense 18-minute video explaining the geology and botany of the region (£2.50, daily March–May and Oct 10:00–17:00, June–Sept 9:30–18:00, closed Nov–Feb, tel. 065/708-8030). You'll see copies of a fine eighth-century golden collar and ninth-century silver brooch (now in Dublin's National Museum). The ruined church next door has a couple of 12th-century crosses but isn't much to see. Mass is still held in the church, which claims the Pope as its bishop. (In the 16th century, when the Anglican English were taking over Ireland, the Pope defended the town as best he could—

by personally declaring himself its bishop.) For lunch in Kilfenora consider the cheap and cheery Burren Centre lunchroom or the more atmospheric Vaughan's Pub (tel. 065/708-8004).

At **Leamaneh Castle,** a ruined shell of a fortified 17th-century house not open to anyone these days, turn north on R480 (direction: Ballyvaughan). After about five miles you'll hit the start of the real barren Burren and see a stone table a few hundred yards off the road (to the east, toward an ugly gray metal barn building).

This is the **Portal Dolmen** (also called the Poulnabrone Dolmen—a stone table). Two hundred years ago, locals called this a "druid's altar." Four thousand years ago it was a grave. Wander over for a look. (It's crowded in midday with tour buses, but it's all yours early or late.)

Be a geologist. Wander for some quiet time with the wildflowers. You're walking across a former seabed. Look for fossils: white smudges were coral. Scratches on rocks were ground by other rocks in a retreating glacier. The boulder debris was left by the glaciers. V-shaped valleys were carved by glacial runoff.

The **Cahercommann ring fort** (one of 500 or so in the area) can be seen on the crest of a hill just off the road about a half mile south of the Portal Dolmen. (You can park at the intersection and walk up the gray farm's driveway and through the gate marked "stone fort" for a look, but there's little to see.) The stretch from Portal Dolmen north to Ballyvaughan offers the starkest scenery.

The **Aillwee Caves** are touted as "Ireland's premier showcave." I couldn't resist a look. While fairly touristy and not worth the time or money if you've seen a lot of caves, they offer your easiest look at the massive system of caves that underlie the Burren. Your guide walks you 300 yards into the plain but impressive cave, giving a serious 30-minute geology lesson. During the Ice Age underground rivers carved countless caves like these. Brown bears, which became extinct a thousand years ago in Ireland, found this cave great for hibernating. But at a constant 50 degrees, I needed my sweater (£5, £14 family deal, open early March–early Nov at 10:00, last tour at 18:30 July–Aug, otherwise 17:30, Dec–Feb call ahead for limited tours, clearly signposted just south of Ballyvaughan, tel. 065/707-7036).

In Ballyvaughan, **Burren Exposure** is your best first stop if you're entering the Burren from Galway. In a modern little building overlooking Galway Bay at the edge of the bleakness, its excellent three-part audiovisual presentation tells the geological, human, and floral story of this unique chunk of Ireland (£3.50, shows start every 12 minutes, April–Oct 10:00–17:30, closed in winter, plush sea-view cafeteria, tel. 065/707-7277, fax 065/707-7278).

Kinvarra

This 10-pub town, between Ballyvaughan and Galway (half an hour from each), is waiting for something to happen in its minuscule harbor. It faces the Dunguaire Castle, a four-story tower house from 1520 standing a few yards out in the bay. (For B&Bs, see "Sleeping," below.)

The **Dunguaire Medieval Castle Banquet** is Kinvarra's most tourist-worthy sight. The 500-year-old Dunguaire Castle hosts a touristy but fun medieval banquet (£30, May–Oct almost nightly at 17:30 and 20:30, CC:VM, reservations tel. 061/360-788, castle tel. 091/637-108). The evening is as intimate as 55 tourists gathered under one time-stained barrel vault can be. You get a decent four-course meal with wine (or mead if you ask sweetly) served amid an entertaining evening of Irish tales and folk songs. Remember that in medieval times it was considered polite to flirt with wenches. It's a small and multitalented cast: one harpist and three singer/actors who serve the "lords and ladies" between tunes. The 40-minute medieval stage show that comes with dessert is the highlight (but the Ruthin banquet in North Wales is better).

Sleeping in Kinvarra (area code: 091): Cois Cuain B&B is a small but stately house with a garden overlooking the square and harbor of the most charming village setting you'll find. Mary Walsh rents three superhomey rooms for nonsmokers (Db-£40, The Harbour, tel. & fax 091/637-119).

Ennis

This bustling market town, the main town of County Clare (pop: 25,000), provides those relying on public transit with a handy transportation hub (good connections to Limerick, Dublin, and Galway; see "Transportation Connections," below) and a chance to wander around a workaday Irish town that is not reliant upon the tourist dollar (though not shunning it either). The new TI is just off O'Connell Street Square (Mon–Fri 9:30–17:30, closed for lunch 13:00–14:00, tel. 065/682-8366) in a large building that will also house the county museum.

The Franciscan monks arrived here in the 13th century. The town grew up around their friary. The Ennis Friary, from 1300, with some fine limestone carvings in its ruined walls, is worth a look (£1, sometimes includes tour, May–Sept daily 9:30–18:30, closed off-season, tel. 065/682-9100). Ask the guide to fully explain the crucifixion symbolism in the 15th-century *Ecce Homo* carving.

The town has its history, but apart from the friary, it's best simply wandered through. If you spend the night (see "Sleeping," below), you'll find live traditional music in the pubs. The tops is Cruise's, on Abbey Street, with music nightly year-round and good food (bar cheaper than restaurant, tel. 065/684-1800).

Other pubs offering traditional music are Quinn's on Lower Market Street (Sat year-round, tel. 065/682-8148), the rough-and-tumble Kelly's on Carmody Street (Sat–Sun in summer, Sat in winter, at intersection with Dumbiggle Road, tel. 065/628-8155), and May Kearney's, across the bridge from the Friary (Thu, Fri, Sun, 100 yards up Newbridge Road, tel.065/682-4888). The Old Ground Hotel hosts live music year-round at its pub (Thu–Sun, open to anyone); though tour groups stay at the hotel, the pub is low-key and feels like a pub, not a stage act. For an easy pub-free place for dinner, try the simple Numero Uno Pizzeria, on Old Barrack Street off Market Place. The White Knights self-service laundrette is also on Old Barrack Street.

Sleeping in Ennis (area code: 065): These three places, all with parking, are on Station Road, clustered a block or two toward the town center from the train/bus station. **Greenlea B&B** is a charming little place with three spacious and comfy rooms run by Mary Conway (S-£16, D-£30, £1.50 less per person with a continental breakfast instead of a full fry, Station Road, tel. 065/682-9049). **Grey Gables B&B,** just across the street, is a bit more upscale and has nine rooms (2 small D-£34, 7 large Db-£38, 2 with kitchenettes, Station Road, tel. 065/682-4487, e-mail: marykeane@eircom.net, Mary Keane). **Rockfield B&B,** a bit nearer to town on Station Road, has four decent, simple rooms (S-£18, Db-£36, tel. 065/682-4749, Pauline O'Driscoll).

For fancier places (that you'll share with tour groups), try the stately, ivy-covered, 18th-century **Old Ground Hotel,** which has a family feel (85 rooms, Sb-£70–90, Db-£88–115, suite-£110–140, rates vary with season, 2-night weekend stays include a dinner, CC:VM, at intersection of Station Road and O'Connell Street, a few blocks from station, tel. 065/682-8127, fax 065/682-8112, e-mail: oghotel@iol.ie) or the modern, less personal **Temple Gate Hotel** (Db-from £95, CC:VMA, nonsmoking floor, O'Connell Street Square, in courtyard with TI, tel. 065/682-3300, fax 065/682-3322, e-mail: templegh@iol.ie).

Transportation Connections—Ennis

By train to: Limerick (6/day, 40 min), **Dublin** (7/day, 3 hrs). Train info: tel. 065/684-0444.

By bus to: Galway (6/day, 1 hr), **Dublin** (5/day, 4 hrs), **Rosslare** (7/day, 5 hrs), **Limerick** (5/day, 70 min), **Doolin/Lisdoonvarna** (2–4/day, 1 hr/1.5 hrs), **Tralee** (6/day, 3 hrs). Bus info: tel. 065/682-4177.

By car: For ideas on driving from Galway to Portrush in Northern Ireland, see the Antrim Coast chapter.

NORTHERN IRELAND

Ireland was once part of Great Britain—a colony made more distant from London than its Celtic cousins not so much by the Irish Sea as by its Catholicism. Protestant settlers from England and Scotland were "planted" in Ireland to help assimilate the island into the British economy. These "Scotch-Irish" established their own cultural toehold on the island, but the Catholic Irish held strong to their culture.

Over the centuries, British rule was never easy. But in the beginning of the 1900s the sparse Protestant population could no longer control the entire island. Ireland won its independence, but the northern six counties (the only ones with a Protestant majority) voted to stay with Britain.

With 94 percent of the Republic of Ireland Catholic and only 6 percent Protestant, there was no question who was dominant. But in the North, the Catholic minority was a sizable 35 percent that demanded attention. Discrimination was considered necessary to maintain the Protestant status quo in the North, and this led to "The Troubles" that have filled headlines since the late 1960s.

It is not a fight over Catholic and Protestant religious differences. It's whether Ireland will be free or part of Britain. And the indigenous Irish, who generally want a united and independent Ireland, happen to be Catholic.

When Ireland won its independence (a 1921 treaty gave it dominion status within the British Commonwealth—like Canada), the issue of unity with the North had to be dealt with. It was uncertain what the final arrangement would be. In the North the long-established Orange Order and the newly mobilized Ulster Volunteer Force (UVF) worked to defend the union with Britain. The UVF became the military muscle of the Unionists. This would be countered on the Catholic side by the Irish Republican Army (IRA). With the Republic's neutrality and the North's enthusiastic support of the Allied cause in World War II, Ulster won a spot close to London's heart. After World War II the split seemed permanent, and Britain invested heavily in Northern Ireland to bring it solidly into the United Kingdom fold.

With the Civil Rights movement of the 1960s, Irish rights needed to be addressed. Extremists polarized issues, and demonstrations became violent. As Protestants and Catholics clashed in 1969, the British Army entered the fray. They've been there ever since. In 1972, a watershed year, combatants moved from petrol bombs to guns. A new, more violent IRA emerged. In the most recent 25-year chapter in the struggle for an independent and united Ireland, more than 3,000 people have been killed.

A 1985 agreement granted Dublin a consulting role in the Northern Ireland government. Unionists bucked this, and violence escalated. In that same year, the Belfast City Hall draped a huge and defiant banner under its dome proclaiming "Belfast Says No."

In 1994 the banner came down. In the 1990s, with Ireland's membership in the European Union, the growth of its economy, and the weakening of the Catholic Church's influence, the consequences of a united Ireland were less threatening to the people of the north.

In 1994 the IRA declared a cease-fire. The Protestants followed suit. Talks are still underway. The Republicans want British troops out of Ireland and political prisoners released. The Unionists want the IRA to turn in its arms and figure their prisoners are terrorists and jail is where they belong. Optimists hail the signing of the Good Friday Accord in 1998. Major hurdles to a solid peace persist, but the downtown checkpoints are history, "bomb damage clearance sales" are over, and more tourists than ever are venturing to Belfast.

Terminology

Ulster consists of nine counties in the northern part of the island of Ireland. Six of those make up Northern Ireland (three counties remain part of the Republic). **Unionists** want the North to remain with Britain. **Republicans** (and **Nationalists**) want a united and independent Ireland ruled by Dublin. **Sinn Fein** is the political wing of the **Irish Republican Army** (IRA). In 1996 Sinn Fein (whose leader is Gerry Adams) got its best election ever, with 15 percent of the vote in Northern Ireland. Orange, and the red, white, and blue of the Union Jack, are the favored colors of the Unionists. Green is the color of the Republicans.

Northern Ireland Is a Different Country

When you leave the Republic of Ireland and enter Northern Ireland, you are crossing an international border. You change money, stamps, phone cards—and your Eurailpass is no longer valid. The Irish punt (while worth nearly 1 British pound sterling) must be changed. Northern Ireland issues its own Ulster pound and also uses English pounds. Like the Scottish pound, Ulster pounds are interchangeable with English pounds. But it's best to change your Ulster pounds into English ones before returning to England (free at any bank in either region).

Safety

Tourists in Northern Ireland are no longer considered courageous (or reckless). Traveling there is as safe as traveling in England. You really have to look for trouble to find it here. Just don't seek out spit-and-sawdust pubs in working-class Protestant neighborhoods and sing Catholic songs. Tourists would notice the tension mainly during the marches. July 12 is Orange Day, when Protestants parade and flex in favor of remaining separate from the Republic of Ireland. For Catholics, it's August 16. Lie low if you stumble onto any big green or orange parades.

BELFAST

Seventeenth-century Belfast was only a village. With the influx, or "plantation," of Scottish and English settlers, Belfast boomed, spurred by the success of the local linen, rope-making, and shipbuilding industries. The Industrial Revolution took root with a vengeance. While the rest of Ireland remained rural and agricultural, Belfast earned its nickname, "Old Smoke," when many of the brick buildings you'll see today were built. The year 1888 marked the birth of modern Belfast. After Queen Victoria granted city status to this boomtown of 300,000, its citizens built the city's centerpiece, City Hall.

Belfast is the birthplace of the *Titanic* (and many ships that didn't sink). The two huge, mustard-colored cranes (the biggest in the world, nicknamed Samson and Goliath) rise like skyscrapers above the harbor as a reminder of this town's shipbuilding might.

It feels like a new morning in Belfast. It's hard to believe that the bright and bustling pedestrian zone was once a subdued, traffic-free security zone. Now there's no hint of security checks, once a tiresome daily routine. On my last visit, the children dancing in the street were both Catholics and Protestants. They were part of a community summer-camp program giving kids from both communities reason to live together rather than apart.

Still, it's a fragile peace and a tenuous hope. Mean-spirited wall murals, hateful bonfires built a month before they're actually burned, and pubs with security gates are reminders that the island is split and about a million Protestants prefer it that way.

Planning Your Time

Big Belfast is thin on sights. For most, a day of sightseeing is plenty.

Day trip from Dublin: With the handy two-hour Dublin–

Belfast train (and its cheap £19 day-return tickets, £29 on Fri or Sun) you could make Belfast a day trip: 7:40-Catch the early morning train from Dublin; 10:30-City Hall tour, browse the pedestrian zone, lunch, ride a shared cab up Falls Road; 15:00-Visit Ulster Museum or side-trip to the Ulster Folk and Transport Museum; Evening-Return to Dublin (last train Mon–Sat at 20:10, Sun at 18:15). Confirm train times at local stations. Note that on Saturday, there's a morning market (at St. George's), a town walk offered by the TI (at 14:00), and only one City Hall tour (at 14:30).

Staying overnight: Belfast makes a pleasant overnight stop, with plenty of cheap hostels, reasonable B&Bs, hotel deals (on Fri, Sat, and Sun), and a resort neighborhood 30 minutes away in Bangor with B&Bs.

Two days in Belfast: Splice in the Living History bus tour, Ulster Museum, and Botanic Gardens, or take a day-trip tour to the Antrim Coast.

Two days in small-town Northern Ireland: From Dublin (via Belfast), take the train to Portrush for two nights and a day to tour the Causeway Coast (castle, whiskey, Giant's Causeway, resort fun), then follow the Belfast-in-a-day plan above.

Coming from Scotland: With good ferry connections (from Stranraer and Troon, both in Scotland, details in "Transportation Connections," below), it's easy to begin your exploration of the Irish isle in Belfast, then head south to Dublin and the Republic.

Orientation (area code: 028)

For the first-time visitor in Belfast for a quick look, the town is pretty simple. There are three zones of interest: central (Donegall Square/City Hall/pedestrian shopping/TI), southern (Ulster Museum/Botanic Gardens/university), and western (working-class sectarian neighborhoods east of the freeway). Belfast's "Golden Mile"—stretching from Hotel Europa to the university district—connects the central and southern zones with many of the best dinner and entertainment spots.

Tourist Information: This modern TI has fine free city maps and an enjoyable bookshop (Mon–Sat 9:00–19:00, Sun 12:00–16:00; Sept–May closes at 17:15 and Sun; north edge of city center at 59 North Street—may relocate in 2001 near City Hall, tel. 028/9024-6609, www.gotobelfast.com). For the latest on evening fun, get *The List* free at the TI or *That's Entertainment* at newsstands (50p).

Arrival in Belfast: Arriving by fast train, you'll go direct to Central Station (with ATMs and free city maps at ticket counter). From the station, a free Centerlink bus loops to Donegall Square, stops near Shaftesbury Square (recommended hostels), the bus station (recommended hotels), and stops near the TI (free with any train or bus ticket, 4/hrly, never on Sun, during morning rush hour bus runs only between station and Donegall Square).

Slower trains arc through Belfast, stopping at several downtown stations, including Central Station, Great Victoria Station (most central, near Donegall Square and most hotels), Botanic (close to the university, Botanic Gardens, and some recommended hostels), and Adelaide (near several recommended B&Bs). It's easy and cheap to connect stations by train (75p).

Helpful Hints

U.S. Consulate: On Queen Street, north of intersection with College Street (Mon–Fri 13:00–16:00, tel. 028/9032-8239).

Phone Tips: To call the Republic of Ireland from Northern Ireland, dial 00-353-area code and local number. To call Northern Ireland from the Republic of Ireland, dial 048, then the local eight-digit number.

Irish Tourist Board: Traveling on to Ireland, are ye? If it's information you'll be wanting, drop by (Mon–Fri 9:00–17:00, plus Sat 9:00–12:30 May–Sept, Castle Street, off Donegall Place, tel. 028/9032-7888).

Post Office: The main P.O., with lots of fun postcards, is at the intersection of Castle Place and Donegall Place (2 long blocks north of Donegall Square, Mon–Sat 9:00–17:30).

Internet Access: Revelations Internet Café is at 27 Shaftsbury Square, near the City Hostel (£5/hr, Mon–Fri 10:00–22:00, Sat 10:00–18:00, Sun 11:00–19:00, tel. 028/9032-0337).

Laundry: The Laundry Room is at 37 Botanic Avenue (£4.40-self-serve, £6-drop-off, Mon–Fri 8:00–21:00, Sat 8:00–18:00, Sun 12:00–18:00). For the B&B neighborhood south of town, the closest is Cleanerette (£5 drop-off, Mon–Fri 8:30–18:00, Sat 9:00–17:00, 160 Lisburne Road, at intersection with Eglantine Avenue, tel. 028/9038-1297).

Bike Rental: McConvey Cycles is at 10 Pottingers Entry, off High Street near Lagan Lookout (£7/24 hrs, Mon–Sat 9:00–17:30, CC:VM, tel. 028/9049-1163).

Market: On Saturday morning, St. George's Market is a commotion of clothes, produce, and seafood (at corner of Oxford and East Bridge Streets, 5 blocks east of Donegall Square).

Getting around Belfast

If you line up your sightseeing logically, you can do most of the town on foot.

By Bus: Handy buses go from Donegall Square East to Malone Road and recommended B&Bs (#70 and #71, 3/hrly, 95p, all-day £2.60 pass).

By Taxi: Taxis are reasonable and should be considered. Rather than use their meters, many cabs charge a flat £3 rate for any ride up to two miles. It's £1 per mile after that. Ride a shared cab if you're going up Falls Road (explained below).

Tours of Belfast

▲**Walking Tour**—Offered Saturdays at 14:00, a Town Walk takes you through the historic core of town (£4, 90 min, departs from TI, sometimes more tours added—check with TI, tel. 028/9024-6609).

▲**Big Bus Tours**—Citybus offers two different bus tours: Their "Belfast: A Living History" tour offers the best introduction to the city's recent and complicated political and social history. You'll cruise the Catholic and Protestant working-class neighborhoods with a commentary explaining the political murals and places of interest—mostly dealing with "The Troubles" of the last 25 years. You see things from the bus and get out only for a tea break (Thu and Sun at 13:00, 2.5 hrs). Their "City Tour," free of politics and religion, takes you on a 40-mile loop of Belfast's sights, with stops at the Parliament and Zoo, and a guide to point out the difference (Wed and Sat at 13:00, 3.5 hrs). Both tours depart from Castle Place (2 blocks north of Donegall Square) and cost £8.50 apiece (pay driver or book by phone to use CC, tel. 028/9045-8484).

Minibus Tours: Rodney's Tours leave from Belfast International City Hostel daily at 10:30 and 14:00 to cover the troubled areas in more depth, with time for photo stops (£7.50, 2 hrs, book in advance, tel. 028/9032-4733). Rodney also offers a variety of minibus tours, including the Antrim Coast (£16, rope bridge, Giant's Causeway, Bushmills Distillery—admission of £3.50 not included—and Dunluce Castle, April–Oct daily 9:30–17:45 depending on demand, book through and depart from hostel, tel. 028/9032-4733). Rodney also works as a private guide (tel. 028/9086-3976, cellular 0783-667-6258, www.minicoachni.co.uk). Or consider **Alternative Tours** (£7.50, 2 hrs with "walkabouts," will pick up on request, tel. 028/9061-1738 or cellular 0787-926-8153, e-mail: alternative_tours@hotmail.com).

Catholic and Protestant Neighborhoods

It will be a happy day when the sectarian neighborhoods of Belfast have nothing to be sectarian about. For a look at a couple of the original home bases of the "The Troubles," explore the working-class neighborhoods of the Catholics' Falls Road and the Protestants' Shankhill Road and Sandy Row.

▲▲**Falls Road**—At the end of Castle Street you'll find a square filled with old black cabs—and the only Gaelic-language signs in downtown Belfast. These shared black cabs efficiently shuttle residents from outlying neighborhoods up and down Falls Road and to the city center. This service originated when the troubles began and locals would hijack city buses and use them as barricades in the street fighting. When bus service was discontinued, local paramilitary groups established the shared taxi service. Any cab (except those in the "Whiterock" line) goes up Falls Road and past Sinn

Belfast

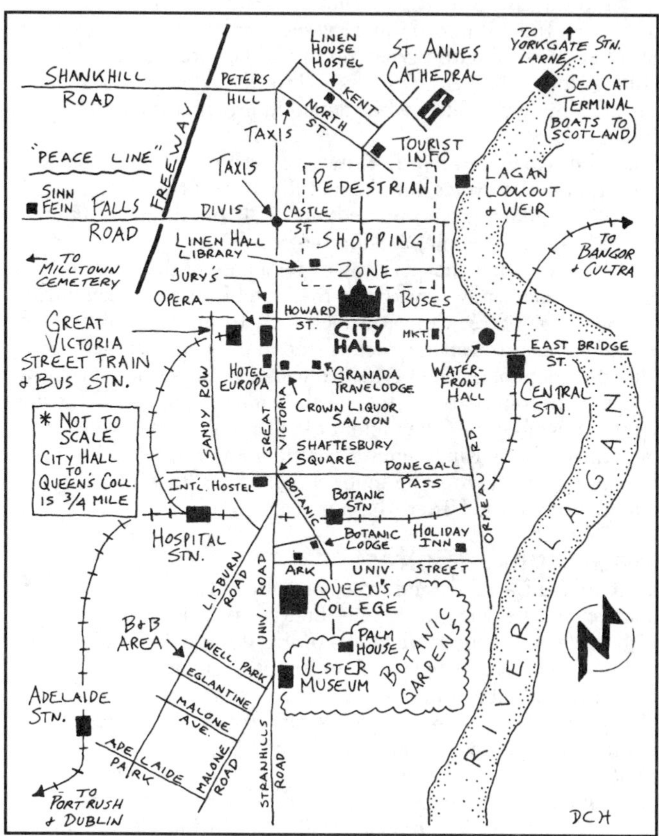

Fein headquarters and lots of murals to the Milltown Cemetery (70p, sit in front and talk to the cabbie). Hop on and off. Easy-to-flag-down cabs run every minute or so in each direction on Falls Road. Twenty trained-guide cabbies do one-hour tours for £15 (cheap for a small group).

The Sinn Fein (pron: shin fayn) office and bookstore are near the bottom of Falls Road. The bookstore is worth a look. Page through books featuring color photos of the political murals that decorate the buildings. Money raised here supports families of imprisoned members of the IRA.

A sad corrugated wall called the Peace Line runs a block or so north of Falls Road, separating the Catholics from the Protestants in the Shankill Road area.

At the Milltown Cemetery walk past all the Gaelic crosses down to the far right-hand corner (closest to the highway), where the IRA "Roll of Honor" is set apart from the thousands of other graves by little green railings. They are treated like fallen soldiers. Notice the memorial to Bobby Sands and the 11 other hunger strikers who starved in protest for a united Ireland in 1981.

Shankhill Road and Sandy Row—You can ride a shared black cab through the Protestant Shankill Road area (departing from end of North Street, 30-minute loop-£1.20, or take a 60-minute tour-£12 for 1–2 people, £15 for 3–6 people).

An easier (and cheaper) way to get a dose of the Unionist side is to walk Sandy Row. From the Hotel Europa, walk a block down Glengall Street, then turn left for a 10-minute walk along a working-class Protestant street. A stop in the Unionist memorabilia shop, a pub, or one of the many cheap eateries here may give you an opportunity to talk to a local. You'll see murals filled with Unionist symbolism. The mural of William of Orange's victory over the Catholic King James II (Battle of the Boyne, 1690) thrills Unionist hearts. (From the south end of Sandy Row, it's a 10-minute walk to the Ulster Museum, below.)

More Sights—Belfast

▲▲City Hall—This grand structure, with its 173-foot-tall copper dome, dominates the town center. Built between 1898 and 1906, with its statue of Queen Victoria scowling down Belfast's main drag and the Union Jack flapping behind her, it's a stirring sight. In the garden you'll find memorials to the *Titanic* and the landing of the U.S. Expeditionary Force in 1942—their first stop en route to Berlin. Take the free 45-minute tour (June–Sept usually at 10:30, 11:30, and 14:30, Sat at 14:30; Oct–May only Sat 14:30; for Sat tours, enter back of building—south side, otherwise enter front; call to check schedule and book, tel. 028/9027-0456). If you can't manage a tour, at least step into the interior, with its marble swirl staircase, and drop into the "What's on in Belfast" room just inside the front door.

The tour gives you a rundown on city government and an explanation of the decor that makes this an Ulster political hall of fame. Queen Victoria and King Edward VII look down on city council meetings. The 1613 original charter of Belfast granted by James I is on display. Its Great Hall—bombed by the Germans in 1941—looks as great as it did the day it was made.

Linen Hall Library—Across the street from City Hall, the 200-year-old Linen Hall Library welcomes guests. It has a fine, hard-bound ambience, a coffee shop, and a royal newspaper reading room (Mon–Sat 9:30–17:30, Sat 9:30–16:00, get free visitor's pass at entrance,17 Donegall Square North, tel. 028/9032-1707).

Golden Mile—This is the overstated nickname of Belfast's liveliest dining and entertainment district, which stretches from the Opera House to the university district.

The **Grand Opera House,** originally built in 1891, bombed and rebuilt in 1991 and bombed and rebuilt again in 1993, is extravagantly Victorian and the place to take in a concert, play, or opera (closed to sightseers, ticket office across street, CC:VM, tel. 028/9024-1919). **Hotel Europa,** next door, while considered the most bombed hotel in the world, feels pretty casual (listed under "Sleeping," below).

Across the street is the museum-like **Crown Liquor Saloon**. Built in 1849, it's now a part of the National Trust. A wander through its mahogany, glass, and marble interior is a trip back into the day of Queen Victoria (although the privacy provided by the snugs—private booths—allows for un-Victorian behavior; Mon–Sat 11:30–24:00; consider a lunch stop, see "Eating," below). Upstairs, **Flannigan's Bar** serves pub grub, is decorated with historic photos, and is the starting point for the **Bailey's Historical Belfast Pub Walk** (£5, May–Sept, Thu at 21:00, Sat at 16:00, 2 hrs, stops at 6 pubs—drinks not included, book in advance, tel. 028/9268-3665, Judy Crawford).

Lagan Lookout Visitors Centre—This center shows off the fruits of the city's £750 million investment in its harbor. The tides of the River Lagan left the town with daily unsightly mud flats. The weir, built in 1994, controls the tides, stabilizing the depth of the harbor. It also doubles as a free pedestrian bridge over the river, affording walkers a fine view of the harbor area, including the big cranes and the new convention center. The Visitors Centre, while mildly entertaining and enthusiastically "interactive," is not worth the £1.50 entry fee (Mon–Fri 11:00–17:00, Sat 12:00–17:00, Sun 14:00–17:00, closed Mon in winter, a short walk from TI, just past the tipsy—four feet off center—Albert clock tower, tel. 028/9031-5444).

▲**Ulster Museum**—While mediocre by European standards, this is Belfast's one major museum. It's free and pretty painless: Ride the elevator to the top floor and follow the spiraling exhibits downhill—there's a cheery café halfway down. You'll find an interesting *Made in Belfast* exhibit just before an arch that proclaims "Trade is the golden girdle of the globe." The delicately worded history section is given an interesting British slant (such as the implication that the famine was caused by the Irish population doubling in 40 years—without a mention of various English contributions to the suffering). After a wander through the *Early Medieval Ireland* exhibit and a peek at a pretty darn good mummy, top things off with the Girona Treasure. Soggy bits of gold, silver, leather, and wood were salvaged from the Spanish Armada's shipwrecked *Girona*—lost off the Antrim

Coast north of Belfast in 1588 (free, Mon–Fri 10:00–17:00, Sat 13:00–17:00, Sun 14:00–17:00, tel. 028/9038-3000).

▲Botanic Gardens—This is the backyard of Queen's University. On a sunny day, you couldn't imagine a more relaxing park setting. On a cold day, step into the Tropical Ravine for a jungle of heat and humidity. Take a quick walk through the Palm House, reminiscent of the Palm House in London's Kew Gardens, but smaller (free, Mon–Fri 10:00–12:00, 13:00–17:00, Sat–Sun 13:00–17:00, less in winter, tel. 028/9032-4902).

Odyssey—A new, huge complex offers a 12-screen cinema plus IMAX, a food pavilion, and science center (2 Queen's Quay, tel. 028/9045-1055).

Sights—Near Belfast

▲▲Ulster Folk and Transport Museum—This 180-acre, two-museum complex straddles the road and rail at Cultra, midway between Bangor and Belfast (8 miles east of town).

The Folk Museum, an open-air collection of 34 reconstructed buildings from all over the nine counties of Ulster, showcases the region's traditional lifestyles. After wandering through the old town site (church, print shop, schoolhouse, humble Belfast row house, and so on), you'll head off into the country to nip into cottages, farmhouses, and mills. Most houses are warmed by a wonderful peat fire and a friendly attendant. It can be dull or vibrant, depending upon when you visit and your ability to chat with the attendants. Drop a peat brick on the fire.

The Transport Museum (downhill, over the road from the folk section) consists of three buildings. Start at the bottom and trace the evolution of transportion from 7,500 years ago—when people first decided to load an ox—to modern times. The lowest building holds an intriguing section on the sinking of the Belfast-made *Titanic*. In the next two buildings you roll through the history of bikes, cars, and trains. The car section rumbles from the first car in Ireland (an 1898 Benz) through the "Cortina Culture" of the 1960s to the local adventures of John De Lorean and a 1981 model of his car. (£4, £11 for families, CC:VM, July–Aug Mon–Sat 10:30–18:00, Sun 12:00–18:00; April–June and Sept Mon–Fri 9:30–17:00, Sat 10:30–18:00, Sun 12:00–18:00; Oct–March closes daily at 16:00; check schedule for special events on the day of your visit, allow 3 hours, tel. 028/9042-8428, www.nidex.com/uftm.) Expect lots of walking. Drivers can drive from one section to the next.

From Belfast reach **Cultra** by taxi (£8), bus #1 or #2 (2/hrly, 30 min from Laganside Bus Centre), or train (2/hrly, 15 min, from any Belfast train station or Bangor). Trains and buses stop right in the park. Public transport schedules get skimpy on Saturday and Sunday.

Sleeping in Belfast
(£1 = about $1.60, country code: 44, area code: 028; to call Belfast from the Republic of Ireland, dial 048 before the local number)

Sleep Code: **S** = Single, **D** = Double/Twin, **T** = Triple, **Q** = Quad, **b** = bathroom, **t** = toilet only, **s** = shower only, **CC** = Credit Card (Visa, MasterCard, Amex).

Many of Belfast's best budget beds cluster in a comfortable area just south of the Ulster Museum and the university. Two train stations (Botanic and Adelaide) are nearby, and buses zip down Malone Road every 20 minutes. Any bus on Malone Road goes to Donegall Square East. Taxis, cheap in Belfast, zip you downtown for £3 (your host can call one). Belfast is more of a business town than a tourist town, so business-class room rates are lower or soft on weekends.

Ulster People's College Residential Centre rents 28 beds in eight rooms year-round on a quiet street near the stop for the bus into town (S-£18, D-£34, £2 per bed cheaper with a continental rather than Irish breakfast, free use of laundry facilities, 30 Adelaide Park, tel. 028/9066-5161, fax 028/9066-8111, e-mail: upc@cinni.org).

Malone Guest House is a classy stand-alone Victorian house fronting the busy Malone Road. It's homey and well run by Mrs. Millar who rents two spacious singles and six large, pastel twins (Sb-£37–40, Db-£50–55 with this book, 79 Malone Road, at intersection with Adelaide Park and bus stop, Belfast BT9 6SH, tel. 028/9066-9565, fax 028/9022-3020).

Camera Guest House rents large smoke-free rooms and comes with an airy, hardwood feeling throughout (Sb-£38, Db-£55, CC:VM, 44 Wellington Park, Belfast BT9 6DP, tel. 028/9066-0026, fax 028/9066-7856, e-mail: pauldrumm@hotmail.com, Paul Drumm).

Windermere House rents 11 rooms, including several small but pleasant singles, in a large Victorian house (S-£22, very small D-£30, D-£44, Db-£46, T-£47, 60 Wellington Park, tel. 028/9066-2693).

Malone Lodge Hotel, by far the classest listing in this neighborhood, provides slick, business-class comfort and spacious rooms in a charming environment on a quiet, leafy street (Sb-£75, Db-£100, superior Db-£110, weekend deals, includes breakfast, CC:VMA, elevator, 60 Eglantine Avenue, Belfast BT9 6DY, tel. 028/9038-8000, fax 028/9038-8088, www.malonelodgehotel.com).

On the same quiet street you'll find: **The George B&B** (6 fine smallish rooms, Db-£44, 9 Eglantine Avenue, tel. 028/9068-3212, Hugh McGuinness), **Eglantine Guest House** (7 pleasant rooms, S-£22, D-£40, T-£57, Lou Cargill will mother you—even do your laundry for a small charge, 21 Eglantine Avenue, tel. 028/9066-7585, fax 028/9066-8203), and the grand old **Marine House B&B** (11 high-ceilinged rooms, S-£22, Sb-£27, D-£38, Db-£45, 30 Eglantine Avenue, tel. & fax 028/9066-2828).

Botanic Lodge rents 20 decent rooms on a lively but stylish "University Ave"–type street with lots of fun eateries nearby (D-£40, Db-£45, CC:VM, 10-minute walk to City Hall at 87 Botanic Avenue, Belfast BT7 1JN, tel. & fax 028/9032-7682).

Sleeping in Hotels

The first three are big, modern, inexpensive chain hotels; the last is a splurge.

Jurys Inn, a huge American-style place that rents its 190 identical modern rooms for one simple price, is perfectly located two blocks from the City Hall (up to 3 adults or 2 adults and 2 kids for about £69, breakfast-£6.50, CC:VMA, nonsmoking floor, Fisherwick Place, tel. 028/9053-3500, fax 028/9053-3511, e-mail: info@jurys.com).

Granada Travelodge is a basic Jurys-style business hotel with 83 cookie-cutter rooms high on value, low on character (Db-£60, often huge weekend discounts—such as Db-£40 for Fri, Sat, or Sun nights, no breakfast, CC:VMA, quiet but extremely central, a block from Hotel Europa and City Hall at 15 Brunswick Street, Belfast BT2 7GE, tel. 0800-850-950 or 028/9033-3555, fax 028/9023-2999).

Belfast Holiday Inn Express is cheaper but not as central as Jurys Inn, with the same basic formula (Db-£70, often weekend deals, kids free, includes continental breakfast, CC:VMA, nonsmoking floors, elevator, 106 University Street, tel. 028/9031-1909, fax 028/9031-1910, e-mail: express@holidayinn-ireland.com).

Hotel Europa is Belfast's landmark hotel—fancy, comfortable, and central—with four stars and good weekend rates. Modern yet elegant, this was Clinton's choice when he visited (Db-£170 Mon–Thu, Db-£95 on Fri, Sat, or Sun; President Clinton's suite-£350, $44 million to uncover what he did there; CC:VMA, 4 nonsmoking floors, Great Victoria Street, tel. 028/9032-7000, fax 028/9032-7800, www.hastingshotels.com).

Sleeping in Hostels and Dorms

Belfast International City Hostel, providing the best value among Belfast's hostels, is big and creatively run with 40 twins and quads. It's located near the Botanic train station in the heart of the lively university district and close to the center. Features include free lockers, left luggage, videos, self-serve laundry for £3, a cheap cafeteria, an elevator, 24-hour reception, and no curfew (S-£17, D-£24, beds in quad-£12, includes breakfast, CC:VM, 22 Donegall Road, tel. 028/9032-4733, fax 028/9043-9699, www.hini.org.uk, e-mail: info@hini.org.uk). Paul, the manager of the hostel, is a veritable TI with a passion for his work. Sometime later in 2001, the hostel will double in size with more doubles added to attract the B&B crowd—worth checking out (or better yet, checking in). The hostel is the starting point for Rodney's Tours (see "Tours of Belfast," above).

The Ark, a smaller, more hip, youthful, and easygoing hostel, is in the university district near the Botanic train station (£7.50 per bed in 4-bed dorms or D-£28, kitchen, 18 University Street, tel. 028/9032-9626, fax 028/9024-5160).

Linen House Youth Hostel fills an old linen factory with a 150-bed industrial-strength hostel. It's on a dark, scary-at-night street in a very central location (£8 dorm beds, S-£12, D-£20, no breakfast, plenty of facilities, kitchen, Internet access, 18 Kent Street, tel. 028/9058-6400, fax 028/9058-6444, e-mail: info@belfasthostel.com).

Queen's Elms Halls of Residence is a big brick Queen's University dorm renting 300 basic institutional rooms, mainly s ingles, to travelers during summer break. Singles should book in advance and ask for a "self-catering room" to snare a spot in the newer building (mid-June–early-Sept only, S-£12, D-£20, cheaper for students, CC:VM, free laundry service, self-serve kitchen, building is set back about 250 yards from street, 78 Malone Road, tel. 028/9038-1608, fax 028/9066-6680, e-mail: qehor@qub.ac.uk).

Eating in Belfast

Downtown: If it's £5 pub grub you want, consider the woody, elegant **Morning Star** (Mon–Sat 10:00–23:00, closed Sun, restaurant upstairs, CC:VM, 17 Pottinger's Entry, tel. 028/9023-5986), the very Irish **Kellys Cellars** (Mon–Sat 11:30–21:00, closed Sun, live traditional music Sat at 15:30, restaurant upstairs, 32 Bank Street, behind Tesco supermarket, tel. 028/9023-4177), or the small, antique **Crown Liquour Saloon,** mentioned in "Sights," above, for its mesmerizing mishmash of mosaics and shareable snugs (booths), topped with a smoky tin ceiling (Mon–Sat lunch only—12:00–15:00, closed Sun, 46 Great Victoria Street, across from Hotel Europa, tel. 028/9027-9901).

For cafés, consider any of many popular eateries in the streets north of Donegall Square. **Bewley's,** popular in Ireland, offers a good-value cafeteria with seating under a conservatory-style roof (Mon–Sat 8:00–17:30, Thu until 21:00, closed Sun, north end of Donegall's Arcade, skip Coffee House with table service, choose cafeteria). **Coffee Metz** has a sleek, light-wood design and £4 meals, including salads (Mon–Sat 9:00–17:00, 12 Queen Street, at intersection with College Street, next door to U.S. Consulate, tel. 028/9024-9484).

Marks & Spencer has an easy coffee shop—serving skinny lattes—and a supermarket in its basement (Mon–Sat 9:00–18:00, closed Sun, WCs on second floor, Donegall Place, a block north of Donegall Square). **Tesco,** another supermarket, is a block north of M&S and two blocks north of Donegall Square (Mon–Sat 8:00–19:00, Thu until 21:00, Sun 13:00–17:00, Royal Avenue and Bank Street). Picnic on the City Hall green.

Near Shaftesbury Square and Botanic Station: Maggie May's serves hearty, inexpensive meals (£4–5, Mon–Sat 8:00–22:30, Sun 10:00–22:30, 50 Botanic Avenue, a block south of Botanic Station, tel. 028/9032-2662), and **Bishop's** is the locals' choice for fish and chips (daily 9:00–01:00, pasta and veggie options, classier side has table service, CC:VM, Bradbury Place, just south of Shaftesbury Square, tel. 028/9043-9070). **Villa Italia** packs in crowds hungry for linguini and *bistecca*. With its checkered tablecloths and a wood-beamed ceiling draped with grape leaves, it's a little bit of Italy in Belfast (£7–10, Mon–Sat 17:00–23:30, Sun 16:00–22:00, CC:VM, 37 University Road, 3 long blocks south of Shaftesbury Square, at intersection with University Street, tel. 028/9032-8356).

Sleeping and Eating in Bangor

(£1 = about $1.60, country code: 44, area code: 028)

To stay in a laid-back seaside hometown—with more comfort per pound—sleep 30 minutes south of Belfast in Bangor (pron: bang-grr). Formerly a slick Belfast seaside escape, Bangor is now sleepy and almost residential feeling. But with easy train connections to downtown Belfast (2/hrly, 30 min, £3.50), elegant old homes facing its newly spruced-up harbor, and the lack of even a hint of big-city Belfast, Bangor appeals. The harbor is a five-minute walk from the train station. (Bangor TI: 34 Quay Street, tel. 028/9127-0069.)

Pierview House B&B is a chandeliered winner, with three of its five spacious rooms overlooking the sea (D-£34, grand Db-£36, family room, CC:VM, 28 Seacliff Road, tel. 028/9146-3381, Mr. and Mrs. Watts). **Battersea Guest House,** one of a row of tall, stately homes overlooking the yacht basin, rents four rooms (small D-£35–37, grand sea-view double-£37–45, 47 Queen's Parade, tel. & fax 028/9146-1643, Rene and John Brann, e-mail: jandar@rannlie.freezone.co.uk). **Royal Hotel** is a fine old place right on the harbor with good weekend rates on its 50 rooms (Db-£75 weekdays, £65 on weekends, view rooms are £10 pricier, CC:VMA, 26 Quay Street, BT20 5ED, tel. 028/9127-1866, fax 028/9146-7810, e-mail: royalhotel@compuserve.com).

Eating: Your hosts can direct you to their favorite eatery. For good £6 meals, try the **Lord Nelson** bistro in the Marine Court Hotel (facing harbor, 18–20 Quay Street) or the bar next door at the **Royal Hotel**. For a tasty break from pub grub, consider **Ganges** for Indian food (Bingham Street) or **Los Amigos** for the whole enchilada (9 Crosby Street, tel. 028/9124-7060).

Transportation Connections—Bangor

By train to Belfast: Trains go from Bangor station (the end of the line, don't use Bangor West) into Belfast via Cultra (Ulster Folk and Transport Museum). The journey (2/hrly, 30 min) gives you a good close-up look at the giant Belfast harbor cranes. Get off at Belfast Central, which has a free Rail-Link shuttle bus to the town center (4/hrly, not Sun) or stay on until the Botanic train station for the Ulster Museum, the Golden Mile, and Sandy Row.

Transportation Connections—Belfast

By train to: Dublin (8/day, 2 hrs), **Larne** (hrly, 1 hr), **Portrush** (7/day, 2 hrs). Train info: tel. 028/9089-9411.

By bus to: Portrush (6/day, 2 hrs), **Glasgow** (2/day, 6 hrs, £32), **Edinburgh** (2/day, 8 hrs), **London** (2/day, 12 hrs, £35). The Europa Bus Centre is behind the Europa Hotel (CC:VM, Ulsterbus tel. 028/9033-7003).

By plane: British Air flies to **Glasgow** (6/day, 45 min, as low as £65 round-trip, must book in advance to get the cheapest fares) and **London** (5/day, 1.25 hr, £139 one-way, £120 round-trip). One-way trips often cost more than a round-trip, but you can forget to return—it's allowed (British Air's Belfast office tel. 0845-606-0747 or central booking at tel. 0345-222-111).

By ferry to Scotland: There are a number of options, ports, and companies. You can sail between Belfast and **Stranraer** (1.25-hr crossing, via SeaCat catamaran or Stena Line ferry—£30, tel. 028/9074-7747) or between Belfast and **Troon** (2/day, 2.5-hr crossing, year-round, £20–25, also takes cars, CC:VMA, Troon-Glasgow trains 2/hrly, 30 min; easy connections from Glasgow to most anywhere in Britain, British tel. 0870-552-3523, www.seacat.co.uk). P&O Ferry goes from **Larne** (20 miles north of Belfast, hrly trains, TI: 028/2826-0088) to **Cairnryan** (tel. 0870-2424-777).

By ferry to England: Consider sailing overnight from Belfast to **Liverpool**—with a bed, dinner, and breakfast—for £40 via North Irish Ferries (8.5 hrs, nightly, CC:VMA, tel. 0870-600-4321).

ANTRIM COAST AND PORTRUSH

The Antrim Coast—the north of Northern Ireland—is one of the most interesting and scenic coastlines in Britain and Ireland. Within a few miles of the train terminal of Portrush, you can visit some evocative castle ruins, tour the oldest whiskey distillery, risk your life on a bouncy rope bridge, and hike along the famous Giant's Causeway—a World Heritage Site.

The homely seaside resort of Portrush used to be known as "the Brighton of the North." While it's seen its best days, it retains the atmosphere and buildings of a genteel, middle-class seaside resort. Portrush fills its peninsula with family-oriented amusements, fun eateries, and B&Bs. Summertime fun seekers promenade along the toy harbor and tumble down to the sandy beaches, which extend in sweeping white crescents on either side.

Superficially, it has the appearance of any small British seaside resort, but its history and high population of young people (students from the University of Coleraine) give Portrush a little more personality. Along with the usual arcade amusements, there are nightclubs, restaurants, summer theater in the town hall, and convivial pubs that people from Belfast travel for. At the end of the train line and just a few miles from several important sights, it's an ideal base for exploring the highlights of the Antrim Coast.

Planning Your Time

You need a full day to explore the Antrim Coast, so allow two nights in Portrush. An ideal day might be a bike tour lacing together Dunluce Castle, Old Bushmills Distillery, and the Giant's Causeway, followed by nine holes on the Portrush pitch-and-putt course. Consider this side trip north from Dublin.

Day 1: 11:00–16:00–Train from Dublin to Portrush.

Day 2: All day for Antrim Coast sights and Portrush.
Day 3: 8:00–10:00–Train to Belfast, all day in Belfast; 19:00–21:00–Train back to Dublin.

Orientation (area code: 028)

Portrush's pleasant and easily walkable town center features sea views in every direction. On one side is the harbor and restaurants, and on the other are Victorian townhouses and vast salty views. The tip of the peninsula is marked by a lighthouse and a park filled with tennis courts, lawn-bowling greens, and putting greens.

The city is busy with students during the school year. July and August are beach resort boom time. June and September it's laid-back and lazy. Families pack Portrush on Saturdays, and revelers from Belfast pack its hotels on Saturday nights.

Tourist Information: The TI, more generous and helpful than those in the Republic, is in the big, modern Dunluce Centre (mid-June–Aug daily 9:00–19:00, otherwise Mon–Fri 9:00–17:00, Sat–Sun 12:00–17:00, closed in winter, tel. 028/7082-3333). Get their free North Ireland driving map, the "Places to Visit" brochure, and a free Belfast map if you're Belfast-bound.

Arrival in Portrush: The train tracks stop at the base of the tiny peninsula that Portrush fills. (The small station has no bag check.) The TI is three long blocks from the train station (follow signs down Eglinton Street and turn left at fire station). All listed B&Bs are within a five-minute walk of the train station (see "Sleeping," below). The bus stop is two blocks from the train station.

Getting around the Antrim Coast

By Bus: In July and August, open-top "Bushmills" buses connect Portrush, Dunluce Castle, Old Bushmills Distillery, and the Giant's Causeway every two hours (maybe hourly in summer, weather permitting). You could spend two hours at Bushmills and the causeway, but you'd be bored at the castle (£3.20 round-trip, buy ticket from driver, pick up a schedule at TI).

By Car: Distances are short, and parking is easy. Don't miss the treacherously scenic coastal route down to the Glens of Antrim.

By Taxi: Groups (up to four) go reasonably by taxi, which costs only £7 from Portrush to Giant's Causeway.

By Bike: Portrush's only bike-rental place has closed. Ask around if anyone's renting bikes.

Sights—Portrush

Barry's Old Time Amusement Arcade—This is a fine chance to see Northern Ireland at play (open weekends and summer only). Just below the train station on the harbor, it's filled with candy floss (cotton candy) and little kids learning the art of one-armed bandits—2p at a time. Get £1 worth of 2p coins from the machine and go wild.

Portrush

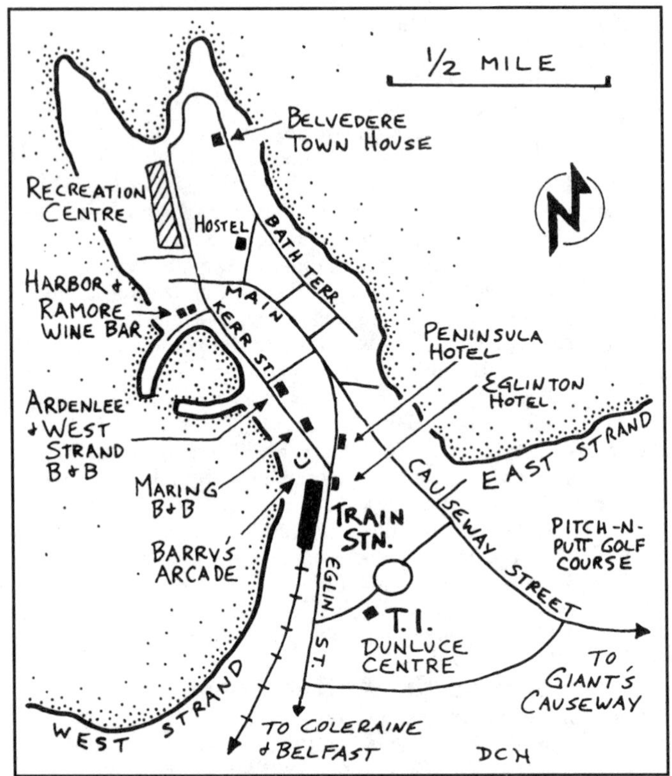

Pitch-and-Putt at the Royal Portrush Golf Course—Irish courses, like those in Scotland, are highly sought after for their lush but dry greens in glorious settings. While serious golfers can get a tee time at the Royal Portrush, rookies can get a smaller dose of this wonderful golf setting at the neighboring "Skerry 9 Hole Links" pitch-and-putt range. You get two clubs and balls for £4.50, and they don't care if you go around twice (April–Sept daily 8:30–19:30, five-minute walk from station, tel. 028/7082-2285).

Portrush Recreation Grounds—For some easygoing exercise right in town, this well-organized park offers lawn-bowling greens (£3/hr with gear), putting greens, tennis courts, a great kids' adventure play park, and a café (tennis shoes, balls, rackets, etc., all rented for a small price, daily Easter–Sept Mon–Sat 10:00–dusk, Sun 13:00–dusk, tel. 028/7082-4441). Other major Portrush amusements include the **Dunluce Center** and **Waterworld**.

Sights—Antrim Coast

▲**Dunluce Castle**—These romantic ruins, perched dramatically on the edge of a rocky headland, are a testimony to this region's turbulent past. During the Middle Ages it resisted several sieges. But on a stormy night in 1639 dinner was interrupted as half the kitchen fell into the sea, taking the servants with it. That was the last straw for the lady of the castle. The Countess of Antrim packed up and moved inland, and the castle "began its slow submission to the forces of nature." While it's one of the largest castles in Northern Ireland and is beautifully situated, there's precious little to see among its broken walls.

Expansion of the castle was financed by the salvaging of a shipwreck. In 1588 the Spanish Armada's *Girona*—returning home after an aborted English mission and laden with sailors and valuables of three abandoned sister ships—sank. More than 1,300 drowned, and only five washed ashore. The shipwreck was excavated in 1967, and a bounty of golden odds and silver ends ended up in Belfast's Ulster Museum.

Castle admission includes a little impromptu guided tour of the ruins and a 15-minute video that's interesting for its effort to defend the notion of "Ulster, a place apart—facing Scotland, cut off from the rest of Ireland by dense forests and mountains . . ." (£1.50, April–Sept Tue–Sat 10:00–18:00, Sun 14:00–18:00, closed Mon; in winter 10:00–16:00, with shorter hours on Sun, tel. 028/2073-1938).

▲▲**Old Bushmills Distillery**—Bushmills claims to be the world's oldest distillery. While King James I (of Bible fame) granted their license to distill "Aqua Vitae" in 1608, whiskey has been made here since the 13th century. Distillery tours waft you through the process, making it clear that Irish whiskey is triple distilled—and therefore smoother than Scotch whiskey (distilled merely twice). The 45-minute tour starts where the mash pit is filled with a porridge that eventually becomes whiskey. (The leftovers of that porridge are fed to the county's particularly happy cows.) You'll see thousands of oak casks—the kind used for Spanish sherry—filled with aging whiskey. The finale, of course, is the tasting in the 1608 Bar—the former malt barn. When your guide asks for a tasting volunteer, raise your hand quick and strong. Two volunteers per tour get to taste test eight different whiskeys (Irish versus Scotch and bourbon). Everyone else gets a single glass of their choice. Nonwhiskey enthusiasts might enjoy their cinnamon and cloves hot toddy. To see the distillery at its lively best, visit when the 100 workers are manning the machinery—Monday morning through Friday noon (weekend tours see a still still). Tours are limited to 35 and book up. In summer call in your name to get a tour time before you arrive (£3.50, daily April–Oct, tours depart on the half hour from 9:30, last tour at 16:00, Sun from 12:00; in winter only Mon–Fri, 5 tours daily at 10:30, 11:30, 13:30, 14:30, and 15:30, tel. 028/2073-1521). The

Northern Ireland's Antrim Coast

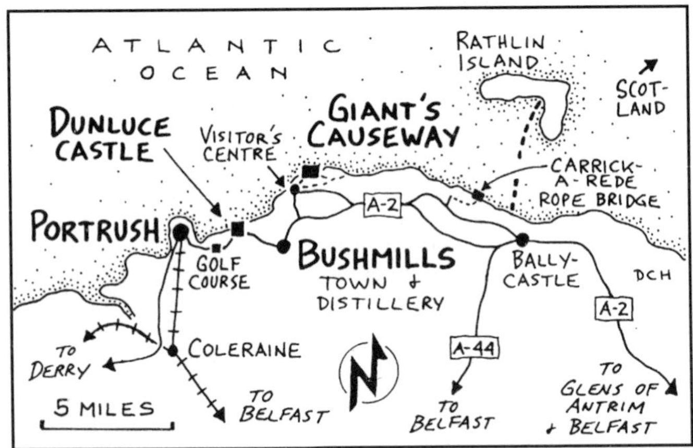

distillery is a signposted quarter mile from Bushmills town center. (Valley View Farm B&B rents rooms at 6a Ballyclough Road, Bushmills, tel. 028/2074-1608).

▲▲Giant's Causeway—This four-mile-long stretch of coastline is famous for its bizarre basalt columns. The shore is covered with hexagonal pillars that stick up at various heights. It's as if earth is offering God his choice of 37,000 six-sided cigarettes.

Geologists claim the Giant's Causeway was formed by volcanic eruptions 60 million years ago. As the lava surface cooled, it contracted and cracked into hexagonal shapes. As the layer of hardened but alligatored rock settled, it broke into its many stair steps.

In actuality, the Giant's Causeway was formed by an Ulster warrior giant named Finn MacCool who wanted to reach his l ove on the Scottish island of Staffa. At that time the causeway stretched to Scotland, way back when the two lands were connected. Today, while the foundation has settled, the formation still extends undersea to Staffa, just off the Scottish coast. Finn's causeway was ruined (into today's "remnant of chaos") by a rival giant. As the rival fled from ferocious Finn back to his Scottish homeland, he ripped up the causeway so Finn couldn't chase him.

For cute variations on the Finn story, as well as details on the ridiculous theories of modern geologists, start your visit in the Visitors Centre (should reopen in spring of 2001 after being damaged by fire last year). The worthwhile video gives a history of the Giant's Causeway and a regional overview (£1, 4/hrly, 12 min). The real information is on the walls of the exhibition. A gift shop and cafeteria are standing by.

A minibus (60p each way, 4/hrly) zips lazy ones a half mile

directly to the Grand Causeway, the highlight of the entire coast. For a better dose of the causeway, consider this plan: follow the high cliff-top trail from the Visitors Centre 10 minutes to a great viewpoint, then five minutes farther on you reach the Shepherd's Stairway. Zigzag down to the coast; at the T junction, go 100 yards right to the towering pipes of "the Organ." Then retrace your steps and continue left to the "Giant's Boot" for some photo fun and the dramatic point where the stairs step into the sea. Just beyond that, at the asphalt turnaround, you'll see the bus stop for the lift back to the Visitors Centre. You could walk the entire five-mile Giant's Causeway. The 75p hiking guide points out the highlights named by 18th-century guides (Camel's Back, Giant's Eye, and so on). The causeway is always free and open (Visitors Centre daily 10:00–17:00, until 19:00 July–Aug, £3 to park, tel. 028/2073-1855).

Causeway Coast Bike Ride—(At last check, no one was renting bikes in Portrush—ask around.) It's an eight-mile, one-hour pedal from Portrush past Dunluce Castle and Bushmills to the Giant's Causeway Visitors Centre. From Portrush to Dunluce Castle, allow 20 minutes. Bike along the Royal Portrush Golf Course and past some beautiful beach scenery (a bike-friendly sidewalk keeps timid riders away from traffic). It's another 20 minutes to Bushmills; the distillery is a quarter-mile detour inland from the town square. Bushmills is a good place for a lunch break; choose among the fancy Bushmills Inn, several pantries, and a happy Hip Chip chippie. From Bushmills the Giant's Causeway is 20 minutes farther over gentle hills.

▲▲Carrick-a-Rede Rope Bridge—For 200 years fishermen have strung a narrow 80-foot-high bridge (planks strung between wires) across a 65-foot-wide chasm between the mainland and a tiny island. The bridge (not the original) still gives access to the salmon nets that are set during the summer months to catch the fish turning the coast's corner. (The complicated system is described at the gateway.) The island affords fine views and, especially during nesting season, great seabird-watching (free, April–Sept daily 10:00–18:00, July–Aug until 20:00, gone in winter, 15-min walk from the £2 car park).

▲Antrim Mountains and Glens—Not particularly high (never more than 1,500 feet), the Antrim Mountains are cut by a series of large glens running northeast to the sea. Glenariff, with its waterfalls, especially the "Mare's Tail," is the most beautiful of the nine glens.

Sleeping in Portrush

(£1 = about $1.60, country code: 44, area code: 028, zip code: BT56 8DG)

Sleep Code: **S** = Single, **D** = Double/Twin, **T** = Triple, **Q** = Quad, **b** = bathroom, **t** = toilet only, **s** = shower only, **CC** = Credit Card (**V**isa, **M**asterCard, **A**mex).

Portrush's many B&Bs all seem well worn. But small-town well worn is better than big-town well worn. August and Saturday nights can be tight. Otherwise it's a "you take a half a loaf when you can get it" town. Rates vary with the view and season—probe for softness. Each listing faces the sea, though sea views are worth paying for only if you get a bay window. Ask for a big room (some doubles can be very small; twins are bigger). Lounges are invariably grand and have bay-window views. All places listed have lots of stairs but are perfectly central and within a few minutes' walk of the train station. Parking is easy.

Peninsula Hotel is a big, new place right in the town center with huge, fresh rooms, modern decor, and comforts. Ask for a room far from its disco, which can be a problem on party nights (Db-£60, Tb-£75, breakfast-£5—eat better and cheaper down the street, CC:VMA, elevator, 15 Eglinton Street, BT56 8DX, tel. 028/7082-2293, fax 028/7082-4315, e-mail: reservations @peninsulahotel.co.uk).

Eglinton Hotel, Portrush's smoky old-time hotel, is central but noisy and impersonal. It's a dark place with small doubles and bigger twins (Db-£60–70 with demand, CC:VMA, across the street from train station, 49 Eglinton Street, BT56 8DZ Portrush, tel. 028/7082-2371, fax 028/7082-3155).

Belvedere Town House, a stately place on the quiet side of town with 13 spacious, relatively well-appointed rooms, is the best value in town (S-£17, Sb-£21, D-£34, Db-£40, 5 percent extra for CC, farthest from station but ideal for drivers, at 15 Lansdowne Crescent, tel. 028/7082-2771, Sammy and Winnie Dunn).

Ardenlee B&B is enthusiastically run by Rodney Montgomery and has six bigger-than-average rooms and a fine location near the station (S-£15, Db-£35–40, £5 discount for 2-night stays, 10 percent discount with this book, 19 Kerr Street, Portrush BT56 8DG, tel. 028/7082-2639).

Harbor Heights B&B rents 14 cramped, well-worn rooms (S-£15, Sb-£20–25, D-£35, Db-£35–40, 10 percent discount with this book, family loft room, CC:VMA, 17 Kerr Street, tel. & fax 028/7082-2765, Anne and Robin Rossborough).

West Strand Guest House has 15 tight, musty rooms, none with private bathrooms (S-£15–17.50, D-£30–34, fine view lounge, 18 Kerr Street, tel. 028/7082-2270, Muriel Robinson).

MacCool's Portrush Youth Hostel is a friendly and laid-back place with 20 beds in four rooms (2, 4, 6, and 8 beds each, £7 per bed, one tiny £16 double, one all-girls' room, lockers, guests' kitchen, game-stocked lounge, nonsmoking, Internet access, bike rental to residents only, 5 Causeway View Terrace, midway between station and tip of peninsula, tel. 028/7082-4845).

Drivers may want to stay just out of town at **Glenkeen Guest House** (10 rooms, Sb-£27, Db-£38–42, some smoke-free rooms, CC:VMA, 7-minute walk from the station, 59 Coleraine Road, tel. 028/7082-2279, Mrs. Little) or **Summer Island House** (4 rooms, Sb-£20, Db-£35–40, family room, 5-minute walk from station, 14 Coleraine Road, tel. 028/7082-4640, Vivian Shields).

Eating in Portrush

Being a university town and a get-away-from-Belfast town, Portrush has more than chips joints. Eglinton Street is lined with cheap and cheery eateries. For pub grub consider the **Eglinton Hotel** or **Peninsula Hotel**. **Don Giovanni** serves decent Italian.

Three restaurants within 50 yards of each other, all under the same ownership and overlooking the harbor, are just about everyone's vote for the best eating values in town.

Ramore Restaurant, dressy black and white, is the spot for fine dining (£10–15 main courses, full dinners for £20–30, Tue–Sat 18:15–22:15, closed Sun–Mon, CC:VM, reservations wise, tel. 028/7082-4313).

While the Ramore Restaurant upstairs is exclusive and pricey, the salty, mod, and much-loved **Ramore Wine Bar** is bursting with happy eaters enjoying the same quality cooking at half the price. The most inviting menu I've seen in Ireland offers huge £5–12 meals ranging from steaks to vegetarian. Their good red wine (from £1.80 glass) is a welcome break after all the Guinness. Come early for a table or sit at the bar (£5.50 lunch specials, dinner 17:00–22:00, daily, no CC, tel. 028/7082-3444).

The **Harbor Restaurant** (run by the Ramore folks with the same winning formula) offers a more subdued, darker bistro ambience and meals for a few pounds more than the wine bar (£5.25 lunches 12:30–14:30, £7–10 dinners 17:30–22:00, closed Mon, tel. 028/7082-2430).

The **Harbor Bar,** upstairs from the Harbor Restaurant, is a plush, overstuffed lounge with a toasty fire and grand views—a great place to enjoy a drink.

Transportation Connections—Portrush

By train to: Coleraine (2/hrly, 12 min, sparse on Sunday morning), **Belfast** (7/day, transfer in Coleraine, 4/Sun, 2 hrs), **Dublin** (7/day, 1/Sun, 5 hrs, several tight but easy connections, £21 one-way, £28 round-trip with Belfast stopover, buy ticket in Coleraine).

By bus to: Belfast (along scenic coast, 2/day, 3.5 hrs, £6).

Driving from Galway to Portrush

Allow a long day for the drive from Galway to Portrush with these interesting stops along the way (leave Galway heading north on N17):

Knock—In 1879 the Virgin Mary and Joseph appeared to locals atop the church in the tiny town of Knock. Word of miraculous healings turned the trickle of pilgrims into a flood and put Knock solidly on the pilgrimage map. Today you can visit the shrine. At the edge of the site a small but interesting folk museum shows "evidence" of the healings, photos of a papal visit, and interesting slices of traditional life.

Belleek Pottery Visitors Centre—After a stretch of scenic coastline and just over the Northern Ireland border you reach the cute town of Belleek, famous for its pottery. The Belleek Parian China factory welcomes visitors with a small gallery and museum (daily 9:00–18:00, less on weekends and off-season), a video, a cheery cafeteria, and fascinating 30-minute tours of its working factory (£2 tours, Mon–Fri 9:30–16:15, call to confirm schedule and reserve a spot, tel. 028/6865-8501).

Ulster American Folk Park—North of Omagh, this museum shows life before emigration, on the boat, and in America for the many Irish who left their homeland during hard times in the 19th century (£4, £2.50 for children, seniors, students; April–Sept Mon–Sat 10:30–16:30, Sun 11:00–17:00, Oct–March Mon–Fri 10:30–15:30, Sat–Sun closed, tel. 028/8224-3292, e-mail: uafp@iol.ie).

Derry—The town of Derry (or Londonderry to Unionists) is the mecca of Ulster unionism. The Foyle River was the logical border between the North and the Republic. Unfortuately, Derry (occupying a bit of land over the river) was kept by the north for sentimental reasons. Consequently, it's been much contested throughout "the Troubles." Get specifics from the helpful TI as you enter the town. You can walk the ramparts of the finest walled town in Ireland, study the political murals, and chat with locals in pubs that rarely see a tourist. Visit the Tower Museum Derry for more city history and excellent audiovisual displays (£4, Mon–Sat 10:00–17:00, Sun 14:00–17:00, Union Hill Place, tel. 028/372-411). Stephen McPhilemy does great city tours (tel. 028/7128-9051, e-mail: nirelandtours@wiredup.net). Park House Hotel has the only real restaurant in the town center.

From Derry it's less than an hour's drive to Portrush, a town much more clearly British.

APPENDIX

BRITAIN

Britain was created by force and held together by force. It's really a nation of the 19th century. Its traditional industry, buildings, and the popularity of the notion of "Great" Britain are a product of the wealth derived from the empire that was at its peak through the Victorian age... the 19th century. Generally, the nice and bad stories are not true and the boring ones are. To best understand the many fascinating guides you'll encounter in your travels, have a basic handle on the sweeping story of this land.

What's So Great about Britain?

Regardless of the revolution we had 200 years ago, many American travelers feel that they "go home" to Britain. This most popular tourist destination has a strange influence and power over us.

Britain is small (about the size of Uganda or Idaho)—600 miles long and 300 miles at its widest point. Its highest mountain is 4,400 feet, a foothill by our standards. The population is a quarter that of the United States. Politically and economically, Great Britain closed out the 20th century only a weak shadow of the days when it boasted that "the sun never sets on the British Empire."

At one time Britain owned one-fifth of the world and accounted for more than half the planet's industrial output. Today the Empire is down to token and troublesome scraps, such as the Falklands and Northern Ireland. Great Britain's industrial production is about 5 percent of the world's total, and Italy has a higher per-capita income.

Still, Britain is a world leader. Her heritage, her culture, and her people cannot be measured in traditional units of power. The United Kingdom is a union of four countries—England, Wales, Scotland, and Northern Ireland. Cynics call it an English Empire ruled by London, and there is some tension between the dominant Anglo-Saxon English (46 million) and their Celtic brothers and sisters (10 million).

In the Dark Ages the Angles moved into this region from Europe, pushing the Celtic inhabitants to the undesirable fringe of the islands. The Angles settled in Angle-land (England), while the Celts made do in Wales, Scotland, and Ireland.

Today Wales, with 2 million inhabitants, struggles with a terrible economy, dragged down by the depressed mining industry. A great deal of Welsh pride is apparent in the local music and the bilingual signs—some with the English spray-painted out. The Welsh language is alive and well.

Scotland is big, accounting for one-third of Great Britain's land area, but sparsely inhabited, with only 5 million people. Only about 80,000 speak Gaelic, but the Scots enjoy a large measure of autonomy with their separate Church of Scotland, their own legal system, and Scottish currency (interchangeable with the British). In a 1998 vote, Scotland decided to "devolve" further. In 2000 it pulled its members of Parliament from Westminster and, for the first time in nearly 300 years, reestablished its own parliament. International affairs will still be decided in London, but Edinburgh will call most of the local shots.

Ireland is divided. Most of it is the completely independent Catholic Republic of Ireland. The top quarter is Northern Ireland, ruled from London. Long ago the Protestant English and Scots moved into the north—the Catholic, industrial heartland of Ireland—and told the Catholic Irish to "go to hell or go to Connaught." The Irish moved to the bleak and less productive parts of the island, like Connaught, and the seeds of today's "Troubles" were planted. There's no easy answer or easy blame, but the island has struggled—its population (3 million) is only one-third of what it used to be—and the battle continues. Recently the moderate center (which, in spite of what the headlines imply, is the vast majority) has voted major concessions to each side. Protestants acknowledged Catholics have equal rights in the North, and Catholics removed the lines from the Republic's constitution refusing to recognize British rule in Ulster.

Just as the United States Congress is dominated by Democrats and Republicans, two parties dominate Britain's Parliament: Labor and Conservatives. (Ronald Reagan would fit the Conservative Party and Bill Clinton the Labor Party like political gloves.) Today Britain's Labor Party, currently in charge, is shoring up a social service system undercut by years of Conservative rule (Thatcher, Major). While in charge, the Conservatives (who consider themselves proponents of Victorian values—community, family, hard work, thrift, and trickle-down economics) took a Reaganesque approach to Britain's serious problems.

This eventually led to a huge Labor victory and the prime ministership of Tony Blair. He's the most popular PM in memory, and his party rules Parliament with a vast majority. Blair's Labor Party is "New Labor"—akin to Clinton's "New" Democrats. It's fiscally conservative but with a keen sense for the needs of the people. Conservative Party fears of old-fashioned, big-spending, bleeding-heart, Union-style liberalism have proven unfounded. The Liberal Parliament is more open to integration with Europe. The economy is booming, and inflation, unemployment, and interest rates are all low. Social programs such as health, education, and the minimum wage are being bolstered but in ways more measured than Conservatives predicted. It looks like Britain is in for a long period of Labor rule.

Basic British History for the Traveler

When Julius Caesar landed on the misty and mysterious isle of Britain in 55 B.C., England entered the history books. The primitive Celtic tribes he conquered were themselves invaders who had earlier conquered the even more mysterious people who built Stonehenge. The Romans built towns and roads and established their capital at "Londinium." The Celtic natives in Scotland and Wales, consisting of Gaels, Picts, and Scots, were not subdued so easily. The Romans built Hadrian's Wall near the Scottish border to consolidate their rule in the troublesome north. Even today, the Celtic language and influence are strongest in these far reaches of Britain.

As Rome fell, so fell Roman Britain, a victim of invaders and internal troubles. Barbarian tribes from Germany and Denmark, called Angles and Saxons, swept through the southern part of the island, establishing Angle-land. These were the days of the real King Arthur, possibly a Christianized Roman general fighting valiantly, but in vain, against invading barbarians. The island was plunged into 500 years of Dark Ages—wars, plagues, and poverty—lit only by the dim candle of a few learned Christian monks and missionaries trying to convert the barbarians. The sightseer sees little from this Saxon period.

Modern England began with yet another invasion. William the Conqueror and his Norman troops crossed the English Channel from France in 1066. William crowned himself king in Westminster Abbey (where all subsequent coronations would take place) and began building the Tower of London. French-speaking Norman kings ruled the country for two centuries. Then followed two centuries of civil wars, with various noble families vying for the crown. In one of the most bitter feuds, the York and Lancaster families fought the War of the Roses, so-called because of the white and red flowers the combatants chose as their symbols. Battles, intrigues, kings, nobles, and ladies imprisoned and executed in the Tower—it's a wonder the country survived its rulers.

England was finally united by the "third-party" Tudor family. Henry VIII, a Tudor, was England's Renaissance king. He was handsome, athletic, highly sexed, a poet, a scholar, and a musician. He was also arrogant, cruel, gluttonous, and paranoid. He went through six wives in 40 years, divorcing, imprisoning, or beheading them when they no longer suited his needs.

Henry also "divorced" England from the Catholic Church, establishing the Protestant Church of England (the Anglican Church) and setting in motion years of religious squabbles. He also "dissolved" the monasteries (around 1540), leaving just the shells of many formerly glorious abbeys dotting the countryside and pocketing their land and wealth for the crown.

Henry's daughter, Queen Elizabeth I, who reigned for 45 years, made England a great trading and naval power (defeating the Spanish Armada) and presided over the Elizabethan era of great writers (such as Shakespeare) and scientists (Francis Bacon).

The long-standing quarrel between England's "divine right" kings and nobles in Parliament finally erupted into a civil war (1643). Parliament forces under the Protestant Puritan farmer Oliver Cromwell defeated—and beheaded—King Charles I. This civil war left its mark on much of what you'll see in England. Eventually, Parliament invited Charles' son to take the throne. This "restoration of the monarchy" was accompanied by a great colonial expansion and the rebuilding of London (including Christopher Wren's St. Paul's Cathedral), which had been devastated by the Great Fire of 1666.

Britain grew as a naval superpower, colonizing and trading with all parts of the globe. Her naval superiority ("Britannia rules the waves") was secured by Admiral Horatio Nelson's victory over Napoleon's fleet at the Battle of Trafalgar, while the Duke of Wellington stomped Napoleon on land at Waterloo. Nelson and Wellington—both buried in London's St. Paul's—are memorialized by many arches, columns, and squares throughout England.

Economically, Britain led the world into the industrial age with her mills, factories, coal mines, and trains. By the time of Queen Victoria's reign (1837–1901), Britain was at the zenith of power, with a colonial empire that covered one-fifth of the world.

The 20th century was not kind to Britain. Two world wars devastated the population. The Nazi blitzkrieg reduced much of London to rubble. The colonial empire has dwindled to almost nothing, and Britain is no longer an economic superpower. The "Irish Troubles" are constant, as the Catholic inhabitants of British-ruled Northern Ireland fight for the independence their southern neighbors won decades ago. The war over the Falkland Islands in 1982 showed how little of the British Empire is left but also how determined the British are to hang on to what remains.

But the tradition (if not the substance) of greatness continues, presided over by Queen Elizabeth II, her husband Prince Philip, and Prince Charles. With economic problems, the turmoil of Charles and the late Princess Diana, the Fergie fiasco, and a relentless popular press, the royal family is having a tough time. But the queen has stayed above it all, and most British people still jump at an opportunity to see royalty. With the death of Princess Diana and the historic outpouring of grief, it's clear that the concept of royalty is alive and well as Britain enters the third millennium.

Britain's Royal Families

802–1066	Saxon and Danish kings
1066–1154	Norman invasion (William the Conqueror), Norman kings
1154–1399	Plantagenet
1399–1461	Lancaster
1462–1485	York
1485–1603	Tudor (Henry VIII, Elizabeth I)

1603–1649	Stuart (civil war and beheading of Charles I)
1649–1659	Commonwealth, Cromwell, no royal head of state
1660–1714	Stuart restoration of monarchy
1714–1901	Hanover (four Georges, Victoria)
1901–1910	Edward VII
1910 to present	Windsor (George V, Edward VII, George VI, Elizabeth II)

Architecture in Britain

From Stonehenge to Big Ben, travelers are storming castle walls, climbing spiral staircases, and snapping the pictures of 5,000 years of architecture. Let's sort it out.

The oldest ruins—mysterious and prehistoric—date from before Roman times back to 3000 B.C. The earliest sites, such as Stonehenge and Avebury, were built during the Stone and Bronze Ages. The remains from these periods are made of huge stones or mounds of earth, even man-made hills, and were created as celestial calendars and for worship or burial. Britain is crisscrossed with lines of these mysterious sights (ley lines). Iron Age people (600 B.C.–A.D. 50) left desolate stone forts. The Romans thrived in Britain from A.D. 50 to 400, building cities, walls, and roads. Evidence of Roman greatness can be seen in lavish villas with ornate mosaic floors, temples uncovered beneath great English churches, and Roman stones in medieval city walls. Roman roads sliced across the island in straight lines. Today, unusually straight rural roads are very likely laid directly on ancient Roman roads.

As Rome crumbled in the fifth century, so did Roman Britain. Little architecture survives from Dark Ages England, the Saxon period from 500 to 1000. Architecturally, the light was switched on with the Norman Conquest in 1066. As William earned his title "the Conqueror," his French architects built churches and castles in the European Romanesque style.

English Romanesque is called Norman (1066–1200). Norman churches had round arches, thick walls, and small windows; Durham Cathedral and the Chapel of St. John in the Tower of London are typical examples. The Tower of London, with its square keep, small windows, and spiral stone stairways, is a typical Norman castle. You'll see plenty of Norman castles—all built to secure the conquest of these invaders from Normandy.

Gothic architecture (1200–1600) replaced the heavy Norman style with light, vertical buildings, pointed arches, soaring spires, and bigger windows. English Gothic is divided into three stages. Early English (1200–1300) features tall, simple spires; beautifully carved capitals; and elaborate chapter houses (such as the Wells Cathedral). Decorated Gothic (1300–1400) gets fancier, with more elaborate tracery, bigger windows, and ornately carved pinnacles, as you'll see at Westminster Abbey. Finally, the Perpendicular style (1400–1600, also called "rectilinear") returns to square towers and emphasizes straight, uninterrupted vertical lines from ceiling to floor, with vast windows and exuberant decoration, including fan-vaulted ceilings (King's College Chapel at Cambridge). Through this evolution, the structural ribs (arches meeting at the top of the ceilings) became more and more decorative and fanciful (the most fancy being the star vaulting and fan vaulting of the Perpendicular style).

As you tour the great medieval churches of England, remember that nearly everything is symbolic. For instance, on the tombs, if the figure has crossed legs, he was a Crusader. If his feet rest on a dog, he died at home, but if the legs rest on a lion, he died in battle. Local guides and books help us modern pilgrims understand at least a little of what we see.

Wales is particularly rich in English castles, which were needed to subdue the stubborn Welsh. Edward I built a ring of powerful castles in Wales, including Caernarfon and Conwy.

Gothic houses were a simple mix of woven strips of thin wood, rubble, and plaster called wattle and daub. The famous black-and-white Tudor, or half-timbered, look came simply from filling in heavy oak frames with wattle and daub.

The Tudor period (1485–1560) was a time of relative peace (the War of the Roses was finally over), prosperity, and renaissance. Henry VIII broke with the Catholic Church and "dissolved" (destroyed) the monasteries, leaving scores of England's greatest churches gutted shells. These hauntingly beautiful abbey ruins (Glastonbury, Tintern, Whitby) surrounded by lush lawns are now pleasant city parks.

Although few churches were built during the Tudor period, this was a time of house and mansion construction. Warmth was becoming popular and affordable, and Tudor buildings featured small square windows and many chimneys. In towns where land was scarce, many Tudor houses grew up and out, getting wider with each overhanging floor.

The Elizabethan and Jacobean periods (1560–1620) were followed by the English Renaissance style (1620–1720). English architects mixed Gothic and classical styles, then Baroque and classical styles. Although the ornate Baroque never really grabbed England, the classical style of the Italian architect Andrea Palladio did. Inigo Jones (1573–1652), Christopher Wren (1632–1723), and those they inspired plastered England with enough columns, domes, and symmetry to please a caesar. The Great Fire of London (1666) cleared the way for an ambitious young Wren to put his mark on London forever with a grand rebuilding scheme, including the great St. Paul's and more than 50 other churches.

The celebrants of the Boston Tea Party remember England's

Georgian period (1720–1840) for its lousy German kings. Georgian architecture was rich and showed off by being very classical. Grand ornamental doorways, fine cast-ironwork on balconies and railings, Chippendale furniture, and white-on-blue Wedgewood ceramics graced rich homes everywhere. John Wood Jr. and Sr. led the way, giving the trend-setting city of Bath its crescents and circles of aristocratic Georgian row houses. "Georgian" is English for "neoclassical."

The Industrial Revolution shaped the Victorian period (1840–1890) with glass, steel, and iron. England had a huge new erector set (so did France's Mr. Eiffel). This was also a Romantic period, reviving the "more Christian" Gothic style. London's Houses of Parliament are neo-Gothic—just 100 years old but looking 700, except for the telltale modern precision and craftsmanship. Whereas Gothic was stone or concrete, neo-Gothic was often red brick. These were England's glory days, and there was more building in this period than in all previous ages combined.

The architecture of modern times obeys the formula "form follows function"—it worries more about your needs than your eyes. England treasures its heritage and takes great pains to build tastefully in historic districts and to preserve its many "listed" buildings. With a booming tourist trade, these quaint reminders of its—and our—past are becoming a valuable part of the British economy.

British TV

British television is so good—and so British—that it deserves a mention as a sightseeing treat. After a hard day of castle-climbing, watch the telly over tea in the living room of your village B&B.

England has five channels. BBC-1 and BBC-2 are government regulated, commercial free, and traditionally highbrow. Channels 3, 4, and 5 are private, are a little more Yankee, and have commercials—but those commercials are clever and sophisticated and provide a fun look at England. Broadcasting is funded by an £80-per-year-per-household tax. Hmmm, 35 cents per day to escape commercials and public television pledge drives.

Britian is about to leap into the digital age ahead of the rest of the TV-watching world. Ultimately every house will enjoy literally hundreds of high-definition channels with no need for cable or satellites.

Whereas California "accents" fill our airwaves 24 hours a day, homogenizing the way our country speaks, England protects and promotes its regional accents by its choice of TV and radio announcers. Commercial-free British TV, while looser than it used to be, is still careful about what it airs and when.

American shows (such as *Frasier* and *ER*) are very popular. The visiting viewer should be sure to tune the TV to a few typical

English shows, including a dose of English situation and political comedy fun and the top-notch BBC evening news. Quiz shows are taken very seriously here. Michael Parkinson is the Johnny Carson of Britain for late-night talk. For a tear-filled, slice-of-life taste of British soap dealing in all the controversial issues, see the popular *Brookside*, *Coronation Street*, or *Eastenders*.

Benny Hill comedy has become politically incorrect but is rumored to be coming back. And if you like Monty Python–type comedy, you've come to the right place.

IRELAND

Irish History

One surprising aspect of Ireland is the richness of its history. While the island is not particularly well endowed with historic monuments, it is soaked in history. Here's a thumbnail overview.

The story of Ireland can be broken into four sections:

500 B.C.–A.D. 500	Iron Age
500–900	"Age of Saints and Scholars"
900–1900	Age of invasions and colonization
20th century to present	Independence and the question of a united Ireland

The Celtic people left the countryside peppered with thousands of ancient sights from the Iron Age. While most of what you'll see will be little more than rock piles that take a vigorous imagination to reconstruct (ring forts, wedge tombs, monumental stones, and so on), just standing next to a megalith that predates the pharaohs while surrounded by lush Ireland is evocative. The finest gold, bronze, and ironwork of this period is in the National Museum in Dublin.

The Romans called Ireland Hibernia, or "Land of Winter"; it was apparently too cold and bleak to merit an attempt to take over and colonize. The biggest nonevent in Irish history is that the Romans never invaded. While the mix of Celtic and Roman contributes to what makes the French French and the English English, the Irish are purely Celtic. If France is *boules* and England is cricket, then Ireland is hurling. This wild Irish national pastime (like airborne hockey with no injury time-outs) goes back to Celtic days, more than 2,000 years ago.

Celts worshipped the sun. Perhaps St. Patrick had an easy time converting the locals because they had so little sun to worship. Whatever the case, a former Roman slave boy, Patrick helped Christianize Ireland in the fifth century. From this period on, monks established monastic centers of learning that produced great Christian teachers and community builders. They traveled, establishing monastic communities all over Ireland, Britain, and Europe. One of the monks, St. Brandon, may have even sailed to America.

While the collapse of Rome left Europe a mess, it meant nothing to Ireland. Ireland was and remained a relatively cohesive society based on monastic settlements rather than cities. While Europe was rutting in the Dark Age mud, the light of civilization shone brightly in Ireland during a Golden Age that lasted from the fifth through the ninth centuries. Irish monks—such as those imported by Charlemagne to help run his Frankish kingdom in 800—actually carried the torch of civilization back to Europe. Perhaps the greatest works of art of Dark Age Europe are the manuscripts (such as the ninth-century *Book of Kells*, which you'll see in Dublin) illuminated, or richly illustrated, by Irish monks. Impressive round towers dot the Irish landscape—silent reminders of this impressive age.

Viking invasions of the ninth century wreaked repeated havoc on the monasteries and shook Irish civilization. Vikings established trading towns (such as Dublin) where before there had been only Celtic settlements and monasteries.

The Normans, who invaded and conquered England after the Battle of Hastings (1066), were Ireland's next uninvited guests. In 1169, the Anglo-Normans invaded Ireland. These invaders, big-time organizers, ushered in a new age in which society (government, cities, and religious organizations) was organized on a grander scale. Individual monastic settlements (the basis of Irish society in the Age of Saints and Scholars) were eclipsed by monastic orders just in from the Continent, such as the Franciscans, Augustinians, and Cistercians.

The English made a concentrated effort to colonize Ireland in the 17th century. Settlers were "planted," and Irish society was split between an English-speaking landed gentry and the local Irish-speaking landless or nearly landless peasantry.

During the 18th century Ireland thrived under the English. Dublin was Britain's second city. Over time, greed on the top and dissent on the bottom required colonial policies to become more repressive. The Enlightenment provided ideas of freedom, and the Revolutionary Age emboldened the Irish masses. (Even the non-Catholic Dubliner Jonathan Swift—dean of St. Patrick's cathedral in the early 18th century—declared "Burn all that's British, except its coal.")

To counter this Irish feistiness, English legislation became an out-and-out attack on the indigenous Gaelic culture. The harp, symbol of Irish culture, was outlawed. Written and unwritten laws made life for Catholics and Irish-speakers very difficult.

The potato famine of 1845 to 1849 was a pivotal event in Irish history. The stature of Ireland and its language never recovered. In a few years Ireland's population dropped from 8 million to 5 million (3 million either starved or emigrated). Ireland's population has not grown since. Britain's population, on the other hand, has grown from 12 million in 1845 to around 60 million today. (During this period, Ireland's population, as a percent of England's, has dropped from 67 percent to about 8 percent.)

While the English are likely to blame the famine on overpopulation (Ireland's population doubled in the 40 years leading up to the famine), many Irish say there actually was no famine—just a calculated attempt to starve down the local population. In fact, there was plenty of food grown on the island for export. It was only the potato crop that failed...and that happened to be what the Irish subsisted on.

The average farmer grew fancier export products for his landlord and was paid in potatoes, which, in good years, he grew on the side. (If this makes you mad at the English landlords, consider American ownership of land in Central America, where the landlord takes things one step further by not growing the local staple at all. He devotes all the land to more profitable cash crops for export and leaves the landless farmer no alternative but to buy his food—imported from the United States—at plantation wages, in the landlord's grocery store.)

The famine was a turning point in Irish history. Before the famine, land was subdivided—each boy got a piece of the family estate (which grew smaller with each generation). After the famine, the oldest son got the estate and the younger siblings, with no way to stay in Ireland, emigrated to Britain, Australia, Canada, and the United States. Today there are 40 million Irish Americans.

After the famine, Irish became the language of the peasant. English was for the upwardly mobile. Because of the huge immigration to the United States, Ireland began to face west, and American influence increased. (As negotiations between Northern Ireland and the Irish Republic continue, American involvement in the talks is welcomed and considered essential by nearly all parties.)

The tragedy of the famine inflamed the nationalist movement. Uprising after uprising made it clear that Ireland was ready to close this thousand-year chapter of invasions and colonialism. Finally, in 1919, Ireland declared its independence. While the northern six counties (the only ones without a Catholic majority) voted to stay with Britain, the independent Republic of Ireland was born. (For a review of the ongoing "Troubles" between the North and the Republic, see the Northern Ireland chapter.)

The Irish Pub

When you say "a beer, please" in an Irish pub, you'll get a pint of Guinness (the black beauty with a blonde head). If you want a small beer, ask for a half pint. Never rush your bartender when he's pouring a Guinness. It takes time—almost sacred time. If you don't like Guinness, try it in Ireland. It doesn't travel well and is better in its homeland. Murphy's is a very good Guinness-like stout but a bit smoother and milder.

In an Irish pub you're a guest on your first night; after that you're a regular. Women traveling alone need not worry—you'll become part of the pub family in no time.

It's a tradition to buy your table a round and then for each person to reciprocate. If an Irishman buys you a drink, thank him by saying, "*Guh rev mah a gut*." Offer him a toast in Irish—"*Slahn chuh!*" A good excuse for a conversation is to ask to be taught a few words of Gaelic.

Craic (crack), the art of conversation, is the sport that accompanies drinking in a pub. People are there to talk. If you feel a bit awkward, remind yourself of that.

Here's a goofy excuse for some *craic*: Ireland—small as it is—has many dialects. People from Cork are famous for talking very fast (and in a squeaky voice)—so fast that some even talk in letters alone. ABCD fish? (Anybody see the fish?) DR no fish. (There are no fish.) DR fish. (There are fish.) CDBD Is? (See the beady eyes?) OIBJ DR fish. (Oh aye, be Jeeze, there are fish.) For a possibly more appropriate spin, replace the fish with "bird" (girl). This is obscure, but your pub neighbor may understand and enjoy hearing it. If nothing else, you won't seem so intimidating to him anymore.

You might ask if the people of one county are any smarter than the next. Kerry people are considered by some of their neighbors to be a bit out of it.

Traditional Irish Music

Traditional music is alive and popular in pubs throughout Ireland. "Sessions" (musical evenings) may be planned and advertised or impromptu. Traditionally, musicians just congregate and jam. There will generally be a fiddle, a flute or tin whistle, a guitar, a bodhran (goatskin drum), and maybe an accordion. Things usually get going around 21:30 or 22:00. Last call for drinks is around 23:30.

The bodhran is played with a small two-headed club. The performer's hand stretches the skin to change the tone and pitch. The wind and string instruments embellish melody lines with lots of improvised ornamentation. Occasionally the fast-paced music will stop and one person will sing an a cappella "lament." This is the one time when the entire pub will stop to listen as sad lyrics fill the smoke-stained room. Stories—ranging from struggles against English rule to love songs—are always heartfelt. Spend a lament enjoying the faces in the crowd. A *ceilidh* (kay-lee) is an evening of music and dance . . . an Irish hoedown.

The music comes in sets of three songs. Whoever happens to be leading determines the next song only as the song the group is playing is about to be finished. If he wants to pass on the decision, it's done with eye contact and a nod.

A session can be magic or lifeless. If the chemistry is right, it's one of the great Irish experiences. The music churns intensely while the group casually enjoys exploring each other's musical style. The drummer dodges the fiddler's playful bow with his cigarette sticking half-ash straight from the middle of his mouth. Sipping their pints, they skillfully maintain a faint but steady buzz. The floor on the musicians' platform is stomped paint-free, and barmaids scurry artfully through the commotion, gathering towers of empty cream-crusted glasses. Make yourself right at home, drumming the table or playing the 10-pence coins. Talk to your neighbor. Locals often have an almost evangelical interest in explaining the music.

Let's Talk Telephones

Here's a primer on making direct phone calls. For more information, see "Telephones" in the Introduction.

Dialing Direct

Calling between Countries: First dial the international access code, then the country code, the area code (if it starts with zero, drop the zero), and the local number.

Calling Long Distance within a Country: First dial the area code (including its zero), then the local number.

Europe's Exceptions: France, Italy, Spain, Portugal, Norway, and Denmark have dispensed with area codes entirely. To make an international call to these countries, dial the international access code (usually 00), the country code (see chart below), and then the local number in its entirety (OK, so there's one exception: for France, drop the initial zero of the local number). To make long-distance calls within any of these countries, simply dial the local number.

International Access Codes

When dialing direct, first dial the international access code of the country you're calling from. For the U.S. and Canada, it's 011. Virtually all European countries use "00" as their international access code; the only exceptions are Finland (990), Estonia (800), and Lithuania (810).

Country Codes

After you've dialed the international access code, then dial the code of the country you're calling.

Austria—43
Belgium—32
Britain—44
Canada—1
Czech Republic—420
Denmark—45

Estonia—372
Finland—358
France—33
Germany—49
Greece—30
Ireland—353
Italy—39
Netherlands—31
Norway—47
Portugal—351
Spain—34
Sweden—46
Switzerland—41
U.S.A.—1

Calling-Card Operators

You can call direct much more cheaply by using a British or Irish phone card from any phone booth, but if you'd prefer to use an AT&T, MCI, or Sprint calling card, these are the numbers you'd use:

	AT&T	MCI	Sprint
Britain	0800-89-00-11	0800-89-02-22	0800-89-08-77
Ireland	1800-55-00-00	1800-55-10-01	1800-55-20-01

Useful Numbers in Britain

Emergency (police and ambulance): 999
Operator Assistance: 100
Directory Assistance: 192 (free from phone booth, otherwise expensive)
International Info: 153 (80p)
International Assistance: 155
United States Embassy: 020/7499-9000
Eurostar (Chunnel Info): 08705-186-186 (www.eurostar.com)
Trains to all points in Europe: 08705-848-848 (www.raileurope.com)

Note: Understand the various prefixes: 0891 numbers are telephone sex–type expensive. Prefixes 0845 and 0870 are local calls nationwide. And 0800 numbers are toll free. If you have questions about a prefix, call 100 for free help.

Useful Numbers in Ireland

Emergency: 999
Operator Assistance: 10 for Ireland, 114 to call outside Ireland
Directory Assistance within Ireland: 11811 (free from phone booth, or 34p)
International Assistance: 11818 (free from phone booth)

London's Airports and Airlines

Airports

For online information on the first three airports, check www.airwise.com/airports/europe.
Heathrow (switchboard): 0870-000-0123

Gatwick (general info): 01293/535-353 for all airlines, except British Airways—0870-551-1155 (flights) or 0845-773-3377 (booking)
Stansted (general info): 01279/680-500
Luton: (general info): 01582/405-100 (www.london-luton.com)

Airlines

Aer Lingus: 020/8899-4747 (www.aerlingus.ie)
Air Canada: 0870-524-7226, (www.aircanada.ca)
Alitalia: reservations 0870-544-8259, Heathrow 020/8745-8400, Gatwick 01293/569-926 (www.alitalia.it)
American: 0345-789-789 (www.aa.com)
British Airways: reservations 0845-773-3377, flight info 0870-551-1155 (www.britishairways.com)
British Midland: reservations 0870-607-0555, info 020/8745-7321 (www.britishmidland.com)
Canadian Airlines: 0845-761-6767, 0181/577-7722 (www.cdnair.ca)
Continental Airlines: 0800-776-464 (www.continental.com)
EasyJet: 0870-600-0000, Luton 01582/445-354 (www.easyjet.com)
KLM Royal Dutch Airlines: 0870-507-4074 (www.klm.com)
Lufthansa: 0345-737-747 (www.lufthansa.co.uk)
Ryanair (cheap fares): 0870-333-1231 (www.ryanair.com)
Scandinavian Airlines System (SAS): 0845-607-27727, 020/8990-7122 (www.scandinavian.net)
United Airlines: 0845-844-4777 (www.ual.com)
Virgin Express: 020/7744-0004 (www.virgin-express.com)

Climate

The first line is the average low, the second line is the average high, and the third line is number of days with no rain.

	J	F	M	A	M	J	J	A	S	O	N	D
LONDON												
	36°	36°	38°	42°	47°	53°	56°	56°	52°	46°	42°	38°
	43°	44°	50°	56°	62°	69°	71°	71°	65°	58°	50°	45°
	16	15	20	18	19	19	19	20	17	18	15	16
CARDIFF (South Wales)												
	35°	35°	38°	41°	46°	51°	54°	55°	51°	46°	41°	37°
	45°	45°	50°	56°	61°	68°	69°	69°	64°	58°	51°	46°
	13	14	18	17	18	17	17	16	14	15	13	13
YORK												
	33°	34°	36°	40°	44°	50°	54°	53°	50°	44°	39°	36°
	43°	44°	49°	55°	61°	67°	70°	69°	64°	57°	49°	45°
	14	13	18	17	18	16	16	17	16	16	13	14

J	F	M	A	M	J	J	A	S	O	N	D
EDINBURGH											
34°	34°	36°	39°	43°	49°	52°	52°	49°	44°	39°	36°
42°	43°	46°	51°	56°	62°	65°	64°	60°	54°	48°	44°
14	13	16	16	17	15	14	15	14	14	13	13
DUBLIN											
34°	35°	37°	39°	43°	48°	52°	51°	48°	43°	39°	37°
46°	47°	51°	55°	60°	65°	67°	67°	63°	57°	51°	47°
18	18	21	19	21	19	18	19	18	20	18	17

Numbers and Stumblers

- Europeans write a few of their numbers differently than we do. 1 = 1 , 4 = 4 , 7= 7. Learn the difference or miss your train.
- In Europe, dates appear as day/month/year, so Christmas is 25-12-01.
- Commas are decimal points and decimals commas. A dollar and a half is 1,50 and there are 5.280 feet in a mile.
- When pointing, use your whole hand, palm downward.
- When counting with fingers, start with your thumb. If you hold up your first finger to request one item, you'll probably get two.
- What we Americans call the second floor of a building is the first floor in Europe.
- Europeans keep the left "lane" open for passing on escalators and moving sidewalks. Keep to the right.
- And please... don't call your waist pack a "fanny pack."

Weights and Measures

1 British pint = 1.2 U.S. pints
1 imperial gallon = 1.2 U.S. gallons or about 4.5 liters
1 stone = 14 pounds (a 168-pound person weighs 12 stone)
28 degrees Centigrade = 82 degrees Fahrenheit
Shoe sizes = about .5 to 1.5 sizes smaller than in the United States

British-Yankee Vocabulary

advert advertisement
afters dessert
anticlockwise counterclockwise
aubergine eggplant
Balloons Belgians
banger sausage
bangers and mash sausage and mashed potatoes
bank holiday legal holiday
bap hamburger-type bun
billion a thousand of our billions (a million million)
biro ballpoint pen
biscuit cookie
black pudding sausage made from dried blood
bobby policeman ("copper" is more common)
Bob's your uncle there you go (with a shrug), naturally
bomb success
bonnet car hood
boot car trunk
braces suspenders
bridle way path for walkers, bikers, and horse riders
brilliant cool
bubble and squeak cold meat fried with cabbage and potatoes
bum bottom or "backside"
candy floss cotton candy
car boot sale temporary flea market with car trunk displays (a good place to buy back your stolen goods)
caravan trailer
cat's eyes road reflectors
ceilidh (kay-lee) informal evening of song and folk fun
cheap and nasty cheap and bad quality
cheerio good-bye
chemist pharmacist
chicory endive
chips french fries
chock-a-block jam-packed
cider alcoholic apple cider
clearway road where you can't stop
coach long-distance bus
concession discounted admission
cotton buds Q-tips
courgette zucchini
cos romaine lettuce
craic (crack) good conversation (Irish and spreading to England)
crisps potato chips
cuppa cup of tea
dear expensive
dicey iffy, risky
digestives round graham crackers
dinner lunch or dinner
diversion detour
donkey's years until the cows come home
draughts checkers
dual carriageway divided highway (four lanes)
elvers baby eels
face flannel washcloth
fag cigarette
fagged exhausted
faggot meatball
fanny vagina
fell hill or high plain
first floor second floor
football soccer
force waterfall (Lake District)
fortnight two weeks
Frogs French people
Full Monty The whole shebang. Everything.
gallery balcony
gammon ham
gangway aisle
gaol jail (same pronunciation)
give way yield
glen Scot. narrow valley
goods wagon freight truck
grammar school high school
half eight 8:30 (not 7:30)
heath open treeless land
holiday vacation
homely likable or cozy
hoover vacuum cleaner
ice lolly Popsicle
interval intermission
ironmonger hardware store
jacket potato baked potato
jelly Jell-O
Joe Bloggs John Doe
jumble sale, rummage sale
jumper sweater
just a tick just a second
keep your pecker up be brave

kipper smoked herring
knackered exhausted (Cockney: cream crackered)
knickers ladies' panties
knocking shop brothel
knock up wake up or visit
ladybird ladybug
lady fingers okra
left luggage baggage check
lemon squash lemonade
let rent
loo toilet or bathroom
lorry truck
mac mackintosh coat
mate buddy (boy or girl)
mean stingy
mews courtyard stables, often used as cottages
minced meat hamburger
mobile (pron. MOH-bile) cell phone
nappy diaper
natter talk and talk
neep Scottish for turnip
nought zero
noughts & crosses tic-tac-toe
off license store selling take-away liquor
pasty crusted savory (usually meat) pie
pavement sidewalk
petrol gas
pissed (rude), paralytic, bevvied, wellied, popped up, ratted, pissed as a newt drunk
pillar box postbox
pitch playing field
plaster Band-Aid
poppers snaps
publican pub manager
public convenience toilets
public school private "prep" school (Eton)
put a sock in it shut up
queue line
queue up line up
quid pound (money, worth about $1.60)
randy horny
redundant, made fired
Remembrance Day Veterans' Day
return ticket round-trip
ring up call (telephone)
roundabout traffic circle
rubber eraser
sanitary towel sanitary pad
sausage roll sausage wrapped in a flaky pastry
Scotch egg hard-boiled egg wrapped in sausage meat
self-catering apartment with kitchen
sellotape Scotch tape
serviette napkin
single ticket one-way ticket
sleeping policeman speed bumps
smalls underwear
snogging kissing cuddling
solicitor lawyer
starkers buck naked
starters appetizers
stone 14 pounds (weight)
subway underground pedestrian passageway
sultanas golden raisins
surgical spirit rubbing alcohol
suss out figure out
swede rutabaga
ta thank you
taxi rank taxi stand
telly TV
theater live stage
tick a check mark
tight as a fish's bum cheapskate (water-tight)
tights panty hose
tipper lorry dump truck
tin can
to let for rent
top hole first rate
topping excellent
top up refill a drink
torch flashlight
towpath path along a river
tube subway
twee quaint, cute
underground subway
vegetable marrow summer squash
verge grassy edge of road
verger church official
way out exit
Wellingtons, wellies rubber boots
wee urinate
whacked exhausted
witter on gab and gab
yob hooligan
zebra crossing crosswalk
zed the letter "z"

Faxing Your Hotel Reservation

Faxing is more accurate and cheaper than telephoning. Use this handy form for your fax (or find it online at www.ricksteves.com/reservation). Photocopy and fax away.

One-Page Fax

To: ______________________ @ ____________________
hotel *fax*

From: ______________________ @ ____________________
name *fax*

Today's date: ___ /____ /___
day *month* *year*

Dear Hotel ______________________________,

Please make this reservation for me:

Name: __________________________________

Total # of people: ____ # of rooms: ____ # of nights: ____

Arriving: ___ /____ /____ My time of arrival (24-hr clock): _____
day *month* *year* (I will telephone if I will be late)

Departing: ___ /____ /____
day *month* *year*

Room(s): Single___ Double___ Twin___ Triple___ Quad___

With: Toilet___ Shower___ Bath___ Sink only___

Special needs: View___ Quiet___ Cheap___ Ground Floor___

Credit card: Visa___ MasterCard___ American Express___

Card #: __________________________________

Expiration date: __________________________

Name on card: ____________________________

You may charge me for the first night as a deposit. Please fax, e-mail, or mail me confirmation of my reservation, along with the type of room reserved, the price, and whether the price includes breakfast. Thank you.

____
Signature

____
Name

____
Address

____
City *State* *Zip Code* *Country*

____
E-mail Address

Road Scholar Feedback for GREAT BRITAIN & IRELAND 2001

We're all in the same travelers' school of hard knocks. Your feedback helps us improve this guidebook for future travelers. Please fill this out (or use the on-line version at www.ricksteves.com/feedback), attach more info or any tips/favorite discoveries if you like, and send it to us. As thanks for your help, we'll send you our quarterly travel newsletter free for one year. Thanks! ***Rick***

Of the recommended accommodations/restaurants used, which was:

Best ______________________________

Why? ______________________________

Worst ______________________________

Why? ______________________________

Of the sights/experiences/destinations recommended by this book, which was:

Most overrated ______________________________

Why? ______________________________

Most underrated ______________________________

Why? ______________________________

Best ways to improve this book:

____

____

I'd like a free newsletter subscription:

____ Yes ____ No ____ Already on list

____
Name

____
Address

____
City, State, Zip

____
E-mail Address

Please send to: ETBD, Box 2009, Edmonds, WA 98020

INDEX